RECENT SOCIOLOGY TITLES FROM W. W. NORTON

TO LEARN MORE ABOUT NORTON SOCIOLOGY, PLEASE VISIT:
WWNORTON.COM/SOC

Core Fourth Edition

You May Ask Yourself

AN INTRODUCTION TO THINKING LIKE A SOCIOLOGIST

Dalton Conley

NEW YORK UNIVERSITY

W. W. NORTON
NEW YORK | LONDON

W. W. Norton & Company has been independent since its founding in 1923, when William Warder Norton and Mary D. Herter Norton first published lectures delivered at the People's Institute, the adult education division of New York City's Cooper Union. The firm soon expanded its program beyond the Institute, publishing books by celebrated academics from America and abroad. By midcentury, the two major pillars of Norton's publishing program—trade books and college texts—were firmly established. In the 1950s, the Norton family transferred control of the company to its employees, and today—with a staff of four hundred and a comparable number of trade, college, and professional titles published each year—W. W. Norton & Company stands as the largest and oldest publishing house owned wholly by its employees.

Editor: Karl Bakeman
Associate Editor: Nicole Sawa
Project Editor: Jennifer Barnhardt
Editorial Assistant: Lindsey Thomas
Managing Editor, College: Marian Johnson
Managing Editor, College Digital Media: Kim Yi
Production Manager: Eric Pier-Hocking
Media Editor: Eileen Connell
Associate Media Editor: Laura Musich
Media Editorial Assistant: Michael Jaoui
Marketing Manager, Sociology: Julia Hall
Book Designer: Kiss Me I'm Polish LLC, New York
Design Director: Rubina Yeh
Photo Editor: Stephanie Romeo
Permissions Manager: Megan Jackson
College Permissions Associate: Bethany Salminen
Composition: Jouve
Manufacturing: Transcontinental Interglobe

Permission to use copyrighted material is included in the credits section of this book, which begins on page A-25.

ISBN: 978-0-393-93774-9 (pbk.)

W. W. Norton & Company, Inc., 500 Fifth Avenue, New York, NY 10110-0017
wwnorton.com
W. W. Norton & Company Ltd., Castle House, 75/76 Wells Street, London W1T 3QT

1 2 3 4 5 6 7 8 9 0

BRIEF CONTENTS ←

CONTENTS

$\longrightarrow$

→

PREFACE

I came to sociology by accident, so to speak. During the 1980s, there were no sociology courses at the high-school level, so I entered college with only the vaguest notion of what sociology—or even social science—was. Instead, I headed straight for the pre-med courses. But there was no such thing as a pre-med major, so I ended up specializing in the now defunct "humanities field major." This un-major major was really the result of my becoming a junior and realizing that I was not any closer to a declared field of study than I had been when arriving two years earlier. So I scanned a list of all the electives I had taken until then—philosophy of aesthetics, history of technology, and so on—and marched right into my advisor's office, declaring that it had always been my lifelong dream to study "art and technology in the twentieth century." I wrote this up convincingly enough, apparently, because the college allowed me to write a senior thesis about how the evolution of Warner Brothers' cartoon characters—from the stuttering, insecure Porky Pig to the militant Daffy Duck to the cool, collected, and confident Bugs Bunny—reflected the self-image of the United States on the world stage during the Depression, World War II, and the postwar period, respectively. Little did I know, I was already becoming a sociologist.

After college, I worked as a journalist but then decided that I wanted to continue my schooling. I was drawn to the critical stance and reflexivity that I had learned in my humanities classes, but I knew that I didn't want to devote my life to arcane texts. What I wanted to do was take those skills—that critical stance—and apply them to everyday life, to the here and now. I also was rather skeptical of the methods that humanists used. What texts they chose to analyze always seemed so arbitrary. I wanted to systematize the inquiry a bit more; I found myself trying to apply the scientific method that I had gotten a taste of in my biology classes. But I didn't want to do science in a lab. I wanted to be out in the proverbial real world. So when I flipped through a course catalog with these latent preferences somewhere in the back of my head, my finger landed on the sociology courses.

Once I became a card-carrying sociologist, the very first course I taught was Introduction to Sociology. I had big shoes to fill in teaching this course at

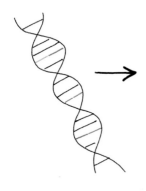

Yale. Kai Erikson, the world-renowned author of *Wayward Puritans* and *Everything in Its Path* and the son of psychologist Erik Erikson, was stepping down from his popular course, "The Human Universe," and I, a first-year assistant professor, was expected to replace him.

I had a lot of sociology to learn. After all, graduate training in sociology is spotty at best. And there is no single theory of society in the same way one might learn, for example, the biochemistry of DNA transcription and translation as the central dogma of molecular biology. We talk about the sociological imagination as an organizing principle. But even that is almost a poetic notion, not so easily articulated. Think of sociology as more like driving a car than learning calculus. You can read the manual all you want, but that isn't going to teach you how to do it. Only by seeing sociology in action and then trying it yourself will you eventually say, "Hey, I've got the hang of this!"

Hence the title of this book. In *You May Ask Yourself,* I show readers how sociologists question what most others take for granted about society, and I give readers opportunities to apply sociological ways of thinking to their own experiences. I've tried to jettison the arcane academic debates that become the guiding light of so many intro books in favor of a series of contemporary empirical (gold) nuggets that show off sociology (and empirical social science more generally) in its finest hour. Most students who take an introductory sociology class in college will not end up being sociology majors, let alone professional sociologists. Yet I aim to speak to both the aspiring major and the student who is merely fulfilling a requirement. So rather than having pages filled with statistics and theories that will go out of date rather quickly, *You May Ask Yourself* tries to instill in the reader a way of thinking—a scientific approach to human affairs that is portable, one that students will find useful when they study anything else, whether history or medicine.

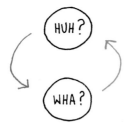

To achieve this ambitious goal, I tried to write a book that was as "untextbook"-like as possible, while covering all the material that a student in sociology needs to know. In this vein, each chapter is organized around a motivating paradox, meant to serve as the first chilling line of a mystery novel that motivates the reader to read on to find out (or rather, figure out, because this book is not about spoon-feeding facts) the nugget, the debate, the fundamentally new way of looking at the world that illuminates the paradox. Along with a paradox, each chapter begins with a profile of a relevant person who speaks to the core theme of the chapter. These range from myself to Angelina Jolie to a guy who declared himself king of an offshore platform, battling the British government for sovereignty. In addition, to show the usefulness of sociological knowledge in shaping the world around us, each chapter also culminates in a Policy discussion and Practice section where the reader gets a chance to show his or her sociological imagination in action (rather than just regurgitate facts).

WHAT'S NEW IN THE FOURTH EDITION

Higher education is in rapid transition, with online instruction expanding in traditional institutions, in the expanding for-profit sector, and in the new, open-courseware movement. With these changes, textbooks must also reinvent and reorient themselves. Students now expect, I believe, an entire multimedia experience when they purchase a textbook.

I was not sure how we were going to top the popular Paradox Animations for the Third Edition. Well, the answer turned out to be that we filmed "Sociology on the Street" assignment videos in addition to a new round of interviews with sociologists. For the chapter on deviance, for example, we sent students out to perform one of Harold Garfinkel's "breaching experiments," in which they purposely break a social norm and document the responses of those around them. To illustrate this (and other assignments), I went on camera to explain and/or perform them myself. It has been years since I had been as nervous speaking on camera as I was the day I walked—barefoot but dressed in a suit—into W. W. Norton's conference room filled with unsuspecting volunteers and proceeded to clip my toenails while I explained the plan for the day and we surreptitiously filmed their (surprisingly unflinching) response.

In addition to crazy videos like this—which also included me rummaging through a garbage can to discuss the environment chapter assignment—I made in-studio videos to further explain some of the trickier concepts in the book, ranging from "correlation" to "total institution." Like the expert interviews and the animations, these "Sociology on the Street" videos are a tradition I expect to continue in future editions to further develop the multimedia aspects of the text, with the goal of reaching learners who prefer all sorts of modalities.

In addition to the new videos, we revised every chapter in the book. Here are some of the highlights:

Chapter 1

In a new interview, sociologist Julia Adams talks about the difference between historians and sociologists.

Chapter 2

The chapter now begins with the research of computational/social media sociologist danah boyd, who integrates multiple research methods to yield dynamic results. A new example of participant observation focuses on Mary Pattillo's study of the interactions between black residents of differing economic classes in gentrifying neighborhoods. The policy box now takes on the political issues associated with population sampling, specifically the proposed readjustments of the U.S. Census.

Chapter 3

A new chapter opener describes the experience of transgender activist Samantha Lauzon, and explores how media has both reflected and enacted change in America's views on the LGBT community. A new example of the control of messages in the media focuses on the policies of Apple's iTunes app store. The policy box has been updated with a discussion of baby-naming trends, particularly unique names and gendered names.

Chapter 4

New data on the relationship between education and leisure time has been included. An updated policy box focuses on the decreasing randomness of roommate pairings in college dorms and how differences between roommates can lead to varying socializations.

Chapter 5

Michael Gaddis's study on how different social networks result in varying social capital has been included, as has Eric Klinenberg's research on the effects of living alone. The discussion of the power elite has been expanded with further examples.

Chapter 6

This chapter includes updated data on the estimated total loss from robbery, burglary, larceny-theft, and motor vehicle theft; crime rates in the United States, including total violent crime rates and murder rates; and incarceration rates and prison populations. Notably, the total violent crime rate and the size of the prison population have been slowly decreasing since 2005. Exonerations due to DNA evidence have led to the abolition of the death penalty in seven states since 2007. The policy box spotlights the debate over whether prisons serve as punishment or rehabilitation.

Chapter 7

A new chapter opener discusses the ties between surnames and intergenerational social mobility. An updated version of the Index of Occupational Status has been included. The policy box now features a discussion of class-based affirmative action. An updated poll by the Pew Charitable Trusts finds that Americans are no longer positive about the possibility of upward mobility.

Chapter 8

Statistics on LGBT populations in the United States, and on women in higher education and the workforce, have been updated. Additional research on gendered professions and industries and an excerpt from an interview with former model and sociologist Ashley Mears on men in the fashion industry have been included. The policy box "Women in Combat" has been updated with information on the Pentagon's decision to lift the ban on women in combat positions, and the effects of sexual assault in the military.

Chapter 9

Demographic data on Native American, African American, Latino, Asian American, and Middle Eastern American populations have been updated. New research on double segregation by race and by income in schools has been included. The updated policy box discusses reverse migration from the United States to other countries, along with the obstacles that accompany it.

Chapter 10

Statistics on household composition, marriage, divorce, and adoption in the United States have been updated. Kathryn Edin's research on the elements of family life in poor African American communities sheds further light on African American family structures. Updated information on the legalization and perceptions of gay marriage in the United States and the repeal of the Defense of Marriage Act has been included.

ACKNOWLEDGMENTS

You May Ask Yourself originated in the Introduction to Sociology course that I have taught on and off since the mid-1990s at New York University, Yale University, and Columbia University. However, the process of writing it made me feel as if I were learning to be a sociologist all over again. For example, I never taught religion, methodology, or the sociology of education. But instructors who reviewed the manuscript requested that these topics be covered, so with the assistance of an army of graduate students who really ought to be recognized as coauthors, I got to work. The experience was invaluable, and in a way, I finally feel like a card-carrying sociologist, having acquired at last a bird's-eye view of my colleagues' work. I consider it a great honor to be able to put my little spin (or filter) on the field in this way, to be able not just to influence the few hundred intro students I teach each year, but to excite (I hope) and instill the enthusiasm I didn't get to experience until graduate school in students who may be just a few months out of high school (if that).

I mentioned that the graduate students who helped me create this book were really more like coauthors, ghost writers, or perhaps law clerks. Law clerks do much of the writing of legal opinions for judges, but only a judge's name graces a decision. I asked Norton to allow more coauthors, but they declined—perhaps understandably, given how long such a list would be—so I will take this opportunity to thank my students and hope that you are still reading this preface.

The original transcription of my lectures that formed the basis of this text was completed by Carse Ramos, who also worked on assembling the glossary and drafted some parts of various chapters, such as sections in the economic sociology chapter, as well as some text in the chapters on authority and deviance. She also served as an all-around editor. Ashley Mears did the heavy lifting on the race, gender, family, and religion chapters. Amy LeClair took the lead on methods, culture, groups and networks, socialization, and health. Jennifer Heerwig cobbled together the chapter on authority and the state and deviance (a nice combo), while her officemate Brian McCabe whipped up the chapter on science, technology, and the environment and the one on social movements. Melissa Velez wrote the first draft of the education chapter (and a fine one at that). Michael McCarthy did the same for the stratification chapter. Devyani Prabhat helped revise the social movements chapter. My administrative assistant, Amelia Branigan, served as fact checker, editor, and box drafter while running a department, taking the GREs, and writing and submitting her own graduate applications. When Amelia had to decamp for Northwestern University to pursue her own doctorate, Lauren Marten took over the job of chasing down obscure references, fact-checking, and proofreading. Alexandre Frenette drafted the questions and activities in the Practice sections at the end of each chapter.

For the Second Edition, much of the work to integrate the interview transcripts and update material based on reviewer feedback fell to a great extent on the shoulders of Laura Norén, a fantastic New York University graduate student who has worked on topics as far ranging as public toilets (with my colleague Harvey Molotch) to how symphonies and designers collaborate (as part of her dissertation). I hope Laura will find her crash-course overview of sociology useful at some point in what promises to be a productive and exciting scholarly career.

When it was time to begin the Third Edition, the updating of all the statistics, fact-checking, and so on that is the bread and butter of a revision fell upon the capable shoulders of Emi Nakazato, who though trained as a social worker in graduate school, adeptly pivoted to that field's cousin, sociology.

For the Fourth Edition, Laura Norén returned as the research assistant. With her prior experience she picked up the task ably without dropping a beat.

In addition to the students who have worked with me on the book, I need to give shouts out to all the top-notch scholars who found time in their busy schedules to sit down with me and do on-camera interviews: Julia Adams, Andrew Cherlin, Nitsan Chorev, Susan Crawford, Matthew Desmond, Mitchell Duneier, Paula England, John Evans, Michael Gaddis, David Grusky, Michael Hout, Shamus Khan, Annette Lareau, Jennifer Lee, Ka Liu, Douglas McAdam, Ashley Mears, Steven Morgan, Alondra Nelson, Devah Pager, Nathan Palmer, C. J. Pascoe, Frances Fox Piven, Allison Pugh, Jen'nan Read, Victor Rios, Jeffrey Sachs, Mario Luis Small, Duncan Watts, and Robb Willer. The filmmaking, editing, and postproduction were done by Erica Rothman at Nightlight Productions with the assistance of Jim Haverkamp, Kevin Wells, Saul Rouda, Dimitriy Khavin, and Arkadiy Ugorskiy. This was no easy task, because we wanted a bunch of cuts ranging from 30-second sound bites to television-show-length segments of 22 minutes. Although a bunch of interviews with academic social scientists on topics ranging from estimating the effects of Catholic schools on student outcomes to the political economy of global trade to the social contagion of autism are not likely to win any Emmys or rock the Nielsens (with the possible exception of the one on college sex), it was certainly one of the most exciting highlights in my sociological career to host this makeshift talk show of sorts on such a wide range of interesting topics. (If only more of our public discourse would dig into issues in the way that we did in these interviews, our society and governance would be in better shape—if I do say so myself!)

Meanwhile, many thanks to Kendall and Annie Madden, who did the transcriptions of the interviews so that they could be seamlessly migrated from video to the pages herein.

I also relied on a number of scholars who generously read chapters of this book and offered valuable feedback, criticisms, and suggestions:

REVIEWERS FOR THE FOURTH EDITION

Mark Austin, University of Louisville

Tamara Luque Black, University of California, Los Angeles

David Brunsma, Virginia Polytechnic Institute and State University

Walter Carroll, Bridgewater State University

Susan Cody-Rydzewski, Georgia Perimeter College

Nicole Cousin-Gossett, University of Maryland, Baltimore County

April Cubbage-Vega, Saddleback College

Amy Donley, University of Central Florida

Gianna Durso-Finley, Mercer County Community College

Michael Fraleigh, Bryant University

Selina Gallo-Cruz, College of the Holy Cross

Matthew Green, College of DuPage

Peter Hart-Brinson, University of Wisconsin–Eau Claire

Kathleen Holmes, Darton State College

Amy Holzgang, Cerritos College

Joyce Johnson, Santa Rosa Junior College

Tracy Xavia Karner, University of Houston

Zeynep Kilic, University of Alaska, Anchorage

Kyle Knight, University of Alabama in Huntsville

Jason Leiker, Utah State University

Olena Leipnik, Sam Houston State University

Michael P. Masters, Montana Tech

Nels Paulson, University of Wisconsin–Stout

Laura Pecenco, University of California, San Diego

Andrew Prelog, Sam Houston State University

Elizabeth Scheel-Keita, St. Cloud State University

Richard Sullivan, Illinois State University

Melissa Swauger, Indiana University of Pennsylvania

Lisa Tracy, Rhodes State College

Jonathan Varhola, Wright State University

Tim Wadsworth, University of Colorado, Boulder

Christine Winter, Southwestern College

REVIEWERS FOR THE THIRD EDITION

Orit Avishai, Fordham University

Carl Backman, Auburn University

Nielan Barnes, California State University, Long Beach

Renee Beard, College of the Holy Cross

Gayle Gordon Bouzard, Texas State University

Andrea Brenner, American University

Jeneve Brooks, Troy University

Victoria Carty, Chapman University

Susan Cody-Rydzewski, Georgia Perimeter College

Carolyn Corrado, State University of New York–Albany

John Curra, Eastern Kentucky University

Gayle D'Andrea, J. Sargeant Reynolds Community College

Regina Davis-Sowers, Santa Clara University

Sophia DeMasi, Montgomery County Community College

Daniel Dexheimer, Santa Clara University

Lynda Dickson, University of Colorado

Gianna Durso-Finley, Mercer County Community College

Kathryn Fox, University of Vermont

Duane Gill, Oklahoma State University

Keisha Goode, City College of New York

Heather Griffiths, Fayetteville State University

Charles Hanna, Duquesne University

Bruce Haynes, University of California, Davis

Kalyn Heald, Northwest Arkansas Community College

Druann Heckert, Fayetteville State University

Larry Hunt, University of Maryland, College Park

Jack King, Northern Illinois University

Roger Klomegah, Fayetteville State University

Rosalind Kopfstein, Western Connecticut State University

Jamee Kristen, Portland Community College

Timothy Kubal, California State University, Fresno

Liza Kuecker, Western New Mexico University

Jenifer Kunz, West Texas A&M University

Jennifer Lerner, Northern Virginia Community College

Ho Hon Leung, State University of New York–Oneonta

Carlos Lopez, Chemeketa Community College

Clara Magliola, Chapman University

Helen Mederer, University of Rhode Island

Joan Meyers, Rutgers University

Linda Morrison, Duquesne University

Geoffrey Moss, Temple University

Ryan Orr, Millersville University

Aurea Osgood, Winona State University

Joshua Packard, Midwestern State University

Nathan Palmer, Georgia Southern University

Paul Prew, Minnesota State University, Mankato

Rachel Zimmer Schneider, University of Akron

Jerald Schrimsher, Southern Illinois University Carbondale

Ben Shirley, Alamance Community College

Sheryl Skaggs, University of Texas at Dallas

Carrie Smith, Millersville University

Tomecia Sobers, Fayetteville Technical Community College

Ann Stein, College of Charleston

Cat Steinhauer, South Plains College

Ann Strahm, California State University, Stanislaus

Linda Vang, Fresno City College

Steven Vassar, Minnesota State University, Mankato

Robert Wahl, Pennsylvania State University

Angela Ware, Auburn University

Sharon Weiss, Truckee Meadows Community College

KC Williams, Coastal Carolina University

Robert Wonser, College of the Canyons

James Wright, Chattanooga State College

Luis Zanartu, Sacramento City College

REVIEWERS FOR THE SECOND EDITION

Christopher Armstrong, Bloomsburg University

Ingrid Castro, Northeastern Illinois University

Jennifer Chernega, Winona State University

Stacia Creek, Southern Illinois University

Michael Cuckler, Asbury College

Marianne Cutler, East Stroudsburg University

Martine Delannay, Madison Area Technical College

James Dowd, University of Georgia

Mark Edwards, Oregon State University

James Elliott, University of Oregon

Colleen Eren, Hunter College

Sally Gallagher, Oregon State University

Fang Gong, Ball State University

Edward Gott, Northeast Wisconsin Technical College

Jennifer Hartsfield, University of Oklahoma

Bruce Haynes, University of California, Davis

Gesine Hearn, Idaho State University

Teri Hibbert, University of Texas, El Paso

Lori Hunter, University of Colorado, Boulder

Susan Janssen, University of Minnesota, Duluth

Laura Jennings, University of South Carolina, Upstate

Ellis Jones, University of California, Davis

Eric Kaldor, State University of New York–Brockport

Rosalind Kopfstein, Western Connecticut State University

Annette Lareau, University of Pennsylvania

Kevin Leicht, University of Iowa

Jennifer Lena, Vanderbilt University

Steve Lippman, Miami University

D. A. Lopez, California State University, Northridge

Robert Mackin, Texas A&M University

Cheryl Maes, University of Nevada, Reno

Joan Manley, Florida Gulf Coast University

Joan Meyers, University of California, Davis

Wendy Moore, Texas A&M University

David Nicholson, University of Oklahoma

Donald Nielsen, College of Charleston

Marjukka Ollilainen, Weber State University

Michael Perez, California State University, Fullerton

Richard Petts, Ball State University

Nancy Plankey Videla, Texas A&M University

John Poindexter, West Shore College

Gabrielle Raley, University of California, Los Angeles

Julie Rauli, Wilson College

Alden Roberts, Texas Tech University

Olga Rowe, Oregon State University

Jennifer Schultz, University of Arizona

Julie Setele, University of California, Davis

Linda Sibler, Union College

Kathleen Slevin, College of William and Mary

Marshall Smith, University of Colorado, Boulder

Katherine Stovel, University of Washington

Steve Swinford, Montana State University

Ronald Thrasher, Oklahoma State University

Amy Traver, Queensborough Community College

Diana Tumminia, California State University, Sacramento

Glenda Walden, University of Colorado, Boulder

Melissa Weiner, Quinnipiac University

Susan Wortmann, University of Nebraska, Lincoln

REVIEWERS FOR THE FIRST EDITION

Rebecca Adams, University of North Carolina at Greensboro

Robert Aponte, Indiana University–Purdue University Indianapolis

Nina Bandelj, University of California, Irvine

Donna Barnes, University of Wyoming

Nielan Barnes, California State University, Long Beach

Marshall Battani, Grand Valley State University

Joel Best, University of Delaware

Melissa Bonstead-Bruns, University of Wisconsin–Eau Claire

Dan Brook, San José State University

Ernesto Bustillos, Pasadena City College

Patricia Campion, Tennessee Tech University

Victoria Carty, Chapman University

Ursula Castella, Ohio University

Pam Chao, American River College

Brenda Chappell, University of Central Oklahoma

Theresa Davidson, Samford University

Patricia Ewick, Clark University

Kathleen J. Fitzgerald, Columbia College

Nicole Flynn, University of South Alabama

Doug Forbes, University of Wisconsin–Stevens Point

David Friedrichs, University of Scranton

Bob Girvan, Clarion University of Pennsylvania

Jeremy Hein, University of Wisconsin–Eau Claire

Christopher Henke, Colgate University
Terrence Hill, University of Miami
Sue Hinze, Case Western Reserve
Robert Hironimus-Wendt, Western Illinois
    State University
Abdy Javadzadeh, Florida International
    University
Robert Keel, University of Missouri–
    St. Louis
Markus Kemmelmeier, University of
    Nevada, Reno
Jerry Koch, Texas Tech University
Samantha Kwan, University of Houston
Bill Lockhart, New Mexico State University
    at Alamogordo
Gerardo Marti, Davidson College
Michael Massoglia, Pennsylvania State
    University
Dennis McGrath, Community College of
    Philadelphia
Edward Morris, Ohio University
Michael Oldani, University of Wisconsin–
    White Water
Kirsten Olsen, Anoka-Ramsey Community
    College
Colin Olson, University of New Mexico
Paul Olson, Briar Cliff University
Krista Paulsen, University of North Florida

Christine Plumeri, Monroe Community
    College
Brian Powell, Indiana University
    Bloomington
Ralph Pyle, Michigan State University
John S. Rice, University of North Carolina
    at Wilmington
Bryan Robinson, State University of
    New York–Albany
Sarah Rusche, North Carolina State
    University
Luis Salinas, University of Houston
Lafleur Small, Wright State University
Regina Smardon, University of
    Pennsylvania
Travis Vande Berg, Ithaca College
Sandra Way, New Mexico State University
Michael Weissbuch, Xavier University
William J. Weston, Centre College
Jerry Williams, Stephen F. Austin University
Howie Winant, University of California,
    Santa Barbara
Rowan Wolf, Portland Community College
Robert Wood, Rutgers University–Camden
Matt Wray, University of Nevada, Las
    Vegas
Richard Zamoff, George Washington
    University

As you can see, it took a village to raise this child. But that's not all. At Norton, I need to thank, first and foremost, Karl Bakeman, the editor into whose lap this project landed (after having passed through the hands of Steve Dunn and Melea Seward). He deserves great credit for brainstorming with me how to do something novel for the fourth edition (hence the "Sociology on the Street" videos) and then convincing the Norton board to dive headfirst into this multimedia experiment of sorts. In addition, I am grateful to associate editor Nicole Sawa, editorial assistant Lindsey Thomas, project editor Jen Barnhardt, and production manager Eric Pier-Hocking, who handled every stage of the manuscript and managed to keep the innumerable pieces of the book moving through production. I also must thank Norton's sociology marketing manager Julia Hall and the social science sales specialists Jonathan Mason, Roy McClymont, and Julie Sindel. Much of *You May Ask Yourself*'s success is due to their boundless energy and enthusiasm. Finally, I owe a special thanks to Eileen Connell, Laura Musich, Michael Jaoui, and Alice Garrard. They are responsible for putting together all of the video and electronic resources that accompany *You May Ask Yourself*. When it comes to developing new digital products to help instructors teach in the classroom or teach online, they are the most creative and resourceful folks working in college publishing today.

Core Fourth Edition

You May Ask Yourself

AN INTRODUCTION
TO THINKING LIKE
A SOCIOLOGIST

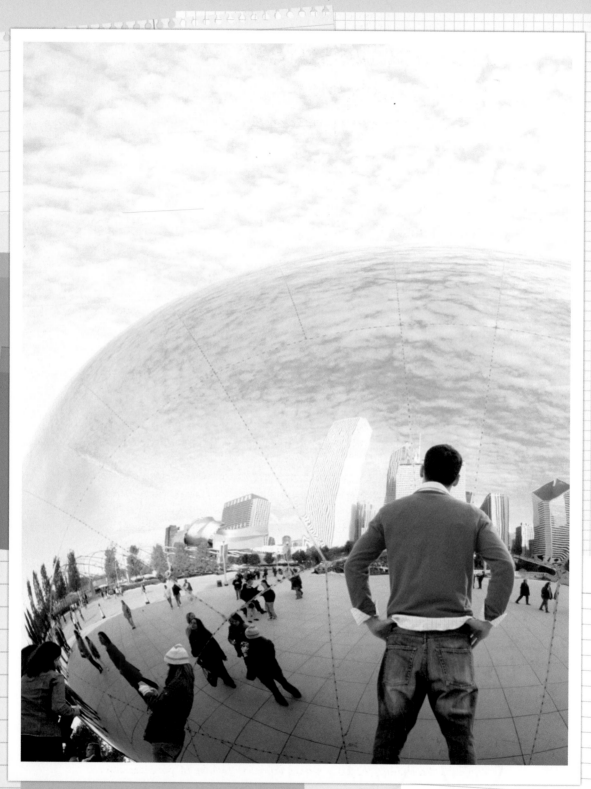

Thinking like a sociologist means looking at the world around you in a new way. Challenge conventional wisdom and question what most people take for granted.

1 The Sociological Imagination: An Introduction

If you want to understand sociology, why don't we start with you. Why are you taking this class and reading this textbook? It's as good a place to start as any—after all, sociology is the study of human society, and there is the sociology of sports, of religion, of music, of medicine, even a sociology of sociologists. So why not start, by way of example, with the sociology of an introduction to sociology?

For example, why are you bent over this page? Take a moment to write down the reasons. Maybe you have heard of sociology and want to learn about it. Maybe you are merely following the suggestion of a parent, guidance counselor, or academic advisor. The course syllabus probably indicates that for the first week of class, you are required to read this chapter. So there are at least two good reasons to be reading this introduction to sociology text.

Let's take the first response, "I want to educate myself about sociology." That's a fairly good reason, but may I then ask why you are taking the class rather than simply reading the book on your own? Furthermore, assuming that you're paying tuition, why are you doing so? If you really are here for the education, let me suggest an alternative: Grab one of the course schedules at your college, decide which courses to take, and just show up! Most introductory classes are so large that nobody notices if an extra student attends. If it is a smaller, more advanced seminar, ask the professor if you can audit it. I have never known a faculty member who checks that all class attendees are legitimate students at the college—in fact, we're happy when students *do* show up to class. An auditor, someone who is there for the sake of pure learning,

Sociology the study of human society.

and who won't be grade grubbing or submitting papers to be marked, is pure gold to any professor interested in imparting knowledge for learning's sake.

You know the rest of the drill: Do all the reading (you can usually access the required texts for free at the library), do your homework, and participate in class discussion. About the only thing you won't get at the end of the course is a grade. So give yourself one. As a matter of fact, once you have compiled enough credits and written a senior thesis, award yourself a diploma. Why not? You will probably have received a better education than most students—certainly better than I did in college.

But what are you going to do with a homemade diploma? You are not just here to learn; you wish to obtain an actual college degree. Why exactly do you want a college degree? Students typically answer that they have to get one in order to earn more money. Others may say that they need credentials to get the job they want. And some students are in college because they don't know what else to do. Whatever your answer, the fact that you asked yourself a question about something you may have previously taken for granted is the first step in thinking like a sociologist. "Thinking like a sociologist" means applying analytical tools to something you have always done without much conscious thought—like opening this book or taking this class. It requires you to reconsider your assumptions about society and question what you have taken for granted in order to better understand the world around you. In other words, thinking like a sociologist means *making the familiar strange*.

This chapter introduces you to the sociological approach to the world. Specifically, you will learn about the *sociological imagination*, a term coined by C. Wright Mills. We'll return to the question "Why go to college?" and apply our sociological imaginations to it. You will also learn what a social institution is. The chapter concludes by looking at the sociology of sociology—that is, the history of sociology and where it fits within the social sciences.

The Sociological Imagination

Sociological imagination the ability to connect the most basic, intimate aspects of an individual's life to seemingly impersonal and remote historical forces.

More than 50 years ago, the sociologist C. Wright Mills argued that in the effort to think critically about the social world around us, we need to use our sociological imagination, the ability to see the connections between our personal experience and the larger forces of history. This is just what we are doing when we question this textbook, this course, and college in general. In *The Sociological Imagination* (1959), Mills describes it this way: "The first fruit of this imagination—and the first lesson of the social science that embodies it—is the idea that the individual can understand his own experience and gauge his own fate only by locating himself within his period, that he can know his own chances in life only by becoming aware of those of all individuals in his circumstances. In many ways it is a terrible lesson; in many ways a magnificent one." The terrible part of the lesson is to make our own lives ordinary—that is, to see our intensely personal, private experience of life as typical of the period and place in which we live. This can also serve as a source of comfort, however, helping us to realize that we are not alone in our experiences, whether they involve our alienation from the increasingly dog-eat-dog capitalism of modern America, the peculiar combination of intimacy and dissociation that we may experience on the Internet, or the ways that nationality or geography affect our life choices. The sociological imagination does not just leave us hanging with these feelings of recognition, however. Mills writes that it also "enables [us] to take into account how individuals, in the welter of their daily experience, often become falsely conscious of their social positions." The sociological imagination thus allows us to see the veneer of social life for what it is, and to step outside the "trap" of rapid historical change in order to comprehend what is occurring in our world and the social foundations that may be shifting right under our feet. As Mills wrote after World War II, a time of enormous political, social, and technological change, "The sociological imagination enables us to grasp history and biography and the relations between the two within society. That is its task and its promise. To recognize this task and this promise is the mark of the classic social analyst."

Mills offered his readers a way to stop and take stock of their lives in light of all that had happened in the previous decade. Of course, we almost always

Sociologist C. Wright Mills commuting to Columbia University on his motorcycle. How does Mills's concept of the sociological imagination help us make the familiar strange?

Have you ever been to a foreign country, noticed how many little things were different, and wondered why? Have you ever been to a church of a different denomination—or a different religion altogether—from your own? Or have you been a fish out of water in some other way? The only guy attending a social event for women, perhaps? Or the only person from out of state in your dorm? If you have experienced that fish-out-of-water feeling, then you have, however briefly, engaged your sociological imagination. By shifting your social environment enough to be in a position where you are not able to take everything for granted, you are forced to see the connections between particular historical paths taken (and not taken) and how you live your daily life. You may, for instance, wonder why there are bidets in most European bathrooms and not in American ones. Or why people waiting in lines in the Middle East typically stand closer to each other than they do in Europe or America. Or why, in some rural Chinese societies, many generations of a family sleep in the same bed. If you are able to resist your initial impulses toward xenophobia (feelings that may result from the discomfort of facing a different reality), then you are halfway to understanding other people's lifestyles as no more or less sensible than your own. Once you have truly adopted the sociological imagination, you can start questioning the links between your personal experience and the particulars of a given society without ever leaving home.

In the following excerpt of dialogue from Quentin Tarantino's 1994 film *Pulp Fiction*, the character Vincent tells Jules about the "little differences" between life in the United States and life in Europe.

VINCENT: It's the little differences. A lotta the same shit we got here, they got there, but there they're a little different.

JULES: Example?

VINCENT: Well, in Amsterdam, you can buy beer in a movie theater. And I don't mean in a paper cup either. They give you a glass of beer, like in a bar. In Paris, you can buy beer at McDonald's. Also, you know what they call a Quarter Pounder with Cheese in Paris?

JULES: They don't call it a Quarter Pounder with Cheese?

VINCENT: No, they got the metric system there, they wouldn't know what the fuck a Quarter Pounder is.

JULES: What'd they call it?

VINCENT: Royale with Cheese.

Vincent Vega (John Travolta) describes his visit to a McDonald's in Amsterdam
to Jules Winnfield (Samuel L. Jackson).

JULES: (repeating) Royale with Cheese. What'd they call a Big Mac?
VINCENT: Big Mac's a Big Mac, but they call it Le Big Mac.
JULES: What do they call a Whopper?
VINCENT: I dunno, I didn't go into a Burger King. But you know what
             they put on french fries in Holland instead of ketchup?
JULES: What?
VINCENT: Mayonnaise.
JULES: Goddamn!
VINCENT: I seen 'em do it. And I don't mean a little bit on the side of
             the plate, they fuckin' drown 'em in it.
JULES: Uucccch!

Your job as a sociologist is to get into the mind-set that mayonnaise on
french fries, though it might seem disgusting at first, is not strange after
all, certainly no more so than ketchup.

feel that social change is fairly rapid and continually getting ahead of us. Think of the 1960s or even today, with the rise of the Internet and global terror threats. In retrospect, we consider the 1950s, the decade when Mills wrote his seminal work, to be a relatively placid time, when Americans experienced some relief from the change and strife of World War II and the Great Depression. But Mills believed the profound sense of alienation experienced by many during the postwar period was a result of the change that had immediately preceded it.

Another way to think about the sociological imagination is to ask ourselves what we take to be natural that actually isn't. For example, let's return to the question "Why go to college?" Sociologists and economists have shown that the financial benefits of education—particularly higher education—appear to be increasing. They refer to this as the "returns to schooling." In today's economy, the median (i.e., typical) annual income for a high-school graduate is $33,176; for those with a bachelor's degree, it is $54,756 (2011 data; Bureau of Labor Statistics, 2013a). That $21,580 annual advantage seems like a good deal, but is it really? Let's shift gears and do a little math.

What Are the True Costs and Returns of College?

Now that you are thinking like a sociologist, let's compare the true cost of going to college for four years to calling the whole thing off and taking a full-time job right after high school. First, there is the tuition to consider. Let's assume for the sake of argument you are paying $8,000 per year for tuition and another $9,000 for fees and room and board. That's a lot less than what most private four-year colleges cost, but about average for in-state tuition at a state school. (Community colleges, by contrast, are usually much cheaper, especially because they tend to be commuter schools whose students live off-campus, but they typically do not offer a four-year bachelor's degree.)

In making the decision to attend college, you are agreeing to pay $17,000 this year, something like $17,680 next year, 4 percent more the following year, and another 4 percent on top of that amount in your senior year. The $17,000 you have to pay right now is what hurts the most, because costs in the future are worth less than expenses today. Money in the future is worth less than money in hand for several reasons. The first is inflation. We all know that money is not what it used to be. In fact, taking into account the standard inflation rate—as measured by the government's Consumer Price Index—it took about $16 in 2011 to equal the buying power of a single dollar back in 1940 (Sahr, 2010). The second reason that money today is worth more than money tomorrow is that we could invest the money today to make more tomorrow.

Using a standard formula to adjust for inflation and bring future amounts into current dollars, we can determine that paying out $17,000 this year and the higher amounts over the next three years is equivalent to paying $70,023 in one lump sum today; this would be the direct cost of attending college. Indirect costs—so-called opportunity costs—exist as well, such as the costs associated with the amount of time you are devoting to school. Taking into account the typical wage for a high-school graduate, not counting differences by gender, age, or level of experience, we can calculate that if you worked full time instead of going to college, you would make $33,176 this year. Thus, we find that the present value of the total wages lost over the next four years by choosing full-time school over full-time work is $132,704. Add these opportunity costs to the direct costs of tuition, and we get $202,727.

Next we need to calculate the "returns to schooling." For the sake of simplicity, we will ignore the fact that the differences between high-school graduates and college graduates change over time—given years of experience and the ups and downs of the economy. Instead, we will regard the $54,756 annual earnings figure for college graduates as fixed and subtract from that amount the $33,176 earned by the typical high-school graduate, which yields a net difference of $21,580. But remember, you would not start earning this money for four years. So the real difference is $21,580 four years from now plus $21,580 five years from now and so on, until you leave the labor force. Assuming that you attend college for only four years and retire at 65, you will have worked 43 years (high-school grads will be in the work force for 47 years because they get a four-year head start). When we compare your college-degree-holding lifetime earnings to the lifetime earnings of someone who has only a high-school education, we find that with a college degree you will make $795,236 more than someone who went straight to work after high school (Figure 1.1). (To make matters more straightforward, we are conveniently ignoring the fact that future money is inherently worth less than present money in economic decision making.) On top of this substantial financial return to schooling, one economist found that those with college degrees were happier, healthier, and less likely to get divorced than their high-school-educated peers, even after controlling for income (Oreopoulos & Salvanes, 2009).

But wait a minute: How do we know for sure that college really mattered in the equation? Individuals who finish college might earn more because they actually learned something and obtained a degree, or—a big or—they might earn more regardless of the college experience because people who stay in school (1) are innately smarter, (2) know how to work the system, (3) come from wealthier families, (4) can delay gratification, (5) are more efficient at managing their time, or (6) all of the above—take your pick. In other words, Yale graduates might not have needed to go to college to earn higher wages; they might have been successful anyway.

Maybe, then, the success stories of Mark Zuckerberg, Steve Jobs, Lady Gaga, and other college dropouts don't cut against the grain so sharply after all. Maybe they were the savvy ones: Convinced of their ability to make it on their own, thanks to the social cues they received (including the fact that they had

Figure 1.1: Returns to Schooling

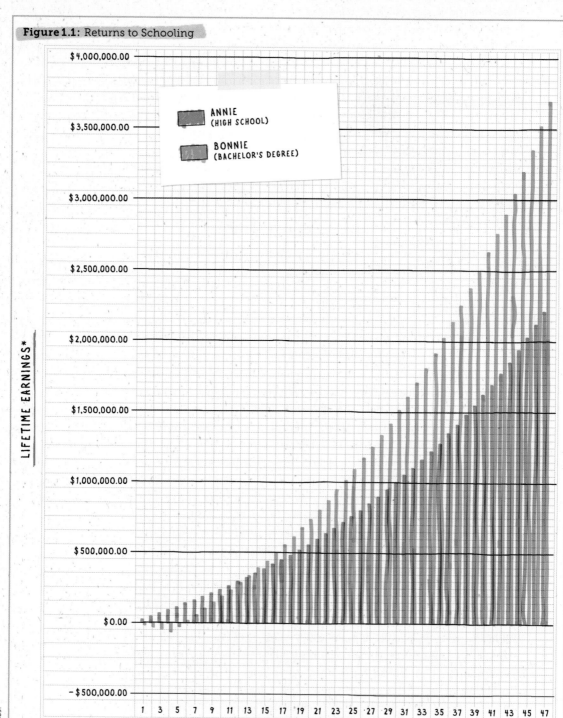

LIFETIME EARNINGS*

ANNIE
(HIGH SCHOOL)

BONNIE
(BACHELOR'S DEGREE)

$4,000,000.00

$3,500,000.00

$3,000,000.00

$2,500,000.00

$2,000,000.00

$1,500,000.00

$1,000,000.00

$500,000.00

$0.00

– $500,000.00

1 3 5 7 9 11 13 15 17 19 21 23 25 27 29 31 33 35 37 39 41 43 45 47

NUMBER OF YEARS SINCE HIGH SCHOOL GRADUATION

* This set of hypothetical women–Annie and Bonnie–live in a world that is not quite like reality. We did not flatten Annie's trajectory to account for the fact that high school diploma holders are more likely to experience periods of forced part-time work and/or unemployment. We also assumed the same rate of income increase over time (i.e.,raises) for these two, although high school diploma holders are more likely to experience wage stagnation than college degree holders.

Source: Murray, 2009.

Two famous college dropouts. Facebook CEO Mark Zuckerberg (left) attended Harvard but dropped out before graduating. John Mackey (right) quit university before founding Whole Foods.

been admitted to college), they decided that they wouldn't wait four years to try to achieve success. They opted to just go for it right then and there. College's "value added," they might have concluded, was marginal at best.

Getting That "Piece of Paper"

Even if college turns out to matter in the end, does it make a difference because of the learning that takes place there or because of our credentialist society that it aids and abets? The answer to this question has enormous implications for what education means in our society. Imagine, for example, a society where people become doctors not by doing well on the SATs, going to college, taking premed courses, acing the MCATs, and then spending more time in the classroom. Instead, the route to becoming a doctor—among the most prestigious and highly paid occupations in our society—starts with emptying bedpans as a nurse's aide and working your way up through the ranks of registered nurse, apprentice physician, and so forth; finally, after years of on-the-job training, you achieve the title of doctor. Social theorist Randall Collins has proposed just such a medical education system in the controversial *The Credential Society: A Historical Sociology of Education and Stratification* (1979), which argues that the expansion of higher education has merely resulted in a ratcheting up of credentialism and expenditures on formal education rather than reflecting

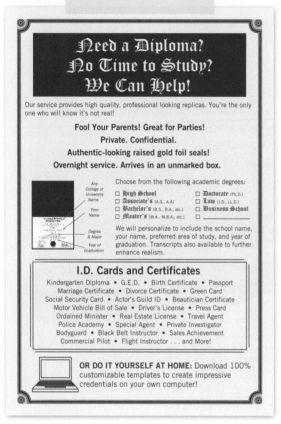

College-campus bulletin boards are covered with advertisements like this one promoting websites that generate diplomas. Why are these fake diplomas not worth it?

any true societal need for more formal education or opening up opportunity to more people.

If Collins is correct and credentials are what matter most, then isn't there a cheaper, faster way to get them? In fact, all you need are $29.95 and a little guts, and you can receive a diploma from one of the many online sites that promise either legitimate degrees from nonaccredited colleges or a college diploma from any school of your choosing. Thus, why not save four years and lots of money and obtain your credentials immediately?

Obviously, universities have incentives to prevent such websites from undermining their monopoly on degree-conferring ability. So they rely on a number of other social institutions, ranging from copyright law to the local police force, to enforce this monopoly power. However, I have no knowledge of anyone—employer, school, landlord—ever verifying my educational claims. That is, no one has ever checked to make sure that I attended college or graduate school. They have taken my résumé at face value. (On the other hand, colleges do check that applicants have completed high school.)

But there are also informal mechanisms by which universities are protected that may be more important than any formal checks. First, there is the university's alumni network. Potential employers rarely call a university's registrar to make sure you graduated, but they will expect you to talk a bit about your college experience. If your interviewer is an alumnus or otherwise familiar with the institution, you might also be expected to talk about what dorm you lived in, reminisce about a particularly dramatic homecoming game, or gripe about an especially unreasonable professor. If you slip up on any of this information, suspicions will grow, and then people might call to check on your graduation status. Perhaps there are some good reasons not to opt for that $29.95 degree and to pay the costs of college after all.

→ What Is a Social Institution?

The university, then, is more than just a printing press that churns out diplomas, and, for that matter, it does not merely impart formal knowledge. It fulfills a variety of roles and provides links to many other societal institutions. For example, a college is an institution that acts as a gatekeeper to what are considered legitimate forms of educational advantage by certifying what is legitimate knowledge. It is an institution that segregates great swaths of the population by age. (You won't find a more age-segregated environment than a four-year college; it even beats a retirement home in having the smallest amount of age variation in its client population.) A college is a proprietary brand that is marketed on sweatshirts and mugs and through televised sporting events. Last but not least, it is an informal set of stories told within a social network of students, faculty, administrators, alumni, and other relevant individuals.

This last part of the definition is key to understanding one of sociology's most important concepts, the social institution. A social institution is a complex group of interdependent positions that, together, perform a social role and reproduce themselves over time. A way to think of these social positions is as a set of stories we tell ourselves; social relations are a network of ties; and the social role is a grand narrative that unifies these stories within the network. In order to think sociologically about social institutions, you need to think of them not as monolithic, uniform, stable entities—things that "just are"— but as institutions constructed within a dense network of other social institutions and meanings. Sound confusing? Bear with me as I provide an example: I teach at New York University, or NYU. What exactly is the social institution known as NYU? It is not the collection of buildings I frequent. It certainly cannot be the people who work there, or even the students, because they change over time, shifting in and out through recruitment and retirement, admission and graduation. We might thus conclude that a social institution is just a name. However, an institution can change its name and still retain its social identity. Duke University was once called Normal College and then Trinity College, yet it remains the same institution.

Of course, all such transitions involving a change of name, location, mission, and so on require a great deal of effort and agreement among interested parties. In some cases, changes in personnel, function, or location may be too much for a social institution to sustain, causing it to die out and be replaced by something that is considered new. Sometimes institutions even try to rupture their identity intentionally. Tobacco company Philip Morris had received such bad press as a cigarette manufacturer for so long that it changed its name to Altria, hoping to start fresh and shake off the negative connotations of its previous embodiment. For that effort to succeed, the narrative of Philip Morris circulating in social networks had to die out without being connected to Altria.

This grand narrative that constitutes social identity is nothing more than the sum of individual stories told between pairs of individuals. Think about your relationship to your parents. You have a particular story that you tell if asked to describe your relationship with your mother. She also has a story. Your story may change slightly, depending on whom you are talking to; you may add some details or leave out others. Your other relatives have stories about your mother and her relationship to you. So do her friends and yours. Anyone who

Social institution a complex group of interdependent positions that, together, perform a social role and reproduce themselves over time; also defined in a narrow sense as any institution in a society that works to shape the behavior of the groups or people within it.

Tobacco company Philip Morris changed its name to Altria at a stockholders' meeting in January 2003.

knows her contributes to her social identity. The sum total of stories about your mom is the grand narrative of who she is.

All of this may seem like a fairly flimsy notion of how things operate in the social world, but even though any social identity boils down to a set of stories within a social network, that narrative is still hearty and robust. Imagine what it would take to change an identity. Let's say your mom is 50 years old. You want to make her 40 instead. You would not only have to convince her to refer constantly to herself as ten years younger; you would also have to get your other relatives and her friends to abide by this change. And it wouldn't stop there. You'd have to change official documents as well—her driver's license, passport, and so on. This is not so easily done. Even though your mother's identity (in this case her age, although the same logic can be extended to her name, ethnicity, and many other aspects of her identity) could be described as nothing more than an understanding between her, everyone who knows her, and the formal authorities, the matter is a fairly complicated one. If that sounds hard, just think about trying to change the identity of a major institution such as your university. You'd have to convince the board of directors, alumni, faculty, students, and everyone else who has a relationship to the school of the need for a change. Altering an identity is fairly difficult, even though it is ultimately nothing more than an idea.

I mentioned that if you wanted to change your mother's age, name, or race, you'd have to convince not only her friends but also the formal authorities, which are social institutions with their own logics and inertias. Let's take the example of college once again. Other than the informal ties of people who have a relationship to the grand narrative of a particular college, a number of social structures exist that make colleges, which are themselves made up of a series of stories within social networks, possible:

1. The *legal system* enforces copyright law, making fake diplomas illegitimate.

2. The *primary and secondary educational system* (i.e., K–12 schooling) prepares students both academically and culturally for college, as well as acting as

an extended screening and sorting mechanism to help determine who goes to college and to which one.

3. The *Educational Testing Service* and *ACT* are private companies that have a duopoly on the standardized tests that screen for college admission.

4. The *wage labor market* encompasses the entire economy that allows your teacher to be paid, not to mention the administrators, staff, and other outside contractors who maintain the intellectual, fiscal, and physical infrastructure of the school you attend.

5. *English*, although not the official language of the United States (there isn't one!), is the language in which instruction takes place at the majority of U.S. colleges. Language itself is a social phenomenon; some would argue that it is the basis for all of social life. But a given language is a particular outcome of political boundaries and historical struggles among various populations in the world. It is often said the only difference between a language and a dialect is that a language has an army to back it up. In other words, deciding whether a spoken tongue is a language or merely a dialect is a question of power and legitimacy.

Trying to understand social institutions such as the legal system, the labor market, or language itself is at the heart of sociological inquiry. Although social institutions shape every aspect of our behavior, they are not monolithic. In fact, every day we construct and change social institutions through ordinary interactions and the meanings we ascribe to them. By becoming aware of the intersections between social institutions and your life, you are already thinking like a sociologist.

The Sociology of Sociology

Now that we have an idea of how sociologists approach their analysis of the world, let's turn that lens, the sociological imagination, to sociology itself. As a formal field, sociology is a relatively young discipline. Numerous fields of inquiry exist, such as molecular genetics, radio astronomy, and computer science, that could not emerge until a certain technology was invented. Sociology might seem to fall outside this category, but to study society, we need not only a curious mind and a certain willingness but also the specific frame of reference—the lens—of the sociological imagination. The sociological imagination is a technology of sorts, a technology that could have developed only during a certain time. That time was, arguably, the nineteenth century, when the French scholar Auguste Comte (1798–1857) invented what he called "social physics" or "positivism."

Auguste Comte and the Creation of Sociology

According to Comte, positivism arose out of a need to make moral sense of the social order in a time of declining religious authority. Comte claimed that a secular basis for morality did indeed exist—that is, we could determine right and wrong without reference to higher powers or other religious concepts. And that was the job of the sociologist: to develop a secular morality. Comte further argued that human society had gone through three historical, epistemological stages. In the first, which he referred to as the theological stage, society

TWO CENTURIES OF SOCIOLOGY

| 1780 | 1785 | 1790 | 1795 | 1800 | 1805 | 1810 | 1815 |

1776–81
American War of Independence

1789–99
French Revolution

1802
Harriet Martineau born

1780s
Industrial Revolution begins

1798
Auguste Comte born

American War of Independence

Industrial Revolution

French Revolution

seemed to be the result of divine will. If you wanted to understand why kings ruled, why Europe used a feudal and guild system of labor, or why colonialism took root, the answer was that it was God's plan. To better understand God's plan and thus comprehend the logic of social life, scholars of the theological period might consult the Bible or other ecclesiastical texts. During stage two, the metaphysical stage according to Comte, Enlightenment thinkers such as Jean-Jacques Rousseau, John Stuart Mill, and Thomas Hobbes saw human-kind's behavior as governed by natural, biological instincts. To understand the nature of society—why things were the way they were—we needed to strip

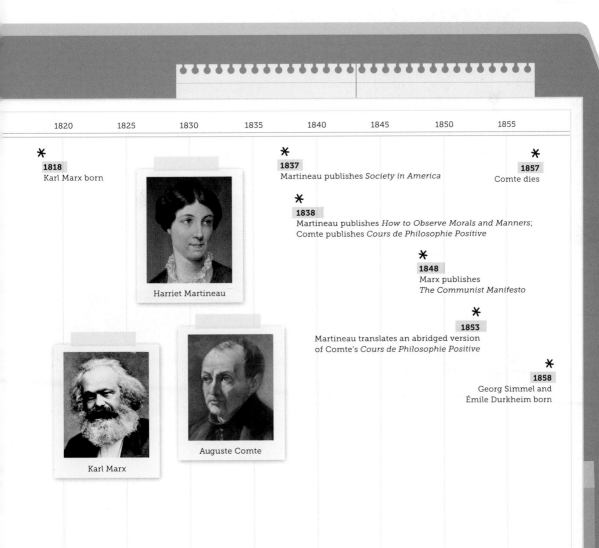

1820   1825   1830   1835   1840   1845   1850   1855

1818
Karl Marx born

1837
Martineau publishes *Society in America*

1857
Comte dies

1838
Martineau publishes *How to Observe Morals and Manners*; Comte publishes *Cours de Philosophie Positive*

1848
Marx publishes *The Communist Manifesto*

1853
Martineau translates an abridged version of Comte's *Cours de Philosophie Positive*

1858
Georg Simmel and Émile Durkheim born

Harriet Martineau

Karl Marx

Auguste Comte

away the layers of society to better comprehend how our basic drives and natural instincts governed and established the foundation for the surrounding world. Comte called the third and final stage of historical development the scientific stage. In this era, he claimed, we would develop a social physics of sorts in order to identify the scientific laws that govern human behavior. The analogy here is not theology or biology but rather physics. Comte was convinced that we could understand how social institutions worked (and didn't work), how we relate to one another (whether on an individual or group level), and the overall structure of societies if we merely ascertained their

TWO CENTURIES OF SOCIOLOGY

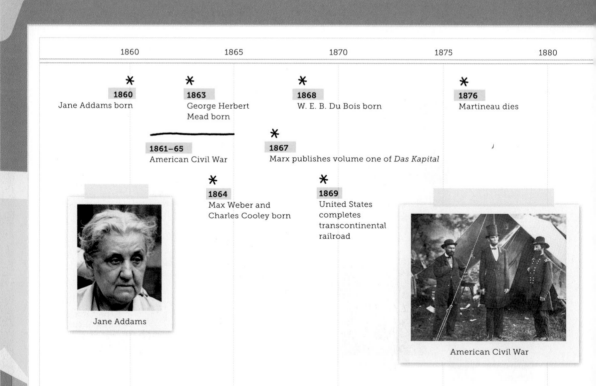

| 1860 | 1865 | 1870 | 1875 | 1880 |

1860
Jane Addams born

1863
George Herbert Mead born

1868
W. E. B. Du Bois born

1876
Martineau dies

1861–65
American Civil War

1867
Marx publishes volume one of *Das Kapital*

1864
Max Weber and Charles Cooley born

1869
United States completes transcontinental railroad

Jane Addams

American Civil War

"equations" or underlying logic. Needless to say, most sociologists today are not so optimistic.

Harriet Martineau Harriet Martineau (1802–1876), an English social theorist, was the first to translate Comte into English. In fact, Comte assigned her translations to his students, claiming that they were better than the original. She also wrote important works of her own, including *Theory and Practice of Society in America* (1837), in which she describes our nation's physical and social aspects. She addressed topics ranging from the way we educate children (which, she

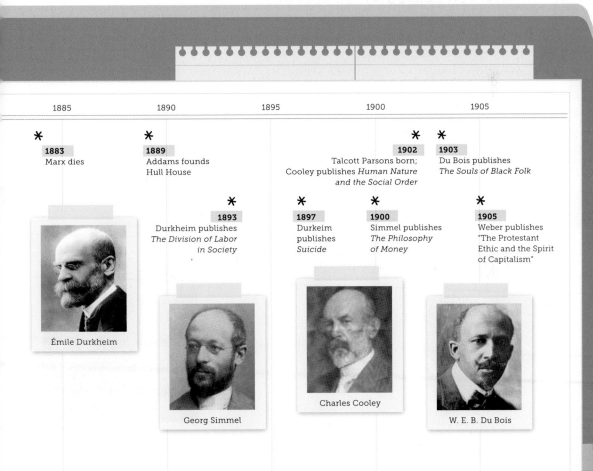

| 1885 | 1890 | 1895 | 1900 | 1905 |

1883
Marx dies

1889
Addams founds
Hull House

1902
Talcott Parsons born;
Cooley publishes *Human Nature
and the Social Order*

1903
Du Bois publishes
The Souls of Black Folk

1893
Durkheim publishes
*The Division of Labor
in Society*

1897
Durkeim
publishes
Suicide

1900
Simmel publishes
*The Philosophy
of Money*

1905
Weber publishes
"The Protestant
Ethic and the Spirit
of Capitalism"

Émile Durkheim

Georg Simmel

Charles Cooley

W. E. B. Du Bois

attests, affords parents too much control and doesn't ensure quality) to the relationship between the federal and state governments. She was also the author of the first methods book in the area of sociology, *How to Observe Morals and Manners* (1838), in which she took on the institution of marriage, claiming that it was based on an assumption of the inferiority of women. This critique, among other writings, suggests that Martineau should be considered one of the earliest feminist social scientists writing in the English language.

TWO CENTURIES OF SOCIOLOGY

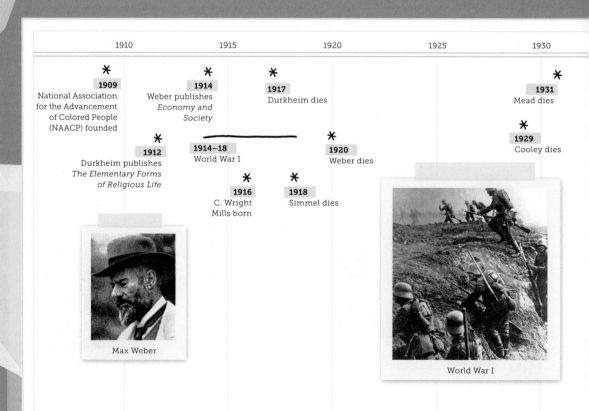

| 1910 | 1915 | 1920 | 1925 | 1930 |

1909
National Association for the Advancement of Colored People (NAACP) founded

1914
Weber publishes *Economy and Society*

1917
Durkheim dies

1931
Mead dies

1912
Durkheim publishes *The Elementary Forms of Religious Life*

1914–18
World War I

1920
Weber dies

1929
Cooley dies

1916
C. Wright Mills born

1918
Simmel dies

Max Weber

World War I

Classical Sociological Theory

Although Comte and Martineau preceded them, Karl Marx, Max Weber, and Émile Durkheim are often credited as the founding fathers of the sociological discipline. Some would add a fourth classical sociological theorist, Georg Simmel, to the triumvirate. A brief overview of each of their paradigms follows. We will return to the work of these thinkers throughout the book.

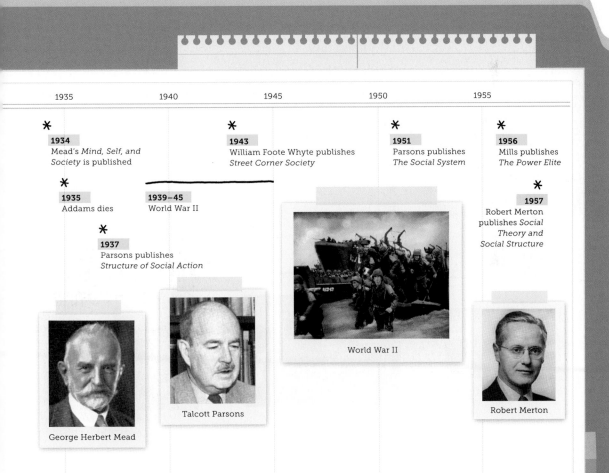

1935　　　　　1940　　　　　1945　　　　　1950　　　　　1955

1934
Mead's *Mind, Self, and Society* is published

1943
William Foote Whyte publishes *Street Corner Society*

1951
Parsons publishes *The Social System*

1956
Mills publishes *The Power Elite*

1935
Addams dies

1939–45
World War II

1957
Robert Merton publishes *Social Theory and Social Structure*

1937
Parsons publishes *Structure of Social Action*

World War II

George Herbert Mead

Talcott Parsons

Robert Merton

Karl Marx Karl Marx (1818–1883) is probably the most famous of the three early sociologists; from his surname the term *Marxism* (an ideological alternative to capitalism) derives, and his writings provided the theoretical basis for Communism. When Marx was a young man, he edited a newspaper that was suppressed by the Prussian government for its radicalism. Forced into exile, Marx settled in London, where he wrote his most important works. Marx was essentially a historian, but he did more than just chronicle events. He elaborated a theory of what drives history, now called historical materialism. Marx believed that it was primarily the conflicts between classes that drove social

TWO CENTURIES OF SOCIOLOGY

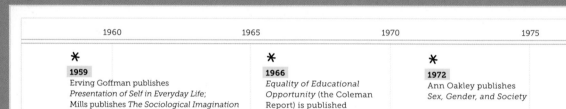

1960	1965	1970	1975

✳ 1959
Erving Goffman publishes
Presentation of Self in Everyday Life;
Mills publishes *The Sociological Imagination*

✳ 1966
*Equality of Educational
Opportunity* (the Coleman
Report) is published

✳ 1972
Ann Oakley publishes
Sex, Gender, and Society

✳ 1962
Mills dies

✳ 1963
Du Bois dies;
the March on
Washington;
Betty Friedan publishes
The Feminine Mystique

✳ 1967
Elliott Liebow publishes *Tally's Corner*;
Peter M. Blau and Otis Dudley Duncan
publish *The American Occupational
Structure*

✳ 1973
Daniel Bell publishes
*The Coming of the
Post-Industrial Society*

✳ 1969
Woodstock

✳ 1977
Paul Willis publishes
Learning to Labor

Erving Goffman

C. Wright Mills

March on Washington

Ann Oakley

change throughout history. Marx saw history as an account of man's struggle to gain control of and later dominate his natural environment. However, at a certain point—with the Industrial Revolution and the emergence of modern capitalism—the very tools and processes that humans embraced to survive and to manage their surroundings came to dominate humans. Instead of using technology to master the natural world, people became slaves to industrial technology in order to make a living. In Marx's version of history, each economic system, whether small-scale farming or factory capitalism, had its own fault lines of conflict. In the current epoch, that fault line divided society into

1980	1985	1990	1995

✱
1978
William Julius Wilson publishes
The Declining Significance of Race

✱
1984
Pierre Bourdieu publishes *Distinction*;
Anthony Giddens publishes *The Constitution of Society*

✱
1991
James Coleman publishes *Foundations of Social Theory*

✱
1979
Parsons dies

1989
Arlie Hochschild publishes *The Second Shift: Working Parents and the Revolution at Home*

✱
1993
Douglas S. Massey and Nancy A. Denton publish *American Apartheid*

Anthony Giddens

William Julius Wilson

James Coleman

Arlie Hochschild

a small number of capitalists and a large number of workers (the proletariat) whose interests were opposed. This political struggle, along with escalating crises within the economic system itself, would produce social change through a Communist revolution. In the ensuing Communist society, private property would be abolished and the resulting ideology governing the new economy would be "from each according to his abilities, to each according to his needs" (Marx & Engels, 1848/1998). We will explore Marx's theories in depth in Chapter 7 on social stratification.

Max Weber If Marx brought the material world back into history, which had been thought of as mostly idea-driven until then, Max Weber (1864–1920), writing shortly after Marx, is said to have brought ideas back into history. Weber and others believed Marx went too far in seeing culture, ideas, religion, and the like as merely an effect and not a cause of how societies evolve. Specifically, Weber criticized Marx for his exclusive focus on the economy and social class, advocating sociological analysis that allowed for the multiple influences of culture, economics, and politics. Weber is most famous for his two-volume work *Economy and Society* (published posthumously in 1922), as well as a lengthy essay titled "The Protestant Ethic and the Spirit of Capitalism" (1904/2003). In the latter, he argued that the religious transformation that occurred during the Protestant Reformation in the sixteenth and early seventeenth centuries laid the groundwork for modern capitalism by upending the medieval ethic of virtuous poverty and replacing it with an ideology that saw riches as a sign of divine providence. *Economy and Society* also provided the theories of authority, rationality, the state (i.e., government), and status and a host of other concepts that sociologists still use today.

Verstehen German for "understanding." The concept of *Verstehen* comes from Max Weber and is the basis of interpretive sociology in which researchers imagine themselves experiencing the life positions of the social actors they want to understand rather than treating those people as objects to be examined.

One of Weber's most important contributions was the concept of *Verstehen* ("understanding" in German). By emphasizing *Verstehen*, Weber was suggesting that sociologists approach social behavior from the perspective of those engaging in it. In other words, to truly understand why people act the way they do, a sociologist must understand the meanings people attach to their actions. Weber's emphasis on subjectivity is the foundation of interpretive sociology, the study of social meaning.

Émile Durkheim Across the Rhine in France, the work of Émile Durkheim (1858–1917) focused on themes similar to those studied by his German colleagues. He wished to understand how society holds together and how modern capitalism and industrialization have transformed the ways people relate to one another. Durkheim's sociological writing began with *The Division of Labor in Society* (1893/1997). The division of labor refers to the degree to which jobs are specialized. A society of hunter-gatherers or small-scale farmers has a low division of labor (each household essentially carries out the same tasks to survive); today the United States has a high degree of division of labor, with many highly specialized occupations. What made the substance of Durkheim's work sociology, rather than economics, was the fact that he argued (and substantiated through legal evidence) that the division of labor didn't just affect work and productivity but had social and moral consequences as well. Specifically, the division of labor in a given society helps to determine its form of social solidarity—that is, the way social cohesion among individuals is maintained. Durkheim followed this work with *Suicide* (1897/1951), in which he shows how this individual act is, in reality, conditioned by social forces: the degree to which we are integrated into group life (or not) and the degree to which our lives follow routines. Durkheim argues that one of the main social forces leading to suicide is the sense of normlessness resulting from drastic changes in living conditions or arrangements, which he calls anomie. He also wrote about the methods of social science as well as religion in *The Elementary Forms of Religious Life* (1917/1995). Although the concept originated with Comte, Durkheim is often considered the founding practitioner of positivist sociology, a strain within sociology that believes the social world can be described and predicted by certain observable relationships.

Anomie a sense of aimlessness or despair that arises when we can no longer reasonably expect life to be predictable; too little social regulation; normlessness.

Positivist sociology a strain within sociology that believes the social world can be described and predicted by certain describable relationships (akin to a social physics).

Georg Simmel Historically, Georg Simmel (1858–1918) has received less credit as one of the founders of sociology, although as of late he is gaining wider recognition. In a series of important lectures and essays, Simmel established what we today refer to as formal sociology—that is, a sociology of pure numbers. For example, among the issues he addressed were the fundamental differences between a group of two and a group of three or more (independent of the reasons for the group or who belongs to it). His work was influential in the development of urban sociology and cultural sociology, and his work with small-group interactions served as an intellectual precedent for later sociologists who came to study microinteractions. He provided formal definitions for small and large groups, a party, a stranger, and the poor. (These are antecedents of network theory, which emerged in the latter half of the twentieth century.)

American Sociology

Throughout the history of sociology, the pendulum has tended to swing back and forth between a focus on big, sweeping theories and on more focused empirical research. The emergence of American sociology was characterized by the latter, applied perspective, and was best embodied by what came to be referred to as the Chicago School, named for many of its proponents' affiliation with the University of Chicago. If the Chicago School had a basic premise, it was that humans' behaviors and personalities are shaped by their social and physical environments, a concept known as social ecology.

Chicago, which had grown from a middle-sized city of 109,260 in 1860 to a major metropolis by the beginning of the twentieth century, when these scholars were writing, served as the main laboratory for the Chicago School's studies. Chicago proved to be fertile ground for studying urbanism and its many discontents. Immigration, race and ethnicity, politics, and family life all became topics of study, primarily through a community-based approach (i.e., interviewing people and spending time with them). Robert Park (1864–1944), for example, exhorted scholars to "go and get the seat of [their] pants dirty in real research." This was a time of rapid growth in urban America thanks to a high rate of foreign immigration as well as the Great Migration of African Americans from the rural South to the urban North. The researchers of the Chicago School were concerned with how race and ethnic divisions played out in cities: how Polish peasants and African American sharecroppers adapted to life in a new, industrialized world, or how the anonymity of the city itself contributed to creativity and freedom on the one hand, and to the breakdown of traditional communities and higher rates of social problems on the other. For example, in the classic Chicago School essay "Urbanism as a Way of Life" (1938), Louis Wirth—himself an immigrant from a small village in Germany—described how the city broke down traditional forms of social solidarity while promoting tolerance, rationality (which led to scientific advances), and individual freedom. Much of the work was what would be called cultural sociology today. For example, in their studies of ethnicity, Park and others challenged the notion inherited from Europe that ethnicity was about bloodlines and instead showed ethnicity "in practice" to be more about the maintenance of cultural practices passed down through generations. Likewise, the stages of immigrant assimilation into American society (contact, then competition, and finally assimilation), which are today regarded as common knowledge and indeed part of our national ideology, were first described by Park.

If there was a theoretical paradigm that undergirded much of the research of the Chicago School, it would be the theory of the "social self" that emerged from the work of the social psychologists Charles Horton Cooley (1864–1929) and George Herbert Mead (1863–1931). Taking up the theme, manifest in the Chicago School's community studies, of how the social environment shapes the individual, Cooley and Mead incorporated some of the key ideas of the pragmatist school of philosophy (which argues that inquiry and truth cannot be understood outside their environment—i.e., that environment affects meaning). Cooley, who taught at the University of Michigan, is best known for the concept of the "looking-glass self." He argued that the self emerges from an interactive social process. We envision how others perceive us; then we gauge the responses of other individuals to our presentation of self. By refining our vision of how others perceive us, we develop a self-concept that is in constant interaction with the surrounding social world. Much of Cooley's work described the important role that group dynamics played in this process. (See Chapter 5 on groups and networks.)

In his classic *Mind, Self, and Society* (1934), George Herbert Mead, a social psychologist and philosopher at the University of Chicago, described how the "self" itself (i.e., the perception of consciousness as an object) develops over the course of childhood as the individual learns to take the point of view of specific others in specific contexts (such as games) and eventually internalizes what Mead calls the "generalized other"—our view of the views of society as a whole that transcends individuals or particular situations. (Mead's theories are discussed in depth in Chapter 4 on socialization.) Key to both Cooley's and Mead's work is the notion that it is through social interaction that meaning emerges. This theoretical paradigm is perhaps best summarized by another Chicago scholar, W. I. Thomas, who stated that "if men define situations as real they are real in their consequences" (Thomas & Thomas, 1928, p. 572). This was an important precursor to the notion of the social construction of reality.

W. E. B. Du Bois However, even as the Chicago School questioned essentialist notions of race and ethnicity (and even the self), the community of scholars was still dominated by white men. The most important black sociologist of the time, and the first African American to receive a PhD from Harvard, W. E. B. Du Bois (1868–1963) failed to gain the renown he deserved. The first sociologist to undertake ethnography in the African American community, Du Bois made manifold contributions to scholarship and social causes.

W. E. B. Du Bois (second from right) at the office of the NAACP's *Crisis* magazine.

Double consciousness
a concept conceived by W. E. B. Du Bois to describe the two behavioral scripts, one for moving through the world and the other incorporating the external opinions of prejudiced onlookers, which are constantly maintained by African Americans.

He developed the concept of double consciousness, a mechanism by which African Americans constantly maintain two behavioral scripts. The first is the script that any American would have for moving through the world; the second is the script that takes the external opinions of an often racially prejudiced onlooker into consideration. The double consciousness is a "sense of always looking at one's self through the eyes of others, of measuring one's soul by the tape of a world that looks on in amused contempt and pity" (1903, p. 2). Without a double consciousness, a person shopping for groceries moves through the store trying to remember everything on the list, maybe taste-testing the grapes, impatiently scolding children begging for the latest sugary treat, or snacking on some cookies before paying for them at the register. With a double consciousness, an African American shopping for groceries is aware that he or she might be watched carefully by store security and makes an effort to get in and out quickly. He or she does not linger in back corners out of the gaze of shopkeepers and remembers not to reach into a pocket lest this motion be perceived as evidence of shoplifting. Snacking on a bag of chips before reaching the register or sampling a tasty morsel from the bulk bins is totally out of the question. Those operating with a double consciousness risk conforming so closely to others' perceptions that they are fully constrained to the behaviors predicted of them. Du Bois was also interested in criminology, using Durkheim's theory of anomie to explain crime rates among African Americans. Specifically, Du Bois theorized that the breakdown of norms resulting from the sudden and newfound freedom of former slaves caused high crime rates among blacks (at least in the South). He also analyzed the social stratification among Philadelphia's black population and argued that such class inequality was necessary for progress in the black community. African Americans, he argued, would be led by what he coined "the talented tenth," an elite of highly educated professionals. In addition to being a major academic sociologist, Du Bois worked to advance a civil rights agenda in the United States. To this end, he co-founded the National Association for the Advancement of Colored People (NAACP) in 1909.

Jane Addams Among sociologists, women, much like African Americans, didn't always receive the respect they deserved. For example, Jane Addams (1860–1935) was considered a marginal member of the Chicago School, yet many of the movement's thinkers drew some of their insights from her applied work. Addams founded the first American settlement house, Hull House, an institution that attempted to link the ideas of the university to the poor through a full-service community center, staffed by students and professionals, which offered educational services and aid and promoted sports and the arts. It was at Hull House in Chicago that the ideas of the Chicago School were put into practice and tested. Although many of Addams's observations and experiences at Hull House were influential in the development of the Chicago School's theories and Addams herself was a prolific author on both the substance and methodology of community studies, she was regarded as a social worker by the majority of her contemporaries. This label, which she rejected, partly resulted from the applied nature of her work, but undoubtedly gender also played a role in her marginalization: Many of the men of the Chicago School also engaged in social activism yet retained their academic prestige.

Modern Sociological Theories

Although it was born in a tradition of community studies that avoided grand theory and drew its insights from the careful observation of people in their environments, American sociology was largely characterized by the concept of functionalism for much of the twentieth century. Drawing on the ideas of Durkheim and best embodied by the work of Talcott Parsons (1902–1979), functionalism derived its name from the notion that the best way to analyze society was to identify the roles that different aspects or phenomena play. These functions may be manifest (explicit) or latent (hidden). This lens is really just an extension of a nineteenth-century theory called *organicism*, the notion that society is like a living organism, each part of which serves an important role in keeping society together. The state or government was seen to be the brain; industry was the muscular system; media and mass communications were the nervous system; and so on.

Functionalism the theory that various social institutions and processes in society exist to serve some important (or necessary) function to keep society running.

Twentieth-century sociologists had moved beyond such simplistic biological metaphors, yet the essential notion that social institutions were present for a reason persisted. Hence, analysis by Parsons and others sought to describe how the various parts of the whole were integrated with, but articulated against, one another. Almost every social phenomenon was subjected to functionalist analysis: What is the function of schooling? The health-care system? Even crime and the Mafia were seen to play a role in a functioning society. For example, functionalists view social inequality as a "device by which societies ensure that the most important positions are conscientiously filled by the most qualified persons" (Davis & Moore, 1944).

Although associated with mid-twentieth-century sociology, the functionalist impulse originated in the nineteenth century, most notably in the work of Durkheim, who in 1893 wrote, "For, if there is nothing which either unduly hinders or favours the chances of those competing for occupations, it is inevitable that only those who are most capable at each type of activity will move into it. The only factor which then determines the manner in which work is divided is the diversity of capacities" (1972). Functionalism was still being applied into the late twentieth century by Richard J. Herrnstein and Charles Murray, who argued in *The Bell Curve* that "no one decreed that occupations should sort us out by our cognitive abilities, and no one enforces the process. It goes on beneath the surface, guided by its own invisible hand" (1994, p. 52).

Female textile workers struggle with a national guardsman during a 1929 strike in Gastonia, North Carolina. How might a conflict theorist interpret labor unrest?

Conflict theory the idea that conflict between competing interests is the basic, animating force of social change and society in general.

Conflict Theory Even though functionalism continues to reappear in many guises, its fundamental assertions have not gone unchallenged. Sociologists such as C. Wright Mills, writing from 1948 through 1962, criticized Parsons and functionalist theory for reinforcing the status quo and the dominant economic system with its class structures and inequalities rather than challenging how such systems evolved and offering alternatives. Functionalism also took a beating in the turbulent 1960s, when its place was usurped by a number of theories frequently subsumed under the label Marxist theory or conflict theory. Whereas functionalists painted a picture of social harmony as the well-oiled parts of a societal machine working together (with some friction and the occasional breakdown), conflict theory viewed society from exactly the opposite perspective. Drawing on the ideas of Marx, the theory—as expressed by Ralph Dahrendorf, Lewis Coser, and others—stated that conflict among competing interests is the basic, animating force of any society. Competition, not consensus, is the essential nature, and this conflict at all levels of analysis (from the individual to the family to the tribe to the nation-state), in turn, drives social change. And such social change occurs only through revolution and war, not evolution or baby steps.

According to conflict theorists, inequality exists as a result of political struggles among different groups (classes) in a particular society. Although functionalists theorize that inequality is a necessary and beneficial aspect of society, conflict theorists argue that it is unfair and exists at the expense of less powerful groups. Thus, functionalism and conflict theory take extreme (if opposing) positions on the fundamental nature of society. Today most sociologists see societies as demonstrating characteristics of both consensus and conflict and believe that social change does result from both revolution and evolution.

Feminist Theory Emerging from the women's movement of the 1960s and 1970s, feminist theory shares many ideas with Marxist theory—in particular, the Marxist emphasis on conflict and political reform. Feminism is not one idea but a catchall term for many theories. What they all have in common is an emphasis on women's experiences and a belief that sociology and society in general subordinate women. Feminist theorists emphasize equality between men and women and want to see women's lives and experiences represented in sociological studies. Early feminist theory focused on defining concepts such as sex and gender, and on challenging conventional wisdom by questioning the meanings usually assigned to these concepts. In *Sex, Gender, and Society* (1972), sociologist Ann Oakley argued that much of what we attribute to biological sex differences can be traced to behaviors that are learned and internalized through socialization (see Chapter 8 on gender).

In addition to defining sex and gender, much feminist research focuses on inequalities based on gender categories. Feminist theorists have studied women's experiences at home and in the workplace. They have also researched gender inequality in social institutions such as schools, the family, and the government. In each case, feminist sociologists remain interested in how power relationships are defined, shaped, and reproduced on the basis of gender differences.

Symbolic Interactionism A strain of thought that developed in the 1960s was symbolic interactionism, which eschewed big theories of society (macrosociology) and instead focused on how face-to-face interactions create the social world (microsociology). Exemplified most notably by the work of one of George Herbert Mead's students, Herbert Blumer, this paradigm operates on the basic premise of a cycle of meaning—namely, the idea that people act in response to the meaning that signs and social signals hold for them (e.g., a red light means stop). By acting on perceptions of the social world in this way and regarding these meanings as *sui generis* (i.e., appearing to be self-constituting rather than flimsily constructed by ourselves or others), we then collectively

Symbolic interactionism a micro-level theory in which shared meanings, orientations, and assumptions form the basic motivations behind people's actions.

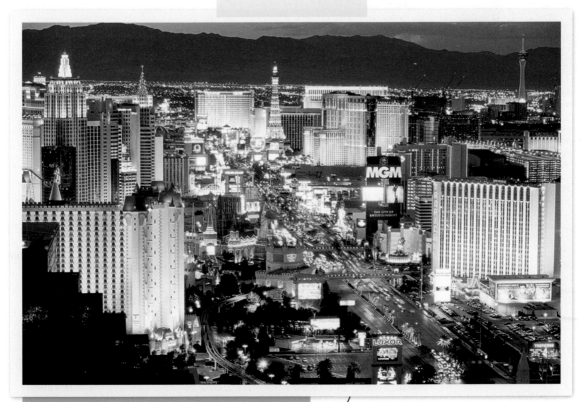

Las Vegas, the ultimate postmodern city, borrows from various regions, times, and cultures to shape its constantly changing landscape.

make their meaning so. In other words, John G. Roberts, Jr. is Chief Justice of the U.S. Supreme Court because we all act as if he is and believe that it is an objective fact he is (even if that belief is the creation of our somewhat arbitrary collective thinking). We then act in ways that reify, or make consequential, this consensus and arrive at our calculations based on the supposed objectivity of this "fact."

The groundwork for symbolic interactionism was laid by Erving Goffman's dramaturgical theory of social interaction. Goffman had used the language of theater to describe the social facade we create through such devices as tact, gestures, front-stage (versus backstage) behavior, props, and scripts. For example, in *The Presentation of Self in Everyday Life* (1959), Goffman explored how our everyday personal encounters shape and reinforce our notions about class and social status. According to Goffman, we make judgments about class and social status based on how people speak, what they wear, and the other tiny details of how they present themselves to others, and at the same time, they rely on the same information from our everyday interactions with them to classify us, too.

Postmodernism If symbolic interactionism emphasizes the meanings negotiated through the interaction of individuals, postmodernism can perhaps be summarized succinctly as the notion that these shared meanings have eroded. A red light, for instance, may have multiple meanings to different groups or individuals in society. There is no longer one version of history that is correct. Everything is interpretable within this framework; even "facts" are up for debate. It's as if everyone has become a symbolic interactionist and decided that seemingly objective phenomena are social constructions, so that all organizing narratives break down. Postmodernists may not feel compelled to act on these shared meanings as seemingly objective, because the meanings aren't, in fact, objective. The term itself derives from the idea that the grand narratives of history are over (hence, "after" modernism, *postmodernism*).

Midrange Theory Although many sociologists have taken to the postmodernist project of deconstructing social phenomena (i.e., showing how they are created arbitrarily by social actors with varying degrees of power), most sociologists have returned, as the pendulum swings yet again, to what sociologist Robert Merton called for in the middle of the last century: midrange theory. Midrange theory is neither macrosociology (it doesn't try to explain all of society) nor microsociology. Rather, midrange theory attempts to predict how certain social institutions tend to function. For example, a midrange theorist might develop a theory of democracy (under what political or demographic conditions does it arise?), a theory of the household (when do households expand to include extended kin or nonkin, and when do they contract to the nuclear family unit or the individual?), or a theory explaining the relationship between the educational system and the labor market. The key to midrange theory is that it generates falsifiable hypotheses—predictions that can be tested by analyzing the real world. (Hypothesis generation is covered in Chapter 2.)

Postmodernism a condition characterized by a questioning of the notion of progress and history, the replacement of narrative within pastiche, and multiple, perhaps even conflicting, identities resulting from disjointed affiliations.

Social construction an entity that exists because people behave as if it exists and whose existence is perpetuated as people and social institutions act in accordance with the widely agreed-upon formal rules or informal norms of behavior associated with that entity.

Midrange theory a theory that attempts to predict how certain social institutions tend to function.

Sociology and Its Cousins

We have already noted that a sociology of sports exists, as can a sociology of music, of organizations, of economies, of science, and even of sociology itself. What then, if anything, distinguishes sociology from other disciplines? Certainly overlap with other fields does occur, but at the same time, there is something distinctive about sociology as a discipline that transcends the sociological imagination discussed earlier. All of sociology boils down to comparisons across cases of some form or another, and perhaps the best way to conceptualize its role in the landscape of knowledge is to compare it with other fields.

History

Let's start with history. History is concerned with the *idiographic* (from the Greek *idio*, "unique," and *graphic*, "depicting"), meaning that historians, at least traditionally, have been concerned with explaining unique cases. Why did Adolf Hitler rise to power? What conditions led to the Haitian slave revolt 200 years ago (the first such rebellion against European chattel slavery)? How did the Counter-Reformation affect the practices of lay Catholics in France? What was the impact of the railroad on civilization's sense of time? How did adolescence arise as a meaningful stage of life? Historians' research questions center on the notion that by understanding the particularity of certain past events, individual people, or intellectual concepts, we can better understand the world in which we live.

Sometimes historians use comparative frameworks to situate their analysis— for example, comparing Hitler's rise and Mussolini's to examine why the Third Reich pursued a genocidal agenda, whereas the Italian fascists had no such agenda and, in fact, somewhat resisted cooperating with Germany's deportation of Jews. Another strategy historians often use, although it is sometimes frowned on, is the notion of the counterfactual: What would have happened had Hitler been killed rather than wounded in World War I? Would World War II have been inevitable even if the victors in World War I had not pursued such a punitive reparations policy after defeating Germany?

The preceding description is, of course, an oversimplification of a diverse field. History runs the gamut from "great man" theories (a focus on figures like Hitler) to people's histories (a focus on the lives of anonymous, disempowered people in various epochs, or on groups traditionally given short shrift in historical scholarship, such as women, African Americans, and subaltern colonials) to

Italian dictator Benito Mussolini (on the left) and Nazi leader Adolf Hitler at a 1937 rally in Munich. How do different disciplines provide various tools to analyze the rise of fascism under these leaders?

historiography (in essence, metahistory examining the intellectual assumptions and constraints on knowledge entailed by the subjects and methods historians choose) in which historians rely on archival material and primary resources.

Sociology, by contrast, is generally not concerned with the uniqueness of phenomena but rather with commonalities that can be abstracted across cases. Whereas the unique case is the staple of the historian, the comparative method is the staple of sociologists. Historical comparative sociologist Julia Adams explained what makes her work different from what a historian would do: "If you define the difference according to whether one is engaged in primary archival research or not, I would . . . also be an historian as well as a sociologist," but the big difference is that, historical sociologists are "consciously theoretical" and "very keen to explain and illuminate" historical patterns (Conley 2013a). Whether looking at contemporary American life, the formation of city-states in medieval Europe, or the origins of unequal economic development thousands of years ago, sociologists formulate hypotheses and theorems about how social life works or worked.

Instead of inquiring why Hitler rose to power, the sociologist might ask what common element allowed fascism to arise during the early to mid-twentieth century in Germany, Italy, Spain, and Japan and not in other countries such as France, Great Britain, or the Scandinavian nations. Of course, sociologists recognize that there is no one-size-fits-all hypothesis that will explain all these cases perfectly, but the exercise of considering competing explanations is illuminating in and of itself. Instead of asking what specific conditions led to the Haitian slave revolt in 1791, the sociologist might ask under what general conditions uprisings have occurred among indentured populations. Instead of asking how the Counter-Reformation affected the practices of lay Catholics in one region of Europe, the sociologist might ask what aspects of the conditions in various regions of Europe made the reaction to the Catholic Church's reforms different. This is a subtle but important difference in focus. Instead of examining the impact of the railroad on our sense of time, the sociologist might compare the railroad to other forms of transportation that both collapsed distances and opened up the possibility of more frequent and longer migrations. And finally, instead of asking how adolescence arose as a meaningful stage of life, the sociologist might compare various societies that have distinct roles for individuals ages 13 to 20 to examine how those labor markets,

How does anthropologist Natasha Dow Schüll's research on slot-machine gamblers challenge the traditional boundaries between anthropology and sociology?

educational systems, family arrangements, life expectancies, and so on lead to different experiences for that age group.

Whether sociologists are comparing two tribes that died out 400 years ago, two countries today, siblings within the same family, or even changes in the same person over the course of his or her life, they are always seeking a variation in some outcome that can be explained by variation in some input. This holds true, I would argue, whether the methods are interviews, research using historical archives, community-based observation studies of participants, or statistical analyses of data from the U.S. census. Sociologists are always at least implicitly drawing comparisons to identify abstractable patterns.

Anthropology

The field of anthropology is split between physical anthropologists, who resemble biologists more than sociologists, and cultural anthropologists, who study human relations similarly to the way sociologists do. Traditionally, the distinction was that sociologists studied "us" (Western society and culture), whereas anthropologists studied "them" (other societies or cultures). This distinction was helpful in the early to mid-twentieth century, when anthropologist Margaret Mead studied rites of passage in Samoa and sociologists interviewed Chicago residents, but it is less salient today. Sociologists increasingly study non-Western social relations, and anthropologists do not hesitate to tackle domestic social issues.

Take two recent examples that confound this division from either side of the metaphorical aisle: Caitlin Zaloom is a cultural anthropologist whose "tribe" (she likes to joke) is the group of commodities traders who work on the floor of the Chicago Mercantile Exchange. Natasha Dow Schüll, another anthropologist, has studied gamblers in Las Vegas and how they lose themselves and their money in the machine zone. Meanwhile, recent sociological scholarship includes Stephen Morgan's study of African status attainment and patronage relations. Another project, spearheaded by business-school professor Doug Guthrie in 2006, investigated the way informal social connections facilitate business in China. Given the era of globalization we have entered, it is appropriate that division on the basis of "us" and "them" has diminished. Many scholars now question the legitimacy of such a division in the first place, asking whether it served a colonial agenda of dividing up the world and reproducing social relations of domination and exclusion—accomplishing on the intellectual front what European imperialism did on the military, political, and economic fronts.

What then distinguishes sociology from cultural anthropology? Nothing, some would argue. However, although certain aspects of sociology are almost indistinguishable from those of cultural anthropology, sociology as a whole has a wider array of methods to answer questions, such as experimentation and statistical data analysis. Sociology also tends more toward comparative case study, whereas anthropology is more like history in its focus on particular circumstances. This does not necessarily imply that sociology is superior; a wider range of methods can be a weakness as well as a strength, because it can lead to irreconcilable differences within the field. For example, demographic and ethnographic studies of the family may employ different definitions of what a household is. This makes meaningful dialogue between the two subfields challenging.

The Psychological and Biological Sciences

Social, developmental, and cognitive psychology often address many of the same questions that sociologists do: How do people react to stereotypes? What explains racial differences in educational performance? How do individuals respond to authority in various circumstances? Ultimately, however, psychologists focus on the individual, whereas sociologists focus on the supra-individual (above or beyond the individual) level. In other words, psychologists focus on the individual to explain the phenomenon under consideration, examining how urges, drives, instincts, and the mind can account for human behavior, whereas sociologists examine group-level dynamics and social structures.

Biology, especially evolutionary biology, increasingly attempts to explain phenomena that once would have seemed the exclusive dominion of social scientists. There are now biological (evolutionary) theories of many aspects of gender relations—even rape and high-heeled shoes (Posner, 1992). Medical science has claimed to identify genes that explain some aspects of social behavior, such as aggressiveness, shyness, and even thrill seeking. Increasingly, social differences have been medicalized through diagnoses such as attention-deficit hyperactivity disorder and the autistic spectrum of diseases. The distinction between these areas of biology and the social sciences lies not so much in the topic of study (or even the scientific methods in some cases), but rather in the underlying variation or causal mechanisms with which the disciplines are concerned. Sociology addresses supra-individual-level dynamics that affect our behavior, psychology addresses individual-level dynamics, and biology typically deals with the intra-individual-level factors (those within the individual) that affect our lives, such as biochemistry, genetic makeup, and cellular activity. So if a group of biologists attempted to explain differences in culture across continents, they would typically analyze something like local ecological effects or the distribution of genes across subpopulations.

Economics and Political Science

The quantitative side of sociology shares many methodological and substantive features with economics and political science. Economics traditionally has focused on market exchange relations (or, simply, money). More recently, however, economics has expanded to include social realms such as culture, religion, and the family—the traditional stomping ground of sociologists. What distinguishes economics from sociology in these contexts is the underlying view of human behavior. Economics assumes that people are rational utility maximizers: They are out to get the best deal for themselves. Sociology, on the other hand, has a more open view of human motivation that includes selfishness, altruism, and simple irrationality. (New branches of economics are moving, however, into the realm of the irrational.) Another difference is methodological: Economics is a fundamentally quantitative discipline, meaning that it is based on numerical data.

Similarly, political science is almost a subsector of sociology that focuses on only one aspect of social relations—power. Of course, power relations take many forms. Political scientists study state relations, legal structure, and the nature of civic life. Like sociologists, political scientists deploy a variety of methods, ranging from historical case studies to abstract statistical models. Increasingly, political science has adopted the rational actor model implicit in economics in an attempt to explain everything from how lobbyists influence legislators to the recruitment of suicide bombers by terrorist groups.

Having explained all of these distinctions, we should keep in mind that disciplinary boundaries are in a constant state of flux. For example, Stanford English professor Franco Moretti argues that books should be counted, mapped, and graphed. In his research, Moretti statistically analyzes thousands of books by thematic and linguistic patterns. Economist Steven Levitt has explored how teachers teach to the test (and sometimes cheat) and how stereotypically African American names may or may not disadvantage their holders. Historian Zvi Ben-Dor Benite has assembled a global, comparative history of how different societies execute criminals. It all sounds like sociology to me! For now, let's just say that significant overlap exists between various arenas of scholarship, so that any divisions are simultaneously meaningful and arbitrary.

Divisions within Sociology

Even if sociologists tend to leverage comparisons of some sort, significant fault lines still persist within sociology. Often, the major division is perceived to exist between those who deal in numbers (statistical or quantitative researchers) and those who deal in words (qualitative sociologists). Another split exists between theorists and empiricists. These are false dichotomies, however; they merely act as shorthand for deeper intellectual divisions for which they are poor proxies. A much more significant cleavage exists between interpretive and positivist sociology. Positivist sociology is born from the mission of Comte—that mission being to reveal the "social facts" (to use the term Durkheim later coined) that affect, if not govern, social life. It is akin to uncovering the laws of "social physics," although most sociologists today would shun Comte's phrase because it implies an overly deterministic sense of unwavering, time-transcendent laws.

To this end, the standard practice is to form a theory about how the social world works—for instance, that members of minorities have a high degree of group solidarity. The next task is to generate a hypothesis that derives from this theory, perhaps that minority groups should demonstrate a lower level of intragroup violence than majority groups. Next, we make predictions based on our hypotheses. Both the hypotheses and predictions have to be falsifiable by an empirical, or experimental, test; in this case, it might involve examining homicide rates among different groups in a given society or in multiple societies. And last comes the acceptance or rejection of the hypothesis and the revision (or extension) of the theory (in the face of contradictory or confirming evidence). These scientific methods are the same as in any basic science. For that reason, positivism is often called the "normal science" model of sociology.

Normal science stands in contrast to interpretive sociology, which is much more concerned with the meaning of social phenomena to individuals (remember Weber's *Verstehen*). Rather than make a prediction about homicide rates, the interpretive sociologist will likely seek to understand the experience of solidarity among minority groups in various contexts. An interpretive sociologist might object to the notion that we can make worthwhile predictions about human behavior—or more precisely, might question whether such an endeavor is worth the time and effort. It is a sociology premised on the idea that situation matters so much that the search for social facts that transcend time and place may be futile. Why measure the number of friends we have by the number of people we see face to face every day, given the existence of the Internet and how it has redefined the meaning of social interaction so completely?

Microsociology and Macrosociology

A similar cleavage involves the distinction between *microsociology* and *macrosociology*. Microsociology seeks to understand local interactional contexts—for example, why people stare at the numbers in an elevator and are reluctant to make eye contact in this setting. Microsociologists focus on face-to-face encounters and the types of interactions between individuals. They rely on data gathered through participant observations and other qualitative methodologies (for more on these methods, see Chapter 2).

Macrosociology is generally concerned with social dynamics at a higher level of analysis—across the breadth of a society (or at least a swath of it). A macrosociologist might investigate immigration policy or gender norms or how the educational system interacts with the labor market. Statistical analysis is the most typical manifestation of this kind of research, but by no means the only one. Macrosociologists also use qualitative methods such as historical comparison and in-depth interviewing. They may also resort to large-scale experimentation. That said, a perfect overlap does not exist between methodological divisions and level of analysis. For example, microsociologists might use an experimental method such as varying the context of an elevator to see how people react. Or they might use statistical methods such as conversation analysis, which analyzes turn taking, pauses, and other quantifiable aspects of social interaction in localized settings.

Microsociology a branch of sociology that seeks to understand local interactional contexts; its methods of choice are ethnographic, generally including participant observation and in-depth interviews.

Macrosociology a branch of sociology generally concerned with social dynamics at a higher level of analysis—that is, across the breadth of a society.

→ ## CONCLUSION

The bottom line is that anything goes; as long as you use your sociological imagination, you will be asking important questions and seeking the best way to answer them. As you read the subsequent chapters, keep in mind that a sociologist "makes the familiar strange." The first six chapters in this book introduce the methodological and theoretical tools that you need in order to think like a sociologist. Chapters 7 through 10 ask you to study the inequalities and differences that divide people in our society.

→ PRACTICE

SOCIOLOGY ON THE STREET

The neighborhood where you grow up exerts a significant effect on the rest of your life. How did your house, neighbors, street, and town influence you? Watch the Sociology on the Street video to find out more: wwnpag.es/SOS1.

QUESTIONS FOR REVIEW

1. Some people accuse sociologists of observing conditions that are obvious. How does looking at sociology as "making the familiar strange" help counter this claim? How does sociology differ from simple commonsense reasoning?

2. What is the sociological imagination, and how do history and personal biography affect it? If a sociologist studies the challenges experienced by students earning a college degree, how could the lessons gained be described as "terrible" as well as "magnificent"?

3. What is a social institution, and how does it relate to social identity? Choose a sports team or another social institution to illustrate your answer.

4. A sociologist studies the way a group of fast-food restaurant employees do their work. From what you read in this chapter, how would Max Weber and Émile Durkheim differ in their study of these workers?

5. Compare functionalism and conflict theory. How would the two differ in their understanding of inequality?

6. You tell a friend that you're taking a class in sociology. There's a chance they know about sociology and are quite jealous. There's also a chance they're confusing sociology with the other social sciences. How would you describe sociology? How does sociology differ from history and psychology?

7. Sociology, like any discipline, features some divisions. What are some of the cleavages in the field, and why might these be described as false dichotomies?

8. Why do people go to college, and how does Randall Collins's book *Credential Society* make the familiar reality of college education seem strange?

PARADOX

A SUCCESSFUL SOCIOLOGIST MAKES THE FAMILIAR STRANGE.

WATCH THE ANIMATED SHORT ABOUT THE SOCIOLOGICAL IMAGINATION PARADOX AT

WWNPAG.ES/PX1

WHAT'S A TRADITIONAL FAMILY?

WHY GO TO COLLEGE?

How is it possible to study something as rapidly evolving as technology? Social scientists utilize standardized research methods to ensure their information is as relevant and accurate as possible.

2 Methods

danah boyd (yes, all lowercase) grew up in Lancaster, Pennsylvania, during a period in which the region was trying to adapt to the decline of the farming economy by reinventing itself as an industrial center. The bad news for central Pennsylvania was that factory employment in the United States had already had its heyday, so by the time Lancaster tried to invigorate its economy with manufacturing, the odds were stacked against it. Though Lancaster would later find its economic footing, other towns in the region would not be as lucky.

Raised by a single mother, danah saw her own financial fortunes ebb and flow with the transformation of the American economic landscape. For example, her mother supported herself by running a local franchise of the direct mail coupon company, Valpak. Of course, direct mail has also now been largely displaced by online marketing.

danah's own intellectual trajectory reflects all the subtleties of this background. Though she was taught some computer programming as a young child in school, her interest in this new technology really took off thanks to her brother's hogging of the home phone line. Back in the days of dial-up connections, her brother would take over the family phone line to communicate with other users on various online bulletin boards. Little is more annoying to a teenage girl, danah says, than a younger brother bogarting the telephone, but when she realized that there were actually other people whose computers were deciphering the clicks, beeps, and screeches emanating from her line, that's when the die was cast. Computing was social. And it was cool.

At Brown University danah combined her varied interests by concocting a hybrid concentration: computational gender studies. Her senior thesis research involved studying how sex hormones affect depth cue prioritization in virtual reality spaces by investigating the changes that transgendered people experience while undergoing hormone therapy as part of their sex reassignment. Evidently, the retina of the eye is the place in the body with the most sex hormone receptors outside of our reproductive system (who knew?), so how we see the world—quite literally—is shaped by sex.

She continued her cross-disciplinary studies at MIT's Media Lab, where she showed how to graph the social networks of individuals without ever seeing their electronic communications but rather only observing those of their friends. It was during a gap year between completing her master's degree and starting her PhD studies at the University of California that she bluffed her way into conducting her first real independent qualitative study. Her subject was early Friendster adopters. (Friendster was among the first social network sites, followed later by MySpace and ultimately Facebook.)

As an early adopter herself, she managed to gain incredible access to both Friendster and MySpace. Although many researchers study youth culture ethnographically by talking to kids and hanging out at malls and other spaces where teenagers congregate, and others perform "content analysis" of online interactions such as Twitter feeds, blogs, and so on, few have combined the two so deftly as danah. Access to online social networks allows her to draw samples of users to contact both online and offline in order to make sure that her interviews and participant observation is not only deep but also broad. She can cover not only different groups based on race, class, gender, and sexuality, but also different cliques that are not so easily categorized by demographers. This dual online–offline approach makes her ethnography more generalizable than the typical approach.

The face-to-face interviews and "hanging out" that she does is critical to understanding the social lives of teens, and is getting more so. This is because teens often speak in code online to avoid being understood by their parents or other adult figures who may be observing them. At other times, what teens say face to face is belied by what danah observes online. For example, although some teens talk about racial integration and cross-race friendships, she can observe very segregated social networks and push her real-life subjects on this matter. Understanding who is left out of social networks—distinguishing between exes and outcasts, for instance—can be just as important as mapping who is included in them.

As more and more social life takes place across platforms, we need more researchers like danah who carefully stitch the domains of our fragmented lives together and help us make sense of them. In the meantime, when danah is not busy doing research at Microsoft Research or running the Data & Society Research Institute, she has helped her mother build a company painting houses in response to her mother's request for "a job the Internet can't take away." Maybe we could all use danah's wise counsel on that front.

As social scientists, we have a set of standard approaches that we follow in investigating our questions. We call these rules research methods. They're

Research methods approaches that social scientists use for investigating the answers to questions.

the tools we use to describe, explore, and explain various social phenomena in an ethical fashion. There are two general categories of methods for gathering sociological data: quantitative and qualitative.

Quantitative methods seek to obtain information about the social world that is already in or can be converted to numeric form. This methodology then uses statistical analysis to describe the social world that those data represent. Some of this analysis attempts to mimic the scientific method of using treatment and control (or placebo) groups to determine how changes in one factor affect another social outcome, while factoring out every other simultaneous event. Such information is often acquired through surveys but may also include data collected by other means, ranging from sampling bank records to weighing people on a scale to hanging out with teens at the mall.

Qualitative methods, of which there are many, attempt to collect information about the social world that cannot be readily converted to numeric form. The information gathered with this approach is often used to document the meanings that actions engender in social participants or to describe the mechanisms by which social processes occur. Qualitative data are collected in a host of ways, from spending time with people and recording what they say and do (participant observation) to interviewing them in an open-ended manner to reviewing archives.

Both quantitative and qualitative research approaches provide ways to establish a causal relationship between social elements. Researchers using quantitative approaches, by eliminating all other possibilities through their study's design, hope to state with some certainty that one condition causes another. Qualitative methodology describes social processes in such detail as to rule out competing possibilities.

This chapter gives examples of sociological research conducted using different methods, starting with the various theoretical viewpoints from which social scientists approach research. We'll then examine some techniques used by researchers to tell causal stories and give examples of specific studies that have employed these methods. Finally, we'll talk about the ways that social research can be used for ends other than filling textbooks and keeping sociologists busy.

Quantitative methods
methods that seek to obtain information about the social world that is already in or can be converted to numeric form.

Qualitative methods
methods that attempt to collect information about the social world that cannot be readily converted to numeric form.

→ Research 101

The general goal of sociology is to allow us to see how our individual lives are intimately related to (and, in turn, affect) the social forces that exist beyond us. Good sociological research begins with a puzzle or paradox and asks, "What causes such and such a thing to happen?" Once you pick a question to investigate, there are two ways to approach research: *deductively* and *inductively*. A deductive approach starts with a theory, forms a hypothesis, makes empirical observations, and then analyzes the data to confirm, reject, or modify the original theory. Conversely, an inductive approach starts with empirical

Deductive approach a research approach that starts with a theory, forms a hypothesis, makes empirical observations, and then analyzes the data to confirm, reject, or modify the original theory.

Inductive approach a research approach that starts with empirical observations and then works to form a theory.

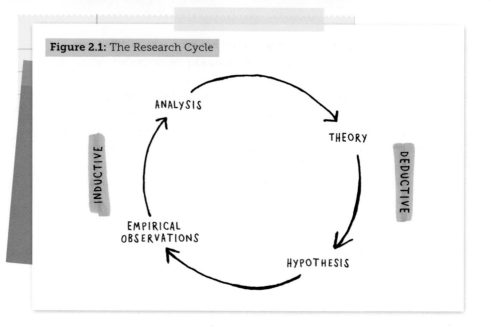

Figure 2.1: The Research Cycle

ANALYSIS

THEORY

INDUCTIVE

DEDUCTIVE

EMPIRICAL
OBSERVATIONS

HYPOTHESIS

observations and then works to form a theory. These different approaches are represented in the research cycle shown in Figure 2.1.

Causality versus Correlation

Correlation or **association**
simultaneous variation in two
variables.

Regardless of which method we use, social research is about telling a story. The goal is to recount the story as completely as possible so we're fairly certain it can't be told any other way. Let's take an example using the relationship between income and health. We know that a correlation (or association) exists between income and health; that is, they tend to vary together. For example, people with higher levels of income tend to enjoy better overall health. But to say two things are correlated is very different from stating that one causes the other. In fact, there are three possible causal stories about the relationship between income and health. We might reasonably assert that bad health causes you to have a lower income—because when you get sick you can't work, you lose your job, and so forth. If we drew a diagram of such a scenario, it would look like this:

POORER HEALTH ⟶ LOWER INCOME

However, we could just as easily tell the opposite story—that higher income leads to better health because you can afford better doctors; you have access to fresh, healthful foods in your upscale neighborhood; and there's a gym at the office. The diagram of this story would look like this:

POORER HEALTH ⟵ LOWER INCOME

Finally, we could conclude that a third factor causes both income and health to vary in the same direction. For the sake of argument, we will call this factor "reckless tendencies"—a love of fast cars, wine, and late nights. Such shortsighted behavior could negatively affect our health (especially the wine). And it could also affect our income. Maybe we are unable to get to work on time or are spending too much money on those fast cars instead of investing it in the stock market. In that case, the causal diagram would look like this:

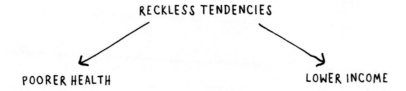

In this scenario, if we merely observe health and income, it may appear as if one causes the other, but the truth of the matter is that they are not related in the slightest apart from being connected through a third factor.

How can we arrive at any conclusions with respect to the health–income correlation? We can't randomly assign people to different jobs at various pay levels and see what happens, nor can we independently affect people's health and (ethically) observe what happens to their income, and it is certainly difficult to curb or instill reckless tendencies on a random basis. Thus, we can't really rule out any of the arrows, but we can confirm some of them. We can rule out many third factors by measuring them and then comparing individuals who are similar in that particular respect (like education level) but differ in other key regards (say, income). Other factors may not be so easy to measure, and in these cases we might look for a natural experiment—that is, an event or change in the real world that affects the factor we believe causes an outcome but does not affect the outcome in any way other than through that factor. For example, some researchers have used lottery winnings as a natural experiment, comparing the health of winners who won a significant sum with those who won only a token amount. The assumption, based on how lotteries work, is that the amount won is not determined by the winner's health, but that subsequent changes in health may well be driven by the money won.

Although few certain answers exist in social science, we can safely conclude that low income does contribute to poor health, at least to some extent in specific contexts. (We can also be fairly sure that bad health has a negative effect on income.) However, our case would be stronger if we knew exactly what effect low income has on health. In other words, we don't know the causal mechanism. Is it that low-wage jobs are stressful? (It is well known that certain types of chronic stress are bad for you.) If so, does such stress cause these workers' behavior to change, perhaps by increasing their consumption of fast food, smoking rates, or alcohol intake? Or is there a more direct, psychobiological pathway—say, the stress of a verbally abusive boss that can cause higher

How did studying lottery winners help sociologists understand the relationship between wealth and health?

corticosteroid levels in the bloodstream? Or is it all of these factors and more? The more dots we can connect, the stronger our causal story becomes and the better prepared we are to intervene.

Causality the notion that a change in one factor results in a corresponding change in another.

Remember, it is very difficult, especially in social science, to assert causality—that change in one factor causes a change in another. It's much easier to say two things are correlated, which just means that we observe change in both. For example, as race varies (across individuals), so does average life expectancy. Likewise, as nutrition changes across or within populations, so does average height, but can we say that better nutrition causes some populations to be taller? Maybe, but maybe not. Let's further examine this.

To establish causality, three factors are needed: correlation, time order, and ruling out alternative explanations. We've already covered correlation. We notice variations in nutrition across countries and simultaneously observe different average heights across the same countries that tend to correspond statistically to those differences in nutrition. Now we need to establish time order. Have people in country A always been taller than those in country B (a bad sign for the "better nutrition causes height" case)? Or did changes in nutrition occur before increases (or decreases) in height? We can imagine a situation where a drought, flood, frost, or some other environmental factor destroyed a main food source in country B, leading to dramatic changes in people's diet and altering average heights in that nation. Finally, we have to rule out alternative explanations for the variations observed in both nutrition and height. Is a third factor responsible for changes in both? The groundwater supply perhaps? Groundwater supply could lead to better nutrition through higher crop yields (which turns out not to matter for height, let's say), but it could also lead to cleaner drinking water and thus less infection (which turns out to matter for height, again for the sake of argument). If this were the case, then the relationship between nutrition and height would be termed spurious or false, whereas the relationship between infection and height might be described as a "true" causal relationship. Figure 2.2 illustrates this possibility.

The Problem of Reverse Causality Reverse causality is just what it sounds like: You think A is causing B when, in fact, B is causing A. Let's look at the relationship between income and health. We know that people who are sick often have less income. But which one is causing the other to happen? Is it that when you're sick, you miss lots of school, don't receive as much education, must take off more time from work, are passed over for promotions, and ultimately remain stuck in a lower-level job and therefore have a lower income than your comparatively healthy neighbor? Or is it that when you're employed in a lower-paying job, you may experience more on-the-job stress and more stress as a result of worrying about money, which has a negative impact on your health by putting you at higher risk for cardiovascular disease? On top of that, you can't afford good health care, a gym membership, or fresh, nutritious food. The problem of reverse causality is why it's so important to establish time order. If a person's income drops only after they get sick, we can be surer that it was sickness that led to the decline in income.

However, we should also note that time order is no guarantee by itself: People may alter their current behavior based on future expectations. Perhaps, for example, I choose to save less today because I assume that my children will become rich adults on their own and support me in my old age. Strict reliance on time order—observing current savings behavior and children's income

> **Reverse causality** a situation in which the researcher believes that A results in a change in B, but B, in fact, is causing A.

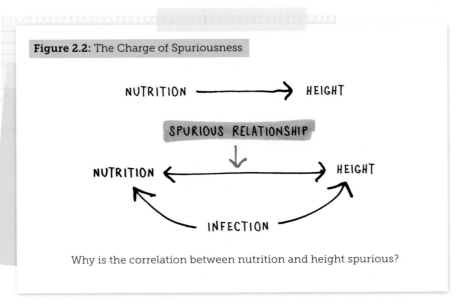

Figure 2.2: The Charge of Spuriousness

NUTRITION ⟶ HEIGHT

SPURIOUS RELATIONSHIP

NUTRITION ⟷ HEIGHT

INFECTION

Why is the correlation between nutrition and height spurious?

30 years later—would lead me to the wrong conclusion—namely, that all the things I bought for my kids which put me into debt caused my children's success later in life, when it was actually the other way around. Their future success caused me to spend wantonly, assuming that they would bail me out once they got their six-figure salaries. One way to fix this, of course, would be to directly measure my expectations for my children's future income to resolve the matter of time order.

Variables

In research we talk a great deal about variables. Simply put, you should always have one dependent variable, which is the outcome you are trying to explain, and one or more independent variables, which are the measured factors that you believe have a causal impact on the dependent variable. Because it's possible to have more than one independent variable, we will call the most important one the *key independent variable*. The difference between the independent and the dependent variables is that change in your dependent variable depends on change in your independent variable. Knowing which variable is which is important for complying with mandates for establishing causality. Often, when we establish correlation but can't do the same for causality, it's because we don't know which variable is causing change in the other—we can't establish time order, for example, so we don't know which variable is the independent and which is the dependent.

In high-school science class, you may have learned that a hypothesis is an educated guess. In social research, we use the term *hypothesis* to refer to a proposed relationship between two variables, usually with a stated direction. The *direction* of the relationship refers to whether your variables move in the same direction (positive) or in opposite directions (negative).

Let's take some examples. We know that income is positively related to education: As people's education increases, usually so too does their income. Overt prejudice, on the other hand, is negatively related to education: As people's educational levels increase, generally their levels of expressed prejudice decrease.

Hypothesis Testing

Are you starting to see how these pieces fit together in the design of a research project? Perhaps we have a special interest in one concept, say, poverty. Poverty is a broad concept, so we need to specify what we mean by poverty in this particular study. The process of assigning a precise method for measuring a term being examined for use in a particular study is called operationalization. When you read a study, it's important to understand how the author is operationalizing his or her concept. If I do a study on poverty among Americans who fall below the official U.S. poverty line, and someone else completes a study that

Dependent variable the outcome that the researcher is trying to explain.

Independent variable a measured factor that the researcher believes has a causal impact on the dependent variable.

Hypothesis a proposed relationship between two variables.

Operationalization the process of assigning a precise method for measuring a term being examined for use in a particular study.

examines poverty using the United Nations definition of it—namely, subsistence on less than $1.25 per day—we're discussing two very different concepts of poverty. As the old adage says, we're comparing apples and oranges. Once I decide how I'm defining poverty, I can begin to consider all the variables related to my concept. In the case of poverty, we might take a look at education, employment status, race, or gender.

It's time to make some decisions. First of all, is poverty my dependent or independent variable? Am I thinking about poverty as the cause of something else (poor health) or its result (lack of formal education)? Let's say I want to examine the factors that cause poverty, and I'm especially interested in the effect of parental education on children's poverty levels, because theory tells me that a link exists. Assuming that I've defined educational level (number of years in school? grades or degrees completed? scores on a certain test? prestige of any college attended?), now I'm ready to pose my research question: What effect do parents' educational levels have on children's chances of living in poverty as adults? And I can form a hypothesis:

> Hypothesis: The lower the educational level of the parents, the greater the chance that their children will be poor as adults.

Also for each hypothesis, an equal and opposite alternative hypothesis exists:

> Alternative hypothesis: There is a positive relationship between parental education and children's likelihood of living in poverty as adults.

Parental education is my key independent variable, but I also believe that race and family structure may affect how my independent variable matters. In this example, race and family structure would be moderating variables—that is, they affect the relationship between my independent and my dependent variables. (Children's education or test scores in this example would be mediating variables that are positioned between the independent and dependent variables but do not interact with either to affect the relationship between them.)

I am not quite ready to test my hypotheses, however. First, I need to tell stories—that is, causal stories about why I would expect the hypotheses to be true. In support of the hypotheses, I might say that parents who are more educated have acquired more confidence and skills for succeeding in our economy and that they are then more likely to pass on some of this knowledge and positive outlook to their kids at home. In support of my alternative hypothesis, parents who have spent a great deal of money on their own education may have less left over to help their children. Establishing the groundwork for a reasonably "fair fight" between main and alternative hypotheses is important so we do not spend time discovering trivialities that are already well known (e.g., low-income individuals tend to be poor). So how good were my guesses or hypotheses?

Validity, Reliability, and Generalizability

Validity, reliability, and generalizability are simple but important concepts. To say a measure has validity means that it measures what you intend it to. So if you step on a scale and it measures your height, it's not valid. Likewise, if I ask you how happy you are with your life in general, and you tell me how happy you are with school in particular, at this exact moment my question isn't a valid measure of your life satisfaction. Reliability refers to how likely you are to obtain the same result using the same measure the next time. A scale that's off by ten pounds might not be totally valid—it will not give me my actual weight—but the scale is reliable if every time I step on it, it reads exactly ten pounds less than my true weight. Likewise, a clock that's five minutes fast is reliable but not valid. But if I ask you to rate your overall satisfaction with your life so far, and you honestly tell me you would give yourself a 10 out of 10, and then a week from now I ask you to rate your overall satisfaction with life so far, and you honestly tell me you'd give yourself a 7 out of 10 (because that first time you had just found $10 on the floor), then that measure (my question) is valid but not reliable. Ideally, we'd like our measures to be both valid and reliable, but sometimes we have to make trade-offs between the two. Keep this in mind as we discuss the various methods of data collection.

Finally, generalizability is the extent to which we can claim that our findings inform us about a group larger than the one we studied. Can we generalize our findings to a larger population? And how do we determine whether we can?

Validity the extent to which an instrument measures what it is intended to measure.

Reliability the likelihood of obtaining consistent results using the same measure.

Generalizability the extent to which we can claim our findings inform us about a group larger than the one we studied.

Role of the Researcher

Experimenter Effects As if social research weren't hard enough already, there are also "white coat" effects—that is, the effects that researchers have on the very processes and relationships they are studying by virtue of being there. Often, subjects change their behavior, consciously or not, just because they are part of a study. Have you ever been in a classroom when the teacher is being observed? It might prove to be the best class the teacher has ever taught, even if she didn't mean to put on the charm for the observer.

When we do qualitative fieldwork (interviews, ethnography, or participant observation) we talk about reflexivity, which means analyzing and critically considering the white coat effects you may be inspiring with your research process. What is your relationship to your research subjects? Frequently, research focuses on groups that are disadvantaged relative to the researcher in one way or another. Researchers might have more money, more education, or more resources in general. How does that shape the interactions between researcher and subjects, and ultimately the findings?

Urban ethnographer Mitchell Duneier spent five years hanging out with booksellers on the sidewalks of Sixth Avenue in Manhattan. He wanted to

Reflexivity analyzing and critically considering our own role in, and effect on, our research.

understand how these street vendors and their groups of friends, many of them homeless, functioned in the community. During the course of his research, Duneier became friends with many of these people, which was apparent when he and I talked about how he made sure he was not exploiting his subjects. Duneier's firm belief in the researcher's responsibility to his or her subjects is not always easy for him. He told me that "in the process of doing my research, before I publish my work, I make an effort to try to show the research that I'm going to publish to the people who are depicted in it. . . . Doing this is a very stressful process. Sometimes you have to read people things that are very unflattering to them. And for me, it has taken a lot of courage to sit in a room with someone, with a manuscript, and to read those things to them. Sometimes I can be shaking when I do it because I'm so afraid of the way people are going to respond. But I feel that if I am going to be writing something about people, and I'm going to be putting it out there for the public to read, whether it's with their name on it or not, then they deserve the basic respect of hearing it from me in advance." Even after the private reading and scrutiny of the work for its most important audience—the subject—Duneier notes that the researcher must show ongoing respect for subjects:

> One of the most basic things that one can do, is to try really hard, to make sure that people don't feel used by you, after you leave the field. It's very easy given the constraints of our lives and the academy, and the great pressures we are under within our own universities, running departments, engaging in teaching, supervising students in research, it's very possible that given those demands that when we leave the field site that we can walk away from our subjects' lives and not stay in touch with them. Not ever send them any acknowledgment of the time that they spent with us. Not ever send them the results of the research. Especially if we end up moving to other parts of the country from where they live, and it's hard to stay in touch with them. It's very easy for them to get the impression that we have just walked away, benefited at their expense. They have given us their emotions, we have appropriated their lives for our sociological purposes, and then have gone on with ours. (Conley, 2009a)

As researchers, we're supposed to remain objective, but even if you want to (and some people may not want to remain impartial in certain situations), it's not always possible. One day an incident occurred between the police and the street vendors when Duneier was there (with his tape recorder running in his shirt pocket, unbeknownst to the police). He defended his friends to the officers. Because he was a white, well-spoken, and highly educated professional, his interactions with police probably differed significantly from those between the typical African American street vendor and the police. Duneier could speak his mind with a bit less fear of arrest and with the knowledge that he could afford a competent lawyer to defend himself. How did Duneier's presence change the interaction that transpired? Most social scientists would

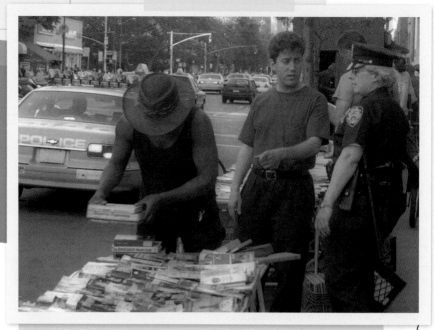

What is the white coat effect? Sociologist Mitch Duneier (center), who studied street-side book vendors for his book *Sidewalk*, talks with a police officer. To see an interview with Duneier, go to wwnpag.es/SC2a.

argue that once subjects become accustomed to the researcher's presence, they again behave as normal, but we don't have any real way to determine this. When we're engaged in qualitative research, we may find ourselves in situations where we have to choose whether objectivity and distance are more important than standing up for what we believe is right. At these times, we need to take a step back and think about our own role as both researcher and participant, because it is our perception and experience of events that eventually become the data from which we make our claims. Duneier acknowledges that ethnographers are not perfect observer-reporters whose presence has absolutely no effect on subjects' attitudes and behavior. The ethnographer, like any other scientist, has a responsibility to readers to make his or her data collection methods public. Furthermore, readers "have to have a sense for how the conclusions were drawn . . . by [researchers] making the lens through which the reality is being refracted apparent. That means telling them something about who we are, not only our race, not only our class or our gender, but a number of other fundamental things."

Power: In the Eyes of the Researcher, We're Not All Equal

Along these lines, it is worth asking the following: What role does power play in research? As social researchers, we're not supposed to make value judgments; we should put aside our personal biases, strive for neutrality, and remain impartial and objective. The truth, however, is that we make judgments all the time, beginning at the most basic level of deciding what to study. What does the field in general deem worthy of scholarly attention? What topics am I sufficiently interested in to spend two, five, or ten years, or my entire career studying? What research do grant-making institutions regard as important enough to fund? What does the social scientific community more broadly view as problematic or interesting and in need of explanation?

Historically, sociology, like most sciences, has been male dominated. But it's also a discipline founded on the idea of making the natural seem unnatural, so it's a good place from which change can percolate. Following the feminist movement of the late 1960s, a growing stream of thought within sociology sought to turn a critical, feminist lens on the discipline itself. Because research ultimately forms the foundation of our work, methods became a key site of debate, and thus the concept of feminist methodology was born. What do feminist research methods look like? First, it's important to understand that there is no one feminist research method, just as there is no single school of feminism. Feminist researchers use the same techniques for gathering data as other sociologists, but they employ those techniques in ways that differ significantly from traditional methods. As Sandra Harding explains it, feminist researchers

> listen carefully to how women informants think about their lives and men's lives, and critically to how traditional social scientists conceptualize women's and men's lives. They observe behaviors of women and men that traditional social scientists have not thought significant. They seek examples of newly recognized patterns in historical data. (1987, p. 2)

Feminist methodology a set of systems or methods that treat women's experiences as legitimate empirical and theoretical resources, that promote social science *for* women (think public sociology, but for a specific half of the public), and that take into account the researcher as much as the overt subject matter.

The feminist part doesn't lie in the method per se, or necessarily in having women as subjects. Rather, Harding proposes three ways to make research distinctly feminist. First, treat women's experiences as legitimate empirical and theoretical resources. Second, engage in social science that may bring about policy changes to help improve women's lives. Third, take into account the researcher as much as the overt subject matter. When we enter a research situation, an imbalance of power usually exists between the researcher and the research subjects, and we need to take this power dimension seriously. The point of adopting feminist methods isn't to exclude men or male perspectives: It's not *instead of*; it's *in addition to*. It means taking all subjects seriously rather than privileging one type of data, experience, or worldview over another.

Creating and Testing Theory

Good research is usually guided by theory, but there are different types of theories. Which theory best fits your subject? In Chapter 1, I described the differences between positivist and interpretive sociology. As distinct as they are in their focus, they also lend themselves to different methodological approaches to research. Because positivists are concerned with the factors that influence

For her research on neighborhoods in Philadelphia, sociologist Alice Goffman did immersive fieldwork as well as quantitative research to collect the data she needed to answer her research questions.

social life, they tend to rely more heavily on quantitative measures. If, however, you're more concerned with the meanings actors attach to their behavior, as interpretive sociologists are, then you'll likely be drawn to more qualitative measures.

Ultimately, the distinction between quantitative and qualitative methods is a false dichotomy: The most important thing is to determine what you want to learn and then contemplate the best possible way to collect the empirical data that would answer your question—that is, deploy whatever tool or set of tools is called for by the present research problem. That's why getting the research question right is so important to the entire endeavor. Once the question is precisely operationalized, the method to answer the question should be obvious. If the question still could be approached in several ways, then you probably haven't refined it enough. Figure 2.3 gives an overview of the entire process.

Data Collection

Remember that social science research is largely about collecting empirical evidence to generate or test empirical claims. So how do we go about collecting the evidence needed to support our claims? Let's use case studies—that is, particular examples of good research—and see what these researchers wanted to know, how they obtained their data, and what they found.

Participant Observation Neighborhoods rise and fall and (sometimes) rise again. Often these changes in fortune are accompanied by racially tinged dynamics: white flight in one direction and, when the tides turn again, (white) gentrification. But sometimes neighborhoods are reshaped by class dynamics

Figure 2.3: The Research Process

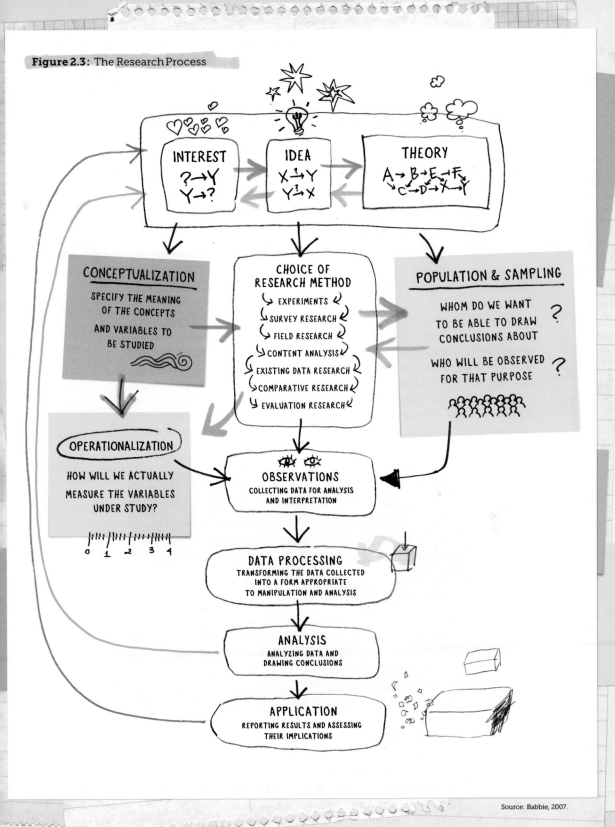

SAMPLES: THEY'RE NOT JUST THE FREE TASTES AT THE SUPERMARKET

People use the word *sample* in many different ways, but in social research it has a very specific and important meaning. You are always studying a population. It could be the entire U.S. population, gay fathers, public schools in the rural South, science textbooks, gangs, Fortune 500 companies, or middle-class, Caucasian, single mothers. Most of the time it's too time consuming and expensive to collect information about the entire population you want to study, so instead you focus on a sample. Your sample, then, is the subset of the population from which you are actually collecting data. (If you do collect information on the entire population, it's called a census.)

How you go about collecting your sample is probably one of the most important steps of your research. Let's say I want to study attitudes toward underage drinking in the United States and hand out a survey to your sociology class. Based on the findings of that survey, I make claims on how the entire U.S. population feels about underage drinking: They're in favor of it. Would you believe my claims? I hope not! Your sociology class is probably not representative of the U.S. population as a whole. Age would be the most important factor, but differences in socioeconomic status, education, race, and the like would exist. In other words,

Population an entire group of individual persons, objects, or items from which samples may be drawn.

Sample the subset of the population from which you are actually collecting data.

Volunteer Phyllis Evans (center) questions a homeless man about his living situation and encourages him to seek help while conducting a survey with team members in New York City.

the results I would obtain from a survey of a college sociology class would not be generalizable to the U.S. population and probably not even to college students as a whole—maybe not even to students at your school (the students next door in organic chemistry might have very different thoughts about underage drinking). I would be "speaking beyond my data."

Although the issues of generalizability are always at play, they become particularly acute when social scientists use case studies. A case study, often used in qualitative research, is an in-depth look at a specific phenomenon in a particular social setting. If we wanted to understand the interaction among parents, teachers, and administrators in the American public school system, we might do a case study of your high

Census taker talking with Charles F. Piper as he works on his car.

Case study
an intensive investigation of one particular unit of analysis in order to describe it or uncover its mechanisms.

school. How representative of all U.S. high schools do you think your school is? Does your town have a higher or lower average household income than the United States as a whole? Is the PTA particularly vocal? Is yours a regional high school whose students travel long distances to attend? All of these factors—these variables—are important, and if your town isn't typical (statistically speaking), we'd question the usefulness of the findings. This is perhaps the main drawback of the case study method. The findings have very low generalizability. One benefit, however, is that we typically obtain very detailed information. So there is often a trade-off between breadth (i.e., generalizability) and depth (i.e., amount of information and nuanced detail). A case study can serve as a useful starting point for exploring new topics. For example, researchers often use case studies to develop hypotheses and to generate and refine survey questions that the researchers will then administer to a much larger sample. Likewise, qualitative case studies are sometimes used to try to understand causal mechanisms that have been indicated in large-scale survey studies.

within racial groups. With the rise of a black professional class since the civil rights era, gentrification—the movement of higher-income individuals into once-distressed inner-city neighborhoods—can be an entirely black affair. But does that create the same tensions as cross-race urban transitions? Or does it provide its own set of unique problems?

To answer this (and other) questions, sociologist Mary Pattillo studied the Chicago neighborhood of North Kenwood–Oakland using the method called participant observation. This approach aims to uncover the meanings people give to their own social actions (and those of others) by observing their behavior in practice, in contrast to just asking them about it after the fact. This strategy is predicated on the notion that surveys, interviews, and other approaches are more easily "managed" by the respondents. That is, studying racial attitudes by surveying respondents, for instance, may lead to subjects telling the researcher what they think is the "right" answer and what the researcher wants to hear. But by hanging out in a given community over a long period, integrating into its daily fabric, and letting the dramas of everyday life unfold with minimal intrusion, participant observers are more likely to capture what folks actually think, feel, and do rather than what they would like to think they do.

This type of sociology typically involves a significant time investment, because the participant observer must gain access to a given community, learn its local norms and logic of behavior, and then watch social dynamics unfold. Often it can take years to do an ethnographic study of this nature. In Pattillo's case, she moved into the community right as other professional blacks were as well. She attended local community board meetings, went to block parties, socialized with neighbors—basically she hung out like everyone else. But the difference was that she was engaging her sociological imagination and took extensive field notes about what was unfolding around her.

What she found was that unlike in typical cross-race situations of gentrification, the middle-class blacks who moved in and revitalized the area occupied a "middleman" status. They offered social resources to their lower-class neighbors—helping them navigate city politics and bureaucracy, for example. But the role came with costs and conflicts as well: Residents of different classes disagreed about the proper use of space, such as whether the front porch was a proper hangout or where barbecuing should take place (in the front or back-yard). There were also more consequential struggles, such as those over local schools. In the end, Pattillo's combination of historical analysis and time spent "hanging out" in the neighborhood painted a rich portrait of class and race as it plays out in Chicago's South Side.

Interviews Want to know how and why someone does something? Why not just ask them to tell you all about it? Interviews are one common form of gathering qualitative data. For her book *Money, Morals, and Manners* (1992), sociologist Michèle Lamont interviewed upper-middle-class men in France and the United States about their tastes. She chose the men in her sample based on their social status—they were employed as managers, professionals, and

Participant observation a qualitative research method that seeks to uncover the meanings people give their social actions by observing their behavior in practice.

entrepreneurs—arguing that these people hold enormous power in their jobs and communities, and consequently their tastes are influential in shaping the culture around them. Lamont conducted more than 160 interviews, trying to determine how the people in her sample defined what it means to be a "worthy person" and analyzing "the relative importance attached to religion, honesty, low moral standards, cosmopolitanism, high culture, money, [and] power" (Lamont, 1992). The comparative aspect of her research design allowed her to identify some of the cultural differences between American and French tastes. For example, she ascertained that the French men valued art more than their American counterparts, whereas the Americans cared more about money than their French counterparts.

By using unstructured, open-ended interviews, Lamont allowed her subjects to go off on tangents, to vent, and to share intimacies that might not appear at first glance to be related to the study. But she also did probe—that is, she pushed subjects past their initial, comfortable answers on somewhat delicate, controversial issues. Knowing how and when to probe and when to back off is part of the art of interviewing that results from practice. Other researchers may rely on semi-structured or structured interviews—that is, interviews in which the researchers have more than just a set of topics to cover in no preset order; rather, the researchers develop a specific set of questions to address with all respondents in a relatively fixed sequence. If an interview becomes very structured, it falls into the next category: survey research.

Survey Research Chances are you've filled out a survey at some point. One customarily receives them from the manufacturers and retailers of electronics and from restaurants and hotels. Surveys are an ordered series of questions intended to elicit information from respondents, and they can be powerful methods of data collection. Surveys may be done anonymously and distributed widely, so you can reach a much larger sample than if you relied solely on interviews. At the same time, however, you have to pay attention to your response rate. Out of all the surveys you distributed, how many were actually completed and returned to you? Lately, we have been bombarded with more and more surveys soliciting our opinions about everything from what soap we prefer to how to stop global warming. It has become increasingly difficult for researchers to get their surveys answered amid the din of our information society, and response rates, in general, continue to fall.

Survey an ordered series of questions intended to elicit information from respondents.

Why does this matter? If those who answered your survey or tore it up were truly random, then the only concern would be the cost in time and money to obtain, say, 200 completed surveys. But, as it turns out, who responds and who doesn't is not random. As a researcher, you need to consider the ways that selection bias can enter your sample. Are the people who completed the survey different in some significant way from the people who didn't complete it? If your survey is about the sacrifices respondents would be willing to make to slow global warming and the only folks who bother to respond are environmentalists, your results will likely indicate that the population is willing to sacrifice far more than it actually would. In fact, the nonrespondents were not even willing to sacrifice the ten minutes to take the survey. Surveys can also be done in person or over the phone. This method of survey design differs from interviews in that a set questionnaire exists. Surveys are generally converted into quantitative data for statistical analysis—everything from simple estimates (How many gay policemen are there in America?) to comparisons of averages across groups (What proportion of gay policemen support abortion rights, and what proportion of retired female plumbers do?) to complex techniques such as multiple regression, where one measured factor (such as education level) is held constant, or statistically removed from the picture, to pin down the effect of another factor (such as total family income) on, say, reported levels of happiness.

The General Social Survey (GSS) run by the National Opinion Research Center of the University of Chicago is one of the premier surveys in the United States. Since 1972, the GSS has asked respondents a battery of questions about their social and demographic characteristics and their opinions on a wide range of subjects. Conducted every other year, the GSS includes some new questions, but many are the same from one survey to the next. This has allowed researchers to track American attitudes about a range of important issues, from race relations to abortion politics to beliefs about sexual orientation, and to see how the beliefs of different demographic subgroups have converged or diverged over four decades. The GSS is an example of a repeated cross-sectional survey. That is, it samples a new group of approximately 2,000 Americans in each yearly survey wave. Each sample should represent a cross-section of the U.S. population of that particular survey year.

A cross-sectional study stands in contrast to a panel survey, also known as a longitudinal study, which tracks the same individuals, households, or other social units over time. One such survey, the Panel Study of Income Dynamics (PSID), run by the Institute for Social Research at the University of Michigan, has followed 5,000 American families each year since 1968. (Recently, the PSID had to trim back to every other year because of budget cutbacks.) It even tracks family members who have split off and formed their own households and families. In this way, the survey has taken on the structure of a family tree. The PSID has contributed to important research on questions about how families transition in and out of poverty, what predicts if marriages will last, and how much economic mobility exists in the United States across generations— just to name a few of the topics that PSID analysis has illuminated.

Historical Methods, Comparative Research, and Content Analysis
How do we study the past? We can't interview or survey dead people, and we certainly can't observe institutions or social settings that no longer exist. What researchers employing historical methods do is collect data from written reports, newspaper articles, journals, transcripts, television programs, diaries, artwork, and other artifacts that date back to the period they want to study. Researchers often study social movements using historical

Historical methods research that collects data from written reports, newspaper articles, journals, transcripts, television programs, diaries, artwork, and other artifacts that date back to the period under study.

methods, because the full import of the movement may not be apparent until after it has ended.

How did America end up with a relatively weak welfare state and a high tolerance for inequality, particularly in the context of race, compared with other industrialized democracies? To answer this question, sociologist Jill Quadagno went back to the archives to research what had been said officially (in regulations and other government documents) and unofficially (in the press) about the passage and implementation of the New Deal in the 1930s and the War on Poverty in the 1960s (Quadagno, 1996).

Quadagno took into account many different explanations: timing (the United States industrialized early, before the adequate development of protective political institutions), institutions (the United States has one of the most fragmented political systems in the developed world, making it comparatively difficult to marshal large-scale government programs), and "American exceptionalism" (the notion that our culture, lacking a history of feudalism, was uniquely individualistic and nonpaternalistic).

> **Comparative research** a methodology by which two or more entities (such as countries), which are similar in many dimensions but differ on one in question, are compared to learn about the dimension that differs between them.

Finally, the issue on which Quadagno focused her research was the looming shadow of racism in America. According to Quadagno, in order to prevent blacks from participating fully in the American social contract, authority devolved from the federal government to state and local authorities, which could then exclude blacks overtly or covertly. The result was a much weaker safety net and one that, for a long time, excluded minorities disproportionately. For example, to ensure that congressional committees controlled by racist southern Democrats passed Social Security, President Franklin D. Roosevelt had to agree to exclude agricultural and domestic workers when the system was established in 1935. This exception was made purposely to exclude African Americans, who were disproportionately employed in these two sectors. Thus, by conducting historical, archival research, Quadagno and others have been able to show the relevance of race in explaining the particularities of the social safety net in the United States.

Whereas the example above focuses on one case, sometimes sociologists compare two or more historical societies; we call this "comparative historical" research. For example, Rogers Brubaker compared the conceptions of citizenship and nationhood in France and Germany (Brubaker, 1992). Comparative research is a methodology by which a researcher compares two or more entities with the intent of learning more about the factors

Children of a plantation sharecropper preparing food on a wood stove in a sparsely furnished shack in 1936. How did Jill Quadagno use historical methods to analyze the ways in which people like these children were excluded from the benefits of the New Deal?

that differ between them. By examining official documents and important texts written over a period of many years leading up to, during, and after the formation of the German and French states, Brubaker showed that their historical circumstances led to very different visions of citizenship in each nation. France was formed from a loosely knit group of powerful duchies and principalities. There was no preexisting French nation or nationality before the creation of the French government. The idea of nationhood—that is, of French identity—had to be forged by the state itself, and this led to a very inclusive notion of citizenship. Germany, by contrast, grew out of an already well-refined, tribal sense of Prussian nationality. Thus, Germany's citizenship policy was based on excluding others rather than including them.

The general approach to comparative research is to find cases that match on many potentially relevant dimensions but vary on just one, allowing researchers to observe the effect of that particular dimension. Although all social science research makes inferences based on implicit or explicit comparison, comparative research usually refers to cross-national studies. For example, in studying the effects of universal health care, it would be better to compare the United States (which is still getting used to running a more universal health care apparatus) with Canada (which has had universal care for decades) than to compare South Africa (which doesn't) with Sweden (which does), because the latter two countries are so different from each other geographically and culturally.

Content analysis a systematic analysis of the content rather than the structure of a communication, such as a written work, speech, or film.

One distinct subtype of historical methods research, content analysis, is a systematic analysis of the content in written or recorded material. Race scholar Ann Morning (2004) used content analysis to investigate depictions and discussions of race in American textbooks across academic disciplines over time. Morning analyzed both manifest and latent content on race in a sample of 92 high-school textbooks published in the United States between 1952 and 2002 in the fields of biology, anthropology, psychology, sociology, world culture, and world geography. *Manifest content* refers to what we can observe; Morning's study included overt discussions and definitions of race and images of different races. *Latent content* refers to what is implied but not stated outright; Morning looked for sections of the texts where race was directly implied, even if the word *race* wasn't used. She chose her sample from all high-school textbooks published in the United States between 1952 and 2002.

Ultimately, Morning's analysis disputed earlier findings that biology textbooks no longer discuss race. Her findings showed that only social sciences texts employed constructivist approaches (i.e., the

Greek miners seeking work in the German Ruhr Basin in 1960 after West Germany began a guest worker program. What did Roger Brubaker's comparative research about European immigration policies reveal about definitions of citizenship?

belief that race is a social construct), whereas biology books reinforced essentialist conceptualizations (i.e., the belief that race is innate and genetic). However, contrary to her original hypotheses, social sciences textbooks also used biological components in their definitions of race, and only the fields of anthropology and sociology critiqued the traditional concept of race. Why does all this matter? As Morning points out, if textbooks aren't changing, how are students supposed to learn new concepts or viewpoints? Anthropology and sociology aren't widely taught at the high-school level, whereas biology is mandatory in most public school systems.

Experimentation Because social scientists deal with people, the controlled environment of a laboratory-based experiment is not always an option. For example, I dream of randomly assigning the students in one of my classes to married or single life in order to examine marital status on some dimension. Assuming seating is random, I'd just draw a line straight down the middle of the lecture hall; all the students on one side would have to marry, while those on the other side would have to remain single. Think of the possibilities! For better or worse, however, I'm not allowed to perform such experiments.

Some sociologists do use experimental methods, however. For instance, sociologist Duncan Watts conducted an experiment to find out the extent to which taste in cultural products like music and movies is determined by what other people think. Watts speculated that "when we look at cultural markets it's very clear that the successful ones are many times more successful than average, so you see things like Harry Potter books have sold probably about 400 million copies around the world. . . . What was puzzling to us about this fact, is that nobody seems to be able to predict which movies, books, albums, etc., are going to be these massive hits" (Conley, 2009b). Watts hypothesized that it was not just the innate cultural quality of a product but the luck of catching on through peer-to-peer influence that determined success in film, music, or publishing. Along with his co-researchers Matthew Salganik and Peter Dodds, Watts tested his hypothesis by creating an online site called Music Lab where they posted mp3s from unknown bands (Salganik et al., 2006). Visitors to the site could download songs and rate how much they liked the music. Some of the 14,341 downloaders saw how many times these previously unheard-of songs from unknown bands had been downloaded by the previous downloaders; some were

Experimental methods methods that seek to alter the social landscape in a very specific way for a given sample of individuals and then track what results that change yields; often involve comparisons to a control group that did not experience such an intervention.

To learn more about Duncan Watts's Music Lab experiment, you can watch my interview with him at **wwnpag.es/SC5**.

unable to see download traffic; and still others could see the song rankings but they had been altered, unbeknownst to the subjects. What the researchers found was that the best songs in one condition rarely did poorly in another condition and the worst rarely did well, but that the songs in the middle could be heavily influenced by how they were rated (if, that is, the downloaders could see those ratings). I asked Watts if his Music Lab experiment could explain other social phenomena. He explained that we can see the same kinds of social influence in the recent housing bubble and recession. According to Watts, "If you look at the recent financial crisis many things went wrong, right? But the big things that went wrong on the way up were this belief that housing prices could not go down, and on the way down a real collapse of our trust in the financial system. Both of them are driven by people thinking whatever they think because of what other people think. These are not fundamentally financial phenomena or economic phenomena even, they're really social phenomena" (Conley, 2009b).

Ethics of Social Research

At the beginning of this chapter, I mentioned the contributions feminists made to research methods with their emphasis on examining relationships between power and the process of knowledge generation. Today, we have more codified standards that must be met by all researchers. Many professional associations have their own ethical standards—doctors, lawyers, journalists, psychologists, and sociologists, just to name a few. Colleges and universities, too, often have guidelines for research conducted with humans (as well as animals, particularly vertebrates). As a professional sociologist, I am beholden to the ethical guidelines established by my peers and the American Sociological Association. As a professor, I am also responsible to my home institution. And as a researcher, I am ultimately responsible to my research subjects. I work with already-collected statistical information (or secondary data) for the most part, which makes the process a little easier, but that doesn't mean I don't have to pay careful attention to the ethical standards of my discipline.

A few golden rules exist in research. The first is "Do no harm." This may seem obvious; you don't want to cause physical harm to your subjects. But what about psychological or emotional harm? What if you want to interview men and women on their attitudes toward abortion, and a respondent becomes very upset because he or she cares deeply about the subject? The initial charge not to do harm seems a little more complicated now. Often, we try to design research projects so that subjects will encounter no more harm than they are likely to experience in everyday life.

The second rule is informed consent. Subjects have a right to know they are participating in a study and what that study will consist of. If you're interviewing people or asking them to complete a survey, this makes sense. But how far do you take the rule of informed consent in participant observation?

Generally, you have to obtain permission to be at your chosen site, but do you remind every person you bump into that you're doing research? What's more, sometimes mild forms of deception are necessary for the sake of research. In Duncan Watts's research about the way a song's rating influenced the way a new listener would rate it, he could not tell his subjects that the ratings they saw were fake. This small amount of deception is usually considered ethically acceptable, but because deception is a slippery slope, panels of academic peers review all research designs to ensure that subjects are protected. If researchers deceive subjects, the deception had better be absolutely necessary to obtain the results, and above all else, the subjects better be safe.

The third rule is voluntary participation, which usually goes hand in hand with informed consent. People have a right to decide if they want to participate in your study. They can also stop participating at any point with no penalty. If you're interviewing someone who doesn't want to answer a question, he or she doesn't have to; if the interviewee wants to stop for whatever reason or no reason, that's his or her prerogative. Ethically, the researcher cannot badger respondents into participating in the study or completing it once they have started. There are also certain protected populations—minors, prisoners and other institutionalized individuals, pregnant women and their unborn fetuses, people with disabilities—whom you often need additional approval to study. As danah boyd's research with teens shows, it's not impossible to study these populations, it just requires additional effort and caution.

Find out if your college or university has an institutional review board and what the requirements are to gain approval for a research project before you start your budding career as a sociologist. And then, never forget, question everything, and make the familiar strange. Good luck!

The Political Battle over Statistical Sampling

You might think that sampling is an arcane, unsexy concern of nerdy researchers trying to make sure their results apply to the population as a whole. In most cases, you would be right. But for almost 30 years, the notion of statistical sampling was a red-hot political issue. At one point, some Republican members of Congress talked about shutting down the government over it.

It all started in 1937, when the Census Bureau used statistical sampling methods to survey unemployment. Of course, knowing the rate of unemployment was of utmost importance during the economic crisis of the Great

Depression. The idea of sampling a portion of the population was then deployed in the 1940 Census, when enumerators asked a random subset of the population (approximately 5 percent) additional questions. They wanted to get more detailed information about what Americans' lives were like without the cost and burden of asking everyone. This was the origin of the so-called census long form (which was eliminated in 2010 after being replaced by the yearly American Community Survey).

So far, so good.

The problems started in 1980 with post-enumeration sampling. Official census counts are based on a mail-in survey and in-person follow-up to addresses that do not respond. In 1980, census officials randomly selected (i.e., sampled) certain blocks and went back and redid the counts there to see if some people were missed or double-counted. In fact, the post-enumeration count showed that the U.S. population was indeed undercounted, by about 1.2 percent. The more troubling aspect of the undercount was that certain groups were more likely to be missed than others. For example, African Americans were undercounted at a rate that was 3.7 percent higher than other races.

This result prompted a fight. It started when the City of Detroit sued to require adjustment of the overall census by the purported under (and over) counts revealed by the sampling. Soon other plaintiffs seeking the same redress also sued, including, most notably, the City and State of New York. This kind of "reweighting" is a common, relatively uncontroversial adjustment done by researchers using survey studies. But when the apportionment of congressional seats is at state—not to mention all of the federal dollars that are divided up by population size—then sampling-based adjustments become *very* political.

The Commerce Department (in which the Census Bureau is based) decided not to readjust the "raw" census figures, and the Supreme Court ultimately upheld this decision. The same statistical question had another trip through the courts after the 1990 count, and then again in preparation for the 2000 Census. Groups that tend to be undercounted also tend to vote for Democratic candidates, so it did not come as a surprise that the Clinton administration hoped to use the sampling-adjusted count following the 2000 Census. Meanwhile, in Congress, the issue caused the usually routine budget appropriation for census operations to stall until a compromise two-track planning approach was adopted. Ultimately, the Supreme Court ruled that not only did the Census Bureau not have to adjust its counts to better reflect the actual population numbers and composition, it could not legally do so even if the Clinton administration wanted the adjustment made. Regardless of the political implications, many statistical and social scientists were unhappy with this outcome because they knew the adjusted counts were more accurate.

Even today, the issue refuses to die. The Court's decision left some wiggle room with respect to adjusting census numbers for the purposes of more accurately distributing the population within states (but not between them). This possibility caused the issue to surface once again during the confirmation hearing of sociologist Robert Groves as President Barack Obama's first Census Bureau director.

Senator Susan Collins from Maine asked Groves, "Will you advocate for the statistical adjustment or use of sampling during the 2010 Census?"

It was, after all, a fair question, because Groves had dissented during George H. W. Bush's presidency from the administration's decision to ignore post-enumeration sampling.

"No, Senator," the University of Michigan professor now responded.

Senator Collins pushed him on the issue with respect to the plans for the 2020 Census.

"I have no plans to do that for 2020," was Groves's response (U.S. Department of Commerce, 2009).

After a hint of doubt, Groves ended up being confirmed and served for three years. Today the post-enumeration sampling approach is used, but only to improve methods for reaching those undercounted populations in future census counts.

→ <u>CONCLUSION</u>

Sociology is a field that deploys a variety of methodologies from survey research to participant observation to historical approaches. Therefore, we sociologists often feel that we have to defend our very identity as scientists. Indeed, even some sociologists would argue that sociology is not a science. I would assert, however, that sociology is among the most difficult sciences of all. Sociology is a science in which you can't complete the controlled experiments that are the staple of most bench science. Perhaps zoology and paleontology are other examples of fields in which the scientist is called on to piece together observational data without the ability to run experiments. Nonetheless, sociologists also must face the task of imputing causal processes, not just describing or classifying the world.

How does one assess causality with only observational data to go by, especially when there are multiple factors to analyze—factors that may all interact with one another? And add to that this complication: Reality changes as you study it and by virtue of the fact that you study it. Our basic units of analysis, such as the family, and our conceptual frameworks, such as race and class, are always shifting as we study them. On top of that, the fact remains that many of the topics we study—gender and sexuality, race and class, family life, politics, and so on—are, by design, the most politically charged and most personally sensitive topics in our society. This doesn't make research easy. So what we sociologists are trying to do in this difficult field is to inch our way toward causality.

PRACTICE

SOCIOLOGY ON THE STREET

There are many ways to research a sociological issue. How might your choice of research methods, subjects, and even your perspective alter your results? Watch the Sociology on the Street video to find out more: wwnpag.es/SOS2.

QUESTIONS FOR REVIEW

1. What is the difference between causality and correlation? Use the example from the beginning of the chapter, on the link between health and income, to illustrate this difference.

2. Describe one of the studies discussed in this chapter, its methodology (e.g., interviews), and its general findings. Then imagine how an additional study using a different methodology (e.g., comparative research) might build on these findings and generate new questions.

3. A sociologist observes the work-seeking habits of welfare recipients. After weeks of observation, trends emerge and the researcher forms a theory about the behaviors of this group. Is the sociologist in this example using a deductive or inductive approach? How would the sociologist study this phenomenon using the other approach?

4. Participant observation research is often long, painstaking, and personally demanding for the sociologist. Why bother with this data collection method? Use the example of Mary Patillo's research to support your answer.

5. Surveys are complicated to design, costly to administer, and potentially suffer from response bias with respect to who answers them. Why use this data collection method? Draw on the case of the General Social Survey to support your answer.

6. Why do sociologists have to run their projects by institutional review boards? What are the "golden rules" sociologists should keep in mind when conducting research?

PARADOX

IF WE SUCCESSFULLY ANSWER ONE QUESTION, IT ONLY SPAWNS OTHERS. THERE IS NO MOMENT WHEN A SOCIAL SCIENTIST'S WORK IS DONE.

WATCH THE ANIMATED SHORT ABOUT THE METHODS PARADOX AT

WWNPAG.ES/PX2

How does culture simultaneously reflect and create our world?
Protests by Israeli religious leaders resulted in a more modest version
of actor Sarah Jessica Parker's dress for this Tel Aviv billboard.

3 Culture and Media

PARADOX

DO MASS MEDIA CREATE SOCIAL NORMS
OR MERELY REFLECT THEM?
CULTURE IS LIKE TWO MIRRORS
FACING EACH OTHER:
IT SIMULTANEOUSLY REFLECTS AND
CREATES THE WORLD WE LIVE IN.

Samantha Lauzon started freshman year of high school as a boy, went home for winter break, and came back as a girl. Other students did not understand— they bullied Lauzon almost every day. Recalling her high school experience in a video posted to YouTube, she said, "More often than not I went home crying. . . . I think it might have been easier knowing I wasn't the only one sitting at home in my bedroom crying." Lauzon is a transgender activist in her thirties now. There was no gay–straight alliance or LGBT (lesbian, gay, bisexual, transgender) support group at her school. There wasn't even YouTube, Twitter, or an online community she could join as a teen, back before the Internet was widely available.

She posted a video about her own crappy high school experience as part of the It Gets Better Project. The thousands of It Gets Better videos target LGBT teens for whom suicide risk is twice as high as for straight teens (Russell & Joyner, 2001). The message is simple: For many LGBT people, high school is the worst part of a life that will get better. Lauzon's message to young people struggling with depression and bullying is supportive but blunt: "Ending your life now is never the answer. If I would have done it when I was 13 years old, when I was bullied in school, I would have never gotten to experience the amazing life that I have now." Anthropologist Mary Gray has found that online communities are particularly important for LGBT young people living in rural areas, for whom local role models might be lacking (2009).

But if online support is so critical for LGBT youth, why did the It Gets Better campaign take so long to emerge? Some might argue that the delay—and clearly Lauzon's high school experience decades ago shows that

Go Online

Someone Out There Feels Like You

I'M NOT A JOKE
DANIEL ARZOLA

Find Community

IT GETS BETTER
PROJECT

The It Gets Better project offers LGBT teens role models and support that they might not otherwise have in real life or see in the mainstream media.

LGBT bullying has been a problem for a long time—is evidence that media are merely a reflection of larger cultural trends. Before it would have been possible to get gay, lesbian, transgender, and straight people to feel safe enough to publicly proclaim their support for LGBT youth, broader social changes had to occur. Since Lauzon's high school years, prohibitions against homosexuals in the military, against gay marriage, and against adoption of children by homosexual parents have been struck down in many places. But wait a second. Weren't some of these legal challenges successful in part because there have been more positive depictions of gays and lesbians in the media? If Lauzon watched the television shows *Northern Exposure* or *Roseanne* when she was young, she would have seen the first (fictional) gay marriages. The movie *Boys Don't Cry* garnered an Oscar win for Hilary Swank who played Brandon Teena, a transgender character based on a man whose murder motivated lawmakers to pass hate crime legislation.

What Lauzon's participation in the It Gets Better campaign demonstrates is the porous—sometimes leading, sometimes following—relationship between culture and media. Media and culture have always been closely related, drawing on one another for meaning in contexts where there are shifting power differences between producers and consumers. In this chapter, we will explore their relationship. Do producers, consumers, advertisers, or some complicated mixture of all three determine what we read, hear, and see in the media-saturated environment? In this chapter we first take a look at culture to explain what this sometimes slippery term has meant for social scientists. Then we look at how culture and the media intersect to shape values, beliefs, and practices in contemporary America.

→ Definitions of Culture

Culture is a vague term that we use to rationalize many behaviors and describe all sorts of peoples and patterns. We talk about a culture of poverty in the United States. We hear about corporate cultures and subcultures, culture wars, the clash of cultures, culture shock, and even cultural conflicts on a global scale. Culture is casually used as shorthand for many things, ranging in meaning from innate biological tendencies to social institutions, and everything in between.

Culture = Human − Nature

We might say that culture is the sum of the social categories and concepts we recognize in addition to our beliefs, behaviors (except the instinctual ones), and practices. In other words, culture is everything but nature.

Culture a set of beliefs, traditions, and practices; the sum of the social categories and concepts we embrace in addition to beliefs, behaviors (except instinctual ones), and practices; everything but the natural environment around us.

The last sentence captures exactly how culture has been defined through the ages—in opposition to nature. The word *culture* derives from the Latin verb *colere* ("to cultivate or till"), suggesting the refinement of crops to meet human needs. (We still use *culture* as a verb in a similar sense, as when we culture bacteria in a petri dish.) The more common meaning of *culture* as a noun developed from the same kind of human control and domination over nature. We could say that culture began when humans started acting as the architects of nature by growing crops rather than hunting and gathering, hence the terms *agriculture* and *aquaculture* (growing fish and other aquatic organisms for human consumption). Dating back centuries, the term *culture* has referred to the distinction between what is natural—what comes directly from the earth and follows the laws of physics—and what is modified or created by humans and follows (or breaks) the laws of the state. That said, culture is both the technology by which humans have come to dominate nature and the belief systems, ideologies, and symbolic representations that constitute human existence.

In the fifteenth century, when European nations organized expeditions to extend commerce and establish colonies in North America, Africa, and Asia, Western peoples confronted non-Western natives. The beliefs and behaviors of these peoples served as a foil to European culture. Today, we recognize that culture is always relative. We cannot talk about culture without reference to the global world, but the definitions, practices, and concepts that we use in this chapter largely emanate from a Western viewpoint. It may also be easier to identify cultural elements when they are different from our own. The challenge in this chapter will be to take what we see as natural and view it as a product of culture. We'll also explore the media and the role they play in the birth and dissemination of culture.

Culture = (Superior) Man − (Inferior) Man

As colonialism led to increased interaction with non-Westerners, Europeans came to recognize that much of what they took for granted as natural was not. Alternative ways of living existed, as manifested in a variety of living arrangements and marital rules, different styles of dress (or lack thereof), other ways of building cities, and other kinds of foodstuffs. Take, for example, the fact that American architecture of the nineteenth and twentieth centuries tended to use the three major Greek styles of columns: Doric, Ionic, and Corinthian. This was merely a product of tradition: There's nothing natural about these columnar styles that made them the dominant choices in the American architecture of those centuries. And if you traveled to non-Western cities, you would encounter examples of other columnar styles—for instance, the columns in the Blue Mosque in Istanbul, Turkey, or the Toltec columns in Tula, Mexico. Such differences may not seem so striking to us now, but think about what it was like for Westerners who rarely came into contact with non-Westerners.

In the wake of these colonial encounters with the New World, philosophers began to define culture in contrast not just to nature but also to what other peoples do, realizing that the way they performed tasks or lived life

U.S. Capitol, Washington, D.C.

Lincoln Memorial, Washington, D.C.

Toltec columns, Tula, Mexico

Blue Mosque, Istanbul, Turkey

was a historical product of specific cultural influences. People started to contemplate why their traditions, beliefs, styles of art, and other ways of living arose. There was nothing inevitable about them, and valid alternative approaches to interacting with the world existed. Coming face to face with these alternative ways of living caused Westerners to question the culture that they had so far taken for granted. Philosophers such as Jean-Jacques Rousseau idealized non-Western "savages" in contrast to corrupt and debased Europeans; others declared their own culture superior, going so far as to claim that non-Western peoples didn't have culture. Ethnocentrism is a term that encapsulates the sense of taken-for-granted superiority in the context of cultural practices and attitudes. It is the belief that one's own culture or group is superior to others, and the tendency to view all other cultures from the perspective of one's own. At the time, some even believed that non-Westerners did not have souls and weren't human, and this notion was used to justify slavery, violence, and oppression. Such claims obviously weren't true (and we owe a lot to anthropologists for disproving them), but the long history of racism with which we still struggle does have some of its roots in these ideas.

A sixteenth-century Aztec's drawing of the conquistador Hernán Cortés. Why did Western definitions of culture change during the age of exploration?

Ethnocentrism the belief that one's own culture or group is superior to others, and the tendency to view all other cultures from the perspective of one's own.

Culture = Man – Machine

Not long after European empires began to emerge and spread, new technologies and forms of business upended European definitions of culture at home. Beginning in the eighteenth and nineteenth centuries, goods that were previously expensive and handcrafted began to be mass-produced and priced within the reach of the average European. New industries and a growing middle class of merchants and industrialists started to transform the political and social climate of Europe, particularly in Great Britain. In response to these rapid social changes, the poet and cultural critic Matthew Arnold (1822–1888) redefined culture as the pursuit of perfection and broad knowledge of the world in contrast to narrow self-centeredness and material gain. Intellectual refinement was the "pursuit of our natural perfection by means of getting to know, on all the matters which most concern us, the best which has been thought and said in the world." Arnold's definition of culture in his book *Culture and Anarchy* (1869) elevates it beyond dull, middle-class institutions such as religion, liberal economics, and political bureaucracy.

Arnold's definition of culture was an extension of views advanced in Plato's *Republic*, which argues that culture is an ideal standing in opposition to

Jean Auguste Dominique Ingres' *La Grande Odalisque* (1814).

the real world. Plato argues that God is the ideal form of anything. A carpenter, for example, tries to construct a material embodiment of that ideal form. He starts with a vision, the divine vision of what a chair or table should look like, and he works his hardest to bring that vision to fruition. Of course, it can never be perfect; it can never approximate the platonic ideal.

The artist's job, in contrast, is to *represent* the ideal within the realm of the real. In fact, there's a long history of artists attempting to represent the ideal female in sculpture and painting, but in reality, no woman could ever exist as a flawless object, content to be gazed upon. Jean Auguste Dominique Ingres' *La Grande Odalisque* has an unrealistically long spine, allowing her to appear smooth, supple, and gracefully elegant as she shows us her backside but turns her face to meet the viewer's gaze with a hint of a smile. In this conception of art—and this understanding of culture—there is a single, best example of any element in the world, from the ideal woman to the ideal form of government to the ideal citizen, which humanity ought to emulate. Furthermore, we see that the ideal woman (and meal and family and governmental structure) is a fluid notion, changing from one place to another and across time periods. Can an ideal be discovered, as Plato believed, or is it constructed?

→ Material versus Nonmaterial Culture

Nonmaterial culture values, beliefs, behaviors, and social norms.

Today, we tend to think that everything is a component of culture. Culture is a way of life created by humans, whatever is not natural. We can divide culture into nonmaterial culture, which includes values, beliefs, behaviors, and social norms, and material culture, which is everything that is a part of our constructed, physical environment, including technology. Well-known monuments, such as the Statue of Liberty or Mount Rushmore, are part of our culture, but so are modern furniture, books, movies, food, magazines, cars, and fashion. Of course, a relationship exists between nonmaterial culture and material culture, and that can take many forms. When someone conjures up a concept like a portable computer, such an invention flows directly from an idea into a material good. Other times, however, it is technology that generates ideas and concepts, values and beliefs. Take, for example, the invention of emoticons or other slang used in instant messaging. *ROFL* (rolling on the floor laughing) and *POS* (parent over shoulder) are part of the Internet lexicon, as are emoticons—symbols constructed from colons, semicolons, parentheses, dashes, and other marks of punctuation (Table 3.1).

Material culture everything that is a part of our constructed, physical environment, including technology.

Language, Meaning, and Concepts

Another way to contemplate culture is the following: It is what feels normal or natural to us but is, in fact, socially produced, like saying "Bless you" when someone—even a stranger—sneezes. Another way to put it is this: Culture is what we do not notice at home but would spot in a foreign context (although remember, the sociologist's job is to notice these things at home, too). In France,

Table 3.1: Emoticons

:-)	=]	:)	=)	:]	:^)	:D	(^.^)	Smile or happy
:-(	:(	=(	(<_>)					Frown or sad
;-)	:P							Wink and tongue sticking out (used to show a joke or sarcasm)
>:0	:-@							Yelling
\(^o^)/								Very excited
%-(	:-S							Confused
~(_8^(l)								Homer Simpson

no one says "*Santé*" when a stranger sneezes in the grocery store. In meeting someone for the first time, but holding packages in your right hand, have you instead extended your left in greeting? In Saudi Arabia, this action would be construed as highly disrespectful. Have you ever taken public transportation during rush hour? Do the passengers waiting to board generally move aside to let people off the train first? In Moscow, nobody steps aside; in Japan, people wait so long that they practically miss the train! In England, pants are called "trousers," women's underwear "pants," suspenders "braces," and garter belts "suspenders." You can imagine the confusion that would ensue if an American businessman told his English client he needed to find a shop where he could buy new pants and suspenders because his luggage had been lost. The Englishman would either assume the American was a cross-dresser or send him to a lingerie shop to buy something special for his wife. Even your sociology class probably has a different culture—language, meanings, symbols—from a biology or dance class.

Another way to think about culture is that it is a way of organizing our experience. Take our symbols, for example. What does a red light mean? It could mean that an alarm is sounding. It could mean that something is X-rated (the "red-light" district in Amsterdam, for instance). It could mean "stop." There is nothing inherent about the meaning of the red light. It is embedded within our larger culture and therefore is part of a web of meanings. You cannot change one without affecting the others.

Culture even includes our language. According to the Sapir-Whorf thesis in linguistics, the language we speak directly influences (and reflects) the way we think about and experience the world. On a more concrete level, if you speak another language, you understand how certain meanings can become lost in translation—you can't always say exactly what you want. Many English words have been adopted in other languages, often as slang, such as *hamburger* and *le weekend* in French. Some staunch traditionalists are opposed to such borrowing because they regard it as a threat to their culture. How many words do we have for college? How central does that make higher education to our society? Many words describe the state of being intoxicated. What does that say about our culture?

Concepts such as race, gender, class, and inequality are part of our culture as well. If you try to explain the American understanding of racial differences to someone from another country, you might feel frustrated, because it may not resonate with him or her. That's because meanings are embedded in a wider sense of cultural understanding; you cannot just extract concepts from their context and assume that their meanings will retain a life of their own. In some cases, when opposing concepts come into contact, one will necessarily usurp the other. For example, when Europeans first encountered them, Native Americans believed that owning land was similar to the way Americans now feel about owning air—a resource that was very difficult to put a price on and

There are no inherent meanings behind a red light; its symbolism varies depending on context.

best understood as a collective responsibility. From a real-estate perspective, the Europeans must have been very excited. ("All this land and *nobody* owns it?") The issue was not a language barrier: Native Americans had a social order that had nothing to do with assigning ownership to pieces of the earth. Acting on their concepts of ownership, Europeans thus began the process of displacing native peoples from their homelands and attacking them when they resisted.

Ideology

Nonmaterial culture, in its most abstract guise, takes the form of ideology. Ideology is a system of concepts and relationships, an understanding of cause and effect. For example, generally on airplanes you're not allowed to use the toilets in the first-class cabin if you have a coach-class ticket. Why not? It's not as if the lavatories in first class are that much better. What's the big deal? We subscribe to an ideology that the purchase of an airline ticket at the coach, business, or first-class fare brings with it certain service expectations—that an expensive first-class ticket entitles a passenger to priority access to the lavatory, more leg room, and greater amenities, such as warm face towels. The ideology is embedded within an entire series of suppositions, and if you cast aside some of them, they will no longer hold together as a whole. If everyone flying coach started to hang out in first class, chatting with the flight attendants and using the first-class toilets, the system of class stratification (in airplanes at least) would break down. People would not be willing to pay extra for a first-class ticket; more airlines might go bankrupt, and the industry itself would erode.

Even science and religion, which may seem like polar opposites, are both ideological frameworks. People once believed that the sun circled around the earth, and then, in the late fifteenth and early sixteenth centuries, along came Copernicus, Kepler, and Galileo, and this system of beliefs was turned inside

Ideology a system of concepts and relationships, an understanding of cause and effect.

out. The earth no longer lay at the center of the universe but orbited the sun. This understanding represented a major shift in ideology, and it was not an easy one to make. In a geocentric universe, humans living on earth stand at its center, and this idea corresponds to Christian notions that humans are the lords of the earth and the chosen children of God. However, when we view the earth as a rock orbiting the sun, just like seven other planets and countless subplanetary bodies, we may feel significantly less special and have to adjust our notion of humanity's special role in the universe. People invest a lot in their belief systems, and those who go against the status quo and question the prevailing ideology may be severely punished, as was Galileo.

More recently, the 2000 presidential election had the potential to shatter the ideology of democracy—that is, the belief that the candidate who receives the most votes ascends to power. The winner of the popular vote, Al Gore, was in fact defeated by George W. Bush, who accumulated the requisite number of Electoral College votes after the Supreme Court interceded on the matter of voter irregularities in Florida, the tie-breaker state. The concept of the Electoral College soon became a hot topic of debate, but the final election result did not prompt riots in the street. As it turned out, the entire ideology of American democracy did not crumble.

Of course, on occasion ideologies do shatter. The fall of the former Soviet Union, for example, marked not just a transition in government but the shattering of a particular brand of Communist ideology. Similarly, when apartheid was abolished in South Africa, more than just a few laws changed; a total reorganization of ideas, beliefs, and social relations followed. Often, ideological change comes more slowly. The fight for women's rights, including equal pay, is ongoing even today, but women won the right to vote way back in 1920.

Studying Culture

The scholarly study of culture began in the field of anthropology in the United States. Franz Boas founded the first PhD program in anthropology at Columbia University in the early 1930s and developed the concept of cultural relativity. Ruth Benedict, following Boas, her teacher and mentor, coined the term *cultural relativism* in her book *Patterns of Culture* (1934). Cultural relativism means taking into account the differences across cultures without passing judgment or assigning value. For example, in the United States you are expected to look someone in the eye when you talk to him or her, but in China this is considered rude, and you generally divert your gaze as a sign of respect. Neither practice is inherently right or wrong. By employing the concept of cultural relativism, we can understand difference for the sake of increasing our knowledge about the world. Cultural relativism is also important for businesses that operate on a global scale.

Cultural relativism taking into account the differences across cultures without passing judgment or assigning value.

But what should one's position be when local traditions conflict with universally recognized human rights? For example, should Western businesspeople condone the cutting of the clitoris in young girls as a local cultural practice, something to be respected, as they go about their business in parts of Africa? There are, of course, limits to cultural relativism. In some countries, it is both legal and socially acceptable for a man to beat his wife. Should we accept that wife beating is part of the local culture and therefore conclude we are not in a position to judge those involved? In the United States, some Jehovah's Witnesses reject blood transfusions because they believe blood to be sacred and not for "consumption" by Christians. If parents refuse a potentially lifesaving surgery for their child because it will require a transfusion, do we respect their right to religious freedom or arrest them for neglect? Where we draw the lines is a difficult matter to decide and sparks a great deal of political debate on topics such as domestic violence, female genital mutilation, and medical practices versus religious beliefs in treating the critically ill.

Margaret Mead with two Samoan women, 1926.

Margaret Mead, Benedict's student, wrote *Coming of Age in Samoa* (1928), which has become part of the canon of anthropology and cultural studies. Based on her ethnographic fieldwork among a small group of Samoans, she concluded that women there did not experience the same emotional and psychological turmoil as their American counterparts in the transition from adolescence to adulthood. She found that young women engaged in and enjoyed casual sex before they married and reared children. The book, published in 1928, caused quite an uproar in the United States and eventually contributed to the feminist movement. The validity of Mead's findings has been disputed, but her work continues to be a landmark of early anthropology for introducing the idea that cultural scripts, modes of behavior and understanding that are not universal or natural, shape our notions of gender. This concept stands in opposition to the belief that such ideas derive from biological programming.

Cultural scripts modes of behavior and understanding that are not universal or natural.

Cockfighting and Symbolic Culture
Clifford Geertz, another American anthropologist, was famous for his studies of and writings on culture, one of which concerned the meaning of cockfighting in Bali. Cockfighting involves placing two roosters together in a cockpit, a ring especially designed for the event, and watching them fight. The meaning of cockfighting varies, however. Some see it as one of the basest forms of cruelty to animals. Others attach religious and spiritual meaning to the event. In the Balinese village where Geertz lived, cockfighting was primarily a vehicle for gambling, but it was also an important cultural event. Very few men are allowed to referee these fights, and their decisions are treated with more regard than the law. People bet a lot of money, often forming teams that pool their resources. Bettors profess themselves to be "cock crazy."

The owners of the prized cocks expend an enormous amount of time caring for them. They feed them special diets, bathe them with herbs and flowers,

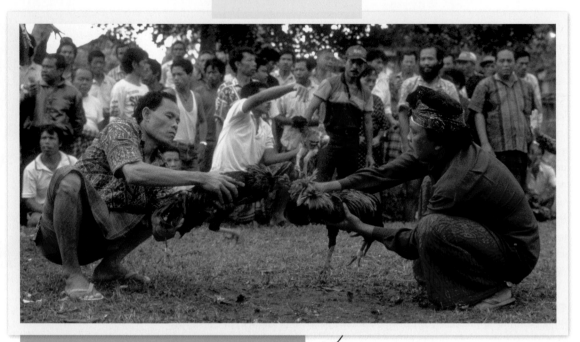

and insert hot peppers in their anuses to give them "spirit." The cock takes on larger symbolic meaning within Balinese society. According to Geertz,

> The language of everyday moralism is shot through, on the male side of it, with roosterish imagery. *Sabung*, the word for cock, is used metaphorically to mean "hero," "warrior," "champion," "man of parts," "political candidate," "bachelor," "dandy," "lady-killer," or "tough guy." . . . Court trials, wars, political contests, inheritance disputes, and street arguments are all compared to cockfights. Even the very island itself is perceived from its shape as a small, proud cock, poised, neck extended, back taut, tail raised, in eternal challenge to large, feckless, shapeless Java. (1973, pp. 412, 454)

In the United States, cocks do not have much symbolic meaning. A more central metaphor in American society is baseball. According to anthropologist Bradd Shore (1998), baseball serves a function in the United States similar to cockfighting's in Bali. We call baseball America's favorite pastime and regularly use baseball metaphors in our daily conversations. If your parents inquire about how you're doing in school this semester, you might say you're "batting a thousand." If you ask your friend how it went the other night at a party when she spoke to the smart guy from your sociology class, and she says she "struck out," you know not to ask, "So when's your first date?" We could learn a lot about American culture by studying baseball, how people watch the game, and what symbolic meanings they attach to it, just as Geertz learned such things about the Balinese by using cockfights as the center of his analysis.

In *The Interpretation of Cultures* (1973), perhaps his most famous book, Geertz wrote, "Culture is a system of inherited conceptions expressed in symbolic forms by means of which people communicate, perpetuate, and develop their knowledge about and attitudes toward life" (p. 89). He was trying to get away from a monolithic definition of culture. So for some, culture is watching players hit a small, hard ball into a field and run around a diamond; for others, it's squatting down in the dust beside a ring and watching two roosters brawl. One pastime isn't inherently better than the other. They're both interesting in their own right, and by understanding the significance of these events for the local people, we can better understand their lives.

Subculture

Like culture, subculture as a concept can be a moving target: It's hard to lock into one specific definition of the term. Historically, subcultures have been defined as groups united by sets of concepts, values, symbols, and shared meaning specific to the members of that group. Accordingly, they frequently are seen as vulgar or deviant and are often marginalized. Part of the original impetus behind subculture studies was to gain a deeper understanding of individuals and groups who traditionally have been dismissed as weirdos at best and deviants at worst.

For example, many music genres have affiliated subcultures: hip-hop, hardcore, punk, Christian rock. High-school cliques may verge on subcultures—the jocks, the band kids, the geeks—although these groups don't really go against the dominant society, because athleticism, musical talent, and intelligence are fairly conventional values. But what about the group of kids who dress in black and wear heavy eyeliner? Maybe teachers simply see them as moody teenagers with a penchant for dark fashion and extreme makeup just seeking to annoy the adults in their life, but perhaps their style of self-presentation means more to them.

Goth culture has its roots in the United Kingdom of the 1980s. It emerged as an offshoot of post-punk music. Typified by a distinctive style of dress— namely, black clothing with a Victorian flair—and a general affinity for gothic and death rock, goth culture has evolved over the last three decades, with many internal subdivisions. Some goths are more drawn to magical or religious aspects of the subculture, whereas others focus mainly on the music. Even the term *goth* has different meanings to people within the subculture: Some see it as derogatory; some appropriate it for their own personal meaning. An internal struggle has grown over who has the right to claim and define the label.

What makes today's goths a subculture? They are not just a random group of people in black listening to music (classical musicians usually wear black

Subculture the distinct cultural values and behavioral patterns of a particular group in society; a group united by sets of concepts, values, symbols, and shared meaning specific to the members of that group distinctive enough to distinguish it from others within the same culture or society.

Goths in Germany (left) and Japan. What characteristics of goth culture make it a subculture?

when they perform, but we don't consider them gothic). Certain words and phrases are unique to goth communities, such as *baby bat* (young goth poseur) and *weekend goth* (someone who dresses up and enters the subculture only on the weekends). Goths in Germany may look very different from those in the United Kingdom, and norms even differ among U.S. cities, so each is a distinct branch of the subculture. Yet as a whole, goths do have their own shared symbols, especially with regard to fashion, so they are visible as a subculture. (Not all subcultures, however, adopt characteristic dress or other easily identifiable features. For example, black men on the down low [secretly seeking sex with men] by definition do not want to be identifiable.)

Cultural Effects: Give and Take

How does culture affect us? As we've discussed, culture may be embedded in ideologies. Our understanding of the world is based on the various ideologies we embrace, and ideologies tend to be culturally specific. Culture also affects us by shaping our values, our moral beliefs. The concept of equal opportunity is a good example of this. The majority of us have been taught that everybody should have an equal shot at the "American dream": going to college, obtaining a job, and becoming economically self-sufficient. This is a relatively recent cultural conception. In England 600 years ago, there was no such culture of equal opportunity but rather a feudal system. If you had asked someone in the government of that period, a social elite, if he (and it would definitely have been a man) believed that everyone should have equal opportunity, he would probably have rejected such a claim. He would have likely insisted that the elite, the nobles, should have more rights, privileges, and opportunities than everybody else. Class mobility simply wasn't a concept that existed. Similarly, the way the concept of equal opportunity is expressed in the contemporary United States has a particularly American flavor. We have a very individualistic culture, meaning that we hold dear the idea that everyone should have the opportunity

Values moral beliefs.

to advance, but we believe people should do it on their own—"pull yourself up by your bootstraps," as we say. Americans hold tightly to the rags-to-riches dream of triumph over adversity, of coming from nothing and becoming a success despite hardship. The problem with this cultural trope is that, as sociologists like to point out, the larger, structural, macro-level forces—general social stratification, racial segregation, sexism, differential access to health care, and education—keep the concept of equal opportunity more fiction than reality. As a culture, Americans tend to suffer a bit from historical amnesia. Slavery was abolished in 1863, and legal segregation lasted until the 1960s. Historically speaking, this is not very long ago. Our notion of equal opportunity often fails to take into account the very unequal starting positions from which people set out to achieve their goals.

If values are abstract cultural beliefs, norms are how values are put into play. We value hygiene in our society, so it is a norm that you wash your hands after going to the bathroom. When you are little, your parents and teachers must remind you, because chances are you haven't yet fully internalized this norm. Once you're an adult, however, you are in charge of your own actions, yet others may still remind you of this norm by giving you a dirty look if you walk from a stall straight past the sinks and out the door of a public restroom. In an office, people might gossip about the guy who doesn't wash his hands— they are shaming him for not following this norm. When you arrive at college, you enter a new culture with different norms and values, and you must adjust to that new environment. If you're attending a school with a major emphasis on partying, you might be reading this textbook secretly because the cultural norm in that kind of environment is not to buy the assigned books or even go to class on a regular basis. If you are enrolled at a community college, commuting may be the main cultural practice. You go there for class and then leave shortly thereafter.

Norms how values tell us to behave.

Reflection Theory

Culture affects us. It's transmitted to us through different processes, with socialization—our internalization of society's values, beliefs, and norms— being the main one. But how do we affect culture? Let's start with reflection theory, which states that culture is a projection of social structures and relationships into the public sphere, a screen onto which the film of the underlying reality or social structures of our society is shown. For example, some people claim that there is too much violence in song lyrics, particularly in rap music. How do hip-hop artists often respond? "I live in a violent world, and I'm like a reporter. I'm telling it like it is; so if you want to fix that, then fix the problems of violence in my community. I'm just the messenger." They are invoking reflection theory.

Socialization the process by which individuals internalize the values, beliefs, and norms of a given society and learn to function as members of that society.

Reflection theory the idea that culture is a projection of social structures and relationships into the public sphere, a screen onto which the film of the underlying reality or social structures of a society is projected.

Why might performers like Lil' Wayne use reflection theory to defend their lyrics? What are some of the limitations to this theory?

A different version of reflection theory derives from the Marxist tradition, which says that cultural objects reflect the material labor and relationships of production that went into them. Earlier in this chapter, we discussed the distinction between material and nonmaterial culture. Karl Marx asserted that it is a one-way street—from technology and the means of production to belief systems and ideologies. According to Marx's view of reflection theory, our norms, values, sanctions, ideologies, laws, and even language are outgrowths of the technology and economic means and modes of production. Likewise, for Marx, ideology has a very specific definition: culture that justifies given relations in production.

By way of example, consider the creation of limited liability partnerships. The concept of limited liability emerged in the nineteenth century during the Industrial Revolution, when new technologies enabled the growth of factories and long-distance travel. At the same time, European countries such as Great Britain were colonizing regions all over the world and establishing large global trade networks. As merchants and factory owners tried to expand, they needed more capital from investors. To attract the most money, they came up with the idea of limited liability partnerships. Limited liability means that when you invest money in a publicly traded corporation, you are not responsible for its debt (you can't lose more than what you paid for your shares) or its actions (unless you are on the board of directors). So if you have stock in a cereal company and it goes bankrupt, the farmers who supply the grain can't hit you up for unpaid bills. Likewise, if several small children choke on the prize included in their boxes of cereal, you cannot be held personally responsible for this tragedy. All you lose is the money you invested in the shares. Even if you didn't know what limited liability meant before you read this paragraph, the legal concept is something we take for granted as part of our common understanding of how capitalism works. Historically, however, it arose from a choice made in England in a specific context. Marx would argue that the combination of factory labor and global trade relations between England and its colonies necessitated and inevitably led to these kinds of legal structures.

Like most theories, reflection theory has its limitations. It does not explain why some cultural products have staying power, whereas others fall by the wayside. Why is it that *The Cuckoo's Calling* by Robert Galbraith had terrible sales until it was leaked that the actual author was J. K. Rowling, who wrote the Harry Potter series? Conversely, Wolfgang Amadeus Mozart was a popular composer in his own day. Why is he still so popular today? Clearly, the relations of production and underlying social structures—indeed, Western society as a whole—have drastically changed since the late eighteenth century, yet the appeal of Mozart's music is as strong as ever. If culture is just a reflection of the state of society in a given epoch, then Mozart should have fallen completely out of favor and we would no longer be interested in him or his music, but this doesn't seem to be the case.

Likewise, if reflection theory is true, why do some products change their meaning over time? Shakespeare is a good example. In nineteenth-century America, Shakespeare was the poet of the people, the playwright for the common man. Scenes from various Shakespearean plays were performed during the intermissions of other events. Conversely, during the intermissions for a full-length Shakespearean play, carnival-like entertainment for the masses called spectacles would be presented. Shakespeare was the most widely performed playwright in England's former colonies, but not revered in terms of high culture. This is not quite what we associate Shakespeare with today, correct? It's just the opposite, in fact: His work is now considered high art. In this instance, the same product changed its meaning over time, and reflection theory doesn't help us understand that change.

Most importantly, reflection theory has been rejected largely because it is unidirectional—that is, it basically buys the rappers' defense that culture has no impact on society. Do we really believe that the media have no impact on the way we live or think? Do we really believe that ideologies have no effect on the

How has the cultural significance of Shakespeare's plays changed over the last 400 years? Compare the poster for an 1884 performance of *Macbeth* (left) with a 1944 photo of Laurence Olivier as Henry V.

choices we make? No. Most people now understand that an interactive process exists between culture and social structure. Most would agree that culture has an impact on society and is not just a unidirectional phenomenon.

Media

Media any formats, platforms, or vehicles that carry, present, or communicate information.

Among the most pervasive and visible forms of culture in modern societies are those produced by the mass media. We might define media as any formats or vehicles that carry, present, or communicate information. This definition would, of course, include newspapers, periodicals, magazines, books, pamphlets, and posters. But it would also include wax tablets, sky writing, web pages, and the children's game of telephone. We'll first discuss the history of the media and then tackle theory and empirical studies.

From the Town Crier to the Facebook Wall: A Brief History

When we talk about the media, we're generally talking about the mass media. The first form of mass media was the book. Before the invention of the printing press, the media did exist—the town crier brought news, and royal messengers traveled by horseback, every now and then hopping off to read a scroll—but they did not exactly reach the masses. People passed along most information by word of mouth. After the 1440s, when Johannes Gutenberg developed movable type for the printing press, text could be printed much more easily. Books and periodicals were produced and circulated at much greater rates and began to reach mass audiences. Since that time the terms *media* and *mass media* have become virtually synonymous.

  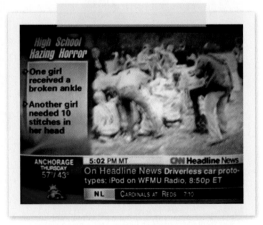

Innovations in mass media include the invention of the printing press and movable type in the fifteenth century, the creation of moving pictures at the turn of the twentieth century, and the adoption of the scrolling ticker by today's 24-hour news channels.

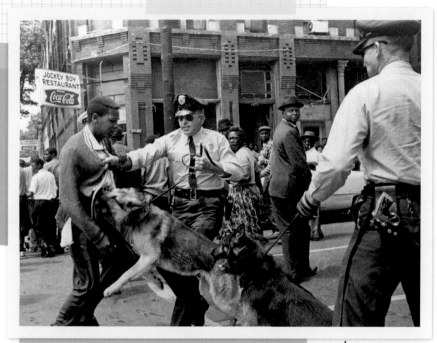

In 1963, for the first time, televisions beamed images such as this photo of police officers attacking a student in Birmingham, Alabama. How did television influence the reaction to events such as the civil rights movement?

The innovations didn't stop there, however. In the 1880s along came another invention: the moving picture or silent film. Its quality was not the best at first, but it improved over time. In the 1920s sound was added to films. For many, this represented an improvement over the radio, which had come along about the same time as the silent film. Television was invented in the 1930s, although this technology didn't make its way into most American homes until after World War II. During the postwar period, new forms of media technology quickly hit the market, and the demand for media exploded: glossy magazines; color televisions; blockbuster movies; Betamax videos, then VHS videos, then DVDs; vinyl records, then eight-track tapes, then cassette tapes, then CDs—and once the Internet came along, the sky was the limit! In 2013, 70 percent of the American population had broadband at home, with access clustered among the younger, wealthier, and better educated (Zickuhr & Smith, 2013).

You're well aware of all the forms the media come in, but let's stop for a minute and contemplate the impact certain forms, such as television, have had on society. Again, televisions didn't become household items in the United States until after World War II. From 1950, the year President Harry S. Truman first sent military advisors to South Vietnam, to 1964, when Congress approved the Gulf of Tonkin Resolution calling for victory by any means necessary, the share of American households with television sets increased from

9 to 92 percent. During the Vietnam War, the American public witnessed military conflict in a way they never had before, and these images helped fuel the antiwar movement. Likewise, television played a large role in the civil rights movement of the 1950s and 1960s. It was one thing to hear of discrimination secondhand, but quite another to sit with your family in the living room and watch images of police setting attack dogs on peaceful protesters and turning fire hoses on little African American girls dressed up in their Sunday best.

Hegemony: The Mother of All Media Terms

All of us might be willing to agree that, on some level, the media both reflect culture and work to produce the very culture they represent. How does this dynamic work? Antonio Gramsci, an Italian political theorist and activist, came up with the concept of hegemony to describe just that. Gramsci, a Marxist, was imprisoned by the Fascists in the 1920s and 1930s; while in jail, he attempted to explain why the working-class revolution Marx had predicted never came to pass. He published his findings in his "prison notebooks" of 1929–35 (Gramsci, 1971). In this vein, then, hegemony "refers to a historical process in which a dominant group exercises 'moral and intellectual leadership' throughout society by winning the voluntary 'consent' of popular masses" (Kim, 2001). This concept of hegemony stands in contrast to another of Gramsci's ideas, *domination*. If domination means getting people to do what you want through the use of force, hegemony means getting them to go along with the status quo because it seems like the best course or the natural order of things. Although domination generally involves an action by the state (such as the Fascist leaders who imprisoned those who disagreed with them), "hegemony takes place in the realm of private institutions . . . such as families, churches, trade unions, and the media" (Kim, 2001). For example, if free-market capitalism is the hegemonic economic ideology of a given society, then the state does not have to explicitly work to inculcate that set of principles into its citizenry. Rather, private institutions, such as families, do most of the heavy lifting in this regard. Ever wonder why children receive an allowance for taking out the trash and doing other household chores? Gramsci might argue that this is the way capitalist free-market ideology is instilled in the individual within the private realm of the family.

Hegemony a condition by which a dominant group uses its power to elicit the voluntary "consent" of the masses.

The concept of hegemony is important for understanding the impact of the media. It also raises questions about the tension between structure and agency. Are people molded by the culture in which they live, or do they actively participate in shaping the world around them? As we discussed earlier in the chapter, it's not an either/or question. Below we'll talk about some of the debates between structure and agency with regard to the media, look at some examples of hegemony in practice, and discuss the possibilities for countercultural resistance.

The Media Life Cycle

We live in a media-saturated society, but one of the most exciting aspects of studying the media is that it allows us to explore the tensions and contradictions created when large social forces conflict with individual identity and free will. We see how people create media, how the media shape the culture in which people live, how the media reflect the culture in which they exist, and how individuals and groups use the media as their own means to shape, redefine, and change culture.

Texts

Why do the adventures in a fairy tale often begin once a mother dies? Are blacks more often portrayed as professionals or criminals in television sitcoms? How often are Asians the lead characters in mainstream films? Who generally initiates conversation, men or women, in U.S. (or Mexican) soap operas? These questions are all examples of textual analysis, analysis of the content of media in its various forms, one of the important strands of study to materialize in the wake of Gramsci's work.

During the 1960s and 1970s, academic studies focused almost solely on texts—television talk shows, newspapers, magazine pages. Finally, scholars recognized the importance of finding out how people read and interpret, and are affected by, these texts: Audience studies were born. The field of psychology has expended a lot of time investigating claims about the effects of television on children, and the debate continues. Sociologists have explored the way women read romance novels or how teenage girls interpret images of superthin models in magazines. For example, in *Reading the Romance: Women, Patriarchy, and Popular Literature* (1987), Janice Radway argues that women exhibit a great deal of individual agency when reading romance novels, which helps them cope with their daily lives in a patriarchal society by providing both escapes from the drudgery of everyday life and alternative scripts to their readers. We are not just passive receptors of media; as readers or viewers, we experience texts through the lens of our own critical, interpretive, and analytical processes.

Back to the Beginning: Cultural Production

The media don't just spontaneously spring into being. They aren't organic; they're produced. You may have heard the expression "History is written by the winners." Well before something becomes history, it has to happen in the present. Who decides what's news? How are decisions made about the content of television shows? To write his classic *Deciding What's News* (1979a), Herbert

In studying newsrooms, Herbert Gans found that many players influenced news production, and he analyzed how journalists internalized those unspoken rules.

Gans went inside the newsrooms at *CBS Evening News*, *NBC Nightly News*, *Newsweek*, and *Time* in the late 1970s. He paid careful attention to the processes by which these news outlets made their decisions on editorial content, "writing down the unwritten rules of journalism," because rules, sociologists know, contain values. Journalists are supposed to be objective, but Gans illustrated the ways in which the mainstream American values journalists had internalized biased the finished product—the news. The notion of "the facts, just the facts, and nothing but the facts" is a worthy idea but to a large degree a farce. Powerful boards of directors regulate the various media; writers, casting agents, directors, and producers decide what goes into sitcoms, soap operas, and after-school specials. Even the huge cache of secret government documents made available on the Internet by WikiLeaks in 2010 were prescreened by individual hackers and researchers. The media are produced by human beings, all of whom have their own biases. Professional journalists may try to minimize the extent to which their own beliefs affect their work, but it is important to keep in mind these "invisible" influences on the media.

Media Effects

In considering the media, mass culture, and subcultures, we can plot the media's effects in a two-dimensional diagram, as shown in Figure 3.1. The vertical dimension indicates if the effect is intended (i.e., deliberate) or unintended. The horizontal axis depicts whether it is a short- or long-term effect. A short-term, deliberate media effect (section A in the illustration) would be advertising. As a kid, you may have watched Saturday morning cartoons; watch them now and keep track of the number of advertisements for children's food. A child today might see an ad for Cocoa Puffs and that same afternoon go grocery shopping with his or her parents. That child is possibly on a sugar crash from an early-morning bowl of Super Frosted Mega Marshmallow Crackle Blasts and is really clamoring for a box of Cocoa Puffs. The advertisers timed it just right, with the pressure on mom or dad to buy that cereal.

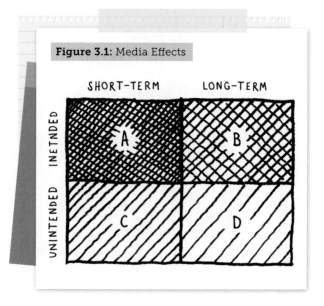

Figure 3.1: Media Effects

Section B of Figure 3.1, on the other hand, represents a deliberate, long-term media campaign. Here, a single theme is reinforced through repeated exposure, as in public service announcements. These are generally used by not-for-profit organizations to educate the public. Classic examples include Smokey the Bear (created in 1944, "Only you can prevent forest fires"), Woodsy Owl (created in 1970, "Give a hoot, don't pollute"), and the "This is your brain on drugs" commercials from the Partnership for a Drug-Free America (the original fried egg aired in 1987, and the sequel frying-pan smash aired a decade later). In a public service campaign the New York City Department of Public Health asked, "Are you pouring on the pounds?" next to an image of a glass full of human fat in an attempt to fight obesity (2009). There also have been long-standing campaigns against drug use and smoking. Of course, not all attempts at deliberate, long-term effects are a success. Often, an issue must be framed as a problem before solutions can be advocated, and that can take a long time in a media campaign. For instance, various environmental groups have advocated for taking measurable action to reduce the release of greenhouse gases. However, only in 2013 did the Environmental Protection Agency feel it had enough support in Congress to propose greenhouse gas emission limits for power plants.

Section C of Figure 3.1 represents media with short-term, unintended consequences. An example might be when teenagers play violent video games and then go out and commit crimes almost identical to those portrayed in the game, or when a kid listens to heavy metal music with violent lyrics and then commits a school shooting. You hear of such events every so often, and sometimes the media's creator will use the defense that the short-term response was not intended. In an interview, for example, the software producer or musician might be asked, "Did you know that your music is causing teenage boys to

THE RACE AND GENDER POLITICS OF MAKING OUT

"When I'm good, I'm very good, but when I'm bad, I'm better."
—ACTRESS MAE WEST

The movie industry's Production Code enumerated three "general principles":

1. No picture shall be produced that will lower the moral standards of those who see it. Hence the sympathy of the audience should never be thrown to the side of crime, wrongdoing, evil, or sin.
2. Correct standards of life, subject only to the requirements of drama and entertainment, shall be presented.
3. Law, natural or human, shall not be ridiculed, nor shall sympathy be created for its violation.

Specific restrictions were spelled out as "particular applications" of these principles:

- Nudity and suggestive dances were prohibited.
- The ridicule of religion was forbidden, and ministers of religion were not to be represented as comic characters or villains.
- The depiction of illegal drug use was forbidden, as well as the use of liquor, "when not required by the plot or for proper characterization."
- Methods of crime (e.g., safe-cracking, arson, smuggling) were not to be explicitly presented.
- References to "sex perversion" (such as homosexuality) and venereal disease were forbidden, as were depictions of childbirth.
- The language section banned various words and phrases considered to be offensive.
- Murder scenes had to be filmed in a way that would not inspire imitation in real life, and brutal killings could not be shown in detail. "Revenge in modern times" was not to be justified.
- The sanctity of marriage and the home had to be upheld. "Pictures shall not infer that low forms of sex relationship are the accepted or common thing." Adultery and illicit sex, although recognized as sometimes necessary to the plot, could not be explicit or justified; they were never to be presented as an attractive option.
- Portrayals of interracial relationships were forbidden.
- "Scenes of passion" were not to be introduced when not essential to the plot. "Excessive and lustful kissing" was to be avoided, along with any other physical interaction that might "stimulate the lower and baser element."
- The flag of the United States was to be treated respectfully, as were the people and history of other nations.

Lucille Ball and Desi Arnaz in the 1950s hit television comedy *I Love Lucy*. Even though their characters were married, they still did not share a bed.

- "Vulgarity," defined as "low, disgusting, unpleasant, though not necessarily evil, subjects," must be treated "subject to the dictates of good taste." Capital punishment, "third-degree methods," cruelty to children and animals, prostitution, and surgical operations were to be depicted with similar sensitivity and discretion.

"Rules were made to be broken," the old saying goes, and the film industry did its best to prove the maxim true. Filmmakers like Alfred Hitchcock pushed the boundaries of a ten-second time limit for kisses by filming a lip-lock for the maximum allotted time, panning away, and then returning to the couple still passionately embracing. Rules such as this were slow to change, but not as slow as others. For one thing, you can be sure that the people kissing were a man and a woman, and they were both white. In fact, in the beginning they would have been married, too, but that ideology—the sanctity of marriage—fell away more quickly on the silver screen than did notions about racial and gender hierarchies and stereotypes. The first on-screen interracial kiss, between Sidney Poitier and Katharine Houghton in *Guess Who's Coming to Dinner*, didn't occur until 1967, the same year the U.S. Supreme Court ruled that state laws preventing interracial marriage were unconstitutional. And in a 1968 episode of *Star Trek*, William Shatner and Nichelle Nichols boldly ventured where no one had gone before with the first black–white lip-lock televised in the United States. The first homosexual kiss between two women hit prime time in 1991 (on the TV show *L.A. Law*, which received backlash from advertisers), while the first same-sex kiss between two men did not happen until 2001 on *Will and Grace*. Change in the media takes time; as society's ideologies about what constitutes good and bad love change, the media will reflect those changes by portraying more positive images of people loving whomever they choose.

Jesse Tyler Ferguson and Eric Stonestreet play gay parents Mitchell and Cameron on ABC's *Modern Family*.

commit violent crimes?" And the response will be, "That is not my intention at all. I use violence as a metaphor." Scientific research hasn't yet ruled definitively one way or the other on this controversial subject, but many believe that the media occasionally have short-term, unintended effects.

Finally, section D of the illustration represents the long-term, unintended effects of the media. Many people, not just cultural conservatives, argue that we have been desensitized to violence, sexual imagery, and other content that some people consider inappropriate for mass audiences. In the film industry, for example, the Production Code, also known as the Hays Code, was a set of standards created in 1930 (although it wasn't officially enforced until 1934) to protect the moral fabric of society. The guidelines were fairly strict, and they were a testament to the mainstream ideologies of the time (see the box on pages 96–97). Slowly, however, the power of the code began to erode because of the influence of television, foreign films, and the fact that being condemned as immoral didn't prevent a film from becoming a success. In 1967 the code was abandoned for the movie rating system. Over time, we have grown accustomed to seeing sexually explicit material in films, on television, and on the Internet. Those who lament this desensitization seek to reinstitute controls over media content.

→ Mommy, Where Do Stereotypes Come From?

Racism in the Media

On December 22, 1941, two weeks after the Japanese attack on Pearl Harbor, *Time* magazine ran an article titled "How to Tell Your Friends from the Japs." There were annotated photographs to help readers identify characteristics that would distinguish, for instance, friendly Chinese from the Japanese, America's enemies during World War II. The magazine offered the following rules of thumb, although it admitted that they were "not always reliable":

- Some Chinese are tall (average: 5 ft. 5 in.). Virtually all Japanese are short (average: 5 ft. 2-½ in.).

- Japanese are likely to be stockier and broader-hipped than short Chinese.

- Japanese—except for wrestlers—are seldom fat; they often dry up and grow lean as they age. The Chinese often put on weight, particularly if they are prosperous (in China, with its frequent famines, being fat is esteemed as a sign of being a solid citizen).

- Chinese, not as hairy as Japanese, seldom grow an impressive mustache.

- Most Chinese avoid horn-rimmed spectacles.

- Although both have the typical epicanthic fold of the upper eyelid (which makes them look almond-eyed), Japanese eyes are usually set closer together.

- Those who know them best often rely on facial expression to tell them apart: the Chinese expression is likely to be more placid, kindly, open; the Japanese more positive, dogmatic, arrogant.

The controversial O.J. Simpson arrest photo. *Time* magazine was accused of darkening his features for their cover.

How can Gramsci's concept of hegemony help us understand this piece from *Time*? Does this article tell us more about the physical differences between Japanese and Chinese, or about the state of mind of the American public at the time? What values are reflected and projected? Are the descriptors empirical (based on fact) or normative (based on opinion)? This is what racism looks like on paper, and it clearly illustrates America's fear and hatred of the Japanese at that time.

The media continue to reflect and perpetuate racist ideologies, even if such examples are not usually as blatant as the 1941 article in *Time*. Sometimes the racism is obvious, and these instances present us with the opportunity to discuss racism in the media. In June 1994 the front cover of both *Time* and *Newsweek* showed the police mug shot of former NFL star O.J. Simpson, who had been arrested for allegedly killing his ex-wife and her friend. *Time* was accused of darkening its image, perhaps implying that those with darker skin are more dangerous, criminal, and evil. In a case whose trial months later would prove to be a racially charged event—Simpson's ex-wife was white, and the police detective overseeing the case had a long history of racial prejudice—the media added fuel to the fire. What purpose was served by darkening Simpson's image? Did the stir surrounding these photos affect the eventual outcome of the trial? Again, we can't state with certainty how one questionable instance in the media affects society, but we can look at the continued negative portrayals of minorities and hypothesize about the cumulative effects of those images.

In early September 2005, just days after Hurricane Katrina had devastated the areas surrounding the Mississippi River basin, two photos quickly began to circulate on the Internet amid discussion of racism and the role it played in the reaction (or inadequate government response) to the catastrophe. The first photo, published by the Associated Press, showed a young African American wading through chest-high water toting groceries; the caption proclaimed that the man had just been "looting a grocery store." The second, which pictured a Caucasian couple doing the same thing, stated that the two were photographed "after finding bread and soda at a local grocery store" (Ralli, 2005). The conclusion these images and their captions conveyed was this: White looters, in their struggle to survive the catastrophe, were not committing a crime, whereas blacks resorting to the same behavior were. Indeed, much of the coverage in the wake of Katrina focused on the looting, vandalism, and other criminal acts

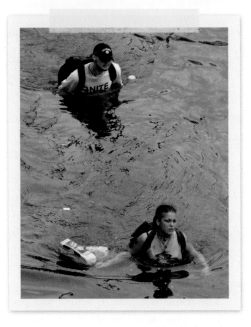

The photo above, published by the Associated Press, shows a young African American wading through chest-high water toting groceries; the caption proclaimed that the man had just been "looting a grocery store." The second photo, which pictures a Caucasian couple doing the same thing, stated that the two were photographed "after finding bread and soda at a local grocery store."

that took place. What critics have pointed out, however, is that these people did what most of us would logically do—try to obtain food and water for our suffering families in the absence of competent government assistance and disaster relief. Because the city of New Orleans, which received the majority of the media attention, was 78 percent nonwhite, the victims were frequently portrayed as criminals.

The coverage of Hurricane Katrina, which was exceptional in the amount of criticism that was publicly levied against such racially charged portrayals (unlike, for example, the December 1941 *Time* piece), supports the main thesis of Barry Glassner's *The Culture of Fear: Why Americans Are Afraid of the Wrong Things* (1999). Glassner asserts that, as a culture, we grossly exaggerate the frequency of rarely occurring events, often through amplification of a single instance through media repetition. We tend to divert or redirect our attention from political, economic, and cultural issues that are either taboo or simply too difficult to talk about toward sensational, but rare, events like school shootings and terrorist attacks. The media are the main vehicles through which this process occurs. In the case of Katrina, we blame the victims, the poorest of the poor, for not leaving the city, rather than asking how the government could leave its own citizens stranded like refugees without access to life's basic necessities.

Sexism in the Media

A frequent critique of the media centers on the representation of women. American media in particular, and Western media more generally, are charged with glamorizing and perpetuating unrealistic ideals of feminine beauty. Some argue that repetitive bombardment by these images decreases girls' self-esteem and contributes to eating disorders. Women's magazines have been heavily criticized, although some researchers (such as Angela McRobbie from the United Kingdom) have taken care to show that women who are active, critical readers still enjoy reading women's magazines. However, as the Canadian sociologist Dawn Currie points out (1999), although girls can choose which magazines, if any, to read and how to critically read them, they can't control the images available to them in those and other texts.

Another focus of feminist media critiques has been images of violence against women. Jean Kilbourne has become one of the most popular lecturers at college and university campuses across America. In 1979 she released a film titled *Killing Us Softly: Advertising's Image of Women*, in which she examines the ways in which women are maimed, sliced, raped, and otherwise deformed in advertising images. One classic example is a photo that shows the image of a woman's body in a garbage can, with only her legs and a fantastic pair of high heels on her feet visible. The message is clear: These shoes are, literally, to die for. Kilbourne's point is clear, too: Such images help sustain a kind of symbolic violence against women. In this critique, advertising does not just reflect the underlying culture that produced it but also creates desires and narratives that enter women's (and men's) lives with causal force.

Of course, there's always room for innovation. Some girls (with the help of their parents) have responded by creating their own magazines that focus on topics other than makeup, clothing, and boys, as mainstream teenage magazines do. For example, *New Moon Girls* is written and edited by girls aged 8 to 13 and contains no advertisements. Likewise, magazines exist for adult women that have more pro-woman messages; *Ms. Magazine* was founded in 1971 during the feminist movement to give voice to women and explore women's issues. Because such magazines don't accept advertising from huge makeup companies and designer fashion houses, however, they are often less economically viable than mainstream women's magazines, which carry ads on as many as 50 percent of their pages. *Bitch* magazine ("It's a noun; it's a verb; it's a magazine"), which has been around since 1996, is a self-declared feminist response to pop culture. It is supported by advertisers but is a not-for-profit publication.

Some advertisers have responded to feminist critiques of the media with new approaches. In 2005 Dove, a manufacturer of skin-care products, launched a new series of ads backed by a social awareness program called the Campaign for Real Beauty. Instead of models, the ads featured "real" women complete with freckles, frizzy hair, wrinkles, and cellulite. The images were intentionally meant to offer a contrast to the images we're accustomed to seeing. And, as Dove's advertisers have said, "firming the thighs of a size 2 supermodel is no challenge" (Triester, 2005). The latest version of Dove's Real Beauty campaign shows side-by-side sketches of the same woman as drawn by a sketch artist. The first image is drawn based on the woman's description of herself and

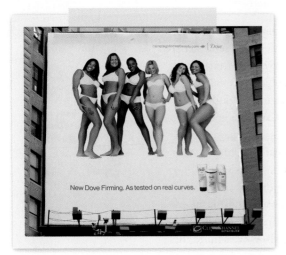

A 2005 billboard from Dove's Real Beauty advertising campaign, featuring women who are not professional models.

is always less attractive than the second image, which is drawn based on someone else's description of the woman, revealing women's inner negative body images. But can calling attention to the way women describe themselves change this inner dialogue? Or will it simply point out another unattractive flaw—low self-esteem?

On the one hand, a pessimist might point out that these "real beauty" ads use nontraditional models merely as a way to be novel; typical models are all so uniformly perfect, they've become boring. Also, Dove isn't telling women that they're beautiful whether or not they have dimpled thighs and therefore they don't need firming lotion. Rather, the manufacturer's message is that it's okay to need firming lotion because you're not the only one who does. Furthermore, the women in the campaign are never overweight, yet 69 percent of adult Americans *are* overweight or obese (Centers for Disease Control and Prevention, 2012a). An optimist, on the other hand, might view this ad campaign as Dove's effort to be socially responsible and to provide alternative images of beauty that aren't based on the stick-thin, perfect bone structure, wrinkle-free, supermodel ideal. Because you're an active, critical reader, not a passive receptor of the media, I'll let you decide.

Political Economy of the Media

In the United States, we (politicians especially) spend a lot of time talking about freedom, particularly freedom of the press. The freedom to say whatever you want is often upheld as one of the great markers of the "land of the free." The press, however, is hardly free. Most broadcasting companies are privately owned in the United States, are supported financially by advertising, and are therefore likely to reflect the biases of their owners and backers. (Compare this model with the United Kingdom's, where the British Broadcasting Company [BBC] cannot accept private funding; households must pay fees for owning television sets; and these fees help cover the BBC's operating costs. This system is beginning to change, however, because of increasing economic pressures, such as competition from satellite television.)

In the United States today, six major companies—Disney, Viacom, Time Warner, News Corporation, CBS, and Comcast—own more than 90 percent of the media. Ownership alone does not equal censorship, but when the majority of the media lie in the hands of a few players, it is easier to ignore or purposely suppress messages that the owners of the media don't agree with or support.

For example, Apple's iTunes app store is the dominant player in the sales of apps for smartphones. Apple demands to review every app to ensure that the content is not something that they "believe is over the line," which they go on to explain is something developers will just know when they cross it. This type of vague policy tends to promote a "chilling effect" whereby developers—not knowing where this mystical "line" is—choose to avoid any content they think might be at all objectionable. Receiving Apple's approval is important because once developers have made an app for Apple's iOS platform, they cannot sell it anywhere but the iTunes store. Is Apple protecting its shoppers or ruling the app developers through a combination of monopoly power and shadowy threats? As corporate control of the media becomes more and more centralized (owned by fewer and fewer groups), the concern is that the range of opinions available will decrease and that corporate censorship (the act of suppressing information that may reflect negatively on certain companies and/or their affiliates) will further compromise the already-tarnished integrity of the mainstream media.

The Internet, to some extent, has balanced out communications monopolies. It's much easier to put up a website expressing alternative views than it is to broadcast a television or radio program suggesting the same. The MIT Center for Future Civic Media, led by Ethan Zuckerman, works to leverage the Internet for the promotion of local activism. One of the MIT projects—VGAZA or Virtual Gaza—allowed Palestinians in the Gaza Strip to document crises and share local stories globally while under embargo. But not even the Internet is beyond the realm of political economy. Smaller sites, for example, cannot afford to have sponsored links on Google's search pages.

Consumer Culture

America is often described as a consumer culture, and rightly so. In my interview with sociologist Allison Pugh, she pointed out that "corporate marketing to children is a 22 billion dollar industry." She then added, "Children 8 to 11 ask for between two and four toys [for Christmas], and they receive eleven on average!" (Conley, 2011a). Sales on major patriotic holidays (Veterans Day, Memorial Day, Presidents' Day) thrive as a result of the notion that it is our duty as American citizens to be good shoppers. As Sharon Zukin points out in her book on shopping culture, *Point of Purchase: How Shopping Changed American Culture* (2003), 24 hours after the terrorist attacks of September 11, 2001, Mayor Rudy Giuliani urged New Yorkers to take the day off and go shopping. It's the tie that binds our society; everyone's got to shop. Malls are our modern-day marketplaces—they are where teenagers hang out, where elderly suburbanites get their exercise, and where Europeans come as tourists to see what American culture is all about. The term *consumerism*, however, refers to more than

Consumerism the steady acquisition of material possessions, often with the belief that happiness and fulfillment can thus be achieved.

To see my interview with Allison Pugh,
go to **wwnpag.es/SC3a**.

just buying merchandise; it refers to the belief that happiness and fulfillment can be achieved through the acquisition of material possessions. Versace, J. Crew, and realtors in certain hip neighborhoods are not just peddling shoes, jeans, and apartments. They are also selling a self-image, a lifestyle, and a sense of belonging and self-worth. The media, and advertising in particular, play a large role in the creation and maintenance of consumerism.

Advertising and Children

The rise of the consumer-citizen has met with increasing criticism, but how does our society produce these consumer-citizens? The Canadian author and activist Naomi Klein published *No Logo: Taking Aim at the Brand Bullies* in 2000; in this book Klein analyzes the growth of advertising in schools. Pepsi and Coca-Cola now bargain for exclusive rights to sell their products within schools, and brand-name fast foods are often sold in cafeterias. The logos of companies that sponsor athletic fields are displayed prominently. This has been commonplace in many colleges and universities for some time now, but the increasing presence of advertising in middle and high schools should also be noted.

One striking example is Channel One, which has been airing in schools around the United States since 1990 (Rhode Island was the only state to refuse Channel One funding). In exchange for television sets, video equipment, and satellite dishes, schools are required to show 12 minutes of prepackaged programming every day. Although Channel One provides news and public affairs information, its programming also includes two minutes of commercials per 12-minute segment. One analysis found that only 20 percent of airtime is devoted to "recent political, economic, social, and cultural stories"; the remaining 80 percent of the prepackaged programming includes sports, weather, and other topics, as well as advertisements for Channel One itself. Studies have found that Channel One cost taxpayers $1.8 billion a year in lost school time; of that amount, $300 million was lost to commercials alone (Molnar & Sawicky, 1998). Meanwhile, Channel One charges advertisers almost $200,000 for each 30-second segment. Channel One is disproportionately found in lower-income school districts that struggle with funding for books and technology, meaning disadvantaged students in these schools are exposed to more advertisements and fewer academic lessons than their peers in systems that can afford to forgo this kind of sponsorship.

The result of all of this advertising is the creation of a self-sustaining consumer culture among children—albeit one that plays out differently for low-income and high-income families. Let's hear Pugh discuss her research with me again on this point:

> I found, for low-income parents, a practice of what I ended up calling "symbolic indulgence." They couldn't afford everything that a middle-class family might consider part of an adequate resource to childhood. So, they might not have blocks, or a bike. They might not have those basics, but they would have the thing that kind of gave the child something to talk about at school [such as a Gameboy]. And so it would be these highly [socially] resonant items [that parents would purchase]. (Conley, 2011a)

In other words, these highly symbolic purchases of "in" toys or devices gave low-resource families an avenue to feel as though they were able to participate in the broader American consumer culture. Meanwhile, ironically, middle-class parents downplayed their consumerism:

> "I'm not materialistic. I'm not one of those bad parents you read about on TV . . . never being able to say no to my kids," [they would say]. So what I found for them is the systematic practice of "symbolic deprivation." The kid would have an enormous amount of stuff. There would be mostly yeses in that child's life. But there would be particular things that that child didn't have, so that they [the parents] could really kind of convince me, convince themselves that they were honorable people. (Conley, 2011a)

Pugh emphasizes that these dynamics are not just about corporate advertising but about the local social systems in which kids and their families find themselves. So to fix the problem, we have to change that dynamic by (somehow) making people less afraid of being different, or perhaps more realistically by diminishing difference itself through sameness—by students wearing school uniforms, for example.

Culture Jams: Hey Calvin, How 'Bout Giving That Girl a Sandwich?

People can take back the media or use the media for their own ends. In that sense, the It Gets Better campaigners we met at the beginning of the chapter are flooding social media with pro-gay messages to override the lack of healthy homosexuality on prime-time TV. Culture jamming (a term that evolved from radio jamming, another form of guerrilla cultural resistance that involves seizing control of the frequency of a radio station) is the act of turning media against themselves. Part of a larger movement against consumer culture and

Culture jamming the act of turning media against themselves.

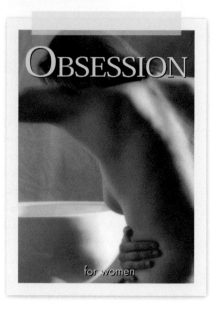

Two satirical ads from *Adbusters* magazine. How do these ads critique or subvert the tobacco and fashion industries?

consumerism, it's based on the notion that advertisements are basically propaganda. Culture jamming differs from appropriating advertisements for the sake of art and sheer vandalism (where the sole goal is destruction of property), although advertisers probably don't care too much about this latter distinction. Numerous anticonsumerist activist groups have sprung up, such as *Adbusters*, a Canadian magazine that specializes in spoofs of popular advertising campaigns. For example, it parodied a real Calvin Klein campaign (which advanced the career of Kate Moss and ushered in an age of ultra-thin, waiflike models) with a presumably bulimic woman vomiting into a toilet. *Adbusters* also sponsors an annual Buy Nothing Day (held, with great irony, on the day after Thanksgiving, known in retail as "Black Friday," the busiest shopping day of the year), which encourages people to do just that—buy nothing on this specific day of the year, encouraging them to reclaim their buying power and focus on the noncommercial aspects of the holiday, such as spending time with family and friends.

Another *Adbusters* spoof caricatured the legendary Joe Camel, the anthropomorphic advertising icon of Camel cigarettes from 1987 until 1997, when R. J. Reynolds, the tobacco firm that conjured up the character, voluntarily stopped using his image after receiving complaints from Congress and various public-interest groups that its ads primarily targeted children. (In 1991, a *Journal of the American Medical Association* study found that more five- and six-year-old kids recognized Joe Camel than Mickey Mouse or Fred Flintstone [P. M. Fischer et al., 1991].) In the *Adbusters* spoof, "Joe Chemo" is walking down a hospital hallway with an IV, presumably dying of cancer caused by smoking.

What's in a Name?

I named my kids E and Yo Xing Heyno Augustus Eisner Alexander Weiser Knuckles, so forgive me if I didn't see what all the fuss was about when Kanye West and Kim Kardashian named their daughter North (West). After all, unlike in countries such as France or Japan, there is no U.S. law that constrains what we can name our offspring; only names that would be considered abusive can be stopped. Names present a unique measure of culture: There are few rules, and no institutions attempt to directly influence our choices, unlike almost every other aspect of culture from food to film to fashion. Thus, trends in names are as close to a pure, unmediated, reflective mirror of societal culture as we can get.

In that light, one could say it was almost inevitable that West and Kardashian chose a unique name for their child. On the one hand, there's a long tradition of celebrities marking their status by giving atypical names to their children. Remember Moon Unit Zappa? Born in 1967, she was perhaps one of the first notable celebrity offspring given a "weird" moniker. The 1960s was the Age of Aquarius, after all. Besides her own siblings, she was followed by uncapitalized "america," the child of Abbie Hoffman; and Free, the spawn of Barbara Hershey and David Carradine, just to mention a few. Fast forward to Gwyneth Paltrow's daughter, Apple Martin, and it should come as no surprise that celebrities do things differently.

The more interesting sociological phenomenon that North West embodies, as the daughter of a black man, is the rise of unique black names. Around the same time celebrities started thinking up names that otherwise served as nouns, verbs, or adjectives, African Americans began to abandon long-standing naming patterns. Until the civil rights movement, a typical black name might have been Franklin or Florence. But then black power happened. Blacks wanted to assert their individuality and break ties from the dominant society, so the proportion of unique names—those that appear in birth records only once for that year—shot up.

Until about 1960, the proportion of unique names for white Americans hovered around 20 percent for girls. For blacks it had always been higher— around 30 percent. During the 1960s, the number of white girls with unique names started to inch up to about 25 percent, but for blacks, it literally sky-rocketed, peaking around 1979 at more than 60 percent for girls and reaching almost 40 percent for boys in 1975 (based on Illinois data). Harvard sociologists Stanley Lieberson and Kelly S. Mikelson, who examined this trend in a

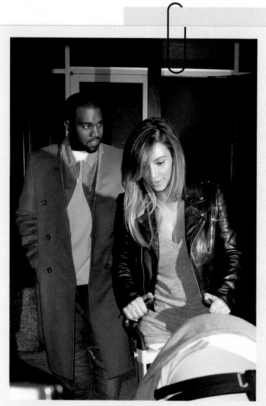

Kim Kardashian and Kanye West's decision to name their daughter "North" represents a larger sociological trend of parents giving their children unique names.

1995 paper, followed it only through the 1980s. But I'd be willing to guess that the practice has continued at a similar rate (Lieberson & Mikelson, 1995).

You might think that all this name coinage would lead to gender confusion in kindergartens. Though I am not advocating gender rigidity, there is some evidence that gender-ambiguous names can cause problems for boys. Economist David Figlio found that "boys named Sue" tend to get into more trouble at school around sixth grade, when puberty hits (2007).

But it turns out that even unique names are gendered. When Lieberson and Mikelson gave a list of unique names they found in the Illinois database to respondents, the vast majority identified the gender of the actual child—for example, Cagdas (boy) or Shameki (girl)—correctly. My own experience mirrors this. Nobody mistakes Yo for a girl's name. Meanwhile, three other Es, who heard about my daughter's name from my public musings, wrote to me. (So much for unique . . .) Two of them were female, bringing the total to 75 percent female. I only wish I had 25 other kids so I could test the gender of every letter in the alphabet. If you think I'm crazy, move to Paris.

→ CONCLUSION

The chapter opened with a description of how several suicides gave rise to a frenzy of YouTube videos and may have even made it easier for President Barack Obama to finally follow through on his campaign promise to do away with the "Don't ask, don't tell" segregation policy in the U.S. military. Now perhaps you can see why that circuitous story is part of a discussion of culture and media. But the fact that YouTube's parent company, Google, is making money off all of the traffic associated with the It Gets Better Project speaks to the fundamental nature of media and culture in our society. Remember that one job of the sociologist is to see as constructed what is usually taken for granted. In a way, It Gets Better disrupted the media flow; the campaign makes media producers out of people who are typically consumers of the largely gay-invisible media on prime-time television and even victims of the thug-like behavior of social media trolls. Are the campaigners just getting on the celebrity-driven bandwagon to increase their own reputations? Or are they meaningful produc-ers of media, reshaping and remixing the messages and materials available to them to produce their new, noncommercial message?

This chapter has presented some new ways of looking at culture: how we construct it, how it affects us, and what this means for understanding ourselves and the world in which we live. Do you now have a new understanding of culture? Can you now see your own culture through a critical lens? What have you previously taken for granted that you can now view as a product of our culture? Can you now look at the media in a different way? Don your critical thinking cap and put some of the stuff you've just learned into practice.

PRACTICE

SOCIOLOGY ON THE STREET

How can we make assumptions about a person before we even meet them? What assumptions do you make if you know a person's name? Watch the Sociology on the Street video to find out more: wwnpag.es/SOS3.

QUESTIONS FOR REVIEW

1. Thinking about "reality" television shows and people who are well-known primarily on social media platforms, define *celebrity* and *cultural icon*. Are people celebrities because they are talented, or can anyone achieve this status? How might this question parallel debates about high culture versus low culture?

2. How does Herbert Gans's *Deciding What's News* (1979) help us understand the way that cultural production simultaneously reflects and creates our world?

3. Goths are visible as a subculture, in part because of their taste in music and fashion. Using these criteria, identify another subculture. In which ways might this group's values oppose the dominant culture?

4. A student holds the widespread cultural belief in upward social mobility through education and therefore studies thoroughly before an upcoming sociology exam. How might this represent an example of hegemony?

5. The term *culture* is complex, in part because it is used in numerous (sometimes contradictory) ways. Use three of the definitions of culture from this chapter to illustrate how a Shakespearean play might be considered "culture."

6. Let's consider how we are part of a consumer culture. Think about a consumer good you recently acquired and care about, such as an item of clothing. Does this item in any way help establish or demonstrate who you are, what you are about, and how you perceive yourself?

7. How do blogs and YouTube potentially change the dynamics of media coverage in the context of a system controlled by a few large companies? Could bloggers and YouTube posters like the It Gets Better campaigners be considered culture jammers?

PARADOX

DO MASS MEDIA CREATE SOCIAL NORMS OR MERELY REFLECT THEM? CULTURE IS LIKE TWO MIRRORS FACING EACH OTHER: IT SIMULTANEOUSLY REFLECTS AND CREATES THE WORLD WE LIVE IN.

WATCH THE ANIMATED SHORT ABOUT THE CULTURE AND MEDIA PARADOX AT

WWNPAG.ES/PX3

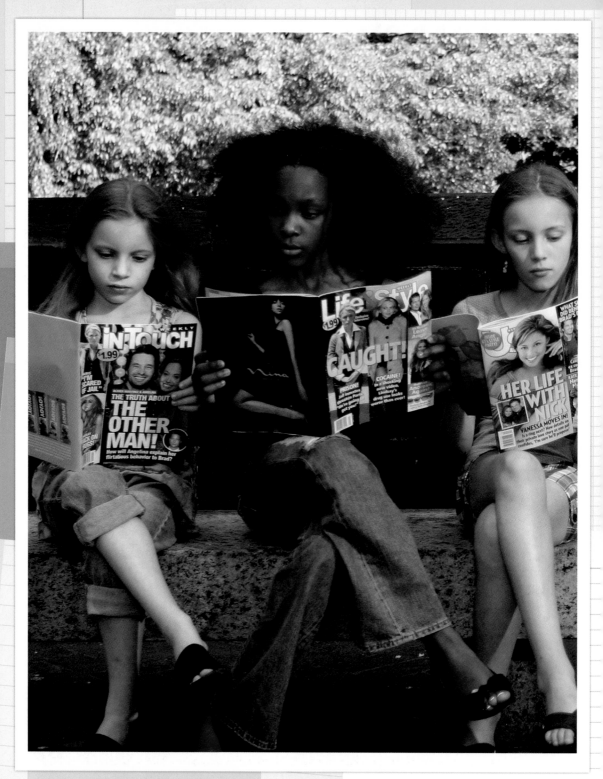

How do socializing factors like friends, family, school, and the media shape our behavior?

4 Socialization and the Construction of Reality

PARADOX

THE MOST IMPORTANT ASPECTS OF SOCIAL LIFE ARE THOSE CONCEPTS WE LEARN WITHOUT ANYONE TEACHING US.

113

Think back to your first day of college. What did you do upon arriving at the classroom? Presumably, you sat in a chair. You probably opened a notebook and took out either a pen or a pencil, or maybe you fired up a laptop. When the professor walked in and called the class to attention, you stopped talking to the person next to you (or, if you didn't, you at least knew that you should). When handed a stack of syllabi, you took one and passed along the rest. You did not sit on anyone's lap. A million dollars says that you were wearing clothes. Another safe bet is that you did not physically assault anyone. Is all of this an accurate description of what occurred? Congratulations! You've been properly socialized.

So how did I know what you did, and more important, how did you know what to do? Why did you sit in a chair and not on the floor? What if no furniture had been in the room? If a blackboard hung on one wall, you probably sat facing it in the absence of desks. Why? How did you know enough to bring paper and something with which to write? Did you receive an e-mail earlier in the week with explicit instructions telling you to do so? Why did you put on clothes this morning? When someone hands you a stack of papers, he or she might say, "Take one and pass them along," but even if that person doesn't, you still know what to do. You've internalized many unwritten rules about social behavior and public interaction. We call the process by which you learn how to become a functioning member of society socialization.

Imagine Mr. Spock, Tarzan, or an android trying to disguise himself as a college freshman. The droid would have to be programmed in minute detail with an endless list of possible reactions to potential situations. Think for a

Socialization the process by which individuals internalize the values, beliefs, and norms of a given society and learn to function as members of that society.

moment about the differences between your knowledge of how to respond to the following situations versus the responses of our droid: knowing how to answer when someone asks "What's up?"; knowing to shift one's knees when someone else needs to slip in or out of a row of seats in the lecture hall; knowing to wait your turn when asking a question in the lecture or discussion section; knowing how to react when someone yells "Fire!" during class and then screams, versus a student shouting the same word during a final exam and then laughing. Consider the difference between these two possible scenarios at a pizzeria: (1) Someone asks for dough, holding out a $5 bill to the cashier; (2) someone asks for "dough," pointing a gun at the same cashier. You know that in the second scenario it is not a wheat-based product to which that person refers. The droid doesn't. He hasn't been socialized. Think how much you have needed to learn, how much knowledge you have internalized and processed, in order to understand that making direct eye contact with someone in a crowded elevator is inappropriate, whereas such behavior at a crowded party might be acceptable. The former might be considered creepy, the latter flirting.

One famous test in the computer science field of artificial intelligence is the Turing Test, in which a subject is asked to have two parallel conversations. One exchange occurs with an actual human, the other with a computer. Both are conducted by instant messaging or some other text-based platform. If the subject can't reliably distinguish the computer from the living human, then the computer is said to have passed the Turing Test (named for the scientist Alan Turing, who first proposed the test in a 1950 research paper). No computer has yet passed the test for very long. Now imagine adding facial expressions, body language, and other nonverbal communication cues to the test criteria. It quickly becomes clear why to be human is to be socialized and that true artificial intelligence is still a long way off.

Socialization: The Concept

Socialization, then, as defined by Craig Calhoun in the *Dictionary of the Social Sciences*, is "the process through which individuals internalize the values, beliefs, and norms of a society and learn to function as its members" (2002, p. 47). Starting from when you were born, the interactions between you and the rest of the world have shaped who you are. Presumably, as a baby, you were wrapped in either a pink or a blue blanket to signify your being a girl or a boy. At some point, you were potty trained—a critical expectation of our society. For babies, the primary unit of socialization is generally the family. As children grow older and enter the educational system, school becomes a key location in their socialization. This is where you probably learned to sit facing the front of the classroom. You learned to raise your hand before asking or answering a question. You learned not to talk when the teacher was speaking and what the punishment would be if you failed to follow this rule. By the time you entered college, you did not have to be told explicitly to do these things because you had *internalized* the rules that govern situations in which the people we designate students and teachers operate. As the examples that open this chapter illustrate, however, we learn more than explicit sets of rules. We learn how to interact on myriad levels in an endless number of situations.

You recognize the limits of your socialization when you find yourself in a new situation and aren't quite sure how to behave. If you've been shy and bookish in high school and you find yourself among a new set of party-going friends at a raucous fraternity party in college, you may not know just what to wear or how to behave. You may take as your model what you've seen on television and in the movies, but the party you are attending may not be quite the same. If, on the other hand, you've been going to similar parties, maybe even at the very same fraternity, with an older brother or sister for the past year or two, this particular party will not present any sort of anxiety. You'll know what to wear, which bathroom to use, whether or not it is cool to post photos of the event on Facebook, what music to like, and which songs deserve an eye-rolling. Your previous experience as a tag-along may now make you a leader among your freshman peers.

Early in elementary school you were taught to raise your hand to speak in class. Can you think of other examples of internalized behavior?

→ Limits of Socialization

Although socialization is necessary for people to function in society, they are not simply blank slates onto which society transcribes its norms and values. Twins are often used to support one or the other side of the nature-versus-nurture debate, because they allow us to factor out genetics. Twins living hundreds or even thousands of miles apart may simultaneously experience the same pain in their right arms—score one point for nature. Take another set of twins, however, who were separated at birth in the early 1900s. One of them was raised as a Jew and the other became a Nazi—score one for nurture. So which theory is correct? Both and neither. In sociology, we tend to think less about right and wrong and more about which theories are more or less helpful in explaining and understanding our social world. The concept of socialization is useful for understanding how people become functioning members of society. Like most theories, however, socialization can be limited in its explanatory power. Have you ever heard someone discussing a "problem child"? The conversation might go something like this: "I just don't know what's wrong with him. He comes from such a nice family. And his older brothers are such nice, respectful boys." How did this child go astray? The primary unit of socialization, the family, seems to have been functional. The other children went on to lead happy and productive lives. What else might explain the youngest son's delinquency? For starters, human beings have agency. This means that, while we operate within limits that largely are not of our own making (e.g., we cannot choose our parents or siblings, and U.S. law requires that all children receive schooling), we also make choices about how to interact with our environment. We can physically walk out of the school, fall asleep in class, or run away from home.

"Human" Nature

Is there such a thing as human nature? It's physiology that prompts you to urinate, but it's socialization that tells you where and when to do so. We are largely shaped by interaction, such that without society the human part of human nature would not develop. We can observe this in children raised by animals or denied human contact. Take the case of "Anna," a young girl whose true age was unknown but estimated at about five years and who had been found in torturous conditions, bound to a chair in an attic, where she had been left almost completely alone in the dark since birth. Her nutritional requirements had been minimally met, and it is believed that her only regular human contact was when her mother delivered these small meals. She could not properly speak or use her limbs, or even walk, when she was discovered. She did not respond to light or sounds the way children normally do. With some care and attention, the nurses at the treating hospital were able to provoke some giggles and coos by tickling her. Eventually, she was able to make speechlike sounds and gain more control of her body, but she never developed to the level of most children her age and died a few years later. Some of the doctors examining her wondered if she had been born mentally retarded, but ultimately, they opined that she could not have survived such an environment unless she had been healthy at birth.

The professionals who cared for Anna and followed her case reached five general conclusions:

1. Her inability to develop past an "idiot level of mentality . . . is largely the result of social isolation."

2. "It seems almost impossible for any child to learn to speak, think, and act like a normal person after a long period of isolation."

3. When she is compared with other cases of isolated children, the similarities "seem to indicate that the stages of socialization are to some extent necessarily related to the stages of organic development."

4. "Anna's history . . . seems to demonstrate that human nature is determined by the child's communicative social contacts as much as by his organic equipment and that the system of communicative symbols is a highly complex business acquired early in life as the result of long and intimate training."

5. Theories of socialization are neither right nor wrong in this case, "but simply inapplicable." (Davis, 1940, pp. 554–65)

What this case illustrates is that "human nature" is a blend of "organic equipment," the raw materials we are physically made of, and social interaction, the environment in which we are raised. In what other ways can we look at the role of socialization and social structures in shaping our behaviors?

Theories of Socialization

Now that we have identified this process called socialization, we can turn to some of the theories about how it works.

Me, Myself, and I: Development of the Self and the Other

Have you ever seen a little girl cover her eyes with her hands and declare, "You can't see me now!" She does not realize that just because she cannot see you doesn't mean you cannot see her. She is incapable of distinguishing between *I* and *you* and has not yet formed an idea of her individual self. How does the concept of the self develop? Sociologists would argue that it emerges through a social process. Perhaps the first full theory of the social self was developed by Charles Horton Cooley, who coined the term *the looking glass self*. According to Cooley in *Human Nature and the Social Order* (1902/1922), the self emerges from our ability to assume the point of view of others and thereby imagine how they see us. We then test this "theory" of how we are perceived by gauging others' reactions and revise our theory by fine-tuning our "self concept."

In the 1930s, George Herbert Mead further elaborated the process by which the social self develops (Figure 4.1). Infants only know the I—that is, one's sense of agency, action, or power. Through social interaction, however, they learn the me—that is, the self as a distinct object to be perceived by others (and by the I). Imagine, for example, that you are taking care of your two-year-old cousin, Joey. He wants a cookie. You explain to him that you will happily give him a cookie just as soon as you go to the bathroom. He starts shouting, "I want cookie! I want cookie!" And you are ready to scream, "But I have to pee!" In a more rational moment, you might argue with your adorable cousin: "How would you feel if I demanded a cookie immediately when you entered the house after a six-hour car ride with no rest stops along the way and your bladder was about to explode?" Although such a line of logic might work with your cousin's seven-year-old sister, it will not work with little Joey because he has yet to develop a sense of the other—that is, someone or something outside

Self the individual identity of a person as perceived by that same person.

I one's sense of agency, action, or power.

Me the self as perceived as an object by the "I"; the self as one imagines others perceive one.

Other someone or something outside of oneself.

How does a small child playing peekaboo demonstrate the social process of creating the self?

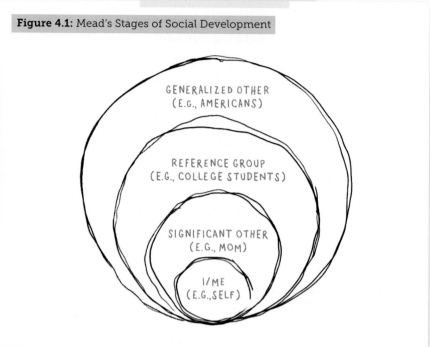

Figure 4.1: Mead's Stages of Social Development

GENERALIZED OTHER
(E.G., AMERICANS)

REFERENCE GROUP
(E.G., COLLEGE STUDENTS)

SIGNIFICANT OTHER
(E.G., MOM)

I/ME
(E.G., SELF)

of oneself. In Joey's mind, there is no *other*, the *you* who hasn't seen a toilet in six hours; there is only the *self* who wants a cookie. This is why we allow children a certain amount of leeway. If your best friend behaved like this, however, you would accuse him or her of being childish, and you would be correct.

How do we move beyond the self? To function as fully adult members of society, we need to be able to recognize that other people have wants, needs, and desires that are sometimes similar to and sometimes different from our own. Thus, imitation, play, and games are important components of childhood development. When a child imitates, he or she is just starting to learn to recognize an other. That's what peekaboo is all about. Eventually, kids understand that you are still there when they cover their eyes. They can then advance to play, according to Mead. During play, children are able to make a distinction between the self and the other. Suppose that you are playing with your cousin Joey, who is now five years old, and he says, "I'll be the cop, and you be the bad guy." He's recognizing you as the other, the bad guy, who has a different set of motives, responses, and actions from the good guy, the cop. Eventually, children move beyond play to formal games.

Games involve a more complex understanding of multiple roles; indeed, you must be able to recognize and anticipate what many other players are going to do in a given situation. Have you ever watched a swarm of toddlers try to play soccer? It's a mess. They're content to kick the ball; that's enough for them. They can't pass, let alone coordinate an offensive attack on an empty goal. It takes an understanding of the other to coordinate passing: You have to consider where to place the ball and calculate whether your teammate can make it to that spot in time for the pass to occur. Games such as soccer involve more than just hand-eye (or foot-eye) coordination. They involve a sophisticated understanding of the various positions others can occupy—that is, they require a theory of social behavior, knowing how others are likely to react to different situations. The goalie is not likely to leave the box in front of the goal, even if I tempt him or her with the ball. But a defender or midfielder is likely to pursue me if I am not controlling the ball very well. We have learned to anticipate these behaviors from repeated experience in the context of a particular sort of constrained social interaction—namely, a soccer game.

Why are games an important part of child development? What do team sports like soccer teach us about multiple roles?

As our parents, siblings, friends, teachers, and Little League coaches socialize us, we learn to think beyond the self to the other. According to Mead, however, that brings us only halfway to being socialized. The final step is developing a concept of the generalized other, which represents an internalized sense of the total expectations of others in a variety of settings—regardless of whether we've encountered those people or places before. In this way, we should be able to function with complete strangers in a wide range of social settings. For example, it is the perception of the generalized other that keeps you from taking off your pants to more comfortably lounge in the park on hot summer days, that keeps you from singing on the bus no matter how much you are enjoying the song on your iPod, and that keeps you from extracting an uncomfortable wedgie in public. We can, and do, continually update our internal sense of the generalized other as we gather new information about norms and expectations in different contexts.

Generalized other an internalized sense of the total expectations of others in a variety of settings—regardless of whether we've encountered those people or places before.

For instance, as a child, you may have been chided by your parents not to pick your nose. You have to be taught that this is unacceptable behavior, because otherwise it might seem perfectly reasonable. You have something in your nose, it's bothering you, you want to remove whatever is stuck there, and, lo and behold, your finger is just the right size. It's remarkably convenient. However, you learn not to pick your nose because it's a socially unacceptable action. But wait! Sometimes you might catch your dad picking his nose in the bathroom at home. Now you revise the original lesson and realize what is most important: not to pick your nose in public. You may even have been taught explicitly that certain activities that are acceptable in private are unacceptable in public. The concept of the generalized other shapes our actions by our internalization of what is, and is not, acceptable in different social situations. Some of us may have internalized the notion that nose picking is inherently disgusting and should never be done anywhere. Some of us may have internalized the notion that nose picking is a little gross but believe it's okay when done in private; the action should just not be performed in public. If you walked outside right now and saw a child picking his nose, you might think, "Eww," but laugh because he is, after all, a child. On the other hand, if his mom was picking her nose, too, you might give her a look of disapproval for violating an established social norm.

People may also intentionally violate established norms. It is not uncommon for children to touch their genitalia in public (watch any group of four- or five-year-olds and you will quickly spot who needs to go to the bathroom). As a society, however, not touching or exposing your genitals in public is a well-established norm (a law, in fact). The exhibitionist who exposes himself or masturbates in public does so not because he was poorly socialized. He has a keen understanding of the generalized other and violates the norm with the explicit purpose of soliciting a reaction from a generalized other (or a very specific other, in some cases).

Agents of Socialization

Families

For most individuals, the family is the original source of significant others and the primary unit of socialization. If you have siblings, you may develop the sense that older and younger children are treated differently. The general impression is that the younger siblings get away with more. Parents, having already gone through the experience of child rearing, may relax their attitudes and behaviors toward later children (even if unconsciously). Note, too, that socialization can be a two-way street. Information doesn't always flow from the older to the younger family members. As computers and other technology become more ubiquitous in our society, children may need to socialize their parents in terms of how to use such technology. For example, the children of immigrants—who are immersed in the U.S. school system while their parents may maintain less contact with mainstream American communities—are likely to take on the role of an agent of socialization instead of the other way around, teaching their parents the language and other tools of cultural assimilation. In a similar vein, a study by economist Ebonya Washington (2008) showed that members of Congress who had daughters were more likely to vote for feminist measures. Perhaps daughters socialize their parents into being more sensitive to women's concerns. Alternatively, it could be that when legislators have their own daughters' future to worry about, they vote for legislative changes that will help them (and, by extension, women in general). So it's hard to say whether this is really socialization at work or merely a change in rational, selfish calculations.

The socialization that occurs within the family can be affected by various demographics. Parents of different social classes socialize their children differently. For example, when asked what values they want their children to have, middle-class parents are more likely to stress independence and self-direction, whereas working-class parents prioritize obedience to external authority (Kohn & Schooler, 1983). Indeed, sociologists have long recognized that parents' social class matters, but how exactly this privilege is transmitted to children (beyond strictly monetary benefits) has been less clear. To better understand this process, ethnographer Annette Lareau spent time in both black and white households with children approximately ten years of age. She found that middle-class parents, both black and white, are more likely to engage in what she calls "concerted cultivation." They structure their children's leisure time with formal activities (such as soccer leagues and piano lessons) and reason with them over decisions in an effort to foster their kids' talents.

Working-class and poor parents, in contrast, focus on the "accomplishment of natural growth." They give their children the room and resources to develop but leave it up to the kids to decide how they want to structure their free time. A greater division between the social life of children and that of the adults exists in such households (Lareau, 2002). Whereas middle-class parents send their kids off to soccer leagues, music lessons, and a myriad of other after-school activities, kids in poor families spend a disproportionate

According to Annette Lareau, how do working-class and middle-class families structure their children's free time differently? What are the results of these different socializing behaviors?

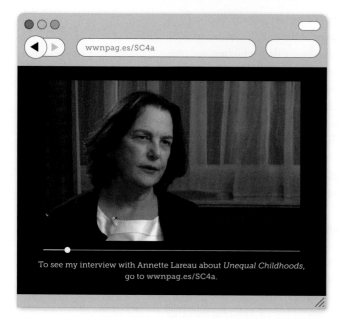

To see my interview with Annette Lareau about *Unequal Childhoods*, go to **wwnpag.es/SC4a**.

amount of time "hanging out," as has been observed by Jason DeParle in *American Dream* (2004), his chronicle of three families on public assistance struggling through the era of welfare reform in Milwaukee. Likewise, a 2006 study by Annette Lareau, Eliot Weingarter, and this author shows the same statistical results: Outside of school, disadvantaged children spend 40 percent more time in unstructured activities than their middle-class counterparts.

Middle-class kids, on the other hand, spend their days learning how to interact with adult authority figures, how to talk to strangers, and how to follow rules and manage schedules. From a very young age, they are taught to use logic and reason to support their choices by mirroring their parents' explanations of why they can or cannot get what they want. Low-income parents, Lareau found, were more likely to answer their children with "Because I said so," instilling respect for authority but missing an opportunity to help their children develop logical reasoning skills commonly used in adult interactions. Middle-class kids discover the confidence that comes with achievements such as learning to play the piano or mastering a foreign language. Whether they actually have fun is unknown, but they are certainly socialized into the same kind of lifestyles that their parents hope them to have as adult professionals. In fact, it should be no surprise that the rise of the "overscheduled" child comes during a period when, for the first time in history, higher-income Americans work more hours than lower-income Americans. If we flip the equation and look at leisure time, it seems that getting lots of education might limit your fun time. Highly educated women spend the fewest hours at leisure (30.3 hours every week), and men with a high-school education or less spend the most leisure time (39.1 hours), though half of the leisure gap is due to the difficulty less-educated men and women have finding full-time jobs (Attanasio et al., 2013). Professional parents familiarize their children with the kind of lives they expect them to lead as adults.

An important question, however, is how these different parenting strategies may or may not affect the long-term outcomes of kids. Luckily, I was able to speak to Annette Lareau upon the publication of her updated edition of *Unequal Childhoods* (2003), for which she went back and followed up with many of the families she had originally studied. Here's what she told me:

> There really were no surprises. I would say it was sad. Many of the working-class and poor children had wanted to do well, their parents had wanted

them to do well, but things had not worked out. So many of them dropped out of high school; some of them had graduated from high school, but they were all in blue-collar jobs or unemployed. Not one was in the professional sector. [For] the middle-class families, it wasn't always easy sailing [either]. Garrett Talinger got his heart broken. Melanie Hamlin had a friend killed in a car accident. It's not that bad things don't happen to middle-class kids; they do. But in terms of being launched, in terms of their life chances, they were much more likely to go to college, and their parents helped them and supervised them in college. So their parents helped them choose their college classes, they gave them advice on their majors, and so the parents continued to provide guidance and help as they went into adulthood. Alexander Williams, the middle-class African American boy, is now going to become a doctor. Garrett Talinger became a high-level manager. He has a suit and tie, his face is shining. (Conley, 2011b)

This was so interesting, so I probed further: What exactly happened in the poor and working-class families' lives that caused the kids, despite their high aspirations, to drop out of high school or go no further than a high-school diploma?

Well, one thing that was very important was the schools that they attended. Schools are very unequal in America. And they [working-class parents] tried to get them into other [better] high schools, but that often didn't work out. And private school is expensive, and they [had] scarce resources. The other thing that happened is that many of the parents wanted their children to go to college. But college [involves] a very complicated set of institutions. To apply to college involves many, many, many steps. If they wanted to go to college, did you take, say, advanced algebra? Did you take the [other] classes you needed to apply to college? Then did they take the SAT and the ACT? Did they apply to college? And if they got in, did they go? And so by the end you have these diversions in pathways between the parents who are middle class and the parents who are working class, despite the aspirations.

Lareau went on to provide a concrete example of these hurdles:

One of the girls who was actually not featured in the book, named Tara Carroll, was dropped for space reasons. She is an African American young woman. Her mother dropped out of high school, [and was from a] deeply religious family, raised by a grandmother. She really wanted to go to college. She applied to eight colleges, but her SAT scores under the old system were a combined score of 700. So, they were really about as low as you can get. But that's a very typical SAT score in urban America. And then she applied to colleges, but she applied to colleges that were two and three hundred points above her SAT. Now, if she had been my daughter, could I have gotten her into a school? Probably. I would have found a school that would have taken a child who had a learning disability, or had low scores, and I could have placed her in college. It would have taken a lot of work. But in her system, her mother depended on the [high] school to help her daughter go to college. So the mother didn't see the applications, and the mother had a car, but she didn't go on college tours. It was up to her daughter and the school. And that is a reasonable decision. Her daughter was rejected everywhere, and she ended up going to community college for a semester and dropping out. And [her experience follows] a very typical pattern for working-class families.

Though Lareau can't definitively discern cause and effect here—What if Tara's SAT scores had been higher? Or if she had lucked out with a fabulous guidance counselor?—things might have turned out differently for Tara, despite the "natural growth" strategy her mother followed. But by showing how social stratification actually worked on the ground, Lareau tells a pretty convincing—if depressing—story.

School

When children enter school, the primary locus of socialization shifts to include reference groups such as peers and teachers. In addition to helping you learn the three *R*s, one of the teacher's main goals is to properly socialize you—teaching you to share, take turns, resolve conflict with words, be quiet when necessary, and speak when appropriate. Walk into any kindergarten classroom and compare it with a third-grade class. What are the main differences? For starters, there is probably a lot more order, and less noise, among the third graders. When you were young and needed to leave the classroom as a group (whether for recess, gym, or music class), you probably had to line up and follow your teacher. Did you have to do this in high school? Highly unlikely, because teenagers are able to get themselves from one classroom to the next, whereas five-year-olds are not. Think about how all those years prepared you for college: Your teachers taught you that you need to have something to take notes on and with, whether it be a pen and notebook or a laptop. You learned to sit at a desk, and if there was a clear front of the room, to face it.

Schools, however, teach us more than how to show up prepared for class, and all schools are not created equal. In *Preparing for Power*, Peter W. Cookson, Jr. and Caroline Hodges Persell explore how private prep schools indoctrinate the students who attend them into a world of social status and privilege. The researchers "document how the philosophies, programs, and lifestyles of boarding schools help transmit power and privilege and how elite families use these schools to maintain their social class" (1985). Admission to these schools is highly competitive and far from democratic. "Legacies" (children who come from families where at least one other member has attended the same school)

CHEERLEADERS

Bush, Booth, Sartore, Brown, Greene, Cowen, Townend, Franchot, Gonzalez.

What advantages do students at elite private schools, such as the young men pictured above in this 1964 Philips Academy yearbook photo, have over those who attend public schools? How do elite schools prepare students differently?

make up more than half (54 percent) of the attendees on average and as many as 75 percent at some schools. The nonacademic part of the curriculum ranges from upper-class sports such as crew and sailing to cultural education in the form of study abroad and smaller field trips overseas. Probably the most important aspect of prep-school education is that it links students into social networks—helping them get into the top colleges and hobnob with students from wealthy and powerful families—that they will have access to and benefit from for the rest of their lives.

Peers

Once we reach school age, peers become an important part of our lives and function as agents of socialization. Adolescents, in particular, spend a great deal of their free time in the company of peers. Peers can reinforce messages taught in the home (even the most liberal of friends will probably expect you to wear clothing when you hang out with them after school) or contradict them. Either way, conformity is generally expected; hence, the term *peer pressure*. Walk into any high-school cafeteria and you'll observe the power of conformity among peer groups. If you have ever tried drugs or alcohol, did you do so by yourself? Probably not. Even when we are being deviant, we often do so in the company (and often at the suggestion) of others. This is why parents express concern about their children hanging out with the "wrong crowd." They're not just being paranoid.

Adolescents do tend to be more open to their friends' advice than to their parents'. A 2002 study of young adolescents (by Wood et al.) found, on the one

Research on television shows such as *Sesame Street* shows that they help children develop math and verbal skills.

hand, that friends were a major source of information on dating and sex. This makes sense. No matter how cool your parents are (or try to be), when you're 15, you probably don't want to talk to them about your love life. On the other hand, the same study found that even though adolescents obtained much of their information on sex from friends, they didn't necessarily believe it. In fact, they were less likely to believe what they learned from friends and the media and more likely to name parents and sex educators as sources of reliable information. It seems as if most adolescents have already learned that they shouldn't believe everything they hear.

Media

Ongoing is a debate about the impact the media have on us. Do violent video games desensitize children to violence and socialize them to become criminals? The jury is still out on that question, but the media can indeed serve as socializing agents. Some television shows are designed with that explicit purpose. *Sesame Street* was created with the intent of providing educational programming for low-income children who didn't have the same opportunities for day care and preschool as their wealthier peers. Guess what—this approach works!

Adult Socialization

The socialization we receive as children can never fully prepare us for the demands that we will face as adults. *Adult socialization* simply refers to the ways in which you are socialized as an adult. When you work at a restaurant, you learn, for instance, what your job responsibilities are, how to take orders and place them in the kitchen, and how to carry a tray full of drinks. As a result of your prior socialization, you probably already knew that you should not talk back to customers. Similarly, your plans upon graduation from college might include moving out of your parents' house, finding a job, and maybe starting a family. Right now, you may not know everything you need to in order to function in each of those situations, but you will learn. Some roles, like some jobs, take more preparation than others—you have to go to law school to become an attorney and medical school to become a doctor. Did you ever wonder why parenting schools don't exist?

Resocialization the process by which one's sense of social values, beliefs, and norms are reengineered, often deliberately, through an intense social process that may take place in a total institution.

Resocialization is a more drastic form of adult socialization. When you change your environment, you may need some resocialization. If you plan to live in another country, you may have to learn a new language and new ways of eating, speaking, talking, listening, or dressing. If you went to a single-sex high school and are attending a co-ed college or university, this change will probably require some resocialization, depending on the extent to which you interacted with the opposite sex during your high-school years. The most drastic case of resocialization would be necessary if you had suffered a terrible accident and lost all of your memory. You would need to relearn everything—how to hold a fork and knife, how to tie your shoes, how to engage in conversation. You would be completely childlike once again—and any inappropriate nose picking would be forgiven.

Total Institutions

The term total institution refers to an institution that controls all the basics of day-to-day life. Members of the institution eat, sleep, study, play, perhaps even bathe and pray together. Boarding schools, colleges, monasteries, the army, and prisons are all total institutions to varying degrees—prisons being the most extreme (see Chapter 6). Sociologist Gwynne Dyer's *War* (1985) provides some insight into the total institution of the U.S. Marine Corps. Marine boot camp strips down much of the prior socialization of recruits and resocializes them to become Marines. Think about how boot camp treats new enlistees: Certain parts of their identity are erased. Uniforms are handed to them and males' heads are shaved. Enlistees live, eat, sleep, bathe, exercise, and study together. Their every move is watched and critiqued, from how they hold a weapon to how they tuck in the corners of their bedsheets. New Marines—and recruits

Total institution an institution in which one is totally immersed and that controls all the basics of day-to-day life; no barriers exist between the usual spheres of daily life, and all activity occurs in the same place and under the same single authority.

in all branches of the armed forces—also must be resocialized to accept the notion that it is okay, even necessary, to kill. Most of us have learned quite the opposite, of course—that under no circumstances should we kill another person. Basic training is not only about teaching recruits new skills; it's about changing them so that they can perform tasks they wouldn't have dreamed of doing otherwise. It works by applying enormous physical and mental pressure on men and women who have been isolated from their normal civilian environment and constantly placed in situations where the only right way to think and behave is that espoused by the Marine Corps. For people to be effective soldiers, they must learn a new set of rules about when it is okay and/or necessary to kill (that is, when they are on active duty, not on leave and at the pizza parlor with their family).

Marines training at Parris Island. How is Marine boot camp an example of a total institution?

Social Interaction

To talk about how institutions and society as a whole socialize us, we need a language to describe social interaction. Robert Merton's role theory provides just such a vocabulary. The first key concept for an understanding of role theory is status, which refers to a recognizable social position that an individual occupies. The person who runs your class and is responsible for grading each student has the status of professor. Roles, then, refer to the duties and behaviors associated with a particular status. You can reasonably expect your professor to show up on time, clothed, and prepared for class. You can also expect that he or she has a fair amount of education, often a PhD, and is knowledgeable about the material. This may not always be true, but it is a fairly standard set of role expectations for someone with the status of professor. Roles are complicated, however, and relatively few of them materialize with handbooks and clear sets of expectations. Sometimes we experience role strain, the incompatibility among roles corresponding to a single status. An example of this is the old dictum for university faculty, particularly young professors, to publish or perish. On the one hand, they need to stay on top of their research, write articles, give lectures, and attend conferences to stay abreast of current topics and remain active in the academic world. On the other hand, they have to teach and perform all the teaching roles that come with the status of professor—preparing lectures, running class sections, meeting with students, grading papers, and writing letters of recommendation.

When your professor arrives at class tomorrow morning with bags under her eyes and a look on her face that seems to say, "No amount of coffee will help me at this point," you may be tempted to conclude, "Oh, she's experiencing role strain." But what if her exhaustion results not from the time demands of simultaneously correcting her midterms and preparing for an upcoming research conference, but rather from the turmoil that ensued last night when

Status a recognizable social position that an individual occupies.

Role the duties and behaviors expected of someone who holds a particular status.

Role strain the incompatibility among roles corresponding to a single status.

the family dog destroyed her daughter's biology project and she had to stay up all night helping her daughter redo it? In this case, role conflict is the culprit. It is not the roles within her status as professor that are the root of her problems, but rather the tensions between her role as professor and her role as mother. Whereas *role strain* refers to conflicting demands within the same status, *role conflict* describes the tension caused by competing demands between two or more roles within different statuses. Each one of us, at any given time, enjoys numerous statuses. These statuses (and their corresponding roles) can and do change over time and between places. When you started college, how did your status change? The obvious answer is that you went from being either a high-school student or perhaps an unskilled worker to becoming a college student. If you graduated from high school and went straight to college, you traded in one status for another. If you still maintain a full- or part-time job, you have added another status. The term *status set* refers to all the statuses you have at any given time.

To obtain a better sense of how roles and statuses function, try the following experiment: Write down as many answers to the question "Who am I?" as you can. Compare your answers with your classmates'. With remarkable similarity, the lists will include statuses such as brother, sister, daughter, boyfriend, student, lifeguard, babysitter, roommate, and so forth. This occurs because we know ourselves in our social roles, in the ways in which we relate to others. You most likely will have listed the key components of your status set.

There are some other key terms that you must learn to understand role theory. Sociologists often make a distinction between an ascribed status and an achieved status, which basically amounts to what you are born with versus what you become. Another way to think about it is in terms of involuntary versus voluntary status. Your age, race, and sex are all largely *ascribed statuses*, whereas your status as a juggler, drug dealer, peace activist, or reality television junkie is an *achieved status*. Sometimes, one status within our status set stands out or overrides all the others. This is called a master status. Examples might

Role conflict the tension caused by competing demands between two or more roles pertaining to different statuses.

Status set all the statuses one holds simultaneously.

Ascribed status a status into which one is born; involuntary status.

Achieved status a status into which one enters; voluntary status.

Master status one status within a set that stands out or overrides all others.

Who are you? What are the different roles in your status set? For example, singer Beyoncé's statuses include mother, daughter, and partner.

include being unemployed, being lesbian, being disabled, or any status that overshadows other statuses. Master status roles can be ascribed, like disability, or achieved, like being a celebrity. The key characteristic of a master status is that people tend to interact with you on the basis of that one status alone.

Gender Roles

Gender roles sets of behavioral norms assumed to accompany one's status as male or female.

One of the most popular strains of thought to evolve from role theory has been the concept of gender roles, sets of behavioral norms assumed to accompany one's status as male or female. In their critiques of role theory, gender theorists such as Candace West and Don Zimmerman (1987) have argued that the statuses of boy/girl and man/woman have distinct power and significance that role theory doesn't adequately capture (you can read more about this in Chapter 8 on sex and gender). If we were to put West and Zimmerman's ideas into the language of role theory, we could argue that sex constitutes a master status in our society. We can see how this fits into larger theories of socialization. From the moment they leave the womb, babies usually wear either pink or blue to designate their sex. There are signs, balloons, greeting cards, and e-cards announcing "It's a boy!" or "It's a girl!" These seemingly silly differences—babies don't care if they wear blue or pink—create a context for older kids and adults to treat babies not as an undifferentiated group of babbling incoherents but as boys and girls. Studies (Lewis et al., 1992) have shown that people interact with babies differently based on whether they are boys or girls, commenting on how "big" and "strong" baby boys are and how "pretty" baby girls may be, or by closely snuggling with female babies rather than holding them facing outward, as with male babies, so that they might see the world.

Not just family members but the larger social world interact with boys and girls very differently and, consequently, socialize them into different roles. Take a stroll through your local toy store, and you will glimpse the function of toys and play—both very important to the development of children—in creating and maintaining gender roles. The toys for playing house will likely be displayed in boxes showing images of little girls pushing and pulling pink irons and purple vacuum cleaners. The boxes for toy stoves will depict girls cooking. Baby dolls will be wrapped in pastel colors, and their packaging will show little girls cradling them. Now meander through the section of the store displaying tool sets, workbenches, and toys related to outdoor activities. On the packages, you will note little boys dressed in bright primary colors,

How do the displays at this New York City toy store serve as an example of the ways that we learn gender roles through socialization?

wielding hammers and fishing poles. The action-figure aisle will be similarly gendered (think Barbie versus G.I. Joe). (Admittedly, these are generalizations. Some images will show boys playing house and girls constructing a bridge, but the vast majority will adhere to what we perceive as traditional gender roles.)

In high school, gender-role socialization continues as peers police each other. Sociologist C. J. Pascoe spent a year in a working-class high school in California finding out just how teens enforce gender norms on one another. She discovered what she calls "fag discourse," a term that describes the near-continuous use of the term *fag* or *faggot* as an insult teenage boys use against one another to curtail improper behavior. She explained in a recent interview how it worked. Someone could get called a fag "if you danced, if you cared about your clothing, if you were too emotional, or if you were incompetent." What's more, actually being gay turned out to be beside the point. As Pascoe explained: "What I came to realize was that they used *fag* as an insult to police the boundaries of masculinity. It wasn't about same-sex desire. In fact, when I asked them about same-sex desire, one boy said, 'Well being gay is just a lifestyle; you can still throw a football around and be gay.'" This "masculinity policing" is no joking matter. A boy she called Ricky was "targeted so relentlessly that he dropped out of school" (Conley, 2009c).

If boys are constantly policing the boundaries of masculinity with homophobic insults, how are girls being socialized into their gender roles? At the school in Pascoe's study, girls did not insult each other. Instead they had to put up with constant sexual harassment from the boys. As the boys looked for behaviors that would prove they were not "fags," they used girls as unwitting resources with which to perform aggressive sexuality by describing to one another either how they could "get" girls or the outlandish and often violent sexual escapades that would then follow. Further, they engaged in rituals of forceful touching, often physically constraining girls' movements. Pascoe describes one hallway scene in which she "watched one boy walk down the hallway jabbing a girl in the crotch with his drum stick yelling, 'Get raped, get raped'" (Conley, 2009c). In this case, gender socialization looks a lot like gender-based bullying. Do these scenes remind you of high school? Was your gender performance policed by your peers?

For some, constant gender-boundary policing has catastrophic effects. Ricky was subject to the steadiest, most virulent "fag discourse" in Pascoe's study and he

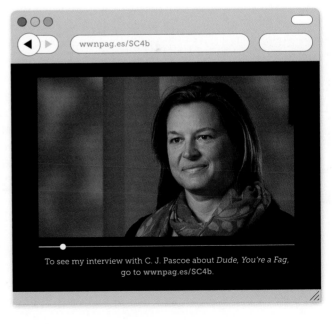

To see my interview with C. J. Pascoe about *Dude, You're a Fag*, go to **wwnpag.es/SC4b**.

dropped out. An 11-year-old in Massachusetts committed suicide after being relentlessly teased; many of the insults he received were part of "fag discourse." And Pascoe points out that 90 percent of school shooters who go on rampage school shootings have been subject to homophobic harassment and teasing (Conley, 2009c).

The Social Construction of Reality

In a February 19, 2006, *New York Times* op-ed essay titled "Mind over Splatter," Vassar professor Don Foster commented on the debate surrounding a Jackson Pollock painting that was recently alleged to be a fake. Is the painting any less artistic for not being a real Pollock when it was, after all, good enough to fool so many people for so long? In a similar vein, Shakespeare's Juliet once inquired, "What's in a name? That which we call a rose by any other name would smell as sweet." The implication is that something is what it is, apart from what we call it or who made it. But do we agree? This question speaks less to the essential nature of things and more to the social construction of reality. Something is real, meaningful, or valuable when society tells us it is.

So what does it mean to say that something is socially constructed? This question is less a debate about what is real versus fake and more an explanation of how we give meanings to things or ideas through social interaction. Two good ways of understanding how we socially construct our reality are to compare one society over different time periods and to compare two contemporary societies. Let's look at some examples.

In U.S. society we take for granted that childhood is a developmental stage. It wasn't always considered so, however; this view came about through a series of cultural, political, and economic changes. In preindustrial times children were expected to care for younger siblings and contribute to the household in other ways as soon as they were physically capable. Toys specifically for children, one of the cultural markers of childhood, did not exist. The early years of one's life were not regarded as a time for play and education. They represented a time of work and responsibility, like most of life's course. However, the development of the industrial factory led to the need for schools, a place where children might spend their days, because parents now left home to go to work. This change in parents' lifestyles meant that a separate sphere had to be created for children. People's lives became more segregated by age, and because of this separation, childhood began to be taken seriously and protected. For example, child labor laws sprang up to protect children from hazardous working conditions.

Adolescence has had a similar history. The notion that a distinct phase exists between childhood and adulthood is relatively new. This important change evolved during the 1950s. After decades of financial hardship and war, America's booming economy led to a new freedom in the popular culture. Access to higher education broadened as well. For many Americans, this extension of educational opportunity delayed the onset of adult responsibilities—such as employment and raising families. With the possibility of an extended adolescence, teenagers (biologically able to reproduce but delayed in their assumption of adult sexual roles) emerged as a discrete social category. Concurrently, cultural changes were marked by the advent of rock and roll, doo-wop, and other popular forms of music. With more access to radios and, to a lesser extent, televisions, and with more free hours after school, teens found the time and means to consume this emerging music culture. Today we can see the life course becoming even further subdivided, with the advent of terms such as *tween*, which refers to the time between childhood and one's teenage years (roughly, ages 10 to 12) and *emerging adulthood*, which is between age 18 and the late twenties.

Which one of these paintings is a "real" Jackson Pollock? Does it matter? (For the record, the real one is on the bottom.) How is the controversy over the Pollock paintings an example of the social construction of reality?

As an example of cross-cultural differences in the social construction of reality, consider the following question: What constitutes food? We tend to think of insects as interesting, necessary to the ecosystem, annoying, or maybe simply gross. However, we generally do not regard them as food. In other cultures, dishes such as fried grasshoppers and chocolate-covered ants are considered a delicacy. Which perspective is "right"? In fact, Americans may be an exception in not eating insects, which, I am told, are delicious. Insects are nutritious (high in protein, low in fat and calories, and a good source of many vitamins and minerals) and economical, but they are inherently neither gross nor delicious. The point is that foods, which we take for granted as natural or self-evident, are assigned meanings and values in different cultural contexts.

We might call the process by which things—ideas, concepts, values—are socially constructed symbolic interactionism (see Chapter 1), which suggests that we interact with others using words and behaviors that have symbolic meanings. This theory has three basic tenets:

Symbolic interactionism a micro-level theory in which shared meanings, orientations, and assumptions form the basic motivations behind people's actions.

1. Human beings act toward ideas, concepts, and values on the basis of the meaning that those things have for them.

2. These meanings are the products of social interaction in human society.

3. These meanings are modified and filtered through an interpretive process that each individual uses in dealing with outward signs.

Lunch? Cicadas, grasshoppers, and other insects on skewers for sale in Donghuamen Night Market in Beijing, China.

Symbolic interactionism can be very useful in understanding cultural differences in styles of social interaction. A classic example of this would be the distance two people stand from one another when conversing. Just because these boundaries are symbolic does not mean that they aren't real. In an interaction between a tourist and a local, standing too close or too far away may make one of the parties feel uncomfortable, but in an international business meeting or in peace talks between nations, symbolic interactions take on a greater level of importance. Similarly, in our culture, we generally believe that looking someone in the eye while talking to them indicates respect and sincerity. In some other cultures, however, it is considered extremely rude to look someone directly in the eye. When you raise your glass in a toast with others and say, "Cheers," you can generally focus your eyes wherever you want. In many European countries, however, it is highly impolite and may be regarded as a sign of dishonesty not to establish eye contact while touching glasses.

Comprehending the three basic tenets of symbolic interactionism listed above is key to seeing how the process of social construction is both ongoing and embedded in our everyday interactions. Symbolic interactionism as a theory is a useful tool for understanding the meanings of symbols and signs and the way shared meanings—or a lack thereof—facilitate or impede routine interactions. Let's look at another theory of human interaction, Erving Goffman's dramaturgical theory of society, which laid the groundwork for symbolic interactionism by using the language of theater as a paradigm to formally describe the ways in which we interact to maintain social order.

How does symbolic interactionism help us understand the differences in greetings among various cultures? Pictured here are Bedouins touching noses, Malian men with their arms around each other, and the Belgian royal family celebrating the prince's eighteenth birthday.

Dramaturgical Theory

All the world's a stage,
And all the men and women merely players.

—William Shakespeare, *As You Like It*

We might say that the dramaturgical theory of society has its roots in William Shakespeare, but we generally credit Goffman with expounding this theory in *The Presentation of Self in Everyday Life* (1959). He argued that life is essentially a play—a play with a moral, of sorts. And this moral is what Goffman and social psychologists call "impression management." That is, all of us actors on the metaphorical social stage are struggling to make a good impression on our audience (who also happen to be actors). What's more, the goal is not just to make the best impression on others; we often actively work to ensure that others will believe they are making a good impression as well. This helps keep society and social relations rolling along smoothly (without the need for too many retakes).

Because we are all actors with roles, according to Goffman's dramaturgical theory, we also need scripts, costumes, and sets. Think again about your first day in this college classroom. You knew your role was student, and presumably

Dramaturgical theory the view (advanced by Erving Goffman) of social life as essentially a theatrical performance, in which we are all actors on metaphorical stages, with roles, scripts, costumes, and sets.

the professor understood his or her role as well. The professor handed out the syllabus (a prop), talked about the general outline of the class for the semester (a script), and maybe gave a short lecture (a performance). What if he had instead started talking about his love for Batman and all things related to Batman? You might have indulged him briefly, thinking that he seemed a bit loony but would eventually relate this tangent to sociology. If your professor, however, had spent the entire lecture talking about Batman, how would you feel? Shocked? Confused? The professor would have deviated from the script generally followed in a college classroom. Was anyone wearing a tuxedo or dressed like an action hero? Probably not, because those are not the costumes we wear to a sociology lecture. Think back to your status set for a minute and ask yourself what the stages, costumes, scripts, and other props associated with each of your roles are. For some, the answer is fairly clear.

We act out some of our roles much more intentionally than others, such as when we are a member of a sports team. If you are on the basketball team, you play on a basketball court (the stage or set), wear a uniform (the costume), follow the rules (the script), and play with a ball (a prop). Often, we play several roles simultaneously, and if we have been properly socialized and don't suffer from too much role conflict, we can transition in and out of roles with a certain amount of ease. Presumably, you understand that the classroom is not the appropriate stage on which to act out an intimate scene with your partner. If you did, one of your classmates might heckle you to "get a room." In dramaturgical theory, the translation would be, "This is the wrong stage. Find the right one."

Another important part of Goffman's theory is the distinction between front-stage and backstage arenas. If you've ever participated in a school play or some other type of performance, you know all about front stage and backstage. Here the meanings are quite literal—a curtain separates these areas, so the border between the front stage and the backstage is clearly delineated. If you've ever worked in a restaurant, you see very clearly a similar line of demarcation. As a waiter you are all smiles out in the dining room. Whenever the customer asks for something, you reply politely with a "Yes, ma'am" or "Right away, sir." Back in the kitchen, however, you might complain loudly to the rest of the staff, criticizing your customer's atrocious taste for ordering escargot with his cheeseburger.

For people in certain professions, the distinction between front stage and backstage is more literal. In the news we sometimes hear about celebrities who have been caught saying something inappropriate because they thought the camera or microphone was off—they believed they were comfortably backstage. Whoops! The higher your profile, particularly if you have a master status such as a celebrity or politician, the greater the portion of your daily world that takes on the designation of front stage. You are always under close scrutiny, so you are always expected to perform your role. In other situations, the lines between front stage and backstage become more blurred. Has a professor ever caught you off guard while you were talking with friends about her class? You might have thought that you were backstage when joking with your friends in the student union, but the unfortunate, unexpected appearance of your professor turned the situation into a front-stage experience.

Face, according to Goffman, is the esteem in which an individual is held by others. We take this notion very seriously; hence, the idea of saving face, which is essentially the most important goal of impression management. If your best friend walked into the classroom right now and sat down beside you with a big smear of chocolate on his face, you would tell him. If the professor walked in sporting the same chocolate smear, however, you might not say anything. Because of the difference in status, and therefore power, between you and the professor, you may decide it's not your place, your role, to say something. If few students are in the class and the professor is your advisor with whom you have a fairly amicable relationship, you might indicate to him that he's got a little something on his cheek. Have you ever encountered a stranger with toilet paper stuck to the bottom of her shoe or with the fly of his pants unzipped? Did you say something? If you did, you were probably motivated by the thought that, if it were you, you would want someone to say something. If you didn't, perhaps you thought calling attention to the toilet paper or exposed underwear would embarrass the person. Or maybe you just simply felt it wasn't any of your business to interfere with a stranger. So you can see how no absolute, fixed scripts exist. (That said, one common rule of thumb is to speak up if the person can do something about it. For example, you would tell a man that he has chocolate on his face because he can wipe his face and remove the chocolate. On the other hand, you would not tell him that his shirt is ugly, because he probably cannot change his shirt at that moment.)

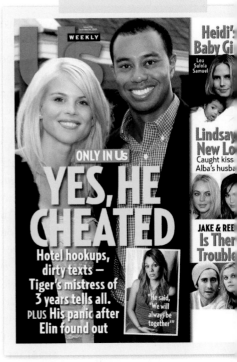

Celebrities such as Tiger Woods suffer from tabloid scandals when their backstage lives become public, but we all make distinctions in our lives between front-stage and backstage behaviors.

Face the esteem in which an individual is held by others.

Similarly, if your professor walked in tomorrow with a black eye, you might ask him what happened. Not wanting to admit he fell asleep grading papers and smacked his face on the desk, he might simply say, "You should see the other guy." This is a common joke people make to save face in light of injuries about which they do not wish to speak. There are many subtleties to learn in life, and nobody explicitly teaches us all of these things. Like driving a car, we generally learn by doing and by sometimes making mistakes.

Indeed, mistakes, called breaches, are themselves an important part of the game. When there's a breach in an established script, we work hard to repair it and move forward. Humor is a useful tool in getting the script back in place. So if your professor lets out an enormous belch in the middle of a lecture, how would you react? You might be horrified; you might laugh nervously. You might delight a little because she has been so arrogant all semester and you are pleased to see her off script, not the perfectly polished professor. If the professor manages to recover and says, "Note to self: Skip the Mountain Dew before lecture next time!" it may smooth over the situation a little (but just a little, because let's face it, what happened was funny) and allow class to continue without a hitch. If the same thing happens during your next class, however, you are just going to assume that your professor is either poorly socialized and extremely uncouth or has severe gastrointestinal problems and needs to scale back on carbonated beverages.

Sometimes, the stakes are so high or the situation is so new that we seek explicit guidance. People can and do make careers out of negotiating social scripts and methods for saving face—think about Miss Manners, Emily Post, or Dear Abby. Not wanting to act inappropriately but unsure of how to behave in situations where we lack a script, we may appeal to professional etiquette experts to coach us through a scene and give stage directions. The truth is, however, that human social interaction is too complex for a single script to work universally.

The art of tact even involves, on occasion, breaking the rules to make others feel comfortable. One particular fable tells the story of a peasant who is invited to the palace for dinner. Unknowingly, she picks up the bowl of water meant for hand washing and begins to drink from it. Many of the nobles at the table chuckle and mutter disparaging comments under their breath. But the queen, who invited the poor woman to dine with her, instead picks up her own silver finger bowl and drinks the water from it. She breaks a formal rule to preserve the face of the invited guest. Moreover, the social situation dictates that only the queen herself, as the most powerful figure at the table, can do that to repair the situation and save face for everyone.

There are some ways to generalize, however. For example, we almost always need to begin our scripts in specific ways; we generally can't just plunge into our lines. (Imagine a colleague getting on the elevator, not saying hello or even looking directly at you, but launching straight into the story of what happened to her on the way to work that day while staring up at the floor number indicators.) Goffman uses the term *opening* to signal the start of an encounter— that is, the first bracket. The closing bracket marks the end of an encounter. Sometimes, we need a nonverbal bracket to commence an encounter, a signal to cease our civic inattention. *Civil inattention* means refraining from directly interacting with someone, even someone you know, until an opening bracket has been issued. For example, you might clear your throat before speaking to somebody. You might catch his or her eye. You might stand up. You might purposely go to the bathroom first, so you can pass that person on the way back and start a conversation. You hope that you will bump into the person and catch his or her eye. We have to signal to people; we have to warn them that we are going to break civil inattention and initiate an encounter.

Openings can be awkward, but it may be even more difficult to end situations. How many times have you gotten off the phone saying, "I should get going." Where? To do what? Or you may say, "Well, I should let you go." Maybe you do hear sirens and screams in the background and you are genuinely concerned that your conversation is keeping the person on the phone from more pressing matters. Under less extreme circumstances, you may be phrasing your desire to end the conversation as a kind gesture to your interlocutor. Sometimes, we resort to formal closings. A ringing bell often indicates the end of a class period. In the absence of a bell, or even prior to its ringing, however, you may close your notebook, start to pack your books, and pick up your coat to signal to the professor that, although the lecture on socialization is fascinating, you have another class in 10 minutes that is a 15-minute walk away. There are *given gestures* that signal a closing, such as putting on your coat. Or, at the end of a meal, you may rub your stomach and say, "Boy, that was delicious. I'm stuffed!" to indicate that you have finished eating but did very much enjoy the food. However, *given off gestures* also exist, unconscious signals of our true feelings. If you grimace every time your fork reaches your mouth, you communicate something else entirely regarding your thoughts about the meal. Many of our gestures and brackets are nonverbal. This is why it is often more difficult to end a conversation on the phone than in person: Much of our toolbox is not available to us.

Ethnomethodology

At this point, you should be *thinking* more critically about the everyday interactions that we often (necessarily) take for granted. In the 1950s and 1960s Harold Garfinkel developed a method for studying social interactions, ethnomethodology (Garfinkel, 1967), that involves *acting* critically about them. Ethnomethodology literally means "the methods of the people" (from *ethnos*, the Greek word for "people"). Garfinkel and his followers became famous for their "breaching experiments." He would send his students into the social world to see what happened when they breached social norms. In one example, Garfinkel sent his students home for the weekend and told them to behave as if their parents' home were a rooming house where they paid rent. Imagine what would happen if you sat down at the kitchen table and demanded to know when dinner was typically served and what days of the week the bed linens were changed. Similarly, a New York City professor instructed his students to ask people on the subway for their seats without offering any reason. Some students simply could not take this action. Others did it, but lied and said that they were not feeling well when they asked for the seat. Try your own breaching experiments. What do you normally do when you get in an elevator? You face forward and watch the numbers above the door. Next time you get into an elevator, face backward. See how the other people in the elevator react. A few weeks into the semester, students tend to sit in the same seats in the same class, particularly if it's a small group, even if they do not have assigned

Ethnomethodology literally "the methods of the people"; this approach to studying human interaction focuses on the ways in which we make sense of our world, convey this understanding to others, and produce a shared social order.

A scene from the film *Borat*. What established scripts did Sacha Baron Cohen's character Borat violate by going on an elevator naked? How did the unsuspecting woman on the elevator try to cope with the breach?

seats. The next time you are in such a situation, take someone else's usual seat and see how he or she reacts. (Come on, that's an easy one!)

Let's think through some of the reactions to breaches. Take the example of the student on the subway asking a stranger to give up his seat. What would you do if this happened to you? Would you give up your seat to the student? You might just get up and offer it to him, because you assume he would not ask for it unless he had a good reason (even if you don't see a cast on his leg). If the stranger were elderly, on crutches, or pregnant or had a small child, you might be more willing to get up—in fact, on most forms of public transportation, seats are marked as reserved for exactly these kinds of people. When this class assignment was originally handed out, note that some of the students simply could not bring themselves to do it. Others lied, saying they were sick, because being ill provides a valid excuse to sit down. Why is that? What's the big deal in asking someone to give you a seat? Well, you might decide, you just don't typically do such a thing. It's not normal behavior. But note that as a society, we construct rules and meanings for what constitutes normal.

Now contemplate the previously mentioned elevator scenario. How would you react if you stepped into an elevator and the only other person inside was facing away from the door (assuming the elevator only opens on one side)? You might look at the wall to see if something is there at which the person is looking and that you can't see. You might try to stand farther away from that person. If someone else gets on the elevator, maybe you would gauge her reaction. If she gave you a look that said, "What's this guy doing?" you might give a sympathetic look, even the hint of a smile, to indicate your agreement: "Yeah, crazy, huh?" Then you could breathe a little easier, knowing that the guy facing backward in the elevator is abnormal, and you, the other passenger, and anyone else who steps inside and faces forward are normal, although there's no social imperative to face forward rather than backward in an elevator.

If you walked into the classroom today and someone was sitting in the seat you consider "yours," how would you feel? Maybe you wouldn't think twice about it, but chances are you would notice, have an emotional reaction—be it annoyance, confusion, even anger—and get to class earlier the next time to claim what's rightfully yours.

New Technologies: What Has the Internet Done to Interaction?

What happens when we are faced with entirely new situations? We have no rules, no scripts, no established social norms. How do people know what to do, or what constitutes appropriate behavior? Usually, some continuity exists between situations, so we can draw on our previous knowledge (just as you could anticipate the norms of a college classroom even though you had never been in one before). But what about something like the Internet, something that humans created, which in turn creates social situations never before possible? Let's think about what happens.

Take online chat rooms, for example. Chat rooms present an interesting test of the dramaturgical model. The potential anonymity of the Internet allows us to present ourselves however we choose. Online I can play the role of a 57-year-old stay-at-home mom who was an international college badminton champ and who enters semiannual pesto-making competitions. Is that who I am? Some online dating and networking websites allow us to craft our own presentation of self, alter our identities, and thereby create new "realities." We've largely removed the stage, costumes, props, vocal inflections, and other nonverbal cues, so we must depend entirely on the scripts with which we are presented. We even develop new ways of communicating. Typing in capital letters can constitute online "yelling." New lexicons are developed: LOL (laugh out loud) and BRB (be right back) are semiverbal cues to our cyber interlocutor. But the technology may also, like the phone, make it difficult to deploy end brackets, to close interactions.

The Internet has changed society in other ways, such as forcing us to develop new technologies to prevent identity theft and create secure online transactions for shopping and banking. Certain aspects of the Internet have also altered the nature and details of crime. Software that allows for music sharing necessitates the development of a new set of ethics. Is it okay to download music free from the Internet? It's illegal in most cases, for sure, but is it unethical? Are there certain circumstances in which it might be okay? For example, when Radiohead made its album *In Rainbows* available for download and left the amount of payment up to customers, should folks have paid or was it just fine to download without donating? The new technologies are changing what we as a society mean by the term *stealing*. Other websites, such as eBay, allow for the sale of stolen goods in ways previously unforeseen. Intentionally or not, people may foster underground economies by purchasing stolen goods in a way not possible before the advent of online auctions. Clicking on an item and entering your credit card number is a completely different social interaction than walking into a dark alley and buying something that literally fell off the back of a truck.

POLICY:

Roommates with Benefits

Eager to throw off my nerdy past and reinvent myself at college, I wrote "party animal" on my roommate application form where it asked incoming freshmen whether they wanted to bunk with a smoker or a nonsmoker. When I told my mother about this later, she laughed and bought me a T-shirt that sported the image of Spuds MacKenzie, the 1980s Budweiser beer mascot, under the words "The original party animal."

I ended up with Tony from Sacramento, a very quiet, Republican son of a judge. (I suppose it's good policy to separate the party animals from those who request them.) I learned to appreciate his taste in music (U2 and The Smiths, as opposed to my predilection for reggae and jazz), and we agreed to disagree about politics during the reelection campaign of Alan Cranston, then one of the most liberal members of the U.S. Senate. I had never met anyone like Tony. And I'm pretty sure he hadn't come across many half-Jewish, Democratic children of New York artists. We learned to get along that first year at Berkeley, and every now and then even tried on each other's values and beliefs, just to see how they fit.

Today I am sad that most of my students will not experience what I did back when Facebook CEO Mark Zuckerberg was in diapers. While the Internet has made it easy to reconnect with the lost Tonys of our lives, it has made it a lot more difficult to meet them in the first place, by taking a lot of randomness out of life. We tend to value order and control over randomness, but when we lose randomness, we also lose serendipity.

As soon as today's students receive their proverbial fat envelope from their top choice college, they are on Facebook meeting other potential freshmen. They are on websites like Roomsurf and RoomSync, scoping out prospective friends. By the time the roommate application forms arrive, many like-minded

Patti Kilroy, right, and Bliss Baek in their dorm room at NYU after first contacting each other through Facebook. Does this process of connecting online reduce the diversity and randomness of the college experience?

students with similar backgrounds have already connected and agreed to request one another.

It's just one of many ways in which digital technologies now spill over into non-screen-based aspects of social experience. I know certain people who can't bear to eat in a restaurant they haven't researched on Yelp. And Google now tailors searches to exactly what it thinks you want to find.

But this loss of randomness is particularly unfortunate for college-age students, who should be trying on new hats and getting exposed to new and different ideas. Which students end up bunking with whom may seem trivial at first glance. But research on the phenomenon of peer influence—and the influences of roommates in particular—has found that there are, in fact, long-lasting effects based on whom you end up living with your first year.

David R. Harris, a sociologist at Cornell, studied roommates and found that white students who were assigned a roommate of a different race ended up more open-minded about race (Harris & Sim, 2002). In a 2000 study, the economist Bruce Sacerdote found that randomly assigned roommates at Dartmouth affected each other's G.P.A.'s (2001).

(Of course, influences can sometimes be negative. Roommates can drive each other's grades up or down. In 2003, researchers at four colleges discovered that male students who reported binge drinking in high school drank much more throughout college if their first-year roommate also reported binge drinking in high school [Duncan et al., 2005; Eisenberg et al., 2013; Kremer & Levy, 2008].)

These studies are important because we know that much education takes place outside the formal classroom curriculum and in the peer-to-peer learning that occurs in places like dorm rooms.

Other than prison and the military, there are not many other institutions outside of college that shove two people into a 100-square-foot space and expect them to get along for nine months. Can you think of any better training for marriage? In fact, in my research with Jennifer A. Heerwig (2011), we have found that Vietnam-era military service actually lowers the risk of subsequent divorce. It's possible that the military teaches you how to subsume your individual desires for the good of the collective—in other words, how to get along well with others.

The drive to tame randomness into controllable order is a noble impulse, but letting a little serendipity flourish isn't such a bad thing. Nor is getting to know someone different from yourself. All colleges should follow the lead of Hamilton College in New York, where roommate choice is not allowed. And if you end up with the roommate from hell? You'll survive, and someday have great stories to tell your future spouse, with whom you'll probably get along better.

→ ## CONCLUSION

In the nature-versus-nurture debate, sociologists have generally fallen firmly on the side of nurture. At least that's what most of us study. Socialization helps us understand and explain how it is that babies—those wrinkled, sometimes alien-looking creatures newly emerged from their mothers' wombs—become people who attend college. How much stake do we put in preserving normality, the status quo? We already talked about tact. Little children are tactless all the time. I once handed my grandfather a wrapped present and said, "Happy Father's Day! It's a shirt!" It was cute because I was 5, but what if I had done the same thing at 15? Would it have been cute? Somewhere along the way, we learn the unwritten rules.

On May 23, 1999, the World Wrestling Federation (WWF) aired a live pay-per-view event called "Over the Edge." When a harness malfunctioned, wrestler Owen Hart, who was being lowered into the ring, fell 78 feet to his death. Although television viewers did not see the live footage of his death, once Hart was removed and sent to the hospital (he was pronounced dead upon arrival), the program continued. The decision to go forward with the event sparked conversation and criticism far beyond the wrestling world. Some were shocked, even outraged, that the producers did not cancel the program, whereas others stood by the old adage, "The show must go on." Why the radically different reactions? Well, for starters, we do not have a social script for this type of incident. Death is a serious matter, to be sure, but how should death be handled when it occurs on live television? We tend to seek a return to normalcy when things do not go as planned. Trying to quickly transition the situation back to normal (and probably to keep their paying customers happy), the WWF continued the live event. Others were disgusted by this seeming insensitivity. The following night the association aired a two-hour tribute to the fallen wrestler.

This is an extreme example and a tragic one, but we witness more mundane, even comical, breaches on a fairly regular basis. When someone important commits them, they draw yet more attention. The point is that we all have a stake in things going a certain way. When things don't go according to plan, depending on the severity, nature, and context of the deviation, we must find some way to recover, and recover we usually do. Whether it is a small breach

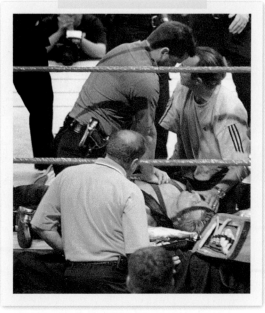

Paramedics try to resuscitate professional wrestler Owen Hart after a deadly fall in Kansas City, Missouri.

in our shared understanding of turn-taking etiquette or a major rupture to the fabric of society, people work hard to broker consensus with respect to shared meaning. The alternative is nothing less than chaos and social insanity.

→ PRACTICE

SOCIOLOGY ON THE STREET

Why does breaking social norms make others uncomfortable or even hostile? Watch the Sociology on the Street video to find out more: wwnpag.es/SOS4.

QUESTIONS FOR REVIEW

1. How does George Herbert Mead's concept of "generalized other" explain why, at the beginning of class, you became silent when your professor started speaking?

2. How does the case of "Anna" affect your assessment of early-socialization programs like Head Start?

3. School plays an important role in our socialization. Think about the way socialization works: What are some of the things we learn from schooling (e.g., the first years in elementary school), and how does this learning differ from what we are taught by our teacher? How are things like gender performance shaped in school?

4. Parents of different social classes socialize children differently. For example, middle-class parents are more likely to stress independence and self-direction, whereas working-class parents prioritize obedience to external authority. Using this example, how does socialization through families potentially reproduce social inequality?

5. You are a university student, but you also wait tables at a restaurant. One evening, one of your professors happens to come in for a meal (seemingly, on a date!). Use role theory to describe the interaction (and possible role conflict) that ensues.

6. What do sociologists mean by "social construction of reality"? How does the idea of social construction bring into question certain elements of everyday life, like gender roles?

7. Let's imagine you use file-sharing networks for music downloading and to discuss your favorite music subgenres with people throughout the world. How does this differ from, for example, speaking only with employees at your local music store? Think about the way technology affects how you interact, the characteristics of the people with whom you're interacting, and how different ways of interacting might affect socialization.

PARADOX

THE MOST IMPORTANT ASPECTS OF SOCIAL LIFE ARE THOSE CONCEPTS WE LEARN WITHOUT ANYONE TEACHING US.

WATCH THE ANIMATED SHORT ABOUT THE SOCIALIZATION PARADOX AT

WWNPAG.ES/PX4

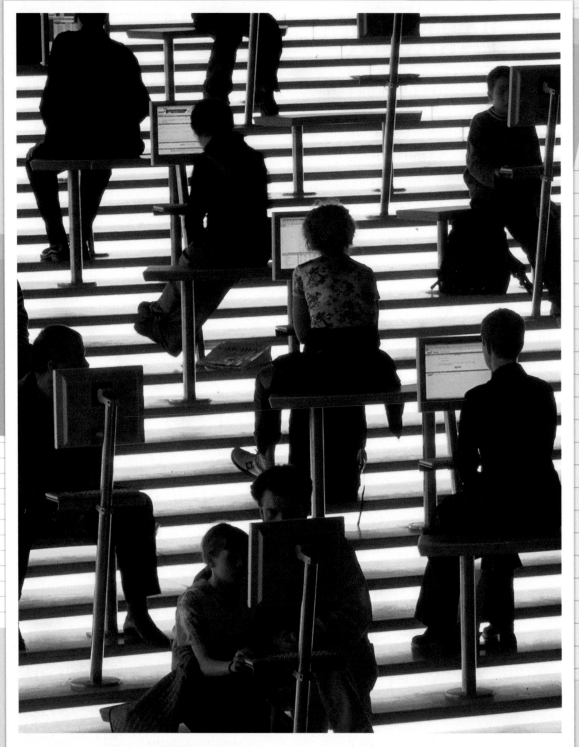

An Internet café in Hanover, Germany. How has technology transformed social interaction?

5 Groups and Networks

PARADOX

THE STRENGTH OF WEAK TIES:
IT IS THE PEOPLE WITH
WHOM WE ARE THE LEAST
CONNECTED WHO OFFER US
THE MOST OPPORTUNITIES.

It would seem that we are living in the age of social networks. Facebook, Pinterest, Twitter, and other social networking sites suck an ever-increasing proportion of the world's population into their virtual landscapes, along with, of course, more and more of our free time, as social life and leisure move online. But other than getting in touch with long-lost high-school buddies, what good are social networks anyway? Sure, you might be able to use Evite or Facebook as a virtual social secretary if you are organizing a baby shower or dorm party. But a good old-fashioned address book and rotary phone could have done the trick (even if it took longer).

Kate Rich, an Australian artist who has made a habit of digging tunnels through the invisible social structures most of us take for granted, has found a practical application for social networks. When she's not working for an anonymous, multinational collective with the ominous title The Bureau of Inverse Technology, she's climbing trees with friends in the English countryside. Or perhaps she's perfecting the recipe for Cube-Cola (http:// sparror.cubecinema.com/cube/cola/), an open-source cola whose motto is "Standing on the hands of giants." The beverage takes its name from the Cube Cinema, a workers' collective located in downtown Bristol, United Kingdom, where the drink is served to patrons.

As manager of the Cube's bar and café since 2003, Kate first looked into ordering only "fair trade" products when confronted with the need for a reliable source of good coffee for her patrons. But she found herself "unsure about the promises and threats made on the packet, almost inevitably happy farmers testifying as if at gunpoint that they use the money for their children's

Infused grappa from local vineyards in Croatia, distributed through Feral Trade.

education" (Conley, 2010). So she decided to put her own social networks to work and created what would soon become Feral Trade (www.feraltrade.org). The premise is simple. Pulling it off was not. The basic idea is that while we cannot quite trust packaging labels, we should be able to trust the firsthand reports of our close friends and colleagues.

To solve her coffee problem, she got in touch with fellow artist Amy Balkin, who was living in San Francisco and who had a sister working in the Peace Corps in El Salvador. The sister, in turn, put Kate in touch with a coffee co-op for which she could vouch. It took about three months to negotiate the first shipment of 30 bags of coffee (the chain of e-mails is documented on the Feral Trade website). From there the business slowly moved into import and distribution of other food products and utilities: tea from Bangladesh, sweets from Iran, Turkish delight from Montenegro, electric rice-cookers from Iran, and so on.

Kate explains her hand-to-hand shipping methodology:

> People sometimes point to the similarities between Feral Trade and the drug trade: Some methods might be similar but the structures of economy and ownership are totally different. Drug running being more or less a mafia version of normal corporate relations, workers alienated from production, etc. With Feral Trade, the couriers are exclusively unpaid; they are peers; they are uncontrollable: coaxed, convinced, and occasionally spontaneously offering their services. I have entirely no leverage over them, other than their own interest or investment in the shipment. (Conley, 2010)

Though Feral Trade has been up and running for almost a decade and Kate has carefully documented every transaction and shipment online for public consumption, it took almost that long for the "authorities" to notice and contact her. Some officials from the U.K. government's Trading Standards Service Public Protection Group and its Environmental Health office dropped by the Cube unannounced. Kate explained to them that there was actually no consumer for them to protect, and that these were the peer-to-peer transactions of the social economy that most people enact when they bring gifts back from vacation for their friends and family, with the key differences that cash is exchanged and that everything is publicly documented. The officials shifted their questions to the fact that many of the products depicted on the Feral Trade website appeared to be "brightly coloured" and therefore might involve dyes that are banned in the United Kingdom. They also admitted that they had made inquiries to Her Majesty's Custom and Excise on the legality of the commercial use of personal import food products and had been "unable to get a straight answer"—which Kate, of course, took as a clear precedent to continue trading.

Kate finds these interactions with official bureaucracies slightly terrifying, even if they make for great Web documentation after the fact. The people she actually finds more frustrating are the "clients" who think she can take very specific retail-level orders.

> It's not about providing a global service to bring in desired items to an individual consumer. It's about coordinated social movement. Can I shift 20 boxes of Iranian sweets from Yazd to Bristol to distribute them amongst friends pre-Xmas? These went fridge-to-fridge—the couriers were me, an Egyptian musician friend, an Iranian art student I met at a party, a Russian professor I know in London and her four-year-old kid, and an IT guy from Hewlett Packard I'd never met before, along with various onlookers and companions. (Conley, 2010)

To someone who might request one very specific T-shirt from Ecuador, she says, "Get your own extended social network!"

> There's a moment where you're in the canopy suspended with your weight spread out over 10 or 20 twiglets of one tree and reaching for a handful of tendrils of the neighbouring tree; that's all your means of support. It always seems impossible, totally terrifying, then you just have to move and you're suddenly safe, grabbing onto one of tree two's branches. The shipping manoeuvres are like that, at their best. Total hazard then the thrill of things moving and cooperating in unplannable ways. (Conley, 2010)

This chapter explores some of the basic theories about group interaction and how it shapes our social world. We'll look at the connections between groups: how size and shape matter, what roles group members play, and how the power of groups works compared with individuals and other institutions. We'll also discuss organizations and how they both react to and create social structure.

Social Groups

Unless you live alone in the woods, and perhaps even then, you are a member of many social groups. Social groups form the building blocks of society and most social interaction. In fact, even the self evolves from groups. Let's start by talking about the various types and sizes of groups. In his classic work "Quantitative Aspects of the Group," sociologist Georg Simmel (1950) argues that without knowing anything about the group members' individual psychology or the cultural or social context in which they are embedded, we can make predictions about the ways people behave based solely on the number of members, or "social actors," in that group. This theory applies not just to groups of people but also to states, countries, firms, corporations, bureaucracies, and any number of other social forms.

Just the Two of Us

Dyad a group of two.

Triad a group of three.

Simmel advances the notion that the most important distinction is that between a relationship of two, which he calls a dyad, and a group of three, which he calls a triad. This is the fundamental distinction among most social relations, he argues, and it holds regardless of the individual characteristics of the group's members. Of course, personality differences do influence social relations, but there are numerous social dynamics about which we can make predictions that have nothing to do with the content of the social relations themselves.

The dyad has several unique characteristics. For starters, it is the most intimate form of social life, partly because the two members of the dyad are mutually dependent on each other. That is, the continued existence of the group is entirely contingent on the willingness of both parties to participate in the group; if either person leaves, the dyad ceases to be. This intimacy is enhanced by the fact that no third person exists to buffer the situation or mediate between the two. Meanwhile, the members of a dyad don't need to be concerned about how their relationship will be perceived by a third party.

For example, we might consider a couple the most intimate social arrangement in our society. Both people must remain committed to being in the dyad for it to exist, and if one partner leaves, the couple no longer exists. There can be no secrets—if the last piece of chocolate cake disappears and you didn't eat it, you know who did. You could withhold a secret from your dyadic partner, but in terms of the actions of the group itself, no mystery lingers about who performs which role or who did what. Either you did it, or the other person did.

In a dyad, symmetry must be maintained. There might be unequal power relations within a group of two to a certain extent, but Simmel would argue that in a group of two an inherent symmetry exists because of the earlier stipulation of mutual dependence—namely, that the group survives only if both members remain. Even in relationships where the power seems so clearly unequal—think of a master and a servant or a prisoner and his captor—Simmel argues that there's an inherent symmetry. Yes, the servant may be completely dependent on the master for his or her wages, sustenance, food, and shelter, but what happens to the master who becomes dependent on the labor that the servant performs? Of course, forcible relationships might develop in which one of two parties is forced to stay in the dyad, but to be considered a pure dyad, the relationship has to be voluntary. Because a dyad could fall apart at any moment, the underlying social relation is heightened.

Dyads are the foundation of all social relationships. Why are they the most intimate relationship, according to Georg Simmel?

The dyad is also unique in other ways. Because the group exists only as long as the individuals choose to maintain it in a voluntary fashion, the group itself exerts no supra-individual control over the individuals involved. For example, whereas a child might claim, "She made me do it" and shamelessly tell on her older sister, a member of a dyad is less likely to say, "I was just following orders" or "The whole group decided to go see *Mission: Impossible 7*, and I really didn't want to, but I went anyway." The force of a group is much stronger when three or more individuals are part of the group.

Let's take a real-life example of how the characteristics of a dyad play out and see why they matter. Think about divorce. One point in a marriage at which the divorce rate is especially high is when a first child is born (and not just because of the parental sleep deprivation that arrives with a newborn). The nature of the relationship between the two adults changes. They have gone from being a dyad to becoming a triad. Perhaps the parents feel a sudden lack of intimacy, even though the baby is not yet a fully developed social actor. On the flip side, a husband or wife might begin to feel trapped in a marriage specifically because of a child. All of a sudden, group power exists—a couple has evolved into a family, and with that comes the power of numbers in a group.

And Then There Were Three

This brings us to the triad, distinguished by characteristics you can probably infer by now. In a triad, the group holds supra-individual power. In other words, in a group of three or four, I can say, "I'm really unhappy, I hate this place,

In what ways are triads more complex than dyads? What are the possible roles of triad members?

I hate you, and I'm leaving," but the group will go on. The husband may walk out on his wife and children, but the family he's abandoning still exists. He's ending his participation in the group, but the group will outlast his decision to leave it. Therefore, the group is not dependent on any one particular member.

What's more, in a triad, secrets can exist. Who left the cap off the toothpaste? If more than two people live under the same roof, you can't be sure. Politics is another aspect inherent in a group of three or more. Instead of generating consensus between two individuals, now you have multiple points of view and preferences that need to be balanced. This allows for power politics among the group's members. Simmel refers to three basic forms of political relations that can evolve within a triad depending on what role the entering third party assumes (Figure 5.1). The first role is that of mediator, the person who tries to resolve conflict between the other two and is sometimes brought in for that explicit purpose. A good example would be a marriage counselor. Rather than go to therapy, couples having marital problems often start a family because they believe a baby will bring them back together. Unfortunately, as most couples come to realize sooner rather than later, a baby cannot play the role of a mediator. Rather, the dynamics of the unhappy family may turn into a game of chicken: Which parent is more devoted to the child? Which dyad forms the core of the group, and which person will be left out or can walk away more easily?

Mediator the member of a triad who attempts to resolve conflict between the two other actors in the group.

A second possible role for the incoming third member of a triad is that of *tertius gaudens* (Latin for "the third that rejoices"). This individual profits from the disagreement of the other two, essentially playing the opposite role from the mediator. Someone in this position might have multiple roles. In the previous example, the marriage counselor plays the part of the mediator, but she is also earning her wages from the conflict between the couple. Maybe she encourages continued therapy even after the couple appear to have resolved all their issues, or perhaps she promotes their staying together even though they've already decided to get a divorce.

Tertius gaudens the member of a triad who benefits from conflict between the other two members of the group.

The third possible role that Simmel identifies for a third party is *divide et impera* (Latin for "divide and conquer"). This person intentionally drives a wedge between the other two parties. This third role is similar to *tertius gaudens*, the difference between the two being a question of intent and whether the rift preexisted. (If you've ever seen or read Shakespeare's *Othello*, there is no better example of *divide et impera* than the way Iago, counselor to Othello, uses the Moor's insecurities to foster a rift between him and his wife Desdemona in order to strengthen Iago's own hand in court politics. The play ends tragically, of course.)

Divide et impera the role of a member of a triad who intentionally drives a wedge between the other two actors in the group.

To take an example with which millions of Americans are familiar, let's return to the case of the triad formed when a romantic couple has a child

Figure 5.1: Political Relations within a Triad

MEDIATOR
The mediator attempts to resolve conflict between the other two members of the triad, and is sometimes brought in for that explicit purpose.

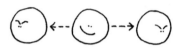

TERTIUS GAUDENS
Latin for "the third that rejoices." This individual profits from the disagreement of the other two actors, essentially playing the opposite role from the mediator.

DIVIDE ET IMPERA
Latin for "divide and conquer." This person intentionally drives a wedge between the other two parties.

but experiences strife and separates. What happens when the couple divorces? What role does the child play? A child could play any of the roles mentioned above. In the original dyad of the biological parents, the child can be a mediator, forcing his or her parents to work together on certain issues pertaining to his or her care. A child can be "the third who rejoices" from the disagreement of the two, profiting from the fact that he or she might receive two allowances or extra birthday presents because each parent is trying to prove that he or she loves the child more. A complicated *divide et impera* situation could develop if one of the child's parents enters into a second marriage, in which the kid remains the biological child of one parent and becomes the stepchild of the other. In this case, all sorts of politics arise because of the biological connection between the one parent and the child versus the marital love relationship between the two adults. The relationship between the nonbiological parent and the stepchild, who have the weakest bond, may be difficult. The situation could unfold in any number of ways. Many domestic comedies (think *The Parent Trap*) are based on the premise of a young, angst-ridden prankster playing the role of *divide et impera* between his or her parent and the new stepmother or -father.

When contemplating how these theoretical concepts work within actual social interaction, keep in mind that these groups—dyads and triads—don't exist in a vacuum in real life. In discussing the politics of a stepfamily, we're talking about a household where there's a stepparent, a biological parent, and a child. Beyond our textbook example, in real life, this triad probably doesn't function so independently. There is probably another biological parent living elsewhere, maybe another stepparent, maybe siblings. Most social groups are very complex, and we need to take that into consideration when we attempt to determine how they operate. This is why we start with Simmel's purest forms. The interactions that take place in groups of two and three become the building blocks for those in much larger groups.

Size Matters: Why Social Life Is Complicated

One key insight is that as the number of people in the group increases geometrically ($2 + 1 = 3$; $3 + 1 = 4$; $4 + 1 = 5$), the complexity of analyzing that group's ties increases exponentially ($2 \times 2 = 4$; $4 \times 4 = 16$; $5 \times 5 = 25$). A two-person group has only one possible and necessary relationship; it must exist for there to be a group. In a triad, a sum of three relationships exists, with each person within the group having two ties. And again, for it to be a group of three, we're not talking about possible connections but actual ones. Each person in the triad has to have two ties—breaking a single tie turns the triad into two dyads. Even if one of the ties between two members is weaker, it is so well-reinforced by the remaining two ties that it is unlikely to fade away, a feature known as the "iron law" of the triad. When you move beyond triads to groups of four or more, something different happens. To create a group of four, there must be at least four relationships, but you can have as many as six. Figure 5.2 shows this exponential rise in possible relationships graphically.

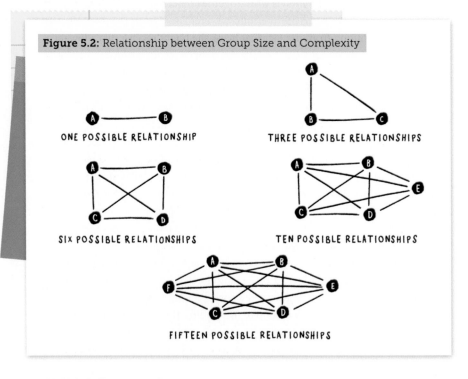

Figure 5.2: Relationship between Group Size and Complexity

ONE POSSIBLE RELATIONSHIP

THREE POSSIBLE RELATIONSHIPS

SIX POSSIBLE RELATIONSHIPS

TEN POSSIBLE RELATIONSHIPS

FIFTEEN POSSIBLE RELATIONSHIPS

In a diagram with four people (A, B, C, and D), we can cross out the diagonals and the group will still exist. Everyone may have only two relationships as opposed to three (the number of possible relationships). A and D might never have spoken to each other, but the group will continue to function. The tendency, however, is for these possible relationships to become actual relationships. You and your roommate are in separate chemistry classes, but your lab partners happen to be roommates. If you both become friendly with your lab partners outside of class, chances are that you will meet your roommate's lab partner and vice versa. Such social ties between friends of the same friend tend to form. This can be good or bad. You may form a study group and, if your roommate's lab partner's boyfriend is a chemist, you (and everyone else) may benefit from his help. On the other hand, if the two break up and you start dating the chemist, it might make future labs a little uncomfortable for your roommate.

Let's Get This Party Started: Small Groups, Parties, and Large Groups

Groups larger than a dyad or triad, according to Simmel, can be classified into one of three types: small groups, parties, and large groups. A small group is characterized by four factors. The first is *face-to-face interaction*; all the members of the group at any given time are present and interact with one another. They are not spread out geographically. Second, a small group is *unifocal*, meaning that there's one center of attention at any given time. Turn taking among speakers occurs. A classroom, unless it's divided and engaged in group work, should be unifocal.

Small group a group characterized by face-to-face interaction, a unifocal perspective, lack of formal arrangements or roles, and a certain level of equality.

What makes the study group on the left a small group, and how is it different from the cocktail party on the right?

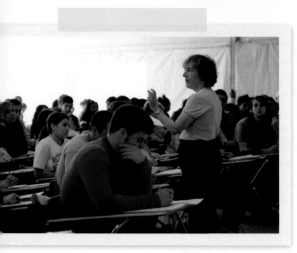

How is this classroom an example of a large group?

Classes usually don't qualify as small groups because a third characteristic of small groups is a *lack of formal arrangements* or *roles*. A study group, though, might qualify if you decide shortly before an exam to meet with some of your classmates. You need to agree on a place and time to meet, but otherwise there is no formal arrangement. In the classroom, however, a professor is in attendance, as are teaching assistants and students—all of whom play official roles in the group. The roles generally encountered in classes also contradict the fourth defining characteristic of a small group, *equality*. After all, you won't be giving your professor a grade, nor will she get into trouble, as you might, for arriving late at a planned lecture. Yours isn't a reciprocal and equal relationship. Within a small group, as in a dyad, there is a certain level of equality. Only in a dyad can pure equality exist, because both members hold veto power over the group. However, in a small group, even if the group will continue to exist beyond the membership of any particular member, no particular member has greater sway than the others. No one member can dissolve the group. If someone in your study group gets tired and falls asleep on his book, you and your classmates can continue to study without him.

When does a small group become a party? If you have ever hosted a party, you know that the worst phase is the beginning. You're worried that people might not show up: The party has started, only three people are there (everyone, after all, tends to arrive fashionably late), and you start to wonder, "Is this going to be it?" You have to keep a conversation going among three people; you refill their glasses as soon as they take one sip. If you're drinking alcohol (only if you're of legal drinking age, of course), you may consume more at the beginning of the party because you are nervous about it not going well. When does your small gathering officially evolve into a party, so that you can relax and enjoy yourself? Simmel would say that a party, like a small group, is characterized by face-to-face interaction but differs in that it is *multifocal*. Going back to the example of your sociology study group, if two people begin to talk about Margaret Mead's theory of the self while the rest of you discuss the differences between role conflict and role strain, then it is bifocal; if another subgroup splits off to deliberate on reference groups, then it has become multifocal. According to Simmel, you've got yourself a party! So when you're hosting your next party, you'll recognize when it has officially started.

Party a group that is similar to a small group but is multifocal.

Large group a group characterized by the presence of a formal structure that mediates interaction and, consequently, status differentiation.

The last type of group to which Simmel makes reference is the large group. The primary characteristic of a large group is the presence of a *formal structure* that mediates interaction and, consequently, *status differentiation*. When you enter a classroom, it should be clear who the teacher is, and you comprehend that she has a higher status than you have in that specific social context.

The professor is an employee of the university, knows more than you know about the subject being taught, and is responsible for assigning you a grade based on your performance in the course. You might be asked to complete a teacher evaluation form at the end of the semester, but it's not the same thing as grading a student. You and your professor aren't equals. The point is that the inherent characteristics of a group are determined not just by its size but also by other aspects of its form. Whether a group stays small, becomes a party, or evolves into a large group may depend on numbers, but it also may depend on the size and configuration of the physical space in which the social actors are assembled, preexisting social relationships, expectations, and the larger social context in which that group is embedded.

Primary and Secondary Groups

Simmel wasn't the only one who tried to describe the basic types of groups. The sociologist Charles Horton Cooley (1909) emphasized a distinction between what he called primary and secondary groups. Primary groups are *limited in the number of members*, allowing for face-to-face interaction. The group is an end unto itself, rather than a means to an end. This is what makes your family different from a sports team or small business: Sure, you want the family to function well, but you're not trying to compete with other families or manufacture a product. Meanwhile, primary groups are *key agents of socialization*. Most people's first social group is their family, which is a primary group. Your immediate family (parents and siblings) is probably small enough to sit down at the same dinner table or at least gather in the same room at the same time. Loyalty is the primary ethic here. Members of a primary group are *noninterchangeable*— you can't replace your mother or father. And while you have strong allegiances to your friends, your primary loyalty is likely to be to your family. Finally, the relationships within a primary group are *enduring*. Your sister will always be your sister. Another example of a primary group might be the group of your closest friends, especially if you've known each other since your sandbox years.

Primary groups social groups, such as family or friends, composed of enduring, intimate face-to-face relationships that strongly influence the attitudes and ideals of those involved.

The characteristics of secondary groups, such as a labor union, stand in contrast to those of primary groups. The group is *impersonal*; you may or may not know all of the members of your union. It's also *instrumental*; the group exists as a means to an end, in this case for organizing workers and lobbying for their interests. In a secondary group, affiliation is *contingent*. You are only a member of your union so long as you hold a certain job and pay your dues. If you change jobs or join another union, your membership in that earlier group ends. Because the members of a secondary group change, the roles are more important than the individuals who fill them. The shop steward, the person chosen to interact with the company's management, may be a different person every year, but that position carries the same responsibilities within the group regardless of who fills it. A sports team is another example of a secondary

Secondary groups groups marked by impersonal, instrumental relationships (those existing as a means to an end).

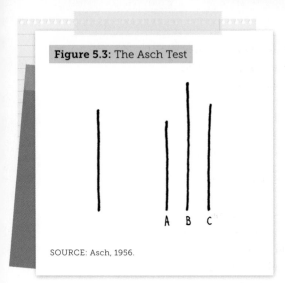

Figure 5.3: The Asch Test

A   B   C

SOURCE: Asch, 1956.

group, although if you're also close friends with your teammates and socialize with them when you're not playing sports, the line between a primary and secondary group can become blurred.

Group Conformity

Although we tend to put a high value on individuality in American culture, our lives are marked by high levels of conformity. That is, groups have strong influences over individual behavior. In the late 1940s the social psychologist Solomon Asch carried out a now-famous series of experiments to demonstrate the power of norms of group conformity. He gathered subjects in a room under the pretense that they were participating in a vision test, showed them two images of lines, and asked which ones were longer than the others and which were the same length (Figure 5.3).

The trick was that only one person in each room was really a research subject; the rest of the people had been told ahead of time to give the same incorrect answer. While a majority of subjects answered correctly even after they listened to others give the wrong answer, about one-third expressed serious discomfort—they clearly struggled with what they thought was right in light of what everyone else was saying. Subjects were the most confused when the entire group offered an incorrect answer. When the group members gave a range of responses, the research subjects had no trouble answering correctly. This experiment demonstrates the power of conformity within a group. More troubling instances of group conformity may be seen in cases of collective violence such as gang rape, which tends to occur among tightly knit groups like sports teams or fraternities (Sanday, 1990).

In-Groups and Out-Groups

In-group another term for the powerful group, most often the majority.

Out-group another term for the stigmatized or less powerful group, the minority.

In-groups and out-groups are another broad way of categorizing people. The in-group is the powerful group, most often the majority, whereas the out-group is the stigmatized or less powerful group, usually the minority (though the numbers don't have to break down this way). For example, in the United States, heterosexuals are the in-group in terms of sexuality (both more powerful and numerically greater), whereas homosexuals, bisexuals, and those who have other nonnormative sexual identities fall into the out-group. However, in South Africa, despite being a minority group, whites are the in-group because of their enormous political and economic power (the legacy of colonialism and apartheid), whereas blacks are the out-group despite their greater numbers. The significance of in-groups and out-groups lies in their relative power to define what constitutes normal versus abnormal thoughts and behavior.

Reference Groups

We often compare ourselves to other groups of people we do not know directly in order to make comparisons. For example, your class might compare itself to another introduction to sociology class, which has a take-home midterm and an optional final. If your class has a 20-page term paper and a two-hour comprehensive final exam, you might feel as if you face an unfair amount of work. If your class has no external assignments, however, and your final grades are based on self-assessment, you might feel comparatively lucky. In either case, the other class serves as a reference group. Reference groups help us understand or make sense of our position in society relative to other groups. The neighboring town's high school or even another socioeconomic class can serve as a reference group. In the first instance, you might compare access to sporting facilities; in the second, you might compare voting patterns.

Reference group a group that helps us understand or make sense of our position in society relative to other groups.

From Groups to **Networks**

Dyads, triads, and groups are the components of social networks. A social network is a set of relations—a set of dyads, essentially—held together by *ties* between individuals. A tie is the content of a particular relationship. One way to think about "the ties that bind" is as a set of stories we tell each other that explain a particular relationship. If I ask you how you know a specific person, and you explain that she was your brother's girlfriend in the eighth grade, and the two of you remained close even after her relationship with your brother ended, that story is your tie to that person. For every person in your life, you have a story. To explain some ties, the story is very simple: "That's the guy I buy my coffee from each morning." This is a uniplex tie. Other ties have many layers. They are multiplex: "She's my girlfriend. We have a romantic relationship. We also are tennis and bridge partners. And now that you mention it, we are classmates at school and also fiercely competitive opponents in Trivial Pursuit."

A narrative is the sum of stories contained in a set of ties. Your university or college is a narrative, for example. Every person with whom you have a relationship at your university forms part of that network. For all your college-based relationships—those shared with a professor, your teaching assistant, or classmates—your school is a large part of the story, of the tie. Without the school, in fact, you probably wouldn't share a tie at all. When you add up

Social network a set of relations—essentially, a set of dyads—held together by ties between individuals.

Tie the connection between two people in a relationship that varies in strength from one relationship to the next; a story that explains our relationship with another member of our network.

Narrative the sum of stories contained in a set of ties.

the stories of all the actors involved in the social network of your school—between you and your classmates, between the professors and their colleagues, between the school and the vendors with whom it contracts—the result is a narrative of what your college is. Of course, you may have other friends, from high school or elsewhere, who have no relationship to your school, so your college is a more minor aspect of those relationships.

In Chapter 4 we talked about the power of symbols. What would you need to do if you wanted to change the name of your school? You and your friends could just start calling it something else. But you'd probably have to hire a legal team to alter the contracts (a form of tie that is spelled out explicitly in a written "story") that the school maintains with all its vendors. You would need to alert alumni and advise the departments and staff at school to change their stationery, websites, and any marketing materials. You would have to advise faculty to use the new name when citing their professional affiliation. You would need to contact legacy families (let's say a family whose last seven generations have attended this college) and inform them of the name change. Do you now have a sense of how complicated it would be to change this narrative? If you try to make a change that involves a large network, the social structure becomes very powerful. Ironically, something abstract like a name can be more robust than most of the physical infrastructure around us.

Embeddedness: The Strength of Weak Ties

Embeddedness the degree to which ties are reinforced through indirect paths within a social network.

One important dimension of social networks is the degree to which they are embedded. **Embeddedness** refers to the degree to which ties are reinforced through indirect paths within a social network. The more embedded a tie is, the stronger it is. That is, the more indirect paths you make to somebody, the stronger the relationship. It may feel less dramatic and intimate, but it's robust and more likely to endure simply by virtue of the fact that it's difficult to escape. You will always be connected to that person—if not directly, then through your "mutual" friends. However, the counterpoint to this dynamic lies in what sociologist Mark Granovetter (1973) calls the **strength of weak ties**, referring to the fact that relatively weak ties—those not reinforced through indirect paths—often turn out to be quite valuable because they bring novel information. Let's say you're on the track team and that's your primary social group. An old classmate from high school whom you didn't really know (or run in the same circles with) back then, you now see occasionally because he also attends your college, but he's on the volleyball team. If the track team isn't doing anything on Friday night but the volleyball team is having a party, you've got an "in" through this relationship that's much weaker than the ones you've got with the other members of the track team. That "in" is the strength of the weak tie you maintain with the classmate from home. If you end up taking your friends

Strength of weak ties the notion that relatively weak ties often turn out to be quite valuable because they yield new information.

from the track team to the volleyball party and they become friends with your old friend, the tie between you and your old classmate is no longer "weak" because it is now reinforced by the ties between your old friend and your new track friends—regardless of whether you are actually more intimate with him or not. This example helps explain why the structure of the network is more complicated than the tie from one individual to another. Even though your friendships did not change at the volleyball party, the fact that people in your social network befriended others in your social network strengthens the ties between you and both of the individuals.

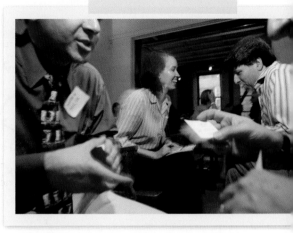

Jena McGregor (center) takes part in a speed networking event in New York City. Participants chat about their businesses and make contacts with as many people as they can in multiple four-minute sessions.

The strength of weak ties has been found especially useful in job searches (Granovetter, 1974). In a highly embedded network, all the individuals probably know the same people, hear of the same job openings, maintain the same contacts, and so on. However, your grandparents' neighbor, whom you see every so often, probably has a completely different set of connections. The paradox is that this weak tie provides the most opportunities. When Granovetter interviewed professionals in Boston (1973), he determined that among his 54 respondents who found their employment through personal network ties, more than half saw this contact person "occasionally" (less than once a week but more than once a year). Perhaps even more surprising was the fact that the runners-up in this category were not people whom the respondents saw "often" (once a week or more); it was those they saw "rarely" (once a year or less), by a factor of almost two to one. Additional research finds that weak ties offer the greatest benefits to job seekers who already have high-status jobs, suggesting that social networks combine with credentials to sort job applicants and that strong ties may be more useful in low-status, low-credential job markets (Wegener, 1991).

In Figure 5.4, by linking two otherwise separate social networks, the weak tie between Natalie and Emily provides new opportunities for dating—not only for them but for their friends as well. Their tie bridges what we call a structural hole between the two cliques, a gap between network clusters, where a possible tie could become an actual tie or where an intermediary could control the communication between the two groups on either side of the hole. In the figure, Jenny is a social entrepreneur bridging a structural hole because the people on the left side of the network diagram (Emily and Jason) have no direct ties with the people on the right (Michael, Doug, and Jeff). Their ties are only indirect, through Jenny. Assuming that the two sides have resources (romantic or otherwise) that would complement each other's, Jenny is in a position to mediate by acting as a go-between for the groups. When a third party

Structural hole a gap between network clusters, or even two individuals, if those individuals (or clusters) have complementary resources.

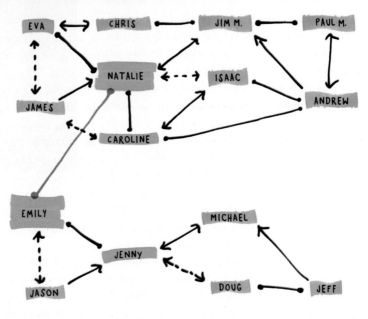

Figure 5.4: The Strength of Weak Ties

Natalie and Emily are social entrepreneurs; they command information to which the rest of their respective social networks do not have access.

connects two groups or individuals who would be better off in contact with each other, that third party is an "entrepreneur," and he or she can profit from the gap. (Sound like the *tertius gaudens* in the triad? It should.)

When sociologist Ronald Burt studied managers in a large corporation (1992), he found that those with the most structural holes in their social networks were the ones who rose through the company ranks the fastest and farthest. This notion can be expanded to explain how a great deal of profit making occurs in today's economy. At one extreme is the totally free market, in which there are no structural holes; no restriction on information exists, and all buyers and sellers can reach one another—think eBay. At the other extreme is the monopoly, in which one firm provides necessary information or resources to a multitude of people (that is, maintains and profits from a gaping structural hole). And then there is everything in between these extremes: everyone from shipping magnates to spice traders to mortgage brokers to feral traders. Take real estate agents as an example. They earn their money by contractually maintaining (or creating) a structural hole. By signing up sellers, the real estate agents prevent the sellers from directly engaging in a transaction with potential buyers. Recently, the social network possibilities facilitated by the Internet (discussed below) have done much to erode the power of brokers—for example, by driving once-powerful travel agents into near extinction (ditto for stockbrokers).

Six Degrees

You have probably heard the term "six degrees of separation" and wondered if it is really true that each one of us is connected to every other person by social chains of no more than six people. The evidence supporting the six degrees theory came out of research undertaken in the 1960s by Stanley Milgram, whose colleagues were pestering him about why it always seemed like the strangers they met at cocktail parties turned out to be friends of a friend. Milgram decided to test the reach of social networks by asking a stockbroker in Boston to receive chain letters from a bunch of folks living in Lincoln, Nebraska. The Lincolnites could only send letters to friends or relatives who they believed would be likely to know someone who might know someone who might know the guy in Boston. About 20 percent of the letters eventually made it to Boston, and the average trip length was just over five people, hence the summary that in the United States there are no more than five people between any set of strangers, or six degrees of separation.

Duncan Watts (2003) noticed that Milgram's findings applied only to the letters that made it to their final destination. What about the letters that did not complete the journey? Were their chains quite a bit longer than six steps, thus making our six-degree theory more like a twelve-degree theory? Watts set up a similar, this time worldwide, experiment using e-mail and statistical models to estimate global connectedness and found that Milgram was not quite right. In Watts's words, "It's not true that everyone is connected to everyone else, but at least half the people in the world are connected to each other through six steps, which is actually kind of surprising" (Conley, 2009b). Furthermore, Watts was able to test the commonsense notion that there are some people out there who just seem to know everyone and that it must be through these superconnected people that the rest of us are able to say we're only six degrees from Kevin Bacon (or whomever). But instead he found that when it comes to whom we know, "the world's remarkably egalitarian," and that superconnectors played almost no role in getting the e-mail forwarded all the way to its destination (Conley, 2009b).

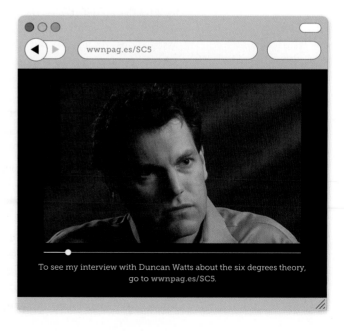

wwnpag.es/SC5

To see my interview with Duncan Watts about the six degrees theory, go to wwnpag.es/SC5.

Social Capital

Having many weak ties is one form of what sociologists call *social capital*. Like human capital, the training and skills that

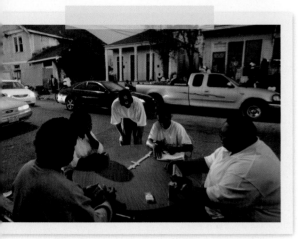

Neighbors in the Central City section of New Orleans gather for their weekly domino game. Communities with thick webs of connection tend to thrive, with lower crime rates and more volunteer involvement.

Social capital the information, knowledge of people or things, and connections that help individuals enter, gain power in, or otherwise leverage social networks.

make individuals more productive and valuable to employers, social capital is the information, knowledge of people or things, and connections that help individuals enter preexisting networks or gain power in them. Consider the importance of networking in endeavors such as preventing neighborhood crime or obtaining a good job. As it turns out, the cliché holds a lot of truth: It's not just what you know but whom you know. But whereas weak ties may be the most advantageous for an individual, for a community, many dense, embedded ties are generally a sign of high levels of social capital.

This concept makes sense when you think about it. Dense social capital means that people are linked to one another through a thick web of connections. As a result of these connections, they will feel inclined—perhaps even impelled—to help each other, to return favors, to keep an eye on one another's property. The more connections there are, the more norms of reciprocity, values, and trust are shared. After all, there is no such thing as total anonymity: Even if you don't know someone directly, chances are that you are only one or two degrees removed from him or her.

In this way, strong social capital binds people together; it weaves them into a tight social fabric that can help a community thrive. "You tell me how many choral societies there are in an Italian region," notes social capital scholar Robert Putnam, "and I will tell you plus or minus three days how long it will take you to get your health bills reimbursed by its regional government" (Edgerton, 1995). After years of research in Italy, Putnam determined that different regions of the country varied widely in their levels of participation in voluntary associations. As it turns out, the strength of participation in a region was a fairly good predictor of the quality and efficiency of its regional government (and, in turn, its economic growth).

The United States and Social Capital If it's true that social capital is correlated with economic and political health, some critics would say that the United States is in big trouble. Voluntary participation in civic life has taken a turn for the worse, and as a result, the nation's stock of social capital is at risk. In his best seller *Bowling Alone: The Collapse and Revival of American Community* (2000), Putnam traces the decline of civic engagement in the last third of the twentieth century. We are more loosely connected today than ever before, he says, experiencing less family togetherness, taking fewer group vacations, and demonstrating little civic engagement.

In *Loose Connections: Joining Together in America's Fragmented Communities* (1998), Robert Wuthnow finds that people are worried about what they see as a breakdown of families and neighborliness and a concurrent rise in selfishness. When

Wuthnow surveyed a random sample of Americans, fewer than half believed that their fellow citizens genuinely cared about others. Even worse, some studies suggest that more and more people think their neighbors are inherently untrustworthy (Lasch, 1991). A considerable majority of Americans believe that their communities are weaker than ever before (Wuthnow, 1998). Without communal ties of civic and religious participation, Americans have lost trust in their neighbors. Interpersonal trust matters; it is essential for building the complex social structures necessary for a functioning democracy and economy.

Bowling alone? Although the overall number of bowlers has increased, the number of people bowling in groups has dropped. Are we seeing a decline in social engagement?

Indeed, more and more people are bowling alone. Actual bowling activity was on the rise at the end of the twentieth century, when Putnam and Wuthnow were writing—the total number of bowlers in America increased by 10 percent from 1988 to 1993—but *league* bowling dropped a whopping 40 percent in the same time frame. This is no good for bowling-lane owners, but it's also bad news for democracy in America. Bowling alone is part of a more general trend of civic disengagement and a decline in social capital. It's happening in PTAs, the Red Cross, local elections, community cleanups, and labor unions. Even membership in the Boy Scouts has decreased by 26 percent since the 1970s. More people live alone. Some go so far as to say that friendships have become shallower, and the phenomenon of BFF (best friends forever) is an increasing rarity (Wuthnow, 1998). As civic participation withers, activities once performed by communities have moved toward private markets.

Who's to blame for America's fading civic life? The social entrepreneur who has too many structural holes to maintain? Parents? Our school systems, television, the Internet? A combination of all these and other factors works in conjunction with broad social trends, creating an increasingly differentiated, specialized, urbanized, and modern world. Social institutions must adjust to the flexibility, sometimes called the liquidity, of modernity by becoming more fragmented, less rigid, and more "porous" (Wuthnow, 1998). It becomes easier to come and go, to pass through multiple social groups such as churches, friends, jobs, and even families. Gone is the rigid fixity of finding and holding onto a lifelong "calling." Similarly, a majority of graduating college students (60 percent) attend more than one school before receiving a degree (Zernike, 2006).

This mobility and flexibility take a toll on people's lives. More than in previous eras, people report feeling rushed, disconnected, and harried, so it's no surprise that civic responsibilities are pushed aside. It's not that Americans don't care. In fact, they join more organizations and donate more money than ever before. They just don't give their time or engage in face-to-face activities (Skocpol, 2004). But before we blame the Internet, note that the trend toward

Pennsylvania's Lancaster County attracts more than 5 million visitors a year with its Pennsylvania Dutch country charm. Horse-drawn wagons carry visitors over covered bridges toward historic museums, colonial homes, and restaurants. Lancaster thrives on tourists' curiosity about the Amish, who first settled the land in 1693. Today about 59,350 Amish live in nearby homogenous farm communities. As far as appearances go, they certainly meet tourists' expectations.

Wearing straw hats and black bonnets, riding horse-drawn buggies, the Amish provide great photo opportunities. Children are taught in private schoolhouses, typically one room, only until the eighth grade, at which point they work full time on the family farm. The lives of the Amish revolve around going to church, tilling the earth, and working for the collective good. They value simplicity and solidarity. How, visitors wonder, have Amish communities in Pennsylvania and other states survived in our fast-paced society?

The Amish certainly appear to be relics of the past, but looks can be deceiving. Although the Amish place primary importance on agriculture, they do so in anything but a premodern fashion. The Amish, especially those living close to urban areas, have adopted farming innovations such as the use of insecticides and chemically enhanced fertilizers. Their homes are stylishly modern, with sleek kitchens and natural gas–powered appliances.

Because Lancaster County has experienced a certain degree of urban growth and sprawl, the Amish are not immune to the hustle and bustle of commerce. In fact, many Amish are savvy business owners. The number of Amish-owned microenterprises more than quadrupled between 1970 and 1990. By 1993 more than one in four Amish homes had at least one nonfarm business owner (Kraybill and Nolt, 1995). The result of this economic growth is a curious mix of profit-seeking entrepreneurship with a traditional lifestyle. Imagine finding out that your local rabbi, priest, or imam doubled as a high-rolling stock trader during the week.

How can these seemingly incompatible spheres of religious tradition and commerce coexist? This is the question Donald Kraybill set out to answer when he studied 150 Amish business entrepreneurs in Lancaster County (1993; in 1995 with Nolt). Not only do the Amish trade with outsiders, Kraybill documented, but they do so quite successfully: About 15 percent of the businesses he studied had annual sales exceeding half a million dollars. Their success rate is phenomenal: Just 4 percent of Amish start-ups fail within a decade, compared with the 75 percent of all new American firms that fail within three

An Amish barn raising in Tollesboro, Kentucky.

years of opening. That is, in a time when the majority of new American business ventures flop, virtually all Amish businesses succeed. Are the Amish just naturally better at conducting commerce? Is it something in their faith, or self-discipline? Perhaps the answer lies in the community's hand-pumped water?

The answer is, none of the above. The secret to Amish success turns out to be the way they strategically combine their traditions with the rest of the modern world. As the Amish have become increasingly entangled in the economic web of contemporary capitalism, they have held onto their cultural traditions by maintaining an ideologically integrated and homogenous community. They are distinctly premodern and un-American in that they believe in the subordination of the individual to the community. They have rejected the prevalent American culture of rugged individualism, the notion of "every man for himself," often said to be the basis for successful entrepreneurship, in favor of "every man for the greater good." Individuals are expected to submit not only to God but also to teachers, elders, and community leaders. Their social fabric firmly binds people together. Whereas fashion for many people is a means of self-expression, the dark, simple clothing of the Amish signals membership in and subordination to the community. They have no bureaucratic forms of government or business; rather, they operate in a decentralized, loose federation of church districts. They reject mass media and automobiles and limit their exposure to diverse ideas and lands. The outcome is homogeneity of

Kimberly Hamme works on billing for her online business, Plainly Dressed, in her Paradise Town, Pennsylvania, home office. Hamme sells what most people would call Amish clothing. She does most of her business over the Internet.

belief, unified values, and not surprisingly, dense social capital. Amish businesses, like the people themselves, are tightly enmeshed in social networks, such as church and kinship systems, that provide economic support. The typical Amish person has more than 75 first cousins, most of whom shop in the same neighborhood. Add to that the taboo on bankruptcy within the community, and Amish businesses would be a dream come true for investors—that is, if the Amish were to accept outside capital (they don't).

Rather than marvel at how this culture maintains its centuries-old traditions while functioning in the business world, we should look at how they succeed in business regardless of being Amish. Kraybill and Nolt found that the cultural restraints of being Amish do indeed thwart business opportunity to some extent. Amish business owners aren't allowed to accept financial capital from outsiders or to prosecute shoplifters (to do so would single out lawbreakers and go against community solidarity). The success of Amish entrepreneurship is a telling example of the power of social capital.

giving more but showing up less predates the Web. It is probably more a result of increased work hours and other pressures to keep up in an age of rising inequality.

The social pendulum swinging between loneliness and unity may be starting to turn back toward togetherness, with slightly different characteristics than we are used to seeing. Sociologist Eric Klinenberg set out to study people who live alone, trying to understand the costs and benefits of leaving some of the ties that bind dangling free (Klinenberg, 2013). He found that being old and living alone is indeed a lonely reality and a growing problem for women, who have always tended to outlive their husbands but are now aging alone in neighborhoods that their children have left for jobs and lives elsewhere. But for young and middle-aged people, living alone is a lifestyle frequently filled with friends, dates, coworkers, volunteer work, and plenty of socializing. People who live alone are more likely to volunteer than people the same age who are living with partners or families. Maybe civic participation is not dying, after all.

But the news may not be all bad on the social capital front: Following the events of September 11, 2001, Putnam noticed a revival of civic engagement among young people who were at or near college age during the terrorist attacks. He found that among 18- to 24-year-olds, voting rates have increased by 23 percent since 2001, following a quarter-century of declining

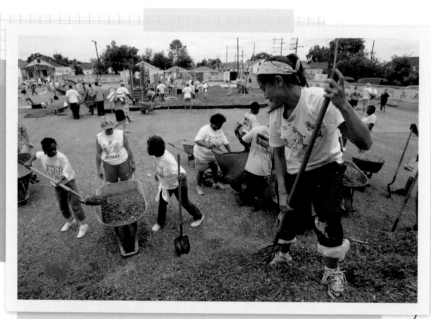

Volunteers build an elementary school playground in New Orleans. After Hurricane Katrina devastated the Gulf Coast in 2005, thousands of college volunteers participated in the rebuilding efforts.

participation in national politics. Another positive sign is that college freshmen are increasingly talking about politics and volunteering in their communities. As a "teachable moment," Putnam argues, 9/11 revealed how interconnected our individual fates are—a point often missed in the anonymity of the daily grind: "We learned that we need to—and can—depend on the kindness of strangers who happen to be near us" (Sander & Putnam, 2005).

Understandably, Putnam's claims have ignited much controversy. Some researchers have noted that even if an increase in participation occurred after 9/11, it was short-lived among adults (Sander & Putnam, 2010). Others claim the opposite, insisting that social capital never declined as Putnam declared. Rather, it has simply become more informal. Wuthnow, for example, argues that modernization brings about new forms of "loose connection" but hardly a disappearance of all connection. Nor does it necessarily follow that modern Americans are any worse off than when connections were tight. Things change, but that does not always mean they change for the worse. Though Putnam laments the loss of face-to-face communal ties, in the past three decades we've witnessed an explosion of non-place-based connections: Think of the rich social life ongoing on social media, including Twitter, blogs, and Facebook.

With the exit of the old (such as the Elks, Rotary, and other fraternal and civic organizations), in have come new kinds of clubs—large national groups like the National Organization of Women, which one can join by mail or online, and informal support groups like Weight Watchers. Furthermore, the trend of declining social capital is falsely linear, as if from the 1970s to today civic society has moved in one simple direction (downhill). More probable is that civic engagement moves like a pendulum, swinging back and forth between privatism (as in the 1920s) and heightened public consciousness (as in the 1930s). Right now may feel like the end of social capital, but perhaps we're just at a low point on a constantly shifting trend line. The calls to save social capital may be a form of projected nostalgia, a misplaced romanticizing of the past.

Sociologist Michael Gaddis has been using network structure to look at another challenging aspect of social capital: Even for people with a healthy number of ties to friends, family, and community, not all social capital is equal. As Gaddis points out, "Everyone knows friends, coworkers, family members, but the important part of social capital . . . is the resources that are linked to you through these networks. Do I know someone who knows someone

wwnpag.es/SC5b

To see my interview with Michael Gaddis about the impact of social networks on low-income children, please go to wwnpag.es/SC5b.

who has a job opening and could refer me? Can I access those resources?" He looked at kids growing up in "low-income families, one-parent families" who applied to the Big Brothers Big Sisters program where they hoped to be assigned an adult mentor with whom to spend time. Because of high demand, only some students got to participate, making it possible for Gaddis to compare students who got mentors with those who wanted them but were not able to get them. It turned out that "mentors with higher education levels, higher income" were "able to make greater changes" amongst the little brothers and sisters (Conley, 2013b). It is not how many people you know that gives you greater social capital, but the resources associated with the people you know and their willingness to share those resources with you that increases your social capital.

The picture we've arrived at is that of a complex social world where the decay of some forms of civic life is accompanied by the eventual emergence of new ways of building communities. Americans living in modern, urban, anonymous, and loosely connected communities carve out new social spaces, in turn creating a different kind of social fabric that holds together our republic. People adapt to what's new, retain what they can of the old, and negotiate within global forces and local communities.

→ Network Analysis in Practice

Researchers take the concepts we've discussed so far—embeddedness, the iron law of the triad, and network position—and apply them to real-world contexts in order to understand how group life shapes individual behavior. Network analysts also map out social relationships to better understand transmission phenomena such as the spread of disease, the rise and fall of particular fads, the genesis of social movements, and even the evolution of language itself.

The Social Structure of Teenage Sex

According to a *New York Times Magazine* article (Denizet-Lewis, 2004), contemporary American teenagers supposedly approach their love lives with a blasé attitude. "Hooking up" has replaced going steady; "friends with benefits" are preferred over girlfriends and boyfriends, with all their attendant demands and the corresponding commitment. The good news is that more reputable studies, including one using network analysis, refute this image of 1970s hedonism being re-created in the contemporary American high school. The bad news is that, even so, the sexual mores of American adolescents are putting them at greater risk of contracting sexually transmitted infections (STIs) than ever before.

Here are some more trustworthy numbers: About 50 percent of American teenagers over the age of 15, when interviewed by researchers, have admitted to engaging in sexual intercourse. (Boys probably tend to exaggerate their sexual experience, and girls probably downplay it.) A good number of those who have not yet had intercourse are still sexually active in other ways: Approximately one-third have "had genital contact with a partner resulting in an orgasm in the past year." Bluntly put, what this means is that a good two-thirds of American teens are having sex or participating in some form of sexual activity. Teenagers' romantic relationships tend to be short term compared with adults', averaging about 15 months, so there is a fair amount of partner trading. Survey research among students in college, where "hookup culture" is prevalent, found that 70 percent use condoms when they engage in vaginal/penile intercourse. That 70 percent is "a lot less than a hundred, but a lot more than zero," notes principal investigator Paula England (Conley, 2009d). To top that off, most adolescents with a sexually transmitted infection "have no idea that they are infected." All of these factors combine to make American teenagers a breeding ground for STIs, which have increased dramatically in this age group in the last decade.

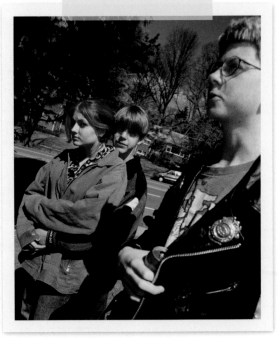

Despite sensational media reports about teenage hookups, monogamous couples such as J.D. and Elysia, both 14, of Yorktown High School in Arlington, Virginia, are more typical. What else does research reveal about high-school sexual relationships?

So what's a public health officer to do? During the administration of George W. Bush, the religious right and conservative policy makers suggested the "virginity pledge" and other abstinence policies as a solution. As it turns out, the pledge does delay the onset of sexual activity on average, but when the teenagers who take it eventually do have sex, they are much more likely to practice unsafe sex (Bearman & Brückner, 2001; Brückner & Bearman, 2005). Among the many problems in designing safe-sex or other programs to reduce the rate of STIs among teenagers is the fact that we knew very little about the sexual networks of American adolescents until quite recently. It would not be far off to say that we knew more about the sexual networks of aboriginal tribes on Groote Island than we did about those of American teenagers.

One component of the National Longitudinal Survey of Adolescent Health, conducted by J. Richard Udry, Peter Bearman, and others from 1994 to 1996, investigated the complete sexual network at 12 high schools across the nation, including the pseudonymous Jefferson High School, whose 1,000-person student body is depicted in Figure 5.5 (Bearman et al., 2004).

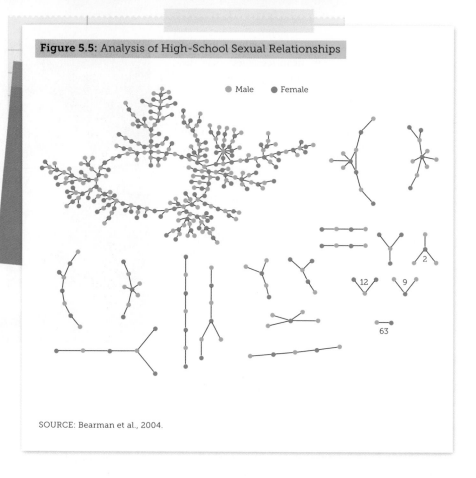

Figure 5.5: Analysis of High-School Sexual Relationships

● Male ● Female

2

12 9

63

SOURCE: Bearman et al., 2004.

They focused their analysis on Jefferson, because its demographic makeup, although almost all white, is fairly representative of most American public high schools and, more important, it is in a fairly isolated town, so less chance exists of the sexual networks spilling over to other schools.

The pink dots represent girls and the blue ones boys. The dyad in the lower right-hand corner tells us that there are 63 couples in which the partners have only had sex with each other. There are small, comparatively isolated networks consisting of ten or fewer people, and then one large ring that encompasses hundreds of students. Preventing the transmission of infection in the small networks is much simpler than preventing the spread in the large ring. One young man in the ring has had nine partners, but even if you persuaded him to use condoms or practice abstinence, you still wouldn't address most of the network. Your action might positively impact the people immediately around him. But to the extent other origin points of infection exist within the network, it is going to be very difficult to stop transmission. One practice that would slow the spread of STIs is lengthening the gap between partners: Sleeping with more than one person at a time increases the rate of transmission. The fuzzy

Panel A: core infection model

Panel C: inverse core model

Panel B: bridge between
disjointed populations

Panel D: spanning tree

SOURCE: Bearman et al., 2004.

ring structure represents a type of network called a circular spanning tree—a spanning tree being one of four ideal types of sex networks hypothesized by Peter Bearman and other epidemiologists (scientists who study the spread of diseases).

Figure 5.6 illustrates the four different possible models of contact and spread for STIs. Panel A represents a core infection model, where the dark, filled-in circles representing infected people are all connected to this core group. Therefore, the infection circulates through everyone in the group, but they're also connected outward to other partners. If you mapped out a sexual network like this, with the objective of stopping diseases from being sexually transmitted, you would try to isolate that core network and either cut them off from sexual relations with others or at least ensure that when they came into contact with uninfected partners, they practiced safe sex. Panel B shows a possible structural hole. Imagine an infected group and an uninfected group, but one person bridges them. Theoretically, such a circumstance is fairly easy to address, in that all you have to do is cut the tie or persuade that one person to engage in safe sex, and you've thus protected the uninfected population. Panel C depicts an inverse core model, representing the way much of the AIDS transmission occurs in populations where men routinely spend long periods of time away from their families, such as long-haul truckers and some men from African villages. The traveling men visit prostitutes in the city or at truck stops, acquire the virus from one, transmit it to another, and then bring the virus back home. The infected members are not connected directly with one another (that is, the prostitutes are not having sex with each other); rather, the individuals at the periphery of the core (the men who solicit the prostitutes) connect the core members to each other and possibly beyond the group to other populations. The last network model, illustrated in panel D, is the spanning tree model, in linear rather than circular form. This is essentially how power grids are laid out: There's a main line, and branches develop off of that line. It is difficult to completely stop transmission along a spanning tree model. That's why we design electrical grids to be a series of spanning trees so that if one circuit fails the power can continue to flow around it, although as anyone who has experienced a blackout knows, specific sections can be left without power if they are severed from the rest of the tree. In terms of STI transmission, you could initiate some breaks that would split the tree into two groups, but that's not going to completely isolate the infection. If you attack something on a branch, you're not doing anything to the rest of the network. There's no key focal point that allows you to stop the spread.

Romantic Leftovers

When Peter Bearman and his colleagues analyzed the sexual habits of teenagers, they uncovered another rule that governed this social network. They found lots of examples of triads, where partners are traded within groups. But the main rule that seemed to govern these relationships was "no cycles of four," which means you do not date the ex of your ex's current boyfriend or girlfriend. The most interesting aspect of the rule, sociologically speaking, is that no one was consciously aware of this pattern. The researchers interviewed many students, and not one of them directly stated, "Of course not, you don't date the ex of your ex's new flame." Yet it's the single taboo that governs everyone. Figure 5.7 illustrates this rule of thumb graphically.

At time 1, Matt and Jennifer are dating, as are Jareem and Maya. At time 2, Jennifer and Jareem date. The rule suggests that Matt and Maya will never date. Why is that? Once Jennifer and Jareem start dating, if Matt and Maya decide to date each other, they are relegating themselves to secondary social status, as if they were "leftovers." The practical, take-home lesson in all of this is that if you want to date the ex of your ex's new crush, act before your ex does. If you're Jennifer and you wish to prevent your old boyfriend Matt from going out with Maya, quickly start dating Jareem, because then Maya and Matt will never date. But extend the "no seconds" rule to thirds or more, and the taboo erodes. The fact that no students in the high school studied were

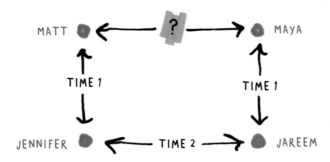

Figure 5.7: Romantic "Leftovers"

MATT

TIME 1

JENNIFER — TIME 2 → JAREEM

MAYA

TIME 1

SOURCE: Bearman et al., 2004.

aware of the rule is what makes this kind of social norm possible: It's not conscious. This is a good example of how social structures govern individual-level behavior, and it speaks to some of the limitations of interpretive sociology. If the researchers had taken a more Weberian approach and asked students how they choose partners and, more important, why they don't date certain people, they probably wouldn't have discovered this rule. The researchers could see it only by taking a bird's-eye view and analyzing this structure with mathematical tools.

Organizations

I've mentioned several times that sociology—here network analysis—can be applied not just to individuals but to all social actors, which may include school systems, teams, states, and countries. In the contemporary United States, companies and organizations are important social actors. In fact, thanks to the Fourteenth Amendment, they have identities as legal persons: They sponsor charitable causes; they can sue and be sued; they even have birthdays.

Organization is an all-purpose term that can describe any social network—from a club to a Little League baseball team to a secret society to your local church to General Motors to the U.S. government—that is defined by a common purpose and that has a boundary between its membership and the rest of the social world. *Formal* organizations have a set of governing structures and rules for their internal arrangements (the U.S. Army, with its ranks and

Organization any social network that is defined by a common purpose and has a boundary between its membership and the rest of the social world.

rules), whereas *informal* organizations do not (the local Brangelina fan club). Of course, a continuum exists, because no organization has absolutely no rules, and no organization has a rule for absolutely everything. Therefore, the study of organizations focuses mainly on the social factors that affect organizational structure and the people in those organizations.

Organizational Structure and Culture

Have you ever heard the phrase the "old boys' club"? The term is used to refer to exclusive social groups and derives literally from fraternities, businesses, and country clubs that allowed only men—specifically, certain groups of elite men—to join. These groups have their own customs, traditions, and histories that make it difficult for others to join and feel as if they belong, even when the "boys" aren't being deliberately hostile. The term organizational culture refers to the shared beliefs and behaviors within a social group and is often used interchangeably with *corporate culture*. The organizational culture at a slaughterhouse—where pay is low, employees must wear protective gear, the environment is dangerous, and animals are continuously being killed—is probably very different from the organizational culture at a small, not-for-profit community law center. The term organizational structure refers to how power and authority are distributed within an organization. The slaughterhouse probably has a hierarchical structure, with a clear ranking of managers and supervisors who oversee the people working the lines. The law center, however, might be more decentralized and cooperative, with five partners equally co-owning the business and collaborating on decisions. How an organization is structured often affects the type of culture that results. If a business grants both parents leave when a new child enters the home, allows for flextime or telecommuting, or has an on-site child-care center, those structural arrangements will be much more conducive to creating a family-friendly organizational culture than those of a company that doesn't offer such benefits.

The growth of large multinational corporations over the course of the last 100 years has affected organizational structure. One example of this impact can be seen in *interlocking directorates*, the phenomenon whereby the members of corporate boards often sit on the boards of directors for multiple companies. In 2013, for example, the boards of insurance companies such as AIG, Humana, MetLife, and Travelers frequently had board members who also served on the boards of drug and medical device makers such as Johnson & Johnson, DuPont, Abbott Laboratories, and Dow Chemical. (The website www.theyrule.net allows you to create an interactive map of companies' and institutions' boards of directors.) Does it matter that these people sit together on the same boards? The problem, critics argue, is that we then allow a select group of people—predominantly rich, white men—to control the decisions

Organizational culture the shared beliefs and behaviors within a social group; often used interchangeably with *corporate culture*.

Organizational structure the ways in which power and authority are distributed within an organization.

made in thousands of companies. Such people also have ties to research institutions and elected officials that may compromise their objectivity and create
conflicts of interest. Capitalism, after all, is based on competition, but if board
members on interlocking directorates favor the other companies to which they
are connected, suppliers may not be competing on a level playing field when
bidding for contracts. Or worse, take the situation that might develop when a
board member of a drug maker asks his friend and fellow board member at
a health insurance company to give preferential coverage to his companies'
drugs over a competitors' drugs. This can lead to higher prices for consumers
who need to purchase the competitors' drugs. Another situation might arise
in which one of these two board members knows a former member of Congress through board service together who they can use as a lobbyist to see
that federal health programs like Medicare and Medicaid also give preferential
treatment to a particular drug, costing taxpayers more than they would have
paid without the pressure arising from these relationships. This type of situation can lead to what sociologist C. Wright Mills called a "power elite" or aristocracy. (Concern over the consolidation of control in the media industry, for
example, is discussed in Chapter 3.)

Institutional Isomorphism: Everybody's Doing It

Networks can be very useful. They provide information, a sense of security and community, resources, and opportunities, as we saw illustrated by
Granovetter's concept of weak ties. Networks can also be constraining, however. Paul DiMaggio and Walter Powell, focusing on businesses, coined the
phrase *institutional isomorphism* to explain why so many businesses that evolve
in very different ways still end up with such similar organizational structures
(1983). Isomorphism, then, is a "constraining process that forces one unit in
a population to resemble other units that face the same set of environmental conditions" (Hawley, 1968). With regard to organizations, this means that
those facing the same conditions (say, in industry, the law, or politics) tend to
end up like one another.

Isomorphism a constraining
process that forces one unit in
a population to resemble other
units that face the same set of
environmental conditions.

Let's consider a hypothetical case: A new organization that enters into
a fairly established industry but wants to approach it differently, perhaps
a bank that wants to distinguish itself from other banks by being more
casual or more community oriented. The theory of isomorphism suggests that
such a bank, when all is said and done, will wind up operating as most other
banks do. It's locked into a network of other organizations and therefore will
be heavily influenced by the environment of that network. The same is true
for new networks of organizations. A group of not-for-profits might spring
up in a specific area. Because all will face the same environmental conditions,
they will likely be, in the final analysis, more similar than different, no matter

how diverse their origins. DiMaggio and Powell are part of a school of social theory referred to as the new institutionalism, which essentially tries to develop a sociological view of institutions (as opposed to, say, an economic view). In this vein, networks of connections among institutions are key to understanding how the institutions look and behave. These theorists would argue that all airlines raise and lower their fares at the same time, for example, not because they are independently reacting to pure market forces but because symmetry, peer pressure, social signaling, and network laws all govern the organizational behavior of these Fortune 500 companies to the same extent that these forces affect the sex lives of seniors at Jefferson High School. Pretty scary, huh?

 POLICY:

The 1965 Hart-Cellar Act

Since 1921 the United States has maintained strict quotas on the number of legal immigrants from specific countries. These quotas were originally based on the proportion of non-U.S.-born residents from each country of origin at the time of the 1910 Census. That original system evolved over the course of the twentieth century. For example, a law passed in 1924 shifted the basis for quotas from the 1910 Census to the 1890 Census, thereby curtailing the numbers of eastern and southern Europeans who could enter the United States. That same law capped overall immigration from the Eastern Hemisphere at about 150,000, essentially cutting off immigration for many years. During the Great Depression, government officials also limited the number of immigrants to avoid competition in the labor market, given the high rates of domestic unemployment. The law was tweaked again in the 1950s. However, it was the Immigration and Nationality Act Amendments of 1965, otherwise known as the Hart-Cellar Act, that changed the face of immigration as we know it today.

Most important, the Hart-Cellar Act eliminated quotas on national origin, replacing this approach with a system of family preferences. Immigrants could sponsor their family members, so immigration suddenly became a network phenomenon. At the time, Senator Edward M. Kennedy of Massachusetts (then in his first term of office) said, "The bill will not flood our cities with immigrants. It will not upset the ethnic mix of our society. It will not relax the standards of admission. It will not cause American workers to lose their jobs" (U.S. Senate, 1965). Although many have debated in the years since whether our cities have become flooded with immigrants, standards of admission have been relaxed, or immigration has caused American workers to lose their jobs, no doubt exists that the ethnic mix of society has changed as a result. How might family networks have shifted the makeup of the immigrant population? And how has this changed national and local politics as of late?

→ <u>CONCLUSION</u>

What do we learn from the formal analysis of group characteristics and social networks? Simply knowing the formal characteristics of a group helps us understand much of the social dynamics within it. Is it a dyad or a triad? What is the proper reference group for a particular social process? Is this group a primary or secondary group—and what does that mean for my obligations to it? Likewise, we can use network analysis in micro- and macro-level studies. You could carefully weigh the potential consequences of dating your best friend's ex by mapping out your social network and anticipating shifts in ties that might transpire. Or you could analyze President Richard Nixon's strategy of "triangulation" of the Soviet Union and Communist China during the early 1970s using the iron law of the triad. Sociologists use network analysis to study everything from migration to social movements to cultural fads to global politics.

→ PRACTICE

SOCIOLOGY ON THE STREET

How has social media significantly changed the number and strength of our weak ties? Watch the Sociology on the Street video to find out more: wwmpag.es/SOS5.

QUESTIONS FOR REVIEW

1. Consider Feral Trade—do you think it relies more on strong or weak ties? Why?

2. The Hart-Cellar Act brought a system of family preferences to the immigration process. Why might a network of family members make it easier for new immigrants to support themselves in the new country they call home?

3. If getting a job is "all about connections," how does the work on "the strength of weak ties" round out our understanding of this phenomenon? How does nepotism (hiring family members) fit into this discussion?

4. An undecided voter who knows little about the political candidates reads the result of the latest poll on voting day and sees that other voters seem inclined to choose one of the candidates. According to Asch's work on conformity, how might the poll affect the voter's behavior? Do you think media sources should release polls shortly before an election?

5. If you could choose your position in a social network, would you want to bridge a structural gap? Why might the manager of a company try to prevent the development of structural gaps between the company's various departments? Would a high-school nurse be more likely to encourage or discourage structural gap formation?

6. What is an organizational structure? Describe the organizational structure at your school or workplace and determine how this structure might affect the organizational culture.

7. A new coffee shop opens in your neighborhood, which already has two other coffee shops. The new coffee shop offers free Internet access to customers. Within a few weeks, the two other shops offer free Internet access as well. Explain how this example might illustrate Paul DiMaggio and Walter Powell's concept of institutional isomorphism.

PARADOX

THE STRENGTH OF WEAK TIES: IT IS THE PEOPLE WITH WHOM WE ARE THE LEAST CONNECTED WHO OFFER US THE MOST OPPORTUNITIES.

WATCH THE ANIMATED SHORT ABOUT THE GROUPS AND NETWORKS PARADOX AT

WWNPAG.ES/PX5

This New York City street poster refers to oppressive
surveillance in George Orwell's novel *1984*. What are the
social consequences of this sort of social control?

6 Social Control and Deviance

PARADOX

IT IS THE DEVIANTS AMONG US WHO HOLD SOCIETY TOGETHER.

Smiley got his nickname because he always smiled at the most improbable times. When teachers yelled at him because he had trouble paying attention, he smiled. When his smile upset the teachers and incited more yelling, he kept smiling. When he and a friend broke into a car for a place to sleep after his abusive parents kicked him out, he smiled. He was surely smiling at the pretty girls with lipstick-reddened lips and poofy Aquanet pompadours he and a couple of homies decided to visit in the neighborhood of a rival gang. He was likely still smiling when eight rival gang members showed up, bringing guns to what might have been a fist fight. Smiley was shot in the head. His homie Victor scooped him off the pavement, bits of fresh brain matter clinging to his new sneakers. Victor cradled the dying Smiley in the back seat on the way to the emergency room; there was no time to wait for an ambulance that might never show up at their ghetto address.

When the police arrived at the hospital, they assigned partial blame to Victor, threatening to charge him as an accessory to murder for being present at the scene. Victor, in anger and disbelief, instead demanded that the police find the real shooter. "What for?" one of them replied, "We want you to kill each other off."

Homeboy Victor is now Associate Professor Victor Rios at U.C.-Santa Barbara. The other 67 homies from the original gang have not had Victor's success: four were murdered; nine were permanently injured, most with hand-guns; a dozen became addicted to drugs, sometimes living on the streets and panhandling to survive. Just two graduated from high school; only Victor went on to college. If it is surprising that Victor, a gang member son of a single welfare mother in an impoverished neighborhood, made it into one of the most heavily credentialed occupations, what does that tell us about the relationship between deviance and social mobility?

Because Victor is now a sociologist, I asked him what he has to say about getting out of the ghetto and into the ivory tower. "A lot of times people say to me, 'Oh, Professor Rios, you're so unique. You have all these qualities, you made it out. You pulled yourself up by the bootstrap. You made it out of the ghetto and now you are here.' And my response is, 'Well, part of it is hard work, but everyone works hard.' For example, my mom, she's washed dishes thirty years of her life, working ten hours a day, and she still makes ten, eleven dollars an hour. That's hard work. But she never progressed." He argues that hard work is not enough; there must be an opportunity trajectory leading out of poverty. Victor clearly recalls where his path started: "I was fortunate to find a teacher that cared, and she heard what happened [to Smiley], and she reached out to me and got me mentors from the university—students, college students, that wanted to go help the ghetto kids." These students provided enlightenment through the sociological imagination; they helped Victor see that there was a system at work larger than himself, larger even than his community: "I was actually living in a world of poverty that wasn't necessarily just produced by the way that people in my community acted, but it was also produced by a larger system of racism, classism, and segregation" (Conley, 2009e).

In his book *Punished: Policing the Lives of Black and Latino Boys* (2011), Rios examines the way the current aggressive policing strategies have effectively criminalized young boys in poor neighborhoods. Police and parole officers are stationed in schools and community centers, the spaces in which education and mentoring traditionally occur, creating a self-fulfilling prophecy where teens are assumed to be criminals, treated with suspicion bordering on aggression, and watched closely until caught in some criminal act. Is flooding crime-ridden neighborhoods with aggressive policing the right thing to do? Or does sending more police to a neighborhood where criminal activity is concentrated simply increase the number of people who get caught, closing routes out of that neighborhood by saddling its residents with criminal records?

The goal of this chapter is to examine how society coheres and why some people transgress the boundaries of normality. For starters, how do people who presumably started life as innocent little kids end up in prison? How did Rios, an impoverished

wwnpag.es/SC6a

To see my interview with Victor Rios, author of *Punished,* visit wwnpag.es/SC6a.

gang member growing up amid violence and theft, end up getting a PhD and becoming a professor? We can then turn to broader questions: Why doesn't society at large look like the violence-ridden Oakland, California, neighborhood of Victor's youth? Why do most of us choose to sacrifice some of our personal interests for the sake of the social whole? How can we explain how society achieves predictable order, and what role does the criminal justice system play? Theorists of social deviance have produced various answers to these questions.

What Is Social **Deviance?**

Social deviance, loosely understood, can be taken to mean any transgression of socially established norms. It can be as minor as farting in church or as serious as murder, so long as it consists of breaking the rules by which most people abide. Minor violations are acts of informal deviance, such as picking your nose. Even if no one will punish you, you sense it is somehow wrong. At the other end of the continuum, we have formal deviance, or crime, which is the violation of laws enacted by society. When deviant persons are caught in deviant acts, depending on the seriousness of the offense, they are subject to punishment. For instance, farting in church might result in glares from your fellow churchgoers, whereas a crime like theft may result in formal state-sanctioned punishments such as fines or community service, or for more severe violations, imprisonment, death, or even torture.

Because social norms and rules are fluid and subject to change, the definitions of what counts as deviance are likely to vary across contexts. Even seemingly obvious cases of deviance, such as killing another person, may not be so clear upon further investigation. When a soldier kills an enemy combatant, that act is considered heroic. But if the same soldier kills his or her spouse, the act is considered heinous and punishable by a long prison sentence. Persons and behaviors have been variously called deviant depending on what culture and historical period they happen to fall in. When women engaged in premarital sex in the Puritan colonies, they were subject to social exile; when women do so today in some Islamic countries, they risk public execution by stoning. In contemporary American society, however, sex outside of marriage is common and largely accepted. Similarly, 50 years ago, it was a crime for African Americans to share water fountains and swimming pools with white citizens; most people would consider such legislation unthinkable bigotry today. Just four decades ago, homosexuality was illegal nationwide. Gay bars were frequent targets of police raids, and sexual orientation was grounds for excluding immigrants (a rule that held until the Immigration Act of 1990; Foss, 1994). As recently as 2003, the U.S. Supreme Court struck down Texas's criminalization of homosexual sex in *Lawrence v. Texas*; before the ruling, it was punishable by arrest and

Social deviance any transgression of socially established norms.

Crime the violation of laws enacted by society.

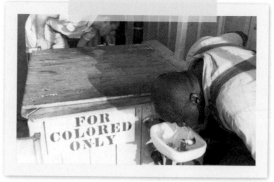

a $500 fine. Changes in laws signal shifting social values and changes in social norms, such as increased tolerance of sexual and racial diversity.

In the popular conception, deviance typically takes the form of blatant rule breaking or lawlessness. But deviance does not necessarily require outlandish activity on the part of social misfits. Deviance is a broad concept covering everything from answering your cell phone during a lecture to murder. Both formal deviance and informal deviance are collectively defined and often subject to a range of punishments. For example, transgender persons—those who do not have a categorical masculine or feminine identity—are often subject to informal and formal punishments for their gender deviance, although most are perfectly law-abiding citizens. The same goes for ethnic minorities, people who bike down crowded city streets, and those who sing along with their iPods on the subway or bus. Even reserved, soft-spoken people, if they find themselves in a noisy crowd, may find that because their behavior goes against the grain, they become, for the moment, social deviants. Yet, deviance is sticky; it cannot be turned off and on so easily. Deviance can be a powerful label, capable of reproducing the entrenched social inequalities that punishment is often supposed to correct.

Functionalist Approaches to Deviance and Social Control

Imagine that society is a single, complex organism with many internal organs that perform specific tasks. The state is society's brain, its decision-making center where legislators contemplate the morality of laws and communicate legislative decisions to other social organs charged with implementation. All of society's organs are necessary to keep the social organism alive and healthy, and these organs are composed of groups of individuals, or cells. A functionalist approach explains the existence of social phenomena by the functions they perform. In this framework, the state develops because society needs a

Social norms and the punishments for violating them change over time and from place to place. Whether it was executing women as witches in the seventeenth century, enforcing Jim Crow laws in the segregated South, or prosecuting John Geddes Lawrence and Tyron Garner for engaging in a same-sex relationship, our definitions of what constitutes deviance change.

decision-making center to help organize and direct social life. All of society's various parts, or organs, are defined by their functions and are arranged according to the needs of the social organism.

Émile Durkheim, author of *The Division of Labor in Society* (1893/1997), utilized such a functionalist approach to explain social cohesion, the way people form social bonds, relate to each other, and get along on a day-to-day basis. Durkheim's thesis is that there are two basic ways society can hold together, or cohere, which he called mechanical and organic solidarity. Mechanical or segmental solidarity—which characterized premodern society—was based on the sameness of the individual parts. In this model, the functional units are like cargo containers; each container is like all the others and can perform the same function as the next. Cohesion stems from the reliable similarity of the parts. In a state of organic solidarity—which characterizes modern society—social cohesion is based on interdependence, because the members in this type of social body perform different, specialized functions, and this increased mutual dependence among the parts is what allows for the smooth functioning of the whole. The physical analogy here is a machine in which each part is different and none would be so meaningful outside the context of the machine.

Social cohesion social bonds; how well people relate to each other and get along on a day-to-day basis.

Mechanical or **segmental solidarity** social cohesion based on sameness.

Organic solidarity social cohesion based on difference and interdependence of the parts.

In premodern society, people were held together by sameness. A peasant farmer in feudal times might have eked out a living by tilling a small plot of land, planting seeds, and then harvesting crops. The peasant next door also eked out a living by tilling, planting, and harvesting. Slight variations existed from one farm to the next, but the farmers' life conditions, and particularly their day-to-day experiences in the field, were roughly the same. The farmers' conversations probably would not have been strained or awkward; the two neighbors would have had plenty of advice and commiseration to share. Such a situation would be an example of mechanical solidarity.

As Western society became more industrialized in the late eighteenth and nineteenth centuries, however, workers developed specialized skills, allowing them to perform particular tasks better and more quickly. This division of labor resulted in a dramatic increase in productivity, but with the efficiency and high productivity of specialization come some negative consequences.

Farmers in premodern society would not have struggled to relate to one another; their sense of sameness bred mechanical solidarity. In contrast, most workers in the industrial and postindustrial economy perform such specialized tasks that they relate to one another through organic solidarity.

Specialized workers have less and less in common with one another, and they may be less able to understand each other. For example, if you held a highly specialized position within the economy as, say, a techno-artist punk rocker, you might find yourself thinking that no one understands what it's like to be you. As a techno-artist punk rocker, you are isolated and alienated because your highly specialized position—your roles within the economy and society more generally—makes it difficult to find common ground with others. If you sit down on a commuter train next to an investment banker and try to talk with her, an awkward conversation might ensue, in which each of you tries to comprehend the daily activities of the other. You may share your morning commute and nothing more. Labor specialization divides us by making it more difficult to form social bonds. However, specialization of tasks enables everyone to do something best. Maybe you are *the best* Japanese humane-certified chicken farm sex determiner (actually called a chick sexer, and yes, they make six figures), because, among other reasons, you don't really have much competition. This high degree of labor specialization makes us all interdependent, creating organic cohesion.

Distinguishing between these two types of social solidarity leads us to our first insight into social deviance. When individuals commit acts of deviance, they offend what Durkheim calls the collective conscience, meaning the common faith or set of social norms by which a society and its members abide. Without a collective conscience—a set of common assumptions about how the world works—there would be no sense of moral unity, and society would quickly dissolve into chaos. So when individuals break from the collectively produced moral fabric, societies are faced with the task of repairing the gash in the fabric by realigning the deviant individual through either punishment or rehabilitation.

The way in which social realignment is achieved, Durkheim concludes, depends on the type of solidarity holding that particular society together. Premodern societies, where people are united by sameness, tend to be characterized by punitive justice: making the offender suffer and thus defining the boundaries of acceptable behavior. Such punishment might involve collective vengeance. If someone in a medieval village committed adultery, stole vegetables, or murdered someone, the villagers would gather together, perhaps in a rowdy, pitchfork-wielding mob, to punish the criminal who had offended the collective conscience. The act of collective, group punishment might have culminated in storming the offender's house or hanging the poor sap in public. In either case, the group punishes the criminal in an act of collective vengeance. The collective probably wasn't interested in hearing the criminal's side of the story: the facts of his personal life, his possible motivations for committing the crime, or the details of his regrettable childhood. Mechanical social sanctions both reinforce the boundaries of acceptable behavior and unite collectivity through actions such as hanging, stoning, or publicly chastising a former member of the community. It is important to note that it is this collective action of vengeance that, by uniting the group through its perpetration and associated emotions of revenge, guilt, and so on, is key to the production of cohesion and unity. (Of course, there are always exceptions, such as the premodern Amish [see Chapter 5] who don't even bother to prosecute shoplifters.)

A similar form of justice can be administered by the state through a more formal process. When the infamous Oklahoma City bomber Timothy McVeigh was put to death, he was, in effect, murdered by the collectivity, by the citizenry of the United States. To opponents of the death penalty, McVeigh's

Two women accused of collaborating with the Nazis are marched through the streets of Paris in the summer of 1944. The mob ripped the women's clothes, then painted swastikas on their shorn heads in order to punish them. How is this an example of a mechanical social sanction?

execution amounted to state-sponsored murder. To others, however, his death signaled that killing innocent people is not acceptable behavior. Although only a small team actually carried out McVeigh's execution, his death was an act in which—theoretically at least—we all participated. When we collectively and publicly put McVeigh to death, we were united in our reinforcement of social norms: Paradoxically, his deviance helped keep our society together.

Organic solidarity, in contrast, by differentiating individuals, produces social sanctions that focus on the individual; that is, they are tailored to the specific conditions and circumstances of the perpetrator. This response to deviance is rehabilitative, meaning that the response is designed to transform the offender into a productive member of society. In the modern mind-set, we care about the rapist's or murderer's motivations and regrettable childhood. We treat the criminal as an individual who can be "fixed" if we can root out the causes of, and triggers for, his or her criminality. For example, what happens if a drug addict steals car radios to support her cocaine habit? The court may order the addict into rehab in hopes of reintegrating her into the productive mainstream.

Punishments may also be restitutive—that is, they attempt to restore the status quo that existed prior to an offense or event. Tort law is an example of restitutive social sanctions. For instance, let's say a negligent contractor doesn't bother to install grating at the bottom of a swimming pool. A little girl playing

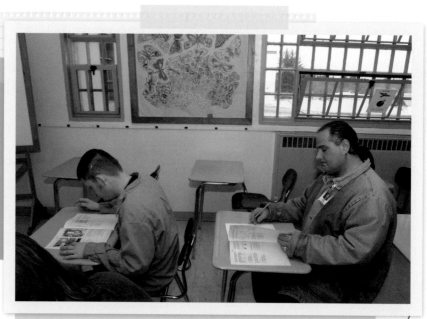

Eric Todaro (left) and Richard Grooms, inmates at a state penitentiary in Oregon, work on a General Education Diploma (GED) test. According to Durkheim, why would prisons provide educational programs and other rehabilitative tools?

at the edge of the pool is sucked into the drain, almost drowns, and ends up with brain damage. Restitutive social sanctions, or tort law, force the contractor (or his insurance company) to pay millions of dollars to the parents of the little girl. The money attempts to reestablish social equilibrium by repaying the parents for what they have lost. (Of course, in this case at least, money is a wholly inadequate salve.)

In the United States, we consider ourselves a modern society, yet both forms of social sanctions, mechanical and organic, still lurk within the U.S. justice system. We don't only try to rehabilitate our criminals and reimburse victims. We also still employ the death penalty in many states. Does Texas, where approximately one-third of the executions in the United States have taken place, have a more premodern division of labor than Wisconsin, which does not punish crimes with the death penalty? Probably not. Did the division of labor revert to primitive, subsistence levels all of a sudden in 1976, when the Supreme Court reinstated the legality of the death penalty? Of course not. Furthermore, some traditionally liberal states such as California and Oregon still have the death penalty on their books. At the same time, we also have a signature form of modern, organic social sanctions as embodied by our elaborate court system. Durkheim doesn't argue that these forms of social sanctions are mutually exclusive—that they can't exist together. In fact, he would expect to find much more of one form of social sanction, but not only one form. Both forms, however, help hold us together by reinforcing the boundaries of normal, socially acceptable behavior.

To make his case, Durkheim analyzed different historical penal and moral codes to discern the ratio of premodern sanctions to modern sanctions throughout history. He examined the Code of Hammurabi in Babylon dating back to 1750 B.C.E. as well as the Pentateuch, the first five books of the Old Testament. He studied more recent sanctions in the Magna Carta, the Napoleonic Code in France, and the South American Drago Doctrine. He argued that, as history progressed and the division of labor developed, the ratio of premodern to modern sanctions changed to favor modern, less-punitive sanctions. So although the United States may still permit its states to apply the death penalty, Durkheim would hypothesize that as our labor market changes to favor even more specialization, we might expect the death penalty to fizzle out. In fact, approximately a dozen states have repealed the death penalty in recent decades, but we should be cautious in drawing overall conclusions about the relationship between division of labor and forms of punishment by focusing on one particular form of sanction.

Social Control

We have explored the paradox of deviance in Durkheim's *The Division of Labor in Society*—the idea that deviance, and specifically the act of collective punishment, holds us together. But what makes us good, law-abiding citizens in the first place? Social control is what sociologists refer to as the set of mechanisms that create normative compliance, the act of abiding by society's norms or simply following the rules of group life. Other sociologists have tried to explain how social control works on individuals to induce compliance to social norms.

Sociologists classify mechanisms of social control into two categories. The first are called formal social sanctions. In most modern societies, these formal sanctions would be rules or laws prohibiting deviant criminal behavior such as murder, rape, and theft. These sanctions are formal, overt "expressions of official group sentiment" (Meier, 1982). Informal social sanctions are based on the usually unexpressed but widely known rules of group membership. Have you ever heard someone use the expression "an unwritten rule"? Informal social sanctions are the unwritten rules of social life. So, hypothetically, if you loudly belch in public, you will probably be the object of scowls of disgust. These gestures of contempt at your socially illicit behavior are examples of informal social sanctions, the ways we keep each other in check by watching and judging those around us. As discussed in Chapter 4, the process of socialization is largely responsible for our acquisition and understanding of these unspoken rules of group social life. Through years of trial and error, we have internalized the rules of the social game.

The idea behind informal social sanctions is that we are all simultaneously enforcing the rules of society and having them enforced upon us. How does this work? At the same time that we are watching or observing others, others are watching us, too. All of us are both spectators and objects of spectacle. We are all the agents of a diffuse, watchful gaze, as in the 1881 painting *Luncheon of the Boating Party* by Pierre-Auguste Renoir, where everyone is gazing at someone else, but no two people make direct eye contact. And beyond watching, all of us can grant rewards for others' good behavior in the form of smiles and encouragement, but we can also sanction with dirty looks, snide comments, and worse. In this way, we are all chipping in our small contributions to the construction of the social whole.

Think about the neighborhood watch groups that preceded the widespread adoption of electronic home security systems. People in a community banded together and agreed to keep out an eye for trespassers, burglars, and suspicious strangers. The idea behind these groups was that neighborhoods could maintain social order by overtly declaring their intention to visually monitor their turf. Sometimes such groups issued signs or decals for doors and windows to signal to unsavory characters that the neighborhood was being "protected" by watchful eyes. But this kind of activity doesn't have to be so formalized. The urban theorist Jane Jacobs coined the term *the eyes and ears of the street* to describe the fact that, ideally, in mixed-use (that is, commercial and residential) neighborhoods, the thread of social control is implicitly woven into daily life (Jacobs, 1961). Through their windows, grandmothers watch children playing baseball

Pierre-Auguste Renoir's *Luncheon of the Boating Party* (1881).

on the street below, on the alert for any trouble. During the course of a busy weekday, a shopkeeper might notice a group of teenagers, who should be at school, loitering outside his store and report this to their parents or the school.

In any society, many agents of both formal and informal social control exist. Our local neighbors act as the primary agents of informal social control, whereas the state, or the government, often has a hand in the construction of formal social sanctions by making laws. The police are an obvious example of an agent of state social control formed for the protection of the public. The police patrol public parks and neighborhoods after nightfall and contain public protests to ensure social order.

Informal social control is the bedrock on which formal social control must rest. If the police go on strike, for example, whether chaos will ensue depends on the degree of social cohesion in a given community. Likewise, without strong informal social norms, the police are relatively helpless. Consider the difficulty police officers have tracking down and arresting those who loot and commit acts of vandalism during an urban riot. Or the difficulty in solving or prosecuting a crime if witnesses are not willing to step forward and testify. If an entire community relaxes its informal social control, formal social control inevitably fails. Lately, the boundary between informal and formal social control is perhaps blurring a bit with the proliferation of surveillance cameras installed by private and public entities.

A Normative Theory of Suicide

After making his observations on social solidarity and social control in *The Division of Labor in Society*, Durkheim next applied his ideas to the sociological study of suicide, perhaps the most personal act of deviance. Or is it? If you were asked to explain what causes a person to die by suicide, you might say mental illness, depression, alcohol or drug addiction, or perhaps a catastrophic event such as a divorce, job loss, or bankruptcy. These are all common, intuitive explanations for suicide. They reflect our automatic perception of suicide as something intensely personal, mediated by individual life circumstances or caused by chemical imbalances and emotional disorders. And all these explanations may contain a piece of the complex answer. However, Durkheim believed these individualistic accounts of suicide were inadequate. What better challenge to a sociologist than taking the most personal act imaginable and explaining it as a "social fact" rather than a result of anguished individual circumstance?

Killing oneself is considered a sin in many religions and a violation of social norms besides. In his 1897 book *Suicide*, Durkheim sought to explain how psychological characteristics in combination with social forces shape suicide rates. According to Durkheim, suicide is, at its root, an instance of social deviance. By observing patterns in suicide rates across Europe (just as he had previously discerned patterns in penal codes), Durkheim developed a normative theory of suicide. His hypothesis is that the social norms of particular groups—the conditions of group life—generate variations in group suicide rates.

What are the social mechanics that cause suicide rates to vary? Durkheim proposed that by plotting social integration on the *y*-axis and social regulation on the *x*-axis of a Cartesian coordinate system, we can construct a theory about how social forces influence suicide rates (Figure 6.1). Social integration refers to the degree to which you are integrated into your social group or community. A tightly knit community in which members interact with each other in a number of different capacities—say the coach of your child's Little League team is also your dentist and you are the dentist's mechanic—is more socially integrated than one in which people do not interact at all or interact in only one role. Social regulation refers to how many rules guide your daily life and what you can reasonably expect from the world on a day-to-day basis. To be at low risk for suicide (and other deviant behavior), you need to be somewhere in the middle: integrated into your community with a reasonable (not oppressive) set of guidelines to structure your life. If you go too far in either direction along either axis, you have either too much or too little of some important facet of "normal" life.

Let's say you drop down the *y*-axis significantly in the direction of egoism. You are not very well integrated into your group. What happens as a result? Durkheim argues that, because others give your life meaning, you would feel hopeless. You wouldn't be part of some larger long-term project,

Social integration how well you are integrated into your social group or community.

Social regulation the number of rules guiding your daily life and, more specifically, what you can reasonably expect from the world on a day-to-day basis.

Figure 6.1: A Normative Theory of Suicide

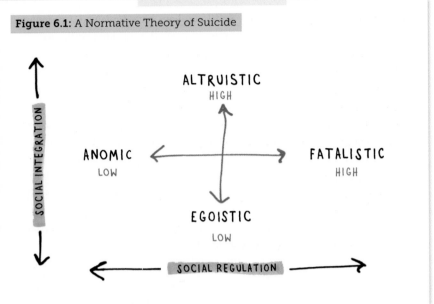

would feel insignificant, and would be at risk of committing egoistic suicide. We all need to feel as if we have made a difference in other people's lives or produced something for their good that will endure after we have died. Durkheim demonstrated the prevalence of this phenomenon by using statistics about suicide rates across different religious groups.

Egoistic suicide suicide that occurs when one is not well integrated into a social group.

Although many Western religions formally prohibit suicide, rates varied substantially across religious affiliations. Durkheim found that throughout Europe, Protestants killed themselves most often, followed by Catholics and then Jews. Why? Protestantism is premised on individualism. When Martin Luther nailed his Ninety-Five Theses to the door of the castle church in Wittenberg, he was directly challenging the authority of the Catholic clergy. As a result of this antiauthoritarian tradition, there isn't an elaborate church hierarchy encumbering most Protestant denominations, and Protestants are encouraged to maintain a direct personal relationship with God. By changing the individual's relationship to God (and therefore of the individual's relationship to the church), Protestantism also stripped away many of the integrative structures of Catholicism. Without the sense of community engendered by the elaborate, communal church rituals, the Protestants slowly drifted down the y-axis of social integration, increasing the chances that individual Protestants might commit egoistic suicide. (More recent research shows that today the greater distinction is between people who are religiously affiliated and those who are not, the latter experiencing significantly higher levels of suicide.)

In Durkheim's era, Catholics killed themselves less often than Protestants, but why did Jews have the lowest suicide rate of any major European religious group, if all these religions prohibited suicide? Judaism may be less structured than Catholicism, but historically speaking, Jews have remained a persecuted minority group. When a social group is persecuted or rejected by the so-called mainstream, its members often band together for protection from persecution. For example, in the United States today, African Americans have one of the lowest suicide rates, probably as a result of their bonding as a minority group, united in a common struggle against a history of oppression.

Too little social integration increases the risk of suicide, but too much social integration can lead to the same result. A person who strays too far up the *y*-axis might commit altruistic suicide, because a group dominates the life of that individual to such a degree that he or she feels meaningless aside from this social recognition. Think about Japanese ritual suicide, sometimes called seppuku (sometimes colloquially known as hara-kiri). In this scenario, samurai warriors who had failed their group in battle would disembowel themselves with a sword rather than continue to live as a disgrace in the community. Durkheim uses the example of Hindu widows in some castes and regions of India, who were expected to throw themselves on their husbands' funeral pyre to prove their devotion. This practice, called suttee or sati, symbolized that a woman properly recognized that her life was meaningless outside her social role as a wife. Official efforts to ban suttee commenced as early as the sixteenth century, and it is now illegal and extremely rare in India.

Altruistic suicide suicide that occurs when one experiences too much social integration.

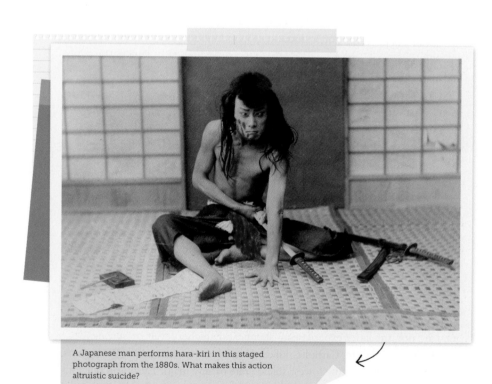

A Japanese man performs hara-kiri in this staged photograph from the 1880s. What makes this action altruistic suicide?

In the preceding examples, the individuals who committed suicide were under some social pressure to do so, but altruistic suicide can be a more personal choice, too. For example, do you think that suicide rates in the military are higher among enlisted soldiers or officers? Enlisted soldiers might be the obvious choice because they experience a lower standard of living and less social prestige, but statistics show that the suicide rate is, in fact, higher among officers. Why? Too much social integration. The identity of the officer—his sense of honor and self-worth—is more completely linked to his role in the military. Enlisted soldiers, in contrast, are not as responsible for group performance. More likely, these soldiers perceive their military service as a job and still identify strongly with their other, civilian roles, so they have a lower risk of altruistic suicide.

As we move to the *x*-axis, social regulation, why or how would social regulation influence the suicide rate? Imagine you commute to school every day. You rise at approximately 7:00 A.M., leave the house by 8:00 A.M., and take the 8:15 A.M. bus to school. But now imagine that some days the bus is late, some days the bus is early, and sometimes it just doesn't come at all. You have no way of knowing when or if the bus will come. You get tired of standing on a cold, lonely corner waiting for a bus that may never come, and after a while you might just stop trying to get to class at all. What's the point of waking up if you won't make it to class on time despite your effort? You have developed a sense of learned helplessness, a depressed outlook in which sufferers lack the will to take action to improve their lives, even when obvious avenues are present.

At the heart of learned helplessness is the sense that we are unable to stave off the sources of our pain, that we have no control of our own well-being. Durkheim studied a similar condition, which he termed *anomie*. Literally meaning "without norms," anomie is a sense of aimlessness or despair that arises when we can no longer reasonably expect life to be more or less meaningful. Our sense of connection between our actions and values is eroded, because too little social regulation exists. Durkheim labeled suicide that resulted from insufficient social regulation anomic suicide. For example, after the stock market crashed in 1929, many businessmen jumped out of skyscraper windows to their deaths. These stockbrokers and investors may have felt that they did everything right and still ended up destitute. For them, the connection between what they thought was the right thing to do—work hard on Wall Street—and just rewards was severed. They had no idea how to cope with the changes.

Durkheim's argument about anomic suicide seems intuitive when it refers to negative events rupturing our everyday lives, but the same principles also hold for positive life events. For example, many lottery winners report spells of severe depression after winning millions of dollars, providing another case of what Durkheim would call anomie (Nissle & Bshor, 2002). If a very poor, frugal man wins the lottery, all of his money-saving habits instantaneously become irrelevant, unnecessary, even a bit silly. Maybe he previously structured his Sundays this way: Walk down to the corner store just as it's about to close

Anomie a sense of aimlessness or despair that arises when we can no longer reasonably expect life to be predictable; too little social regulation; normlessness.

Anomic suicide suicide that occurs as a result of insufficient social regulation.

to pick up a castoff of the Sunday paper, painstakingly cut coupons from the circulars for hours, and then plan a visit to each of three local grocery stores to find the best deals throughout the week. Maybe he always took lunch to work in reused brown paper bags to save money. Now he has $5 million in his checking account and no behavioral template (something that social processes yield) for life as a wealthy man. His difficulties do not revolve around the quantity of material resources or standard of living suddenly available to him. They revolve around the now-absent rules he previously used to give meaning to his life.

Fatalistic suicide suicide that occurs as a result of too much social regulation.

The final coordinate is fatalistic suicide, which occurs when a person experiences too much social regulation. Instead of floundering in a state of anomie with no guiding rules, you find yourself doing the same thing day after day, with no variation and no surprises. In 10 years, what will you be doing? The same thing. In 20 years? The same thing. You have nothing to look forward to because you reasonably expect that nothing better than this will ever happen for you. This type of suicide usually occurs among slaves and prisoners. You might imagine that slaves and prisoners would commit suicide because of their physical hardships, but Durkheim's research suggested that it is more accurate to understand their suicidal deaths as resulting from the suffocating tyranny of monotony.

Early feminists wrote of the "problem that has no name": That life as a 1950s suburban stay-at-home mother was a stifling routine, the same every day, for as long as the imagination could conjure. Sylvia Plath, a feminist poet and writer, committed suicide in 1963 shortly after the publication of her novel *The Bell Jar*, in which the semiautobiographical character Esther's fatalism is palpable: "I saw the days of the year stretching ahead like a series of bright white boxes, and separating one box from another was sleep, like a black shade. Only for me, the long perspective of shades that set off one box from the next had suddenly snapped up, and I could see day after day after day glaring ahead of me like a white, broad, infinitely desolate avenue" (1963/1971, p. 143). Women's roles in society were tightly controlled, and thus they were at higher risk for fatalistic suicide.

According to many theories of deviance, what happens at the group level affects what happens at the individual level. For example, Durkheim hypothesized that members of minority groups were more socially integrated within their group, and therefore Jews in Europe had lower suicide rates. Perhaps minority solidarity inspires feelings of belonging and love between family and nonfamily alike within the group. Because feeling loved and wanted is generally regarded as a good thing, we could say that this solidarity makes group members happy or at least staves off depression. Less depressed, happier people commit suicide less often than those who feel unimportant, worthless, and hopeless. Group dissimilarities start at the macro level (group solidarity), filter down to the individual level (feelings of depression or happiness), and can be detected again in the aggregate (differential suicide rates).

Social Forces and Deviance

In keeping with Durkheim's attempt to discover the social roots of suicide and other forms of deviance, sociologist Robert Merton pioneered a complementary theory of social deviance. Instead of stressing the way sudden social changes lead to feelings of helplessness, Merton argued that the real problem behind anomie occurs when a society holds out the same goals to all its members but does not give them equal ability to achieve these goals. Merton's strain theory, advanced in 1938, explains how society gives us certain templates for acting correctly or appropriately. More specifically, we learn what society considers appropriate goals and appropriate means of achieving them. The strain in strain theory arises when the means don't match up to those ends; hence, Merton's theory is also called the "means-ends theory of deviance." When someone fails to recognize and accept either socially appropriate goals or socially appropriate means (or both), he or she becomes a social deviant.

Strain theory Robert Merton's theory that deviance occurs when a society does not give all of its members equal ability to achieve socially acceptable goals.

If you have decided to pursue a college education, presumably to land a decent job, you are probably what Merton terms a conformist. A conformist accepts both the goals and strategies to achieve those goals that are considered socially acceptable. Your goal is to earn a good living, maybe start a family, and take long, exotic vacations where you will take photos with a fancy camera and then post them online to impress your friends. You've decided to pursue this lifestyle through a better education, deliberate cultivation of the right social network, and hard work.

Conformist individual who accepts both the goals and strategies to achieve them that are considered socially acceptable.

Now let's say that you go to class every day, take minimal notes, and read just enough to earn a passing grade. All you want is to get by and be left alone. You don't care how much money you will earn, as long as it's enough to pay for your studio apartment and other small monthly bills. You've accepted society's acceptable means (you're still going to college, after all), but you've rejected society's goals (the big house, the 2.3 kids, and the new car). You've rejected the idea of getting ahead through hard work, the American dream. You are a ritualist, a person who rejects socially defined goals but not the means.

Ritualist individual who rejects socially defined goals but not the means.

If, however, you yearn to be rich and famous but don't have the scruples, patience, or economic resources to get there by using socially acceptable means, you may be an innovator. Let's say you are particularly interested in buying a mansion and expensive jewelry, and marrying a gorgeous husband or wife. Instead of slaving away on Wall Street for years, you sell drugs, fence stolen goods, and make a few friends in the Mafia.

Innovator social deviant who accepts socially acceptable goals but rejects socially acceptable means to achieve them.

Among those who reject *both* means and goals are retreatists and rebels, although the boundaries between the two are not always so cut and dried. Retreatists completely stop participating in society. This type is perhaps illustrated by adventurer Christopher Johnson McCandless, the subject of the bestselling 1997 book and 2011 film *Into the Wild*, who simply decided not to play the game and moved to the woods where he lived without running water or electricity. (I won't tell you what happens to him in case you plan on reading

Retreatist one who rejects both socially acceptable means and goals by completely retreating from, or not participating in, society.

Conformist

Ritualist

Innovator

Retreatist

Rebel

Which type are you? Do you follow socially accepted means and goals? According to Robert Merton, you're a conformist. Doing the bare minimum? You're probably a ritualist. If you're like WorldCom CEO Bernard Ebbers and want to earn big rewards but have few scruples about how you reach them, you're an innovator. You're a retreatist if you reject all means and goals of society. You're a rebel, like Che Guevara, if you not only reject social means and goals but also want to destroy society itself.

Rebel individual who rejects both traditional goals and traditional means and wants to alter or destroy the social institutions from which he or she is alienated.

the book.) A rebel also rejects both traditional goals and traditional means but wants to change (or destroy) the social institutions from which he or she is alienated. One example is Ernesto "Che" Guevara, the Argentine Marxist who famously fought for communism in Cuba. His disgust at the impoverished conditions he encountered as a doctor traveling through Latin America led to the formation of a guerrilla group. Che chose to fight the government rather than, say, propose new legislation or raise money for a new hospital.

Symbolic Interactionist Theories of Deviance

Whereas Durkheim and Merton focused on the ways different parts of the organic social body function together, another school of sociologists in the 1960s and 1970s took a different approach to the study of deviance. Working in the tradition of symbolic interactionism (see Chapters 1 and 4), a term coined by Herbert Blumer, these sociologists stressed the particular meanings individuals bring to their actions, rather than the broader social structures of which they are unwittingly a part (Blumer, 1969). To determine why people commit crimes, or to seek the root causes of deviance in a given society, a symbolic interactionist would look at the small and subtle particulars of a social context, and the beliefs and assumptions people carry into their everyday interactions. Functionalist theories, such as Durkheim's and Merton's, are sometimes called macro theories because they seek to paint the social world in wide brushstrokes: generalizable trends, global or national forces, and broad social structures. At the opposite end of the spectrum, micro theories such as symbolic interactionism zoom in on the individual. Symbolic interactionism takes seriously our inner thoughts and everyday interactions with one another, including how others see us and how we respond to our surroundings.

Labeling Theory

As a child, did you ever shoplift, trespass, or forge a document? If you were slow and tactless enough to get caught, your parents probably gave you a stern lecture and maybe grounded you. Chances are, however, that over time the incident slowly faded into the background and you stopped feeling guilty. You probably never came to think of yourself as a shoplifter or trespasser, as a criminal or social deviant. You simply made a stupid mistake, never to be repeated. Let me give you an example from my own past. One afternoon when I was in junior high school, a friend and I decided to play "fireman, waterman," a game that required one person (the fireman) to flick lit matches into the air, while the waterman tried to extinguish them with a plant mister. To make a long story short, I was the fireman and I won. As you might expect, the incident ended badly—specifically, one of the stray, airborne matches set my friend's apartment on fire. After extinguishing the blaze, fire department officials questioned me about my role in starting the fire, but ultimately, I was absolved from blame and the fire was declared an accident. My parents, although obviously shaken and disappointed, never formally punished me. The trauma of the incident, they said, was lesson enough. Now imagine that, instead of being pardoned, I was held accountable for my role in starting the fire and sent to a juvenile corrections facility. Do you think I still would have followed the same life trajectory, eventually going to college and graduate school, and becoming a sociology professor and textbook author?

The labeling theory of social deviance offers insight into how people become deviants. According to this theory, individuals subconsciously notice how others see or label them, and their reactions to those labels over time form the basis of their self-identity. It is only through the social process of labeling

Labeling theory the belief that individuals subconsciously notice how others see or label them, and their reactions to those labels over time form the basis of their self-identity.

that we create deviance by assigning shared meanings to acts. We all know that stealing, trespassing, and vandalizing are wrong, abnormal, and criminal behavior, but these acts are considered deviant only because of our shared meanings about the sanctity of private property and our rules about respecting that property. Although the fire caused by my unfortunate stint in pyrotechnics was labeled an accident, it might have been termed a crime just as easily. There was and is nothing inherently deviant about setting an apartment on fire, accidentally or otherwise. In 1963, Howard S. Becker, a proponent of labeling theory, made precisely this point, arguing that individuals don't commit crimes. Rather, social groups create deviance, first by setting the rules for what's right and wrong, and second by labeling wrongdoers as outsiders. Offenders are not born; they are made. They are a consequence of how other people apply rules and sanctions to them.

Social groups create rules about the correct or standard mode of conduct for social actors. When these rules are broken, society's reaction to the act determines if the offense counts as deviance. Becker also argues that not only are deviant acts created by a process of labeling but *deviants* are also created by a process of labeling. If you break a rule—say, accidentally burn down an apartment—but your violation is not labeled a crime or otherwise recognized as deviant, then *you* are not recognized as a criminal or deviant. We become (or don't become) deviant only in interaction with other social actors. It is this social reaction to an act, and the subsequent labeling of that act and offender, that create social deviance.

To illustrate this process of becoming deviant, Becker interviewed 50 marijuana users in "Becoming a Marihuana User" (1953). He began his study with a simple inquiry: Are marijuana users different from nonusers? Is there something about the individual psychology of marijuana users that causes them to smoke marijuana? The answer given by most scientists, politicians, and parents in the 1950s, when Becker was writing, was a hearty *yes*. Certainly, the commonsense conception of marijuana use today assumes that marijuana users are somehow different from nonusers. But Becker argues that chronic marijuana use results from a process of social learning. Before people light up, they must first learn how to smoke marijuana. More important, they must then redefine the sensations of marijuana use as "fun" and desirable. Just as setting an apartment on fire is not inherently a crime, getting high is not "automatically or necessarily pleasurable" (Becker, 1963). According to one novice user in Becker's study, "It started taking effect and I didn't know what was happening, you know, what it was, and I was very sick. I walked around the room, walking around the room trying to get off, you know; it just scared me

How did Howard Becker apply labeling theory to the use of marijuana?

at first, you know. I wasn't used to that sort of thing" (p. 239). Another user never could learn to enjoy pot:

> It [marijuana] was offered to me, and I tried it. I'll tell you one thing. I never did enjoy it at all. I mean it was just nothing that I could enjoy. [Becker: Well, did you get high when you turned on?] Oh, yeah, I got definite feelings from it. But I didn't enjoy them. I mean I got plenty of reactions, but they were mostly reactions of fear. [You were frightened?] Yes. I didn't enjoy it. I couldn't seem to relax with it, you know. If you can't relax with a thing, you can't enjoy it, I don't think. (p. 240)

A person trying marijuana is usually able to redefine the experience when smoking with long-term users who assure the novice that the physical effects are normal, even enjoyable. One of Becker's interviewees, a veteran smoker, recalled how a beginner "became frightened and hysterical" after smoking for the first time. An older user told the newbie, "I'd give anything to get that high myself" (Becker, 1963). This comment and others like it apply new meaning to the sensations of getting high. Marijuana smoking becomes pleasant through a social process, and marijuana becomes an object of desire. How objects and sensations become meaningful (or pleasant) through social processes is the focus of Becker's study, in contrast to explanations that focus on what objects *are*. Similarly, the taste of alcohol probably didn't appeal to your palate when you first tried it; however, because alcohol had a certain social allure, being associated with either adulthood or rebellion, you may have learned to appreciate its taste (even before you reached the legal drinking age of 21).

Another example of a social process may help illustrate the power of labeling theory. As part of a psychology experiment, a group of eight adults with steady employment and no history of mental illness presented themselves at different psychiatric in-patient hospitals and complained of hearing voices (Rosenhan, 1973). Each of the pseudo-patients was admitted after describing the alleged voices, which spoke words like "thud," "empty," and "hollow." In all cases, the pseudo-patients were admitted with a diagnosis of schizophrenia. The researchers instructed the pseudo-patients, once they were hospitalized, to stop "simulating any symptoms of abnormality." Each pseudo-patient "behaved on the ward as he 'normally' behaved." Still, the doctors and staff did not suspect that the pseudo-patients were imposters. Instead, the treating psychiatrists changed their diagnosis of schizophrenia to "schizophrenia in remission." Something even more troubling than the misdiagnosis occurred. Once the pseudo-patients had been labeled insane, all their subsequent behavior was interpreted accordingly. One male pseudo-patient, for example, gave the hospital staff a truthful account of his personal history. During his childhood he had been close to his mother but not his father. Later in life, he became close with his father and more distant from his mother. His marriage was

The force of labels and roles can affect us very quickly. The Stanford Prison Experiment, conducted by Philip Zimbardo in 1971, provides insight into the power of such social labels and how they might explain the incredibly inhumane acts of torture, most involving violence and humiliation, committed at Abu Ghraib, the American-run prison in Iraq. Zimbardo, a psychology professor at Stanford, rounded up some college undergraduate men to participate in an experiment about "the psychology of prison life." Half the undergraduates were assigned the role of prisoner, and half were assigned the role of prison guard. These roles were randomly assigned, so there was nothing about the inherent personalities of either group that predisposed them to prefer one role over the other.

To simulate the arrest and incarceration process, the soon-to-be prisoners were taken from their homes, handcuffed, and searched by actual city police. Then all the prisoners were taken to "prison"—the basement of the Stanford psychology department set up with cells and a special solitary confinement closet.

Philip Zimbardo's Stanford Prison Experiment.

The guards awaited their prisoners in makeshift uniforms and dark sunglasses to render their eyes invisible to inmates. Upon arrival at the prison, all the criminals were stripped, searched, and issued inmate uniforms, which were like short hospital gowns. The first day passed without incident, as prisoners and guards settled into their new roles. But on the morning of the second day, prisoners revolted, barricading themselves in their mock cells and sparking a violent confrontation between the fictitious guards and prisoners that would ensue for the next four days. From physical abuse, such as hour-long counts of push-ups, to psychological

violence, such as degradation and humiliation, the
guards' behavior verged on
sadism, although just days
before these same young
men were normal Stanford
undergrads. The prisoners
quickly began "withdrawing
and behaving in pathological ways," while some of the
guards seemed to relish their
abuse. The original plan was
for the experiment to last 14
days, but after only 6 days it
spiraled out of control and
had to be aborted.

This Iraqi detainee in Abu Ghraib prison was hooked up
to wires after American soldiers made him stand on a box.
How can Zimbardo's experiments help us understand the
torture at Abu Ghraib?

The lesson, claims Zimbardo, is that good people can do terrible
things, depending on their social surroundings and expectations. When
thrown into a social context of unchecked authority, anonymity, and
high stress, average people can become exceptional monsters. It's a
phenomenon Zimbardo calls the "Lucifer effect," and it offers insights
into how the atrocities at Abu Ghraib prison in Iraq became possible
(Zimbardo, 2007). In 2005, when the media made public the horrify-
ing images of Iraqi prisoners being degraded and abused—some naked
and on their knees inches from barking dogs; some wearing hoods
and restrained in painful, grotesque positions; some forced to lie atop
a pile of other naked prisoners—with grinning American soldiers looking on, many commentators (and military officials) sought to explain
the abuses as a case of "bad apples" among otherwise good soldiers.
Bad apples don't just arise out of nowhere, however, nor are people
inherently malicious or brutal by nature. When given limitless power
under the high stakes of uncertainty, as happened to the soldiers at Abu
Ghraib, abuse becomes the norm, and people who are otherwise good
can do evil things.

In experiments such as David L. Rosenhan's or films like *Shock Corridor* (above), people with no history of mental illness are admitted into psychiatric hospitals. These examples raise questions about the stickiness of labels. What are some of the consequences of being labeled a deviant?

"characteristically close and warm," with no persistent problems. He reported rarely spanking his children. Sounds like a fairly typical guy, right? This is how the hospital record described the pseudo-patient's personal history:

> This white 39-year-old male . . . manifests a long history of considerable ambivalence in close relationships, which begins in early childhood. A warm relationship with his mother cools during adolescence. A distant relationship to his father is described as becoming very intense. Affective stability is absent. His attempts to control emotionality with his wife and children are punctuated by angry outbursts and, in the case of his children, spankings. And while he says that he has several good friends, one senses considerable ambivalence embedded in those relationships also. (Rosenhan, 1973, p. 253)

Even though the pseudo-patient was acting "normally" shortly after his admission, the "abnormal" label stuck and continued to color the staff's perceptions and diagnoses. Just in case you are curious, the pseudo-patients were kept by the hospitals for 7 to 52 days, with an average stay of 19 days. Sticky label, indeed.

Labeling theorists believe the fact that deviant labels stick no matter what the circumstances has important consequences for behavior. If, after committing a crime or hearing voices, you were labeled deviant and people treated and thought about you differently, how would you feel? Like the same person but just someone who, say, was arrested for possessing drugs? Or would the criminal label become part of the way you thought about yourself? Labeling theorists call the first act of rule breaking (which can include experiences or actions such as hearing voices, breaking windows, or dyeing one's hair neon orange) primary deviance. After you are labeled a deviant (a criminal, a drug addict, a shoplifter, even a prostitute), you might begin behaving differently as a result of the way people think about and act toward you. Others' expectations about how you *will* act affect how you *do* act. Secondary deviance refers to deviant acts that occur after primary deviance and as a result of your new deviant label. For example, a deviance researcher interviewed a woman in her sixties who had been under psychiatric care for some 20 years (Glassner, 1999). This is how she recalls the process of becoming mentally ill:

> The first time I was taken to a psychiatrist for help was when I was getting depressed over a miscarriage. I had tried for many years to have that baby, and finally I was pregnant and planning to be a mother and all, and then I lost it. Anyhow, they told me I was "deeply depressed," but it didn't really mean much to me. I figured I'd get over it once I got pregnant again or something. But when I went home, everybody treated me differently. My husband and my mother had met with the social worker, who explained that I had this problem, with depression and all. From then on I was a depressive. I mean, that's the way everyone treated me, and I thought of myself in the same way after a while. Maybe I am that way, maybe I was born that way or grew up like that, but anyhow, that's what I am now. (p. 73)

First, the woman sees her experience with depression as a passing phase, something she will recover from in time. Then a psychiatrist labels her "deeply depressed." When she arrives home, family members treat her differently, and "from then on" she is "a depressive." You can see how the woman's initial experience is redefined by her interaction with the psychiatrist and how the psychiatrist's label eventually becomes an integral part of the woman's identity. Of course, these labels themselves are socially structured by group stereotypes that can often serve as default cognitive categories.

Stigma

We've seen how primary deviance can snowball into secondary deviance, whereby a few initial wrong steps or unlucky breaks can define a person's future actions and reactions. It doesn't end there. Secondary deviance can quickly become social stigma. A stigma is a negative social label that not only changes others' behavior toward a person but also alters that person's self-concept and social identity. We frequently say that certain behaviors, groups, identities, and even objects are stigmatized. Mental illness still carries a stigma in our society. Pedophilia carries a bigger one.

Having a criminal record can also carry a stigma, as can a person's race. In 2001 Devah Pager, then a graduate student in sociology, conducted a study

Primary deviance the first act of rule breaking that may incur a label of "deviant" and thus influence how people think about and act toward you.

Secondary deviance subsequent acts of rule breaking that occur after primary deviance and as a result of your new deviant label and people's expectations of you.

Stigma a negative social label that not only changes others' behavior toward a person but also alters that person's own self-concept and social identity.

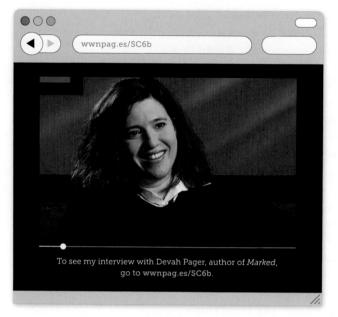

To see my interview with Devah Pager, author of *Marked*, go to wwnpag.es/SC6b.

to determine the effects of race and a criminal record on employment opportunities (Pager, 2003). She dispatched potential job candidates (African American and Caucasian male college students who had volunteered for the experiment) with similar résumés to apply for entry-level service positions. Half the participants of each race were told to indicate a prior felony conviction on their job applications. Pager found that of those with no criminal record, the white applicants were more likely to get a response (34 percent compared with 14 percent), but also that the white men with a supposed felony conviction were more likely to be called back than the black men who did not report a criminal record (17 percent compared with 14 percent). The employers in Pager's study were slightly more willing to consider a white applicant with a felony record than a black applicant with a clean history. So not only is a criminal record a stigma that deters potential employers, but the race of a job applicant continues to matter. One possible explanation, reasoned Pager, is that

employers are attempting to select the best candidate for the job, but are affected by all kinds of pervasive and largely unconscious stereotypes that result in privileging or preferring a white candidate to a black candidate. . . . Employers have these negative stereotypes based on really pervasive media imagery, for example, of young black men involved with the criminal justice system or acting out in some negative way. There's lots of information we get about all of the negative characteristics that we might attribute to the African American population. . . . They talked about black men as being lazy and dangerous and criminal and dressing poorly; they were very candid about all of these negative characteristics that they attributed to black men. But then, right after that, when I asked them about their experiences over the past year with black applicants or black employees, they had a much harder time coming up with concrete examples of those general attitudes, and for the most part, employers reported having very similar kinds of experiences with their black and white employees. (Conley, 2009f)

Pager's research reveals how stigmas have real consequences, shaping the map of opportunities for men with criminal records, and illuminates the challenges faced by black men, whose skin carries a stigma of deviance into the labor market whether they've been in prison or not. Of course, in this case, because the testers were trained with a script, the issue of internalized self-stigma doesn't come up to influence their interactions. But such internalized stigma is itself an important source of disadvantage and stress for marginalized groups.

Broken Windows Theory of Deviance

As labeling theory predicts, the ways other people see you affect your behavior and overall life chances. So, too, does the way you see your social surroundings, according to the broken windows theory. In 1969 Zimbardo conducted another experiment in which he and his graduate students abandoned two cars, leaving them without license plates and with their hoods propped up, in two different neighborhoods (Wilson & Kelling, 1982). The first car was abandoned in a seemingly safe neighborhood in Palo Alto, California, where Stanford University is located. The second car was left in the South Bronx in New York City, then one of the most dangerous urban ghettoes in the country. Unsurprisingly, the abandoned car in Palo Alto remained untouched, whereas the car deposited in the South Bronx lost its hubcaps, battery, and any other usable parts almost immediately. However, it was the next stage in the experiment that offers valuable insight into how social context affects social deviance. Zimbardo went back to the untouched car in Palo Alto and smashed it with a sledgehammer. He and his graduate students shattered the windshield, put some dents in the car's sides, and again fled the scene. What do you think happened to the smashed and dented car in the "safe," rich neighborhood? Passersby began stopping their cars and getting out to further smash the wreck or tag it with graffiti. The social cues, or social context, influenced the way people, even in a rich neighborhood, treated the car.

> **Broken windows theory of deviance** theory explaining how social context and social cues impact whether individuals act deviantly; specifically, whether local, informal social norms allow deviant acts.

In the South Bronx, the overall social context—involving many broken windows, graffiti, and dilapidated buildings—encouraged deviant acts at the outset because the neighborhood setting of decay and disorder signaled to residents that an abandoned car was fair game for abuse. In Palo Alto, where neighborhood conditions were clean and orderly, people were unlikely to vandalize an abandoned car. However, when the vehicle was already mangled, that cue of turmoil signaled to people that it was okay to engage in the otherwise deviant act of vandalism. The broken windows theory of deviance explains how social context and social cues impact the way individuals act; specifically, whether local, informal social

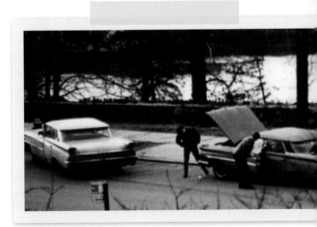

People inspect an abandoned car in the South Bronx. Philip Zimbardo placed this car in New York City and left another near Stanford University in Palo Alto, California. The car near Stanford went untouched for days, but the car pictured above was relieved of its hubcaps and other parts almost immediately.

norms allow such acts. When signals seem to tell us that it's okay to do the otherwise unthinkable, sometimes we do. The broken windows theory of deviance has inspired some politicians to institute policies that target the catalysts for inappropriate behavior (vandalism, burglary, and so forth). In fact, one of Zimbardo's graduate students who participated in the car experiment, George Kelling, later worked as a consultant for the New York City Transit Authority in 1984, devising a plan to crack down on graffiti. The underlying assumption of the plan was that the continued presence of graffiti-covered cars served as a green light for more graffiti and perhaps even violent crimes. The Transit Authority then launched a massive campaign to clean up graffiti, car by car, to erase the signs of urban disorder, in the hope of reducing subway crime. In the mid-1990s New York City mayor Rudy Giuliani also initiated a campaign of "zero tolerance" for petty crimes such as turnstile jumping, public urination, the drinking of alcohol in public, and graffiti. Today, the city's newer subway cars are "graffiti-proof," meaning that spray paint doesn't adhere to the metal exterior of the cars. Indeed, both petty and serious crimes have dropped dramatically in New York City since the 1990s (Kelling & Sousa, 2001), although some criminologists dispute the causal impact of the Giuliani strategy.

Crime

As noted above, crime is a more formal sort of deviance, not only subject to social sanction but also punishable by law. Sometimes an act falls clearly at one end of the spectrum or the other. Situations of self-defense aside, killing a person is generally agreed to be criminal; nose picking, however unpalatable, isn't. In other cases, though, the distinction is not so clear. Whereas you might get strange looks for wearing aluminum-foil hot pants to class, if you show up with no clothes on at all, you will likely be sent to a mental health care provider for assessment, or arrested and thrown in jail for indecent exposure. But what if your hot pants weren't foil at all but just silver paint? Would this be indecent exposure?

Crime runs the gamut in type and degree. Most of us think of violence or drugs when we contemplate crime, but there are many other ways of breaking the law.

Street Crime

> *You don't make up for your sins in church. You do it in the streets.*
> —"Johnny Boy" Civello in *Mean Streets*

Street crime crime committed in public and often associated with violence, gangs, and poverty.

Street crime generally refers to crime committed in public. The term invokes specific images, however, of violent crime, typically perpetrated in an urban landscape. Both historically and today, street crime is often associated with gangs and currently with both disadvantaged minority groups and poverty. Just why people are drawn to a career of street crime has long been a favorite question of social scientists and is still a matter of heated debate. Explanations for the fluctuations and trends in violent crime rates also vary widely. One theory, for example, posits that street crime rises and falls in relation to the availability of opportunity within the legitimate economy. When this is lacking, people turn elsewhere. Expanding on Merton's strain theory and the idea of anomie, sociologists Richard Cloward and Lloyd Ohlin (1960) developed differential opportunity theory, which states that in addition to the legitimate economic structure, an illegitimate opportunity structure also exists that is unequally distributed across social classes. Hence, crime should rise or fall according to the relative returns on opportunities in the legitimate and illegitimate economies.

One way, then, to reduce crime would be to raise the costs in the illegitimate economy, thereby lowering the net returns. Such a strategy lies behind tougher sentencing policies, such as "three strikes" laws (if you are convicted of three felony crimes, you are imprisoned for life), which aim simultaneously to deter criminals and to incarcerate habitual offenders. The focus of such policies tends to be violent crime; lately, however, such laws have been extended to nonviolent crimes, such as drug dealing. Another strategy would be to increase the returns to entry-level opportunities in the legitimate economy; raising the minimum wage is one way to do this. Either strategy—decreasing the returns to the illegitimate economy or increasing the returns to the legitimate economy—shortens the distance, or differential, between the two economies.

Many people attribute the decrease in crime rates to the adoption of a community policing ideology, in which police officers are viewed (and view themselves) as members of the community they serve. Rather than enforce laws from the outside in, members of the police force work to develop reliable relationships and bonds of trust with community residents. On a practical level, this means that greater police presence is felt in areas where community policing is in effect. (However, convincing evidence on this causal claim is still lacking; that said, community policing probably doesn't hurt.)

White-Collar Crime

Bernard L. Madoff rose through the social ranks of wealth on Long Island, then Manhattan, then London, and eventually became the chairman of the NASDAQ exchange, which was based on technology his privately held firm had developed. In 2009, he was sentenced to 150 years in prison—a life sentence for the then-71-year-old. His crime was taking money from investors and fabricating great rates of return to pump up his reputation and keep money coming in when, in fact, his funds were losing money. Returns to investors were paid not from any actual gains their initial investments were accruing, but from the new money coming in the door. Madoff lived an opulent lifestyle,

Bernie Madoff

employing well-connected friends and family to keep a steady stream of new investments coming in. During the economic downturn in 2008, Madoff could not keep up with investors' demands to cash out. An investigation by the Federal Bureau of Investigation (FBI) led to his arrest. Madoff estimated that he had lost $50 billion, making his the largest fraud in American history.

Infractions such as fraud are called white-collar crime, a term coined by sociologist Edwin Sutherland in 1939. It is typically committed by a professional (or professionals) in his or her (or their) capacity in the professional world against a corporation, agency, or other professional entity. According to the FBI,

> [w]hite-collar crimes are categorized by deceit, concealment, or violation of trust and are not dependent on the application or threat of physical force or violence. Such acts are committed by individuals and organizations to obtain money, property, or services, to avoid the payment or loss of money or services, or to secure a personal or business advantage. (2003)

White-collar crime offense committed by a professional (or professionals) against a corporation, agency, or other institution.

Although street crime is the most prevalent type of crime, looking strictly at the numbers, white-collar crime has greater financial impact. It has been estimated in one Cornell University study to cost the United States more than $300 billion a year. In contrast, the FBI has estimated that in 2012 the total loss from robbery, burglary, larceny-theft, and motor vehicle theft was $15.5 billion (2013).

Corporate crime a particular type of white-collar crime committed by the officers (CEOs and other executives) of a corporation.

A particular type of white-collar crime is corporate crime, offenses committed by the officers (CEOs and other executives) of a corporation. In the late spring of 2012, J.P. Morgan trader Bruno Iksil (also known as the London Whale) placed a giant risky trade and ended up losing $6.2 billion for the bank. Losing billions on a trade is bad but not illegal. Iksil was fired, not arrested. But U.S. federal prosecutors have indicted his boss and his boss's deputy for conspiring to cover up the losses by filing false reports. Penalties for their crimes include fines and up to 25 years in prison.

Interpreting the Crime Rate

Although it may seem, after a glance at the gruesome headlines in today's newspapers, that crime is only growing progressively worse, the truth is that deviance has always been present. Kai Erikson, in *Wayward Puritans*, demonstrates how even America's seemingly most upstanding and God-fearing community, the Puritans, produced some bad apples—drunkards, adulterers, and thieves (1966/2005). Erikson's point, however, was that while what is defined as deviant may change over time, deviance is forever with us. For example, Erikson found "crimes against the Church," particularly by Quakers in the late 1650s, to be of central concern to the Puritan community. Religious or moral offenses, such as drunkenness and adultery, were of primary concern over economic or political ones—at least those were the crimes taken most seriously and probably reported most frequently during the Puritan era. Erikson's central thesis is that a relatively stable amount of deviance may be expected in a given community, but what counts as deviance evolves depending on the type of society or historical period we examine. Think back to our early definition of social deviance; it is, after all, a social construct and subject to change over time and across cultural values.

If the definitions of deviance and crime are always changing, how can we discern if the crime rate is going up or down? In 1960, the total crime rate was around 160.9 per 100,000 people. By 1992, that number had soared to a little over 757, but it has now fallen back to around 386. Figure 6.2 shows the violent crime rate in the United States from 1960 to 2012.

How can so much change occur in the crime rate in so little time? Is the situation really rapidly degenerating into complete chaos? Probably not. To make a statement about the crime rate going up or down, we have to know what is factored into the crime rate. For instance, the definition of assault may change to include more minor offenses. Recently, one local government proposed including brawls at sporting events in the assault category. And if the classifications of violent crimes are changing, it's difficult to compare the crime rate over time. It is also possible that levels of crime reporting by victims fluctuate. In times of economic recession, people might be less likely to report

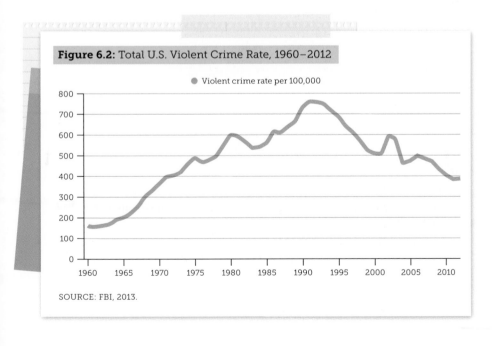

Figure 6.2: Total U.S. Violent Crime Rate, 1960–2012

● Violent crime rate per 100,000

SOURCE: FBI, 2013.

crime because they feel helpless, depressed, or apathetic. Alternatively, a presidential address on fighting terrorism or injustice might make us more diligent in defending the social order.

The point is that the crime rate changes in response to fluctuations in how society classifies and reacts to deviance. In fact, reporting bias may work in the opposite direction from the actual crime rate. Imagine a neighborhood where crime is common. People might be reluctant to report being pickpocketed on the subway when they have just read about three murders the same day. Conversely, in a situation where crime rates are perceived to be low, such as at the opera house, you might be more likely to report a missing wallet. In this way, the reporting of petty crimes may vary inversely to the rate of serious crimes. For these reasons, criminologists (experts trained in studying crime) usually reject the overall crime rate as a reliable indicator of trends in crime. Instead, criminologists use the murder rate to make statements about the overall health of society. Why do they use these statistics instead of violent crime rates? For one thing, it's difficult to fake a murder—either there is a body or there isn't. The murder rate is the best indicator we have of crime in general (Figure 6.3), but even it is not immune to broader changes in society.

For example, if you were shot today in the United States, you would have a much better chance of surviving the gunshot injury than you would have had in 1960. It could be that many more people are arriving at the hospital with bullet wounds, but far fewer of those victims are dying on the operating table thanks to advances in medical technology. The greater survival rate complicates our interpretation of the murder rate (Harris et al., 2002). Has there been

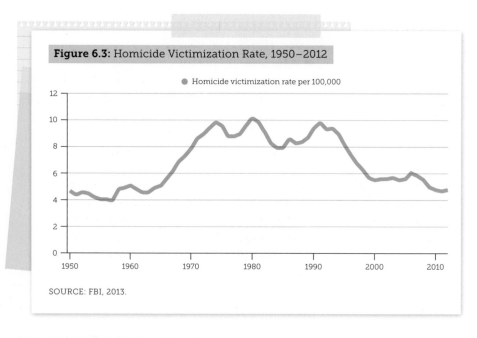

Figure 6.3: Homicide Victimization Rate, 1950–2012

● Homicide victimization rate per 100,000

SOURCE: FBI, 2013.

a decline in the number of murder attempts, or are doctors just better able to treat bullet wounds? It's difficult to say definitively. We can use the murder rate as a gauge to gain a general sense of crime fluctuations, but precise statistics are practically impossible.

→ Crime Reduction

Thus far, we have studied some of the functions and social origins of criminal behavior, as well as the prevalent methods of measuring crime. So how do crime fighters fight crime?

Deterrence Theory of Crime Control

In 1971 President Richard M. Nixon ushered in America's first War on Drugs. Linking drug use to violent crimes and the decay of social order, the federal and state governments instituted an array of harsher penalties for the possession or sale of illegal substances. The philosophy of deterrence, or deterrence theory, suggests that "crime results from a rational calculation of the costs and benefits of criminal activity" (Spohn & Holleran, 2002). If you know you can make a quick buck by selling cocaine (maybe enough to pay your rent, say, or put food on the table), you might be tempted to engage in such illicit activities. But what if, instead of a slap on the wrist, a person caught with small quantities of cocaine is sentenced to a minimum of 15 years in prison? The temptation to sell cocaine might be reduced because you know that the cost of getting caught is higher than the potential benefits of selling drugs. Let's say you are arrested and wind up in prison for 15 years. Would you choose to sell cocaine again? How might the criminal justice system prevent you from doing so?

Deterrence theory philosophy of criminal justice arising from the notion that crime results from a rational calculation of its costs and benefits.

Specific deterrence is what the system attempts when it monitors and tries to prevent known criminals from committing more crimes. An example would be the prison parole system, because the criminal remains under supervision and is being specifically deterred from committing another crime. When he or she is released and freed from direct control after parole has ended, however, the effect is one of general deterrence, whereby criminals who have been punished for a previous offense may opt not to commit more crimes for fear of going back to jail. Another example of general deterrence would be if, from word on the street, you learn that dealing cocaine carries a prison sentence of 15 years and decide not to risk it. Deterrence theory suggests that crime in general, and recidivism in particular, can be reduced through both specific and general deterrence. Recidivism is the "reversion of an individual to criminal behavior" after involvement with the criminal justice system (Maltz, 2001).

Recidivism when an individual who has been involved with the criminal justice system reverts to criminal behavior.

However, deterrence theory—in practice—has other, unintended consequences that may lead to more crime. For one thing, increased supervision and stricter parole codes have made it more likely that offenders will commit technical violations against their parole terms. Because the system has increased its surveillance of former prisoners, requiring time-consuming meetings with parole officers, the system creates better odds for technical slipups and for catching and punishing them. This is suggested by studies showing that rates of new criminal offenses (as opposed to technical violations) for parolees tend to resemble those of people with comparable sociodemographic characteristics who have never been incarcerated. In addition, the prison experience might not have the intended rehabilitative effect. Could prisons make it more difficult for offenders to return to the "straight and narrow"?

Let's first think back to Durkheim and his theory of anomie, which affirms that when our normal lives are disrupted and we can no longer rely on things being relatively stable, we are more likely to commit suicide or engage in other deviant acts. Going to prison for 10 or 15 years might have just this effect; it would be very difficult to "find stable employment, secure suitable housing, or reconcile with . . . family" afterward. Also, reintegration into a community after release from prison is extremely difficult because of "the absence of . . . informal social controls and strong social bonds" (Spohn & Holleran, 2002). Furthermore, while in prison, drug offenders rarely receive the kind of substance abuse treatment that addicts need. They are thus more likely to revert to drug use upon release. Therefore, imprisonment may be particularly counterproductive for drug offenders, and getting tough on crime may inadvertently breed criminals. In addition, as low-level offenders interact daily with serious criminals in prison, they may become socialized by these new peers, adopting their attitudes and behaviors.

Sociologists and geographers have also examined the impact of incarceration on the communities prison inmates call home (Fagan et al., 2003; Williams, 2005). In New York City the incarcerated population is disproportionately drawn from a small handful of neighborhoods, a pattern that is sustained even as crime rates have dropped dramatically. While they are in prison, inmates cannot make positive contributions to the community in terms of providing steady incomes, starting families, or building up social networks that lead to employment in legitimate industries. At the community level, high rates of incarceration among community members create conditions for continued poverty, as those left behind must support families on fewer salaries both

This map of Brooklyn, New York, shows the density of prison admissions in 2003.

during and after incarceration. From Pager's research earlier in the chapter, we know that former felons have a difficult time finding employment. Blocked access to legitimate employment creates conditions for sustained poverty. At the same time, historical crime rates are used to determine current police involvement, which means that once-crime-ridden neighborhoods will continue to receive disproportionate formal surveillance and a higher likelihood that their residents will be arrested.

Goffman's Total Institution

The high rates of recidivism in the United States bring us back to labeling theory, which suggests that the process of becoming a deviant often involves contact with, even absorption into, a special institution such as a prison or mental health institution. And as labeling theorists have shown, our interaction with others very significantly impacts the formation of our personal identity. Erving Goffman, writing in the symbolic interactionist tradition, theorized about how institutions such as prisons and mental health hospitals often become breeding grounds for secondary deviance, providing an important link in the reproduction of deviance through their effects on inmates and patients (Goffman, 1961).

Presumably, most of us sleep, play, and work in different places, with different people and rules structuring our interactions at each location. For example, you probably spend the evening in your home or dorm, relatively undisturbed, and leave in the morning for class, where you are expected to dress appropriately and respect your professors. Total institutions are distinguished by "a breakdown of the barriers separating" these "three spheres of life" (sleep, work, play). In total institutions, "all aspects of life are conducted in the same place and under the same single authority" (Goffman, 1961). In such total institutions as prisons and mental hospitals, life is highly regimented, and the inmates take part in all scheduled activities together. The inmates have no control over the form or flow of activities, which are chosen by the institutional authorities to "fulfill the official aims of the institution." Thus, if the official aim of prisons is rehabilitation, prisoners might be required to attend at least one self-improvement class a day or engage in some sort of productive labor. All of these activities occur in the same place with the same group of people every day.

> **Total institution** an institution in which one is totally immersed and that controls all the basics of day-to-day life; no barriers exist between the usual spheres of daily life, and all activity occurs in the same place and under the same single authority.

In Chapter 4 we examined the various theories of socialization and the development of the self through our interactions with other social actors. All your life you have been slowly accumulating knowledge about who you are in the world. Once you enter a total institution such as a prison, a process that strips away your sense of self begins. As Goffman puts it, "a series of abasements, degradations, humiliations, and profanations" quickly commences. Once people enter a prison or a mental institution, they are closed off from their normal routines and cease to fulfill their usual social roles. Because the

Inmates in an Arizona jail. The local sheriff requires all of the county's inmates to work seven days a week. They are fed only twice a day, are denied recreation, and receive no coffee, cigarettes, salt, pepper, or ketchup.

roles people play are important to the way they perceive themselves, this separation from the world erodes that sense of identity. In the Stanford Prison Experiment, what first occurred when the "inmates" arrived at the "prison" in the basement of the psychology department? They were issued uniforms and given numbers in place of names. The mandated homogeneity of prisoners (and patients) results in an erasure of self. The total institution simultaneously strips away clothes, personal belongings, nicknames, hairstyles, cosmetics, and toiletries—all the tools that people use to identify themselves. The inmates no longer have control over their environment, peer group, daily activities, or personal possessions. It's not hard to see how this process leads to a sense of helplessness. The total institution rapidly destroys a prisoner's sense of self-determination, self-control, and freedom.

The authorities in these total institutions are given the unenviable duty of "showing the prisoners who's boss" and expediting the process of prisoner degradation to ensure "co-operativeness" (Goffman, 1961). Wardens must "socialize" inmates into compliance through informal "obedience test[s]" or "will-breaking contest[s]" until the inmate "who shows defiance receives immediate visible punishment, which increases until he openly 'cries uncle' and humbles himself." When Zimbardo locked a group of seemingly normal college kids into the basement of a Stanford building (discussed in the box on pages 206–207), he found that not only were the inmates affected but the guards also felt impelled to use increasingly violent and inhumane means to solidify their authority and keep the prisoners in check. We can see these patterns in everyday life, too. When given the responsibility of watching younger siblings, have you ever secretly (or not so secretly) delighted in bossing them around? Because the roles we play are important to how we think about ourselves, it is hardly possible for the self-images of both guards and prisoners to remain unaffected by the prison environment.

Foucault on Punishment

> On March 2, 1757, Damiens the regicide was condemned "to make the amende honorable [a kind of ritual abasement] before the main door of the Church of Paris," where he was to be "taken and conveyed in a cart, wearing nothing but a shirt, holding a torch of burning wax weighing two pounds"; then, "in the said cart, to the Place de Greve, where, on a scaffold that will be erected there, the flesh will be torn from his breasts, arms, thighs, and calves with red-hot pincers, his right hand, holding the knife with which he committed the said parricide, burnt with sulfur, and, on those places where the flesh will be torn away, poured molten lead, burning oil, burning resin, wax and sulfur melted together and then his body drawn and quartered by four horses and his limbs and body consumed by fire, reduced to ashes and his ashes thrown to the winds." (Foucault, 1977, p. 1)

Besides possibly turning your stomach, the above passage vividly illustrates the dramatic shift in penal practices from the eighteenth century to the present day. How do we conceive of punishment nowadays? We usually think of prisons, juvenile detention centers, and probation. In *Discipline and Punish* (1977), the French theorist Michel Foucault examines the emergence of the modern penal system and how this system represents a transformation in social control. How did the modern prison system emerge? And what functions does it serve in the disciplining of modern life?

When Robert François Damiens was publicly tortured and then eventually drawn and quartered for trying to kill King Louis XV, the target of punishment was Damiens' body. The entire public spectacle revolved around Damiens suffering for his wrongdoing, culminating in his death. Damiens was even put to death holding the same knife he used to attack the king. According to Foucault, this gruesome "violence against the body" (1977) exemplifies a premodern form of punishment, which is concentrated on the body and associated with the crime committed. So, for example, if you kill someone, you are publicly executed. If you steal something, perhaps your fingers or hand will be cut off. This "eye for an eye" mentality is similar to that represented by Durkheim's mechanical social sanctions.

We might like to believe that modern punishment came about because prison reformers lobbied for more humane penal tactics that aimed to reform

The execution of Robert François Damiens, a French servant who attempted to assassinate King Louis XV at Versailles in 1757.

the criminal through rehabilitation. We no longer (with the exception of the death penalty) publicly violate the criminal's body by, for example, pouring molten lead on his excoriated body. Punishment takes place in private, away from the public eye, and it leaves the criminal's body intact. (Although much violence, including rape, does occur inside prison walls, the state does not formally sanction it and is supposed to protect prisoners from such attacks.) Foucault claims that modern punishment has as its target what he calls "the soul" of the prisoner. The soul, for Foucault, is the sum of an individual's unique habits and peculiarities: what makes me *me* and you *you*. Such a penal system tries to understand the individual and his or her abnormalities to correct or reform bad habits. (Again, this is a highly stylized view of the history of criminal justice, given that in the United States, some jurisdictions still impose the death penalty and our government has even tortured political detainees. At the very least, we have witnessed an incomplete Foucaultian transformation.)

By "reforming the soul," Foucault means the use of experts such as social workers, psychologists, and criminologists to analyze and correct individual behavior. How does a prisoner become eligible for parole? The *New York State Parole Handbook* (New York State Division of Parole, 2007) indicates that "parole 'readiness'" depends on the inmate's "good prison behavior," involvement in "prison programming" for education and skills acquisition, and substance abuse counseling, all to "make important strides in self-improvement." After a criminal leaves prison on parole, the newly released prisoner is assigned a field parole officer who is in charge of monitoring the whereabouts of the parolee and guiding his or her reentry into community life. The handbook also indicates that a parole officer must help parolees "develop positive attitudes and behavior" and "encourage participation in programs for self-improvement." Parolees are, in principle, scrupulously supervised by parole officers and sometimes subject to unscheduled visits at work or home. This is all part of what Foucault would consider the modern face of penal practices.

How did the transformation in penal practice, from punishment targeted at the body to reform of the soul, take place? Foucault believes that this transformation is linked to changes in how social control operates more generally, which in turn leads to innovations in penal practices. Foucault uses the following example to illustrate the way modern punishment is organized and its implications for modern social control:

> The prisoners' day will begin at six in the morning in winter and at five in the summer. They will work for nine hours a day throughout the year. Two hours a day will be devoted to instruction. Work and the day will end at nine o'clock in winter and at eight in summer. . . . At the first drum-roll, the prisoners must rise and dress in silence, as the supervisor opens the cell doors. At the second drum-roll, they must be dressed and make their beds. (Foucault, 1977, p. 6)

Foucault's example, extracted from a contemporary prisoners' timetable in France, contrasts strikingly with the way poor Damiens was punished several centuries earlier. Foucault's point, however, is that this sort of regimentation happens in not only prisons but also society at large. Penal practices are indicative of how social control is exercised outside prison walls. Disciplinary techniques are modes of monitoring, examining, and regimenting individuals that are diffused throughout society. Foucault gives many examples of where and how this discipline takes place both in and out of prisons—in the military, in schools, in medical institutions, and so forth. For example, when you first entered school, perhaps even when you entered college, you were probably required to take a series of standardized tests. You were also required to visit your pediatrician for shots and a checkup in which he or she meticulously documented your growth and health. Once in school, you were made to sit in straight, orderly rows (so the teacher could see all students at all times) and then were issued a report card every term. If you were chronically disruptive or inattentive in class, you might have been sent for special testing by experts to determine if you had a learning or behavioral disorder. These are all examples of how you have been subjected to various modes of discipline that monitor, examine, and regiment individuals.

Foucault articulated the diffusion of disciplinary techniques in society through the concept of panopticism. Jeremy Bentham, an English philosopher, devised the panopticon as an architectural design for a prison. The panopticon is a circular building composed of an inner ring and an outer ring. Prisoners'

Panopticon a circular building composed of an inner ring and an outer ring designed to serve as a prison in which the guards, housed in the inner ring, can observe the prisoners without the detainees knowing whether they are being watched.

The Stateville Penitentiary in Illinois was built along the principles of Bentham's panopticon, a model for a prison in which inmates would always be visible.

cells are located in the peripheral outer ring, and large windows compose the front and back of each cell, allowing ample natural light to flood the rooms. The inner ring is a guards' tower, which also has large windows that open onto the windows of prisoners' cells. The cells "induce in the inmate a state of conscious and permanent visibility." The guards can always see the prisoners, regardless of where they are in their cells, but the prisoners do not know when they are being watched (although the visibility of the central tower serves as a reminder that they are always under scrutiny). Foucault asserts that the "power" of the guards is both "visible and unverifiable" (1977).

Foucault uses the panopticon as a metaphor for the general functioning of disciplinary techniques in society. Therefore, when the modern prison system emerged, based on monitoring, examining, and regimenting individual prisoners, there was a "gradual extension of the mechanisms of discipline," and they "spread throughout the whole social body," which led to "the formation of what might be called in general the disciplinary society." Remember all the steps you had to go through to gain entrance to kindergarten? The tests and checkups? And then the report cards, the parent–teacher conferences, the tidy rows of desks? These are the sorts of panoptic (literally, "all-seeing") disciplinary techniques diffused throughout the social body. In Foucault's words, "our society is one not of spectacle, but of surveillance."

The U.S. Criminal Justice System

At various points in history, the U.S. criminal justice system has fluctuated between two approaches to handling criminals: rehabilitation and punishment. Since the 1890s, argues Frank Allen, the rehabilitative ideal has lost most of its significance and appeal because of shifting cultural values among Americans. Despite what Durkheim predicted, the concept of punishment ("lock 'em up and throw away the key") has largely replaced rehabilitation, winning political and popular favor and influencing criminal justice policy (Allen, 1981).

Today we have the highest rates of incarceration than ever before in American history. At the start of 2002, approximately 5.6 million adults at some point had served time in state or federal prison. That's about 2.7 percent of American adults, up from 1.3 percent in 1974, a difference of 3.8 million people (Bonczar 2003). In 2011 and 2012, slightly more people left incarceration

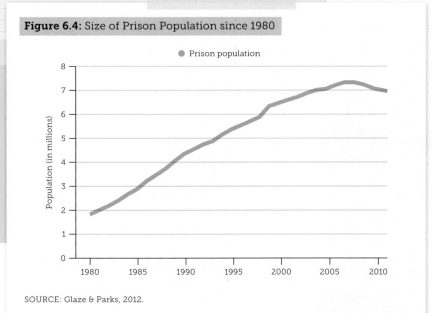

Figure 6.4: Size of Prison Population since 1980

Prison population

Population (in millions)

SOURCE: Glaze & Parks, 2012.

than got locked up, but 1 in 34 Americans is still under correctional supervision (see Figure 6.4). What accounts for the increase? According to the Bureau of Justice Statistics, about two-thirds of the increase occurred as a result of first-incarceration rates, meaning that the system has expanded as a result of arresting first-time offenders, mostly caught in violation of tough new penal codes, such as those expanded in the War on Drugs.

Not all Americans have been affected equally by the tougher laws, however. Among black men, 16.6 percent were current or former prisoners in 2002, compared with 7.7 percent of Hispanic men and 2.6 percent of white men. Among women, a similar pattern holds, although far fewer women are incarcerated (1.7 percent of black women, 0.7 percent of Hispanic women, and 0.3 percent of white women). The lifetime chances of imprisonment for men and women combined are 3.4 percent for whites, 10 percent for Hispanics, and 11.3 percent for blacks. If current incarceration rates don't change, a whopping 32 percent of black males are estimated to serve time in a state or federal prison during their lifetime, compared with 17 percent of Hispanic men and 5.9 percent of white men. These numbers of prisoners are strikingly high for an industrialized democracy, and the United States is the only industrialized nation in the world to use capital punishment (U.S. Department of Justice, 2007).

Similar to imprisonment rates, justice on death row is not color-blind (see Figure 6.5). In 1998 a study of Philadelphia death penalty cases revealed ample evidence of some form of racial discrimination: Either the race of the defendant or the race of the victim came to bear on the outcome of the case

Figure 6.5: Number of Executions and Race of Prisoners Executed, 1976–2012

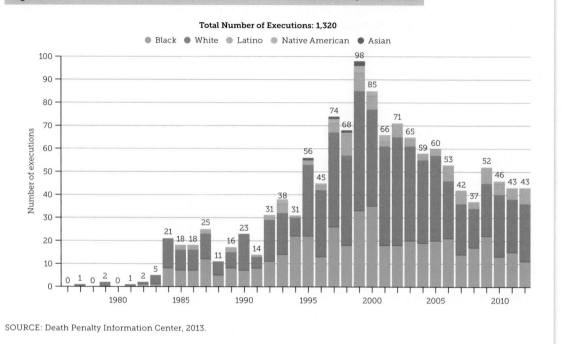

Total Number of Executions: 1,320

● Black ● White ● Latino ● Native American ● Asian

SOURCE: Death Penalty Information Center, 2013.

(Baldus et al., 1998). First, the race of the murder victim matters. For example, in a study of the North Carolina justice system, researchers found that the odds of a murderer receiving a death sentence rose 3.5 times if the victim was white, holding constant other relevant factors (Unah & Boger, 2001). Second and more obviously, the race of the accused matters. Contrary to popular belief about black-on-white violence, interracial murders are fairly rare. As of September 2013, out of 1,347 executions carried out in the United States since 1976 (when the Supreme Court reinstated the death penalty), 273 involved cases of black-on-white homicide, but only 31 involved executions arising from cases of white-on-black murder. One hypothesis would assert that these statistics could result from African Americans committing disproportionately more crime than whites while receiving, on average, appropriate penalties for their criminal behaviors. To make this sort of claim, we would need to have faith in the criminal justice system as a sound entity that generally delivers fair and accurate punishment. However, more than enough data to the contrary exist. Between 1973 and 2009, 138 people were exonerated from death row: Of these, 71 were black, 53 white, and 12 Latino. In 2004 alone, six persons were released from death sentences, some after years behind bars, their careers and families having been permanently altered by the disruption. Many of these exonerations resulted from new DNA evidence. In a sense, the new technology has shed light on the flaws in the system, raising the question: "How many cases were wrongly judged before the deployment of DNA testing?" This evidence of injustice has led to the abolition of the death penalty in Illinois, Connecticut, New Jersey, New York, New Mexico, and Maryland since 2007.

POLICY: Does Prison Work Better as <u>Punishment</u> or <u>Rehab?</u>

With prison overcrowding resulting from our extremely high incarceration rate (see page 224), one of the questions running through criminal justice research is the proper role of time behind bars. Does going to prison give inmates access to services and treatment that makes them better equipped to be productive members of society, thereby reducing the number of crimes they might commit in the future? Is it plausible to think that individuals who are incarcerated may spend their time kicking drug habits, gaining religion, avoiding negative influences in their community, obtaining an education, and emerge less likely to commit crime when they are released?

Or perhaps the very thought of serving hard time works to deter crime? If so, we might expect the strongest deterrent effect to be among those who have already dealt with the harsh realities of prison life. After all, who would want to go back to jail after being released and tasting the freedom that most of us take for granted? This is the principle behind "scared straight" programs for youth who are teetering on the path of righteousness. By showing teenagers in trouble what prison is "really" like, such interventions hope to take any glamorous shine off a life of crime.

But it could also be the case that prison ends up being like "college for criminals"—a chance to network with other convicts, learn new illicit skills, and harden oneself to mainstream social norms, all while missing out on work experience and educational opportunities, and gaining the stigma of having done time. In other words, perhaps prison actually creates crime by increasing recidivism.

At first blush it would seem that prison does indeed breed crime. After all, one of the best predictors of future arrest is past incarceration. However, it could obviously be the case that those criminals sent up the river so to speak

Inmates at San Quentin State Prison in an adult education class. Why do prisons spend taxpayer money to fund educational opportunities for inmates?

are the ones most beyond hope of reform. That is, they would have committed more crimes regardless of whether they went to prison, received probation, or were let off completely. We could, of course, look at offenders who commit the same crime, comparing those who go to prison and those who don't, to see how they fare afterward. But the problem is that there may be subtle differences in the two groups that judges knew about but which we cannot hope to adequately measure from administrative records.

A solution to this problem comes from the fact that some states and localities randomly assign judges to cases. Like anyone else, judges are human beings with certain tendencies. Specifically, some judges are harsher in their sentencing than others. So it's like assigning convicts to a randomized medical treatment: Some get the "treatment" (the harsh judge who sends them to prison) and some get the "placebo" (the more lenient judge who gives them probation). By examining variability in outcomes among convicted criminals based on the type of judge they were assigned (not on their own characteristics), we can identify the effects of incarceration—and, by extension, the effects of the massive investment we've made in the prison system.

As it turns out, for adults, it doesn't make much difference to their probability of committing a future crime (and getting caught) whether or not they go to prison. (This lack of a difference suggests that taxpayers could get roughly the same crime rate but save a bunch of money on prison overhead by sentencing most criminals to house arrest. Of course, for this to work we have to assume that the deterrent effect against first-time offenses is minimal as well.)

For youth, the story is even starker: Across the United States, more than 130,000 juveniles are detained each year, and on any given day 70,000 minors are in formal detention. But as it turns out, locking these kids up makes them less likely to complete high school and more likely to commit crimes as adults (as evidenced from the random assignment to judges). In other words, far from being "scared straight," kids sent to detention are simply prepped for criminal life. Of course, this means that not only is locking kids up expensive, it generates future costs in the form of more crime to deal with when they grow up.

→ CONCLUSION

Training a sociological lens on deviance requires a careful and slow review of not only the immediate causes and effects of deviance but also the broader social forces that undergird and define it. Sometimes, doing so takes us to paradoxical places, such as Emile Durkheim's finding that some degree of crime is healthy for a society, insofar as crime unites the social body by allowing us all to rally against a common enemy. Sometimes, doing so reveals the unintended consequences of labels such as "deviant." And quite often, sociologists study tragedies in order to seek the social answers to violence and death. Sociology does not hope to provide comprehensive accounts of criminal acts or injustice, but it does seek to dig deeper for concrete answers in our social world.

→ PRACTICE

SOCIOLOGY ON THE STREET

Formal and informal social sanctions allow people to coexist with strangers in crowded public spaces. When do people break these sanctions, and how do others enforce sanctions? Watch the Sociology on the Street video to find out more: wwnpag.es/SOS6.

QUESTIONS FOR REVIEW

1. How does Philip Zimbardo's Stanford Prison Experiment help explain the behavior documented at Abu Ghraib prison?

2. Describe two potential roles—as punishment or rehab—that prisons could play in society. What evidence from this chapter suggests that prisons "work" to rehabilitate people? To scare or punish people?

3. Explain the difference between mechanical and organic solidarity. How do deviants hold us together in both types of society?

4. We usually think of suicide as solely the result of an intensely personal decision. What is Émile Durkheim's explanation for suicide? Define egoistic suicide and describe why, according to Durkheim, more Protestants commit suicide than Catholics.

5. A student wants to achieve good grades but is not interested in studying for exams; instead, the student finds various ways to cheat. How does Robert Merton's strain theory explain this behavior, and which "type" does the student exemplify?

6. How does the broken windows theory of deviance support the claim that the definition of *deviant* depends on social context? What happened to social control mechanisms like formal and informal social sanctions in Philip Zimbardo's study involving cars?

7. Why don't criminologists use the crime rate as an indicator of crime trends? What do they use instead, and why?

8. Describe Émile Durkheim's theory of the collective conscience and explain how it is related to punishment. How does Michel Foucault's focus in *Discipline and Punish* (1977) differ from Durkheim's work regarding punishment in premodern and modern societies?

9. Explain how a fraternity house could be considered a total institution.

PARADOX

IT IS THE DEVIANTS AMONG US WHO HOLD SOCIETY TOGETHER.

WATCH THE ANIMATED SHORT ABOUT THE SOCIAL CONTROL AND DEVIANCE PARADOX AT

WWNPAG.ES/PX6

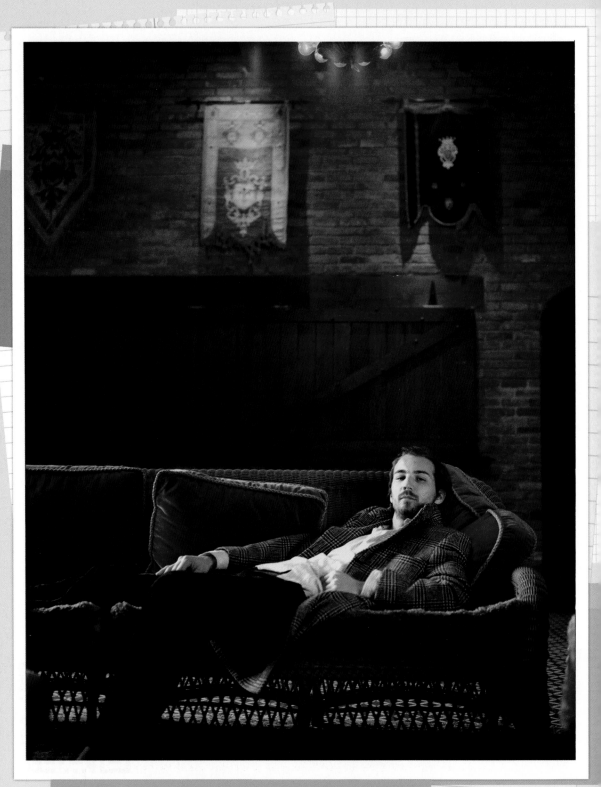

Jamie Johnson, heir to the Johnson & Johnson fortune and director of the 2003 documentary *Born Rich*. To what extent are individuals born into a particular socioeconomic level?

7 Stratification

PARADOX

INEQUALITY IS THE
RESULT OF ABUNDANCE.

Sarah Katz, meet Jeff Rutgers. While it turns out that first names probably don't predict success all that well, last names tell us not only about our
chances for success today, they link us to the successes (or lack thereof) of our
distant ancestors. By analyzing the distribution of last names in the professional directories of lawyers and doctors, economic historian Gregory Clark
is able to assess the degree to which societies demonstrate social mobility or
its opposite, social reproduction (2014).

As it turns out, by being an Ashkenazi Jew (those who populated Europe),
Sarah Katz enjoys about an eight-fold greater chance of being a medical doctor today than does Jessica Smith (Smith being the most common surname
in the United States). Jeff Rutgers, meanwhile, by virtue of being descended
from a male ancestor who attended an Ivy League or similarly old university
sometime between 1650 and 1850, enjoys an approximate three-fold advantage. Also of advantaged pedigree are Hiro Suzuki, by virtue of having a
Japanese surname, and Patricia Winthrop, who shares a name with a rich
family of the 1920s.

Perhaps unsurprisingly, the actor Denzel Washington does not hail from
a family of doctors and lawyers. Washington is among the most common
African American surnames and displays the mark of racial inequality such
that black Washingtons are two-thirds less likely to be represented among the
directory of physicians than they should be based on overall numbers in the
population. Ditto for Annie Begay and John Yazzie, who have the two most
common Native American names and are 94 percent less likely to be doctors
compared with the U.S. average! While racial inequality for these groups is

well known, I'd like to introduce you to Ralph Gagnon, who I bet you didn't know was also disadvantaged even though he is white.

According to Clark, the descendants of New France settlers—that is, the mostly French people who came through Quebec, Canada, and other northern areas—have 40 percent lower odds of becoming a doctor. Though this is, of course, less than the disadvantage of being black, Latino, or Native American, it is also perhaps more surprising because we think of the French as not only white but a relatively high-status group. Indeed, some of our most snooty words come from French (Hors d'oeuvres, anyone?). What's more, people of French origin have been associated with an elite status since the time of the Norman conquest of England in 1066.

More than figuring out what your name says about your postgraduation chances, Clark's analysis is interesting because it challenges some of our most cherished assumptions about social mobility. Through his analysis of names in Sweden, India, medieval Europe, the modern United Kingdom, the United States, Chile, and other societies, Clark finds that the intergenerational correlation in status is much higher than we had previously thought. Typically, sociologists and economists examine the extent to which parent-and-child measures of social class, such as income, are correlated. Zero would mean that it makes no difference whatsoever to your income what your parent earned. One would mean that there was an absolutely rigid caste system where each generation perfectly reflects the success of the prior one. Most societies obviously fall in the middle somewhere. The latest research on income, for example, has busted the myth that the United States, despite being more unequal than most European societies, has higher rates of economic mobility. Indeed, the United States showed a father–son income correlation of .6, among the highest of rich countries.

But Clark's analysis tells us that the U.S. parent–child correlation in "social class" overall is about .84! To explain the discrepancy, he suggests that earlier work focused on one measure of social class, making it look like there's a lot more mobility than there actually is. Take Microsoft founder Bill Gates, Jr., for example. He dropped out of college even though his father graduated from law school, so by education measures Gates, Jr. would seem to be downwardly mobile. But measure income or wealth, of course, and he is upwardly mobile in a huge way. However, Clark's contention is that in some underlying, summary measure of class or status, most of us reflect our parents' social position a lot more than we may care to believe. This, he argues, is the only reason why he would see the effects of what your ancestors did 15 generations ago on what you might be doing for a living now.

Perhaps even more surprising than the fact that the rates of social mobility are higher than we thought they were is that, according to Clark, they don't vary all that much across time and place. Medieval Europe with its feudal system had more or less the same degree of social exchange between classes as does modern Britain today. The unequal, deregulated United States enjoys more or less the same fluidity as social democratic Sweden on the one hand, and on the other hand is not significantly more mobile than India, whose caste system is thought to be the most rigid social structure of all. Even conscious efforts to totally remodel society, including the slaughtering of elites, can only temper slightly the degree of social inheritance. Despite the purges of the Cultural Revolution, massive land redistribution, and complete political transformation, Communist China under Mao Zedong only reduced its intergenerational persistence to about .7, down from .8.

So if we value social mobility, what's a poor old sociologist to do in light of Clark's analysis? Maybe we should all give up and just change our last names to Potros, a Coptic Christian name from Egypt. As it turns out, in the United States at least, Copts are the most successful group of all. One version of Coptic lore claims that they are the true descendants of the pharaohs. If that's right, then maybe the long arm of social history is even stronger than Clark imagined.

Views of Inequality

To answer questions about stratification, we need a conceptual framework through which to view inequality. In the following section, I present three possible frameworks and leave it to you to decide which you think is most appropriate to explain the intersection of various dimensions of stratification. We'll start with the Enlightenment in the eighteenth century and move forward from there.

Jean-Jacques Rousseau

Writing prolifically from 1750 to 1782, Jean-Jacques Rousseau greatly influenced the political ideas of the French Revolution and the development of socialist thought. Seeing humankind as naturally pure and good, Rousseau appealed to biology and human instincts to explain social outcomes. For Rousseau, it is only through the process of building society and repressing this pure natural character that social problems develop. Specifically, Rousseau sees the emergence of private property, the idea that a person has the right to own something, as the primary source of social ills. If we were to strip away the elements of society that result from the institution of private property—the competition, isolation, aggression, and hierarchical organization—only social equality, a condition in which no differences in wealth, power, prestige, or status based on nonnatural bases exist, would remain. According to Rousseau, there are two forms of inequality: physical (or natural), which "consists in a

Jean-Jacques Rousseau

Social equality a condition in which no differences in wealth, power, prestige, or status based on nonnatural conventions exist.

difference of age, health, bodily strength, and the qualities of the mind or of the soul," and social (or political), which

> depends on a kind of conventional inequality and is established or at least authorized by the consent of men. This latter consists of the different privileges which some men enjoy to the prejudice of others, such as that of being more rich, more honored, more powerful, or even in a position to exact obedience. (Rousseau, 1754/2004, p. 15)

Rousseau acknowledges that a certain amount of natural inequality will always exist between people: Someone is always going to be better than someone else at kicking a ball, hunting large game, doing math, or seeing long distances. Some of these inequalities are a simple result of aging, as a basketball player in her twenties will almost certainly have greater physical abilities than a basketball player in her eighties. In contrast, social inequality is a result of privileges and uneven access to resources (i.e., private property) and will eventually lead to social ills. There are only so many resources available in any society and, more broadly, in the world as a whole.

Imagine that all the resources available in a given society are represented in a single pizza, cut into ten slices, and ten hungry people are sitting around the pie. In Rousseau's ideal natural world, where people are inherently good and lack any notion of personal ownership, each individual would get one slice. But in a world where private property is the norm, the division is likely to be significantly less equitable. For whatever reason—maybe some of the ten have more guile, maybe some paid more than others, maybe one person's family owns the pizza parlor—the pie is distributed unevenly among the ten. Rousseau sees such inequality as ultimately detrimental and as a catalyst for social conflict.

Imagine yourself as one of the people who get no pizza, even though there are ten of you and ten slices. Imagine further that you have a hungry family who would certainly have appreciated that slice of pizza. Now imagine watching the person sitting across from you slowly enjoying five steaming slices, one by one. Would this make you jealous? Would it make you spiteful? Would it make you subvert your essentially good nature in trying to steal a slice? Might you even be willing to hurt the pizza hoarder to feed yourself and your family? Might the pizza hoarder then defend his personal property and maybe even hurt you to keep your hands off it? According to Rousseau, he might also buy off the biggest and strongest of those who have no pizza with two slices in order to protect his rights.

The Scottish Enlightenment and Thomas Malthus

Rousseau saw the move away from the pure state of nature as an extremely negative historical development, complaining that "man was born free, and he is everywhere in chains." But thinkers of the later Enlightenment, including Adam Ferguson and John Millar of Scotland and Thomas Malthus of England, saw inequality as good, or at least necessary. These three agreed that inequality arises when private property emerges and that private property emerges when resources can be preserved, because it is only through surpluses that some people are able to conserve and increase their bounty. This leads to the paradox of this chapter: Inequality is a result of surplus.

When individuals or groups in society become more efficient and productive, they can gather, hunt, or grow more than they themselves can consume at a given time. They can then conserve such a surplus, whether that means turning milk into cheese, making berries into preserves, or putting their money into a hedge fund. In whatever way they choose, they can preserve current resources and transform them into assets, a form of wealth that can be stored for the future. (In fact, the word *asset* comes from the French legal expression *aver assetz*, meaning "to have enough.") Whereas previously the incentive might have been to share the wealth when you couldn't store it—to generate reciprocal goodwill for the rainy day when you don't have enough to eat and your neighbor does—now when property can be preserved, the incentive is for individuals to hoard all of it, so that when a rainy day comes along, personal savings are available. Alternatively, if a resource-rich individual decides to distribute surplus wealth, he or she might decide to extract power, promises, and rewards in return for what he or she provides.

For Ferguson and Millar, such social developments resulting from the establishment of private property represent a huge improvement in society, because private property leads to higher degrees of social organization and efficiency: If an individual can preserve and accumulate resources and become more powerful by storing up assets (private property), he or she will have much more incentive to work. Thanks to personal incentives, people won't just slack off after they have accumulated what they need for the day's survival, but will instead work to build up society, and as a by-product they will improve civilization. For the Scottish Enlightenment thinkers, inequality was a prerequisite for social progress, and social progress was a prerequisite for the development of civilization—the greatest goal toward which humankind could strive.

Malthus also had a positive view of inequality, but for a different reason. In 1798, Malthus published an anonymous treatise titled "An Essay on the Principle of Population as It Affects the Future Improvement of Society," arguing that human populations grow geometrically (multiplicatively, like rabbits), while our ability to produce food increases only arithmetically (much more slowly). Simply put, his theory suggests that a rising number of people on the planet will eventually use up all the available resources and bring about mass starvation and conflict. Take the pizza example from above: With ten people and ten slices, the pie could be divided evenly. But what if there were 20 people or 50 people? Or 100 people? As the number of people increases, each person gets less and less, even if the pie is divided evenly. Humankind, Malthus believed, was similarly destined to live in a state of constant near-death misery, as population growth always pushed society to the limits of food availability.

Because of these dire trends, Malthus believed inequality was good, or at least necessary, for avoiding the problem of massive overpopulation and hence starvation. Inequality, from his perspective, kept the population in check. After all, for Malthus, the main problem with the world, especially with England, was the number of people in it, and anything that tended to restrain population growth was supremely good. In this vein, he denounced soup kitchens and early marriages while defending the effects of smallpox, slavery, and child murder (Heilbroner, 1999). Malthus believed that overpopulation would create more and more human misery, and therefore the most logical solution would be to allow the population to thin itself out naturally rather than to exacerbate the problem by reducing the levels of inequality, a measure that would "temporarily" ease the condition of the "masses," thereby causing their numbers to swell even more. Such a condition is today called a Malthusian population trap—a situation in which population growth leads not to abundance but increased poverty.

In an interview for this book, I asked Jeffrey Sachs of the Earth Institute at Columbia University if he thought that Africa might be facing a Malthusian trap as the per capita land available for farming dwindles, and if so, what can be done to get out of the trap. Sachs captured the complexity of the big picture, so I'll let him speak for himself:

> In Africa there's been a partial transition from high mortality to low mortality, from maybe 600 of every 1,000 children dying before their fifth birthday to a situation where it's perhaps around 150 per 1,000 dying. Still remarkably high by global standards, but way down from what it was. But the fertility rates especially in the rural areas remain high—as many as five or six, sometimes even seven per woman. That means rapid population growth. The woman that has six children, [of whom] two die, has on average four children who grow up to adulthood. Two of those will be daughters. Each woman is replacing herself with two daughters in the next generation. That's a doubling of the population from one generation to the next, called a gross population number. That's extraordinary. You can't keep ahead of that in terms of economic development, and certainly not in ecology. So what do you do about that? What do you do to accelerate the reduction of fertility? Save the children. It seems paradoxical. But when the children are staying alive, the families say, "Ah! It's safe to have fewer children. I don't need to have six for insurance. My children will survive."
>
> Make sure the girls stay in school, especially secondary school. A girl who has a chance to go to secondary school will get married several years later. By then she will be more empowered, have a market value in the economy, say, "I'm gonna go out and get a job. I don't want to get married, and also I'm not

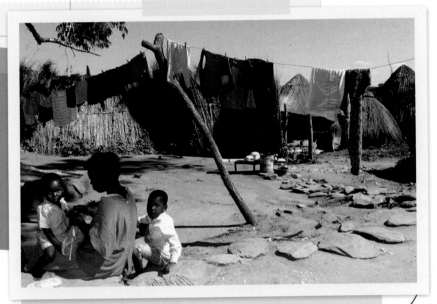

Farmworker Stella Machara and her sons Kudakwachi and Simbaracha in front of their home in Zimbabwe. According to Jeffrey Sachs, why is sub-Saharan Africa stuck in a Malthusian population trap? To see more of the conversation with Sachs, visit **wwnpag.es/SC7b**.

gonna let my father choose to marry me at age twelve," which is how it might be normally. Make sure there are contraceptives available. Family planning is not a freebie. It absolutely requires training, skilled community work, health workers, the physical availability of contraception; and that's more than an impoverished woman, in a patriarchal setting, with lots of children dying in a rural area, is going to somehow find her way to on her own. She may have zero cash. History has shown free availability of family planning and contraceptive services is part of the set of things that are necessary to lower fertility that also includes child survival, girls' education, women's awareness, and community health workers. That can lead to a remarkably accelerated demographic transition, and that's the kind of holistic approach that successful societies have done. (Conley, 2009g)

Georg Wilhelm Friedrich Hegel

A third view of inequality comes from the German philosopher Georg Wilhelm Friedrich Hegel, who viewed history in terms of a master–slave (sometimes called a master–servant) dialectic. The word dialectic means a two-directional relationship—one that goes both ways, like a conversation between two people. One person talks, putting out an idea or thesis. Then the other

Dialectic a two-directional relationship, following a pattern in which an original statement or thesis is countered with an antithesis leading to a conclusion that unites the strengths of the original position and the counterarguments.

responds, pointing out some problems with the thesis or posing a counterposition, an antithesis. Then the original speaker responds, and hopefully the two arrive at a synthetic arrangement constructed from elements of the original position and the strongest counter-points.

In Hegel's master–slave dialectic, the slave is dependent on the master because the master provides food, shelter, and protection. In this way, the slave is akin to a child raised by the master. However, as Hegel observed, the master is also dependent on the slave, who performs the basic duties of survival until the master can no longer function on his own. He doesn't remember how to grow his own food, drive a car, prepare meals, or even get dressed without help. Basically, the master would not be able to function if left to fend for himself. Thus, the master–slave nexus becomes a relationship of mutual dependency.

But Hegel was writing in the early nineteenth century. There really aren't masters and slaves today, are there? In fact, while we think of slavery as a dreadful practice left on the ash heap of the past, researchers of modern human trafficking believe that there are actually more enslaved people now—estimates suggest 27 million people—than there were at the height of the transatlantic slave trade (De Baca, 2011). And, according to the CIA, the United States is no exception to this phenomenon, with forced laborers constituting tens of thousands of entrants to the country each year. Modern human trafficking often involves females who are kept as domestic workers and/or sex workers in cities around the world, but some tomato pickers in Florida and construction workers in Dubai may also be considered part of the modern trade in humans (Ehrenreich & Hochschild, 2004; Estabrook, 2009; Human Rights Watch, 2006).

The path to becoming a slave is often paved with a mixture of deceit and desperation. Poor families in rural areas are perhaps too eager to believe the promises of men traveling through their villages, who offer to find good, safe work for their daughters in the city. Once the girls arrive, they are often raped by these men to "teach" them how to serve clients, given a meager room, watched over to prevent escape, and told they must work to repay the cost of their travel and lodging. Some end up staying this way for life, because the stigma of prostitution is something they cannot bear to take back to their families and they have no other way to make money. In the case of the tomato pickers, the crew bosses who exploit them would simply go out of business

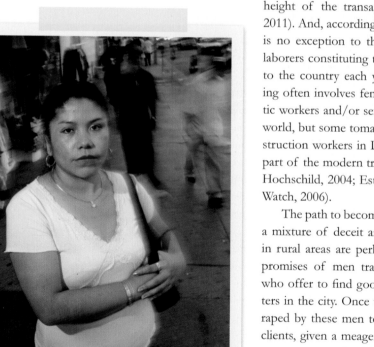

Florencia Molina, a victim of human trafficking, became virtually enslaved at a dressmaking shop on the outskirts of Los Angeles, where she worked up to 17 hours a day, 7 days a week, and lived there, too, without the option of showering or washing her clothes.

if they paid their work forces minimum wage, because 90 percent of the tomatoes grown in America are harvested by underpaid, illegal immigrant workers who risk beatings and deportation if they try to leave (Comisi, 2011). In this sense, the exploited people need their abusers for lodging and protection from the authorities, and the abusers need their workforces to remain captive to ensure the continuation of their way of life.

Hegel views history as marching steadily forward from a situation of few masters and many servants or slaves—such as monarchies and empires, not to mention the entire feudal system—to a society with more and more free men and women, a situation of democracy and equality. His was an optimistic view of history, to say the least. According to Hegel, notions of inequality are constantly evolving in a larger historical arc. He saw this as a trajectory that would eventually lead to equality for all (or very nearly all). We will see later that many sociologists have had a bone or two to pick with this position, as well as with those laid out by Rousseau, Ferguson, Millar, and Malthus.

Standards of Equality

Assuming for the moment that we do value equality in society, what kind of equality do we want? There are different ideologies or belief systems regarding equality, so it's important to recognize that when various groups use the rhetoric of equality, particularly in the political sphere, they may be talking past each other or jostling for advantage. What did Thomas Jefferson mean when he proclaimed in the Declaration of Independence that "all men are created equal"? And what exactly do we mean by equality in the twenty-first century?

Equality of Opportunity

One standard of equality is termed equality of opportunity. Let's think of society as a game of Monopoly, in which all of the players try to maximize their holdings of wealth (the game's houses and hotels) and their income (the rent collected from other players who land on built-up properties after an unfortunate roll of the dice). In this game, the person with the most money in the end is the winner. Monopoly follows the rules of equality of opportunity. Sure, one player may wind up flat broke and another player may control 95 percent of the wealth, but the rules were fair, right? Everyone had an equal chance at the start. Assuming nobody cheated, any differences were a result of luck (the dice) and skill (the players' choices). The same goes for society. The mere existence of inequality is not at issue here. Some people have more wealth and income than others, and some people enjoy greater social prestige or power than others, but the rules of the game are still fair. We all go into the game of society, as

Equality of opportunity the idea that everyone has an equal chance to achieve wealth, social prestige, and power because the rules of the game, so to speak, are the same for everyone.

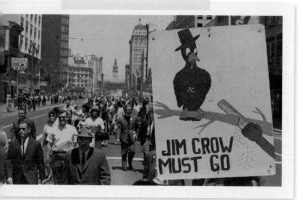

Civil rights activists in San Francisco demonstrate against Jim Crow laws in 1964. Why did the demand for equal opportunity resonate with most Americans?

we do into a game of Monopoly, knowing the rules, and therefore any existing inequality is fair as long as everyone plays by the rules.

This is the standard model for what equality means in a bourgeois society, such as modern capitalist society. Although the word *bourgeois* is often used pejoratively, here I mean it as a neutral description—a society of commerce in which the maximization of profit is the primary business incentive. Almost all modern capitalist societies purport to follow an ideology of equal opportunity. The equal opportunity ideology was adopted by civil rights activists in the 1960s, who argued that the rules were unfair. For instance, the segregation of public spaces and other

Bourgeois society a society of commerce (modern capitalist society, for example) in which the maximization of profit is the primary business incentive.

Jim Crow laws (a rigid set of antiblack statutes that relegated African Americans to the status of second-class citizens through educational, economic, and political exclusion) were seen as incompatible with the bourgeois notion of fairness or equality of opportunity.

The rallying cry for equality of opportunity resonates with our overall capitalist ideology. Unequal opportunity clearly stifles meritocracy, a system in which advancement is based on individual achievement or ability. For example, if you were to have a heart transplant, would you not want the most knowledgeable heart surgeon with the most dexterous hands? Or would you settle for the one born to rich parents who finagled their child's way into medical school? Under a system of equal opportunity, everyone who is willing can compete to become a heart surgeon, and eventually the most talented will rise to fill the most demanding, important positions.

Equality of Condition

Equality of condition the idea that everyone should have an equal starting point.

A second standard of equality is a bit more progressive and is termed equality of condition. Going back to our Monopoly analogy, imagine if at the beginning of the game, two players started out with an extra $5,000 and already owned hotels on Boardwalk and Park Place, and Pennsylvania and North Carolina Avenues, respectively, while the other two players started out with a $5,000 deficit and owned no property. Some would argue that the rules of the game need to be altered in order to compensate for inequalities in the relative starting positions. This is the ideology behind equality of condition. An example of this ideology is affirmative action, which involves preferential selection to increase the representation of women and minorities in areas of employment, education, and business from which they have historically been excluded (for a more thorough discussion, see Chapters 8 and 9). Affirmative action is when a person or group in a gatekeeper position, such as a college admissions office or

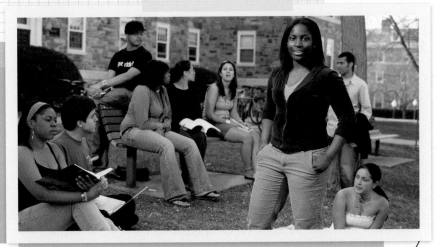

Middlebury College student Laura Blackman received help from the Posse Foundation, which recruits inner-city kids for elite colleges. How are affirmative action policies an example of equality of condition?

the human resources department in charge of hiring new workers, actively selects some applicants who haven't faced an even playing field, often due to racism or sexism in society. Sometimes these policies can enhance efficiency if they result in fairer competition; other times they may result in a trade-off between efficiency and equality in favor of the latter. We may accept that certain groups with slightly lower SAT scores are admitted to colleges because they faced much greater obstacles to attain those SAT scores than other groups of test takers who enjoyed more advantages. Such "social engineering" may be based on race, class, gender, or any other social sorting category, as long as the proponents can make a justifiable claim that the existing playing field is tilted against them.

Equality of Outcome

The final and most radical (or rather most antibourgeois and anticapitalist) form of equality is equality of outcome, the position that each Monopoly player should end up with the same amount regardless of the fairness of the "game." This admittedly would make for a dull round of Monopoly: In this scenario, the players on Baltic Avenue would make just as much as those on Boardwalk, and some mechanism in the game—say, a central banker or all the players pooling their resources—would ensure game play that lived up to Karl Marx's maxim in the *Critique of the Gotha Programme* (1890–91/1999), "From each according to his ability, to each according to his needs." This standard is concerned less with the rules of the game than with the distribution of resources; it is essentially a Marxist (or Communist) ideology. Like Rousseau's

Equality of outcome the idea that each player must end up with the same amount regardless of the fairness of the "game."

idea that there will always be physical inequalities—some will be better at math, others will be better at physical work, and so on—equality of outcome is the idea is that everyone contributes to society and to the economy according to what they do best. For instance, someone who is naturally gifted at math might become an engineer or a mathematician, whereas someone better at physical work might build infrastructure such as roads and bridges. A centrally organized society calls on its citizens to contribute to the best of their ability, yet everyone receives the same rewards. The median income is everyone's income regardless of occupation or position.

Under equality of outcome, or equality of result, the individual incentives touted by the Scottish Enlightenment thinkers are eliminated. Nobody earns more power, prestige, and wealth by working harder. In this system, the only incentive is altruistic; you are giving to society for the sake of its progress and not merely for your own betterment (although arguably, it may be in the self-interest of the individual to see society progress as a whole). Bill Gates would probably have to give up his $120.5 million estate and take a big step down, whereas a single mother working two jobs in order to provide food, shelter, and day care for her children is likely to take a bit of a step up. She might even end up being Bill Gates's neighbor. Critics worry that without the selfish incentives of capitalism, all progress would halt, and sloth might take over. Unless an oppressive rule emanated from some central agency, collective endeavors would

be doomed to failure on account of the free rider problem, the notion that when more than one person is responsible for getting something done, the incentive is for each individual to shirk responsibility and hope others will pull the extra weight. (You might have encountered this sort of situation while collaborating on group projects for school.) Critics of this system argue that even when there is a relatively strong central planning agency to assign each worker a task and enforce productivity, such an administrative mechanism cannot make decisions and allocate resources as efficiently as a more free-market approach does.

Forms of Stratification

Thus far we have discussed standards of equality and inequality only in general terms, but there are many dimensions and forms by which this equality or inequality can emerge in a given society. For example, a society can be stratified based on age. In many tribes, for instance, age determines the social prestige and honor that the group accords an individual. (By contrast, some argue that in the youth-obsessed culture of the United States, age is a source of dishonor.) Those younger than you would place great weight on your words and in some cases treat them as commands. Furthermore, birth order can be the basis of inequality. Such a system was prevalent as late as the nineteenth century in European society, where the first-born male typically inherited the family estate; however, in certain parts of the world, birth order still plays a role in resource distribution. Gender or race and ethnicity also can be the predominant forms social stratification takes. Ultimately, many dimensions exist within which inequality can emerge, and often these dimensions overlap significantly.

Stratified societies are those where human groups within them are ranked hierarchically into strata, along one or more social dimensions. Many sociologists and philosophers believe that there are four ideal types of social stratification—estate system, caste system, class system, and status hierarchy system—although all societies have some combinations of these forms and no type ever occurs in its pure form. In addition to these, some sociologists propose a fifth ideal type, an elite–mass dichotomy. Each system has its own ideology that attempts to legitimate the inequality within it.

In Western Australia, Aboriginal elder Brandy Tjungurrayi wears a pencil through his nose—a sign of his senior status.

Estate System

The first ideal type of social stratification is the estate system. Primarily found in feudal Europe from the medieval era through the eighteenth century, and in the American South before the Civil War, social stratification in estate systems has a political basis. That is, laws are written in a language in which rights and duties separate individuals and distribute power unequally. For example, in the antebellum American South, many states required land ownership for voting privileges. Europe also historically restricted voting rights to landowners. Before reforms, political participation depended on the social group (the estate) to which you belonged. There was limited mobility among the three general estates—the clergy, the nobility, and the commoners (the commoners were typically further divided into peasants and city dwellers)—and each group enjoyed certain rights, privileges, and duties. In certain eras, it was possible for a rich commoner to buy a title and become a member of the nobility. And often, one son or daughter of a noble family would join the clergy and become part of that estate. Therefore, there was some mobility, but social reproduction—you are what your parents were and what your children will be—generally prevailed. (We'll examine the concept of social mobility more closely below.)

Estate system a politically based system of stratification characterized by limited social mobility.

Caste System

Another type of stratification is a caste system. As opposed to having a political basis, the caste system is religious in nature. That is, caste societies are stratified on the basis of hereditary notions of religious and theological purity.

Caste system a religion-based system of stratification characterized by no social mobility.

Today the caste system is primarily found in South Asia. For instance, in India the historical legacy of the caste system, also known as the *varna* system, still dominates. The *varna* system is composed of four main castes: Brahmin, Kshatriya, Vaishya, and Shudra (the Dalits or "untouchables" are a lower order of the Shudra). These divisions correspond loosely to priests, warriors, traders, and workers, respectively. Over the past 5,000 years, however, the caste system in India has evolved into a complex matrix of thousands of subcastes. Each of the major castes is allowed to engage in certain ritual practices from which the others, for better or worse, are excluded. For instance, the Dalits (or "untouchables") are excluded from the performance of *any* rituals that confer purity, which places them at the bottom of the caste system and typically leaves them with occupations seen as impure, such as the cremation of corpses or disposal of sewage.

The castes in India have historically been endogamous—communities in which members generally marry within the group. Although the caste system there remains very powerful at many levels, intermarriage between castes (or exogamy) has begun to erode the system. Because of the resulting problems with classifying children, the caste system would simply fall apart if high levels of exogamy occurred. The strict divisions would begin to look more like a spectrum and would eventually fade away. An additional method of securing the caste hierarchy is *social closure* within Indian society. This means that there has been little to no individual mobility within the caste ranks. If you are born an untouchable, you remain an untouchable, you marry an untouchable, your children are untouchables, and you die an untouchable.

Although there is little to no individual mobility in caste systems, an entire caste can leapfrog over another and obtain a higher position in the hierarchy. This process is called sanskritization. Sometimes such an attempt works, and sometimes it doesn't. During the colonial period, when the British governed South Asia, the Vaishya, the second-lowest caste in Pakistan, adopted Christianity, the religion of the British, in an attempt to jump ahead in the hierarchy. Their attempt was not successful. However, by becoming Christian, the Vaishya caste did enjoy a unique fate after the partition of Pakistan from India. Pakistan became a Muslim state in which Islamic law (the shar'ia) was enforced. One of the rules of the shar'ia is that Muslims are forbidden from imbibing or serving alcohol (or any mind-altering substances). So who got the jobs serving foreigners in the hotel bars? The Vaishya, who were now Christian. Their efforts to jump ahead in the caste system may have failed, but they ended up with fairly decent jobs in a relatively impoverished country.

Islamic law prohibits Muslims from serving or imbibing alcohol, so the Christian Vaishya handle beer distribution in Pakistan. This employee inspects a bottle of vodka at the Murree Brewery Company, Pakistan's oldest public company and only brewery.

Class System

A third type of stratification is the class system, an economically based hierarchical system characterized by cohesive, oppositional groups and somewhat loose social mobility. Class means different things to different people, and there is no consensus among sociologists as to the term's precise definition. For instance, some might define class primarily in terms of money, whereas others see it as a function of culture or taste. Some people barely even notice it (consciously at least), whereas others feel its powerful effects in their daily lives. So what is class? Is it related to lifestyle? Consumption patterns? Interests? Attitudes? Or is it just another pecking order similar to the caste system? Some controversy has existed about whether class is a real category or a category that exists in name only. As in the caste and estate systems, the lines that separate class categories in theory should be clearly demarcated, but there have been problems in drawing boundaries around class categories—for instance, upper class, middle class, and so on. Some scholars have even argued that class should be abandoned as a sociological concept altogether. So let's try to clear up some of the misconceptions.

Unlike other systems, a class system implies an economic basis for the fundamental cleavages in society. That is, class is related to position in the economic market. Notions of class in sociological analysis are heavily influenced by two theorists, Karl Marx and Max Weber. In Marxist sociological analyses, every mode of production—from subsistence farming to small-scale cottage industries to modern factory production to the open-source information economy—has its own unique social relations of production, basically the rules of the game for various players in the process. Who controls the use of capital and natural resources? How are the tasks of making and distributing products divided up and allocated? And how are participants compensated for their roles? In tips? Hourly wages? In-kind goods? Profit or rent? Thus, to talk about class in this Marxist language is to place an individual into a particular group that has a particular set of interests that often stand opposite to those of another group. For example, workers want higher wages; employers (specifically, capitalists) wish to depress wages, which come largely out of profits.

In this sense, class is a relational concept. That is, one can't gain information about a person's class by simply looking at his or her income (as in, "That person made only $13,000 last year; therefore, she is working class"). Class identity, in fact, does not correspond to an individual at all but rather to a role. A person

Class system an economically based hierarchical system characterized by cohesive, oppositional groups and somewhat loose social mobility.

Why is the concept of class problematic? For example, Oseola McCarty, of Hattiesburg, Mississippi, worked as a washerwoman and had only a sixth-grade education. However, she donated $150,000 to the University of Southern Mississippi from her savings.

may pull in a six-figure salary, but as long as he owns no capital (that is, stock or other forms of firm ownership) and earns his salary by selling his labor to someone else, he finds himself in the same category as the lowest-paid wage laborer and antagonistic to "owners," who may net a lot less income than he does. And an individual may, over the course of her career, change class positions as that career evolves. The class positions, the roles with respect to the production process, do not change, however.

Indeed for Marx, it all boils down to two antagonistic classes in a fully mature capitalist society: the employing class (the bourgeoisie or capitalist class) and the working class (the proletariat). The proletariat sells its labor to the bourgeoisie in order to receive wages and thereby survive. But, according to Marx, the bourgeoisie extract surplus value from the proletariat, even when a few of the proletarians make high incomes. As this is a fixed-pie or zero-sum view of economic production, an exploitative and hence inherently conflict-ridden relationship exists between the two classes. The central aspect of Marxist class analysis is this exploitation—capitalists taking more of the value of the work of laborers than they repay in wages.

Because the two-class model does not appear to adequately describe the social world as we find it in most modern capitalist economies, more recent Marxist theorists such as Erik Olin Wright have elaborated this basic model with the concept of contradictory class locations. Wright suggests that people can occupy locations in the class structure that fall between the two "pure" classes. For instance, managers might be perceived as both working class and capitalist class: They are part of the working class insofar as they sell their labor to capitalists in order to live (and don't own the means of production), yet they are in the capitalist class insofar as they control (or dominate) workers within the production process. Conversely, the petit bourgeoisie, a group including professionals, craftsmen, and other self-employed individuals or small-business owners, according to Wright, occupy a capitalist position in that they own capital in the form of businesses, but they aren't fully capitalist because they don't control other people's labor. The issue of class definition could also be further complicated by multiple class locations (multiple jobs), mediated class locations (the impact of relationships with family members, such as spouses, who are in different class locations), and temporally distinct class locations (for instance, many corporations require that all their managers spend a couple of years as a shop floor worker before becoming a manager). Marxists use these distinctions to analyze how various classes rise and fall under the capitalist system.

Max Weber takes an alternative view of class. He argues that a class is a group that has as its basis the common life chances or opportunities available to it in the marketplace. In other words, what distinguishes members of a class is that they have similar value in the commercial marketplace in terms of selling their own property and labor. Thus, for Weber, property and lack of property are the basic categories for all class situations. If you have just graduated from law school, you may have no current income or wealth, but you enjoy a great

Proletariat the working class.

Bourgeoisie the capitalist class.

Contradictory class locations the idea that people can occupy locations in the class structure that fall between the two "pure" classes.

deal of "human capital" (skills and certification) to sell in the labor market, so you would clearly be in a different class from someone with little education but a similar current economic profile. But if you owned a company that you inherited, for instance, you would belong to yet another (higher) class. Weber's paradigm is distinct from the Marxist class framework, where the basic framework is antagonistic and exploitative; rather, for Weber, class is gradated, not relational. Put another way, your class as a newly minted attorney does not affect or determine my class as an accountant, computer programmer, or day laborer.

Status Hierarchy System

The fourth type of stratification system, a status hierarchy system, has its basis in social prestige, not in political, religious, or economic factors. In classical sociology, Weber contributed most heavily to the modern-day sociologist's understanding of status. For Weber, status groups are communities united by either a positive or negative social estimation of their honor. Put more simply, status is determined by what society as a whole thinks of the particular lifestyle of the community to which you belong. In this sense, those with and without property can belong to the same status group if they are seen to live the same lifestyle. Let's use the example of professors. There are certain things that professors typically do in common: They attend conferences to discuss scholarly issues, they teach college courses, and they tend to read a lot. This leads society as a whole to confer a certain status on professors, without placing the sole focus on income, which can vary widely among professors. Likewise, various individuals in a society who earn similar incomes may not have much in common in terms of lifestyles (and therefore status).

Although a status group can be defined by something other than occupation, such as a claim to a specific lifestyle of leisure (skate punks) or membership in an exclusive organization that defines one's identity (the Daughters of the American Revolution), much work by sociologists has been related to occupational status. After all, work is one of the most centrally defining aspects of our lifestyle. In the 1960s, for example, Peter M. Blau and Otis Dudley Duncan created the Index of Occupational Status by polling the general public about the prestige of certain occupations (1967; an abbreviated version based on more recent data appears in Table 7.1). Many folks have since refined this rank ordering, but the story is much the same. What is particularly interesting is that the hierarchy is largely stable over time and across place. Occasionally, new jobs need to be slotted in (there were no Web designers in the 1960s), but they generally are slotted in fairly predictable ways based on the status of similar occupations and do not create much upheaval within the overall rank ordering. The scores on the Duncan scale (as it is known) range from 0 to 96, with 0 being the least prestigious and 96 the most prestigious.

Status hierarchy system a system of stratification based on social prestige.

Table 7.1: The Relative Social Prestige of Selected U.S. Occupations

| OCCUPATION | Blue-Collar Occupation | | | | OCCUPATION | Blue-Collar Occupation | | | |
| | White-Collar Occupation | | | | | White-Collar Occupation | | | |
	Prestige Score		↓	↓		Prestige Score		↓	↓
Physician/surgeon	86	X			Welder	41			X
Lawyer	74	X			Data entry operator	41	X		
Architect	72	X			Farmer/rancher	40			X
Dentist	72	X			Carpenter	39			X
Member of the clergy	68	X			File clerk	36	X		
Reistered nurse	66	X			Child-care worker	35			X
Secondary-school teacher	66	X			Auto body repairperson	32			X
Veterinarian	62	X			Retail salesperson	31	X		
Sociologist	61	X			Truck driver	31			X
Police officer	58		X		Aircraft mechanic	31			X
Actor	55	X			Cashier	30	X		
Firefighter	53		X		Taxi driver/chauffeur	29			X
Realtor	48	X			Waiter/waitress	28			X
Machinist	47		X		Bartender	25			X
Musician/singer	47	X			Door-to-door salesperson	23			X
Construction equipment operator	46		X		Janitor	22			X

SOURCE: Frederick, 2010.

Table 7.1 shows that occupations with very different characteristics may have similar prestige scores. For instance, college presidents are given the same occupational status as instructors despite the huge salary discrepancy between the two. Blau and Duncan observed that five-sixths (just over 83 percent) of the explanation for people's status ratings of occupations was attributed to the education necessary for the position and not the income corresponding to that position.

Although we have emphasized that status may have its basis in occupation, it can also be formed through consumption and lifestyle, though these factors are often closely linked. This means that there should be a tendency for status differences between groups to be finely gradated and not relational: Fundamentally antagonistic status groups such as capitalists and laborers or owners and renters do not exist. Rather, people exist along a status ladder, so to speak, on which there is a lot of social mobility. Often, individuals seek to assert their status or increase their status not just through their occupation but also through their consumption, memberships, and other aspects of how they live. They might try to generate social prestige by driving a fancy car, living in a gated community, wearing stylish clothes, or using a certain kind of language.

Elite–Mass Dichotomy System

The final stratification system is the elite–mass dichotomy system, with a governing elite, a few leaders who broadly hold the power in society. Vilfredo Pareto, in *The Mind and Society* (1935/1983), took a positive view of elite–mass dichotomies, whereas C. Wright Mills saw much to dislike in such systems. For Pareto, when a select few elite leaders hold power—as long as the elites are the most able individuals and know what they are doing—the masses are all the better for it. This imbalance, where a small number of people (say 20 percent) cause a disproportionately large effect (more like 80 percent), has come to be known as the Pareto Principle or the 80/20 rule. The basis for Pareto's argument is that individuals are unequal physically, intellectually, and morally. He suggests that those who are the most capable in particular groups and societies should lead. In this way, Pareto believes in a meritocracy, a society where status and mobility are based on individual attributes, ability, and achievement. Pareto opposed caste systems of stratification that create systematic inequality on the basis of birth into a specific group. He criticized societies based on strict military, religious, and aristocratic stratification, arguing that these systems naturally tend to collapse. Concerning such systems, he argues that aristocracies do not last, and that, in fact, history is a "graveyard of aristocracies" (Pareto & Finer, 1966).

Along these lines, the ideal governing elite for Pareto is a combination of foxes and lions—that is, individuals who are cunning, unscrupulous, and innovative along with individuals who are purposeful and decisive, using action and force. This applies not only to the political realm but also to the economic realm, and the masses will be better off for it. The whole system works over time, in Pareto's view, when there is enough opportunity and social mobility to ensure that the most talented individuals end up in the elite and that it does not become a rusty aristocracy.

Mills takes a much more negative view of the elite–mass dichotomy, arguing that it is neither natural nor beneficial for society. In Mills's view, the elite do not govern the way Pareto claims they do. Mills argues in *The Power Elite* (1956/2000) that there are three major institutional forces in modern American society where the power of decision making has become centralized: *economic institutions* (with a few hundred giant corporations holding the keys to economic decisions), the *political order* (the increasing concentration of power in the federal government and away from the states and localities, leading to a centralized executive establishment that affects every cranny of society), and the *military order* (the largest and most expensive feature of government). According to Mills, "families and churches and schools adapt to modern life; governments and armies and corporations shape it; and, as they do so, they turn these lesser institutions into means for their ends." The elite for Mills are simply those who have most of what there is to possess: money, power, and prestige. But they would not have the most were it not for their positions within society's

Elite–mass dichotomy system a system of stratification that has a governing elite, a few leaders who broadly hold power in society.

Meritocracy a society where status and mobility are based on individual attributes, ability, and achievement.

How does Timothy Geithner embody C. Wright Mills's definition of a power elite?

great institutions. Whereas Pareto views elite status as the reward for the talent that helped certain individuals rise through the ranks of society, Mills sees the unequal power and rewards as determining the positions. And whereas Pareto sees a benefit in having power centralized in a large, otherwise ungovernable society, Mills warns of the dangers. For Mills, such a system hurts democracy by consolidating the power to make major decisions into the hands (and interests) of the few.

The power elite is further stratified for Mills; at the inner core of the power elite are those individuals who interchange commanding roles at the top of one dominant institutional order with those in another. In Mills's view, as the interactions among the big three power elites increase, so does the interchange of personnel among them. For example, after serving as President Barack Obama's budget director, Peter Orszag took a top management position at Citigroup, a firm that benefited substantially from the government bailout after the 2008 financial crisis. Who replaced him in the White House? Jacob Lew, who was budget director under President Bill Clinton and later worked for Citigroup himself. Likewise, back in 1961, Robert McNamara left the presidency of Ford Motor Company to serve as secretary of defense under President John F. Kennedy. The list of people who have gone through the revolving doors of power goes on. This is of central importance to Mills, because as the elite increasingly assume positions in one another's domains, the coordination among the elite becomes more and more entrenched.

The inner core also includes the professional go-betweens of economic, political, and military affairs. These include individuals at powerful legal firms and financial institutions, such as corporate lawyers and investment bankers. The outer fringes of the power elite, which change more readily than the core, are individuals who count in the decisions that affect all of us but who don't actually make those decisions.

Let's take, for example, the business sector in America. Although the White House asserted that corrupt businesses such as Enron and WorldCom were simply isolated cases of "bad apples," this assertion becomes suspect if we analyze the close personal networks and overlap of board members within the American business elite. For instance, more than 80 percent of the 1,000 largest corporations shared at least one director with another large company, and on average any two of the corporations were connected by fewer than four degrees of separation (Davis, 2003). Wall Street is particularly densely connected. Most troubling is the fact that many U.S. Treasury secretaries have come from a single firm: the investment bank Goldman Sachs. As a result of these networks, which Mills both saw and predicted, decisions by various

Income versus Wealth

Most people, when they consider economic status, think of **income**: money received by a person for work, from transfers (gifts, inheritances, or government assistance), or from returns on investments. Recent trends in earnings in the United States suggest that there is an increasing divergence or inequality between the bulk of the people and the rich, but especially between the super-rich and the merely rich. For instance, from 1950 to 1970, for every dollar earned by the bottom 90 percent of the American population, those in the top 0.01 percent earned an additional $162. If that sounds like a big distinction, that's nothing compared with more recent data. Between 1990 and 2002, for every dollar earned by those in the bottom 90 percent, each taxpayer at the top (and this would include Bill Gates) took home $18,000 (Johnston, 2005).

A recent trend in sociological analysis, however, is to analyze stratification in terms of wealth ownership. What is **wealth** in relation to income? Wealth is a family's or individual's net worth (total assets minus total debts). For the majority of American families, assets include homes, cars, other real estate, and business assets, along with financial forms of wealth such as stocks, bonds, and mutual funds. Put simply, wealth is everything you own minus debts such as mortgages on homes, credit card debt, and, as most of you will probably have, debt from student loans. One way to think about the difference between income and wealth is to imagine income as a stream or river of money flowing through a family's hands. Wealth, by contrast, is a pool of collected resources that can be drawn on at specific times, a financial reservoir.

companies become increasingly similar. Many studies have suggested that these elite networks spread practices, principles, and information that account for some of the surprising conformity in approaches to corporate governance and ethics. Rather than "a few bad apples," a better analogy is perhaps a brush fire, where morals, practices, and decisions spread easily across corporate America—especially when like-minded people hold power in government agencies that are meant to monitor business practices. For example, the response to the 2008 financial crisis was evidently mapped out in a room with a dozen or so top bankers and the president of the New York Federal Reserve, Tim Geithner, who later became Treasury secretary in the Obama administration.

Again, because the stratification systems discussed above are all ideal types, these systems are not mutually exclusive. That is, they can overlap in a given society and almost always do, and it would be highly unlikely to find a modern society that is stratified by only one of the systems.

How Is America Stratified Today?

Socioeconomic status an individual's position in a stratified social order.

Sociologists often use the phrase socioeconomic status to describe an individual's position in a stratified social order. When sociologists talk about socioeconomic status, they are referring to any measure that attempts to classify groups, individuals, families, or households in terms of indicators such as occupation, income, wealth, and education. Although the boundaries between socioeconomic categories are not sharply defined, the lay public generally divides society into the upper class, the middle class, the working class, and the poor. Because these are common terms, we need to take them seriously, even if they are not of scientific origin and lack sufficient rigor.

Income money received by a person for work, from transfers (gifts, inheritances, or government assistance), or from returns on investments.

Wealth a family's or individual's net worth (that is, total assets minus total debts).

The Upper Class

Upper class a term for the economic elite.

Generally, the upper class refers to the group of individuals at the top of the socioeconomic food chain. In practice, however, the term is used to describe diverse and complex concepts. Historically, the upper class was often distinguished by not having to work. (The economist and social critic Thorstein Veblen dubbed this group the leisure class.) Its members were able to maintain their lifestyle by collecting rent and/or other investment returns. They were the aristocracy, the wealthy, the elite, the landowners. The only way to join this sphere was by birth or (occasionally) marriage. The upper class was the basis for Marx's capitalist class.

In the United States, "upper class" is associated with income, wealth, power, and prestige. According to some sources, the primary distinguishing characteristic of upper-class individuals is their source of income—generally more from returns on investments rather than wages. Although estimates vary, approximately 1 percent of the U.S. population is considered to fall in this stratum (Figure 7.1). Over the decade leading up through 2008, this group saw its income rise 18 percent, while the average American worker experienced stagnant wages (Saez, 2010). By 2009, the top 1 percent enjoyed a net worth that was 225 times greater than that of the median American family—the highest ratio ever recorded (Allegretto, 2011). In 2010, CEO salaries averaged 263 times that of the average American worker (Anderson et al., 2010). At the same time, in 2010 the nation saw its highest poverty rate since 1993 (U.S. Census Bureau, 2011a). In the period between 2009 and 2012, the top 1 percent of Americans saw their income grow by 31.4 percent, but the income of all other Americans barely grew at all, increasing just 0.4 percent (Saez, 2013). Over and above income levels, the upper class is also distinguished by prestige and power, which can be used to promote personal agendas and influence everything from political decisions to consumer trends. This is of particular importance because, as noted above, members of the upper class often wear many hats. As Dennis

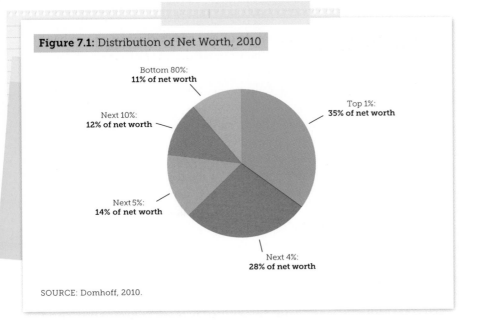

Figure 7.1: Distribution of Net Worth, 2010

Bottom 80%:
11% of net worth

Next 10%:
12% of net worth

Next 5%:
14% of net worth

Next 4%:
28% of net worth

Top 1%:
35% of net worth

SOURCE: Domhoff, 2010.

Gilbert states in *The American Class Structure in an Age of Growing Inequality* (1998),

> The members of the tiny capitalist class at the top of the hierarchy have an influence on economy and society far beyond their numbers. They make investment decisions that open or close employment opportunities for millions of others. They contribute money to political parties, and they often own media enterprises that allow them influence over the thinking of other classes. (p. 286)

Recently we have seen how top bankers' decisions to invest in risky mortgage practices have decimated the net worth of those—mostly in the middle and working classes—who have lost their homes (and home equity) to foreclosure.

The Middle Class

Although those in the upper class have very real influence and control, the effects of this are sometimes limited in the public perception. In the 2007 article "The American People: Social Classes" published in the online magazine *Life in the USA* (a "complete guide to American life for Immigrants and Americans"), Elliot Essman speaks for much of the mainstream media when he asserts that the implications of such power are not far-reaching in our daily lives. "The very rich control corporations and have some political power, but the lifestyle and values of the very wealthy do not have much impact on the country in general," he states. "America is a middle class nation."

The United States is often thought of as a middle-class nation—so much so that depending on how the question is phrased, almost 90 percent of Americans have self-identified with this stratum. That said, there is no consensus on what the term middle class really means. Sociologists, economists, policy makers, think tank analysts, and even the public at large all work with different operating assumptions about the term. The categories become particularly blurry when we attempt to separate the middle class from the working class (or "working families," to use the political campaign euphemism).

So what is middle class? If you look up the term in various dictionaries, you'll encounter myriad definitions. Some refer explicitly to position (that is, below upper class, above lower class); others speak to shared vocational characteristics and values. Still others mention principles. One of the most interesting comes from *Merriam-Webster's Collegiate Dictionary,* which indicates that the middle class is "characterized by a high material standard of living, sexual morality, and respect for property."

The Middle Class and Working Class: Expansion and Retrenchment In the United States, the middle class has historically been composed of white-collar workers (office workers), and the working class composed of those individuals who work manually (using their hands or bodies). However, this distinction eroded with two trends. First, the post–World War II boom led to the enrichment of many manual workers. In those days, most working-class whites, ranging from factory workers to firemen to plumbers, were able to buy their own homes, afford college for their children, and retire comfortably. The working class became the newly expanded middle class.

From the post–World War II era of the late 1940s through the oil crisis of 1973, this middle class was a large and fairly stable group, maintained by corporate social norms emphasizing equality in pay and salary increases (Krugman, 2005). From 1947 through 1979, the average salary increase was fairly stable across all household income levels—in fact, the lowest-earning 20 percent of households showed the highest average earnings increase, 116 percent.

A second, countervailing trend has also eroded the traditional manual–nonmanual distinction between the working and middle classes: The rise of the low-wage service sector. Since 1973, manufacturing has steadily declined in the United States, and the service jobs replacing factory work have generally been either very high skilled (and rewarded) or relatively low skilled (and therefore not paid very well). This new and expanding group of low-wage service workers challenges the notion that working-class status arises from physical labor. Data entry clerks, cashiers, paralegals, and similar occupations are technically white-collar jobs yet pull in working-class wages.

Over the past three decades, the income gap between a corporate CEO and a single-mother waitress has grown exponentially, and the relatively stable middle class of previous decades has become increasingly stratified (Figure 7.2). For example, a CEO who makes at least $184,500 is in the top

Middle class a term commonly used to describe those individuals with nonmanual jobs that pay significantly more than the poverty line— though this is a highly debated and expansive category, particularly in the United States, where broad swathes of the population consider themselves middle class.

Figure 7.2: Average CEO Pay versus Production Worker Pay, 1970–2010

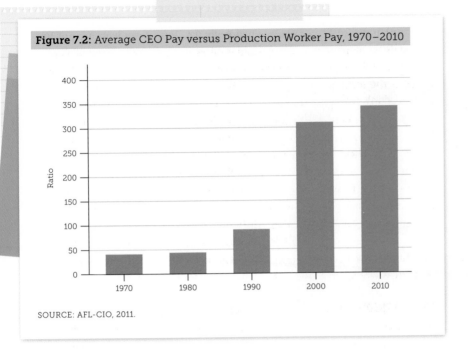

SOURCE: AFL-CIO, 2011.

5 percent of households, and his or her average expected salary increase since 1979 (adjusted for inflation) is an impressive 81 percent. On the other end of the scale, a waitress who makes only $25,600 is in the bottom 20 percent of households, and her income will have decreased by 1 percent over the same period. And if we consider an average family—say, a two-parent household with two kids and a middle-range annual income of $68,000—then this family would probably have experienced an income increase of 15 percent since 1979. (Go to www.inequality.com for more information.)

How and why has this differential income growth happened? One factor may be the changing nature of available employment. As the technological sector expands, the majority of jobs are being created either at very high skill levels with correspondingly high salaries (engineers and hedge fund managers) or at very low levels with little room for upward mobility (baristas at Starbucks who serve lattes to those hedge fund managers). And the fastest-growing job category for those with no more than a high-school education is food preparation and service.

Furthermore, this bifurcated job growth is reflected in the change in educational expectations of potential employers. Whereas for much of the post–World War II period, a high-school diploma could earn a person (a white man, specifically) enough to support a family, a college degree is now often a minimum requirement for decent employment. But although the number of high-school graduates going to college has increased (to roughly 66 percent), bachelor's degree completion rates still stand at approximately 59 percent

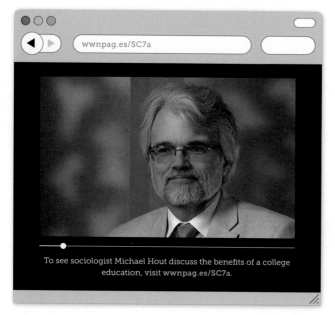

To see sociologist Michael Hout discuss the benefits of a college education, visit wwnpag.es/SC7a.

nationally (i.e., lots of students are not finishing) (Bowen et al., 2009; National Center for Education Statistics, 2013a, 2013b). If a college education is the gateway to becoming middle class and only a quarter of the American population has at least a four-year degree, we can expect the percentage of middle-class Americans to shrink.

In an interview for this book, sociologist Michael Hout helped explain that even though there has been stagnation in the number of people receiving bachelor's degrees, the value of those degrees is increasing. Hout pointed out that part of what is holding students back from getting their degree is that the cost of college is increasing and a larger proportion of the cost is borne by individuals and families rather than states. For example, due to state budget shortfalls, the University of California system—one of the biggest and best—announced a tuition hike of 32 percent for the academic year starting in 2010 that was swiftly followed by another 9.6 percent rise in 2011 (McMillan, 2011). Hout goes on to describe the way that sacrificing to pay for college plays out differently across social classes.

> There is a class-specific preference for these kinds of risks. The sons and daughters of college graduates see the benefit of a college education more clearly. They have had it drummed into them since they could talk. . . . Sons and daughters of people who haven't been to college can exercise a certain skepticism about it, and they see in their neighborhoods evidence that it might not pay off. Who leaves the neighborhood? Somebody who has reaped the full benefit of the college education. They're out of sight and out of mind. Who's back in the neighborhood? That kid who maybe dropped out after three years, with a three-figure loan debt, six-figure loan debt. And the presence of those people makes it look like college doesn't pay off. (Conley, 2009h)

Some argue that along with income inequality, income insecurity (or volatility) has also increased for the middle classes. In *The Great Risk Shift* (2006), Jacob Hacker asserts that the chances of an American family experiencing a 50 percent drop in their annual income from one year to the next were 17 percent in 2002, up from around 7 percent in 1970. A 50 percent salary cut would still leave the CEO mentioned above in the top 40 percent of household incomes, but how about our waitress and our middle-income family? Cutting their salary by half would send either into a major financial crisis, maybe even bankruptcy. However, other researchers argue that income instability is not the result of fluctuating earnings or job insecurity but rather stems from two major changes in family dynamics. First, there are more changes to household structure today because of divorce and remarriage; second, women now play a greater role in breadwinning (even exceeding men as a proportion of the workforce at one point during the recent recession), but they also enter and exit the workforce with greater frequency than men. (See Chapter 8 for more about women in the workforce.)

The Poor

Unlike the fuzzy definitions of other classes, poverty has an official, government definition. In 2013, the poverty line for a family of four was $23,550 (U.S. Department of Health and Human Services, 2013). The poor are, ironically, often said to resemble the rich in being more oriented toward the present and therefore less worried about the future than their middle-class and working-class counterparts (although this is highly debated). Day-to-day survival keeps the poor clearly planted in the present. Of course, like any class, the poor are not a unified group. In fact, one distinction often made in political speeches is that between the "working poor" (those who deserve our assistance) and the "nonworking poor" (those who can work but don't and therefore have a weaker moral claim on assistance). This latter group is sometimes called the "underclass." Of course, even these two categories obscure huge distinctions within either group; in fact, poverty is a state that families usually shift in and out of throughout their history, and often a clear distinction does not exist between the working class and the poor.

Global Inequality

One of the main reasons cited for rising income and wealth inequality in the United States is globalization—the rise in the trade of goods and services across national boundaries, as well as the increased mobility of multinational businesses and migrant labor. If the effect of globalization in the United States has been to bifurcate labor into high-skilled and low-skilled jobs, what has been the effect on worldwide inequality? The answer to that question depends on how you frame the analysis. In the long view, there is no question that global income inequality has been steadily rising over the last few centuries. At the start of the agricultural and industrial revolutions, almost the entire population of the world lived in poverty and misery (see the discussion of Malthus earlier in the chapter). Birthrates were high, but so was mortality. Most people barely survived, no matter where they lived.

But then, thanks to technological innovations, food production started to increase dramatically in some areas of Europe. Soon after—during the Industrial Revolution—large-scale factory production took the place of small cottage industries, resulting in the creation of vast, unequally distributed wealth. Simultaneously, European powers began to explore, conquer, and extract resources from other areas of the globe. Fast-forward a few hundred years to the mid-twentieth century, when the world and most of its wealth were carved up and ruled by major Western powers. Enormous global inequalities had emerged through the combination of colonialism and unequal development. Since around 1950, many of these former colonies have gained political independence, but they have lagged well behind the West in terms of income per capita.

Scholars have long been trying to figure out why Europe developed first. Early explanations, dating back to the French essayist Montesquieu (1748/1750), focused on geographic differences between the peoples of Europe and the global south (as the less-developed regions of the world are sometimes called). Perhaps because of the south's heat or humidity, Montesquieu associated virtue and rationality with the north; the south he associated with vice and passion. Montesquieu's views are now discarded as a racist account of uneven development, but more recent versions of the geographical explanation focus on differences in the length of growing seasons, the higher variability of water supply (because of more frequent droughts), the types of cereal crops that can grow in temperate zones compared with tropical and subtropical regions, the lack of coal deposits (the first fuel that drove industrialization, long before oil), and perhaps most important, the disease burden in warmer climates (Sachs, 2001).

Economist Jeffrey Sachs explains that Africa's geography made it much more difficult for an agricultural revolution to occur. He prods us to understand the complexity of the constraints on Africa's development before pointing fingers:

> Africa is a continent largely of that rain-fed agriculture, whereas the Green Revolution was based first and foremost on irrigation agriculture. Now is that bad governance that Africa does not have vast river systems? Or is that a matter of the Himalayan Tibetan plateau, which creates the Indus, the Punjab (meaning five rivers, after all), the Ganges, the Yangtze, and so forth? These are functions of physical geography. Africa has a savannah region, which means a long dry season together with a single wet season typically. (Conley, 2009g)

So Africa was not fortunate when it came to physical geography and it missed out on the Green Revolution because it could not easily implement irrigation agriculture. But that's not all. If you recall from our discussion of Malthus, Africa also carried a higher disease burden because of the way malaria is transmitted through animal hosts—more deadly in Africa than in Asia. Even with that, Sachs is not through explaining just how Africa came to be so disadvantaged compared with other regions of the world. Important impacts of colonialism would be easy to overlook if we focused only on geography and infectious disease transmission, he says.

> Let's talk more about Africa. Racism. Absolutely pervasive. The slave era, the treatment of white people in the rich north Atlantic vis-à-vis the black people. Let's face it: We want to pretend that's not part of our society, part of our history, part of our view of the hopelessness of regions, part of the way that they were treated unfairly. If you look through the colonial-era memos in Africa about the repression of education levels and so forth by colonial powers, that's also part of the history. Then you come to infrastructure, you come to physical geography, you come to history, and you come to an odd historical context. (Conley, 2009g)

Was the atrocious treatment by colonial powers somehow the fault of African leaders? Does this ever-so-brief primer on the history of African development help you to understand that the sociological imagination cannot function properly without a wide array of information about everything from epidemiology to history to geography and beyond?

Others argue that geography doesn't matter as much as social institutions do. In one version of this line of reasoning, it is a strong foundation of property rights, incorruptible judiciaries, and the rule of law in general that predict economic development (Easterly & Levine, 2002). These, in turn, were institutions "native" to Europe and were transferred to the areas where European colonists settled and lived in significant numbers (Acemoglu et al., 2001), spurring later development in areas such as India and Latin America (compared with much of Africa, where Europeans did not settle, which has lagged in development). Other scholars argue that the types of relationships different colonized regions had with the European powers largely determined their fate today: For example, under the rule of the British Raj, India was endowed with a huge network of railways to move cotton, tea, and other products to market. This network, in turn, helped spur

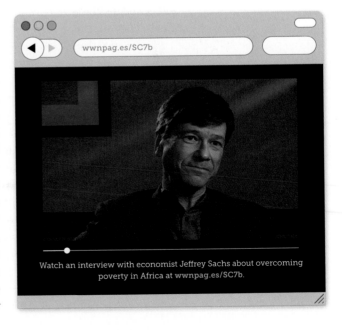

Watch an interview with economist Jeffrey Sachs about overcoming poverty in Africa at wwnpag.es/SC7b.

wwnpag.es/SC7b

Tremendous global inequalities have emerged through the combination of colonialism and unequal development. What are some of the ways that social scientists explain the gap between rich and poor regions of the world?

economic growth once India got over the rocky transition to self-government after gaining its independence. By contrast, because of the disease burden in most sub-Saharan African countries, Europeans didn't stay and invest but rather focused on extractive industries, building railways that ran just to and from mines instead of extensive networks of roads and train tracks.

Today that legacy of unequal starting places and economic potentials means that the latest spurt of globalization has engendered an even greater level of income inequality across the north–south divide while creating huge differences within developing countries. Indeed, some regions, such as sub-Saharan Africa and eastern Europe, have become poorer over the last 25 years, whereas in some previously poor regions, such as South and East Asia, income levels have risen. Considering the net change, the economist Xavier Salai-i-Martin estimates that there were around half a billion fewer poor people in the world by the turn of the twenty-first century than there were in the 1970s (Salai-i-Martin, 2002). Likewise, he claims, "all indexes show a reduction in global income inequality between 1980 and 1998." There have indeed been global reductions in population-weighted between-country differences, which can largely be attributed to the rapid growth of the Chinese and Indian economies over this period. Within individual countries, however, inequality has generally risen over the same time frame. The story of globalization and inequality is thus a complex and constantly changing one.

Social Reproduction versus Social Mobility

Once we begin to understand the basics of stratification—how members of a society are hierarchically organized along different lines—the next issue is the possibility of those members' changing their social position in the hierarchy. This is generally referred to as social mobility, the movement between different positions within a system of social stratification in any given society. Pitirim A. Sorokin (1927/1959) emphasized the importance of not just looking at the mobility of individuals but also examining group mobility. For example, rather than just asking why Ugo, a cashier at Sears, was promoted to regional manager, thereby increasing his income and status, Sorokin suggests we also look at why the group Ugo belongs to—black males of Nigerian descent in their mid-twenties—does or does not appear to be generally mobile.

Sorokin noted that social mobility can be either horizontal or vertical. *Horizontal social mobility* means a group or individual transitioning from one social status to another situated more or less on the same rung of the ladder. Examples of this might be a secretary who changes firms but retains her occupational status, a Methodist person who converts to Lutheranism, a family that migrates to one city from another, or an ethnic group that shifts its typical job category from one form of unskilled labor to another. *Vertical social mobility*, in contrast, refers to the rise or fall of an individual (or group) from one social stratum to another. We can further distinguish two types of vertical mobility: *ascending* and *descending* (more commonly termed *upward* and *downward*). An individual who experiences ascending vertical mobility either rises from a lower stratum into a higher one or creates an entirely new group that exists at a higher stratum. Ugo's promotion to regional manager at Sears is an example of rising from a lower stratum to a higher one. By becoming a manager, he has changed his class position, a change that confers both a higher salary and more prestige. Conversely, imagine that for some reason there was an immediate need for translators of Igbo (or Ibo, the language spoken by the Igbo people based in southeast Nigeria) in the United States. Ugo, who speaks Igbo, along with many other Nigerians who speak the language, would then find better jobs and thereby enjoy higher social status. This would be an example of a new group, Igbo translators, existing in a higher stratum.

Descending vertical mobility can similarly take either of two forms: individual or group. One way to think of these forms is as the distinction between a particular person falling overboard from a ship and the whole ship sinking. Sorokin asserted that "channels of vertical circulation necessarily exist in any stratified society and are as necessary as channels for blood circulation in the body" (1927/1959).

Most sociologists concerned with studying mobility focus on the process of individual mobility. These studies generally fall into two types: mobility

Social mobility the movement between different positions within a system of social stratification in any given society.

tables (or matrices) and status attainment models. Constructing a mobility table is easy, although making sense of it is much more difficult (see Table 7.2 for an example). Along the left-most column of a grid, list a number of occupations for people's fathers (it was traditionally done for males only). Across the top, list the same occupational categories for the sons (the respondents). There can be as many or as few categories as you see fit, so long as they are consistent for the parental and child generations. For example, a five-category analysis might include upper nonmanual occupations (managers and professionals), lower nonmanual occupations (administrative and clerical workers, low-level entrepreneurs, and retail salespeople), upper manual occupations (skilled workers who primarily use physical labor, such as plumbers and electricians), lower manual (unskilled physical laborers), and farmworkers. The number of categories can be expanded, and it is not uncommon to see seven-, nine-, or even fourteen-category tables. The key is filling in the boxes. Probably not many people fall into the cell where the father is upper nonmanual and the son is a farmer. However, because of the decline in the agricultural workforce over the course of the twentieth century, you are likely to observe (at least in the United States) a fair bit of movement from farmwork in the parental generation to other occupations in the children's generation. Changes in the distribution of jobs lead to what sociologists call structural mobility, mobility that is inevitable from changes in the economy. With the decline of farmwork because of technology, the sons and daughters of farmers are by definition going

Structural mobility mobility that is inevitable from changes in the economy.

Table 7.2: Mobility Table: Father's Occupation by Son's First Occupation

FATHER'S OCCUPATION	SON'S OCCUPATION					
	Upper nonmanual	Lower nonmanual	Upper manual	Lower manual	Farm	Total
Upper nonmanual	**1,414**	521	302	643	40	2,920
Lower nonmanual	724	**524**	254	703	48	2,253
Upper manual	798	648	**856**	1,676	108	4,086
Lower manual	756	914	771	**3,325**	237	6,003
Farm	409	357	441	1,611	**1,832**	4,650
Total	4,101	2,964	2,624	7,958	2,265	19,912

SOURCE: Hout, 1983.

to have to find other kinds of work. This type of mobility stands in contrast to exchange mobility, in which, if we hold fixed the changing distribution of jobs, individuals trade jobs not one-to-one but in a way that ultimately balances out.

As most measures of economic inequality have risen each year since the 1960s, Americans have comforted themselves with the thought that they still live in the land of opportunity. Rates of occupational (and income) mobility in the United States have long been thought to have dwarfed those of European societies with their royalty, aristocracies, and long histories. However, recent research suggests that this may be cold comfort: Some economists have argued that U.S. mobility rates have declined significantly since the 1960s. Others go so far as to say that Americans now enjoy less mobility than their European counterparts. A fierce debate has ensued, because many of these studies compare apples and oranges—different measures, different data, different years. However, a consensus seems to be slowly emerging that mobility rates should be broken down into the two components discussed above, structural and exchange mobility. When we do this, it turns out that rates of "trading places" are fairly fixed across developed societies. By contrast, historically the United States has enjoyed an advantage in growth-induced upward mobility; as the farm and blue-collar sectors withered and white-collar jobs expanded, sons and daughters of manual workers have, by necessity, experienced a degree of upward occupational mobility. However, sociologists and economists debate whether economic growth still drives upward mobility, or whether bifurcated job growth means intergenerational stagnation.

Another common methodology for studying social mobility is the status-attainment model. This approach ranks individuals by socioeconomic status, including income and educational attainment, and seeks to specify the attributes characteristic of people who end up in more desirable occupations. The occupational status research of Peter M. Blau and Otis Dudley Duncan (1967), who ranked occupations into a status hierarchy to study social attainment processes, is generally seen as the paradigmatic work in this tradition. Unlike mobility tables, the status-attainment model allows sociologists to study some of the intervening processes. For example, how important is education in facilitating upward occupational shifts in status? How critical is the prestige of a person's first job out of school? How does IQ relate to the chances for upward or downward mobility? The status-attainment model is an elastic one that allows researchers to throw in new factors as they arise and see how they affect the relationships between existing ones, generally ordered chronologically over a typical life course. Generally, it is thought that education is the primary mediating variable between parents' and children's occupational prestige. That said, research shows that parental education and net worth, not occupation or income, best predict children's educational and other outcomes (Conley, 1999). Blau and Duncan didn't measure net worth, but by now it has become a fairly standard factor in many socioeconomic surveys.

Exchange mobility mobility in which, if we hold fixed the changing distribution of jobs, individuals trade jobs not one-to-one but in a way that ultimately balances out.

Status-attainment model approach that ranks individuals by socioeconomic status, including income and educational attainment, and seeks to specify the attributes characteristic of people who end up in more desirable occupations.

Although there is increasing consensus on what aspects of class background matter (and how much they do), there is relatively little understanding of the multiple mechanisms by which class is reproduced (or how mobility happens). For instance, families with a higher socioeconomic status are likely to have more success in preparing their children for school, entry exams, and ultimately the job market because they have greater access to resources that promote and support their children's development. These might include educational toys when the children are very young, tutors in grade school, and expensive test-preparation courses for exams such as the SAT, GRE, LSAT, MCAT, and so on. Once again, let us compare the CEO of a large, profitable U.S. corporation with a single mother working as a waitress at the local diner. The status of the CEO's occupation and his disproportionate income and wealth in relation to the waitress's easily put his socioeconomic status leaps and bounds ahead of hers. Because of this disparity, he can send his children to the top private schools, where they will be funneled toward highly paid positions. In contrast, assuming that the single mother has no other source of income, her children are likely to get a public education without all the extras. This by no means mandates that they are destined for lower-level occupations, but it certainly suggests that if this were a race, the CEO's children started several miles ahead.

Class-Based Affirmative Action

The push for class-based affirmative action (for lack of a better term) is partly a response to the slow decline of race-based affirmative action, as evidenced by the Supreme Court's 2014 ruling to uphold the decision of Michigan's voters to ban race-based affirmative action across the University of Michigan system. In addition to the (legally) declining significance of race in admissions, the call for economic considerations in the college admissions process arises from mounting evidence that class has become an increasingly salient driver of academic opportunity (and success).

The statistics about increasing class stratification on American campuses are alarming: "The college-completion rate among children from high-income families has grown sharply in the last few decades, whereas the completion rate for students from low-income families has barely moved" (Bailey & Dynarski, 2011). Moreover, high-income students make up an increasing share of the enrollment at the most selective colleges and universities (Reardon et al., 2012), even when compared with low-income students with similar test scores and academic records (Bailey & Dynarski, 2011; Belley & Lochner, 2007; Karen, 2002).

Class-based admissions policies, then, offer a way to redress unequal access to selective institutions of higher education while also indirectly tackling racial disparities. Additionally, class-based policies, if well designed, can help address some of the criticisms of traditional, race-based affirmative action.

What challenges do colleges face in promoting diversity through admissions policies?

One of the most common criticisms of race-based affirmative action is that as currently designed, such admissions policies typically help those minorities who least need it. Whereas prior to the 1970s race was seen to trump class in determining the life chances for success for the vast majority of African Americans, today it is the reverse pattern that predominates (Reardon et al., 2012). Back in 1967, Peter M. Blau and Otis Dudley Duncan described the process of stratification in the United States in their landmark book, *The American Occupational Structure* (Blau & Duncan, 1967). In this study, they found that class background mattered little for African Americans compared with whites. Instead, they described a dynamic called "perverse equality": No matter what the occupation of the father of a black man (this was a period of low labor force participation for women overall, even if black women did work at significant rates), he himself was most likely to end up in the lower, manual sector of the labor market. Meanwhile, in each generation a small, new cadre of professional blacks would emerge seemingly randomly through a dynamic they described as "tokenism"—that is, family background mattered little in predicting who emerged into the small, black professional class.

By the mid-1970s, however, this dynamic had changed. In 1978, sociologist William Julius Wilson described a black community where class stratification was increasingly rearing its head (Wilson, 1978). Later work confirmed intergenerationally what Wilson observed cross-sectionally: There were increasing class divisions within the black (and Latino) communities, and class background was an increasingly salient predictor of economic success, not just for whites but for minorities as well (Conley, 1999; Killewald, 2013).

Sean Reardon goes so far as to argue that class disparities have eclipsed racial ones, at least in terms of achievement: "The black-white achievement gap was considerably larger than the income achievement gap among cohorts born in the 1950s and 1960s, but now it is considerably smaller than the income achievement gap. This change is the result of both the substantial progress made in reducing racial inequality in the 1960s and 1970s and the sharp increase in economic inequality in education outcomes in more recent decades" (Reardon, 2013). Economist Roland Fryer, Jr. sums this up nicely: "Relative to the 20th century, the significance of discrimination as an explanation for racial inequality across economic and social indicators has declined" (Fryer, 2010).

In short, although class divisions within historically underrepresented minority groups are increasing, 1960s identity-group policies treat disadvantaged groups uniformly. The result of such a homogenizing admissions policy is that the most disadvantaged minorities are not helped and intra-racial stratification is enhanced. Thus, either in lieu of, or in combination with race-based policies, class-based affirmative action could address these inequalities within minority (and majority) communities.

If one were to decide to design a class-based admissions policy, how would one implement such a scheme? Can we just ask students' parents to self-report their "class" or socioeconomic status by disclosing their income, education, and wealth? Here's where the devil lies in the details. Parental income is the most easily verifiable, because colleges can ask for tax returns. But analysis shows that it matters the least in predicting college enrollment and completion. In other words, by designing admissions policies around income, we would be doing less well in helping those who need it most. Parental education is actually the strongest predictor but the least verifiable. (How can you check that someone has *more* education than they report on a form?) Parental wealth, meanwhile, is the most unequal by race—getting us the most racial bang for the buck, so to speak. The typical African American family has about 10 percent of the net worth of the typical white family. Wealth also predicts college outcomes (though not as strongly as parental education). So it would seem to be an ideal measure for balancing concerns about race and class diversity on campus.

However, parental wealth faces an even greater problem of verification, potential gaming, and perverse incentives against savings. For example, because Medicaid has strict asset limits, many families shift assets from one individual to another (or even get divorced) in anticipation of needing Medicaid's long-term care insurance component. Similar shell games may emerge in response to offspring approaching their senior year of high school. Unlike the case of education, however, where self-reporting is the only metric to go by for parental wealth, we can infer a lot based on a few factors that are less apt to be gamed.

First, we can measure the median housing value of a community in which a student was raised. This has been shown to be a very good proxy for individual wealth level. If it were measured for all years from birth, the incentive to move to a poor-value neighborhood in the period just preceding college applications would be minimized. Second, other forms of wealth can be ascertained or imputed through property tax records, estate tax records, and schedules A through D of the federal income tax return. While these individual-level measures could theoretically be gamed, the fact that they are measured over multiple years (as with the address of the applicant) minimizes such potential threats; and when combined with the neighborhood-level measures, such risk is further minimized.

Or, when all is said and done, if we want to maintain or increase diversity on campus, we can do what we are already doing: just asking applicants to check a box on the race question on their application (never asking for verification), while we hoping that people are honest and the courts are sympathetic.

→ # CONCLUSION

Horatio Alger, Jr. (1832–1899) was an American author of dime novels that told rags-to-riches stories. The narratives typically depicted a plucky young downtrodden boy who eventually achieved the American dream of success and fortune through tenacious hard work while maintaining a genuine concern for the well-being of others. Alger wrote more than 130 novels with titles such as *Sink or Swim* (1870), *Up the Ladder* (1873), *From Boy to President* (1881), *Making His Way* (1901), *A New Path to Fortune* (1903), and *Finding a Fortune* (1904). Works like these contributed to the national ideology that all Americans could make it if they only pulled themselves up by their own bootstraps.

Although more than 100 years old, Alger's novels still resonate with a faith in mobility that is woven into the national fabric and self-image of Americans. Today the majority of Americans are no longer positive about the possibility of upward mobility. A 2013 poll by the Pew Charitable Trusts found that only one-third of Americans thought that their children would be better off than they were, and in 2012 only 24 percent of Americans believed that they themselves have achieved the American dream (Pew Research Center, 2013a; Public Agenda, 2012). What is so striking is that more and more Americans are buying into the Alger myth—more Americans than 20 years ago believe it possible to start at the bottom and work your way to the top. People generally believe that hard work and education are more important than social connections or a wealthy background. Are Americans overly optimistic, or are sociologists just being naysayers? Only more research will tell us for sure.

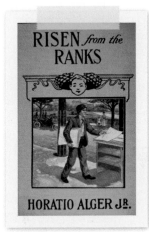

This Horatio Alger, Jr. novel features a newsboy who rises to newspaper editor. Are most Americans today likely to achieve upward mobility?

→ PRACTICE

SOCIOLOGY ON THE STREET

Someone you would consider rich may not think of themselves that way. If the label "rich" is relative, what does it mean to be rich? Watch the Sociology on the Street video to find out more: wwnpag.es/SOS7.

QUESTIONS FOR REVIEW

1. How does the number of doctors with last names from particular ethnic groups demonstrate the lasting influence of history on intergenerational mobility?

2. How does class-based affirmative action continue to help some racial minority students? What does this policy change tell you about the status of various categories of stratification in America?

3. Whereas inequality is the result of abundance, how does the relationship between the bourgeois and proletariat suggest that abundance is the result of inequality?

4. To talk about the rich, the poor, and the way society is economically stratified sounds like the job of economists. Why should sociologists be interested in stratification? How does a better understanding of stratification potentially contribute to the well-being of society?

5. Why, according to Adam Ferguson and John Millar, is inequality necessary? In what way does their argument anticipate the "free rider problem"?

6. What is "equality of condition," and why did Thomas Malthus argue against striving for this form of equality?

7. What are the ideal types of social stratification and how do they differ? Which one, in your opinion, best describes stratification in the United States?

8. What is the difference between income and wealth? Why might certain sociologists prefer to measure inequality based on wealth instead of income?

9. What is structural mobility, and how does this concept describe the decline of manufacturing jobs in the United States since the early 1970s?

10. According to Max Weber, what do being a teacher, having a cool car, and being a member of a prestigious association have in common?

PARADOX

INEQUALITY IS THE RESULT OF ABUNDANCE.

WATCH THE ANIMATED SHORT ABOUT THE STRATIFICATION PARADOX AT

WWNPAG.ES/PX7

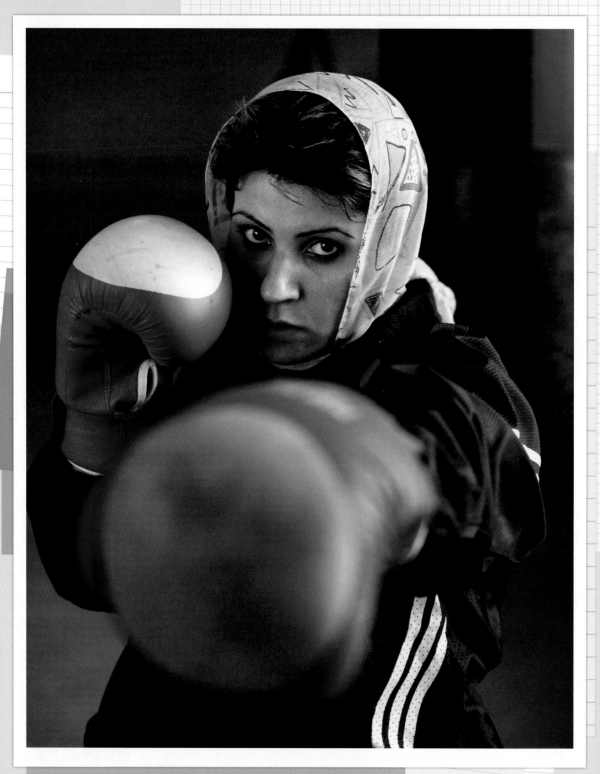

Rosia Rezaee is a member of the Afghan Women's Boxing Club. This organization's twenty members have challenged conservative gender ideology in Afghanistan through their passion for boxing and advocacy for women's freedom to equally participate in society.

8 Gender

PARADOX

THE BIOLOGICAL CATEGORIES OF
SEX STRONGLY INFLUENCE THE
SOCIAL DYNAMICS OF GENDER;
HOWEVER, THE SOCIAL CATEGORIES
OF GENDER CAN SOMETIMES
DETERMINE THE BIOLOGY OF SEX.

In social science, there is a statistical technique called "individual fixed effects." Basically it boils down to comparing an outcome across time as some factor changes. So, for example, if we want to know whether having kids makes people happier and more fulfilled, we might ask them before they have their first child and then again afterward. Fixed effects can be used to look at the effect of marriage and divorce on health; of education on wages; of home ownership on savings rates; and of family income on kids' test scores. However, certain key sociological variables resist fixed effects, simply because they don't change over time. Think race. Think birth cohort. Think parents' age. And, of course, think sex. Very few people get to experience life in both locker rooms, so to speak. Sex isn't a boundary we typically flip back and forth across. However, it has been known to happen. Among the estimated 25,000 or so Americans who have undergone sexual reassignment surgery, few are probably better positioned to report with a scientific eye than Deirdre McCloskey, a Harvard-trained, world-renowned economist who used to be named Donald.

Perhaps it was the combination of her gifts of economic science and beautiful writing style that made McCloskey destined to be the one who would prominently (and touchingly) describe effects of gender (and her associated border crossing) to a wide readership in her memoir, *Crossing*.

"It's strange to have been a man and now to be a woman," she admits. "But it's no stranger perhaps than having been a West African and now being an American, or once a priest and now a businessman. Free people keep deciding to make strange crossings, from storekeeper to monk or from

8 Gender

PARADOX

THE BIOLOGICAL CATEGORIES OF SEX STRONGLY INFLUENCE THE SOCIAL DYNAMICS OF GENDER; HOWEVER, THE SOCIAL CATEGORIES OF GENDER CAN SOMETIMES DETERMINE THE BIOLOGY OF SEX.

In social science, there is a statistical technique called "individual fixed effects." Basically it boils down to comparing an outcome across time as some factor changes. So, for example, if we want to know whether having kids makes people happier and more fulfilled, we might ask them before they have their first child and then again afterward. Fixed effects can be used to look at the effect of marriage and divorce on health; of education on wages; of home ownership on savings rates; and of family income on kids' test scores. However, certain key sociological variables resist fixed effects, simply because they don't change over time. Think race. Think birth cohort. Think parents' age. And, of course, think sex. Very few people get to experience life in both locker rooms, so to speak. Sex isn't a boundary we typically flip back and forth across. However, it has been known to happen. Among the estimated 25,000 or so Americans who have undergone sexual reassignment surgery, few are probably better positioned to report with a scientific eye than Deirdre McCloskey, a Harvard-trained, world-renowned economist who used to be named Donald.

Perhaps it was the combination of her gifts of economic science and beautiful writing style that made McCloskey destined to be the one who would prominently (and touchingly) describe effects of gender (and her associated border crossing) to a wide readership in her memoir, *Crossing*.

"It's strange to have been a man and now to be a woman," she admits. "But it's no stranger perhaps than having been a West African and now being an American, or once a priest and now a businessman. Free people keep deciding to make strange crossings, from storekeeper to monk or from

273

civilian to soldier or from man to woman. Crossing boundaries is a minority interest, but human" (McCloskey, 1999, p. xii).

Written in the third person—certainly rare if not totally unique among memoirs—in order to reconcile the multiple selves that McCloskey experienced over the course of his/her adulthood, *Crossing* details the harrowing journey across the invisible yet robust boundary of sex/gender. This voyage was made all the more improbable by McCloskey's advanced age (52) at the time then-Donald initiated the biological process of the change after decades of cross-dressing, fathering and providing for two children, and serving as a husband and professionally active man. And it was made not only improbable but dramatic by the fact that McCloskey's sister—a professional psychologist—stopped his various surgeries several times by threatening to sue the surgeons and had him committed to a mental hospital against his will. Indeed, she had worked so hard that after his penile removal surgery, he feared waking up "crazy."

Ultimately, however, Deirdre triumphed: After almost $100,000 of uncovered medical expenses, procedures that were performed across North America and even Australia (including facial bone surgery, voice surgery, and hormone therapy, just to name a few), Deirdre emerged happy, if weatherworn, to document the process while beginning a new life. Estranged from his ex-wife and kids, she nonetheless was relieved (not crazy) to engage in the painful process of stretching his neovagina—fashioned from some of his small intestine—for 30 minutes each day; to continue the laborious (and also painful) electrolysis treatments; and to otherwise continue the journey into womanhood—a continent she had previously visited as a cross-dressing tourist, hoping to pass for a native in Donald's dresses.

Along the way, McCloskey indeed chronicles a number of changes that she experienced before and after, as man and then as woman. It's too bad that his ex-wife couldn't stay married to the female McCloskey, because Deirdre speculates that she might, in fact, like this version better: "His wife would become angry if he talked of his Chicago doubt [back when he was deciding whether to leave his faculty position at the prestigious University of Chicago economics department], for it was tedious after a while to listen to the whining. My ex-wife would like Deirdre better if she knew her, she reflected. No angst" (p. 149).

McCloskey also wrote down 41 differences between Donald and Deirdre, some of which fall into the realm of well-worn gender stereotypes. (McCloskey is the first to note that however rigid and

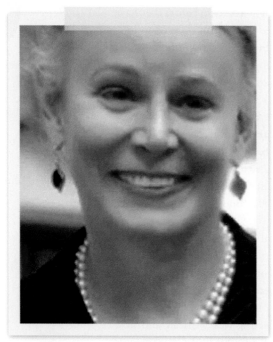

What does economist Deirdre McCloskey's experiences on both sides of the sex/gender divide tell us about the differences between sex, gender, and sexuality?

defended the boundary of sex is, the experience of gender operates along a continuum and consists of a culturally instantiated grab bag of characteristics that are found among individuals of both sexes in varying degrees.) Below are twenty of those differences:

- She cries.

- She sweats less.

- She loses weight less easily.

- Her color memory and color vocabulary are a little better.

- She works at remembering what people wear.

- She likes cooking.

- She listens intently to stories people tell of their lives, and craves detail.

- She is more alert to relational details in stories ("Ah, I see, she's his cousin by marriage"). She finds herself remembering the family trees, the ex-boyfriends, the big events.

- She is less impatient.

- She drives more slowly and less aggressively.

- She can't remain angry for long.

- She feels duty bound to wash the dishes.

- She loves, just loves, the little favors of womankind—getting a card for someone, making meatloaf for Charles up the street, helping someone through a day of his life.

- She assumes a less confident mask for dealings with salespeople and auto mechanics.

- She is uninterested in sports and finds the sports pages pointless.

- She no longer thinks of social life as strict exchange.

- She dotes on every child she meets.

- She has more friends.

- She thinks less about sex.

- She gets as much pleasure from loving as from being loved.

All we need now is a whole group of social scientists to go through this form of participant observation so that we can obtain a statistical distribution of effects! Or maybe not. Actually, sometimes what is gained in narrative is lost in numbers.

Mars and Venus

If you think Deirdre McCloskey's list of differences between herself and her male predecessor is long, that's just a drop in the bucket when it comes to the divergence of men and women, or so says pop psychologist John Gray. Gray argues that men and women differ so fundamentally in their values, attitudes, thought processes, preferences, and behavior patterns that they might as well be from different planets altogether. (Interplanetary travel might explain the exhaustion McCloskey felt after his journey into a she.) Gray writes that men and women don't even speak the same language, but have distinct biologically and psychically driven styles of communication, feeling, and action.

Gray's relationship guidebook *Men Are from Mars, Women Are from Venus* (1992) was a best seller for a decade. It sold more than 14 million copies and inspired nearly a dozen spin-offs, from *Mars and Venus on a Date* to a diet and health book with such recipes as the Mars–Venus supershake. So widely recognized is the book's title that now, when the tricky issue of gender relations rises to the fore, as it so often does in America, we often discuss the matter in terms of the innate differences between Martians and Venusians.

When you deal with the stress of dating and breakups, you might be tempted to use the Mars–Venus framework. It offers the appeal of easy-to-grasp, commonsense generalizations. Men and women are different biological organisms, according to Gray, and their biological differences manifest themselves in the ways men and women behave. By nature, allegedly, men don't like to express their feelings but instead retreat to their "caves" after a hard day at the office. Women are just more expressive and relational, always communicating about their feelings. These things are just biological givens, so individuals must take personal action to navigate what nature's given us, or so the self-help books would have us believe.

If you're a sociologist, this kind of thinking won't get you too far in explaining concepts such as sex, sexuality, gender, and the many messy complications, exceptions, and social patterns that beg for explanations beyond the individual, psychical, or biological levels. In the marketplace of ideas, sociological explanations are always at a disadvantage compared with pop psychological explanations of complex social phenomena. People prefer quick, easy answers to the long and often arduous sociological route. After all, they make more intuitive sense at first blush, they're easier to grasp, and we're accustomed to them. Unfortunately, they are often wrong. On the sociologist's path, you'll have to leave behind your Mars–Venus

Why would a sociologist disagree with the arguments about gender that John Gray poses in *Men Are from Mars, Women Are from Venus*?

guidebooks (including the shortened, illustrated version) and instead take up the sociological imagination. Sex and gender may, in fact, be the most difficult areas to remember that what seems natural is often anything but. The seemingly rigid and innate differences between the "opposite sexes" can turn out to be fluid.

In applying our sociological imaginations to sex and gender, we will come across many feminist strands of thought. Feminism was at first embraced as a consciousness-raising movement to get people to understand that gender is an organizing principle of life; gender matters because it structures relations between people. Further, as gender structures social relations, it does this on unequal ground, so there are real powers and privileges at stake in gender ideology. Neoconservative talk show host Rush Limbaugh would have you believe that feminism "was established to allow unattractive women easier access to the mainstream" (Media Matters for America, 2005). In fact, the basic idea behind feminism is that women and men should be accorded equal opportunities and respect—a position that almost anyone in the contemporary United States would be hard pressed to criticize. Feminists tend to be less interested in erasing the differences between men and women than in uncovering the power stakes behind the socially constructed differences between the genders.

The sociologist's first task is to disentangle the terms *sex, sexuality,* and *gender*. Sex is typically used to describe the biological differences that distinguish males from females. Sexuality refers to desire, sexual preference, and sexual identity and behavior. Far from being strictly natural, how we have sex and with whom vary by time and place. Gender denotes a social position, the set of social arrangements that are built around normative sex categories. It is, you could say, what people do with the physical materials of sex.

No one disputes that biological differences exist between men and women. However, what we make of those differences does not inevitably arise out of the biological. Gender is one set of stories we tell each other and believe in to get by in the world. It's a collectively defined guidebook that humans use to make distinctions among themselves, to separate one being from another, and to comprehend an otherwise fuzzy mass of individuals. But the gender story can change, and we'll see how it has done so throughout history and across cultures. To grasp this insight takes sociological imagination, and it brings us closer to understanding the power of ideas. We consistently behave as though women act a certain way that is distinct from the behavior of men, until those behaviors and attitudes become so ingrained they seem inevitable. Herein lies the paradox: Gender is a social construction, but it is so deeply rooted and seemingly natural that it is a major structure organizing our everyday lives— our goals, our desires, even our bodies. And if gender is a human invention, we have to take it as seriously as we would any other institution, as Judith Lorber argues. In *Paradoxes of Gender* (1994), Lorber claims that gender is a social institution that "establishes patterns of expectations for individuals, orders the social processes of everyday life, is built into the major social organizations

Feminism a consciousness-raising movement to get people to understand that gender is an organizing principle of life. The underlying belief is that women and men should be accorded equal opportunities and respect.

Sex the biological differences that distinguish males from females.

Sexuality desire, sexual preference, and sexual identity and behavior.

Gender a social position; the set of social arrangements that are built around normative sex categories.

of society, such as the economy, ideology, the family, and politics, and is also an entity in and of itself." Although gender is a social construction, it matters in the real world, organizing our day-to-day experiences and having profound consequences for the life chances of men and women. Gender is ultimately about power struggles and how they organize daily life, from household economies and wage labor to birth control and babies' names.

Sex: A Process in the Making

We make sense of much variation between men and women by referring to their biological differences. This can range from the behavioral consequences of hormones (such as premenstrual syndrome), relative physical strength of bodies ("regular" versus "girl" push-ups), brain architecture (subsequent rational or irrational action), and chromosomes (XX or XY). But in so doing, we tend to miss a crucial link between nature and nurture. The study of gender boils down to seeing how the two spheres, nature and nurture, overlap, penetrate, and shape each other. The biological world of sex and bodies does not exist outside of a social world, and the social world of human beings is always made up of human bodies. Studying the links between the two allows us to see the social construction of both gender and sex.

Gayle Rubin, in her influential essay "The Traffic in Women: Notes on the 'Political Economy' of Sex" (1975), called the social construction of gender categories based on natural sex differences the "sex/gender system." Rubin claimed that in every society, a division of labor by gender occurred, one in which men universally performed the kinds of tasks accorded higher value than those done by women. Men did the hunting and the fighting; they ran corporations and governments. But a decade later, scholars paused to consider that perhaps Rubin got it wrong. What's so natural about a sexed body in the first place?

This might strike you as a strange question. Bodies are, so we think, natural, God-given, sacred, hardwired. Human babies come equipped with a set of male or female organs, hormones, and chromosomes—what we might call "the plumbing" that you're equipped with at birth. We think of sex as an either/or binary. You're either male or female. But in fact, there are some peculiar exceptions and blurred lines that have led sociologists to view this model of natural sex as more of an ideal than an absolute.

Consider the story of David Reimer, otherwise known as "John/Joan." In 1976, Reimer was an average baby boy who, at eight months of age, suffered a botched circumcision that left him with virtually no penis. Under the guidance of Dr. John Money at Johns Hopkins University, Reimer's parents agreed to have their son undergo sex reassignment surgery. David was surgically made into a girl, Brenda, who would go on to endure one heck of a tough childhood.

John Money claimed for years that Brenda was a success story of his approach to dealing with intersex children, those who are born with a reproductive or sexual anatomy that doesn't seem to fit the typical definitions of female or male. Here was proof that nurture trumped nature in sexual identity; you could raise a genetic male as a girl and she'd turn out just fine. Sex reassignment surgery was the best solution to cases like David Reimer's, Money argued. As it turns out, Money was wrong. Despite the hormone treatments and her frilly dresses and curly hair, Brenda never did feel comfortable as a girl. When Reimer learned the truth in his adolescence, he made several suicide attempts before eventually changing his sex identity back to that of a male. Later, he underwent reconstructive surgery that enabled him to have a normal sex life (Colapinto, 2000).

John/Joan's story has had little effect on the way physicians treat intersex children. Most notable has been the founding of the Intersex Society of North America (ISNA) in 1993, which advocates reform in the medical practice of sex reassignment (ISNA, 2006). Surgeons today still recommend secretive surgery during infancy to make intersex children conform to an ideal of normal genitalia. About 90 percent of these surgeries reassign an ambiguous male anatomy into a female one because, in the disquieting phrase of the surgical world, "It's easier to make a hole than build a pole." A 2000 American Academy of Pediatrics policy statement on intersex surgery states that "the birth of a child with ambiguous genitalia constitutes a social emergency." To quickly resolve the "emergency," doctors are advised to examine external genitalia "to determine the degree of masculinization." Furthermore, the statement continues, "The size of the phallus and its potential to develop at puberty into a sexually functional penis are of paramount importance." So size does matter, it seems, at least to doctors.

A general rule among doctors is that a phallus less than 2 centimeters in length constitutes a "micropenis" (although that standard changes from time to time), and a male infant would be better off raised as a female rather than suffer the shame of a small penis. While physicians claim to have the interests of the child and the parents at heart, what else is at stake in intersex births? The social notion of a binary sex is also being protected. A binary sex system imposes order in the world and helps us makes sense of an otherwise complicated mass of populations. Yet it also limits our ability to accept difference. It is the goal of ISNA to reduce embarrassment and secrecy over intersex conditions.

Most people think—if they think about it at all—that the medical construction of sex applies only to a handful of individuals. Based on a review of medical literature from 1955 to 1998, Brown University

David Reimer was subjected to gender reassignment surgery at 18 months old. What does his story tell us about the relationship between biological sex and gender identity?

biology researcher Anne Fausto-Sterling estimates that the number of deviations from the binary of male or female bodies may be as high as 2 percent of live births, and the number of people receiving "corrective" genital surgery runs between 1 and 2 in every 1,000 births (Fausto-Sterling, 2000). Just to give you an idea of what 2 in 1,000 looks like, there are now about 2 in 1,000 children born with Trisomy 21 (also known as Down's syndrome), a biological condition that is more visible than intersex. Human variation within and across the two sexes is surprisingly high, and intersex activists point to the fact that social discomfort and fear of difference, rather than medical necessity, may be what pushes parents and surgeons to the operating table.

Surgeons medically construct their version of "proper" or "normal" sex, in conjunction with one on which most of us also agree. What makes a male a male and not a female? To answer this, many people would unhesitatingly mention the presence of testosterone and a penis. But consider for a moment that women also have some testosterone—the chemical boundaries are not as rigid as our socially constructed categories. If you're having trouble with the modern medical definition of sex categories, then perhaps the ancient Greeks can persuade you to consider the sociohistorical production of sex. Our present-day understanding of sex, in fact, goes way back.

Sexed Bodies in the Premodern World

Whereas Dr. John Money operated on a mutually exclusive two-sex model of human body types, a lesser known but equally plausible "one-sex" model dominated Western biological thought from the ancient Greeks until the mid-eighteenth century (Laqueur, 1990). In the old one-sex way of thinking, there was only one body (a male body) and the female body was regarded as its inversion—that is, as a male body whose parts were flipped inside rather than hanging on the outside. People believed that women were a lesser but not so radically different version of men.

Not until the two-sex model of human bodies gained ground did women and men become such radically different creatures in the popular conception. Incidentally, historian Thomas Laqueur shows us that this differentiation of bodies prompted changes in ideas about the female orgasm. In the one-sex model, it was believed that both a man's orgasm and a woman's were requirements for conception. (There is new medical evidence that dual orgasms do increase the chance of conception.) In the mid-1800s, female orgasm was considered unnecessary. Whereas seventeenth-century (female) midwives advised would-be mothers that the trick to conceiving lay in an orgasm, nineteenth-century (male) doctors debated whether it was even possible for women to experience orgasm.

Contemporary Concepts of Sex and the Paradoxes of Gender

The point of all this sex talk is to challenge our tendency to think of bodies as wholly deterministic. This is not to say that biology isn't a driving force, but merely to acknowledge that our understandings of, categorizations of, and behavior toward bodies are not set in stone. By contrast, essentialist arguments, also called essentialism, explain social phenomena in terms of natural ones. The hallmarks of essentialism are fixity, lack of history, absolutism, and biological determinism—meaning that what you do in the social world should be a direct result of who you are in the natural world. If you are born with male parts, essentialists believe, you are essentially and absolutely a man, and you will be sexually attracted to women only, as preordained by nature. Medical experts today maintain the ideal of a dimorphic or binary (either male or female) model of sex by tweaking babies who blur the boundaries. The trick is to recognize that the very boundaries separating male and female bodies are themselves somewhat contested.

This is not to say that there is no biological reality or that everything is a social construction. However, a common assumption we make is that biology comes before or dictates behavior, but sociologists now think of the nature–behavior relationship as a two-way street. Confused yet? Feminist philosopher Elizabeth Grosz (1994) proposes that we view the relationship between the natural and the social (in this case, sex and gender) as existing on a Möbius strip. The Möbius strip is an old math puzzle that looks like a twisted ribbon loop, yet it has just one side and one edge. Biological sex, the plumbing, makes

Essentialism a line of thought that explains social phenomena in terms of natural ones.

Biological determinism a line of thought that explains social behavior in terms of who you are in the natural world.

Elizabeth Grosz uses a Möbius strip, such as this one drawn by M. C. Escher, as a model for sex and gender. Even though the ants appear to be above or below each other, they are really on the same side of the strip.

up the inside of the strip, whereas the social world—culture, experience, and gender—make up the outside. But as happens in the contours of gender, the inside and outside surfaces are inseparable. In thinking or talking about sex and gender, we often switch from one to the other without even noticing that we've changed our focus (Fausto-Sterling, 2000). Some societies in various historical periods have made sense of the plumbing in different ways, and these explanations become the social construction of gender.

Gender: What Does It Take to Be a Woman (or a Man)?

You have now learned about a case in which sex was conferred rather than innate. Medically and historically, biological sex does not exist in the world in some fixed, natural state. Our next step is to trace the different social senses that humans have taken from sex. There are many historical and cross-cultural meanings, roles, and scripts for behavior that we like to think correspond to more or less fixed biological categories. This complete set of scripts is what sociologists refer to as gender, or the division of people, behaviors, and institutions into two categories: male and female.

Much like sex difference, people tend to think that gender difference is a natural cleavage between two static groups—you're either a man or a woman. Why do men tend to fight one another, dominate the hard sciences, and outnumber women in the top political offices? Why do women tend to mother, stay more connected with their families, and outnumber men in occupations that involve caring for others? The short (essentialist) answer is that men and women are naturally (that is, biologically) different, so they behave differently.

The longer, sociological answer is that gender differences are much more fluid and ambiguous than we care to admit. They cannot be so easily explained by appeals to natural differences between the sexes, because gender isn't natural: It's a social institution, as Judith Lorber claimed (1994). Gender establishes patterns of expectations for people, orders our daily lives, and is one of the fundamental building blocks of society—law, family, education, the economy, everything. The process of forming a gendered identity starts before a person is even born, as soon as the fetus is identified. Through socialization and personality development, a child acquires a gendered identity that, in most cases, reproduces the attitudes, values, and actions that his or her social milieu deems suitable for a boy or girl. (Recall our discussion of gender roles in Chapter 4.) We impose rigid boundaries to maintain a gender order, but if we look at how gender systems vary, we can expose those boundaries as social constructions. If gender is a set of stories we tell ourselves to get through the complications of living, those stories are subject to change, but they do have real consequences for us, the actors who star in that story.

Gender Differences in Other Cultures

One crucial part of the story we hear about gender is that only two genders exist, just like our idea about sex. John Gray would surely have been writing a very different book if the title had been *Men Are from Mars, Women Are from Venus, and Everyone in Between Is from Earth*. Many Western cultures struggle to divide the world neatly between men and women with correspondingly clear male and female bodies. Not so, however, for the Navajo society of Native Americans. In Navajo tribes, there are not two but three genders: masculine men, feminine women, and the *nadle*. The *nadle* might be born with ambiguous genitalia at birth or they may declare a *nadle* identity later on regardless of genitalia. The *nadle* perform both masculine and feminine tasks and dress for the moment, according to whatever activity they're doing. Although they are often treated like women, they have the freedom to marry people of any gender, "with no loss of status" (Kimmel, 2000).

Gender scholars have grown somewhat uncomfortable with the search for occurrences of "third genders" among ethnic others, pointing out that gender frameworks can be hard to shake. Serena Nanda (1990) and Gayatri Reddy (2005) studied *hijras* in India, a group that is often included in textbooks like this one to stand in as proof that a binary either/or gender system is not so natural after all. From Reddy we know that "hijras are phenotypic men who wear female clothing and ideally, renounce sexual desire and practice by undergoing a sacrificial emasculation—that is, an excision of the penis and testicles" (Reddy, 2005). To our Western ears, then, these men who renounce manhood but who are not women are actively staking a claim for a third gender. But Reddy goes on to develop the definition of what it means to be a *hijra,* which includes behaviors that may have little to do with gender: dedication to the goddess Bedhraj Mata, conferring fertility to newlyweds and newborns; a sometimes reluctant, sometimes quite dedicated entry into prostitution; communal living; self-sacrifice; and poverty. Thus *hijra* identity is a master status, but it is not experienced by the *hijras* as a fight for turf between gender categories. Like Don Kulick's Brazilian *travesti* (see page 299), the *hijras* may have few qualms about the balance they've struck between gender and sexuality and more fears about the way their poverty will shape their chances in life. To be sure, the widespread stigmatization—both groups are believed to be violent and untrustworthy—is likely related to

Hijras embracing at a wedding.

The Toilette of Venus by Peter Paul Rubens. What explanations do sociologists offer for changing ideals of beauty?

their transgression of the boundaries shaping and containing gender and sexuality practices, but using these two groups as measuring sticks against which the Western sex and gender binaries can be dismantled is a short-sighted exercise of the sociological imagination.

Gender Differences across History

Within a two-gender system, there is enormous variation in what counts as a "good" or "bad" man or woman. For example, how the ideal man or woman looks is itself historically contingent. Specifically, ideal feminine beauty has been a continuous site of change and contestation. Look at the seventeenth-century Rubenesque women, the voluptuous beauties who by today's high fashion standards are simply fat. In traditional economies where food was scarce, a plump woman was a sign of good health, wealth, and attractiveness. The long-standing preference for a robust female body has changed as industrialized societies moved from relative scarcity of food to plenitude. Today the cheaper foods are the fattening ones, and gym membership is only for those with enough disposable income. Contrary to the slogans, bigger isn't better in this economy—not if you're a woman, at least.

Accompanying this economic expansion, the transition to modern Western society also brought advances in medical knowledge and scientific discourse. By the 1920s, the female figure was standardized by the development of norms for healthy weights according to height. The fleshy Rubenses no longer fit a beauty ideal; they don't even look healthy.

Gender Differences Today

Today's idealized (white, middle-class) standards for feminine beauty in the United States present a dilemma for millions of women and girls. Approximately 3 percent of the U.S. population meets the diagnostic criteria for an eating disorder, and 90 percent of that population is female (Swanson et al., 2011). In 2010, women had approximately 8.6 million cosmetic procedures. The top five cosmetic surgical procedures for women were liposuction (also the most popular procedure for men), breast augmentation, eyelid surgery, tummy tucks, and breast reduction. Americans spent almost $12.7 billion on cosmetic procedures in 2010, yet their quest for ideal beauty was likely the pursuit of an illusion. That is, women may come close but will never attain it, as the ideal itself is always evolving (American Society for Aesthetic Plastic Surgery, 2011).

Dominant or "emphasized" definitions of femininity—as embodied by looks—are always undergoing change as well, from the hysterical Victorian housewife to the sporty working girl of the 1980s to today's heroically impossible supermom. This might be an easy point to grasp about femininity, but most people think that masculinity is less subject to such trends and fashions. It is always harder to denaturalize the dominant category; being the norm, it often is invisible. Among social categories, those who go unquestioned tend to be most privileged.

In addition to a dominant image of femininity, some theorists argue that today there exists a hegemonic masculinity as well (Connell, 1987). Hegemony is the complete dominance of a group of people, a type of power so complete that it goes unnoticed by the people who are dominated. Hegemonic masculinity is so dominant that it easily escapes our attention and is regarded as the norm against which all others are judged. Erving Goffman (1963) describes this masculine ideal as a young man who is "married, white, urban, northern, heterosexual, Protestant, father, of college education, fully employed, of good complexion, weight and height, and [with] a decent record in sports."

Hegemonic masculinity the condition in which men are dominant and privileged, and this dominance and privilege is invisible.

Today's ideal man has not always been the hegemonic definition. In *Manhood in America* (1996), Michael Kimmel traces the development of masculinity in the West and finds that in the eighteenth century, the ideal man was not associated with physical fitness, money-making endeavors, or sports. Business endeavors were the boorish concerns of the rude trade classes, and physical strength undermined one's gentlemanly dispositions. Ideal masculinity in the 1700s went hand in hand with kindness and intellect, and preferably a little poetry, a very different image from the modern-day ideal of the "man's man."

Over time and from place to place, gender roles are fluid, changing, and context-specific. Chapter 4 on socialization stated that gender roles are sets of behavioral norms assumed to accompany one's status as a male or female. Many of the differences we observe between men and women do not have much to do with gender differences at all; instead, the behaviors arise as a result of the different positions men and women occupy. Sociologist Cynthia Fuchs Epstein calls these "deceptive distinctions," that grossly exaggerate the actual differences between men and women (1988). What makes a man a man and not a woman? The sociological answer begins with "It depends."

Gender roles sets of behavioral norms assumed to accompany one's status as a male or female.

Many sociologists think of gender as a major building block in the social order and as an integral element in everyday life. It is so fundamental to the way our lives go that it is often viewed as an organizing principle of every interaction with others and even with oneself (Stacey & Thorne, 1985). That is, all social institutions and practices—education, marriage, law, the economy, fashion, health care, even baby names—are in some way tied up with gender norms and expectations. And gender crosses paths with other social statuses, such as race, class, nationality, and even body type, in significant and materially consequential ways. To speak of gender as a social construction is to say that it isn't a given. Gender is a phenomenon that shapes reality and organizes our lives even if we don't realize it, and even when we wish it didn't. Therefore, one goal central to the feminist movement has been to unpack and understand what gender is, how it is constructed, and why it takes the forms it does.

→ The Woman Question

Rubin's Sex/Gender System

At the start of the feminist movement in the 1960s, theorists scrambled to find an answer to the "woman question": What explains the nearly universal dominance of men over women? What is the root of patriarchy, a system involving the subordination of femininity to masculinity? Anthropologist Gayle Rubin was one of the first in a long string of thinkers to argue that the nearly universal oppression of women was in need of an explanation. In the field of anthropology, most scholars studying societies around the world had previously assumed that women's subordination was a given. If such subordination occurred everywhere, it must be fulfilling some function, and it could just as well be passed over in favor of more novel research questions.

Patriarchy a nearly universal system involving the subordination of femininity to masculinity.

Rubin challenged this notion and proposed the "sex/gender system" in which, she argued, every society participates in some form or other (1975). In this system, the raw materials of biological sex are transformed through kinship into asymmetrical gender statuses. She used the structural perspective of Claude Lévi-Strauss, a French anthropologist, to suggest that because of the universal taboo against incest—fathers and brothers cannot sleep with their daughters and sisters—women who start out belonging to one man (their father, or their brother if dad dies) must leave their families of origin and go belong to another man (their husband). Women are treated like valuable property whose trade patterns strengthen relations between families headed by men. This "traffic in women" gives men certain rights over their female kin. The resulting sex/gender system, she argued, was not a given; it was the result of human interaction.

Rubin's theories made waves. Feminist thinkers widely agreed that the task at hand was to explain universal male dominance. Why were women—despite a few token examples of matrifocal or women-led tribes in the anthropology books—always on the bottom of stratification systems? Why did women in almost every society seem to get short shrift? Anthropologist Michelle Rosaldo (1974) answered that it must be women's universal association with the private sphere. Because women give birth and then rear children, they become identified with domestic life, which universally is accorded less prestige, value, and rewards than men's public sphere of work and politics. Another plausible answer to the "woman question" came from fellow anthropologist Sherry Ortner (1974), who claimed that women are furthermore identified with something that every culture defines as lower than itself—nature. A woman, she reasoned, comes to be identified with the chaos and danger of nature because of bodily functions like lactation and menstruation (what feminist philosopher Simone de Beauvoir [1952] has poetically described as "woman's enslavement to the species").

Parsons's Sex Role Theory

Ortner's answer to the "woman question" sounds like a plausible one. But note the binary logic at work in these anthropological accounts: culture versus nature, private versus public, man versus woman. However, the world is less rigid, more nuanced, and certainly less easily molded into binary categories than these theories suggest. What underlies these theoretical approaches is structural functionalism. This theoretical tradition dominated early anthropological thought, and it assumed that every society had certain structures (such as the family, the division of labor, or gender) that existed to fulfill some set of necessary functions. Talcott Parsons, an influential American sociologist of the 1950s, offered a widely accepted functionalist account of gender relations (Parsons, 1951). According to Parsons's sex role theory, the nuclear family is the ideal arrangement in modern societies because it fulfills the function of reproducing workers. With a work-oriented father in the public sphere and a domestic-oriented mother in the private sphere, children are most effectively reared to be future laborers who can meet the labor demands of a capitalist system. Sex, sexuality, and gender are taken to be stable and dichotomous, meaning that each has two categories. Each category is assigned a role and a given script that actors carry out according to the expectations of those roles, which are enforced by social sanctions to ensure that the actors do not forget their lines. Women and men play distinctive roles that are functional for the whole of society; a healthy, harmonious society exists when actors stick to their normal roles. Generally speaking, according to Parsons, social structures such as gender and the division of labor are held in place because they work to ensure a stable society.

Functionalism was a hit in the 1950s; it makes intuitive sense and conveniently explains away otherwise difficult social facts fraught with exceptions. But Parsons's sex role theory falls short on several points. For starters, the argument is tautological—that is, it explains the existence of a structure in terms of its function, essentially claiming that things work the way they do because they work. In explaining a phenomenon in terms of its function, functionalists relied on the presumption that the need for the function preexists the phenomenon, a tricky leap of logical faith. Furthermore, they glossed over the possibility that other structures could fulfill the same functions.

The functionalist sex role story also does not explain how and why structures change throughout history. If traditional husband and wife sex roles were so functional, why did they change drastically in the

Structural functionalism
theoretical tradition claiming that every society has certain structures (the family, the division of labor, or gender) that exist to fulfill some set of necessary functions (reproduction of the species, production of goods, etc.).

Sex role theory Talcott Parsons's theory that men and women perform their sex roles as breadwinners and wives/mothers, respectively, because the nuclear family is the ideal arrangement in modern societies, fulfilling the function of reproducing workers.

In the 1950s, Talcott Parsons advanced the idea that the nuclear family effectively reared children to meet the labor demands of a capitalist system.

1970s? In Parsons's account, gender roles appear to be a matter of voluntarism, as if women and men choose, independently of external power constraints, to be housewives and breadwinners. Finally—and this is a problem with much early feminist thinking as well—sex and gender are regarded as being composed of dichotomous roles, when these categories are, in fact, fuzzy, flexible, and variable in combination with other social positions, such as race and class.

Psychoanalytic Theories

Where functionalism focuses too much, perhaps, on society as a whole, Freudian theorists have provided an overly individualistic, psychoanalytic account of sex roles. The father of psychoanalysis, Sigmund Freud (1856–1939), famously quipped, "Anatomy is destiny." Although biological determinism plays a major role in Freudian theory, so does the idea that gender develops through family socialization.

According to Freud's developmental psychology, girls and boys develop masculine and feminine personality structures through early interactions with their parents. Boys, so the story goes, have a tormented time achieving masculinity because they must resolve the oedipal complex. In this stage of development, around age 3, every normal boy experiences heterosexual love for his attentive mother. But he realizes quickly that he will be castrated (psychologically, not literally) by his father if he continues to fancy his mother. To resolve the oedipal stage, the boy rejects his mother, in turn emulating his emotionally distant father and developing rigid ego boundaries.

Girls do not experience quite the same resolution to their analogous "penis envy." When a little girl realizes that she lacks the plumbing to have sexual relations with her mother, she experiences penis envy toward her father. However, she ultimately realizes that one day she too can have a baby, thus providing feminine gratification. Girls end up identifying with their mothers, growing up with less rigid ego boundaries and more easily connecting with others than boys do.

Feminist psychoanalyst Nancy Chodorow (1978) applied Freud's theory to answer a particular version of the "woman question"—namely, why are women predominantly the caregivers? She reasoned that parents' unequal involvement in child rearing was a partial cause for the universal oppression of women. Her answer was that mothering by women is reproduced in a cycle of role socialization, in which little girls learn to identify as mothers and little boys as fathers. Social structures such as gender roles and the division of labor induce the psychological process of forming a gender identity, and they in turn reproduce themselves when women raise children and men work outside the home. Chodorow argued that egalitarian relations between the sexes would be possible if men shared the mothering.

Carol Gilligan (1982) also adapted Freudian psychology to make the case that men and women have different ways of thinking. By her account, women make major life decisions (such as choosing whether or not to have an abortion) based on what she calls an "ethics of care." Women, she claimed, tend to view the world as composed of human connections and relationships. In contrast, men make decisions by adhering to a system of rules. For them, the world is governed by impersonal, abstract rules and notions of justice.

Gilligan found evidence of men's and women's "different voices" in the playground observations of sociologist Janet Lever. Little boys, observed Lever, tend to play competitive, rule-intensive games (like war), whereas little girls play cooperative and people-based games (like house). Lever also found that when a conflict erupted on the playground, boys argued with appeals to the rules of the game. They made and judged claims such as "It's not fair!" and then were able to continue their game. Girls, however, played shorter and less complex games. When a conflict broke out, they were more likely to bend the rules to spare each other's feelings, or they would just give up and quit (Lever, 1976).

What did sociologist Janet Lever observe about the difference between the types of games that boys play versus those favored by girls?

If the "different" theoretical approaches of Chodorow and Gilligan sound reasonable, let's look at two variations on Freudian explanations for why girls and boys turn out the way they do. Melanie Klein (1882–1960) expanded Freud's account of child development to emphasize the importance of the mother's role. She claimed that boys suffer breast envy (Klein, 1949). Jacqueline Stevens went further, arguing that boys suffer from pregnancy envy on their way to acquiring a masculine identity that focuses on the acquisition of property and territory, through finance and war, in lieu of the baby they secretly lament not being able to have (Stevens, 2006).

Before you see a psychoanalyst to discuss your own penis or pregnancy envy, consider the biological reductionism in all these psychological accounts. For starters, Freud's theories lacked empirical evidence and were based on the model of a two-parent nuclear family. Most of you reading this probably did not grow up in the traditional family setting on which Chodorow and Gilligan based their research—a white, middle-class, nuclear family with a working father and stay-at-home mother. Sociologist Carol Stack underscored this point in her ethnography of a poor black community. In *All Our Kin* (1974), she finds that the division between male and female roles and attitudes is not as clear-cut as Freud would have us think. Caregiving is a valued responsibility for both men and women, who are oriented toward a larger network of community and family.

Moreover, Chodorow, Gilligan, Klein, and Stevens take for granted a binary sex/gender system, whereas we know that those categories are much more fluid in real life. These psychological theories of gender development contain elements of essentialist thinking as well. Recall that in essentialist arguments, social behavior is reduced to natural, biologically determined behavior. On the extreme end of essentialist thought is Freud, who claimed that "anatomy is destiny." Although Chodorow and Gilligan move away from such a reductionist stance by locating the root of gender differences in the household division of labor, they both treat men and women as agents who have inherent and necessary personality traits. Gilligan argues that not only are men and women inherently different, but women are so much the better because they're more relational and connected to others. Feminist historian Joan W. Scott (1988) calls this the "herstory" approach in women's history, in which feminists try so hard to include women's experiences that they end up assessing everything women do as superb. Such theorists fail to recognize that not all women adopt an ethics of care or relational orientation.

Conflict Theories

By the 1980s, another wave of thinkers began to tackle an issue missing from earlier discussions of the "woman question": power. Conflict theorists mixed old-school Marxism with feminism to claim that gender, not class, was the driving force of history. Socialist feminists, also known as radical feminists, claimed that the root of all social relations, including relations of production, stemmed from unequal gender relations.

Economist Heidi Hartmann (1981) and legal theorist Catharine MacKinnon (1983), for example, both analyzed how capitalism combines with patriarchy to make women economically dependent on men's incomes. This means that in a capitalist society, women have a disadvantaged position in the job market and within the family. Capitalists (that is, men) in turn reap all the benefits of women's subordination. When women are subordinate, men benefit. To radical feminists, gender inequality is first and foremost about power inequalities, and gender differences (as in personality development) emerge from there. However, what lies beneath these conflict theories is yet another variant of essentialism. They basically posited that the world is divided into two groups: men and women (red flag number one). These two groups are necessarily pitted against each other in a struggle for resources (red flag number two). Again, men and women are reduced to automatons in a static battle, which women always lose.

"Doing Gender": Microinteractionist Theories

A social theory is useful only if it helps you understand the social world in which you live. Of course, there are power differentials and forces of socialization that operate in the world. But men and women act and interact in a variety

Many conflict theorists argue that patriarchal capitalists benefit through systems that subordinate women. For instance, many cotton mills in the nineteenth and early twentieth centuries hired young, unmarried women and required them to live in company boarding houses in order to regulate their behavior.

of ways and with unlimited possibilities for outcomes. Gender is also a process, as social constructionists have argued. Candace West and Don H. Zimmerman, for example, argue in their influential article "Doing Gender" (1987) that gender is not a fixed identity that we take with us into our interactions. Rather, it is the product of those interactions. In this framework, gender is a matter of active doing, not simply a matter of natural being. To be a man or a woman, they argue, is to perform masculinity or femininity constantly.

The "doing gender" perspective is rooted in Erving Goffman's dramaturgical theory, symbolic interactionism, and ethnomethodology. That is, West and Zimmerman argue that people create their social realities and identities through interactions with one another. Unlike the structural functionalists, psychoanalysts, and conflict theorists, however, social constructionists view gender roles as having open-ended scripts. Perhaps individuals come to the stage situated differently according to their place in power hierarchies or personality development, but their lines and gestures are far from being predetermined. Regardless of social location, individuals are always free to act, sometimes in unexpected ways that change the course of the play. But by and large, as a result of "doing gender," people contribute to, reaffirm, and reproduce masculine dominance and feminine submissiveness.

Black Feminism

If gender is a performance, it is much more than a set of neutral scripts that we voluntarily follow. Our actions are influenced by structural forces that we might not even be aware of, such as class or race privilege. As Patricia Hill Collins (1990) claims, we "do" a lot more than gender; gender intersects with race, class, nationality, religion, and so forth. Black feminists have made the case that early liberal feminism was largely by, about, and for white middle-class women. In trying to answer the "woman question" and explain women's oppression, early feminists assumed that all women were in the same oppressed boat. In so doing, they effaced multiple lines of fragmentation and difference into one simple category: woman. For example, by championing women's rights to work outside the home in *The Feminine Mystique* (1963/1997), leading second-wave feminist Betty Friedan ignored the experiences of thousands of working-class and nonwhite women who were already working, sometimes holding down two jobs to support their families.

"Woman" is not a stable or obvious category of identity. Rather, women are differentially located in what Collins calls a "matrix of domination." A 40-year-old poor, black, and straight single mother living in rural Georgia will not have the same conception of what it means to be a woman as a 25-year-old professional, white, single lesbian in Chicago. More fundamentally, she argues, black women face unique oppressions that white women don't. For instance, black women experience motherhood in ways that differ from the white masculinist

Patricia Hill Collins criticized feminist leaders such as Betty Friedan (pictured above in the red dress), Billie Jean King (in tan pants and a blue shirt on the left), or Bella Abzug (in the gray dress, with the hat) for ignoring the experiences of thousands of working-class and nonwhite women.

ideal of the family, as "bloodmothers," "othermothers," and "community other-mothers," thus revealing that white masculine notions of the world are sometimes irrelevant to the daily lives of black women (Collins, 1990).

Gender, sexual orientation, race, class, nationality, ability, and other factors all intersect. Just as some women enjoy privilege by virtue of their wealth, class, education, and skin color, some men are disadvantaged by their lack of these same assets. As bell hooks (1984) noted, if women's liberation is aimed at making women the social equals of men, women should first stop and consider which men they would like to equal. Certainly, not all men are privileged over all women. Making universal comparisons of men to women misses these nuances and implicitly excludes marginally positioned people from the discussion.

Power comes from many different angles; it doesn't sit evenly on a plane for all women. When the black activist Sojourner Truth (1797–1883) asked, "Ain't I a woman?" (1851), she summed up some elusive philosophical questions: What is woman? Who counts as a woman and why?

Postmodern Theories

As perspectives have expanded and previously rigid categories have begun to crumble, the validity of the "woman question" is itself now in question. For instance, anthropologist Oyèrónké Oyěwùmí argues that the "woman question" is a product of uniquely Western thought and cannot be applied to African societies. In *The Invention of Women* (1997), she presents ethnographic research of Yoruban society in West Africa, which she claims was once a genderless society. In Yoruba, before the arrival of anthropologists, villagers did not group themselves as men or women or use body markers at all. Rather, they ranked themselves into strata by seniority. When Western feminist scholars arrived on the scene, presuming the preexistence of gender relations, they, of course, found a system of gender. But this system of categories—distinct males and females—indicates a Western cultural logic, what Oyěwùmí has termed "bio-logic."

Bio-logic runs deep in our cultural experiences and understandings of gender. It acts as a sort of filter through which all knowledge of the world runs, but in fact there may be different ways of knowing outside such a paradigm. But if "woman" is such an unstable category—one that is merely "performed," as postmodern theorist Judith Butler says, one that is so fragmented and trapped in discourse—how are we supposed to study it? Feminists must have some sturdy ground on which to unite, build coalitions, and tackle injustice. Philosopher Susan Bordo (1990) provides a pragmatic buoy by arguing that there are hierarchal and binary power structures out there that do still oppress women. The postmodern emphasis on fragmented identity, blurring of sex and gender boundaries, and gender skepticism won't get gender theory anywhere when it comes to addressing issues such as the wage gap, eating disorders, or rape.

Sociology in the Bedroom

Sex. You think it's the most personal, intimate act. The bedroom is surely the one place where the sociological imagination is the last thing you'll need. But a sociological approach can reveal some startling insights about the social construction of sexuality. Connections may be found between the sheets and history, desire and science, how we do it and how it in turn organizes what we do, as well as with whom and with what meanings. As expected, an excavation into the social construction of sexuality divulges a surprising amount of variation in what is considered normal bedroom behavior. By exposing different social patterns of sexuality, throughout history and across cultures, the sociologist can trace unequal power relations and show how sexuality expresses, represses, and elucidates those relations.

Sexuality in Other Times and Places

Among the ancient Greeks, for example, homosexual relationships were accepted and supposed to be patterned on an active–passive distinction (although historians have shown that many exceptions existed). The active partner was supposed to be older or higher in status than the passive partner. To flip the rules was a violation, and it was considered shameful for a master or noble to be penetrated by a younger man. A more extreme and brutal example of sexual relations founded on power relations can be found today in the social orders in U.S. prisons, where rape is about power: Who is in charge, who is being penetrated, and who is normal versus deviant. Prison rape may not be primarily about seeking sexual gratification; it is reported that few prison rapists climax during the act. In prison, the homosexual act is often seen as something altogether distinct from homosexual identity.

Or, consider sexual normality among the Sambia, a mountain people in Papua New Guinea. Anthropologist Gilbert Herdt (1981) reported that fellatio played a significant role in a boy's transition into manhood. Young boys are initiated into manhood by a daily ritual of fellatio on older boys and men. By

An ancient Greek image of two male lovers. How can comparing social patterns of sexuality across cultures and throughout history help sociologists understand modern sexuality?

taking in the vital life liquid (semen) of older men, boys prepare themselves to be warriors and sexual partners with women. Fellatio, for Sambia boys, then, is the only way to become "real" men.

Other cultures' attitudes toward homosexuality are on a whole different level. Both the Siwans of North Africa and the Keraki, also in New Guinea, prefer homosexuality to heterosexuality, for fairly straightforward, practical reasons (Kimmel, 2000). Because every male is homosexual during his adolescence and then bisexual after heterosexual marriage, the limited straight sex keeps down the birthrate. In these cultures with scant resources, homosexuality makes practical sense to limit the chances of teen pregnancy and overpopulation.

There is enormous variation in how humans have sex and what it means to them. Mouth-to-mouth kissing, common in Western cultures, is unthinkable among the Thonga and Sirono cultures: "But that's where you put food!" (Kimmel, 2000). American middle-class couples have sex a few nights a week for about 15 minutes a pop; the people of Yapese cultures near Guam engage in sex once a month. Marquesan men of French Polynesia are said to have anywhere from 10 to 30 orgasms a night! Which of these is "normal"?

The Social Construction of Sexuality

By treating sexuality as a social construction—that is, as always shaped by social factors—the sociologist would argue that the notion of normal, especially pertaining to what happens behind closed bedroom doors, is always contested. In other words, there is no natural way of doing it. If an essentially right way existed, we wouldn't be able to find such wild and woolly variation throughout history and across cultures. Starting from the view that sex itself is a social creation, sociologists tend to argue that humans have sexual plumbing and potential but no sexuality until they are located in a social environment. The range of normal and abnormal is itself a construction, a production of society. The study of this range can lead the willing sociologist into an exploration of the social relations on which sex is built.

Sexuality and Power Marxist feminists, for instance, argue that sexuality in America is an expression of the unequal power balance between men and women. Catharine MacKinnon (1983) argued that in male-dominated societies, sexuality is constructed as a gender binary, with men on top and women on the bottom (literally and figuratively). To MacKinnon, sexuality is the linchpin of gender inequality, an expression of male control. In a male-dominated state, where men have the power to create the world from their allegedly more objective point of view, says MacKinnon, sex is rape and rape is sex: "Man fucks woman; subject verb object."

Adrienne Rich (1980) called sexuality in America a "compulsory hetero-sexuality." This "political institution," at least for some, is not a preference but something that has been imposed, managed, organized, and enforced to serve a male-dominated capitalist system in which women's unpaid domestic work is required to support men's paid work outside of the home. Because her work is unpaid, the woman in this situation is unable to leave a bad husband. According to Rich, people come to see heterosexuality as the norm, when it is, in fact, a mechanism integral to sustaining women's social subordination. Although these arguments are provocative, in the end, they also reflect essentialist and reductionist views of sex. Surely not all women are mere objects or are duped into exploitative relations with their oppressive male partners.

Homosexuality The connections between sex and power are best exemplified in the social construction of the homosexual, the social identity of a person who has sexual attraction to and/or relations with other persons of the same sex. For most of the past century, the dominant view has been that individuals are born either homosexual or heterosexual, gay or straight, queer or normal. Sexual orientation was thought of as a kind of personhood automatically acquired at birth or something carried in our genes (despite documented cases of identical twins in which one is straight and the other gay). But recall the ancient Greeks' homosexual love, prison rape, and the Sambian rites of manhood. Men in these cultures engage in homosexual acts without adopting a homosexual identity. When do acts, behaviors, or desires crystallize into identities?

Before 1850, there was no such thing as a homosexual. Sure, people engaged in homosexual behaviors. But around 1850, the homosexual identity was born. The French philosopher Michel Foucault (1926–1984) led the way to poststructuralist notions of the body and sexuality as historical productions. In *The History of Sexuality* (1978), Foucault made the case that the body is "in the grip" of cultural practices. That is, there is no presocial or natural body; instead, culture is always already inscribed on our bodies. It's a by now familiar stance on the social construction of the body and on the permanent intermingling of the biological and the social. But Foucault further argued that the way in which we know our bodies is linked to power, and knowledge and power go hand in hand. As the population expanded in nineteenth-century Europe, newly formed states and their administrators developed a concern for population management. The rise of scientific ways of thinking at the time led to the creation of what Foucault calls "bio-power," the observation and management of populations by influencing patterns in births, deaths, and illnesses.

Discourses of sexuality had by then surfaced. People talked about sex, scientists studied it, and government officials tried to regulate it, whereas a century before, all this sex talk did not exist. With the development of the

Homosexual the social identity of a person who has sexual attraction to and/or relations with other persons of the same sex.

An 1895 cartoon illustrating Oscar Wilde's sodomy trial. Wilde was convicted of gross indecency for his homosexual relationship with Lord Alfred Douglas. He served two years of hard labor in prison.

biological and human sciences in the nineteenth century, doctors wanted to know which kinds of sex were normal and which were deviant, and new attention was paid to policing those differences. By the late 1800s, "Homosexuality appeared as one of the forms of sexuality when it was transposed from the practice of sodomy onto a kind of interior androgyny, a hermaphrodism of the soul" (Foucault, 1978). In Foucault's account, homosexuality comes back to the efforts of government bureaucrats trying to assert their power (that of the state) over human populations.

This new homosexual body that had been constructed became a personality type, and a deviant one at that. The American Psychiatric Association and the American Psychological Association listed homosexuality on their list of mental disorders until 1973. Homosexuals were regarded as needing to be regulated, observed, studied, and most important, controlled. Because everyone was capable of, or in danger of, sexual deviance, the urgency to confess one's sexuality grew, as did the scientific need for public surveillance. Who was gay? How could a homosexual be detected? Anyone could be a pervert—your professor, your roommate, even you!

To regulate potentially perverse bodies, new modes of social control emerged in the transition to modern structures of state power. Coercion and direct force were replaced with more efficient forms of restraint: self-surveillance and what Foucault called *normalization*. Under a sovereign king (that is, before the modern state), discipline was administered on a scaffold or stockade, by direct punitive physical force. In modern society, discipline was administered by the self: "There is no need for arms, physical violence, material constraints. Just a gaze. An inspecting gaze, a gaze which each individual under its weight will end by interiorizing to the point that he is his own overseer, each individual thus exercising this surveillance over, and against, himself." It was, Foucault adds, "a superb formula" (Foucault, 1980).

The act of sodomy became synonymous with the person who performs it. Even our language reflects the way sexual behavior becomes more than a single event among the many other behaviors that make up an individual's life. Here's what I mean. If a man roasts a whole pig—a serious, time-consuming undertaking that requires research, dedication, and planning—he is not known ever after as a "pig roaster" or even as a gourmand. He's still just Bob from down the block who hosted one heck of a barbeque. But if a man has anal sex with another man—something that takes less time and probably less dedication and research than roasting a pig—he becomes a sodomite, a homosexual, gay, or whatever terminology might fit the context. This was not always so. At one point, what happened in the bedroom stayed there. But over the last century what happened behind closed doors was outed and a whole new body and being were produced. Today our society places a huge emphasis—our entire selfhood, according to Foucault—on sexuality. Now what you do (and with whom) defines who you are: Not just how others see you, but how you

experience yourself. The framing of homosexuality as a comprehensive social identity, in fact, produced homosexuals, so that today 3.4 percent of Americans identify themselves as lesbian, gay, bisexual, or trans (Gates & Newport, 2012). There are hundreds of gay pride parades every year all over the country, and gay marriage is legal in many states.

Consider the widely used argument against lesbian and gay couplings: "It's unnatural," meaning that sex is supposed to be about reproduction. This is a popular argument against same-sex marriages, but it also stigmatizes straight couples experiencing or choosing infertility. Besides, homosexuality occurs widely in nature; one of our closest primate cousins, the bonobo, practices homosexuality (Parker, 2007). Though based on questionable data, Alfred Kinsey's 1948 study *Sexual Behavior in the Human Male* suggested that at least 10 percent of men were homosexual. He challenged the psychiatric model of homosexuals as perverse and abnormal and instead viewed sexuality as a continuum (Kinsey, 1948). Most people, he claimed,

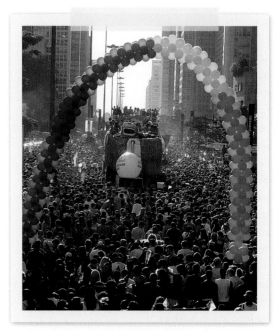

Thousands participate in a 2003 gay pride parade.

experience both heterosexual and homosexual feelings and behaviors. Kinsey's figures have since been disputed—his sampling was not representative of the U.S. population as a whole—but the basic idea holds. Across the globe and throughout history, there has been more or less the same degree of homosexual behavior. Social perceptions of homosexuals, however, are in flux.

Studies of homosexuality today approach the phenomenon not as being located in a unified, stable, or even identifiable type of person, "the homosexual." Rather, this fluid identity intersects with other social positions, such as class, race, age, location, ability, and gender. But how does gender influence sexuality? We've seen already how sex and gender do not match up; female plumbing does not always neatly correspond to a feminine gendered identity. Yale historian George Chauncey makes the case in *Gay New York* (1994) that in early-twentieth-century New York, an emerging working-class gay world was split between masculine men and the effeminate men who solicited them. As long as men stuck to their masculine gender scripts, no matter how often they engaged in gay sex, they were not considered abnormal like the girly men, who were derided for their effeminacy.

How do *travesti* challenge common binary models of understanding gender and sexuality?

The reverse is true among the *travesti,* transgender prostitutes in Brazil. Anthropologist Don Kulick conducted an ethnography of the *travesti*, males who adopt female names, clothing styles, hairstyles, cosmetic practices, and linguistic pronouns; ingest female hormones; and inject industrial silicone directly into their bodies to give themselves breasts and round buttocks or *bunda* (Kulick, 1998). They display all the stereotypically feminine traits, yet they do not self-identify as women. In fact, they think it is both repugnant and impossible for men to try to become women. Kulick argues that in Brazil, gender is determined by sexual practice; "what one does in bed has immediate and lasting consequences for the way one is perceived (and the way one can perceive oneself) as a gendered being. If one penetrates, in this particular configuration of sexuality and gender, one is a 'man.' If one expresses interest in the penis of a male, and especially if one 'gives'—allows oneself to be penetrated by a male—then one is no longer a man." However, the *travesti* do not think they are women; they think of themselves as *travesti,* men who emulate women but are not women. The primacy of penetration as a determinant of gender is common across cultures and challenges Americans to look beyond chromosomes and hormones to practices and cultural context.

Why Not Talk about Teen Sex?

The many ways of doing it—over time and across cultures—complicate the romantic ideal of love in modern America. Arguably, a glaring discrepancy exists between this ideal and reality. In 1948, Kinsey found high rates of bisexual activity—as many as 46 percent of males and between 6 and 14 percent of females engaged in it. He also documented a wide variety of sexual positions, preferences, desires, and extramarital activity among men and women. The Reverend Billy Graham denied the findings and claimed that Kinsey "certainly could not have interviewed any of the millions of born-again Christian women in this country who put the highest price on virtue, decency and modesty." Indeed, Kinsey's sample was biased by the willingness of those who participated. Although this bias calls the exact figure into question, his study was a landmark for bringing to light a wide range of sexual practices and preferences in the U.S. population.

Federal funding for studies of sexual activity has since come under attack in the name of decency. Witness the defunding of the American Teenage Study in 1992, which some politicians called one of those "reprehensive sex surveys undertaken to legitimize homosexuality and other sexually promiscuous lifestyles" (Remez, 2000).

From Hooking up to Virginity Pledges Sometimes the policies meant to achieve one end backfire and cause the opposite outcome, despite the best intentions. Government efforts to influence healthy teen sexuality provide one example. Recent studies have described the blasé attitude that contemporary American teenagers supposedly bring to their love lives. When sociologist Paula England surveyed students at one Midwestern university about their sex lives, half reported that their previous sexual partner was someone they had slept with only once. Here's how she explained hook-up culture, which has replaced dating as the route to romance on college campuses around the country. She did her first surveys at Northwestern, where "before people ever go on a date, they hook up." Lest there be any confusion: a hook-up is not sex . . . unless it is. A hook-up means "something sexual happens, that 'something sexual' is not always

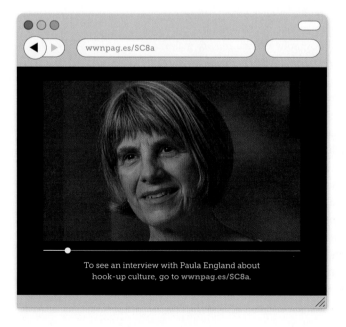

To see an interview with Paula England about hook-up culture, go to wwnpag.es/SC8a.

intercourse, often in fact [in] the majority of cases it isn't, and there is no nec-essary implication that anybody's interested in a relationship, but they *might* be interested." Dating is infrequent, but it is not dead. It is "charged with more meaning now, and it's more likely to be leading to a relationship." Further-more, "there's a strong norm that relationships should be monogamous and marriages should be monogamous and that people eventually want to get to monogamy and a marriage. They're just putting it off a lot longer. That's really what's changed, I think" (Conley, 2009d).

Why so many short-lived hook-ups instead of longer-term relationships? For one thing, the students are not looking to begin families anytime soon. For another, relationships are just more work. England found that heterosexual males are not necessarily expected to sexually satisfy the women they hook up with, but the opposite is true when they are in relationships. In a hook-up, "a real gender inequality is if there's oral sex but they didn't have intercourse; sometimes it's reciprocal, but if it is not reciprocal it's much more likely that the woman is servicing the guy than vice versa. So it seems like the hook-ups are prioritizing male pleasure" (Conley, 2009d). In a hook-up culture, what might determine whether a pair continues to hook up or moves on to new partners? England has a theory that goes like this:

> Partner-specific investment may well be important. In other words, . . . our ability to please partners may not just be generally what have we learned from a lifetime of experience but what have we actually learned about this particular partner and what works for them and what they like and what they need. . . . If it's hook-up number two, she's more likely to have an orgasm than if it's one, and if it's three more likely, and if it's four even more likely. (Conley, 2009d)

She also noted that these hook-ups rarely produce babies—70 percent of stu-dents used a condom the last time they had vaginal sex.

Here are more numbers: Just fewer than 50 percent of American teenag-ers over the age of 14 tell surveyors that they have had sexual intercourse (Figure 8.1), but this rate is not growing; it has remained more or less steady since 2003 (Centers for Disease Control and Prevention, 2010). Boys probably lie more often about the extent of their sexual experience (citing the proverbial girlfriend in a different state), and girls possibly downplay their sexual activity. Many of those who have not had intercourse are still sexually active in other ways. As we learned in Chapter 5, a good two-thirds of American teens are already having sex or are very close to doing it. Teenagers' romantic interludes last about 15 months on average, leaving them plenty of time before mar-riage (average age 25 for women and 27 for men) to have many partners. To top it off, most adolescents with a sexually transmitted disease (STD) don't know that they are infected. All of these factors combine to put American

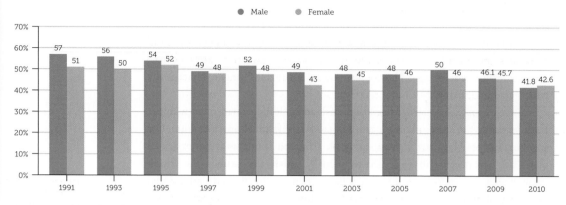

Figure 8.1: Percentage of High-School Students Who Have Had Sex, 1991–2010

● Male   ● Female

SOURCE: Centers for Disease Control and Prevention, 2011a.

teenagers at high risk for STDs, which have been increasing dramatically since the 1970s.

So what's a public health officer to do? During its years in office, the Bush administration (2001–9) advocated a "virginity pledge" and other abstinence policies, and the abstinence advocacy group True Love Waits says that 2.5 million young people have made the virginity pledge since 1993 (Herbert, 2011). As it turns out, the pledge does, on average, delay the onset of sexual activity as well as reduce a teenager's number of sexual partners, according to the National Longitudinal Study of Adolescent Health (Brückner & Bearman, 2005). The study, funded by the Centers for Disease Control and Prevention and the National Science Foundation, followed the sexual activity of 12- to 18-year-olds for six years. It found that teenagers who took the virginity pledge had about the same rates of STDs as those who never made the pledge. So when sex happens (as it almost always does), it's much more likely to come in a rush of surprisingly strong, unfettered desire. Among the pledgers, only 40 percent ended up using a condom during sex—why would they have a condom if they were planning to be virgins until marriage?—compared with 60 percent of teens who had not pledged.

Teenagers at Silver Ring Thing, a faith-based abstinence-only program held at a church in Canton, Ohio. According to research by social scientists, what are the results of abstinence-only programs?

Growing Up, Getting Ahead, and Falling Behind

In January 2005, Harvard president Larry Summers was a guest speaker at a conference called "Diversifying the Science and Engineering Work Force." He was invited to deliver a provocative address, and indeed, his speech was so provocative that it sparked a media frenzy termed "Gendergate" by journalists. Summers stated that at the highest levels of performance, men might have an innate advantage over women in scientific aptitude and that genetic differences could explain the scarcity of female "hard" scientists at elite universities (Atlas, 2005). Critics referred to the speech as a blatant example in academia of sexism, in which a person's sex is the basis for prejudicial discrimination and where sex may matter more than a person's performance or merits.

Sexism occurs when a person's sex or gender is the basis for judgment, discrimination, and hatred against him or her.

Summers's explanation threw his university into turmoil and eventually led to his resignation, and likely prevented him from becoming the chair of the Federal Reserve, but the general problem he described is a real one. In 2000, although 48.2 percent of students who graduated with a bachelor's degree in math from a top-50-ranked university were female, only 8.3 percent of math faculty members were women (Nelson & Rogers, 2004). A flip side to this controversy is that women are overtaking men in college enrollment (Figure 8.2). Fifty-five percent of college students in 2006 were women (Wang & Parker,

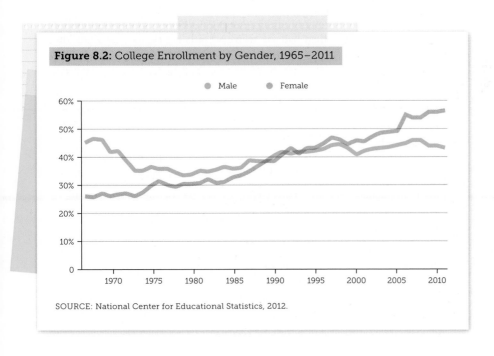

Figure 8.2: College Enrollment by Gender, 1965–2011

● Male   ● Female

SOURCE: National Center for Educational Statistics, 2012.

2011). However, despite their increased enrollment, women remain overrepresented in traditionally feminine fields of study: The arts and the humanities. Men also outnumber women at elite colleges, where they are groomed for high-power professions in finance, law, or politics.

Within academia, men dominate traditionally masculine fields such as math and physics. Not surprisingly, positions in these "hard" sciences pay more than those in "soft" ones. The average engineering college professor begins with a starting salary of about $78,700; the average English/literature professor starts out at $52,000 (Brantley, 2012). Do men become mathematicians and women literary critics because they are hardwired to do so? Not even Larry Summers would attribute gender segmentation in education entirely to genes. He suggested that it may be one of many factors, and even that got him into trouble. In fact, what he argued was that there was greater variance (not a higher average) in math scores for boys. Because the very highest math scorers end up at the top, and because boys had a bigger spread, the very few at the top tended to be male (as well as the few at the bottom end), even if average scores were similar across gender.

Whether or not Summers's argument holds water, we do know that men and women vary in thousands of major and minor measures. It starts at birth. The average male newborn weighs 2 ounces more than the average female newborn. For infant death rates, however, the disadvantage is tilted against males, who are at higher risk of death than females. Psychologist Carol Gilligan contends that by adolescence, the disadvantages are stacked against girls, who "lose their voices" as they suffer blows to their self-confidence. Eating disorders are about twice as likely to affect adolescent and teen girls compared with their male peers. More than half of teenaged girls are on diets or think they should be. What's more, girls more frequently report low self-esteem, more girls attempt suicide, and more girls report experiencing some form of sexual harassment in school. Psychologist Mary Pipher's *Reviving Ophelia* (1994) details the fiery demise of adolescent girls: "Something dramatic happens to girls in early adolescence. . . . They crash and burn in a social and developmental Bermuda Triangle."

Psychologist Christina Hoff Sommers challenges this "girl crisis" in *The War against Boys: How Misguided Feminism Is Harming Our Young Men* (2000). She finds that because they are inadvertently penalized for the shortchanging of girls, boys are the ones suffering in education and adolescent health. For example, although females in general attempt suicide twice as frequently as males, boys ages 15 to 19 succeed in killing themselves four times more often than girls. Teenage girls may sneak more cigarettes than boys, but boys are more likely to be involved in crime, alcohol, and drugs and to be suspended from school or drop out. Male teens are also 40 percent more likely to be victimized by violent crime, and that's even taking rape into account. Being an adolescent stinks, no matter what gender (or sex) you are.

What accounts for the wide range of statistical differences that exist between men and women? Essentialists might refer to natural sex differences, but sociologists are apt to call these same differences "deceptive distinctions," those that arise because of the particular roles individuals come to occupy (Epstein, 1988). Why do men think in the abstract terms of rationality and justice? Because their employment possibilities are more likely to include jobs with these demands. Why are women so good at mothering? Because their bleak employment prospects encourage them to accept domestic roles and rely on a male's salary. Who is more relational and who is more rational? Anthropologists William and Jean O'Barr find that the true test of what type of language an individual uses during testimony in court is the witness's occupation, not gender (O'Barr, 1995; Kimmel, 2000). Physicists tend to speak in more abstract terms, teachers in more relational ones, regardless of gender. Once such deceptive distinctions are revealed, it is easy to flip the essentialist rhetoric to see that gender differences are a product of gender inequality, not the cause. Physicists speak in more abstract terms, teachers in more rational ones because their jobs demand it. The question then shifts to, Why do men and women end up disproportionately split into occupations by gender? We need to peel back another layer of the gender onion.

Gender Inequality in the Classroom

We can find one answer (or onion layer) in the educational system. As we saw in our discussion of gender-role socialization in Chapter 4, the classroom functions as a sort of gender training ground for boys and girls. Not only does the classroom begin training children how to act properly gendered (which toys to play with, what colors to wear), but this is the place where children learn quickly about gender inequality. In *Failing at Fairness,* education professors Myra and David Sadker (1994) report that boys are called on more in class, they interrupt girls (and get away with it) more often than the reverse, and their teachers expect them to be better at math and worse at reading. Girls, the authors show, are frequently bullied out of classroom discussion, put down by their male classmates, and effectively silenced. Boys and girls may share one classroom, but they receive two separate educations.

When students open their schoolbooks or turn on the television set, they may find further representations of gender inequalities. In 1975, when the U.S. Department of Health, Education, and Welfare surveyed children's books, it found that active boys, shown outdoors having exciting and important adventures, populated textbooks. When shown at all, girls remained passive, dependent, and bored (and usually boring). Since then, some changes have been made. For example, representations in the popular media, once highly

As more and more women entered the workforce, one common career for women was secretary. The Olivetti company marketed typewriters for secretaries via the glamorous "Olivetti girls" campaign. If you didn't know that Olivetti made typewriters, based on this ad, what job would you guess "Olivetti girls" had?

reflective of the same stereotypes as in textbooks, have increasingly shown more girls in active roles—engaged in sports, holding careers, and defying traditional stereotypes of homemaking femininity. Girls, so it appears in the media, are catching up. But representations of masculine roles have remained defiantly distant from child rearing, housework, and nurturance.

Inequality at Work

The same trend holds fast in the real world of work and family, where women's roles have expanded into paid work while men's have hardly budged toward more involvement in the domestic sphere (see Chapter 10). The past few decades have brought arguably the biggest change in American gender relations. Since the 1970s, almost 37 million more women have entered the labor force, from 31.5 million in 1970 to 72 million in 2008 (Figure 8.3). Of course, the overall population has increased by 50 percent in that period as well, accounting for part of the rise, but the percentage of women ages 16 to 64 who are in the workforce has risen from approximately 43 to 60 percent. In fact, because the Great Recession of 2008–9 hit male-dominated industries the hardest (such as construction), it helped accelerate the trend toward gender equality in labor force participation. Today there are about the same number of women and men in the workforce. Women even exceeded men for a brief moment at the depth of the economic crisis, though the recovery in male sectors has since outpaced that in predominantly female ones—most notably because women are disproportionately employed in the public sector, and state governments have yet to recover from the twin challenges of economic woes and ballooning budgets (Covert, 2011).

However, the greater number of women entering the labor force has not catapulted them to equality with their male peers in the workplace. Despite the passage of Title VII of the 1964 Civil Rights Act, which declared it unlawful for employers to discriminate on the basis of a person's race, nationality, creed, or sex, women have continued to fare much worse than their male counterparts in the workforce. Although legally entitled to enter all lines of work, women routinely face sexual harassment, an illegal form of discrimination that runs the gamut from inappropriate jokes on the job to outright sexual assault to sexual "barter," in which women workers give sexual favors

Sexual harassment an illegal form of discrimination, involving everything from inappropriate jokes on the job to outright sexual assault to sexual "barter"—all intended to make women feel uncomfortable and unwelcome, particularly on the job.

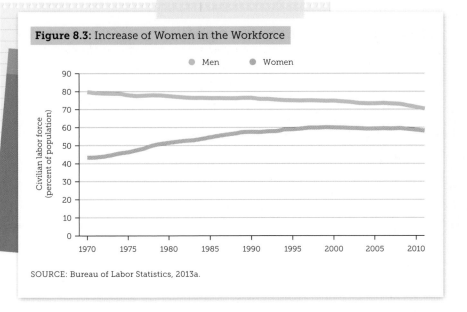

Figure 8.3: Increase of Women in the Workforce

SOURCE: Bureau of Labor Statistics, 2013a.

under the threat of punishment (Kimmel, 2000). Intended to make women feel uncomfortable and unwelcome, sexual harassment occurs across many settings and in all kinds of relationships—walking down the street and having to listen to "Whooo, baby!" is just one annoying everyday example. In the workplace, some argue, sexual harassment is one of the chief ways in which men resist gender equality. In 1982, the U.S. Court of Appeals ruled that sexual harassment is a violation of the Civil Rights Act, because it is a form of discrimination against an individual on the basis of sex. But even though sexual harassment is illegal, it often takes insidious forms not easily detected by everyone or verifiable in court. Most commonly, sexual harassment takes the form of "hostile environments" in which women feel unsafe, excluded, singled out, and mocked.

In addition to working in such hostile environments, women have consistently been paid less than their male peers, earning about 81 cents to every $1 of a man's wage (BLS, 2013a; Figure 8.4). (In some large, economically successful cities, however, the gender gap may be shrinking or even reversing among young adults.) The media touted women's gains in the 1970s and 1980s, when masses of women entered the U.S. labor force. Yet women disproportionately entered the lower rungs of the occupational hierarchy. These feminized jobs, what Louise Howe (1977) calls "pink-collar" jobs, are low-paid secretarial or service industry jobs. Cleaning buildings, filing papers, and making coffee are hardly what women imagine when they dream of independence.

Many new women workers find themselves shuffled into occupations dominated by other women, and women who go into a male-dominated field often find that, soon enough, they are surrounded by women. Like names, jobs

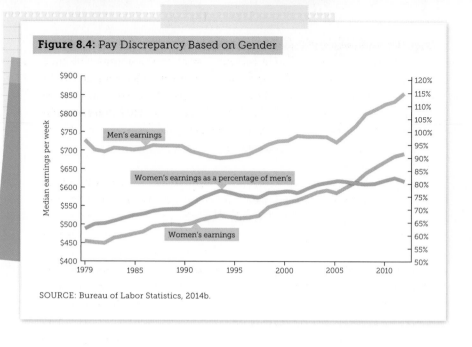

Figure 8.4: Pay Discrepancy Based on Gender

Median earnings per week

$900 — 120%
$850 — 115%
$800 — 110%
$750 — 105%
$700 — 100%
$650 — 95%
$600 — 90%
$550 — 85%
$500 — 80%
$450 — 75%
$400 — 70%

Men's earnings

Women's earnings as a percentage of men's

Women's earnings

1979   1985   1990   1995   2000   2005   2010

SOURCE: Bureau of Labor Statistics, 2014b.

become feminized when too many women hit the scene. This has happened in fields such as real estate sales, clerical work, pharmacy, public relations, bartending, bank telling, and more recently, sociology. In *Job Queues, Gender Queues* (1990), sociologists Barbara Reskin and Patricia Roos argue that women end up in lower-paid jobs because these occupations lose (or have lost) their attractiveness for white men. When a job becomes deskilled and less autonomous, earnings decline, and work conditions in general deteriorate, men flee to better positions, leaving (typically white) women next in line to shuffle into the ranks of men's cast-off work.

Take book editing, which changed from a "gentlemen's profession" to a virtual female ghetto in the mid-twentieth century. Formerly the high-cultural mission of men with elite academic records, book editing evolved into a more commercial enterprise in the 1960s and 1970s. The result was that editorial work took a downturn in autonomy, job security, and importance. As the job lost its attractiveness to male candidates, the female labor supply was increasing on the crest of second-wave feminism. Thus, bookediting jobs, like the other fields that optimists point to as women's inroads into traditionally male-dominated work, became resegregated and ghettoized as women's work. And anything categorized as women's work tends to yield lower pay, prestige, and benefits such as health coverage than men's.

Glass Ceilings When women do enter more prestigious corporate worlds, they often encounter gendered barriers to reaching the very top: the so-called glass ceiling, which effectively is an invisible limit on women's climb up the occupational ladder. Sociologist Rosabeth Moss Kanter argues in her classic

Glass ceiling an invisible limit on women's climb up the occupational ladder.

study *Men and Women of the Corporation* (1977) that the dearth of women in top corporate positions results from a cultural conflation of authority with masculinity. In Indesco, the fictitious name of the corporation Kanter studied, she found another case of deceptive distinctions at work: Most people believe that men and women come to occupy the kinds of jobs for which they are naturally best suited. Secretaries are predominantly women (98.6 percent), according to this belief, because women seem to act the feminine part better than they play the masculine managerial role.

Fourth-grade teacher Ryan Fittje is the only male teacher at his Fremont, Nebraska, school.

To the contrary, Kanter showed, job segregation often works the other way around: The job makes the person; the person doesn't make the job. Employee behavior tends to be determined by job requirements and the constraints of the organizational structure of the company. At Indesco, secretarial positions derived status from that of the boss. The job was also based on principled arbitrariness, meaning that there were no limits to the boss's discretion as to what his secretary should do (type, fax, pick up his dry cleaning, look after his dog when he's away). Furthermore, secretarial work was characterized by fealty, the demand of personal loyalty and devotion of secretary to boss. Under these conditions, secretaries adopted certain behaviors to get through a day's work, including timidity and self-effacement, addiction to praise, and displays of emotion—all qualities that Indesco bosses tended to think of as just the way women are.

What happens when a woman breaks into a top managerial position? She becomes a numerical minority, what Kanter calls a token, a stand-in for all women. Because tokens have heightened visibility, they experience greater performance pressures. Male peers tend to rely on gender stereotypes when interpreting a token's behavior, seeing female managers as "seductresses, mothers, pets," or tough "iron maidens." When a token female manager botches the job, it just goes to show that women can't handle the corporate world and should be kept out of it.

Similarly, Jennifer L. Pierce's study of law firms (1995) showed that sexual stereotypes, as much as organizational structure, are underlying causes of job segregation. Paralegals make up a feminized "semi-profession": About 86 percent of them are women, according to the Bureau of Labor Statistics. Meanwhile, women account for only 16 percent of law firm partners, even though, for the last two decades, the number of women graduating from law school was about 39 to 49 percent of all graduates (Scharf & Flom, 2010).

Paralegals are expected to be deferential (that is, they should not stick up for themselves), caring, and even motherly toward the trial lawyers for whom they work. Given the adversarial model of the U.S. legal system, trial lawyers, in contrast, perform what Pierce (1995) calls masculine emotional labor. To excel in the job takes aggression, intimidation, and manipulation. When a woman joins the higher ranks of trial lawyering, she's likely to face exclusion from informal socializing with her colleagues (no drinks after work), deflation of her job status (frequently being mistaken for a secretary), sexual harassment, and difficulty bringing clients into the firm. Female litigators find themselves in a double bind not experienced by their male counterparts. When deploying courtroom tactics of aggression and intimidation—the very qualities that make a male lawyer successful and respected—women litigators find themselves being called "bitches," "obnoxious," and "shrill." But when they fail to act like proper "Rambo litigators" in the courtroom, women are equally chided for being "too nice" and "too bashful." The trade-off between being a good woman and being a successful lawyer adds yet another obstacle for women to make it to the top in male-dominated jobs.

Glass Escalators Just as the odds are stacked against female tokens, they tilt in favor of men in female-dominated jobs. In *Still a Man's World* (1995), Christine Williams found that male nurses, elementary school teachers, librarians, and social workers inadvertently maintain masculine power and privilege. Specifically, when token men enter feminized jobs, they enjoy a quicker rise to leadership positions on the aptly named glass escalator. These escalators also operate in law firms, where male paralegals, themselves tokens in the overwhelmingly female semi-profession, reap benefits from their heightened visibility (Pierce, 1995). Male paralegals are said to enjoy preferential treatment over their female peers, such as promotions and even the simple (but substantial) benefit of being invited to happy hour with the litigators.

> **Glass escalator** the accelerated promotion of men to the top of a work organization, especially in feminized jobs.

Or at least that is how it used to be. Williams' new research suggests that women are holding a more equitable share of the top spots in nursing, elementary schools, and libraries, but that a larger problem is emerging that hits both men and women: wages in these careers have not kept pace with the cost of living (Williams, 2013). Careers that have traditionally been associated with women are not the only ones that have seen declining wages. Manufacturing, trucking, and warehouse jobs—traditionally dominated by male workers—are also paying less (Mishel & Shierholz, 2013).

In the fashion industry, the escalator reverses the gender filter Williams originally found for women-dominated fields. Aspiring male models are forced off at the second floor while a small number of women models can continue to top model status. I talked to former model Ashley Mears about the wage structure in the

Go to **wwnpag.es/SC8b** to see more of my interview about modeling as an occupation with Ashley Mears, a former fashion model turned Boston University Sociology Professor.

modeling industry. She confirmed that "you see a complete inverse" where "women outearn men by two to one, sometimes much more" and that "there are just more jobs and opportunities for women models." She explained that there are two reasons for this, one cultural and one structural. From a cultural perspective, "for a man to do the work of showing his body, displaying his body, it's read as being less than what we fully expect in a hegemonically masculine way. It's read as being effeminate work." From a structural perspective there simply are no stepping stones to managerial positions or other promotions for models. According to Mears (who became a sociologist), on the models' job escalator, "there's no place to go," because career positions in the fashion industry go to experienced businesspeople and designers (Conley, 2013c).

POLICY: **Women in Combat**

The media made a lot of noise about who was fit to fight in the armed forces during the 1990s. From Bill Clinton's 1993 "Don't ask, don't tell" solution to gays in the military, to Barack Obama's repeal of this policy in 2011, and beyond, debates over women in combat and about sex in the military have been a heated issue. As the policy landscape shifts, the issue is coming back onto the media radar, and it's still a gendered battleground out there.

In 1994, the U.S. Department of Defense enacted a new policy that opened up an array of positions to women, from fighter piloting to commanding warships. In January 2013, the Pentagon took the major step of removing the ban on women serving in combat positions, a step many said would change little for women who are already on the front lines in Iraq and Afghanistan. Army Sergeant Rebekah Havrilla worked in an Ordinance Disposal Unit, technically a noncombat role that frequently put her in combat situations. She explained what went on while she was taking care of improvised explosive devices (IEDs): "I saw combat repeatedly. I went outside the wires six or seven days a week. I was in a couple of firefights; I was hit by IEDs multiple times. We spent days on end near the border with Pakistan engaged in missions. If that's not a front-line experience, I don't know what is" (Fortin, 2013).

So far, more than 280,000 female soldiers have been deployed to Iraq and Afghanistan—far more than the 7,500 who served in Vietnam and the 41,000 who fought in the first Gulf War. During the Iraq conflict, 1 in every

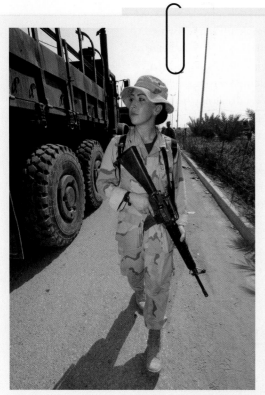

A U.S. soldier prepares to distribute water to Iraqis in Al Faw, Iraq.

10 U.S. soldiers was female (Corbett, 2007). The trouble is, in a counterinsurgency operation like the one in the Iraqi theater, where mortar attacks and roadside bombings occur just about anytime or anywhere, the distinction between combat and support units is virtually nonexistent. Women were essentially serving in combat operations throughout the Iraqi campaign, with some shocking outcomes and implications.

Unofficially, American women have been in combat since the War of Independence, when Margaret Corbin (Molly Pitcher) took over loading a cannon after her husband was shot. Even formally, women have long held dangerous roles in the military. Some 30 military nurses were held as prisoners of war for three years in World War II. About 1,000 women have been killed in action since the Spanish American War (Wilgoren, 2003). But there is something that makes us uncomfortable about women in the military, and the source of our unease boils down to a few potential concerns.

In 1979, Virginia's former-senator Jim Webb wrote an article titled "Women Can't Fight," the central argument of which was that women are weak: They have less bodily strength, they can become pregnant, and they can't emotionally handle the calculated violence of war, thus making them a liability to their units. Second, and related, the presence of women was thought to jeopardize military goals by distracting male soldiers, either through sexual attraction or, more likely, through men's paternal instincts to protect female soldiers from danger and, particularly, rape by the enemy. Women, Webb thought, would make the masculine military organization crumble.

Even though Webb later apologized and proclaimed that "women *can* fight," the pregnancy controversy has continued. An order on November 4, 2009, from Major General Anthony Cucolo considered court-martialing any soldiers under his command who become pregnant or caused someone else to become pregnant while serving a tour of duty. General Cucolo later told the Pentagon he believed that pregnancies had threatened the mission in Iraq, and would punish, though not imprison, pregnant soldiers and their sexual partners for lack of dedication to the mission (Gould, 2010). In other news around the military, recent reports reveal that war is especially dangerous for women, not just on the battlefield but also in the barracks. According to studies of female veterans, women are more likely than men to develop posttraumatic stress disorder (PTSD). The principal source of trauma for male veterans is combat. For women, it is believed, there are two sources of trauma in the military: combat and sexual assault. Women are at high risk of rape or the threat of rape, not just by enemy forces but by their fellow soldiers. As of 2007, the Veterans Administration had diagnosed possible PTSD in some 34,000 Iraq and Afghanistan veterans, and nearly 3,800 of them were women (Corbett, 2007). A debilitating condition that combines depression, anxiety, emotional numbness, and sleeplessness, PTSD can develop after exposure to extreme stress and trauma.

Molly Pitcher at the battle at Monmouth.

According to researchers at the Veterans Affairs Medical Center in Iowa, 79 percent of female veterans in one reliable study reported being sexually harassed during their military service. Fully 30 percent of the women reported an attempted or completed rape (Sadler et al., 2003). In the Iowa study, among those who reported rape, 14 percent reported that they had been gang raped, and 37 percent said they had been raped more than once.

What makes the military an especially dangerous place for women? For one thing, it is a male-dominated organization with a masculine culture. This atmosphere puts newcomer women at an outsider disadvantage. As combat-support specialist Abbie Pickett told the *New York Times,* "You're one of three things in the military—a bitch, a whore, or a dyke. . . . As a female, you get classified pretty quickly" (Corbett, 2007). In addition, the military teaches core values of aggression, insensitivity, and obedience to carry out the violence of war. Add to that the stressful uncertainties of the battlefield, and sexual assault is just a short step up from routine harassment.

Finally, rape is not primarily about sex, pleasure, or desire but power. In the military, women hold less power than men. As subordinates, women enter this male-dominated field already having lesser authority, which increases the likelihood of what is sometimes called "command rape," in which men of rank assault their juniors (Benedict, 2007).

As hundreds more women soldiers have returned from battle showing the effects of trauma from both sexual assault and combat, the issue of women in the military is not likely to remain a quiet one. Ironically, the old debate has taken a new unfortunate turn as women are indeed exposed to the perils of war—not necessarily the danger of sexual predators across enemy lines but rather the risk of sexual predators among their own comrades.

→ CONCLUSION

During World War II, America got a gender makeover. When 6 million American women flooded the factory labor force in response to the nation's call for help, they were galvanized by the now-familiar Rosie the Riveter image. Hollywood discovered Rose Monroe in the 1940s, when she was working at an aircraft parts factory in Michigan; she was quickly remade into a female hero, espousing such empowering slogans as "We can do it!" (Enloe, 2000). Most women taking on men's jobs such as skilled factory work were eager to acquire the new skills and living wages that women's pink-collar jobs had not offered. Some of them were coaxed to the factories by offers of child care and ready-made meals they could take home to their families at the end of the work day. But as Ruth Milkman (1987) argues, the increase in female employment did not lead to gender equity. Far from it. Job segregation by sex did not break down; it just took new forms, redefining women's wartime work as an extension of domesticity, the new but temporary "woman's place." The work of women in factories was revised to be "women's work." It was supposedly light and less strenuous, clean, and even glamorous. Furthermore, it was still segregated by sex, and women earned less than male factory workers.

A World War II poster featuring Rosie the Riveter.

At the end of the war, husbands, brothers, and sons returned, and the nation called on women yet again to make a sacrifice—this time to return to the domestic life. In just four years, millions of women went from their homes to the factories and back again. Occupational segregation by sex persisted throughout, as it still does today. Did Rosie's dramatic moment amount to nothing? Maybe not, as it turns out.

A mother's employment outside the home is known to affect kids in surprising ways. In families where the mother works, even part time, brothers and sisters are more likely to end up as economic equals down the road (Conley, 2004) and adopt more egalitarian attitudes toward gender roles (Kimmel, 2000). The kids may even spend fewer hours watching television (Bianchi & Robinson, 1997). Regardless of early sex role socialization, Rosie's factory days made a ripple in the prevailing gender norms. This ripple was surely felt by her children, who had been exposed to new definitions of what a woman could be. This is just one sociological explanation of women's gains in equality today. Another interpretation is offered by Robert Jackson (1998), who makes the case that women are destined for equality because in a modern economy with rationalized, bureaucratic organizations, it just doesn't make strategic sense to be prejudiced against women. There's something irrational and inefficient, it seems, about sex discrimination. It doesn't make economic sense.

What both explanations underscore is the potential of sociology to account for changes in social structures like gender that too often we take as given and fixed. In the study of sex and gender (as in other "sociologies"), social structures and context matter. What seems to be normal or natural often turns out to be fluid and contingent. The stuff we build up around the plumbing—roles, expectations, psyches, institutions—is not essential. These are socially constructed facts, built less on the biological and more on the existing social structures of relations.

We've traced the intricate details through which a system of sexes, genders, and sexualities has evolved. Can we "undo gender," or are we stuck in the paradox of reproducing our own creation, even if we recognize its inequalities? If we humans have constructed gender as a way to organize, simplify, and control a messy social world, then indeed we can deconstruct it. Judith Lorber (1994) argues that only when we stop using gender as a basis for dividing up the world—in terms of which jobs people hold, what rights they exercise, how much money they earn, how much control they have over their bodies, and with whom they can have sex—will we find true equality in the world.

→ PRACTICE

SOCIOLOGY ON THE STREET

Internet dating is a major resource for people looking for potential partners, with a seemingly unlimited pool. What are the similarities and differences between dating online compared to dating in person? Watch the Sociology on the Street video to find out more: wwnpag.es/SOS8.

QUESTIONS FOR REVIEW

1. How does Gayle Rubin's "sex/gender system" help us understand the differences listed between Donald and Deirdre that economist McCloskey describes at the beginning of the chapter?

2. Women represent a minority group in the military. Men are in the minority as nurses and paralegals. How are women and men treated differently in these positions, and what does this suggest about the way gender structures social relations?

3. How do the cases of the *hijras* and the *travesti*, as described in this chapter, challenge our understanding of sex and gender?

4. How does the case of "John/Joan" (David Reimer) support the view of sex as a category based on nature? How does this case support the view of sex as socially constructed and enforced?

5. What is "essentialism"? Explain how John Gray's book *Men Are from Mars, Women Are from Venus* could be described as essentialist.

6. How does Talcott Parsons describe the role of men and women in his "sex role theory"? Explain how conflict theories can be seen as a critique of structural functionalism, and describe some limitations of each approach.

7. What is the difference between homosexual "acts" and a homosexual "identity"? How did the historical development of the latter, according to Michel Foucault, affect how one sees oneself?

8. More differences seem to exist among boys and girls than between them. Nonetheless, we tend to think of them as different. What are "deceptive distinctions," and how do they create gender differences? Use an example from Rosabeth Kanter's work to support your answer.

PARADOX

THE BIOLOGICAL CATEGORIES OF SEX STRONGLY INFLUENCE THE SOCIAL DYNAMICS OF GENDER: HOWEVER, THE SOCIAL CATEGORIES OF GENDER CAN SOMETIMES DETERMINE THE BIOLOGY OF SEX.

WATCH THE ANIMATED SHORT ABOUT THE GENDER PARADOX AT

WWNPAG.ES/PX8

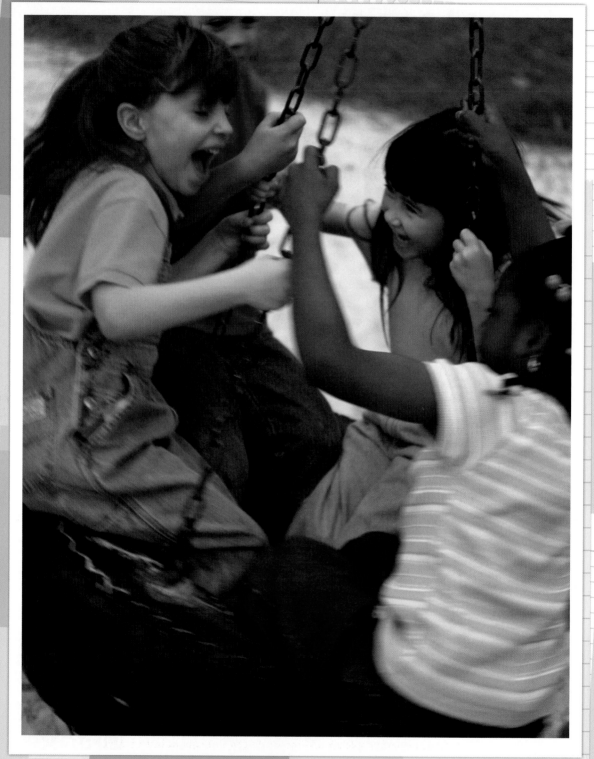

9 Race

PARADOX

RACE AS WE KNOW IT HAS NO
DETERMINISTIC, BIOLOGICAL BASIS:
ALL THE SAME, RACE IS SO
POWERFUL THAT IT CAN HAVE
LIFE-OR-DEATH CONSEQUENCES.

HUMANS

"I found my baby sister!" I declared to my mother, wheeling a carriage around for her to see the newest member of our family whom I had just kidnapped. I was not quite three years old, and the toddler was only a few months younger than that, with cornrows braided so tightly on her little head that they pulled the brown skin of her face tautly upward. I remember that she was smiling up at me, and I must have taken her smile as permission to swipe the unattended stroller from the courtyard of our housing complex.

"No, you haven't!" my mother gasped, putting a hand over her open mouth. The child was quickly returned to her frantically searching mother, despite my tearful protests.

This story fascinates me today: I wanted a baby sister so badly that I kidnapped a black child, not realizing that race is a primary way we divide families. How could I be so oblivious to the meaning of race—something that years later feels so natural, so innate? To my childhood self, race was neither a meaningful category nor a too obvious one. In the largely minority housing project where I grew up in the 1970s, race was not something mutable, like a freckle or hairstyle; it defined who looked like whom, who was allowed to be in the group, and who wasn't. But for my sister and me, as whites, race was turned inside out. We had no idea that we belonged to the majority group, the privileged one. We just thought we didn't belong.

Is race real? You might consider this a paradoxical question. After all, how is a huge part of your identity *not* real? The sociological study of race treats it as a social phenomenon that seems natural but isn't. That is, race is a real social distinction, and people around the world and throughout history have drawn sharp lines between "us" and "them" on the basis of race. But as a biological, genetic, geographic, or cultural category, race has fluid and changeable boundaries. In this sense, race is constructed in the interests of groups that wish to maintain power and social exclusion. To the sociologist, understanding racial differences—including income, educational attainment, crime rates, and teen pregnancy—means treating differences not just as personal matters but as pieces of a larger social picture. Having grown up as a "honky" in the housing projects of New York City's Lower East Side, a fish out of water, I've been looking at race with the sociological imagination ever since my failed kidnapping. Now it's your turn.

The Myth of Race

Race a group of people who share a set of characteristics—typically, but not always, physical ones—and are said to share a common bloodline.

Perhaps you have heard claims that race is fake, that it's "just a myth." Race refers to a group of people who share a set of characteristics—typically, but not always, physical ones—and are said to share a common bloodline. People obviously have different physical appearances, including eye color, hair texture, and skin color, so it's perhaps puzzling to hear that (biological) racial differences somehow do not exist. To speak of the myth of race is to say that it is largely a social construction, a set of stories we tell ourselves to organize reality and make sense of the world, rather than a fixed biological or natural reality. In this sense, it resembles the socially constructed notions of childhood and adolescence that we discussed in Chapter 4. We tell the set of stories over and over and, collectively, believe in it and act on it, therefore making it real through such practices as largely separate marriage and reproductive communities. But we could organize our social distinctions a different way (for example, based on foot size or hair color), and indeed, throughout history, we have told this set of stories in myriad ways.

Take, for example, the following excerpt from an 1851 issue of *Harper's Weekly Magazine*, in which the author describes the physiognomy of a certain racial group. Try to guess which race the author is describing:

> [They are] distinctly marked—the small and somewhat upturned nose, the black tint of the skin. . . . [They] are ignorant, and as a consequence thereof, are idle, thriftless, poor, intemperate, and barbarian. . . . Of course they will violate our laws, these wild bisons leaping over the fences which easily restrain the civilized domestic cattle, will commit great crimes of violence, even capital offences, which certainly have increased as of late.

Most people would guess that the minority group in question here is African Americans. This passage was written, in fact, about Irish immigrants, who in late-nineteenth-century America struggled to assimilate amid fierce and widespread racism (Knobel, 1986). It was believed that the Irish were a distinct category of people who carried innate differences in their blood, differences that made them permanently inferior to their white American neighbors.

When the term *race* comes up in America today, we usually think in two colors: black and white. But, at the turn of the twentieth century, Americans categorized themselves into anywhere from 36 to 75 different races that they organized into hierarchies, with Anglo-Saxon at the top followed by Slav, Mediterranean, Hebrew, and so on down the list (Jacobson, 1998). Even though the United States was a nation of immigrants, many Americans doubted whether "ethnic stock," such as the Irish, were fit for self-governance in the new democracy.

In 1790, Congress passed the first naturalization law, limiting the rights of citizenship to "free white persons." This law strikes us today as both restrictive

THE USUAL IRISH WAY OF DOING THINGS.

An anti-immigration cartoon from an 1871 issue of *Harper's Weekly*. How have attitudes about race changed over the course of American history?

and inclusive. It was restrictive because it granted naturalization only to free whites, thereby coloring American citizenship. Yet it also set up an initially broad understanding of "whiteness," an umbrella term that in common parlance could include not just Anglo but also Slavic, Celtic, and Teutonic (German) Europeans. However, as millions of immigrants surged to the shores of America—25 million European immigrants arrived between 1880 and World War I—the notion of "free white persons" was reconsidered. With an Irish-born population of more than 1 million in 1860, Americans began to theorize racial differences within the white populace. Questions arose in the popular press and imagination, such as "Who should count as white?" "Whom do we want to be future generations of Americans?" "Who is fit for self-governance?" The inclusiveness of "white persons" splintered into a range of Anglos and "barbarous" others, and Americans began to distinguish among Teutons, Slavs, Celtics, and even the "swarthy" Swedes. The Immigration Act of 1924 formalized the exclusive definition of whiteness by imposing immigration restrictions based on a quota system that limited the yearly number of immigrants from each country. The law set an annual ceiling of 18,439 immigrants from eastern and southern Europe, following the recommendation of a report stating that northern and western Europeans were of "higher intelligence" and thus ideal "material for American citizenship" (Jacobson, 1998).

A racist ideology can be seen in this early line of thinking about whiteness. Racism is the belief that members of separate races possess different and unequal traits coupled with the power to restrict freedoms based on those differences. Racist thinking is characterized by three key beliefs: that humans are divided into distinct bloodlines and/or physical types; that these bloodlines or

Racism the belief that members of separate races possess different and unequal traits.

physical traits are linked to distinct cultures, behaviors, personalities, and intellectual abilities; and that certain groups are superior to others.

European immigration slowed during World War I and essentially came to a halt as a result of the 1924 National Origins Act, while internal African American migration from the rural South to the industrial North skyrocketed. These shifts, along with the solidification of the one-drop rule (see below), shifted national attention away from white–nonwhite relations toward white–black relations. Whites of "ethnic stock" were drawn back into the earlier, broad category of white, thereby reuniting Anglos and other Europeans. Public horror at Nazi crimes following the conclusion of World War II further strengthened the idea of whiteness as an inclusive racial category.

Today being of Irish descent is a matter of ethnic—not racial—identification, a reason to celebrate on St. Patrick's Day. I know this firsthand: Being one-eighth Irish and having an Irish-WASP (white Anglo-Saxon Protestant) name like Dalton Conley entitles me to free drinks on the Irish holiday. Irish American is no longer considered a restrictive racial category, as once was the case. Whiteness today is something we take for granted, a natural part of the landscape. But dig just a hundred years back into the unnatural history of race, and you might not even recognize it. Not only have groups of people been categorized differently over time, showing that there is nothing natural about how we classify groups into races today, but the very concept of what a race is has changed over time.

The Concept of Race from the Ancients to Alleles

The idea of race, some scholars have claimed, did not exist in the ancient world (Fredrickson, 2002; Hannaford, 1996; Smedley, 1999; Snowden, 1983). Well, it did and it didn't. It did in the sense that the ancients recognized physical differences and grouped people accordingly. In ancient Egypt, for example, physical markers were linked to geography. Believing that people who looked a certain way came from a certain part of the world, the Egyptians spoke for instance of the "pale, degraded race of Arvad," whereas their darker-skinned neighbors were designated the "evil race of Ish." The Chinese also linked physical variation to geography, as laid out in a Chinese creation myth. As the ancient tale goes, a goddess cooked human beings in an oven. Some humans were burnt black and sent to live in Africa. The underdone ones turned out white and were sent to Europe. Those humans cooked just right, a perfect golden brown, were the Chinese.

However, in the ancient worlds of Greece, Rome, and early Christendom, the idea of race did not exist as we know it today, as a biological package of traits carried in the bloodlines of distinct groups, each with a separate way of being (culture), acting (behavior), thinking (intelligence), and looking (appearance). The Greek philosopher Hippocrates, for instance, believed that physical markers such as skin color were the result of different environmental factors, much as the surface of a plant reflects the constitution of its soil and the amount of sunlight and water it receives. To be sure, the Greeks liked the looks of their fellow Greeks the best, but the very notion of race goes against Aristotle's principle of civic association, on which Greek society was based. The true test of a person was to be found in his (women were excluded) civic actions. Similarly, the Romans maintained a brutal slavery system, but their slaves, as well as their citizens, represented various skin colors and geographic origins. The ancients may have used skin color to tell one person from the next—they weren't color-blind—but they didn't discriminate in the sense of making judgments about people on the basis of their racial category without regard to their individual merit (Hannaford, 1996). The notion has been so thoroughly displaced by racialized thinking that to us moderns, it is impossibly idealistic to imagine a society without our race concept.

Race in the Early Modern World

Modern racial thinking developed in the mid-seventeenth century in parallel with global changes such as the Protestant Reformation in Europe, the Age of Exploration, and the rise of capitalism. For example, European colonizers, confronted with people living in newly discovered lands, interpreted human physical differences first with biblical and later with scientific explanations, and race proved to be a rather handy organizing principle to legitimate the imperial adventure of conquest, exploitation, and colonialism. To make sense of what they considered the "primitive" and "degraded" races of Africa, Europeans turned to a biblical story in the book of Genesis 9, the curse of Ham. According to this obscure passage, when Noah had safely navigated his ark over the flood, he got drunk and passed out naked in his tent. When he woke from his stupor, Noah learned that his youngest son, Ham, had seen him naked, whereas his other sons had respectfully refused to behold the spectacle. Noah decided to curse Ham's descendants, saying, "A slave of slaves shall he be to his brothers" (Gourevitch, 1998). European Christians and scientists interpreted this tale to mean that Ham was the original black man, and all

A medieval illustration depicting Ham as a black man. How did Europeans use the biblical story to defend colonialism?

black people were his unfortunate, degraded descendants. For an expanding Europe and America, the Hamitic myth justified colonialism and slavery.

When the divine right of conquest lost its sway, science led the way as an authority behind racial thinking, legitimating race by scientific mandate. Scientific racism, what today we call the nineteenth-century theories of race, brought a period of feverish investigation into the origins, explanations, and classifications of race. In 1684, François Bernier (1625–1688) proposed a new geography based not on topography or even political borders but on the body, from facial lineaments to bodily configurations. Bernier devised a scheme of four or five races based on the following geographic regions:

- *Europe* (excluding Lapland), *South Asia, North Africa,* and *America:* people who shared climates and complexions

- *Africa proper:* people who had thick lips, flat noses, black skin, and a scanty beard

- *Asia proper:* people who had white skin, broad shoulders, flat faces, little eyes, and no beard

- *Lapps* (small traditional communities living around the northern regions of Finland and Russia): people who were ugly, squat, small, and animal-like

Scientific racism sought to make sense of people who were different from white Europeans—who constituted the norm, according to the French scientist Comte de Buffon (1707–1788). This way of thinking, called ethnocentrism, the judgment of other groups by one's own standards and values, has plagued scientific studies of "otherness." In Buffon's classification schemes, anyone different from Europeans was a deviation from the norm. His pseudoscientific research, like all racial thinking of the time, justified imperial exploits by automatically classifying nonwhites as abnormal, improper, and inferior.

With the publication of *On the Natural Varieties of Mankind* in 1775, Johann Friedrich Blumenbach (1752–1840), widely considered the founder of anthropology, cataloged variation by race, including differences in head formation, a pseudoscience called phrenology. Blumenbach's aim was to classify the world based on the different types of bumps he could measure on people's skulls. Based on these skull measurements, he came up with five principal varieties of humans: Caucasian, Mongoloid, Ethiopian, American, and Malay. Caucasians (named after the people who live on the southern slopes of the Georgian region of eastern Europe), he decided, were the superlatives of the races based on their excellent skull qualities.

Another eighteenth-century thinker, the Swiss theologian Johann Caspar Lavater (1741–1801), popularized physiognomy, which correlated outside appearances to inner virtues. Not surprisingly, light skin and small features signified high intellect and worthy character. Political philosophers were also on board with racial thinking. Charles de Secondat, Baron de Montesquieu, had

Scientific racism nineteenth-century theories of race that characterize a period of feverish investigation into the origins, explanations, and classifications of race.

Ethnocentrism the belief that one's own culture or group is superior to others and the tendency to view all other cultures from the perspective of one's own.

Charts like this one helped phrenologists interpret the shapes of human skulls. How did nineteenth-century theorists use this sort of pseudoscience to justify racism?

already made the connection between climate and certain forms of government in *The Spirit of the Laws* (1748/1750).

Race was now considered not just a set of physical traits but something that comes with social implications. Immanuel Kant (1724–1804) argued for a link between inner character and outside physiognomy and further claimed that these individual markers were also imprinted on an entire nation's moral life.

However, racial differences were still believed by many to be the product of climate (and therefore not immutable or innate to the soul). In fact, in 1787 the Reverend Minister Samuel Stanhope Smith, who was president of what is now Princeton University, wrote an essay in which he proposed that dark skin should be thought of as a "universal freckle." Differences in skin shade, he maintained, were really just like different levels of suntans. It was his belief that if an African from the sub-Sahara were transplanted to Scandinavia, his dark-brown skin would turn lighter over the course of generations (and perhaps the underlying social and cognitive characteristics associated with race would change as well). Notice how Smith's pliable view of race captures a spirit of ontological equality: We are all born the same deep beneath our skin; it just so happens that some of us have been out in the sun a bit longer than others. Ontological equality is the philosophical and religious notion that all people are created equal.

Ontological equality the philosophical and religious notion that all people are created equal.

Herbert Spencer coined the term *survival of the fittest*. How did Spencer draw from the work of Darwin to justify racism?

Social Darwinism the application of Darwinian ideas to society—namely, the evolutionary "survival of the fittest."

Reverend Smith's line of thinking also demonstrates the scientific influence of Lamarckism, now a discredited footnote in the history of scientific thought. The basic tenet of Lamarckism is that acquired traits can be passed down across generations. For example, an acquired attribute such as flexibility, language skill, or sun exposure can be passed down to a person's offspring, affecting generations to come.

Lamarckism was debunked by Charles Darwin, who in 1859 published his theory of natural selection. Darwin argued that acquired attributes could not be transmitted; instead, change can occur only through the positive selection of mutations. Darwin's theory had an enormous impact on how people thought of race. In effect, it called into question the popular belief that climate influenced racial difference and instead offered an account in which racial lineages were much more deeply rooted and long-standing. What's more, humankind was now seen as being on a trajectory in which some groups have advanced (or evolved) more than others. The popular nineteenth-century notion of social Darwinism was the application of Darwinian ideas to society—namely, the evolutionary "survival of the fittest." Social theorist Herbert Spencer (1820–1903) promulgated the idea that some people, defined by their race, are better fit for survival than others and are therefore intended by nature to dominate inferior races. A new puzzle arose with Darwinian ideas: What, if not inherited climate change, could explain the development of humans along such radically different lines?

Eugenics

Scientists now had to arrive at a new explanation of physical difference among humans, and the scientific community confronted a growing debate: monogenism versus polygenism. The debate turned on the origins of the various races of humans. Were humans a united species, or did we come from separate origins? Monogenists, including religious traditionalists, believed that humans were one species, united under God. Polygenists believed that different races were, in fact, distinct species. Darwin sided with the monogenists, claiming that the notion of different species was absurd. (Politics, it is said, makes for strange bedfellows. It certainly did in this case, as Darwinists and religious traditionalists, usually opposed, became allies in arguing that all humans were one species.)

Even though the monogenists won the debate, the notion of separate roots and distinct reproductive genetic histories has had a lasting impact on how we think of human difference. Under the model of natural selection, human difference must have evolved over tens or hundreds of thousands of years (if not millions), not just over a few generations in relative sun or shade. Such a vast time frame was used as evidence that races were very different (and not simply superficially so).

Howard Knox (center), assistant surgeon at Ellis Island from 1912–1916, examined immigrants for diseases and disabilities, including mental illnesses.

A new movement, eugenics, took the idea of very distant origins and ran with it. Eugenicists, led by Sir Francis Galton (1822–1911), claimed that each race had a separate package of social and psychological traits transmitted through bloodlines. Eugenics literally means "well born"; it is the pseudoscience of genetic lines and the inheritable traits they pass on from generation to generation. Everything from criminality and feeblemindedness to disease and intelligence, Galton asserted, could be traced through bloodlines and selectively bred out of or into populations. One of his followers, the American psychologist H. H. Goddard (1866–1957), applied eugenic thinking to generalize findings from his intelligence tests in America. He tested a handful of immigrants arriving at Ellis Island in the early twentieth century and generalized their test scores to whole populations, claiming—and garnering many believers, too—that around 70 percent of the immigrants sailing from eastern and southern Europe were, in his phraseology, "morons" who posed a serious threat to the good of the nation. Goddard supported the immigration exclusion acts that in 1924 largely blocked non-Anglos from immigrating and were intended to improve the "stock" of the nation. This concern about the new and objectionable stock of immigrants, as opposed to "native," more desirable immigrants of an earlier epoch, was the crux of nativism, the movement to protect and preserve indigenous land or culture from the allegedly dangerous and polluting effects of new immigrants. Madison Grant (1865–1937), an influential writer, epitomized the spirit of nativism when he argued that not restricting the immigration of southern and eastern Europeans was "race suicide" for the white race (1916/1936).

The problem with race, for eugenicists, scientists, and politicians, has always been that if race is such an obvious, natural means of dividing the world, why does no foolproof way of determining racial boundaries exist?

Eugenics literally meaning "well born"; a pseudoscience that postulates that controlling the fertility of populations could influence inheritable traits passed on from generation to generation.

Nativism the movement to protect and preserve indigenous land or culture from the allegedly dangerous and polluting effects of new immigrants.

Bhagat Singh Thind

According to the social historian Ian Haney López, the U.S. Supreme Court grappled with this question in the late nineteenth and early twentieth centuries (Haney López, 1995). In a landmark case in 1923, for example, Dr. Bhagat Singh Thind, a high-caste Hindu of full Indian blood, was denied American citizenship. The Supreme Court ruled that he did not qualify as a "free white person," despite being the first Indian Sikh to be inducted into the U.S. Army in World War I. In previous cases, the Court relied on a combination of scientific evidence and "common knowledge" to decide who counted as white. But the Thind case posed a particular challenge because leading anthropologists at the time uniformly classified Asian Indians as members of the Caucasian race. The very notion of whiteness was at stake: If the anthropologists were right, then the commonly accepted conception of whiteness would be radically changed to include dark-skinned immigrants like Thind. The Court therefore decried science as failing to distinguish human difference sufficiently, relying on common knowledge alone to deny Thind's claims to whiteness. As the Court put it, "The words 'free white persons' are words of common speech, to be interpreted in accordance with the understandings of the common man" (Haney López, 1995).

Twentieth-Century Concepts of Race

The judges in the Thind case were not the only people who attempted to define whiteness and nonwhiteness in the absence of a stable scientific taxonomy of race. In Nazi Germany, for example, race posed certain key questions: How can Jewishness be detected? Are Jews a race or a religious group? Both, actually: They are a religious group that has been racialized. Scholars have pointed out that the seeds of racism may be traced to anti-Judaism among early Christians, who forced Jews to convert. Anti-Semitism grew in the eleventh century and was based on the belief that getting rid of Jews was preferable to converting them. But Jewishness was still a social identity at this point—a matter of having religious beliefs that differed from the norm. Anti-Semitism did not turn into racism until the idea took hold that Jews were intrinsically inferior, having innate differences that separated them from their Christian neighbors (Fredrickson, 2002; Smedley, 1999). In Nazi Germany, where Jews were believed to have such innate and inherited differences, the problem remained: How can a person be identified as Jewish? This became an obsession during the Nazis' program of racial purification. They devised a "scientific" way to detect Jewishness by measuring ratios of forehead to nose size to face length, but they had little luck in nailing down a reliable strategy for making such a determination (hence, Jews in Nazi-occupied countries were forced to wear a yellow Star of David as a marker of their identity).

In the 1960s, many whites in rural parts of America similarly failed in trying to distinguish themselves from their mixed Native American and black neighbors (known as "tri-racial isolates") by searching for distinguishing signs on the body, such as differences in fingernails, feet, gums, and lines on the palm of a hand. In exasperation, some whites reported having to rely on good, old-fashioned "instinct" to distinguish themselves from nonwhites (Berry, 1963).

One means (but still not foolproof) of drawing sharp racial boundaries in America was the one-drop rule, asserting that just "one drop" of black blood makes a person black. The rule developed out of the laws passed in many U.S. states forbidding miscegenation, or interracial marriage. By 1910, most whites in the United States had accepted this doctrine. The one-drop rule was integral in maintaining the Jim Crow system of segregation upheld in the 1896 Supreme Court decision in *Plessy v. Ferguson*. In the American South, it was clear that anyone of black lineage fell on the unfortunate side of the racial divide, and the rule essentially cleaved America into two societies: one black, one white. This meant again clumping together all "white ethnics" into one united category. As F. James Davis notes (1991), the one-drop rule was highly efficient, not least because it completely erased stratification *within* the black community that had previously been based on skin tone.

Scientific racial thought slowly passed out of vogue as theories of cultural difference gained momentum among American intellectuals from the 1920s to the 1940s. Anthropologist Franz Boas dismissed the biological bases of discrete races, and sociologists such as Robert Park advanced new ideas about culture's importance in determining human behavior. Race, these thinkers argued, was less about fixed inherited traits than about particular social circumstances. Furthermore, when World War II exposed the kind of atrocities to which scientific racism could lead, it became socially and scientifically inappropriate to discuss race in biological terms, and eugenics came to be considered a dangerous way of thinking. With the decline of scientific racism and the shift toward cultural theories of race and ethnicity, the Immigration Act of 1924 was gradually chipped away at starting in 1959 and then completely repealed in 1965. Don't let the formal denouncement of racial thinking fool you, however. Cultural explanations of race often reflect a disguised racist ideology just as much as biological ones do.

Despite the ideas of scholars such as Boas and Park, the old idea of fixed, biological racial differences remains alive and well today, although in modified form. The search for racial boundaries continues in the twenty-first century with the rise of molecular genetics. DNA research now allows us to look deeper than the bumps on our heads, deeper than skin tone or palm lines. Today you can find a number of DNA testing companies offering

One-drop rule the belief that "one drop" of black blood makes a person black, a concept that evolved from U.S. laws forbidding miscegenation.

Miscegenation the technical term for interracial marriage; literally meaning "a mixing of kinds"; it is politically and historically charged—sociologists generally prefer *exogamy* or *outmarriage*.

Marion West (center) embraces Vy Higgensen (right). The distant cousins discovered their relationship after results of separate DNA tests were entered into a database.

you an inside look at your heritage. You send in $100 to $200; the testing kit arrives in the mail; you swab your mouth according to the directions and then send the swab to the company. Your "real" identity comes back from the lab in about seven weeks.

Wayne Joseph, a 53-year-old Louisiana high-school principal with Creole roots, did just that. Born and raised black, but having light skin, Joseph was mildly curious about the percentages in his veins. He received some unexpected results: His genetic makeup is 57 percent Indo-European, 39 percent Native American, 4 percent East Asian, and zero percent African (Kaplan, 2003). Despite the findings, Joseph continues to embrace his ethnic identity as black. As he put it to reporters, "The question ultimately is, are you who you say you are, or are you who you are genetically?"

Cells, alleles, and gene sequences have become the new tools of science that promise to reveal our racial truths, but the old idea hasn't much changed— that there is a biological and social package of traits inside our bodies that can be traced through our lineage—despite our knowledge that humans are biologically one species. There is no doubt that there exists genetic variation that corresponds to the general geographic origins of what we call race, but the amount of variation is nowhere near as great as most people believe. Further, the relationship between genes and complex social behavior (i.e., intelligence) is not very well understood. Yet when the 2004 General Social Survey asked respondents why, on average, African Americans have worse jobs, income, and housing than white people, about 80 of the 888 respondents, or 9 percent, responded that blacks "have less in-born ability to learn." (Moreover, a whopping 49.7 percent of respondents believed that blacks are worse off because they "just don't have the motivation or will power to pull themselves up out of poverty.") The historical search for difference affects our belief system today.

 ## Racial Realities

The biological validity of discrete racial categories—be it the bumps on your skull or the DNA in your blood—may be debatable, but in social life, race is real, with real consequences. Just ask someone of the Burakumin race in Japan. Today comprising approximately 3 percent of the Japanese population, the Burakumin originated as a group of displaced people during fourteenth-century feudal wars. With no connection other than being Japanese, the Burakumin suddenly shared something undesirable—they were homeless, destitute, and forced to wander the countryside together. Imagine all the homeless people today in Miami or Los Angeles suddenly uniting. The Burakumin formed a distinct social category, with complete social closure, their own reproductive pool, their own occupational pool, and so on, although they were not a distinct group genetically. Today, however, it is commonly believed that the

Burakumin "are descendants of a less human 'race' than the stock that fathered the Japanese nation as a whole" (De Vos & Wagatsuma, 1966). Six hundred years later, the Burakumin still display no physical distinctions from their fellow Japanese citizens. For those people in Japan wishing to avoid interrelations with the Burakumin, this lack of distinctiveness poses a dilemma. So for a hefty price, there are private investigators for hire who will confirm the pedigree of your prospective employee, tenant, or future son-in-law.

In Japan, the Burakumin live in ghettos, called *burakus,* and score lower on health, educational achievement, and income compared with their fellow Japanese citizens. Yet when Japanese and Burakumin immigrate to America, the scoring gap narrows dramatically. The distinction between Burakumin and other Japanese is meaningless outside of the significance bestowed on it in their home country. Again, we see that race is not necessarily just about physical or biological differences.

The Burakumin are a minority who can be distinguished from the rest of the Japanese population only by genealogical detectives. Prejudice against this group often leads to homelessness.

To take an example of racial realities closer to home, consider the consequences of being Arab—or perhaps I should say being perceived as Muslim—in post–9/11 America. In an interview for this book, Jen'nan Read used the image of a Venn diagram to explain that "Arab is an ethnicity; being a Muslim is a religious categorization. In the U.S. context a lot of Muslims and Arabs seem to be the same group. In fact, most Arabs in the United States are Christians who immigrated prior to World War One. And most Muslims are actually not Arab . . . one-third are South Asian, one-third are Arab, and about a quarter are African Americans who have converted to the religion" (Conley, 2009i). In the United States, Muslims are often identified with Islamo-terrorists. Followers of Islam these days are often lumped into a fixed racial category as a dangerous and undemocratic "other," seen as separate from, and inferior and hostile to, Christians.

In the first year after the events of 9/11, the number of anti-Muslim hate crimes shot up 1,600 percent (Read, 2008). And more than a decade later, although reported crimes have dropped, backlash has continued, as in the story of Zaid Ismail, a car salesman in Florida. Things were going fine for Ismail until his new manager took to calling him "little terrorist." One day, while in the restroom, Ismail heard someone knock on the door, asking, "Hey, are you making bombs in there?" Ismail, a Palestinian American, even found a note on his car telling him to go back to the Middle East or face death. "I'm an American like everyone else," he told reporters. "It's not right" (Moskovitz, 2006).

In the wake of terrorist anxiety, and several years into the war on terror, Muslims in America have undergone what scholars call racialization, the formation of a new racial identity by drawing ideological boundaries of

Racialization the formation of a new racial identity by drawing ideological boundaries of difference around a formerly unnoticed group of people.

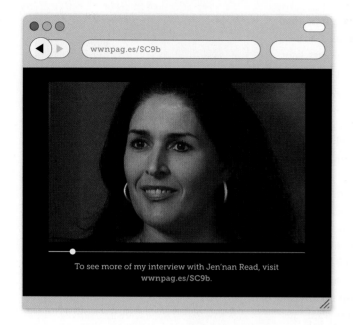

To see more of my interview with Jen'nan Read, visit wwnpag.es/SC9b.

difference around a formerly unnoticed group of people. These days, any brown-skinned man with a beard or woman with a headscarf is subject to threats, violence, and harassment. And men with turbans bear some of the worst discrimination, although nearly all men who wear turbans in the United States are Sikh or Punjabi, members of one of the world's largest religious groups, which originated in India. Four days after 9/11, Balbir Singh Sodhi, a Sikh living in Mesa, Arizona, was shot five times and killed in the gas station he owned. He was the first victim of an anti-Muslim epidemic, and he wasn't even Muslim. In one representative Harvard study, 83 percent of Sikhs interviewed said that they or someone they knew personally had experienced a hate crime or incident, and another 64 percent felt fear or danger for their family and themselves (Han, 2006). Even more striking is what happens to Caucasian Americans who convert to Islam. One woman, despite having fair skin and green eyes, has been categorized by people as Palestinian when she wears the Muslim headscarf, called the *hijab*. She's even been told, "Go back to your own country," although she was born and raised in California (Kuruvil, 2006; Spurlock, 2008). The frequency of such incidents is likely to increase as more people convert to Islam in the United States (Read, 2008).

The racialization of Muslims operates on several flawed assumptions. First, people make stereotyped assumptions based on appearance (turban = Osama bin Laden), even if in their own personal experience they know better (not everyone wearing a turban is a member of al-Qaida). Second, making snap judgments about Muslims requires a gross caricaturization of Islam's followers. Remember, most Arabs in the United States are not Muslim but Christian, and about 23 percent of U.S. Muslims are African American (Pew Research Center, 2011a).

As it turns out, American Muslims are both a highly diverse population and a very mainstream one. Muslims have been in North America since the seventeenth century, when they were transported from Africa as slaves, and about 37 percent of Muslims were born in America (Pew Research Center, 2011a). As a group, they are assimilated with the mainstream, having income and education levels similar to those of the rest of the population. By and large, they hold fast to the ideas that education is important and that hard work pays off in a successful career. Doesn't sound too radical, does it? That's because the overwhelming majority of Muslims in America and throughout the world strongly disagree with Islamic extremism (Pew Research Center, 2011a).

Of course, no racial boundaries are drawn along accurate lines or real differences, but again, once racialized, a group faces real social consequences.

Race versus Ethnicity

What's the difference between race and ethnicity anyway? Some books use the terms interchangeably; most subsume race under the umbrella label of ethnicity. Today's understanding of race is that it is

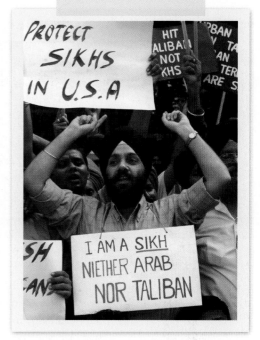

A group of Sikhs protest after the murder of Balbir Singh Sodhi.

- *Externally imposed:* Someone *else* defines you as black, white, or other.

- *Involuntary:* It's not up to you to decide to which category you belong; someone else puts you there.

- *Usually based on physical differences:* Those unreliable bumps on your head.

- *Hierarchal:* Not white? Take a number down the ranks.

- *Exclusive:* You don't get to check more than one box.

- *Unequal:* It's about power conflicts and struggles.

This last point is important for making sense of the Burakumin and Muslim Americans. Racial groupings are about domination and struggles for power. They are organizing principles for social inequality and a means of legitimating exclusion and harassment.

Ethnicity, one's ethnic affiliation, is by contrast

- *Voluntary:* I choose to identify with my one-eighth Irish background (it makes me feel special, so why not?).

- *Self-defined:* It is embraced by group members from within.

- *Nonhierarchal:* Hey, I'm Irish, you're German. *Great!*

- *Fluid and multiple:* I'm Irish *and* German. *Even better!*

- *Cultural:* Based on differences in practices such as language, food, music, and so on.

- *Planar:* Much less about unequal power than race is.

Ethnicity can be thought of as a nationality, not in the sense of carrying the rights and duties of citizenship but in the sense of identifying with a

Ethnicity one's ethnic quality or affiliation. It is voluntary, self-defined, nonhierarchal, fluid and multiple, and based on cultural differences, not physical ones per se.

Crowds line the streets at the St. Patrick's Day Parade in New York City. How is this an example of symbolic ethnicity?

Symbolic ethnicity a nationality, not in the sense of carrying the rights and duties of citizenship but of identifying with a past or future nationality. For later generations of white ethnics, something not constraining but easily expressed, with no risks of stigma and all the pleasures of feeling like an individual.

past or future nationality. For Americans, Herbert Gans (1979b) called this identification symbolic ethnicity. Symbolic ethnicity today is a matter of choice for white middle-class Americans. It has no risk of stigma and confers the pleasures of feeling like an individual. For example, from 2000 to 2010 the second-fastest-growing racial group in the United States was Native Americans. According to the U.S. Census, the American Indian and Alaska Native (alone or multiracial) population grew by 1.1 million, about 39 percent, whereas the entire U.S. population grew during that same time by 9.7 percent (U.S. Census Bureau, 2012a). These numbers are not the outcome of migration or a Native American baby boom, but instead reflect a growing interest in claiming one's heritage, so long as it's not too stigmatizing and brings just the right amount of uniqueness. And claiming American Indian ancestry is more than a matter of checking a box. Membership criteria vary from tribe to tribe but usually there has to be genealogical proof.

These differences between race and ethnicity underscore the privileged position of whites in America, who have the freedom to pick and choose their identities, to wave a flag in a parade, or to whip up Grandma's traditional recipe and freely show their ethnic backgrounds. The surge of ethnic pride among white Americans today implies a false belief that all ethnic groups are the same, but in the very way that symbolic ethnicity is voluntary for white ethnics, it is not so for nonwhite ethnic Americans such as Latinos and Asians. As soon as someone classifies you as different on the basis of your phenotypical (racial) features, you lose the ability to choose your ethnic identity. It becomes racialized—subsumed under a forced identifier, label, or racial marker of "otherness" that you cannot escape. Thus, although it is common to use the term *ethnicity* across the board to refer to Latino, black, Asian, or Irish backgrounds, being Irish in America is something that a person can turn on or off at will. You can never *not* be Asian or black: Your body gives away your otherness, no matter how much you want to blend in.

To be black in America is to be just that—black. Some scholars argue that this is the fundamental issue about race in America. Blacks were considered, until recently, a monolithic group. They were unique among racial groups in that their ethnic (tribal, language group, and national) distinctions were deliberately wiped out during the slave trade in order to prevent social organization and revolt (Eyerman, 2001). Alex Haley's landmark novel *Roots* (1976) raised an awareness among African Americans about tracing their ethnic rather than racial identity. This is changing now as more and more African Americans trace back their roots to specific places in Africa through genealogical research or DNA testing. Likewise, immigration from Africa and the Caribbean has created distinctly recognizable national groups of origin among the U.S. black population. Finally, the presidential campaign of Barack Obama led, perhaps, to a symbolic expansion of who counts as black within the African American community: even the son of a white, Kansan mother and Kenyan father who has half-Asian and fully African half-siblings. Though some African Americans were initially uncomfortable with embracing Obama and his mixed heritage as black like them, their attitudes would have had little impact on the wider perception of Obama as a black man because of the continuing significance of the one-drop rule in America. In the end, these initial misgivings faded and Americans of all races celebrated the inauguration of America's first black president.

Ethnic Groups in the United States

The United States is home to countless ethnicities today. It has such a heterogeneous population, in fact, that it is on its way to having no single numerically dominant group. Until the mid-nineteenth century, ethnic diversity was minimal because immigration rates were relatively low until about 1820. Early in the country's formation, white Anglo-Saxon Protestants dominated over Native Americans as well as black slaves. From that point forward, Anglos secured their place at the top of the cultural, political, and economic hierarchy, prevailing over other immigrant populations. As exemplified in the following snapshot of ethnic groups in America today, these historical hierarchies have remained relatively stable and intact despite drastically changing demographics.

Native Americans

According to archaeological findings, the original settlers of the North American continent arrived anywhere between 12,000 and 50,000 years ago from northeast Asia, traveling by foot on glaciers. This is disputed by some tribes, such as the Ojibwe, who believe that their ancestors came from the east, not the west. Before European explorers arrived in significant numbers for extended periods in the fifteenth century (there is evidence that the Vikings had reached North America before then), the indigenous population was anywhere between 10 and 100 million. The tribes living here when Europeans showed up were geographically, culturally, and physically diverse, but they were categorically viewed as a single uncivilized group by arriving Spanish, French, and British explorers. Even today, "Indians" in America are part of 280 distinct cultural groups (Gray & Nye, 2001). Foreshadowing the lack of respect to come, Columbus called all of the people he met Indians, despite their clear cultural differences, because he thought he was in India. Confronted with foreign

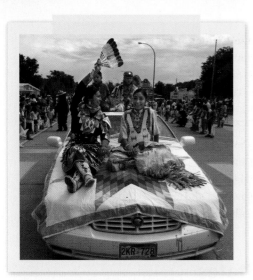

The Oglala Nation Pow Wow and Rodeo parade is a bright spot for the Pine Ridge Indian Reservation, which, like many federal reservations, is plagued by problems linked to low socioeconomic status.

diseases and unfamiliar military technology, the Indians were quickly dominated by white invaders. In Central and South America, the Spanish brutally enslaved them as labor for the mining industry. In the northern parts of North America, French colonialists nurtured their relationships with the Indians in order to cultivate a profitable fur trade. The British, chiefly concerned with acquiring land, settled colonies with the long-term goal of expanding the British state, dispossessing and "civilizing" America's indigenous population in the process (Cornell, 1988).

American Indians' way of life was completely obliterated by the European settlements, as vital land was taken from them and their communal infrastructure disrupted. Most devastating were the newly imported diseases, such as smallpox and cholera, against which the Indians, having no native immunity, were virtually defenseless. There were also grueling forced marches from native lands to dedicated reservations. By the end of the 1800s, the Native American population had dwindled to approximately 250,000 (U.S. Census Bureau, 1993). The Indian Bureau (later called the Bureau of Indian Affairs) was established as part of the War Department in 1824 to deal with the remaining "Indian problem," and its chief means was "forced assimilation." This involved removing Indian children from their families and putting them in government-run boarding schools that taught the superiority of Anglo culture over "primitive" Native culture and religion. Children who refused to adopt Western dress, language, and religion met with harsh physical and emotional punishment (Cornell, 1988). (A similar project was undertaken in British-ruled Australia with the native Aboriginal tribes.) Despite this poor treatment, Navajo men served the United States in World War II, in which 29 "code talkers" used the Navajo language in lieu of cryptography to protect the secrecy of American communications. The work of the code talkers was critically instrumental in the American victory at Iwo Jima and many other battles throughout the war (Bixler, 1992). Today Native Americans number about 5.2 million (U.S. Census Bureau, 2012a). Only about one-fifth of Native Americans live in a designated American Indian area. The largest reservation, Navajoland or Diné Bikéyah, covers approximately 16 million acres of Arizona, New Mexico, and Utah. Reservations are generally impoverished and rife with health problems, domestic abuse, substance abuse, poor infrastructure, and high crime. In fact, Native Americans as a whole are plagued by the lowest average socioeconomic status. They rank among the worst in terms of high-school dropout rates and unemployment, which go hand in hand with poor health outcomes such as alcoholism, suicide, and premature death. Suicide rates are more than double that of the general population and are the second-leading cause of death for Native Americans from ages 15 to 34 (Centers for Disease Control and Prevention, 2012b). Around 33 percent of Native Americans die before age 45, compared with 11 percent of the U.S. population as a whole (Garrett, 1994). As an ethnic group, Native Americans have grown by 39 percent in the recent past (U.S. Census Bureau, 2012a). This increase has resulted from the high birthrate among Native Americans and the increased tendency among whites to embrace their Native roots. Declaring your newfound Native roots is at once a case of symbolic ethnicity and a pragmatic act: Native Americans are eligible for numerous types of federal assistance, ranging from health care services to preferential admission rates at colleges, though a 2004 Civil Rights Commission report found that the federal government spends more per capita for health care for prisoners than for Native Americans (Ho, 2009).

African Americans

The first black people in North America arrived not as slaves but as indentured servants contracted by white colonialists for set periods. They were in the same circumstances as poor, nonfree whites such as those from Ireland or Scotland (Franklin, 1980). The system of slavery, however, evolved to meet colonial labor needs, and the slave trade was a fixed institution by the end of the

Wiley College student body president Kabamba Kiboko dances at a pep rally. Her family came to the United States from the Congo. For the first time, more Africans are entering the country than during the slave trade.

seventeenth century. African Americans have been, all in all, on the bottom of the racial hierarchy ever since.

Just before the American Revolution, slaves made up more than 20 percent of the colonial population (Dinnerstein et al., 1996). Today about 14 percent of the American population is black (U.S. Census Bureau, 2011b). Like the Japanese Burakumin, this minority group has high rates of poverty, health problems, unemployment, and crime. According to the U.S. Census Bureau, the median income of African Americans as a group is roughly 61 percent that of whites. In 2011, more than 6.9 million people in the United States were on probation or parole, in jail, or in prison—that's 2.9 percent of all U.S. adult residents, or 1 in every 34 adults (Glaze and Parks, 2012). Among black men ages 25 to 39, about 7 percent are behind bars compared with 3 percent of black men overall and slightly fewer than 3 percent of Hispanic men in that same age group. Overall, just 0.5 percent of white men are imprisoned. (Glaze and Parks, 2012).

Sociologists and demographers today are beginning to study how new black immigrants are fracturing the holistic conception of "African American." For the first time, more Africans are entering the country than during the slave trade. More than 9 percent of the black population is foreign born (U.S. Census Bureau, 2012b). Afro-Caribbeans such as Cubans, Haitians, and Jamaicans resent being unilaterally categorized as African American, because each of these immigrant groups enjoys a unique history, culture, and language that do not correspond to the American stereotypes of black skin. For this reason, new black immigrant groups would rather not assimilate, but instead retain their distinctive immigrant status, setting themselves apart from the lowest status group in America, blacks (Greer, 2006).

Latinos

Latino, like the term *Hispanic* (the two are often used interchangeably), refers to a diverse group of people of Latin or Hispanic origin. In 2011, the majority of Latinos in the United States were from Mexico (about 65 percent), Puerto Rico (about 9.5 percent), Cuba (3.6 percent), and the Dominican Republic (2.9 percent). (Figure 9.1 provides a breakdown of the U.S. Hispanic population by region of origin.) They are a huge and rapidly expanding segment of the American population; in 2012 they made up approximately 17 percent of the population, surpassing African Americans (U.S. Census Bureau, 2012c). Latinos also live in a wide array of locations, although they have clustered on the West Coast and in the South and Midwest (U.S. Census Bureau, 2011c).

Hispanics are often called an "in between" ethnic group because of their intermediate status, sandwiched between Caucasians and African Americans. Unlike African Americans, the majority of Latinos in America today have come by way of voluntary immigration, particularly during the last four decades of heavy, second-wave immigration. Puerto Ricans are the exception, because they have been able to travel freely to the United States since 1917, when Puerto Rico became an American territory and its inhabitants U.S. citizens. The chief motivation for Latino immigration is economic, because of America's high demand for labor in the service, agriculture, and construction industries.

Mexicans, Puerto Ricans, and Cubans all have diverse phenotypical traits that make racial distinctions of a unified Latino type nearly impossible. Mexicans are generally classified as "mestizos," a term referring to a racially mixed heritage that combines Native American and European traits. For instance, Puerto Ricans are often a mixture of African, European, and Indian backgrounds. So ambiguous is the Latino label that at various times the U.S. Census has classified them as part of the white race and as a separate race. At the moment, being Hispanic or Latino is considered an ethnic identity, not a racial identity.

Most Cubans consider themselves Hispanic whites, although their immigration status has changed drastically in recent years. Following the Communist revolution led by Fidel Castro, the first large wave of Cuban immigrants arrived in southern Florida in the 1960s. These immigrants were upper or middle class, and educated, and perceived as the victims of a Communist regime that came to power during the Cold War. As such, they were welcomed enthusiastically to this country, and their assimilation started smoothly (Portes, 1969). By 1995, however, that warm welcome had faded. The U.S. federal government terminated its 35-year "open door" policy toward Cuban refugees, and the heavy media coverage of Cubans arriving since then in small boats has led to stereotypes of a desperate "wetback" invasion. Arrivals since the 1970s—who generally are from lower socioeconomic backgrounds in Cuban society—have met more resistance from their host society, consequently experiencing higher rates of unemployment, low-wage work, and dependence on welfare and charity than native whites and previous Cuban émigrés (Portes et al., 1985).

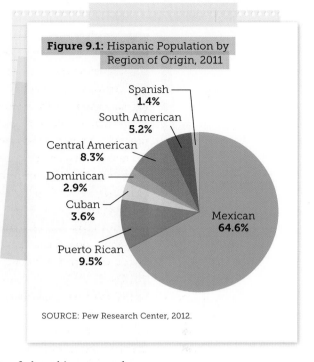

Figure 9.1: Hispanic Population by Region of Origin, 2011

Spanish 1.4%
South American 5.2%
Central American 8.3%
Dominican 2.9%
Cuban 3.6%
Puerto Rican 9.5%
Mexican 64.6%

SOURCE: Pew Research Center, 2012.

Asian Americans

Like *Latino,* the term *Asian American* is very broad, encompassing diverse and sometimes clashing peoples from China, Korea, Japan, and Southeast Asia. The first wave of Asians to arrive in the United States in the mid-nineteenth

Diners eat at a restaurant in Lowell, Massachusetts, which has the second-largest concentration of Cambodian immigrants in the United States. The area has become a tourist draw and economic engine for the old mill city.

century were predominantly laborers of Chinese, then Japanese, then Korean and Filipino origin. A second large wave of immigration is currently under way, mostly made up of well-educated and highly skilled people from all over Asia.

Early Asian immigrants were perceived as a labor threat and therefore met with extreme hostility. The Chinese Exclusion Act of 1882, which led to a ban against the Chinese in 1902, marked the first time in American history in which a group was singled out and barred entry. Urban "Chinatowns" developed out of ghettos in which marginalized Chinese workers, mostly men, were forced to live. Japanese immigrants faced similar hostilities and were formally barred entry by the Oriental Exclusion Act of 1924. By 2010, Asian and mixed-Asian U.S. residents amounted to 4.8 percent of the population. This was a 43.3 percent increase over a decade, making Asian Americans the fastest-growing racial group (U.S. Census Bureau, 2011d). They are most heavily concentrated in California, Hawaii, New York, Illinois, and Washington.

Asian Americans are unique among ethnic minorities because of their high average socioeconomic status, surpassing that of most other ethnic minorities as well as most whites in terms of educational attainment. For example, the median family income for the U.S. population as a whole in 2011 was $51,484, whereas for Asian Americans it was $69,510 (U.S. Census Bureau, 2012d). That said, despite the overall success of Asian Americans, certain groups—notably Cambodians and Hmong (from Laos and Vietnam)—experience very high poverty rates.

Furthermore, Asian Americans overall disproportionately find it difficult to be reemployed once they lose a job. In 2012, the Asian American unemployment rate for those with bachelor degrees or higher was 0.6 percentage points higher than the rate for whites (Bureau of Labor Statistics, 2013b), and Asian Americans and blacks suffer from the longest average duration of unemployment spells. In 2012, unemployed Asian Americans experienced a median 24 weeks before they found work again. For blacks that year, the figure was 24.7 weeks. (Whites and Latinos had 17.6- and 16.7-week median durations between jobs in 2012.) However, these black–Asian and white–Latino similarities obscure different reasons for the long duration for the various groups. Whereas blacks typically face barriers to employment, Asians have more family support and savings and thus are able to wait out a bad labor market for the best possible job.

In recent years, Asians have been applauded for their smooth assimilation as the "model minority," the implication being that if only other ethnic groups could assimilate so well, America would have fewer social problems. Such a view, however, effaces the rather unsmooth history Asian immigrants have faced in this country, as well as the continuing poverty and discrimination faced by some Asian ethnics. Furthermore, "positive" stereotypes of high achievement are not always beneficial and can place enormous pressure on Asian youths to measure up to an impossibly high ideal.

Middle Eastern Americans

Middle Easterners come from places as diverse as the Arabian Peninsula, North Africa, Iran, Iraq, and the Palestinian territories. They established communities in the United States as far back as the late 1800s, but their numbers have swelled since the 1970s as part of the rising tide of non-European immigration. Middle Easterners in this second wave of immigration often arrive from politically tumultuous areas to seek refuge in the United States.

Today about 1.5 million Americans report some Arab origins, and even more Americans have a Middle Eastern heritage, because not all Middle Easterners are Arabic (U.S. Census Bureau, 2013a), despite the fact that most Americans regard anyone from the Middle East as Arab and Muslim. In fact, the largest Middle Eastern population in the United States today is from Iran, and they are Persians, not ethnic Arabs, and do not generally speak Arabic. Similarly, although the majority of new Middle Eastern Americans are Muslim, many of them are Christian, and a small number are Jewish (Bozorgmehr et al., 1996).

Widespread misunderstandings about Middle Easterners derive, in part, from their negative stereotyping in the mainstream media. In one study of television portrayals of Arabs, researchers found four basic myths that continue to surround this ethnic group. First, they are often depicted as fabulously wealthy—as sultans and oil tycoons. Second, they are shown as uncivilized and barbaric. Third, they are portrayed as sex-crazed, especially so that they can be used as underage white sex slaves. Fourth, they are said to revel in acts of terrorism, desiring to destroy all things American (Shaheen, 1984). Little has changed since this study came out nearly 30 years ago, although after 9/11, the emphasis shifted away from stereotypes of Arabs as extremely rich and toward one of Middle Easterners as terrorists.

The Importance of Being White

We've seen some of the trajectories of various ethnic and racial groups in America, but what about the largest racial population, whites? Scholars have begun to pay more attention to what it means to be a white person. Every year on the first day of my introduction to sociology class, I ask my 200 or so students to write down the five social categories that best describe who they are. Black students almost always put their race at or near the top of the list. Latino and Asian American students usually list their ethnicity as well. Until recently, I could be fairly confident that whites would not list their race. Some might identify Polish, German, or another ethnic or national origin, but not one white student would write down Caucasian, white, or even Euro-American. And that was the point of my experiment.

We have already seen how the category of whiteness is socially constructed—first inclusively defined as all "free white persons" in 1790, then restrictively defined as only northern and western European whites in the early twentieth century, and reformulated back to an umbrella category by the mid-twentieth century. We know now that this category, which seems so natural and innate, is actually a flexible label that has expanded over time to include many formerly nonwhite groups such as Jews, Irish, and Italians. Today most white people have little awareness of the meaning of whiteness as a category. As Nell Irvin Painter, the author of *The History of White People*, says, "The foundation of white identity is that there isn't any. You're just an individual" (Schackner, 2002).

Whiteness, argues Peggy McIntosh (1988), is an "invisible knapsack of privileges" that puts white people at an advantage, just as racism places nonwhites at a disadvantage. In her now classic essay "White Privilege: Unpacking the Invisible Knapsack," McIntosh catalogs more than 50 "Daily Effects of White Privilege," ranging from the mundane to the major. Here are just a few McIntosh notices:

- I can go into a music shop and count on finding the music of my race represented, into a supermarket and find the staple foods which fit with my cultural traditions, into a hairdresser's shop and find someone who can cut my hair.
- I can arrange to protect my children most of the time from people who might not like them.
- I do not have to educate my children to be aware of systemic racism for their own daily physical protection.

- I am never asked to speak for all the people of my racial group.
- I am not made acutely aware that my shape, bearing, or body odor will be taken as a reflection on my race.
- I can choose blemish cover or bandages in "flesh" color and have them more or less match my skin. (pp. 3–5)

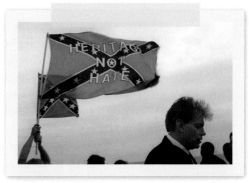

Former Klansman David Duke stands under a Confederate battle flag. How was Duke able to cast the NAAWP as a pro-white movement instead of a racist organization?

Whiteness, then, is about not feeling the weight of representing an entire population with one's successes or failures. It's about not having to think about race much at all.

In recent years, however, awareness of whiteness has been on the rise, as evidenced by the profusion of scholarship on whiteness, the goal of which is to call attention to the social construction and ensuing privilege of the category. Calling attention to whiteness helps whites understand how slanted the playing field really is. It also helps rectify something wrong with the way we study race in America: By traditionally focusing on minority groups, the implicit message that scholarship projects is that nonwhites are "deviant," to borrow from the Comte de Buffon, and that's why we study them. Even popular culture has caught on with memes like "stuff white people like," "columbusing," and "if black people said the stuff white people say," which offer humorous yet pointed critiques of privileges that affluent white people tend to have in America.

But white consciousness may have another, more troubling side. In 1980, before white studies got under way in universities, the white supremacist David Duke left his position as the grand wizard of the Knights of the Ku Klux Klan and founded the National Association for the Advancement of White People (NAAWP), attempting to sugarcoat his racist movement with a seemingly more politically correct approach. In this new framework, Duke presented whites as a besieged minority, writes sociologist Mitch Berbrier (2000), defining the NAAWP's mission as a pro-white heritage movement as opposed to an anti-black one. Sociologist Abby Ferber has analyzed the clever appropriation of civil rights language in Duke's white supremacist discourse. For example, in an article by Duke in the *White Patriot,* Ferber finds the rhetoric of reverse discrimination, victimhood, and the right to cultural difference:

> [O]ur race and all others should have the right to determine their own destiny through self-determination and rule. . . . [E]very people on this planet must have the right to life: the continued existence of its unique racial fabric and resulting culture. (*White Patriot,* no. 56, p. 6, quoted in Ferber, 1999)

Sounds reasonable, right? That's because the new language of white supremacy allows racists to move away from explicitly racist language (of biological inferiority, for example). Duke's NAAWP also co-opts civil rights discourse, as in the organization's original mission statement: "The NAAWP is a not for profit, nonviolent, civil rights educational organization, demanding equal rights for whites and special privileges for none."

Such examples demonstrate one possible outcome of the emergence of white studies: to politically empower extremists by giving them a legitimate language for their racist ends. Note, however, that this rhetoric does not acknowledge the advantages whites typically enjoy. The power of whiteness studies is that it exposes the social construction of a seemingly natural (and neutral) category, giving a sense of the unequal footing beneath the labels "white" and "black." (That is, whites can embrace ethnic identity, but blacks are stuck in a racial category.) But like any new "technology," such discourse can be used for many ends.

Minority–Majority Group Relations

What are the *social* consequences of race? Scholars have defined four broad forms that minority–majority group relations can take: assimilation, pluralism, segregation, and conflict.

In the 1920s, sociologist Robert Park began to wonder what, on the one hand, held together the diverse populations in major American cities and, on the other hand, sustained their cultural differences. He came up with a race relations cycle of four stages: contact, competition, accommodation, and assimilation. His model, called straight-line assimilation, was at first accepted as the universally progressive pattern in which immigrants arrive, settle in, mimic the practices and behaviors of the people who were already there, and achieve full assimilation in a newly homogenous country.

Straight-line assimilation
Robert Park's 1920s universal and linear model for how immigrants assimilate: they first arrive, then settle in, and achieve full assimilation in a newly homogenous country.

Milton Gordon (1964) tweaked Park's model by suggesting multiple kinds of assimilation outcomes. For Gordon, an immigrant population can pass through (or stall in) seven stages of assimilation: cultural, structural, marital, identificational, attitude receptional, behavior receptional, and civic assimilation (Table 9.1).

With Park and Gordon in mind, let's do a thought experiment. Imagine yourself as a Polish immigrant arriving at Ellis Island in 1900. You don't have much money, and you've come to America in search of opportunity; this is the land of plenty, so you've been told. You settle into a Polish enclave of Manhattan, where you connect with friends and maybe some family. You do your best to learn English. You buy a pair of riveted denim pants, popular among American workmen. You secure work in a factory thanks to your connections in the Polish community. After an initial period of tension and conflict stemming from job competition and housing constraints, you eventually are accepted by your Anglo-American neighbors, first by being allowed to join the workers' union and then—and this probably only happens to your children—by being allowed to marry into an Anglo family. By this time, you think of yourself as an American. Congratulations, you have reached Milton Gordon's final stage of civic assimilation.

Table 9.1: Gordon's Stages of Assimilation

STAGES OF ASSIMILATION	CHARACTERISTIC
Cultural assimilation	Change of cultural patterns to those of host society
Structural assimilation	Large-scale entrance into cliques
Marital assimilation	Large-scale intermarriage
Identification assimilation	Development of sense of collective identity based exclusively on host society
Attitude reception assimilation	Absence of prejudice
Behavior reception assimilation	Absence of discrimination
Civic assimilation	Absence of value and power conflict

Harold Isaacs (1975) noticed something that these theories of assimilation could not explain: People did not so easily shed their ethnic ties. Ethnic identification, among white ethnics and everyone else, persisted even after a group attained certain levels of structural assimilation. Clifford Geertz (1973) explained this persistence as a matter of primordialism—that is, the strength of ethnic ties resides in deeply felt or primordial ties to one's culture. Ethnicity is, in a word, *fixed*. If not biologically rooted, it's rooted in some other intractable source that Geertz reasoned must be culture.

The flip side of this argument came from Nathan Glazer and Daniel P. Moynihan in *Beyond the Melting Pot* (1963). Far from being a deeply rooted structure that kept people bonded to their culture, ethnic identification, they reasoned, persisted because it was in an individual's best interest to maintain it. They saw ethnic groups as miniature interest groups—individuals uniting for instrumental purposes, such as fending off job competition. Glazer and Moynihan believed that ethnicity was fluid and circumstantial. More recently, scholars have posited that ethnic identification is both a deeply felt attachment and an instrumental position that can change according to circumstance (Cornell & Hartmann, 1998).

Primordialism Clifford Geertz's term to explain the strength of ethnic ties because they are fixed in deeply felt or primordial ties to one's homeland culture.

Pluralism

For most people, however, assimilation into American society is not so easy, and acceptance varies systematically. At times a pressure cooker has been invoked as a more appropriate metaphor than a melting pot. Park's model was useful in shifting attention away from essentialist explanations of the so-called innate differences among immigrants, but it suffers from several shortcomings.

Figure 9.2: Five Largest Foreign-Born Populations in the United States, 1850 to the Present (in thousands)

1850	1880	1900	1930
FRANCE <<<<<<<<< 54	SWEDEN <<<<<<<< 194	SWEDEN <<<<<<<< 582	POLAND <<<<<<<< 1,269
CANADA <<<<<<<<< 148	CANADA <<<<<<<< 717	GREAT BRITAIN <<<< 1,168	CANADA <<<<<<<< 1,310
GREAT BRITAIN <<<< 379	GREAT BRITAIN <<<< 918	CANADA <<<<<<<< 1,180	UNITED KINGDOM <<< 1,403
GERMANY <<<<<<<< 584	IRELAND <<<<<<<< 1,855	IRELAND <<<<<<<< 1,615	GERMANY <<<<<<<< 1,609
IRELAND <<<<<<<<< 962	GERMANY <<<<<<<< 1,967	GERMANY <<<<<<<< 2,663	ITALY <<<<<<<<<< 1,790
TOTAL: 2.2 million	TOTAL: 6.7 million	TOTAL: 10.3 million	TOTAL: 14.2 million

SOURCE: U.S. Census Bureau, 2011f.

Most obviously, it does not apply to nonwhite immigrants, many of whom are not fully accepted into all areas of American society. Park's model also does not apply to involuntary immigrants, notably African Americans and some refugees. Ernest Barth and Donald Noel (1972) noted that assimilation is not necessarily the end result for immigrants. On the contrary, other outcomes such as exclusion, pluralism, and stratification are possibilities. And as others point out (Lieberson, 1961; Massey, 1995; Portes & Zhou, 1993), some immigrants assimilate more easily than others, depending on a variety of structural factors, like migration patterns; differences in contact with the majority groups; demographics including fertility, mortality rates, and age structure; and

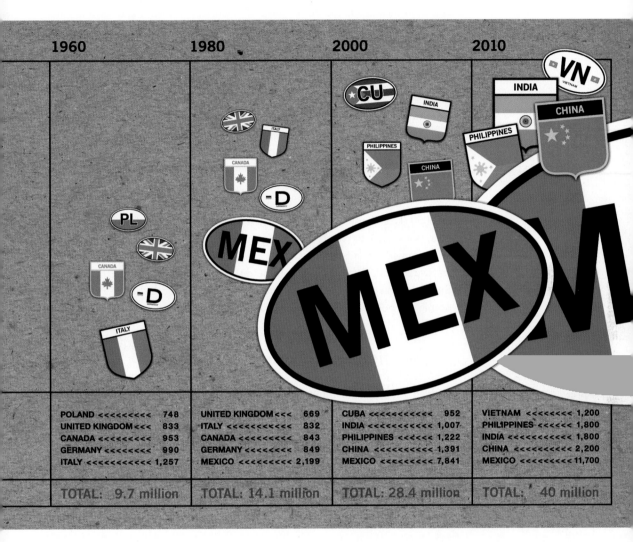

ultimately, power differentials between groups. This is the case for the "new immigration," which, in comparison with the earlier era of European immigration (1901–30), is a large-scale influx of non-European immigration that began in the late 1960s and continues to the present (Figure 9.2).

The new immigrants, largely from Hispanic and Asian countries, are racialized as nonwhites—even though Asians are widely considered a "model minority." They therefore are subject to a different set of conditions for assimilating and face greater obstacles to their upward mobility (Massey, 1995). For example, Portes and Zhou (1993) report that the children of Haitian immigrants living in Miami's Little Haiti are at high risk for downward mobility because they face social ostracism from their own ethnic community if they choose to adopt the outlook and cultural ways of native-born Americans. Among Haitian youth, a common message is the devaluation of mainstream norms, and anyone who excels at school or abides by mainstream rules runs the risk of being shunned for "acting white." This picture of assimilation is much more complex than Park's initial formulation.

A society with several distinct ethnic or racial groups is said to be a **pluralism**, meaning that a low degree of assimilation exists. A culturally pluralistic society has one large sociocultural framework with a diversity of cultures functioning within it. This is the premise of multiculturalism in America. Statistically speaking, in a pluralist country, no single group commands majority status. Switzerland, with its three linguistic groups—German, French, and Italian—is a striking example of ethnic autonomy and balance. Demographic projections suggest that whites will make up about 47 percent of the population by 2050 (U.S. Census Bureau, 2012e). A broader definition of pluralism, however, is a society in which minority groups live separately but equally. Imagine America with no substantial stratification, no oppression, and no domination. In Switzerland, despite slight income differences among ethnic groups (with the exception of recent immigrant groups like the Turkish), no one group dominates politically, but the same cannot be said for America.

Pluralism the presence and engaged coexistence of numerous distinct groups in one society.

Segregation and Discrimination

Segregation the legal or social practice of separating people on the basis of their race or ethnicity.

A third paradigm for minority–majority relations is segregation, the legal or social practice of separating people on the basis of their race or ethnicity. An extreme case of segregation was the southern United States before the civil rights movement. Under the Jim Crow system of segregation, reinforced by the Supreme Court's 1896 ruling in *Plessy v. Ferguson*, a "separate but equal" doctrine ruled the South. Strictly enforced separation existed between blacks and whites in most areas of public life—from residence to health facilities to bus seats, classroom seats, and even toilet seats.

Although the *Plessy* decision ruled that separate facilities for blacks and whites were constitutional as long as they were equal, in real life the doctrine legalized unequal facilities for blacks. The National Association for the Advancement of Colored People (NAACP) has long recognized that segregation and discrimination are inescapably linked. Nowhere is this clearer than in the case of education. Social science data consistently show that an

Black actor, singer, and civil rights leader Paul Robeson leads Oakland dockworkers in singing the national anthem in 1942.

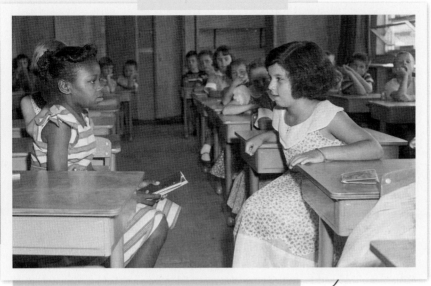

Elementary-school students in Ft. Myer, Virginia, face each other on the first day of desegregation.

integrated educational experience for minority children produces advantages over a nonintegrated school experience. School segregation almost always entails fewer educational resources and lower quality for minority students.

As Anthony Marx (1998) has noted, concern over segregation grew during World War II as America was caught in the embarrassing contradiction of espousing antiracist rhetoric against its Nazi foes while upholding an egregiously racist doctrine at home. America emerged from the war as a global force with heightened stakes for its world reputation; this new status, along with growing public dissent, perhaps helped motivate the Supreme Court's landmark 1954 decision in *Brown v. Board of Education*. The Court's majority opinion that legally segregated public schools were "inherently unequal" is considered the ruling that struck down the "separate but equal" doctrine. It was also the spark that ignited the civil rights movement of the 1960s.

However, school desegregation has been under fire since several Supreme Court decisions in the 1990s (*Dowell*, 1991; *Pitts*, 1992; *Jenkins*, 1995). Two 2007 cases in Louisville, Kentucky, and Seattle, Washington, came the closest to overturning the spirit (if not the letter) of *Brown*. Earlier, former presidents Richard Nixon and Ronald Reagan had both openly attacked desegregation initiatives, especially busing. In 1981, President Reagan's attorney general, William Bradford Reynolds, flatly proclaimed that the "compulsory busing of students in order to achieve racial balance in the public schools is not an acceptable remedy" (Orfield, 1996). Today most U.S. schools are only marginally less segregated than they were in the mid-1960s. Researchers at the University of California, Los Angeles found double segregation by both race and income where "the typical black student is now in a school where almost two of every three classmates (64%) are low-income, nearly double the rates for whites (37%) and Asians (39%) . . . and 80% of Latinos and 74% of blacks attend schools that are majority nonwhite students" (Orfield, et al., 2012). School segregation is invariably linked to poverty, which is perpetuated by residential segregation, and perhaps this issue is the one we should be addressing if we are concerned about mitigating racial disparities.

In 1968, under President Lyndon B. Johnson's initiative, the Kerner Commission reported that despite the civil rights movement sweeping the nation, America was split into two societies: "one black, one white—separate and unequal." The main reason for the fissure was residential segregation, what sociologist Lawrence Bobo has termed the "structural linchpin of American racial inequality" (Bobo, 1989). Residential segregation, scholars argue, maintains an urban underclass in perpetual poverty by limiting its ties to upwardly mobile social networks, which connect people to jobs and other opportunities. When you live in the ghetto, your chances of landing a good job through your social network are indeed slim (Wilson, 1987).

It has also been suggested that residential segregation inflicts poverty through a "culture of segregation" (Massey & Denton, 1993). According to this argument, you live in a ghetto that's extremely isolated from the outside world—no family restaurants like the Olive Garden, no mainstream bank branches, not even a chain grocery store that sells fresh vegetables. You're surrounded daily by the ills that accompany poverty: poor health, joblessness, out-of-wedlock children, welfare, educational failure, a drug economy, crime and violence, and, in general, social and physical deterioration. In the ghetto, the most extreme form of residential segregation, you come to believe that this is all there is to life; the social ills become normative. It's no big deal to sell drugs, drop out of school, depend on welfare, or run with a gang. You slide into the very behaviors that, in turn, reproduce the spiral of decline of your neighborhood.

Whether you buy this line of thought or not (and this viewpoint has been criticized as being overly deterministic), consider how a segregated neighborhood got that way in the first place. It didn't just pop up out of nowhere, nor was it always there. As Douglass Massey and Nancy Denton (1993) have argued, the ghetto was deliberately and systematically constructed by whites to keep blacks locked into their (unequal) place. Before 1900, blacks faced job discrimination but relatively little residential segregation. Blacks and whites lived side by side in urban centers, as the index of dissimilarity numbers in

In 1942, a race riot broke out in Detroit, Michigan, during an attempt by white residents to force African Americans out of the neighborhood.

Figure 9.3 shows. The index of dissimilarity, the standard measure of segregation, captures the degree to which blacks and whites are evenly spread among neighborhoods in a given city. The index tells you the percentage of nonwhites who would have to move in order to achieve residential integration.

Various structural changes—industrialization, urbanization, the influx of southern blacks to the North who competed with huge waves of European immigrants—led to increased hostility and violence toward blacks, who found themselves shut out of both white jobs and white neighborhoods. The color line, previously more flexible and fuzzy, hardened into a rigid boundary between black and white.

The black ghetto was manufactured by whites through a set of deliberate, conscious practices. Boundaries separating black neighborhoods were policed by whites, first with the threat of violence and periphery bombings in the 1920s and then with "neighborhood associations" that institutionalized housing discrimination. Property owners signed secret agreements promising to not allow blacks into their domain. When a black family did move to a neighboring block, whites often adopted the strategy of flight instead of fight, and this process of racial turnover yielded the same result: black isolation. Even today, when a black family moves into a white neighborhood, the property

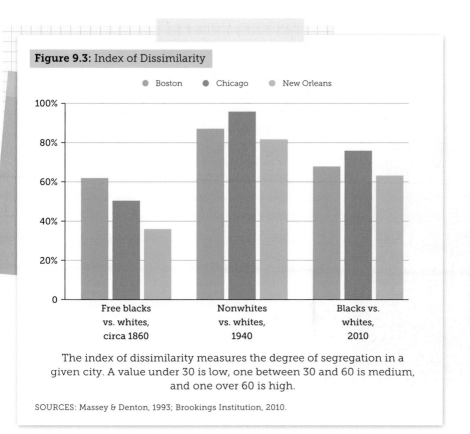

Figure 9.3: Index of Dissimilarity

● Boston   ● Chicago   ● New Orleans

The index of dissimilarity measures the degree of segregation in a given city. A value under 30 is low, one between 30 and 60 is medium, and one over 60 is high.

SOURCES: Massey & Denton, 1993; Brookings Institution, 2010.

value declines slightly, in subtle anticipation of the process of white flight, which leaves behind a run-down, undesirable black neighborhood—a veritable vicious circle. On the other hand, the formerly black neighborhood of Harlem in New York City is now no longer majority black, a consequence of the recent in-migration of whites and Hispanics (Roberts, 2010).

Also helping to create the black ghetto have been specific government policies, such as the Home Owners' Loan Corporation (HOLC), that in the early 1930s granted loans to home owners who were in financial trouble. The HOLC also instituted the practice of "redlining," which declared inner-city, black neighborhoods too much of a liability and ineligible for aid. Following the HOLC's lead, the U.S. Federal Housing Administration and the Veterans Administration—both of which were designed to make home ownership a reality for struggling Americans—funneled funds away from black areas and predominantly into white suburbs. Finally, by the 1950s, urban slums were being razed in the name of "urban renewal," which essentially became a program of removal, as African Americans were relocated to concentrated public housing projects (Massey & Denton, 1993). These deliberately discriminatory policies are perpetuated today by de facto segregation in the form of continued suburban white flight and the splintering of school districts along racial lines.

Some scholars argue that a new form of segregation has emerged in America: The criminal justice system. During the 1960s, blacks were slightly overrepresented in the nation's prisons, but in absolute numbers there were many more white felons, because whites made up a larger percentage of the total U.S. population. Today the racial distribution in jails and prisons is the reverse. Blacks and Latinos now make up the majority of incarcerated people. One in four black men in their twenties is in prison or jail, on probation, or on parole at any given moment (Pettit & Western, 2004). Is imprisonment just another means of confining the black population away from whites? Several scholars make this case, based on changes in drug laws that seem to affect minorities disproportionately.

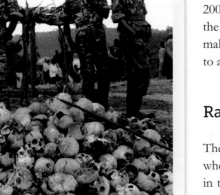

Ethnic Tutsi troops overlook a pile of skulls that will be reburied in a memorial to approximately 12,000 Tutsi massacred by Hutu militias.

Racial Conflict

The final paradigm of race relations is conflict relations, when antagonistic groups within a society live integrated in the same neighborhoods, hold the same jobs, and go to the same schools. This was the volatile scenario in Rwanda in 1994, when roughly 800,000 Tutsi were murdered by Hutu, mostly by machete, in the span of 100 days. That's about 333.3 killings per hour, or five and a half lives every second (Gourevitch, 1998). The killings, as well as the maiming and systematic rape of Tutsi women, were the culmination of more than a century of racial hostility that began with the Belgian colonization of Rwanda.

Belgian explorers, immersed in discourses of scientific racism, confronted two Rwandan tribes, the Hutu and the Tutsi, who for ages had been living and working together and intermarrying. Because of all their shared social, cultural, and genetic heritages, scientists today cannot distinguish Hutu and Tutsi into separate biological populations. But in the late nineteenth century, the Belgians gave preferential treatment to the Tutsi, whom they believed to be superior to the Hutu. What followed was a brutal system of oppression in which the Tutsi dominated the Hutu.

When Rwanda was granted independence in 1962, after a century of hatred brewing between the two groups, the Hutu took power under a dictatorship masked as a democracy, and their long-standing animosity simmered into an explosion in April 1994 after three years of failed crops. The result was genocide, the mass killing of a particular population based on racial, ethnic, or religious traits. The genocide, backed by the government and media, turned neighbors into murderers overnight: Friends killed friends, teachers killed students, and professionals killed coworkers. The Rwandan genocide was a stark reminder that when we speak of the myth or fiction of race, we cannot deny its reality in social life.

> **Genocide** the mass killing of a group of people based on racial, ethnic, or religious traits.

Group Responses to <u>Domination</u>

There are several forms of response to oppression, four of which are briefly outlined below: withdrawal, passing, acceptance, and resistance. Although we tend to think of minority groups as being oppressed by majority groups, keep in mind that sometimes the majority are the oppressed group, as in South African apartheid, where 4.5 million white Afrikaners and British dominated 19 million indigenous people.

Withdrawal

An oppressed group may withdraw, as the Jewish population did after Nazi persecution in Poland. Before World War II, Jews in Poland numbered 3.3 million, the second-largest Jewish population in the world. Eighty-five percent of Polish Jews died in the Holocaust, leaving roughly 500,000. After World War II, violence against Jews continued, and many moved. These conditions, plus the bitter taste of Polish complicity in the Holocaust itself, caused many Jews to leave for good. By 1947, Poland was home to just 100,000 Jews.

Another case of withdrawal was the Great Migration of the mid-twentieth century in the United States. Blacks streamed from the Jim Crow rural South in search of jobs and equality in the industrialized urban North and West; an estimated 1.5 million African Americans left per decade between 1940 and 1970. The North opened opportunities to blacks that previously had been violently denied them in the South, including economic and educational gains as well as the cultural freedom manifested in the Harlem Renaissance. But leaving the South did not always lead to immediate improvements. In their search for a better life, many African Americans found cramped shantytowns on the edge of urban centers, exploitation by factory owners looking for cheap black labor, and increasing hostility from white workers. Racialized competition for housing and employment sometimes led to violent clashes, such as the East St. Louis riots in the summer of 1917. The riots, principally involving white violence against blacks, raged for nearly a week, leaving nine whites and hundreds of African Americans dead. An estimated 6,000 black citizens, fearing for their lives, fled the city, another stark example of withdrawal.

Passing

Another response to racial oppression is passing, or blending in with the dominant group. For example, during his early adulthood, Malcolm X attempted to look more like white men through the painful process of chemically straightening or "conking" his Afro. A more recent example was the pop star Michael Jackson. Passing is not necessarily about physical changes, though. One of the most common ways people have tried to pass has been to change their surnames. The single largest ethnic group in the United States today is German Americans. Not English, but German. Where, do you ask, are all the Schmidts and Muellers? They now go by Smith and Miller, after a huge wave of name changing among German Americans during the world wars—if not during the first one, then often by the second.

Acceptance versus Resistance

Another response is acceptance, whereby the oppressed group feigns compliance and hides its true feelings of resentment. In Erving Goffman's terms, members of this group construct a front stage of acceptance, often using stereotypes to their own advantage to "play the part" in the presence of the dominant group (1959; see Chapter 4). Backstage, however, privately among their subaltern or oppressed group, they present a very different self. Sociologist Elijah Anderson refers to this as "code-switching," a strategy used by African Americans in the presence of dominant white society. In Anderson's ethnography of a black neighborhood in Philadelphia, blacks learn two languages, one of the street and one of mainstream society, and daily survival

Subaltern a subordinate, oppressed group of people.

becomes a matter of knowing which one to speak at the right time. For an inner-city youth, an act of code-switching could be as simple as putting on a leather jacket and concealing his textbook beneath it for the walk home from school (Anderson, 1999). (Code-switching is akin to the double consciousness that W. E. B. Du Bois ascribed to African Americans who maintain two behavioral scripts; see Chapter 1.)

A more overt form of resistance, the fourth paradigm of group responses to domination, would be collective resistance through a movement such as revolution or genocide, or through nonviolent protest as in the U.S. civil rights movement.

Collective resistance an organized effort to change a power hierarchy on the part of a less-powerful group in a society.

Prejudice, Discrimination, and the New Racism

On the individual level, racism can manifest itself as prejudice or discrimination. Prejudice refers to thoughts and feelings about an ethnic or racial group, whereas discrimination is an act. Robert Merton developed a diagram for thinking about the intersections of prejudice and discrimination (Merton, 1949; Figure 9.4). One who holds prejudice and discriminates is an "active bigot." This is the prototypical racist who puts his money (or burning cross) where his (or her) mouth is. Those who are neither prejudiced nor discriminatory are "all-weather liberals," not only espousing ideologies of racial equality or talking the talk, but also walking the walk when faced with real choices.

Prejudice thoughts and feelings about an ethnic or racial group.

Discrimination harmful or negative acts (not mere thoughts) against people deemed inferior on the basis of their racial category, without regard to their individual merit.

Many people fall between these two stances. A "timid bigot" is one who is prejudiced but does not discriminate—a closet racist perhaps, who backs down when confronted with an opportunity for racist action. Conversely, one who is not prejudiced but does discriminate is termed a "fair-weather liberal." Despite the fair-weather liberal's inner ideological stance in favor of racial equality, he or she still discriminates, perhaps without knowing it. For instance, a couple who consider themselves open minded about race relations may feel compelled to sell their home as soon as they are confronted with new black neighbors (white flight, as discussed above). Of course, they do not cite residential integration as their motivation for leaving, but instead offer an excuse that has embedded racist reasons, such as the differences in school districts. In fact, the prime time for families to move out of integrated

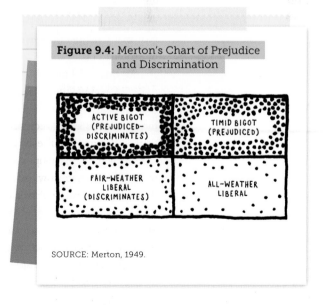

Figure 9.4: Merton's Chart of Prejudice and Discrimination

SOURCE: Merton, 1949.

Right-wing National Democratic Party members protest immigration and refugee policies in Germany. How is this an example of cultural racism?

neighborhoods happens to be around the time when the eldest child of the family turns five and begins school.

Active bigots are hard to come by these days, because prejudicial viewpoints are largely unacceptable in the ostensibly antiracist West. But don't be fooled into thinking that race doesn't matter anymore. It does, and racism is still alive and going strong, although it's veiled in different terms. You just have to know how to look for it. Old-fashioned, overt racism tended to convey three basic ideas: Humans are separable into distinct types; they have essential traits that cannot be changed; and some types of people are just better than others. Not many people openly make such claims in America today, as they tend to be frowned on.

As this old kind of racism declines, race scholars are beginning to find traces of a new kind of racism gaining ground. According to Howard Winant (2001), the new racial hegemony comes with "race neutral" rhetoric and relies more on culture and nationality to explain differences between nonwhites and whites than immutable physical traits. The new line of thinking, called "laissez-faire racism," replaces biology with culture and presumes that there is something fixed, innate, and inferior about nonwhite cultural values. In America, this kinder, gentler antiblack ideology is characterized by the persistence of negative stereotyping, the tendency to blame nonwhites for their own problems, and resistance to affirmative action policy (Bobo et al., 1997). (We'll have more to say about the concept of affirmative action below.) The irony is that since the civil rights triumphs of the 1960s, the official stance of formal equality has brought about subtler forms of prejudice and discrimination, making it harder to tackle racism and inequality. When a state proclaims racial equality, white privilege is let off the hook and goes unnoticed.

Likewise, in the new color-blind Europe, argues Neil MacMaster (2001), a "differentialist" or "cultural" racism has taken hold. Characteristic of cultural racism is the call to protect national (white) identity from "criminal" and polluting cultural outsiders, constructing an image of "fortress Europe." Anti-refugee commentary is one example of the new racist ideology. For example, in a televised speech in 1978, Margaret Thatcher made the following appeal to cultural purity in regard to 4 million immigrants from recently decolonized countries: "Now that is an awful lot, and I think it means that people are really rather afraid that this country might be swamped by people with a different culture" (MacMaster, 2001).

How Race Matters: The Case of Wealth

In *An American Dilemma* (1944), Gunnar Myrdal pointed out that blacks and whites think about equality in different but complementary ways. In his study, whites cared most about intimate relations—they were most adamant about maintaining personal distance from blacks, especially when it came to marriage, but they did not mind so much if blacks had equal chances of earning a living. Blacks valued equal employment and legal rights first; the freedom to marry whites was at the bottom of their list of concerns. These "rank orders of discrimination" gave Myrdal some hope; if economic discrimination was of least concern for whites and greatest for blacks, then maybe African Americans could catch up. But it has not worked out that way.

Nonwhites, especially African Americans, Latinos, and Native Americans, lag behind whites on a number of social outcomes, from income and educational attainment to crime rates and infant mortality rates. For example, blacks are half as likely as whites to graduate from college or hold a professional or managerial job, and are twice as likely to be unemployed and to die before their first year of life. As striking as the figures are, if there is one statistic that captures the persistence of racial inequality in the United States, it is net worth. If you want to determine your net worth, all you have to do is add up everything you own and subtract from this figure the total amount of your outstanding debt. When you do this for nonwhite and white families, the differences are glaring. So while most of America felt the impact of the housing market crash and 2008–9 recession, African Americans and Latinos felt the blow far more sharply than whites. Median wealth for whites fell 16 percent, yet African Americans and Latinos experienced 53 and 66 percent losses, respectively (Pew Research Center, 2011b).

Latinos are a varied group but largely reflect African Americans on wealth measures. The median Latino family in 2009 had just $6,325 in assets, and one-third of these households had zero or negative net worth (Pew Research

Center, 2011b). We know considerably less about Native Americans because reliable data are lacking, but given that they have a poverty rate of 32.2 percent (compared with just 13 percent for whites), their wealth is not likely to be high. Asian Americans, however, have low rates of poverty (12.1 percent) and high rates of home ownership, at about 60 percent (U.S. Census Bureau, 2011e).

This "equity inequality" has grown in the decades since the civil rights triumphs of the 1960s. What's more, the wealth gap cannot be explained by income differences alone. That is, the asset gap remains large even when we compare black and white families at the same income levels. Even among the often-heralded new black middle class, the accumulated assets of a family earning $40,000 a year amount to less than $20,000; a similar white family has a nest egg of around $80,000. For many among the growing black and Latino middle classes, this lack of assets may mean living from paycheck to paycheck, being trapped in a job or neighborhood that is less beneficial in the long run, and not being able to send one's kids to top colleges. Parents' wealth is also a strong predictor of children's teenage and young adult outcomes—everything from teenage premarital childbearing to educational attainment to welfare dependency (Conley, 1999).

Equity inequality captures the historical disadvantage of minority groups and the way those disadvantages accrue over time. The institutional restraints on black property accumulation discussed above were one mechanism for hindering blacks' asset growth. Similar processes and policies have decimated the wealth of Native Americans, who went from living off the land (the entire U.S. territory) to being disproportionately impoverished and dispossessed over the course of a century by exploitative U.S. policies. One of the most telling examples of this sort of institutionalized dispossession happened to Japanese Americans. As skilled farmers, Japanese immigrants accrued enough wealth in the early twentieth century to attract resentment, culminating in the 1924 Alien Land Act, which prohibited noncitizens from owning land. Japanese immigrants then found success in business, running nurseries and selling cut flowers, and amassed considerable wealth by 1941, about $140 million cumulatively (Lui, 2004). When World War II broke out and panic spread over the possibility of a treacherous Japanese population in America, the Roosevelt administration mandated a program of internment by Executive Order 9066. Japanese American citizens were placed into camps in the western part of the United States. They were given only a week to dispose of all their assets, forcing them to sell their homes and businesses to whites at scandalously low prices (Lui, 2004). The result was a huge forced transfer of wealth from Japanese to whites under discriminatory government policy.

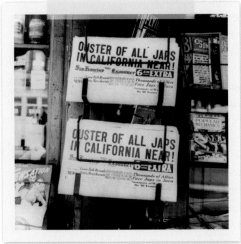

What were the consequences of the Japanese internment camps? How are they an example of equity inequality?

The issue of race barely surfaced in all the discussion over George W. Bush's 2001 tax cuts. Amid his package of tax reductions was the proposed repeal of the federal estate tax, which had been in place since 1916 and affects only the richest 1.4 percent of the deceased. As the law stood at the time of the debate, the first $675,000 per individual ($1.35 million for couples) of net estate value was exempt from tax. Because of a 1997 change in the law, this exemption amount would rise steadily until it reached $1 million for individuals in 2006. The Bush estate tax repeal phased out the entire tax by 2010. When the tax returned in 2011, the exemption had been pushed to $5 million for an individual and $10 million for a couple. Because the number of African Americans who would benefit is extremely small, Bush's ultimate goal of eliminating the tax forever would likely exacerbate the already growing wealth gap between blacks and whites.

In summary, policies intending to address disparities between nonwhites and whites must take into account the extreme wealth gap and its historical trajectory. Affirmative action aimed at improving wages and increasing job openings for blacks, Latinos, and Native Americans can address only a piece of a larger cycle of equity inequality. Income from work provides for the day-to-day, week-to-week expenses; wealth is the stuff long-term upward mobility is made of.

Institutional Racism

Another cause of the asset inequality discussed above is the simple fact that property in black neighborhoods doesn't accrue value at the same rate as that in mostly white areas. Property reflects only the value accorded to it in the market-place. In this vein, when a neighborhood's housing values precipitously decline as the proportion of black residents rises, the price changes provide a record of the economic value of "blackness." And it does not take any "active bigots" or otherwise racist individuals to generate this phenomenon. Namely, aside from any personal ideology, whites have an economic incentive to sell when they sense a neighborhood starting to integrate, as evidence shows that once a neighborhood reaches somewhere between 5 and 20 percent black, it quickly becomes predominantly black due to a rash of selling (with an accompanying drop in values) (Card et al., 2008). This expectation means that it is rational for whites to be the first to sell as blacks increase in numbers in a given area in order to prevent a loss of equity. This, of course, becomes a self-fulfilling prophecy and a vicious circle linking race and property values results—to the disadvantage of blacks. (Meanwhile, property value does not follow the same clear-cut pattern for other ethnic minorities, although minority enclaves generally have lower real estate values than exclusively white neighborhoods.)

The case of race and property values is an example of institutional racism—institutions and social dynamics that may seem race-neutral but actually end up

Institutional racism
institutions and social dynamics that may seem race-neutral but actually disadvantage minority groups.

disadvantaging minority groups. Another example is provided by sentencing laws for dealing or consuming cocaine. At the height of a period of panic over crack cocaine infiltrating neighborhoods, the United State passed the Anti-Drug Abuse Act of 1986. This law declared that for sentencing purposes, 1 gram of crack cocaine was equivalent to 100 grams of powdered cocaine. The result was a mandatory minimum sentence of five years for a first-time possession charge for a typical crack user. Because crack was cheaper and more prevalent in low-income, predominantly black communities, the result was a huge racial disparity in drug sentences by race. President Obama addressed this issue in 2010 by signing the Fair Sentencing Act, which reduced the sentencing ratio between powder cocaine and crack from 100-to-1 to 18-to-1. This ratio, while an improvement, still leaves a significantly disparate impact by race (Davis, 2011).

Yet another example of institutional racism can be found in the case of hiring patterns by employers. With limited information about job applicants, employers may be rational to use social networks to recruit employees since informal ties (i.e., references) can provide more reliable information about individuals than can be gleaned from paper job applications. And because whites tend to hold more managerial positions, and social networks tend to be segregated by race, this need for additional information on the part of employers also perpetuates racial disparities with no racially explicit motivation.

A related dynamic is called statistical discrimination, where firms use race as a shorthand proxy for having attended poorer schools and having experienced other disadvantages that would lead to less productive performance. Although this dynamic is not completely color-blind, it is different from overt racism in that the motivation is not about race per se, but about underlying characteristics that tend to be associated with race. Finally, institutional racism can even be encoded into the educational system through test construction. There has been much debate about cultural bias in testing. Beyond this issue, however, is the effect of stereotypes on performance. The psychologists Claude Steele and Joshua Aronson, for example, have shown that they can drive black students' test scores down just by priming them with negative stereotypes before they sit for the exam (Steele & Aronson, 1998). These are just a few of the ways race can continue to disadvantage certain groups even in an age when overt racial animus may have waned in significance.

Figure 9.5: An Ethnic Snapshot of America Today

White, not Hispanic
63.7%

Each symbol represents 1% of the U.S. population.

SOURCE: U.S. Census Bureau, 2011e.

The **Future** of Race

This brief overview of the history of race and its present-day ramifications allows us to make some guesses about the future of race. For starters, racial and ethnic diversity in America will tend to increase. The 2010 Census data show a 134 percent increase in Americans who identify as multiracial—that is, 9 million people (Pew Research Center, 2011c). The number of foreign-born people in the United States surpassed 37 million (U.S. Census Bureau, 2010a). And according to National Research Council projections, by the year 2050, largely thanks to the most recent wave of immigration (along with differential fertility rates), America's Latino and Asian populations will triple, making up about 28 percent and 9 percent of the U.S. population, respectively (U.S. Census Bureau, 2012e). No longer black and white, America is now a society composed of multiple ethnic and racial groups with an ever-shifting color line marking fuzzy boundaries (Figure 9.5).

In 1996, there was a Multiracial March on Washington in which multiracial activists demanded a separate census category to bolster their political claims and recognition. Although the movement did not result in a multiracial identity category, for the first time ever, the 2000 Census allowed respondents to check off more than one box for racial identity. The resulting multiracial population is currently estimated to be about 9 million, and those are just the self-identified people who checked more than one race box in 2010. The latest census also asks separate questions about race and ethnicity, which means that census data can now be used to examine some of the racial diversity within the Hispanic population, as well as some ethnic diversity among African American and white populations (Figure 9.6).

Figure 9.6: Race Questions from the 2010 U.S. Census

9. **What is Person 1's race?** *Mark ☒ one or more boxes.*

- [ ] White
- [ ] Black, African Am., or Negro
- [ ] American Indian or Alaska Native — *Print name of enrolled or principal tribe.* ↙

- [ ] Asian Indian
- [ ] Chinese
- [ ] Filipino
- [ ] Other Asian — *Print race. for example, Hmong, Laotian, Thai, Pakistani, Cambodian, and so on.* ↙

- [ ] Japanese
- [ ] Korean
- [ ] Vietnamese

- [ ] Native Hawaiian
- [ ] Guamanian or Chamorro
- [ ] Samoan
- [ ] Other Pacific Islander — *Print race, for example, Fijian, Tongan, and so on.* ↙

- [ ] Some other race — *Print race.* ↙

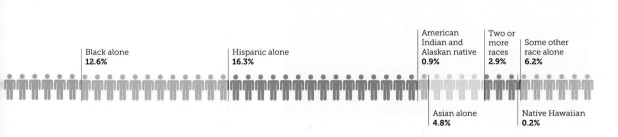

Black alone **12.6%** Hispanic alone **16.3%** American Indian and Alaskan native **0.9%** Two or more races **2.9%** Some other race alone **6.2%** Asian alone **4.8%** Native Hawaiian **0.2%**

This so-called browning of America brings us to a new crossroads. The white–black divide may become the white–nonwhite divide or the black–nonblack divide. Sociologist Jennifer Lee has looked at just this question and her research shows that the experience of first- and especially second-generation Asians and Latinos indicates the new color line is black–nonblack. What does this mean? In the simplest terms, it means that the biggest differences in demographic characteristics like income, educational attainment, and interracial marriage will be between blacks and all other groups while the distinctions between these other groups continue to narrow. Lee notes,

> If you look at rates of educational attainment or interracial marriage or multiracial reporting, Asians and Latinos, their disadvantage stems from their immigrant histories, and so with each generation you see outcomes improving. For African Americans, you see there's some progress, but it's not nearly at the same speed, and so what I see is [that] the divide is really blacks and everyone else. . . . The one caveat I would add is that those Latinos who have darker skin, who are more mistaken for African Americans or black Americans . . . will probably fall on the black side of the divide. In part because of their skin color, but also because their socioeconomic status is not on par with some of the other lighter skin Latino groups like Cubans. (Conley, 2009j)

Lee points out that the biggest losers in this new configuration of race in America are likely to be—no surprise—blacks, who may be blamed for their own poverty when compared with successful Latino and Asian immigrants. Lee cautions, "Someone will look at African Americans who have been here longer and who aren't attaining certain levels of mobility and say, why can't they make it? If race isn't an issue for Asians and Latinos, it shouldn't matter for blacks. What I argue is that the stigma attached to blackness because of the history of blackness is so different, they are not immigrants. To compare African Americans to immigrants is never fair."

How close are we to this new black–nonblack color line? At least four states (California, Texas, Hawaii, and New Mexico) are deemed "majority minority" states, where whites are not the majority of the population within major metropolitan areas (U.S. Census Bureau, 2010b). But

To watch more of my interview with Jennifer Lee about the color line, visit **wwnpag.es/SC9a**.

let's not forget that racial categories are social constructions, not static entities. To claim a multiracial identity presupposes the existence of a monoracial identity, when we know no scientifically pure or distinct race of people exists. Similarly, the notion of a white minority presumes that whiteness is a fixed racial category, whereas whiteness has expanded to include groups that were considered nonwhite in the past and may continue to fold Asians and Latinos into a kind of whiteness that emphasizes symbolic ethnicity. Indeed, as Warren and Twine (1997) point out, as long as blacks are present, a back door is open for nonblacks to slip under the white umbrella. For example, the Asian success story as the "model minority" is made possible by Asians' ability to blend in with whites, because they are unequivocally not black. We are at a point in American history when whiteness may be expanding again, with blacks, as always, serving as the counterweight.

POLICY: Reverse Migration

Many countries sending immigrants to the United States—and asking that America welcome those immigrants—themselves have policies that discourage Americans from moving there. This is a profound unfairness at the heart of our immigration policy, and one that almost no one acknowledges. The first step to domestic immigration reform may be overturning the restrictions that other nations, including Mexico, place on American immigration to their countries.

Mexico, while pressing for its citizens to work and conduct business in the United States, poses Kafkaesque obstacles to foreigners wanting to acquire legal residence and buy desirable property there. For instance, Article 27 of the Mexican constitution states: "Foreign citizens cannot own land within 100 km of the borders or 50 km of the sea; however, foreigners can have a beneficial interest in such land through a trust [*fideicomiso*], where the legal ownership of the land is held by a Mexican financial institution." Of course, Mexican immigrants to the United States can own land outright.

Hurdles to citizenship are higher in Europe than in the United States. For instance, Austria, Italy, Lithuania, Slovenia, and Spain require most applicants to have a decade of legal residency before being able to naturalize, versus the five years or less required of those seeking to naturalize in the United States (Goodman, 2010; U.S. Citizenship and Immigration Services, 2014). Contrast

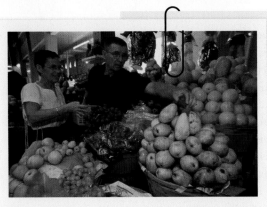

When Len and Sue Breitfeller retired, they moved from Philadelphia to Ajijic, Mexico.

the $2,500 in naturalization fees charged by Switzerland with the $680 application fee charged in the United States.

Many other countries, including China, Egypt, and Haiti, make it tougher for children of U.S. citizens born there to become citizens than vice versa (United Nations High Commissioner for Refugees, 2014; U.S. Citizenship and Immigration Services, 2004). Bilateral agreements for citizenship would be fair, mutually enhance the respective economies, and reduce the xenophobia and antagonisms between nation-states so linked.

Of course, most U.S. citizens would not want to emigrate to Mexico, a country where the average wage is about one-sixth of what it is here. But some Americans might, and some do. Even with the current legal impediments to resettling, one estimate puts the number of Americans seeking to settle in Mexico at 1 million. Think retirees who depend only on their monthly Social Security checks. Or entrepreneurs who want lower taxes. Or poor families in Minnesota who might prefer the climate and lifestyle of Baja, or Alabamans seeking relief from tornadoes.

Although a Mexican citizenship policy change may not mean an immediate queue of American citizens at the Mexican border, over the long term such a policy would chip away at parochialism and leave U.S. citizens, known for high rates of domestic migration, weighing a move to Miami against one to Cancun. This may seem unlikely, but who, during the early years of the Clinton administration, would have predicted that more Americans would emigrate to Ireland in the next 15 years than Irish would emigrate to America? This human tide to Dublin was driven by U.S. citizens of Irish descent favored by Irish citizenship laws. A policy shift that made it easy for Americans to become Mexican might prompt a similar flow.

Most consequential would be the long-term effects from the mobility of Mexican natives, whose ability to move legally between the two countries would change Mexico's demographics and investment patterns. More of its own citizens would remain or return, as occurred in the European Union when, for instance, Portugal and Greece joined: Greeks and Portuguese who had been residing in wealthier countries such as France went home to reap the benefits of the foreign investments the European Union incentivized.

The United States should sign bilateral treaties agreeing to naturalize citizens from other countries on the same terms as the partner countries naturalize Americans. The point is not that most Americans would pursue a *tarjeta verde* (green card), but that just knowing this is possible would make Mexico and its citizens less alien.

Ultimately, a bilateral citizenship treaty with Mexico would further blend the two countries. It's been almost two decades since salsa passed ketchup as the top condiment in the United States. Meanwhile, Coca-Cola and Pepsi drinks dominate the Mexican beverage market. Eventually, Spanglish may become the primary spoken language in some parts of North America, a phenomenon that for many evokes fears of cultural extinction. We should not give in to these collective fears but look at a map of North America from 1700 and recognize that today's nations and nationalities are historical flukes: Spain, France, England, the Chickasaw, and hundreds of other settled nations then prevalent no longer populate the landscape. Why raise a ruckus about keeping people out of a place that was not ours to begin with, when instead we could be snorkeling in Cozumel?

→ CONCLUSION

When you look at race using the sociological imagination, you'll recognize that it's hardly a cut-and-dried issue. You'll see the historical social construction of ideas and identities. You'll see the present-day realities—sometimes monstrosities—of an aspect of our lives so often called a myth or fiction. And you'll be equipped to look at the changing nature of race and race relations that will affect your future.

→ PRACTICE

SOCIOLOGY ON THE STREET

Decades after real estate segregation (or "redlining") became illegal, many Americans still live in communities that are highly segregated by race and/or socioeconomic status. How does unofficial segregation occur? Watch the Sociology on the Street video to find out more: wwnpag.es/SOS9.

QUESTIONS FOR REVIEW

1. What does the childhood anecdote from the beginning of the chapter, about not yet having learned the meaning of race, teach us regarding the nature of race? Would a nonwhite three-year-old have brought home a white "baby sister"? How does this question bring up the "invisible knapsack of privileges" that puts white people at an advantage?

2. What does real estate value have to do with school segregation? With this link in mind, how have inequalities in wealth contributed to long-term inequality between blacks and whites in the United States?

3. Although the validity of "race" is debatable, why do sociologists study race as it relates, for example, to the likelihood of going to prison? What does this mean about what is "real," the way people understand the world, and what sociologists should study?

4. How has science been informed by culture (including racist beliefs), and in turn, how has science fueled racism?

5. As the saying goes, "You can't judge a book by its cover." How do eugenics and physiognomy contradict this saying (in regard to people)? Are the principles behind these pseudosciences still with us today?

6. What is "racialization," and how has it differed between Muslims and the Irish?

7. How is stating your ethnicity more similar to stating that you like the Beatles than describing your race?

8. Which of the four forms of minority–majority group relations has recently been most prevalent in the United States and Rwanda, respectively? How have the minority groups in these countries responded quite differently to domination?

9. Thinking about the history of race, what do you predict for the future of "race" and "ethnicity" as social categories? Will they stay the same? What do demographic trends and history lessons suggest might happen in the coming decades in the United States?

PARADOX

RACE AS WE KNOW IT HAS NO DETERMINISTIC, BIOLOGICAL BASIS: ALL THE SAME, RACE IS SO POWERFUL THAT IT CAN HAVE LIFE-OR-DEATH CONSEQUENCES. →

WATCH THE ANIMATED SHORT ABOUT THE RACE PARADOX AT

WWNPAG.ES/PX9

HUMANS

CIVILIZED

UNCIVILIZED

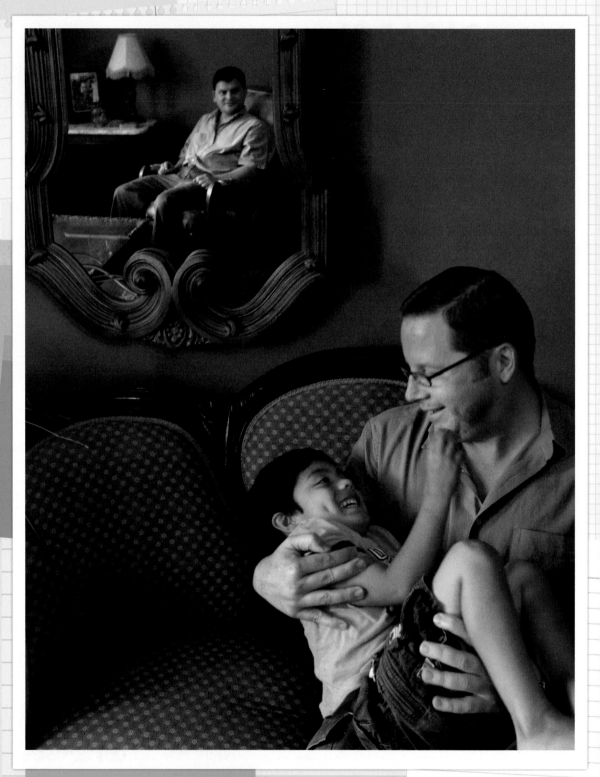

Yossi and his two dads, Ken Bukowski and
Peter Altman, relax at home.

10 Family

PARADOX

WE THINK OF THE FAMILY
AS A HAVEN IN A HARSH WORLD,
BUT IN FACT, INEQUALITY
BEGINS AT HOME.

ELDEST   MIDDLEBORNS

YOUNGEST

In many ways, Ozzie and Harry typify the American ideal of a family. They met while Harry was vacationing in Italy, and it was love at first sight. Harry was 31 and successful; Ozzie was 24, talented, and full of promise. The two quickly initiated a passionate monogamous relationship. Eight years later the couple owned a house in the Los Angeles area, where they lived with their two daughters. Harry worked as a literary agent, supporting Ozzie, a full-time homemaker, and the kids. Theirs is a fairy tale come true.

Yet the story of Ozzie and Harry brings the traditional concept of family into a modern perspective. The two could not come from more dissimilar backgrounds. Harry is white, Jewish, and Ivy League–educated; Ozzie is Afro-Brazilian, Catholic, and less formally schooled. Harry is well off; Ozzie grew up in a poor family and was raised without a father. The couple is "transracial, transnational, cross-class, [and] interfaith" (Stacey, 2004). In fact, they share only one demographic characteristic: They are both male.

Not only is the couple an against-all-odds success story, their story illustrates just how strong our notion of traditional family is. Even in this most progressive of arrangements, the two assume the historically gendered roles that we often associate with family units. Where do these notions of the traditional family come from? To examine this, let's start with the original Ozzie and Harriet: The Nelsons.

There is something inevitably comforting about watching family television shows from the 1950s. It is a glimpse into a foreign yet consoling world where growing boys like Ricky and David Nelson may be viewed dashing into a kitchen, with schoolbooks in hand and a cheerful "Hi, Mom. Hi, Pop!"

Why did the idea of the traditional family—embodied here by the Nelsons from the television show *The Adventures of Ozzie and Harriet*—emerge after World War II?

Their loving parents, Ozzie and Harriet, together listen to their children's problems and together steer them on the right path to adulthood. *The Adventures of Ozzie and Harriet*—the situation comedy that first aired on ABC in 1952—typifies a familiar, traditional form of family that today evokes nostalgia and fuels political debates: the male breadwinner (although no one knows for sure what Ozzie did for a living); the kind, female homemaker; and their nurtured, well-socialized children.

The scenes of 1950s family life can overwhelm the unprepared viewer with a surge of sentiments—everything from the warm fuzzies to bleak loneliness to bitter cynicism. At first blush, the quality of family life today, with widespread divorce, out-of-wedlock births, dual incomes, and ever-increasing work hours, seems to have taken a nosedive. But if the domestic world of Ozzie and Harriet seems too good to be true, that's because, of course, it is. Anyone watching at the time readily acknowledged that such television shows did not reflect how Americans actually lived. Rather, they portrayed American families as people wanted to see them. Millions of viewers turned to the idealized life presented in *The Adventures of Ozzie and Harriet* to be entertained by the dramatization of mundane details of suburban life and soothed by the easy resolution of the day's problems by the end of the episode.

In the postwar era, the traditional family—the idealized model of a male breadwinner, a female homemaker, and their dependent children—emerged as the dominant, normative, and mythical model for domestic life. It was dominant, because indeed many Americans took to it; in the 1950s, 86 percent of children lived in two-parent families, and 60 percent of children were born into homes with a male breadwinner and a female homemaker (Coontz, 2001). It was normative, because it has been hailed, then and now, as the proper form for families, the way things ought to be. Finally, the taken-for-grantedness of the traditional family is mythical, because its existence does not represent a natural, timeless, or universal approach to family arrangements.

In the sociological imagination, the traditional family looks less like a universal norm and more like an ideological construct—and an unusual one at that. Arising out of unique social structural conditions of the 1950s, characters such as the Nelsons are exceptional, not just for their special Christmas décor and family picnics but also because they are, in fact, unique. That is, the so-called traditional family model deviates from both its predecessors and its successors. Yet many of us still idealize this model and miss it terribly. By studying cross-cultural variation in family forms, we'll see that this allegedly traditional family is not always the dominant model. By unpacking the historical development of the traditional family and its subsequent breakdown, we'll come to recognize that this idea of family is not a universal fact. And regardless of what kind of family ties you may deem worth forging, worth loving, and worth defending, as a sociologist your job will be to study all family forms without prejudgment.

Family Forms and Changes

Why do we fall for the people we do? At first thought this might seem like a simple question. You start by envisioning the personal qualities of your lover, perhaps something about his or her physique, personality, sense of humor, or charm. If you take a step back and really try to think about it, you might admit to more practical reasons as well—physical proximity, shared language, financial security—those everyday factors vital to functioning relationships. If you take yet another step back, you face the larger question of mate selection: The phenomenon of human partnering that is patterned by history, culture, and law.

I know this is an unromantic way to view your love life, but consider the host of cultural and legal codes that prohibit you from partnering with, say, your 14-year-old first cousin. In Victorian England or a modern-day Muslim tribe, however, a man's 14-year-old first cousin might be a perfectly good match. Historically, interracial partnerships have also been prohibited. In 1961, when President Barack Obama's parents were married, it was still illegal in 22 different states for a white and a nonwhite to be married. Then in *Loving vs. Virginia* (1967) the U.S. Supreme Court unanimously struck down America's antimiscegenation laws. (See Chapter 9 for a discussion of the one-drop rule.) Similar laws, aimed at maintaining white "racial purity," existed in South Africa during apartheid as well as in Nazi Germany. In the contemporary world, ethnically

The Lovings embrace at a press conference the day after the Supreme Court ruled in their favor in *Loving v. Virginia*, June 13, 1967.

Endogamy marriage to someone within one's social group.

Exogamy marriage to someone outside one's social group.

Monogamy the practice of having only one sexual partner or spouse at a time.

Polygamy the practice of having more than one sexual partner or spouse at a time.

Polyandry the practice of having multiple husbands simultaneously.

Polygyny the practice of having multiple wives simultaneously.

mixed couples are hardly shocking, but 50 years ago in the United States they were almost unthinkable. When a culture maintains either legal or normative sanctions against people marrying outside their race, class, or caste, we call it a rule of endogamy, meaning marriage from within. To some extent, we all practice endogamy—that is, on some level people tend to hook up with similar people, because it makes for easier relations if you and your partner share a social group. In other parts of the world, such as India, historically people haven't had much of a choice: The caste system of India is based on a rigid adherence to endogamy (see Chapter 7).

In much of the contemporary Western world, exogamy, or marriage to someone outside one's social group, is legally possible, if not always culturally acceptable. Consider the following unlikely pair: The African American son of a steel mill worker in Illinois and the only child and sole heir of a mega-millionaire, white, chart-topping rock-and-roll star in Tennessee. The 1994 union of Lisa Marie Presley and Michael Jackson lasted less than two years, but it is an example of a couple who transgressed social, class, and racial groups. However, what is also telling is that by the time they met and fell for each other, they were already both celebrities and social equivalents, despite the gulf between their backgrounds. Total exogamy—when people from completely different social categories get together—is rare.

In addition to codes of endogamy and exogamy, another basic social structure governs your love life: How many partners you're expected to have. In societies that practice monogamy a person can partner with only one other. In societies that practice polygamy people have more than one sexual partner or spouse at a time. This can take the form of a woman having several husbands, called polyandry, as happens in some rural areas of Asia. Or a man can take several wives, called polygyny, the most common form of polygamy, practiced in many contemporary Islamic and African cultures. Although the Mormon Church outlawed polygamy in 1890, some Mormon splinter groups, called fundamentalists, continue the practice of one man supporting several families at the same time (Lee, 2006).

The next time someone asks why you fell for your special someone, keep in mind that the answer could be quite long and sociologically involved. Cultural norms and state regulations play a fundamental, if invisible, role in your love life. These factors first set the limits as to who is even available on your romantic horizon. Once you find that person (or those persons, for you polygamists), your next move will be to form a relationship with him or her, probably in the shape of a family. But just what does the typical traditional family look like?

Malinowski and the Traditional Family

The normative "traditional family" is one in which a heterosexual couple lives with their dependent children in a self-contained, economically independent household. This family is typically a patriarchal one, governed by a male head with a dependent wife and children. In 1913 Bronislaw Malinowski put to rest a long-standing family debate among anthropologists about the universal existence of families. Scholars had argued that traditional tribal societies couldn't possibly have family units because of their egregious nondiscriminating sexual promiscuity. Malinowski, based on his research of Australian Aboriginals (who seemed to have sex with everyone), suggested that these natives did, in fact, form ties indicative of familial arrangements. The Aboriginals, he found, recognized family relations and kept them distinct from other forms of social connection. They maintained a central place, the equivalent of a hearth and home, where the family gathered. And they bestowed feelings of love, affection, and care on each family member. Thus, the dispute was settled: The family was accepted as a universal human institution for most of the twentieth century, and this notion continues to endure today. It is so strong that scientists look for Malinowski's family ties even among rodents. Neurogeneticists have discovered a genetic basis for monogamous coupling in one species of prairie voles and are hard at work trying to determine whether or not humans share the same neurological mechanisms for partner preference (Young & Wang, 2004; Fink et al., 2006; Young & Hammock, 2007).

Malinowski argued that the family, in addition to being a universal phenomenon, was a necessary institution for fulfilling the task of child rearing in society. The influential structural-functional sociologist Talcott Parsons would expand on this notion in the 1950s. As we learned in Chapter 8, according to Parsons, the traditional nuclear family, consisting of a mother and father and their children, was a functional necessity in modern industrial society, because it was most compatible with fulfilling society's need for productive workers and child nurturers. And so the nuclear family reigned supreme, timeless, and universal. (Note that although the nuclear family is a particular form of the traditional model, in this chapter we will use the two terms synonymously.)

The problem with functionalist arguments such as these is that even if one social institution seems to perform some function for society, the function is not necessarily performed only by that particular institution. A functional need is not sufficient cause for the development of an institution, especially not when other kinds of institutions can perform the function just as well. But when you have Western blinders on, as most social scientists following Malinowski did, it becomes difficult to see anything other than the kind of

Nuclear family familial form consisting of a father, a mother, and their children.

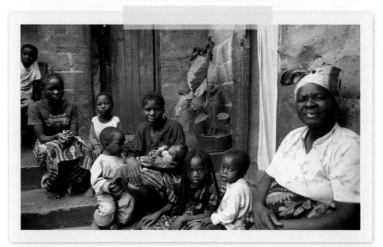

Families come in all different forms. What are some of the ways that family groups can differ from culture to culture? For instance, how does an extended family in the United States (top) differ from the Na in China (middle) or Zambian families in Africa (bottom)?

family life you expect to see. When properly fitted with your sociological lens, however, you can make the familiar strange, and you'll find some colorful variation among familial arrangements.

Take the Mandurucu villagers of South America, for instance. They give new meaning to the hearth-and-home feature of Malinowski's universal family. Mandurucu men and women live in separate houses at different ends of their village; they eat separate meals; they sleep apart. In fact, they only meet up with each other to have sex (Collier et al., 1997). Among the Na people of southern China, who have managed to retain their distinctive culture despite war, Communism, and the onset of quasi-capitalism, the institution of marriage doesn't exist. The Na do not have any practice like it, nor do they put much thought into fatherhood. Children grow up with uncles rather than fathers as the primary males in the home. Sex occurs in the middle of the night, when men visit women for anonymous and spontaneous encounters. There are no social rules restricting who can partner with whom. Yet the Na manage just fine, reproducing from generation to generation and maintaining a stable economy.

If the Na take hands-off fatherhood to the extreme, women in present-day Zambia implode our notions of caring motherhood. Zambian mothers don't nurture their daughters in the way Westerners would expect. When a Zambian girl needs advice, she is expected to seek out an older female relative as a confidante in preference to her mother (Collier et al., 1997). Mothers' "essential" nature has always been defined in the West as nurturing and connected to offspring—presumably ordained by women's biological birthing functions. However, the way motherhood is practiced in Zambian culture suggests that a mother's unconditional warmth, despite the rhetoric, is not necessarily a biological given.

The Family in the Western World Today

Even the modern Western family comes in a variety of forms. The typical American family today is not likely to resemble the Nelsons. In addition to nuclear families, one needs to count the extended family—kin networks that extend outside or beyond the nuclear family. Families with no children also exist (for instance, couples that become "empty nesters" after their children move out), as do two-wage-earner families (dual-income families), single-parent families, blended stepfamilies, and adopted families, to name just a few possibilities. Although the traditional family was the dominant model for a majority of people living in the 1950s, it never described home life for all Americans. And it's increasingly losing its edge today as families take on new shapes and sizes. In 1986, fewer than 10 percent of U.S. families consisted of a male breadwinner, a female housewife, and their children, a figure that has since fallen to 6 percent (Stacey, 1996; U.S. Census Bureau, 2013b). Today only one-fifth of American households consist of a married couple with their own

Extended family kin networks that extend outside or beyond the nuclear family.

children, and 61 percent of households have only one or two people in them (U.S. Census Bureau, 2013b).

In the face of soaring divorce rates, the Ozzie and Harriet way of life is indeed becoming a historical artifact. Nowadays, although the exact figure varies considerably from study to study, approximately 40 percent of all marriages end in divorce (Hurley, 2005). This statistic doesn't seem to discourage too many people, though, because three of four divorced men and two of three divorced women try their hand at marriage again. But alas, the second time around has about the same rate of failure as the first, and those marriages are even a bit more likely to hit the skids (Coontz, 2010). It's commonly thought that divorce has skyrocketed since the 1950s, but actually the divorce rate has been steadily rising since the nineteenth century, as divorce became less and less of a social and religious taboo (see Figure 10.4). Divorce rates seem to have stabilized over the past decade or so, with about 90 percent of marriages making it to the five-year mark and 70 percent making it to 15 years; then, another 1 percent of marriages dissolve each year after that, whether by divorce or death. But rising divorce rates in the United States have not put marriage in any danger of extinction. Eventually, 86 percent of men and 89 percent of women are projected to get married, but men are more likely to remarry after a divorce (U.S. Census Bureau, 2013b).

Given the increased incidence of divorce and remarriage, families are taking on new shapes and sizes, such as single-parent and blended arrangements (Figure 10.1). As of 2009, about 16 percent of children in America lived in a blended family (U.S. Census Bureau, 2011f), which reconfigures the aftermath of divorce into step-relations. (We'll have more to say about the effect of divorce on children below.) Cohabitation, living together in an intimate relationship without formal legal or religious sanctioning, has also emerged as a socially acceptable arrangement; roughly 7 percent of heterosexual American couples live together as opposed to legally tying the knot, a 13 percent increase from 2009 (Fry & Cohn, 2011). However, two-thirds of cohabiters either break up or get married within three years (Centers for Disease Control and Prevention, 2013a). Most cohabiters believe that living together is an effective means of curtailing future divorce. It's the commonsense notion that living together provides a sample of what married life is like and will inform and improve the couple's future marriage. On the opposite side of the debate, conservative supporters of "family values" point to studies showing a higher divorce rate among couples who cohabit before marriage than those who don't (Meckler, 2002). Conservative Christian counselors advise that "living in sin" sets up a rockier road for a marriage, but the actual reason for the higher divorce rate probably has to do more with selection bias: Most people who cohabit are also the kind of individuals who are more likely to flout social conventions and therefore divorce anyway.

Single women are having their days as well, as the proportions of women who never marry and never have children are on the rise. The Census Bureau

Cohabitation living together in an intimate relationship without formal legal or religious sanctioning.

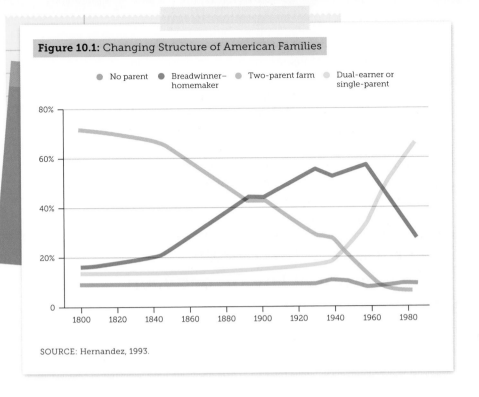

Figure 10.1: Changing Structure of American Families

Legend:
● No parent ● Breadwinner–homemaker ● Two-parent farm ● Dual-earner or single-parent

SOURCE: Hernandez, 1993.

estimates that 40 percent of U.S. women born in the 1980s will never be married with children. Twenty-five percent of American households are headed by single moms (so they have children, but are not married) and twenty percent of women remain child-free (Livingston & Cohn, 2010; Mathur et al., 2013). Women who do have children are doing so at a later age than ever before—now averaging 25.6, up from 21 in the 1970s (Centers for Disease Control and Prevention, 2013b). However, women have been delaying marriage for even longer, tying the knot at 27 years old, on average (Hymowitz et al., 2013). The age when a woman has her first baby varies by subgroup: White professional women, on average, postpone motherhood even longer. Another interesting new twist in American families is the rapid rise in the number of twins. Between the years 1980 and 1997, the number of twin births rose 52 percent, from 68,339 to 104,137 births, and triplet and other higher-order multiple births increased by a staggering 404 percent, from 1,337 to 6,737. This rise took place almost entirely among white women. As professional white women increasingly delay childbearing, they are biologically more likely to give birth to twins, and this trend is compounded by the more widespread use of fertility treatments, which increase the likelihood of a multiple birth (Martin et al., 2010). And then there is adoption. In 2010, approximately 1 percent of children in the United States were adopted (Centers for Disease Control and Prevention, 2011b; Chandra et al., 2005). International adoption rates, which had been climbing since the 1980s, peaked at 22,000 in 2004 and are falling fast. In 2012 only 8,668 children were adopted from foreign countries, in part because of

Single mother Melissa Ludtke holds adopted daughter Maya Xia. Why have stories like Ludtke's become more common over the last few decades?

more rigorous qualifications required of new parents by foreign countries, as well as UN-sanctioned adoption bans on countries like Guatemala (U.S. Department of State, 2013).

Single-parent families, historically the result of death or desertion, are on the rise as more parents never marry or end up divorced. In 1960, 9 percent of U.S. children lived with just one parent; by 1986, that number was 25 percent; by 2013, it was 31 percent, and 80.6 percent of those children lived in single-mother families (Mathur et al., 2013). Single-parent families are also becoming more common worldwide—as of the late 1990s, approximately one-fifth of all families around the globe were headed by women (UNICEF, 2007).

Keeping It in the Family: The Historical Divide between Public and Private

Given the enormous cross-cultural and even within-cultural variation among family forms, you may be wondering how and why the so-called traditional family ever came to be the standard marker of normalcy. The short answer is that the development of the family was tied to the development of modernity, state formation, and the rise of the modern economy. For starters, *traditional family* is a misleading term; this family structure is not characteristic of all tradition, just that of the 1950s. The nuclear model of stay-at-home mom and working father is itself deviant compared with American family arrangements both 50 years before it and 50 years after. It was a historically specific model in a unique era, in which many white city-dwellers moved to the suburbs, married young, and raised three or four children. It was a prosperous era, too: In the 1950s real wages grew more in any single year than they did in the 1980s as a whole. With just a high-school education, an average 30-year-old white man could earn enough at his manufacturing job to buy a median-priced home on 15 percent of his salary (Coontz, 2001). Today, with just a high-school education, an average 30-year-old man is likely to be tenuously positioned in the service sector, making about $15 an hour and probably lacking employer-provided health insurance. But it's not just money that set the 1950s apart. As Stephanie Coontz notes in *The Way We Never Were: American Families and the Nostalgia Trap* (1992), people long for the sense of simplicity, wholesomeness, and ease that 1950s families like the Nelsons are perceived to have enjoyed.

Early Modern Families

The traditional family is a relatively new phenomenon that developed only as complex, state-governed societies emerged. In the preindustrial family of the

Preindustrial families, such as these settlers, operated like a small business. The home was a site for work, and the entire family was involved.

nineteenth century, each household unit operated like a small business—that is, as a miniature family economy. It was a site for both production and consumption, where work was done in the home and the home was a working unit. Families made and used their own food, clothes, and goods, and there was little if any surplus wealth.

Families tended to live near their kin and thus could get help and support from their kinship networks, strings of relationships between people related by blood and co-residence (that is, marriage). Preindustrial communities didn't have huge savings banks, insurance companies, payday lenders, or government agencies to help in hard times; that was the role of family. For example, a down-and-out uncle might have a failed crop of wheat one summer. He could call in an IOU from his luckier cousin across the village, borrowing some of his crop and setting off a reciprocal exchange of food, clothing, and child care. Such families would have a grapevine structure where more lateral kinship ties endured than vertical ones (usually, no more than three generations of one family were alive at a time). Communities cooperated in a noncash economy, using a barter system to swap goods. There was no significant accumulation of goods, no savings, no wealth, and not much beyond what individuals needed to survive. There was also minimal division of labor between the sexes, such that men were involved in child care, and women and children often performed the same manual labor as men. Indeed, in the preindustrial family, children were thought of as "small adults," as Philippe Ariès argued in 1962. They didn't

Kinship networks strings of relationships between people related by blood and co-residence (that is, marriage).

warrant any special treatment or consideration, and childhood was hardly the nurturing period we think of today. In fact, some scholars argue that the whole notion of childhood, or children's special needs, is a relatively recent invention, as is that of motherhood as a full-time occupation. Both have emerged only since the middle of the nineteenth century and have been made possible through industrialization, the rise of the cash economy, formal schooling, and the establishment of privacy in the family.

Families in the Industrial Era

With the Industrial Revolution, the realms of the public and private—previously intertwined as one in the working family—split into separate spheres of work and home, as men left household production for wage work in factories. Families stopped being productive mini-economies for the barter system and instead became strictly sites for consumption. Out went household spinning and weaving, and in came the factory-made sweater. Food, clothing, furniture, decorations, appliances, cosmetics, pharmaceuticals: You name it, the family was there to consume it. Specifically, women made the choices of what and how much their families would consume.

Furthermore, "women's work"—tending the home and raising children—became relegated to the private, domestic sphere, where it went unpaid as a woman relied on a man's wages, at least among the middle classes. All the extra money in the new wage economy passed through the hands of women, who remained in charge of running the home and doing the shopping. Such functions might seem like a move toward women "wearing the pants" in the family, but they, in fact, provided a point of emergence for a new form of gender inequality. Women were in charge of spending the family's money, not earning it, and in our society, work for money is the most highly valued form of labor. Women's work was the unpaid management of the home, and this distinction established unequal positions for men and women in society. At the very least, a man had the chance to spend his wages before they ever reached the other members of his family.

The results of these structural changes were far-reaching. First, a gendered division of labor arose in the household, where women now were in exclusive charge of maintaining the home and rearing children. Second, as the mobility of families searching for paid labor opportunities increased, they became separated from their kinship networks. Family structures changed from grapevine forms to "beanpole" families, in which kinship ties are vertical. Because people didn't live near their siblings, aunts, and uncles, they could depend only on their children and parents who lived with them. As life expectancies increased, up to five generations may have been alive at any given time, but lateral ties (such as those existing between cousins) weakened because of the longer distances separating these kin.

The beanpole family structure is particularly taxing on women today, who, because of delayed childbirth, are likely to find that their parents need assistance just as their own children are leaving home. As a result of declining fertility and longer life expectancies, the U.S. population is growing older, so the problem of elder care (and its disproportionate impact on women) will only get worse. In 2010 the median age in the United States was 37.2 years, with seven states having a median age of 40 or older (U.S. Census Bureau, 2011g).

A third fallout of the new cash economy and the resulting split between public and private realms was the creation of the cult of domesticity, the notion that true womanhood centers on domestic responsibility and child rearing. During the first half of the twentieth century, ideas sprang up surrounding woman's true nature—ideas meant to support her newly created role as housewife. These included the notion that women, more than men, are endowed with the innate emotional qualities required to provide warmth and comfort. According to this ideology, not only are women better suited for home life,

This nineteenth-century painting illustrates the Victorian feminine domestic ideal. How did the Industrial Revolution transform the division of labor between men and women?

their domesticity also comes to be seen as necessary for the survival of society. Women, so the argument goes, are needed to ensure that the home remains a safe haven in the otherwise cold seas of capitalist enterprise. As breadwinners, men struggle in the dog-eat-dog commercial world, whereas women provide the emotional shelter that anchors private life in human sentiment, emotion, care, and love.

Cult of domesticity the notion that true womanhood centers on domestic responsibility and child rearing.

Families after World War II

By the 1950s the model nuclear family had already come to be idealized, although it was mostly attainable only by white middle- and upper-class families (see the section below on racial and ethnic differences in family structure). Most men's earnings were simply not great enough to afford a stay-at-home wife and dependent children. The gap between ideal and real narrowed as real wages (wages adjusted for inflation) increased in the 1950s, making the patriarchal tradition of a male breadwinner and a female homemaker a feasible arrangement for a greater number of families. Still, many nonwhite, non-middle-class families and individuals were excluded from the prosperity of the 1950s (see Chapter 9), and women worked outside the home throughout history, especially nonwhite women.

Textile factory workers in 1949. Why did many women leave their jobs after World War II?

During the post–World War II economic boom, the manufacturing economy thrived with unionized jobs, real living wages, government housing subsidies, and job-training programs. It was a period of great optimism and for good reasons: The Depression was over; America and its allies had won the war; and the United States was now dominant on the world's economic stage. Americans moved en masse to the suburbs—often to homes that required little to no down payment. Meanwhile, many women quit their jobs, if they had them, and returned to cultivating domesticity full time; the divorce rate dropped to just over 1 in 4 marriages; and fertility rates soared during this "baby boom." The Ozzie and Harriet Nelson type of family was in its prime.

As family scholars are quick to point out, however, these trends in families were atypical. Although the divorce rate dipped in the 1950s, it had been on the rise since the end of the nineteenth century, so modern appeals to return to an age when divorce did not exist ring somewhat hollow. Furthermore, the fertility boom following World War II represented an unusual spike in family size, which had otherwise been on the decline since well before the turn of the century. What's more, the 1950s were also an era of rampant teen pregnancies: The teenage birthrate was twice as high in 1957 as in the 1990s. The difference was that pregnant teens in the postwar era had less access to abortion, and when they bore children, they more often got married. In fact, the 1950s marked the twentieth century's youngest national average for age at time of marriage—an average of 20 and 22 years old for women and men, respectively. Finally, the decline in women's workforce participation represented a dip in an otherwise upward trend, especially given women's labor power during

World War II (when women were hired as temporary replacements for men serving in the armed forces).

Although the period was an anomaly in many ways, we tend to look back fondly (and sometimes bitterly) to the 1950s family as the normal and right way for families to be. But Stephanie Coontz found that while children's well-being and family economic security were at an all-time high toward the end of the 1960s, it was also a time of tumultuous struggle for racial and sexual equality (Coontz, 2001). What, then, do we really miss?

Family and Work: A Not-So-Subtle Revolution

Since the 1970s, American men and women have been caught up in what Kathleen Gerson (1985) calls a "subtle revolution" in our way of organizing work and home—even as we fantasize about an imagined time gone by. Women's participation in the labor force has soared, whereas fertility rates have plummeted. By the end of the 1970s, more women were in, rather than out of, the labor force for the first time. In 1950, approximately 30 percent of women worked outside the home; that number more than doubled to 60 percent by 1999 (Francis, 2005). Today, 65.9 percent of all mothers, married or not, are working moms (Bureau of Labor Statistics, 2013c; Figure 10.2).

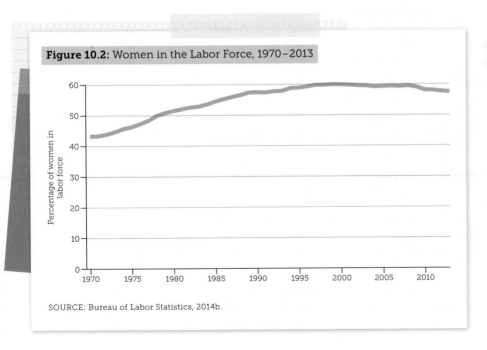

Figure 10.2: Women in the Labor Force, 1970–2013

Percentage of women in labor force

SOURCE: Bureau of Labor Statistics, 2014b.

At the same time, birthrates have dropped, sinking from a baby boom to a baby bust. In the mid-1950s the birthrate was about 106.2 births per 1,000 women. That rate had dropped to just 62.9 in 1980, and as of 2012 it was back down near that low point at 63.2 (Martin et al., 2013). The National Center for Health Statistics reports that marriage rates since the 1960s have also declined, and many adults are postponing marriage until later in life. With the rising divorce rate, marriage is looking less and less like the stable force in women's lives that it was in the postwar era. In fact, by 2007, more Americans age 15 and older were single than married for the first time in a century. The result is that the cult of domesticity is out of the picture for most women, and daughters since the 1970s have increasingly departed from their mother's paths.

The gender revolution in work and family is probably here to stay, and with notable effects on children. Research study after research study has hinged on one basic question: Is maternal employment good, bad, or neutral for kids? There's no shortage of hypotheses. A study published in *Child Development* (Brooks-Gunn et al., 2003) suggests that having a working mother in one's early years can result in lower cognitive achievement and increased behavioral problems for a child. Yet another study published in the prestigious journal *Science* (Chase-Lansdale et al., 2003) claims the opposite: For moms with lower income levels, leaving kids in day care to enter the workforce is beneficial. Hundreds of studies fall on both sides of the argument, with mothers' employment being either disastrous or advantageous to their children. Family situations are just too complex and diverse to generalize. Perhaps, then, this mishmash of results is a consequence of asking the wrong question. Maybe we should instead ask, "How does maternal employment affect children differently within the family?"

In *The Pecking Order* (2004), I found that when a mother worked while raising her children, the adult daughters and sons eventually attained jobs that were more or less equivalent and made about the same income. But in families with a stay-at-home mom, the gender gap widens. When the mother does not work and thus cannot provide a same-sex parental role model in terms of career choices, daughters fare far worse than sons, earning roughly $8,000 less a year than their brothers later in life. And without a working-mother role model, daughters are 15 percent less likely to graduate from college than their brothers (whereas in the general population, more women than men earn college degrees).

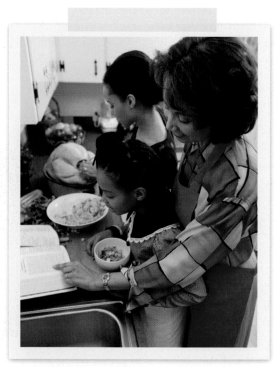

A mother and her daughters prepare dinner. The family is where people first learn how to "do gender" and conform to social norms. What are some of the lessons that we might learn about gender at home?

A <u>Feminist</u> "Rethinking of the Family"

As noted in Chapter 4, the family is the primary unit of socialization for most of us. If family life is structured by larger forces in the social order, such as wage policy and gender inequality at work, then it is also simultaneously a site for the reproduction of these relations. As we have just seen, whether or not a mother works outside the home may affect the outcomes of her sons and daughters differently. Sarah Fenstermaker Berk (1985) has characterized the family as a "gender factory" of sorts, where women and men learn to take on distinct roles paralleling the divide between public and private spheres. The family is where people first learn how to "do gender" in conformity with social rules. Sociologist Marjorie Duvall (1991) shows in *Feeding the Family* that family ties are constructed through women's acts of shopping, preparing meals, and serving them. In everything from the planning of menus to accommodating a child's dislike of lima beans, women are doing gender. As Barbara Risman notes, "It is at home that most people come to believe that men and women are and should be essentially different" (1998). In the act of traditional marriage itself, rituals are gender-stratified: Brides are given away by their fathers, and they take the last name of a husband in patrilineal custom.

The idealized cult of domesticity, although a historical and cultural anomaly among many possibilities, has had powerful and lasting effects on many women's family ideals. Feminist consciousness, raised in the 1960s, led many women to question the ideology of domesticity, finding it "stultifying, infantilizing, and exploitative" of women (Stacey, 1987). In 1963, the feminist writer Betty Friedan led the assault against the limits of being a homemaker with her classic *The Feminine Mystique*. She writes in the introduction:

> The problem lay buried, unspoken, for many years in the minds of American women. It was a strange stirring, a sense of dissatisfaction, a yearning that women suffered in the middle of the twentieth century in the United States. Each suburban housewife struggled with it alone. As she made the beds, shopped for groceries, matched slipcover material, ate peanut butter sandwiches with her children, chauffeured Cub Scouts and Brownies, lay beside her husband at night—she was afraid to ask even of herself the silent question—"Is this all?" (1963/1997, p. 15)

Sociologists elaborated on Freidan's invocation, claiming that what really distinguishes the head of the family is power. The family, as they see it, is a battleground for the power to make collective decisions on everything from who does the laundry to what neighborhood to live in to what college fund to invest in. This is the case, argues sociologist Jessie Bernard in *The Future of Marriage* (1972), even in the comfortable living rooms of traditional nuclear

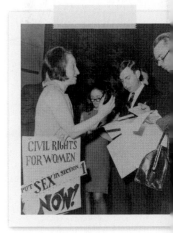

Betty Friedan in 1967, advocating for the addition of an equal rights clause for women in the New York state constitution.

families such Ozzie and Harriet Nelson's. Take, for instance, the tensions that arise from the different ways household members spend money. In studies of welfare recipients, women have been known to spend a greater portion of their welfare benefits on children than fathers do. And in a study of Japanese American families, working wives tended to keep their earnings separate from their husbands' income, and even secret, to preserve their autonomy to spend it how they—and not their husbands—chose (Glenn, 1986).

Furthermore, money is not all the same within the family; rather, husbands', wives', and children's incomes are earmarked in distinctive ways. Women's earnings tend to be spent on extras, so-called luxury items, or otherwise nonessential expenses. Her money is devalued as "fun money." Men's earnings, on the other hand, are earmarked for essentials. When sociologist Margaret Nelson interviewed working wives, one woman explained, "What he makes there is mainly like insurance, taxes, and all that. What I make usually goes for food, clothing—whatever I find necessary . . . or just to take the kids once a week to Middlebury and blow it" (Nelson, 1990). So even a household's income is gendered. As Viviana Zelizer (2005) notes, the distinctions between household incomes help protect a man's status and sense of masculinity when a wife also takes on a breadwinner role in dual-income families. In this way, feminist rethinking of the family urges us not to view the family as a necessarily cohesive, unified whole but to recognize that the family is not immune from socially structured gender relations. And as gender relations change, so too do family forms. As women become less financially dependent on men, for example, more equality slowly develops in other areas of their relationships. Or does it?

When Home Is No Haven: Domestic Abuse

Family life is not always the warm, nurturing environment it appears to be on prime-time television, where moms and dads stand ready with hugs, siblings crack jokes, and grandma is strict but well intentioned. Abuse, neglect, and manipulation happen across all familial relationships—sibling "rivalry" becomes physically aggressive, husbands and wives with powerful tempers hit and control one another, adult children plunder their elderly parents' life savings. The most frequent form of family violence is sibling on sibling (Eriksen & Jensen, 2006). But before you assign all the blame for your current low self-esteem on that time your brother walloped you upside the head with a shoe, note that the strongest two predictors of sibling-on-sibling violence are dads with short tempers and moms who get physical when it comes to punishing the kids (Eriksen & Jensen, 2006). So is it your brother's fault that he learned how to solve problems by mimicking dad's anger management strategy and piggy-backing on mom's heavy hand of authority? This monkey-see, monkey-do explanation has had a long history in the study of domestic violence. Studies have found that abuse transmission is not genetic and that only about one-third of people who are abused as children go on to have a seriously neglectful or abusive relationship with their own children (Oliver, 1993). Broad social factors like poverty, single-parent households, and low levels of educational attainment are associated with higher levels of all types of domestic abuse.

When violence occurs within a couple it's often called IPV, intimate partner violence. More than one-third of women and one-quarter of men have been raped, physically attacked, and/or stalked by an intimate partner at some point in their lives (Centers for Disease Control and Prevention, 2011c). In 2007, IPV resulted in 2,340 deaths, 70 percent of whom were women and 30 percent men. In a given year the health care cost of IPV was an estimated $8.3 billion (Centers for Disease Control and Prevention, 2011d).

Elder abuse is a relatively new field of study that investigates physical, verbal, and financial abuse intentionally or unintentionally perpetrated against people (usually family members) who are at least 57 years old. Estimates suggest elder abuse is not particularly widespread; one-year prevalence was 4.6 percent for emotional abuse, 1.6 percent for physical abuse, 0.6 percent for sexual abuse, 5.1 percent for potential neglect, and 5.2 percent for current financial abuse by a family member (Acierno et al., 2010). The impact of mistreatment in intimate relationships can have serious and long-lasting financial, health, and emotional consequences for individuals, families, and communities.

→ The Chore Wars: Supermom Does It All

One of the main ways that gender is enacted within the family is with respect to the unpaid labor that needs to be done at home. In the case of housework and the chore wars, gender remains a salient social force that shapes family life. The cult of domesticity lingers on, such that even though 60 percent of women participated in the workforce in 2008, domestic duties, such as housework and child care, still fall disproportionately on their shoulders (Francis, 2005). Women return from the office to take up what Arlie Hochschild (1989) calls the second shift: responsibility for housework and child care—everything from cooking dinner to doing laundry, bathing children, reading bedtime stories, and sewing Halloween costumes. Despite women's gains in the public realm of work, the revolution at home has, as Hochschild described it, stalled.

Within a two-career household, parents are likely to spend their at-home time on separate—and unequal—tasks. One study from 1965 to 1966 found

Second shift women's responsibility for housework and child care—everything from cooking dinner to doing laundry, bathing children, reading bedtime stories, and sewing Halloween costumes.

that working women averaged 3 hours each day on housework, whereas men put in a meager 17 minutes. When it comes to leisure activities, however, men surpass their working wives. Working fathers watch an hour more of television per day than working mothers. They also sleep a half hour longer (Hochschild, 2003). The resulting "leisure gap" can brew hostilities between exasperated, exhausted wives and their unresponsive husbands.

Using national studies on time use from the 1960s and 1970s, Hochschild counted the hours that women and men put in on the job in addition to their time spent on housework and child care. She determined that women worked roughly 15 hours longer each week than men (Hochschild, 2003). After 52 weeks, this added up to 780 hours more that women work than men—that's an extra month! This gap appears to be closing, however, as men do more and women do less housework (Figure 10.3). Valerie A. Ramey and Neville Francis (2006) found that as of 2004, women spent roughly 9 hours more per week on what they termed "home production": housework along with child care and homework assistance.

The division of labor in the home refers to not just who does how much but also who does what. As Viviana Zelizer (2005) shows, housework tasks are patterned around gender. When men do housework, their contribution is referred to as "helping out around the house," and their wives zealously thank them. Women who have "helping" husbands in the home consider themselves extremely lucky. Many men, however, never report feeling lucky or extremely

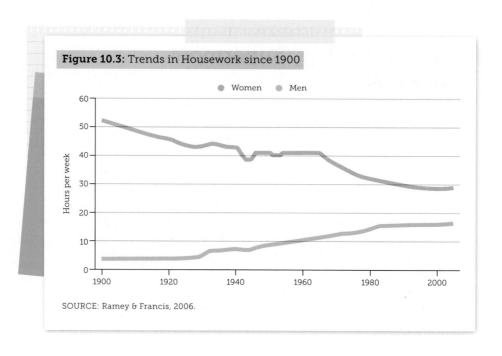

Figure 10.3: Trends in Housework since 1900

SOURCE: Ramey & Francis, 2006.

thankful when their wives do the housework. And women *do* the housework; they don't simply "help out."

In addition, men are typically in charge of outdoor, stereotypically masculine activities, whereas women disproportionately do the work inside. Even cooking is broken down by gender: Men more often cook the meat for a meal when they share work in the kitchen. Men also have more control over when they help out, because they are more likely to be in charge of chores that don't require completion on a daily basis, such as changing the oil in the family car or mowing the lawn. Women are more likely to be locked into a fixed and harried housework routine: Pick up the kids from day care, cook dinner, wash the dishes, administer the bath, and put the baby to bed (Zelizer, 2005).

Yet another male advantage in the division of household labor is that men get to do more of what they like to do, while women are often stuck with the most undesirable chores, such as scrubbing toilets and ironing. The time fathers spend with their children is more likely to be special recreational time, such as trips to the park, rather than more mundane daily baths and feedings. In fact, most of a father's child-care time occurs on the weekends, whereas mothers spend their time with children during the other five days of the week. Finally as children grow up, their care of aging parents takes on gendered patterns. Adult daughters are often the primary caregivers to parents, and they are more likely than their brothers to help an aging parent with housework. Adult sons, in contrast, assist aging parents with appliance repairs and yard work (Zelizer, 2005).

Neoclassical economists typically look at a member's power in the family as a direct expression of that member's utility to the family unit, and that tends to be measured in terms of his or her income. In such a formulation, money talks, and whoever earns the bacon doesn't have to cook it. This is not so for women, whose income goes only so far in increasing their power in the family. The more a wife contributes to the household income, the more her husband is likely to share, or "help out" with, the second shift. That seems to fit the bacon theory. But as soon as the wife's earnings start to overtake her husband's, he drops out of the shared domestic equation, leaving the entire second shift up to her (Bittman et al., 2003). Furthermore, when women earn more than their husbands, the perceived insult to masculinity may make for a tense home environment. Men, it seems, are not willing to let anyone else wear the proverbial pants in the household.

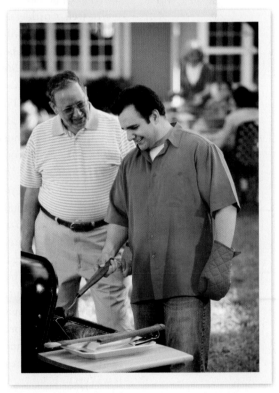

Sociologists have noted a chore gender gap: Men frequently perform intermittent tasks that they enjoy, such as grilling dinner, whereas women often take on undesirable everyday chores.

With all the advances in home cooking and cleaning technology over the past few decades, you might wonder why the second shift can't be handled a little more efficiently than in a whole extra month of labor a year. But, as Ruth Schwartz Cowan reports in *More Work for Mother: The Ironies of Household Technology from the Open Hearth to the Microwave* (1983), all those time-saving devices like the vacuum cleaner and the washing machine have paradoxically increased the amount of time women spend on housework. As Windex, dishwashers, and the Swiffer broom crowded the market, standards of cleanliness rose and even more cleaning was necessary than before. That said, as women have increased their hours in the formal labor market, the gender gap has declined in recent years: Women now do only 1.8 hours of household work for every hour a man completes, compared with the six-fold difference in the 1960s.

The entrepreneur Don Aslett, who built a business around domestic cleaning services, told one sociologist, "The whole mentality out there is that if you clean, you're a scumball" (Ehrenreich, 2001). Although not always so harshly spoken of, housework certainly is overlooked as a worthy or meaningful activity in America. For one thing, it's unpaid labor, and in a cash economy, it seems pretty, well, worthless. For another, it has been construed historically as women's work. A housewife, measured against modern criteria for success such as salaries, pensions, benefits, bonuses, and promotions, is just a housewife. Radical feminists in the 1960s argued that housework should be fairly compensated, because without a woman's labor, the American male workforce would not be able to keep going. This "reproductive labor" argument stressed the value of social reproduction, all the activities and tasks that women performed daily to keep their working husbands' lives running smoothly. The movement for just compensation for women's household labor was one banner galvanizing early radical feminists.

This movement, you've probably figured out, did not catch on immediately. In fact, it took a good four decades and one tragedy. Zelizer (2005) showed that women's unpaid work commanded a price tag in the distribution of monetary rewards for surviving family members of those killed in the September 11, 2001, terrorist attacks. In the aftermath of 9/11, friends and family grappled with the shock and grief of losing loved ones. Some relatives of victims filed wrongful death suits against the airlines of the hijacked planes. To curb individual lawsuits and to spare the airlines from insurmountable litigations, the U.S. government established the September 11 Victim Compensation Fund. Attorney Kenneth Feinberg had the job of administering the $7 billion fund to settle 2,880 death claims and 2,680 personal injury claims (Chen, 2004). It was up to Feinberg to decide, among those injured and the families of those killed, who received what.

As Zelizer notes, at first the fund was distributed to surviving family members in the amount of the deceased's estimated future earnings and made no provision for compensating unpaid household work. Feminists organized and lobbied Feinberg on the issue, arguing that "ignoring the unpaid work performed by full-time workers raises sex discrimination concerns. . . . Women victims, especially mothers, are much more likely to have expended significant time on unpaid work" (Zelizer, 2005). In the end, the Victim Compensation Fund Final Rule allowed for a case-by-case review of compensation claims on the lost economic value of household services that would have been provided by the deceased. Perhaps it takes a national tragedy for people to reevaluate the importance of individual, daily life.

It also takes marginalization to appreciate the center, as Christopher Carrington's study of gay couples in San Francisco demonstrates. Blumstein and Schwartz (1983) have suggested that an egalitarian division of labor is much more likely to exist in the households of gay and lesbian couples. But as Carrington (1999) notes, they also pay much more care and attention to their household chores, spending about two times as long on cleaning as heterosexual couples. The explanation? Homosexual couples see housework as a means of legitimating their households; thus, it is a more central, validating activity for them than it is for the typical working wife.

If, as sociologists argue, the burden of the second shift falls on working mothers in dual-income families, we might expect some nasty consequences. Indeed, Hochschild found that in response to the stalled revolution, some women tried to do it all. This is the supermom strategy. She cooks, she cleans,

Many women juggle full-time jobs with caring for their children and running their home with little help from their spouses. According to Arlie Hochschild, what are the consequences of the supermom strategy?

she climbs the career ladder, all while being a devoted parent and loving partner. Supermoms, of course, don't really exist, but there is a perpetual myth that some women can do it all, and if other women can't, it's a result of some personal flaw.

Women who buy into the supermom myth burn out quickly, and typically their marriages absorb the shock. In one study, Hochschild (1989) found that married women are more likely than men to think about divorce (30 percent of married women have considered divorce versus 22 percent of men). Women are also likely to give a more comprehensive list of reasons for wanting a divorce. In her interviews of dual-income families, Hochschild encountered bitter women, fed up with doing all the work, and puzzled men, confused over their wives' hostilities, or bitter themselves at begrudgingly having to help out more.

Because women still earn less than men, about $0.81 for every dollar that a man earns, a disproportionate financial shock hits women after a divorce (Hegewisch et al., 2013). Given the rampant threat of divorce, some women bite the second-shift bullet, just letting the hostilities simmer. Other women manage by cutting household corners where they can, allowing the dust to pile up and skimping on the children's evening story time. For them, hostilities linger beneath a growing sense of parental guilt.

In households in which men and women genuinely share the second shift, marriages are much more likely to be stable and happy ones. Studies (for example, that conducted by Michael S. Kimmel in 2000) have found that when men share the housework, working wives experience less stress. Barbara Risman (1998) calls these "fair families," where husbands and wives equally split the roles of breadwinner and homemaker. In fair families, couples honor an ideology of gender equality, and both men and women benefit from such an arrangement. Women win the self-respect that comes with being economically independent, and they respond by regarding marriage less as a necessity and more as a voluntary, love-based relationship. Men, by sharing the breadwinner burden, are less stressed and feel freer to find jobs they enjoy. Perhaps most important, Risman speculates about a uniqueness in these sharing couples: They are more often close friends.

Despite these findings, most men simply don't budge on the issue of sharing the second shift. But they should, advises Dr. Benjamin Spock, and not just because it makes for a healthier, happier home environment. Dr. Spock's phenomenally successful parenting guide, *Baby and Child Care*, has sold more than 50 million copies in seven editions since 1946, making it second in sales only to the Bible. Among Spock's child-rearing tips is the suggestion that fathers should be involved parents. Studies consistently find that men who share child rearing and housework have happier marriages, better health, and longer lives (Kimmel, 2000). As Dr. Spock put it, "There is no reason why fathers shouldn't be able to do these jobs as well as mothers" (1946/1998).

Furthermore, studies show that when left to their own devices, men are perfectly fine housekeepers, cooks, and primary parents (Gerson, 1993). Men just don't live up to their potential as often when a woman is around to handle the second shift.

Swimming and Sinking: Inequality and American Families

African American Families

For millions of American households, the idealized traditional family in *The Adventures of Ozzie and Harriet* never even came close to a lived reality. For African American families, who throughout history have combined work and family, the split between the public and private spheres has never made much sense. Neither has the ideal of exclusive, "isolationist" motherhood made sense for women lacking the resources that allow for full-time homemaking. More often, black and poor women have come to rely on extra-familial female networks in order to manage child-care and work responsibilities (Stack & Burton, 1994). If the average American woman has two shifts, then the typical black American mother has three, because she is more often the primary or only breadwinner. This greater importance of women in the black family has unfortunately been conflated with "backward" female domination or matriarchy.

Social scientists in the 1960s made heavy use of the matriarchal thesis to explain social problems in the African American community. In *The Negro Family: The Case for National Action* (1965), Daniel Patrick Moynihan found that 25 percent of black wives out-earned their husbands, versus only 18 percent of white wives. This "pathological" matriarchy, Moynihan argued, undercuts the role of the father in black families and leads to all sorts of problems later in life, such as domestic violence, substance abuse, crime, and degeneracy. You name it, the matriarch caused it. The root of matriarchy, Moynihan asserted, dated back to the days of slavery, which reversed roles for men and women and continued to haunt African Americans up to the time of his report.

According to the Moynihan report and similar arguments, the matriarch is a stereotypically bad black mother. She's domineering and unfeminine, always wearing the pants in the family. She's hefty and gruff. She spends so much time away from the home that she can't supervise her own kids. And when she is at home, she's too bossy and strong; thus, she emasculates her man and drives him away. If only the matriarch could be a little more feminine, a little less strong, a little *whiter,* suggested the report, the black family could lift itself up out of poverty. The image of the matriarch makes it easier to lay the blame on African

American families for their own problems—social ills such as neighborhood decay, stagnating wages, single motherhood, higher divorce rates, and lower school achievement. The matriarch is also a powerful reminder to all women of just what can go wrong when women challenge the patriarchal decree that they be submissive, dependent, and feminine. The Moynihan report's prescription for the social problems of black people was just this: Black women should aspire to the cult of true (white) womanhood.

Scholars like W. E. B. Du Bois had argued all along, however, that African American female-headed families were the outcome, rather than the cause, of racial oppression and poverty. And in 1987 William Julius Wilson graphed a "marriageable Black male index," which highlighted the scarcity of employed, un-incarcerated black men (fewer than 50 marriageable black men per 100 black women back then). In such a context, if black women didn't work to pay the rent, put food on the table, and take care of the kids, who would? As Elaine Kamplain has pointed out, African American mothers were "damned if they worked to support their families and damned if they didn't" (Hochschild, 2003).

Matriarchy is one of many misreadings that social critics have imposed on the black family. But when critics hold fast to the idealized concept of the nuclear family, they are likely to see any model that differs from the traditional yardstick as deviant. The sociologist's trick is to view the traditional family, in which a heterosexual couple lives together with their dependent children in a self-contained, economically independent household, as just one of many potential family forms. After all, this particular kind of family evolved from the socially constructed separation of home and work—a separation rooted in the upper classes—and the experiences of most African American families stray from that norm. In fact, asserts Patricia Hill Collins (1990), women of color have never fit this model. Collins looks at the family with a different set of lenses on—what she calls an Afrocentric worldview—which allows for alternative concepts of family and community. One instance of this worldview is more of a collective effort with strong neighborhood support.

Identifying the traditional family as a specific historical phenomenon that has rarely applied to black families enables us to analyze the black community's unique characteristics in a less judgmental manner. African American communities tend to have an expanded notion of kinship, as denoted by the all-encompassing use of the words *brother* and *sister*. This may have developed out of blacks' historical experience with slavery. Because slaves were separated from their biological families at the auction block by white owners, blacks adapted by expanding the definition of *family* from immediate bloodlines to racial ones. Under slavery, black men and women occupied indistinct work roles, often performing the same labor side by side in plantation fields. The legacy of their shared labor was incompatible with a nuclear family, a model predicated on the differentiation between male and female spheres (Collins, 1990).

As a result of segregation throughout the twentieth century, the particular African American notions of community and family continued to endure. But after World War II, the manufacturing economy took a downturn and many black workers, employed by shrinking industries, found themselves at risk of economic marginalization. Marital rates among blacks have been in decline since the 1960s, and female-headed households have been on the rise among both the poor and middle classes. Kathryn Edin's ongoing research in poor African American communities has found a consistent interest in the elements that constitute family life, such as having children and getting married, though poor-quality schools, lack of jobs, and (sometimes) substance abuse make it difficult to undertake a traditional progression of dating, love, marriage, and childbearing. Childbearing often precedes marriage, but unlike common stereotypes of indifferent cads interested primarily in sex, fathers-to-be are often excited about becom-

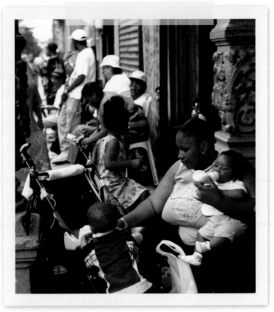

Many African American parents rely on extrafamilial community members to help raise children. What are some of the criticisms of the matriarchal thesis?

ing parents and tend to strengthen their commitment to the baby's mother. Unfortunately, parenting the same child (or children) may not be enough to hold these couples together until they feel financially secure enough to marry. Black children (55 percent) and Hispanic children (31 percent) were more likely to live with a single parent than non-Hispanic white children (21 percent) or Asian children (13 percent) (U.S. Census Bureau, 2013b). This statistic reflects, in part, the high rates of unemployment and incarceration and low rates of education among black men.

Latino Families

According to the 2010 Census, Latinos are the largest minority group in America, making up 16 percent of the U.S. population. The U.S. Census Bureau defines Latino as "a person of Cuban, Mexican, Puerto Rican, South or Central American, or other Spanish culture or origin regardless of race" (2011c). Latinos also live all over the United States, although they have clustered on the West Coast and in the South and Midwest (Hernandez et al., 2007). Given the diverse origins and geography of Latinos, how can we make general claims about the Latino family? Sociologists don't all agree that such a thing exists or that a generic Latino identity is even imaginable (Santa Ana, 2004). But there are a few common threads that run through many Latino families. Their family ties are strong, and family is a top priority to many Latinos—so important, in fact, that individual Latinos often define their self-worth in terms of their family's image and accomplishments (Ho, 1987). Like African American families, Latino families act as safety nets, and members take seriously their responsibilities to help one another, even in long chains of needy extended relations (Skogrand et al., 2004). They have a strong sense of community and allegiance to it (Hurtado, 1995). For example, so many Latino immigrants send remittances, or money, to family members back home that remittances are now one of the largest sources of cash to the Mexican and many other Central American economies.

Traditional rules of gender and authority also loom large in Latino culture. Women listen to their men, and children to their elders, in a clear-cut hierarchy. This should make sense to anyone who's taken a Spanish language class (or studied any other Romance language). The heavy use of titles and ranks in the everyday vocabulary shows that respect and formality are crucial (DeNeve, 1997). Most Latino families are also shaped by a tradition of devout Catholicism. Combine high religiosity with the importance of family honor, and you soon recognize a few tendencies: High rates of marriage and relatively low rates of divorce, high rates of marriage at a young age, and a lot of babies born out of wedlock. This third outcome may seem contradictory, but think about it: If a young Latina does have premarital sex and becomes pregnant without a marriage prospect in sight, she's less likely than her African American or white peers to have an abortion, a worse breach of Catholic culture than an out-of-wedlock birth. Add to that a tight-lipped stance on discussing sex at home, the dwindling of preventive sex education, and the difficulty (not to mention the embarrassment) teens face trying to get their hands on effective and affordable birth control, and you end up with a lot of babies born to single Latina moms. About 53 percent of all Latino babies are born to unwed mothers, compared with 29 percent of non-Hispanic white babies (those numbers are still lower than the nearly 72 percent of African American babies born outside of marriage) (Centers for Disease Control and Prevention, 2013b).

Flat Broke with Children

Single mothers and poverty often go hand in hand in America, and these twin challenges plague nonwhite communities to a greater extent than white Americans. In a shrinking welfare state with widening economic gaps between the rich and the poor, single mothers are faced with tough trade-offs between mothering and work. Single mothers rely on a combination of welfare, family, lovers, luck, and creativity to make ends meet. At any given point in the past few decades, half of all mothers raising children by themselves have relied on welfare to get by. In contrast to the media myth of the "lazy welfare mother"

Jenni McGlaun talks on the phone while her 15-month-old son, Jesse, plays in their Milwaukee home. McGlaun has been on and off welfare for five years. What does Kathryn Edin and Laura Lein's research on single mothers reveal about the choices these women face between welfare and work?

who watches television and buys filet mignon with her food stamps, many of these mothers work hard (often off the books) and desperately want to escape poverty. Welfare critics might be surprised to read *Making Ends Meet: How Single Mothers Survive Welfare and Low-Wage Work* (1997), in which sociologists Kathryn Edin and Laura Lein find that all single mothers prefer self-reliance to welfare dependency. In fact, a majority get off the welfare rolls in two years, and hardly any stay on welfare for more than eight years.

In their study of 379 mothers across four U.S. cities, Edin and Lein traced what happens when poor single mothers are faced with the choice between welfare and work. The word *choice* here is misleading: It implies freedom, as though these women can easily move from dependency to self-sufficiency. However, because single mothers are often unskilled or semiskilled and have less education than average, their employment options are limited to low-wage work that rarely provides benefits (the kinds of jobs listed in the paper Reagan had flashed).

Edin and Lein found that mothers on welfare could cover about three-fifths of their expenses. In low-wage jobs, they faced a larger gap between earnings and expenses, in part to cover the costs of transportation, child-care arrangements, increased rent, and fewer food stamps. (Both the food stamp program and federal housing program consider income when determining benefits; even a father's child support can translate into a rent increase for a single mother.) This system makes a savings account virtually impossible for welfare recipients to maintain and is arguably the real culprit behind the trap of dependency. In fact, leaving welfare for work substantially increases these women's expenses, such that they can cover only two-thirds of those expenses on low wages alone. One working mother voiced her frustrations:

> Ask any politician to live off my budget. Live off my minimum wage job and just a little bit of food stamps—how can he do it? I bet he couldn't. I'd like him to try it for one month. Come home from work, cook dinner, wash clothes, do everything, everything, get up and go to work the next day, and then find you don't have enough money to pay for everything you need. (Edin & Lein, 1997, p. 149)

Barbara Ehrenreich, a sociologist and writer, tried to make ends meet with low-wage work in 1998. That was a year in which the Preamble Center for Public Policy estimated that the odds against a typical welfare recipient's landing a job at a living wage were about 97 to 1. Nationwide, it took an average hourly wage of $8.89 to afford a one-bedroom apartment. Currently, the federal minimum wage is $7.25, which amounts to a full-time yearly salary of $15,080. Only approximately 5 percent of the labor force makes the minimum wage or less, but about 20 percent of the workforce plugs away for $9 an hour or less, and Ehrenreich wanted to figure out just how they did it (Bureau of Labor Statistics, 2013d; Ehrenreich, 2001; Greenhouse, 2013).

Ehrenreich traveled the country working for $6 or $7 an hour as a waitress, hotel maid, and Wal-Mart sales clerk. At these low wages, she had to pay high rates for rent by the week (because she lacked the required one-month security deposit). She had to eat for less than $9 a day, a budget that at best included canned beans, fast food, or noodle soup microwaved at a convenience store, and she supplemented this diet by sponging junk food from charities. All the while, Ehrenreich prayed for her health to keep up (low-wage jobs are often physically taxing), gave up clothes shopping, and juggled two or more jobs. She still could not afford to live off of her wages:

> I grew up hearing over and over, to the point of tedium, that "hard work" was the secret of success: "Work hard and you'll get ahead" or "It's hard work that got us where we are." No one ever said that you could work hard— harder than you ever thought possible—and still find yourself sinking ever deeper into poverty and debt. (2001, p. 220)

Most welfare recipients live with few extras, often in neighborhoods with high poverty concentration and elevated crime rates. Yet politicians and voters alike worry about the cycle of dependency, the so-called welfare trap, and taxpayers deeply resent any person—real or perceived—who gets a free ride. Welfare critic Charles Murray, author of the conservative classic *Losing Ground*

(1984), believes welfare moms are staining the very moral fabric that holds the country together. As he sees it, all economic support should be pulled from under the feet of single mothers, and that would keep poor women and teens from having babies for whom they cannot care.

The 1996 Personal Responsibility and Work Opportunity Reconciliation Act, the national welfare reform enacted during the Clinton administration, didn't go as far as Murray would have liked, but it did make into policy the sentiment common among taxpayers that it was time for lazy welfare moms to get their act together, learn self-sufficiency, and take responsibility for themselves. But responsibility can take on several, often conflicting, meanings for mothers. Faced with either welfare or low-wage work, single mothers find that the government's definition of responsibility is narrowly defined as wage work. In *Flat Broke with Children: Women in the Age of Welfare Reform* (2003), Sharon Hays shows that many of these women are forced to take low-paying jobs with no future and little career stability. As a result, they are frequently driven to marry for financial support. All too often, Hays finds, single mothers (and their children) end up in poverty, homeless, or seeking alternatives to get by, including illicit sources of income.

In *Flat Broke with Children*, Sharon Hays found that many women stayed in abusive relationships or married for financial support to escape poverty. For instance, Marcia Felts Wimberly weathered an abusive husband in order to get a surgical procedure covered by his insurance. Now a single mom, she has no medical insurance and is struggling with debt.

Single mothers' paid labor often requires that they sacrifice responsible parenthood. By forcing welfare moms to enter the workforce while not providing adequate child care, the government encourages women to abandon their children in an unsupervised home. To the single mothers Hays interviewed, real responsibility meant taking care of and supervising their children, looking after their health, and providing them with a safe home environment. According to Hays, for the most desperate women in America, being a responsible worker requires being an irresponsible mother. To manage this tension between being a good worker or a good mother, single mothers may shoot for the nearly impossible strategy of self-reliance, but in reality they often end up depending on cash assistance from family or boyfriends. They barter with sisters, cousins, and kindly neighbors. They also take side jobs (again hiding their income to avoid rent increases or food stamp ineligibility) or go to relief agencies, although this last option proves too humiliating for most to bear. As a last resort, some single mothers turn to criminal activity such as prostitution or drug dealing, where the earnings are high but the moral costs "rob them of the self-respect they gained from trying to be good mothers" (Edin & Lein, 1997).

The Pecking Order: Inequality Starts at Home

By now, you can see that there's no universal family form and that plenty of gender inequality exists in American families. But you might still think that, at least when it comes to the children, the home (no matter who makes up a family) is a haven of equality, altruism, and infinite love in an otherwise harsh world. In *Haven in a Heartless World* (1977), Christopher Lasch paints a rosy portrait of domestic life. To him, the home really is a haven where workers seek refuge from the cold winds of a capitalist public sphere. The family is sacred because it provides intimate privacy, managed by a caring woman who shields male workers from "the cruel world of politics and work." Building on the socially constructed split between the public and private spheres, this idea of the family as insulated from the outside world is deeply entrenched in America.

However, as you might have guessed by now, such ideas give a misleading sense of the family as a harmonious unit, its members altruistically sacrificing for one another to forge a healthy, hearty, and loving private world. As I found while researching my book *The Pecking Order* (2004), a compelling but largely invisible struggle also takes place in the home. In each American family, there exists a pecking order among siblings—a status hierarchy, if you will—that can ignite the family with competition, struggle, and resentment. Parents often abet such struggles, despite their protestations that they "love all their children equally."

Let me illustrate with the story of a future president, William Jefferson Blythe IV, born to a 23-year-old widow named Virginia. Childhood was rough for young Bill, especially after his mother married Roger Clinton, a bitter alcoholic who physically abused his wife. Bill cites the day that he stood up to his stepfather as the most important day in his transition to adulthood and perhaps his entire life. In 1962, when Bill was 16, Virginia finally left Roger, but by then there was another Roger Clinton in the family, Bill's younger half-brother.

Despite the fact that Bill despised his stepfather, he went to the Garland County courthouse and changed his last name to Clinton so that he would have the same surname as the younger brother he cherished. Although they were separated by ten years, were only half-siblings, and ran in very different circles, the brothers were close. The younger Roger probably hated his father more than Bill did, but he nonetheless took on some of the old man's traits as he came of age, most notably substance abuse. By age 18, he was heavily into marijuana. During Bill's first (unsuccessful) congressional run in 1974, Roger spent much of his time stenciling signs while smoking joints at campaign headquarters.

As Bill's political fortunes rose, Roger's prospects first stagnated and then sank. He tried his hand at a musical career, worked odd jobs, and eventually began dealing drugs—and not just pot. In 1984 the Arkansas state police informed then-Governor Bill Clinton that his brother was a cocaine dealer under investigation. After a sting operation, which the governor did not obstruct, Roger was arrested. He was beside himself in tears, threatening suicide for the shame he had brought on his family and especially his brother, the successful politician.

You might be wondering, as Clinton biographer David Maraniss has, "How could two brothers be so different: the governor and the coke dealer, the Rhodes scholar and the college dropout?" (1995). To be sure, a pair of brothers who are, respectively, a former president and an ex-con is a fairly extreme example. But the basic phenomenon of sibling differences in success that the Clintons represent is not all that unusual. In fact, in explaining economic inequality in America, sibling differences represent more than half of all the differences between individuals.

What do sibling disparities as large as these indicate? If asked to explain why one brother succeeded while the other failed miserably, most people would point to different individual characteristics, such as work ethic, responsibility, personal motivation, and discipline. To account for a sibling's failures, people also tend to cite personal reasons, such as "a bad attitude," "poor emotional or mental health," or most commonly, "lack of determination" (Conley, 2004).

Other people will grapple for an explanation by suggesting the role of birth order. The commonly held idea is that firstborns are naturally more driven and successful, if just because they are most favored by their parents. But this is still a form of individual explanation—something unique to the biology or psychology of the sibling—that fails to take into account the role of sociological factors. For example, in families with two kids, birth order doesn't matter that much. Firstborns don't have too much advantage over one younger sibling. For example, slightly fewer than one-fourth of U.S. presidents were firstborns, about what we would expect from chance. Birth position matters only in the context of larger families and limited resources. When family resources are stretched thin, love really does become a pie, as they say. The children born first or last into a large family seem to fare better socioeconomically than those born in the middle. Middle kids feel the effects of a shrinking pie, as they tend to be shortchanged on resources like money for college and parental attention.

Taken as a whole, the facts about intrafamily stratification present a much darker portrait of American family life than we are accustomed to. Sure, we want to think of the home as a haven in a heartless world, but the truth is that inequality starts at home. These statistics also pose problems for media stories and politicians concerned with the erosion of the idealized nuclear family. In fact, they hint at a trade-off between economic opportunity and stable, cohesive families. The family is, in short, no shelter from the cold winds of capitalism; rather, it is part and parcel of that system.

A pecking order emerges during the course of childhood. It both reflects and determines siblings' positions in the overall status ordering that occurs within society. It is not just the will of parents or the "natural" abilities of children (or lack thereof); the pecking order is conditioned by the swirling winds of society, which in turn envelop the family. Furthermore, sibling disparities are much more common in poor families and single-parent homes than in rich, intact families. In fact, when families have limited resources, the success of one sibling often generates a negative backlash among the others. As the parents unwittingly put all their eggs—all their hopes and dreams—in just one basket, the other siblings inevitably are left out in the cold. Americans like to think that their behavior and destiny remain solely in their own hands. But the pecking order, like other aspects of the social fabric, ends up being shaped by social forces.

The <u>Future</u> of Families, and There Goes the Nation!

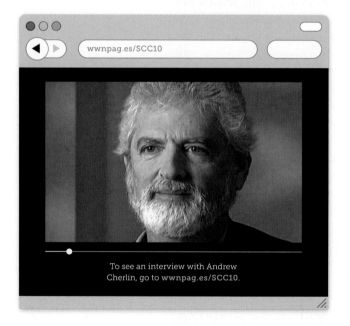

To see an interview with Andrew Cherlin, go to **wwnpag.es/SCC10**.

Divorce

Throughout this chapter we have examined the idealization of monogamous marriage as a key characteristic of American culture. Sociologist Andrew Cherlin writes in *The Marriage-Go-Round: The State of Marriage and the Family in America Today* (2009) about how the idealized conception of marriage is currently helping to delay age at first marriage and otherwise shape contemporary American marital patterns. He finds a paradox. On the one hand, Americans value marriage very highly—85 to 90 percent of us will eventually get married. On the other hand, America has the highest divorce rate of any comparable Western country. How does he explain this love-hate relationship? Cherlin suggests that both the drive to get married and the desire to divorce are rooted in our collective past,

> all the way to the Colonial days when marriage was the nexus of civil society that the early settlers established. It's very important here.... We want to be married. At the same time though, we're very individualistic, and that has deep cultural roots too. Think about the saying "Go west, young man." Think about the rugged individual. We're individualists. And so we want to be married, but we evaluate our marriages in very personal terms. Am I getting the personal growth that I need out of my marriage? And if you think the answer is no, you feel justified in leaving. (Conley, 2009k)

Social science research over the past couple of decades has struggled to establish just how high rates of divorce alter the social fabric. Figure 10.4 illustrates the divorce rate in America since 1920. Adding a layer to the American marriage paradox, it turns out that the most politically and religiously conservative states have the highest rates of divorce: "The states with the top ten divorce rates, eight out of ten of those voted for John McCain in the 2008 election. All ten voted for George Bush in the 2004 election" (Conley, 2009k). Cherlin explains that personal economics, not personal values, may end up contributing to rocky marriages. The states with high divorce rates are relatively poor; a sizable number of their citizens struggle to find jobs with decent wages, which compromises the ideal vision of family as a haven protected from crass financial concerns. Couples who cannot provide themselves a middle-class lifestyle may begin to question the utility of marriage in the first place. They face all of the responsibility of looking out for each other without the means to live the ideal lifestyle to which they aspire. Cherlin also notes that younger people have even more difficulty finding good jobs because they have less work experience, and this may delay their marriage plans (Conley, 2009k). Young couples may live together, even have children together, holding off on long-term personal relationships until after they have established long-term financial relationships with reliable employers.

Much of the debate about divorce follows the children of divorced parents through their educational careers and into their adult relationship choices. The moral and political debate surrounding the long-term consequences of divorce

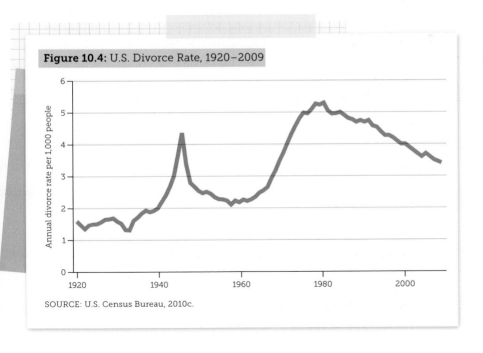

Figure 10.4: U.S. Divorce Rate, 1920–2009

SOURCE: U.S. Census Bureau, 2010c.

has largely treated its effects as uniform for all offspring. In *The Pecking Order* (2004), I paint a more nuanced picture, in which circumstances and context widely vary the impact of divorce on kids—even those in the same family. Everything from the timing of the divorce to a parent's hostility can influence a kid's educational attainment, future earnings, and socioeconomic success. Blanket condemnations of divorce are therefore dangerously naïve, as are those who say that it's no big deal.

For example, in their best seller *The Unexpected Legacy of Divorce* (2000), Judith Wallerstein and her colleagues claim that divorce almost universally damages children's self-esteem and developmental trajectories. Based on interviews with about 50 offspring of divorced parents, they conclude that adult children of divorce suffer from higher rates of depression, endure low self-esteem, and have difficulties forming fulfilling, lasting relationships of their own.

Sociologist Linda Waite and columnist Maggie Gallagher echo this view in *The Case for Marriage: Why Married People Are Happier, Healthier, and Better Off Financially* (2000). (The title, in this case, says it all.) They claim that married parents provide better homes for their children than divorced ones because they have more money and time to spend on the children, enjoy stronger emotional bonds with them, have more social capital (connections) that will be helpful to their children's chances for success, and are physically and mentally healthier. By contrast, they say, divorced families are likely to manifest more child abuse, neglect, and delinquency, and the children will probably attain less education.

On the flip side of the debate are research findings that suggest a less calamitous future for the children of single-parent families, finding that children from divorced households generally do not do much worse than other kids. In *For Better or for Worse: Divorce Reconsidered* (2002), psychologists E. Mavis Hetherington and John Kelly argue that the children of divorce, for the most part, do adjust well to the new reality. Under some conditions, but certainly not all, divorce produces in kids more stress and depression, and lower future socioeconomic success. Continued parental conflict and role reversals in which children "play parent," for example, make divorce potentially destructive. In other cases, however, parents who leave a high-conflict marriage probably spare their children from ongoing family feuds, hostilities, or abuse. At least one study shows that kids from high-conflict marriages that stay together may do worse than kids from high-conflict marriages that break up (Morrison & Coiro, 1999).

Too often, social science research is carelessly picked up in political debates as simple sound bites. Saying kids from divorced families fare worse than kids from intact families is one thing; saying that divorce caused those worse outcomes is quite another matter. That is, we can't really know for sure that had those parents stayed together, the kids would have been better off. We can only say that high levels of parental conflict are bad—with or without divorce in the picture.

Blended Families

As should be clear by this point, the dynamics involved in maintaining a family (both as a whole and in terms of the individual relationships within it) are complicated. This complexity increases drastically when two family units are integrated. As stated on Helpguide.org, "To a child who does not belong to one, stepfamily may suggest Cinderella's family or the Brady Bunch." However, if you are part of a blended family or know someone who is (there's a good chance you do, given that one-third of the children in the United States now fall into this category), you understand that neither extreme reflects reality. As divorce becomes more common, so too does the blended family form. Two people meet, fall in love, get married, have kids—we'll call them family A. Then they decide to split. Another pair does the same (family B). Some time later, Mom A encounters Dad B, and the process repeats. The result is a blended family or stepfamily, with stepparents, stepchildren, and sometimes step-siblings. Blended families are the result of not only divorce but also death. When either partner dies, remarriage is not uncommon. According to the 1990 U.S. Census, 3.6 percent of grooms and 10 percent of brides had previously lost a spouse (Kreider & Ellis, 2011).

In fact, in his book, Cherlin estimates that more than a quarter of American children today experience at least two maternal partner changes, and more than 8 percent experience three or more. Some developmental psychologists worry about this dynamic, as it impacts children's ability to form trusting, stable ties with adult figures in their lives. Others see children as robust and more or less adaptable to most changes that come their way.

Gay and Lesbian Couples

Marriage, divorce, remarriage. Stepfamilies, blended families. Another family arrangement on the rise, as we saw at the beginning of the chapter, is same-sex couples. At present, same-sex marriages are legal in the Netherlands, Belgium, Spain, Norway, Sweden, Canada, Portugal, Iceland, Argentina, Mexico, and a growing number of U.S. states. Thousands of gay and lesbian couples have sworn their marriage vows in these states. As for gay parenting, research consistently finds that lesbian and gay parents are at least as successful as heterosexuals in producing well-adjusted, successful offspring (Stacey, 1997).

But homosexual unions continue to face fierce opposition. More than half of U.S. states have adopted constitutional amendments banning same-sex marriages. In 1996 President Clinton signed into federal law the Defense of Marriage Act (DOMA), which stipulated that federally recognized marriages had to be heterosexual and that states where gay marriage was illegal were not required to recognize same-sex marriages conducted in states where it was legal. But DOMA was struck down in 2013. Now same-sex couples with a legal marriage contract can move to whatever state they like without worrying about losing their marital rights. On the other hand, if they decide to get divorced, they might have to move back to a state where same-sex marriage is legal in order to split. A state that has declared same-sex marriage unconstitutional would be tacitly recognizing the sanctity of that union by allowing it to formally dissolve, or so some states' legal thinking goes.

An old joke goes, "Gays and lesbians getting married—haven't they suffered enough?" That is, if homosexual couples want to marry, why not just let them do it? Opponents of gay marriage—many of whom are strongly religious, "social values" conservatives—argue that nontraditional familial arrangements will wreak social havoc. Let gays get married, so the argument goes, and you effectively destroy the family. Once the family goes, look out—the next step is chaos, no moral order. Furthermore, opponents of gay marriage claim that the purpose of a family is to procreate and raise children into functioning adults, and this is determined by biology. Because gay marriage does not produce the biological children of both parents, such people believe that it is not functional, right, or natural.

According to the Pew Research Center, views are steadily shifting. In 1996, 64 percent of Americans were opposed to gay and lesbian marriage. By 2013, American views were teetering on the brink of majority support, with 50 percent in favor and 43 percent opposed (Pew Research Center, 2013b). Young people are the strongest supporters of same-sex marriage, with 7 in 10 of the millennial generation (born since 1980) supporting same-sex marriage, while the same percentage of people over 70 oppose same-sex marriage. Many demographers predict that as more young people hit voting age (and more of the older cohort dies), same-sex families will eventually be able to get legally married in whatever state they like (Pew Research Center, 2013b; Lifeway Research, 2013).

Multiracial Families

Miscegenation the technical term for interracial marriage, literally meaning "a mixing of kinds"; because the term is politically and historically charged, sociologists generally prefer *exogamy* or *outmarriage*.

Gays have not been the only ones who have faced obstacles to legal marriage. The technical term for interracial marriage is miscegenation, which literally means "a mixing of kinds." This term, however, is politically and historically charged and, as such, should be used with a degree of caution. Sociologists and other social scientists generally prefer the term *exogamy* or *outmarriage*.

Considering the history of race relations in the United States (see Chapter 9), it is not surprising that the idea (and even legality) of interracial marriages and families has been cause for controversy. Although interracial marriage was never illegal at the federal level, from 1913 to 1948, 30 states enforced anti-miscegenation laws. Many of these laws lasted until 1967, when the Supreme Court finally declared them unconstitutional, reversing the restrictions in 16 remaining states.

We have undoubtedly come a long way since 1967. One year after the Supreme Court ruling (1968), a Gallup poll revealed that 80 percent of Americans were opposed to blacks and whites getting married. By 2009 that number had dropped to 17 percent (Wang, 2012). However, attitudes toward exogamy in the United States vary greatly by location, religion, and a host of other factors. And, of course, such polls capture only expressed attitudes, subject to social desirability bias, not actual behavior (i.e., actual intermarriage rates).

In 2010, 15 percent of new marriages were between people of different races or ethnic groups. Asian Americans had the highest rate of outmarriage at 28 percent, followed by 26 percent of Latinos, 17 percent of blacks, and 9 percent of whites (Wang, 2012). These percentages significantly change when gender is taken into account. For example, 36 percent of Asian American women marry someone outside of their race, unlike Asian American men who have only a 17 percent rate of outmarriage. Black men have a 24 percent rate of outmarriage versus black women's rate of 9 percent.

American families are increasingly looking like the family of Robert De Niro and Grace Hightower, pictured above. How are attitudes about multiracial families changing?

Expanding Marriage

When the poet Elizabeth Barrett Browning wrote, "How do I love thee? Let me count the ways," little did she know that a century and a half later the list would extend into the hundreds—at least for married couples. As of 2004, the U.S. General Accounting Office had identified more than 1,000 legal rights and responsibilities attendant to marriage (Shah, 2004). The era of big government is clearly not over when it comes to family policy.

These rights and responsibilities range from the continuation of water rights upon the death of a spouse to the ability to take funeral leave. And that's just the federal government. States and localities have their own marriage provisions. New York State, for example, grants a spouse the right to inherit a military veteran's peddler's license. And Hawaii extends to spouses of state residents lower fees for hunting licenses. No wonder gay and lesbian

Jeanne Fong (left) and Jennifer Lin, a same-sex couple from San Francisco, celebrate during a marriage equality rally in Washington, D.C.

activists put such a premium on access to marriage rights. Some gay marriage advocates want all spousal rights immediately and will settle for nothing less. Others take an incremental approach, aiming to secure first the most significant domestic partner rights, such as employer benefits like health care.

But with all the divorces and blended families, it's unclear if our current legal system is best suited to the task of serving families' needs. Perhaps it is time to consider if we'd be better off by breaking down or unbundling the marriage contract into its constituent parts. Then, applying free-market principles, we could allow each citizen to assign the various rights and responsibilities now connected to marriage as he or she sees fit. In addition to employer benefits, some of the key marital rights include the ability to pass property and income back and forth tax-free, spousal privilege (that is, the right not to testify against one's husband or wife), medical decision-making power, and the right to confer permanent residency to a foreigner, just to name a few. The mutual responsibilities of marriage include parenthood—a husband is the legal father of any child born to his wife regardless of biological paternity—and shared tort liability. Why not allow people to parcel out each of these marital privileges?

Take my own marriage as a case in point: My ex-wife is a foreigner who applied for citizenship, and her marriage to me made that possible. Marrying a foreigner is pretty common—7 percent of married couples in the United States are made up of a U.S.-born spouse and a foreign-born spouse (U.S. Census Bureau, 2013c). As the law now stands, I, as a straight American man, theoretically could become a green card machine. As long as I can convince the overstretched Department of Homeland Security that my penchant for falling in love with foreign women is genuine, I can divorce and remarry as many times as I like, obtaining permanent residency for each of my failed loves along the way. Is this fair to the many Americans who can't sponsor aging grandparents or, in some cases, even parents? Or is it fair even to straight Americans who are happy marrying other Americans and don't want to see the country fill up with my romantic baggage?

Instead, why not give all Americans the right to sponsor one person in their lifetime—a right that they could sell, if they so desire? This would mean that if I wanted to marry a Kenyan after divorcing an Australian, I could, but I would need to purchase, perhaps on eBay, the right to confer citizenship from someone else who didn't need it. Similarly, why not let all Americans name one person (other than their lawyer, priest, or therapist) who can't be forced to testify against them in court? This zone of privacy could be transferred over the course of a lifetime, perhaps limiting such changes to once every five years.

While we are at it, how about allowing each of us to choose someone with whom we share our property, with all the tax (and liability) implications that choice would imply? We might even allow parenthood to become contractual and in multiples greater than two by letting people name individuals they want to be the co-parents to their biological children, even if that means a kid ends up with three or four parents, none of whom are married to each other. This would help grandparents, for instance, have the legal right to act on behalf of the grandchildren in their care.

We could go down the long list of rights and responsibilities embedded in the marriage contract. Ideally, most people would choose one person in whom to vest all these rights, but everyone would have the freedom to decide how to configure these domestic, business, legal, and intimate relationships in the eyes of the law.

Other people have proposed changing marriage by making it more flexible. A prominent group of queer activists (see www.beyondmarriage.org) continues to argue that the law should recognize a variety of households—from conjugal couples to groups of elderly people living collectively—as "legal families." But they have not specified the rights that should go along with such arrangements or addressed the problems and paradoxes that might arise if legal rights and responsibilities were extended to groups of more than two. Unbundling marital rights would achieve the same end without creating new inequities based on group size.

It might also take some of the vitriol out of the marriage debate. Marriage itself could stay in church (or in Las Vegas, as the case may be). And each couple could count their own ways to love.

→ CONCLUSION

By now you should be wary of any social institution that is hailed supreme because it is "more natural." You should be skeptical of any family arrangement that is deemed more functional than another, and you should hold the traditional family at a critical distance, especially considering the experiences of women, African Americans, gays and lesbians, the poor, the mainstream, and the marginalized.

Under the "postmodern family condition," as Judith Stacey calls it, clear rules no longer exist in our complex, diversified, and sometimes messy postindustrial society (1996). Gone are the ruling days of the normative Nelsons. Families today take on many shapes and sizes that best fit their members' needs, and they are defined not by blood ties but by the quality of relationships. Let us count the ways. . . .

PRACTICE

SOCIOLOGY ON THE STREET

It seems like everyone has an opinion on whether women with children—especially young children—should be in the workforce. Why is the conversation over "having it all" still mainly about mothers? Watch the Sociology on the Street video to find out more: wwnpag.es/SOSC10.

QUESTIONS FOR REVIEW

1. The case of Ozzie and Harry at the beginning of the chapter brings to mind the variety of family arrangements. Describe the "nuclear family" and three other family forms. Does sociological research suggest that one such arrangement is necessarily the right one?

2. Think about the discussion regarding rights for same-sex couples. How do the functionalist arguments by Bronislaw Malinowski (1913) and Talcott Parsons (1951) help explain the changes (or lack thereof) in the institution of marriage?

3. How do historical cultural ideals relate to current rates of marriage and divorce in the United States? Name one reason that the likelihood of being currently married might be lower among those with low incomes.

4. Sometimes what's considered "normal" is far from what's most prevalent currently or historically. How does this statement relate to perceptions about the "traditional" family?

5. Describe how a gendered division of labor arose after the Industrial Revolution. How was this change tied to kinship networks?

6. What is the cult of domesticity? How has it changed over the last century?

7. What is the second shift, and how does it relate to a leisure gap between husbands and wives?

8. Are mothers on welfare lazy? Use the findings by Kathryn Edin and Laura Lein (1997) to help answer this question.

9. What is a pecking order, and what does the term mean for children in a family? According to this concept, does your birth position in the family or number of siblings matter to your life chances for success in school and beyond?

PARADOX

WE THINK OF THE FAMILY AS A HAVEN IN A HARSH WORLD BUT IN FACT, INEQUALITY BEGINS AT HOME.

WATCH THE ANIMATED SHORT ABOUT THE FAMILY PARADOX AT

WWNPAG.ES/PXC10

1950s FAMILY

DISADVANTAGED FAMILY

YOUNGEST

ELDEST

MIDDLE-BORNS

ADVANTAGED FAMILY

GLOSSARY

A

Achieved status a status into which one enters; voluntary status.

Altruistic suicide suicide that occurs when one experiences too much social integration.

Anomic suicide suicide that occurs as a result of insufficient social regulation.

Anomie a sense of aimlessness or despair that arises when we can no longer reasonably expect life to be predictable; too little social regulation; normlessness.

Ascribed status a status into which one is born; involuntary status.

Association *see* correlation.

B

Biological determinism a line of thought that explains social behavior in terms of who you are in the natural world.

Bourgeois society a society of commerce (modern capitalist society, for example) in which the maximization of profit is the primary business incentive.

Bourgeoisie the capitalist class.

Broken windows theory of deviance theory explaining how social context and social cues impact whether individuals act deviantly; specifically, whether local, informal social norms allow deviant acts.

C

Case study an intensive investigation of one particular unit of analysis in order to describe it or uncover its mechanisms.

Caste system a religion-based system of stratification characterized by no social mobility.

Causality the notion that a change in one factor results in a corresponding change in another.

Class system an economically based hierarchical system characterized by cohesive, oppositional groups and somewhat loose social mobility.

Cohabitation living together in an intimate relationship without formal legal or religious sanctioning.

Collective resistance an organized effort to change a power hierarchy on the part of a less-powerful group in a society.

Comparative research a methodology by which two or more entities (such as countries), which are similar in many dimensions but differ on one in question, are compared to learn about the dimension that differs between them.

Conflict theory the idea that conflict between competing interests is the basic, animating force of social change and society in general.

Conformist individual who accepts both the goals and strategies to achieve them that are considered socially acceptable.

Consumerism the steady acquisition of material possessions, often with the belief that happiness and fulfillment can thus be achieved.

Content analysis a systematic analysis of the content rather than the structure of a communication, such as a written work, speech, or film.

Contradictory class locations the idea that people can occupy locations in the class structure that fall between the two "pure" classes.

Corporate crime a particular type of white-collar crime committed by the officers (CEOs and other executives) of a corporation.

Correlation or **association** simultaneous variation in two variables.

Crime the violation of laws enacted by society.

Cult of domesticity the notion that true womanhood centers on domestic responsibility and child rearing.

Cultural relativism taking into account the differences across cultures without passing judgment or assigning value.

Cultural scripts modes of behavior and understanding that are not universal or natural.

Culture a set of beliefs, traditions, and practices; the sum of the social categories and concepts we embrace in addition to beliefs, behaviors (except instinctual ones), and practices; everything but the natural environment around us.

Culture jamming the act of turning media against themselves.

D

Deductive approach a research approach that starts with a theory, forms a hypothesis, makes empirical observations, and then analyzes the data to confirm, reject, or modify the original theory.

Dependent variable the outcome that the researcher is trying to explain.

Deterrence theory philosophy of criminal justice arising from the notion that crime results from a rational calculation of its costs and benefits.

Dialectic a two-directional relationship following a pattern in which an original statement or thesis is countered with an antithesis, leading to a conclusion that unites the strengths of the original position and the counterarguments.

Discrimination harmful or negative acts (not mere thoughts) against people deemed inferior on the basis of their racial category, without regard to their individual merit.

Divide et impera the role of a member of a triad who intentionally drives a wedge between the other two actors in the group.

Double consciousness a concept conceived by W. E. B. Du Bois to describe the two behavioral scripts, one for moving through the world and the other incorporating the external opinions of prejudiced onlookers, which are constantly maintained by African Americans.

Dramaturgical theory the view (advanced by Erving Goffman) of social life as essentially a theatrical performance, in which we are all actors on metaphorical stages, with roles, scripts, costumes, and sets.

Dyad a group of two.

E

Egoistic suicide suicide that occurs when one is not well integrated into a social group.

Elite–mass dichotomy system a system of stratification that has a governing elite, a few leaders who broadly hold power in society.

Embeddedness the degree to which ties are reinforced through indirect paths within a social network.

Endogamy marriage to someone within one's social group.

Equality of condition the idea that everyone should have an equal starting point.

Equality of opportunity the idea that everyone has an equal chance to achieve wealth, social prestige, and power because the rules of the game, so to speak, are the same for everyone.

Equality of outcome the idea that each player must end up with the same amount regardless of the fairness of the "game."

Essentialism a line of thought that explains social phenomena in terms of natural ones.

Estate system a politically based system of stratification characterized by limited social mobility.

Ethnicity one's ethnic quality or affiliation. It is voluntary, self-defined, nonhierarchal, fluid and multiple, and based on cultural differences, not physical ones per se.

Ethnocentrism the belief that one's own culture or group is superior to others, and the tendency to view all other cultures from the perspective of one's own.

Ethnomethodology literally "the methods of the people"; this approach to studying human interaction focuses on the ways in which we make sense of our world, convey this understanding to others, and produce a shared social order.

Eugenics literally meaning "well born;" a pseudoscience that postulates that controlling the fertility of populations could influence inheritable traits passed on from generation to generation.

Exchange mobility mobility in which, if we hold fixed the changing distribution of jobs, individuals trade jobs not one-to-one but in a way that ultimately balances out.

Exogamy marriage to someone outside one's social group.

Experimental methods methods that seek to alter the social landscape in a very specific way for a given sample of individuals and then track what results that change yields; often involve comparisons to a control group that did not experience such an intervention.

Extended family kin networks that extend outside or beyond the nuclear family.

F

Face the esteem in which an individual is held by others.

Fatalistic suicide suicide that occurs as a result of too much social regulation.

Feminism a consciousness-raising movement to get people to understand that gender is an organizing principle of life. The underlying belief is that women and men should be accorded equal opportunities and respect.

Feminist methodology a set of systems or methods that treat women's experiences as legitimate empirical and theoretical resources, that promote social science *for* women (think public sociology, but for a specific half of the public), and that take into account the researcher as much as the overt subject matter.

Formal social sanctions mechanisms of social control by which rules or laws prohibit deviant criminal behavior.

Free rider problem the notion that when more than one person is responsible for getting something done, the incentive is for each individual to shirk responsibility and hope others will pull the extra weight.

Functionalism the theory that various social institutions and processes in society exist to serve some important (or necessary) function to keep society running.

G

Gender a social position; the set of social arrangements that are built around normative sex categories.

Gender roles sets of behavioral norms assumed to accompany one's status as male or female.

Generalizability the extent to which we can claim our findings inform us about a group larger than the one we studied.

Generalized other an internalized sense of the total expectations of others in a variety of settings—regardless of whether we've encountered those people or places before.

Genocide the mass killing of a group of people based on racial, ethnic, or religious traits.

Glass ceiling an invisible limit on women's climb up the occupational ladder.

Glass escalator the accelerated promotion of men to the top of a work organization, especially in feminized jobs.

H

Hegemonic masculinity the condition in which men are dominant and privileged, and this dominance and privilege is invisible.

Hegemony a condition by which a dominant group uses its power to elicit the voluntary "consent" of the masses.

Historical methods research that collects data from written reports, newspaper articles, journals, transcripts, television programs, diaries, artwork, and other artifacts that date back to the period under study.

Homosexual the social identity of a person who has sexual attraction to and/or relations with other persons of the same sex.

Hypothesis a proposed relationship between two variables.

I

I one's sense of agency, action, or power.

Ideology a system of concepts and relationships, an understanding of cause and effect.

Income money received by a person for work, from transfers (gifts, inheritances, or government assistance), or from returns on investments.

Independent variable a measured factor that the researcher believes has a causal impact on the dependent variable.

Inductive approach a research approach that starts with empirical observations and then works to form a theory.

Informal social sanctions the usually unexpressed but widely known rules of group membership; the unspoken rules of social life.

In-group another term for the powerful group, most often the majority.

Innovator social deviant who accepts socially acceptable goals but rejects socially acceptable means to achieve them.

Institutional racism institutions and social dynamics that may seem race-neutral but actually disadvantage minority groups.

Isomorphism a constraining process that forces one unit in a population to resemble other units that face the same set of environmental conditions.

K

Kinship networks strings of relationships between people related by blood and co-residence (that is, marriage).

L

Labeling theory the belief that individuals subconsciously notice how others see or label them, and their reactions to those labels over time form the basis of their self-identity.

Large group a group characterized by the presence of a formal structure that mediates interaction and, consequently, status differentiation.

M

Macrosociology a branch of sociology generally concerned with social dynamics at a higher level of analysis—that is, across the breadth of a society.

Master status one status within a set that stands out or overrides all others.

Material culture everything that is a part of our constructed, physical environment, including technology.

Me the self as perceived as an object by the "I"; the self as one imagines others perceive one.

Mechanical or **segmental solidarity** social cohesion based on sameness.

Media any formats, platforms, or vehicles that carry, present, or communicate information.

Mediator the member of a triad who attempts to resolve conflict between the two other actors in the group.

Meritocracy a society where status and mobility are based on individual attributes, ability, and achievement; a society that assigns social status, power, and economic rewards on achievement, not ascribed, personal attributes or favoritism.

Microsociology a branch of sociology that seeks to understand local interactional contexts; its methods of choice are ethnographic, generally including participant observation and in-depth interviews.

Middle class a term commonly used to describe those individuals with nonmanual jobs that pay significantly more than the poverty line—though this is a highly debated and expansive category, particularly in the United States, where broad swathes of the population consider themselves middle class.

Midrange theory a theory that attempts to predict how certain social institutions tend to function.

Miscegenation the technical term for multiracial marriage; literally meaning "a mixing of kinds"; because the term is politically and historically charged, sociologists generally prefer *exogamy* or *outmarriage*.

Monogamy the practice of having only one sexual partner or spouse at a time.

N

Narrative the sum of stories contained in a set of ties.

Nativism the movement to protect and preserve indigenous land or culture from the allegedly dangerous and polluting effects of new immigrants.

Nonmaterial culture values, beliefs, behaviors, and social norms.

Norms how values tell us to behave.

Nuclear family familial form consisting of a father, a mother, and their children.

O

One-drop rule the belief that "one drop" of black blood makes a person black, a concept that evolved from U.S. laws forbidding miscegenation.

Ontological equality the philosophical and religious notion that all people are created equal at birth.

Operationalization the process of assigning a precise method for measuring a term being examined for use in a particular study.

Organic solidarity social cohesion based on difference and interdependence of the parts.

Organization any social network that is defined by a common purpose and has a boundary between its membership and the rest of the social world.

Organizational culture the shared beliefs and behaviors within a social group; often used interchangeably with *corporate culture*.

Organizational structure the ways in which power and authority are distributed within an organization.

Other someone or something outside of oneself.

Out-group another term for the stigmatized or less powerful group, the minority.

P

Panopticon a circular building composed of an inner ring and an outer ring designed to serve as a prison in which the guards, housed in the inner ring, can observe the prisoners without the detainees knowing whether they are being watched.

Participant observation a qualitative research method that seeks to uncover the meanings people give to their social actions by observing their behavior in practice.

Party a group that is similar to a small group but is multifocal.

Patriarchy a nearly universal system involving the subordination of femininity to masculinity.

Pluralism the presence and engaged coexistence of numerous distinct groups in one society.

Polyandry the practice of having multiple husbands simultaneously.

Polygamy the practice of having more than one sexual partner or spouse at a time.

Polygyny the practice of having multiple wives simultaneously.

Population an entire group of individual persons, objects, or items from which samples may be drawn.

Positivist sociology a strain within sociology that believes the social world can be described and predicted by certain describable relationships (akin to a social physics).

Postmodernism a condition characterized by a questioning of the notion of progress and history, the replacement of narrative within pastiche, and multiple, perhaps even conflicting, identities resulting from disjointed affiliations.

Prejudice thoughts and feelings about an ethnic or racial group.

Primary deviance the first act of rule-breaking that may incur a label of "deviant" and thus influence how people think about and act toward you.

Primary groups social groups, such as family or friends, composed of enduring, intimate face-to-face relationships that strongly influence the attitudes and ideals of those involved.

Primordialism Clifford Geertz's term to explain the strength of ethnic ties because they are fixed in deeply felt or primordial ties to one's homeland culture.

Proletariat the working class.

Q

Qualitative methods methods that attempt to collect information about the social world that cannot be readily converted to numeric form.

Quantitative methods methods that seek to obtain information about the social world that is already in or can be converted to numeric form.

R

Race a group of people who share a set of characteristics—typically, but not always, physical ones—and are said to share a common bloodline.

Racialization the formation of a new racial identity by drawing ideological boundaries of difference around a formerly unnoticed group of people.

Racism the belief that members of separate races possess different and unequal traits.

Rebel individual who rejects both traditional goals and traditional means and wants to alter or destroy the social institutions from which he or she is alienated.

Recidivism when an individual who has been involved with the criminal justice system reverts to criminal behavior.

Reference group a group that helps us understand or make sense of our position in society relative to other groups.

Reflection theory the idea that culture is a projection of social structures and relationships into the public sphere, a screen onto which the film of the underlying reality or social structures of a society is projected.

Reflexivity analyzing and critically considering our own role in, and effect on, our research.

Reliability the likelihood of obtaining consistent results using the same measure.

Research methods approaches that social scientists use for investigating the answers to questions.

Resocialization the process by which one's sense of social values, beliefs, and norms are reengineered, often deliberately, through an intense social process that may take place in a total institution.

Retreatist one who rejects both socially acceptable means and goals by completely retreating from, or not participating in, society.

Reverse causality a situation in which the researcher believes that A results in a change in B, but B, in fact, is causing A.

Ritualist individual who rejects socially defined goals but not the means.

Role the duties and behaviors expected of someone who holds a particular status.

Role conflict the tension caused by competing demands between two or more roles pertaining to different statuses.

Role strain the incompatibility among roles corresponding to a single status.

S

Sample the subset of the population from which you are actually collecting data.

Scientific racism nineteenth-century theories of race that characterize a period of feverish investigation into the origins, explanations, and classifications of race.

Second shift women's responsibility for housework and child care—everything from cooking dinner, to doing laundry, bathing children, reading bedtime stories, and sewing Halloween costumes.

Secondary deviance subsequent acts of rule-breaking that occur after primary deviance and as a result of your new deviant label and people's expectations of you.

Secondary groups groups marked by impersonal, instrumental relationships (those existing as a means to an end).

Segmental solidarity *see* mechanical solidarity.

Segregation the legal or social practice of separating people on the basis of their race or ethnicity.

Self the individual identity of a person as perceived by that same person.

Sex the biological differences that distinguish males from females.

Sex role theory Talcott Parsons's theory that men and women perform their sex roles as breadwinners and wives/mothers, respectively, because the nuclear family is the ideal arrangement in modern societies, fulfilling the function of reproducing workers.

Sexism occurs when a person's sex or gender is the basis for judgment, discrimination, and hatred against him or her.

Sexual harassment an illegal form of discrimination, involving everything from inappropriate jokes on the job to outright sexual assault to sexual "barter"—all intended to make women feel uncomfortable and unwelcome, particularly on the job.

Sexuality desire, sexual preference, and sexual identity and behavior.

Small group a group characterized by face-to-face interaction, a unifocal perspective, lack of formal arrangements or roles, and a certain level of equality.

Social capital the information, knowledge of people or things, and connections that help individuals enter, gain power in, or otherwise leverage social networks.

Social class or **socioeconomic status** an individual's position in a stratified social order.

Social cohesion social bonds; how well people relate to each other and get along on a day-to-day basis.

Social construction an entity that exists because people behave as if it exists and whose existence is perpetuated as people and social institutions act in accordance with the widely agreed-upon formal rules or informal norms of behavior associated with that entity.

Social control mechanisms that create normative compliance in individuals.

Social Darwinism the application of Darwinian ideas to society—namely, the evolutionary "survival of the fittest."

Social deviance any transgression of socially established norms.

Social equality a condition in which no differences in wealth, power, prestige, or status based on nonnatural conventions exist.

Social institution a complex group of interdependent positions that, together, perform a social role and

reproduce themselves over time; also defined in a narrow sense as any institution in a society that works to shape the behavior of the groups or people within it.

Social integration how well you are integrated into your social group or community.

Social mobility the movement between different positions within a system of social stratification in any given society.

Social network a set of relations—essentially, a set of dyads—held together by ties between individuals.

Social regulation the number of rules guiding your daily life and, more specifically, what you can reasonably expect from the world on a day-to-day basis.

Socialization the process by which individuals internalize the values, beliefs, and norms of a given society and learn to function as members of that society.

Socioeconomic status *see* social class.

Sociological imagination the ability to connect the most basic, intimate aspects of an individual's life to seemingly impersonal and remote historical forces.

Sociology the study of human society.

Status a recognizable social position that an individual occupies.

Status hierarchy system a system of stratification based on social prestige.

Status set all the statuses one holds simultaneously.

Status-attainment model approach that ranks individuals by socioeconomic status, including income and educational attainment, and seeks to specify the attributes characteristic of people who end up in more desirable occupations.

Stigma a negative social label that not only changes others' behavior toward a person but also alters that person's own self-concept and social identity.

Straight-line assimilation Robert Parks's 1920 universal and linear model for how immigrants assimilate: They first arrive, then settle in, and achieve full assimilation in a newly homogenous country.

Strain theory Robert Merton's theory that deviance occurs when a society does not give all of its members equal ability to achieve socially acceptable goals.

Street crime crime committed in public and often associated with violence, gangs, and poverty.

Strength of weak ties the notion that relatively weak ties often turn out to be quite valuable because they yield new information.

Structural functionalism theoretical tradition claiming that every society has certain structures (the family, the division of labor, or gender) that exist to fulfill some set of necessary functions (reproduction of the species, production of goods, etc.).

Structural hole a gap between network clusters, or even two individuals, if those individuals (or clusters) have complementary resources.

Structural mobility mobility that is inevitable from changes in the economy.

Subaltern a subordinate, oppressed group of people.

Subculture the distinct cultural values and behavioral patterns of a particular group in society; a group united by sets of concepts, values, symbols, and shared meaning specific to the members of that group distinctive enough to distinguish it from others within the same culture or society.

Survey an ordered series of questions intended to elicit information from respondents.

Symbolic ethnicity a nationality, not in the sense of carrying the rights and duties of citizenship but identifying with a past or future nationality. For later generations of white ethnics, something not constraining but easily expressed, with no risks of stigma and all the pleasures of feeling like an individual.

Symbolic interactionism a micro-level theory in which shared meanings, orientations, and assumptions form the basic motivations behind people's actions.

T

Tertius gaudens the member of a triad who benefits from conflict between the other two members of the group.

Tie the connection between two people in a relationship that varies in strength from one relationship to the next; a story that explains our relationship with another member of our network.

Total institution an institution in which one is totally immersed and that controls all the basics of day-to-day life; no barriers exist between the usual spheres of daily life, and all activity occurs in the same place and under the same single authority.

Triad a group of three.

U

Upper class a term for the economic elite.

V

Validity the extent to which an instrument measures what it is intended to measure.

Values moral beliefs.

Verstehen German for "understanding." The concept of *Verstehen* comes from Max Weber and is the basis of interpretive sociology in which researchers imagine themselves experiencing the life positions of the social actors they want to understand rather than treating those people as objects to be examined.

W

Wealth a family's or individual's net worth (that is, total assets minus total debts).

White-collar crime offense committed by a professional (or professionals) against a corporation, agency, or other institution.

BIBLIOGRAPHY

Acemoglu, D., et al. (2001, December). The colonial origins of comparative development: An empirical investigation. *The American Economic Review, 91*(5), 1369–1401.

Acierno, R., et al. (2010). Prevalence and correlates of emotional, physical, sexual, and financial abuse and potential neglect in the United States: The National Elder Mistreatment Study. *American Journal of Public Health, 100*(2), 292–297.

AFL-CIO. (2011). Trends in CEO pay. Retrieved from www.aflcio.org/Corporate-Watch/CEO-Pay-and-the-99/Trends-in-CEO-Pay

Allegretto, S. A. (2011, March 23). *State of working America's wealth.* Economic Policy Institute. Retrieved from www.epi.org/page/-/BriefingPaper292.pdf

Allen, F. A. (1981). *The decline of the rehabilitative ideal: Penal policy and social purpose.* New Haven: Yale University Press.

American Society for Aesthetic Plastic Surgery. (2011, April 4). Demand for plastic surgery rebounds by almost 9%. Retrieved from www.surgery.org/media/news-releases/demand-for-plastic-surgery-rebounds-by-almost-9%25

Anderson, E. (1999). *Code of the street: Decency, violence, and the moral life of the inner city.* New York: W. W. Norton.

Anderson, S., et al. (2010, September). *Executive excess 2010: CEO pay and the great recession.* Institute for Policy Studies. Retrieved from www.ips-dc.org/reports/executive_excess_2010

Ariès, P. (1965; orig. 1962). *Centuries of childhood: A social history of family life.* New York: Vintage.

Arnold, M. (1869). *Culture and anarchy.* London: Smith, Elder & Co.

Asch, S. E. (1956). Studies of independence and conformity: A minority of one against a unanimous majority. *Psychological Monographs, 70*(9, Whole No. 416).

Atlas, J. (2005, February 27). The battle behind the battle at Harvard. *The New York Times.* Retrieved from http://query.nytimes.com/gst/fullpage.html?res=950DE3D8143DF934A15751C0A9639C8B63&sec=&spon=

Attanasio, O., et al. (2013). The evolution of income, consumption, and leisure inequality in the US, 1980–2010. In C. Carroll et al. (Eds.), *Improving the measure of consumer expenditures.* Chicago: University of Chicago Press.

Babbie, E. R. (2007). *The practice of social research* (11th ed.). Belmont, CA: Wadsworth.

Bailey, M. J., & Dynarski, S. M. (2011). Inequality in postsecondary education. In G. J. Duncan & R. J. Murnane (Eds.), *Whither opportunity? Rising inequality, schools, and children's life chances,* (pp. 117–132). New York: Russell Sage Foundation.

Baldus, D. C., et al. (1998). Racial discrimination and the death penalty in the post-*Furman* era. *Cornell Law Review, 83*, 1638. Retrieved from www.lawschool.cornell.edu/research/cornell-law-review/upload/baldus.pdf

Barth, E. A. T., & Noel, D. L. (1972). Conceptual frameworks for the analysis of race relations: An evaluation. *Social Forces, 50*, 333–348.

Bearman, P. S., & Brückner, H. (2001). Promising the future: Virginity pledges and the transition to first intercourse. *American Journal of Sociology, 106*(4), 859–912.

Bearman, P. S., et al. (2004). Chains of affection: The structure of adolescent romantic and sexual networks. *American Journal of Sociology, 110*(1), 44–91.

Beauvoir, S. de. (1952). *The second sex.* New York: Knopf.

Becker, H. S. (1953, November). Becoming a marihuana user. *American Journal of Sociology, 59*, 235–243.

Becker, H. S. (1963). *Outsiders: Studies in the sociology of deviance.* New York: Free Press.

Belley, P., & Lochner, L. (2007, October). *The changing role of family income and ability in determining educational achievement* (NBER Working Paper No. 13527). Retrieved from www.nber.org/papers/w13527

Benedict, H. (2007, March 7). The private war of women soldiers. *Salon.com.* Retrieved from www.salon.com/news/feature/2007/03/07/women_in_military/print.html

Benedict, R. (1934). *Patterns of culture.* New York: Mentor Books.

Berbrier, M. (2000). The victim ideology of white supremacists and white separatists in the United States. *Sociological Focus, 33*, 175–191.

Berk, S. F. (1985). *The gender factory: The apportionment of work in American households.* New York: Plenum Press.

Bernard, J. S. (1972). *The future of marriage.* New York: World Publishers.

Berry, B. (1963). *Almost white.* New York: Macmillan.

Bianchi, S., & Robinson, J. (1997). What did you do today? Children's use of time, family composition, and the acquisition of social capital. *Journal of Marriage and the Family, 59*(2), 332–344.

Bittman, M., et al. (2003). When does gender trump money? Bargaining and time in household work. *American Journal of Sociology, 109,* 186–214.

Bixler, M. T. (1992). *Winds of freedom: The story of the Navajo Code Talkers of World War II.* Darien, CT: Two Bytes.

Blau, P. M., & Duncan, O. D., with collaboration of A. Tyree. (1967). *The American occupational structure.* New York: Wiley.

Blumer, H. (1969). *Symbolic interactionism: Perspective and method.* Englewood Cliffs, NJ: Prentice-Hall.

Blumstein, P. W., & Schwartz., P. (1983). *American couples: Money, work, and sex.* New York: Morrow.

Bobo, L. (1989). Keeping the linchpin in place: Testing the multiple sources of opposition to residential integration. *Revue Internationale de Psychologie Sociale, 2,* 306–323.

Bobo, L., et al. (1997). Laissez-faire racism: The crystallization of a kinder, gentler, antiblack ideology. In S. A. Tuch & J. K. Martin (Eds.), *Racial attitudes in the 1990s: Continuity and change* (pp. 15–42). Westport, CT: Praeger.

Bonczar, Thomas P. (2003). Prevalence of Imprisonment in the U.S. Population, 1974-2001. Bureau of Justice Statistics. Retrieved from http://www.bjs.gov/content/pub/pdf/piusp01.pdf

Bordo, S. (1990). Feminism, postmodernism, and gender skepticism. In L. J. Nicholson (Ed.), *Feminism/postmodernism* (pp. 133–156). New York: Routledge.

Bowen, W., et al. (2009). *Crossing the finish line: Completing college at America's public universities.* Princeton, NJ: Princeton University Press.

Bozorgmehr, M., et al. (1996). Middle Easterners: A new kind of immigrant. In R. Waldinger & M. Bozorgmehr (Eds.), *Ethnic Los Angeles* (pp. 347–378). New York: Russell Sage Foundation.

Brantley, A. (2012). *2011–12 National Faculty Salary Survey executive summary.* Knoxville, TN: College and University Professional Association for Human Resources. Retrieved from www.cupahr.org/surveys/files/salary2012/NFSS12ExecutiveSummary.pdf

Brookings Institution. (2010). 2010 Racial and ethnic distributions of 100 largest metropolitan and 2000–2010 change. Retrieved from www.brookings.edu/%7E/media/Files/rc/papers/2011/0831_census_race_frey/0831_census_race_appendixa.pdf

Brooks-Gunn, J., et al. (2003). Maternal employment and child cognitive outcomes in the first three years of life: The NICHD study of early child care. *Child Development, 73*(4), 1052–1072.

Brubaker, R. (1992). *Citizenship and nationhood in France and Germany.* Cambridge, MA: Harvard University Press.

Brückner, H., & Bearman, P. S. (2005). After the promise: The STD consequences of adolescent virginity pledges. *Journal of Adolescent Health, 36,* 271–278.

Bureau of Labor Statistics (BLS), U.S. Department of Labor. (2013a). Women in the labor force: A databook. BLS Report 1040, p. 57. Retrieved from www.bls.gov/cps/wlf-databook-2012.pdf

Bureau of Labor Statistics (BLS), U.S. Department of Labor. (2013b). Labor force statistics from the Current Population Survey. Retrieved from www.bls.gov/cps/cpsaat07.htm

Bureau of Labor Statistics (BLS), U.S. Department of Labor. (2013c). Employment characteristics of families, summary. Retrieved from www.bls.gov/news.release/famee.nr0.htm.

Bureau of Labor Statistics (BLS), U.S. Department of Labor. (2013d). Characteristics of minimum wage workers: 2012. Retrieved from www.bls.gov/cps/minwage2012.htm.

Bureau of Labor Statistics (BLS), U.S. Department of Labor. (2014a). Labor force statistics from the Current Population Survey. Retrieved from www.bls.gov/cps/cpsaat37.htm

Bureau of Labor Statistics (BLS), U.S. Department of Labor. (2014b). Labor force participation rate—women. Retrieved from http://research.stlouisfed.org/fred2/series/LNS11300002

Burt, R. (1992). *Structural holes.* Cambridge, MA: Harvard University Press.

Calhoun, C. (2002). *Dictionary of the social sciences.* New York: Oxford University Press.

Card, D., et al. (2008). Tipping and the dynamics of segregation. *Quarterly Journal of Economics, 123*(1), 177–218.

Carrington, C. (1999). *No place like home: Relationships and family life among lesbians and gay men.* Chicago: University of Chicago Press.

Centers for Disease Control and Prevention. (2010). Surveillance summaries: Youth risk behavior surveillance. Retrieved from www.cdc.gov/mmwr/pdf/ss/ss5905.pdf

Centers for Disease Control and Prevention. (2011a). National Survey of Family Growth. 2006–2010. Retrieved from www.cdc.gov/nchs/nsfg.htm

Centers for Disease Control and Prevention. (2011b). Key statistics from the National Survey of Family Growth, Table 1, fn 2. Retrieved from www.cdc.gov/nchs/nsfg/key_statistics/a.htm#adoption

Centers for Disease Control and Prevention. (2011c). National Intimate Partner and Sexual Violence Survey: 2010 summary report. National Center for Injury Prevention and Control, Division of Violence Prevention.

Centers for Disease Control and Prevention. (2011d). Understanding intimate partner violence: Fact sheet 2011. Retrieved from www.cdc.gov/violenceprevention/pdf/ipv_factsheet-a.pdf

Centers for Disease Control and Prevention. (2012a). *Health, United States, 2012*, Table 63, p. 205. Retrieved from www.cdc.gov/nchs/data/hus/hus12.pdf#063

Centers for Disease Control and Prevention. (2012b). Suicide: Facts at a glance. Retrieved from www.cdc.gov/violenceprevention/pdf/suicide-datasheet-a.PDF

Centers for Disease Control and Prevention. (2013a, April 4). First premarital cohabitation in the United States: 2006–2010 National Survey of Family Growth. *National Health Statistics Reports, 64*. Retrieved from www.cdc.gov/nchs/data/nhsr/nhsr064.pdf.

Centers for Disease Control and Prevention. (2013b). Births: Final data for 2011. *National Vital Statistics Reports, 62*(1). Retrieved from www.cdc.gov/nchs/data/nvsr/nvsr62/nvsr62_01.pdf

Chandra, A., et al. (2005, December). Fertility, family planning, and reproductive health of U.S. women: Data from the 2002 National Survey of Family Growth. Centers for Disease Control and Prevention, National Center for Health Statistics. Vital and Health Statistics series 23, no. 25. Retrieved from www.cdc.gov/nchs/data/series/sr_23/sr23_025.pdf

Chase-Lansdale, P. L., et al. (2003). Mothers' transitions from welfare to work and the well-being of preschoolers and adolescents. *Science, 299*(5612), 1548–1552.

Chauncey, G. (1994). *Gay New York: Gender, urban culture, and the makings of the gay male world, 1890–1940.* New York: Basic Books.

Chen, D. W. (2004, November 18). $7 billion for the grief of Sept. 11. *The New York Times.* Retrieved from www.nytimes.com/2004/11/18/ntregion/18fund.html

Cherlin, A. J. (2009). *The marriage-go-round: The state of marriage and the family in America today.* New York: Knopf.

Chodorow, N. (1978). *Reproduction of mothering: Psychoanalysis and the sociology of gender.* Berkeley: University of California Press.

Clark, G. (2014). *The son also rises: Surnames and the history of social mobility.* Princeton, NJ: Princeton University Press.

Cloward, R., & Ohlin, L. (1960). *Delinquency and opportunity.* New York: Free Press.

Colapinto, J. (2000). *As nature made him: The boy who was raised as a girl* (1st ed.). New York: HarperCollins.

Collier, J., et al. (1997). Is there a family? New anthropological views. In R. N. Lancaster & M. di Lionardo (Eds.), *The gender/sexuality reader: Culture, history, political economy* (pp. 71–81). New York: Routledge.

Collins, P. H. (1990). Work, family, and black women's oppression. In *Black feminist thought: Knowledge, consciousness and the politics of empowerment* (pp. 45–68). New York: Routledge.

Collins, R. (1979). *The credential society: A historical sociology of education and stratification.* New York: Academic Press.

Comisi, C. (2011). Landmark partnership between the Coalition of Immokalee Workers and Bon Appétit Management Company. *WhyHunger.* Retrieved from www.whyhunger.org/news-and-alerts/48-why-reporter/807-landmark-partnership-between-the-coalition-of-immokalee-workers-and-bon-appetit-management-company.html

Conley, D. (1999). *Being black, living in the red: Race, wealth, and social policy in America.* Berkeley: University of California Press.

Conley, D. (2004). *The pecking order: Which siblings succeed and why.* New York: Pantheon Books.

Conley, D. (2009a). Interview with Mitchell Duneier. New York, NY, October 8.

Conley, D. (2009b). Interview with Duncan Watts. New York, NY, October 8.

Conley, D. (2009c). Interview with C. J. Pascoe. 104th Annual Meeting of the American Sociological Association, San Francisco, CA, August 8.

Conley, D. (2009d). Interview with Paula England. 104th Annual Meeting of the American Sociological Association, San Francisco, CA, August 8.

Conley, D. (2009e). Interview with Victor Rios. 104th Annual Meeting of the American Sociological Association, San Francisco, CA, August 9.

Conley, D. (2009f). Interview with Devah Pager. New York, NY, October 8.

Conley, D. (2009g). Interview with Jeffrey Sachs. New York, NY, October 8.

Conley, D. (2009h). Interview with Michael Hout. 104th Annual Meeting of the American Sociological Association, San Francisco, CA, August 9.

Conley, D. (2009i). Interview with Jen'nan Read. 104th Annual Meeting of the American Sociological Association, San Francisco, CA, August 9.

Conley, D. (2009j). Interview with Jennifer Lee. 104th Annual Meeting of the American Sociological Association, San Francisco, CA, August 9.

Conley, D. (2009k). Interview with Andrew Cherlin. 104th Annual Meeting of the American Sociological Association, San Francisco, CA, August 8.

Conley, D. (2010). Interview with Kate Rich. E-mail interview, January.

Conley, D. (2011a). Interview with Allison Pugh. 106th Annual Meeting of the American Sociological Association, Las Vegas, NV, August 21.

Conley, D. (2011b). Interview with Annette Lareau. 106th Annual Meeting of the American Sociological Association, Las Vegas, NV, August 21.

Conley, D. (2013a). Interview with Julia Adams. 108th Annual Meeting of the American Sociological Association, New York, NY, August 12.

Conley, D. (2013b). Interview with Michael Gaddis. 108th Annual Meeting of the American Sociological Association, New York, NY, August 12.

Conley, D. (2013c). Interview with Ashley Mears. 108th Annual Meeting of the American Sociological Association, New York, NY, August 12.

Conley, D., & Heerwig, J. (2011). The war at home: Effects of Vietnam-era military service on postwar household stability. *American Economic Review, 101*(3), 350–354. doi:10.1257/aer.101.3.350

Connell, R. (1987). *Gender and power.* Stanford, CA: Stanford University Press.

Cookson, Jr., P. W., & Persell, C. H. (1985). *Preparing for power.* New York: Basic Books.

Cooley, C. H. (1909). *Social organization: A study of the larger mind.* New York: Scribner's.

Cooley, C. H. (1922; orig. 1902). *Human nature and the social order.* New York: Scribner's.

Coontz, S. (1992). *The way we never were: American families and the nostalgia trap.* New York: Basic Books.

Coontz, S. (Ed.). (2001). *Historical perspectives on family diversity. Shifting the center: Understanding contemporary families.* Mountain View, CA: Mayfield Publishing Company.

Coontz, S. (2010). How to make it work this time. *The New York Times,* Room for Debate section. Retrieved from www.nytimes.com /roomfordebate/2010/12/19/why-remarry/how -to-make-a-second-marriage-work

Corbett, S. (2007, March 18). The women's war. *The New York Times.* Retrieved from www .nytimes.com/2007/03/18/magazine/18cover .html?scp=1&sq=&st=cse

Cornell, S. (1988). *The return of the native: American Indian political resurgence.* New York: Oxford University Press.

Cornell, S., & Hartmann, D. (1998). Fixed or fluid? Alternative views of ethnicity and race. In *Ethnicity and race: Making identities in a changing world* (pp. 39–71). Thousand Oaks, CA: Pine Forge Press.

Covert, B. (2011, March 8). Prepare for a possible "womancession." *National Public Radio.* Retrieved from www.npr.org/2011/03/08/134357162/the -nation-prepare-for-a-possible-womancession

Cowan, R. S. (1983). *More work for mother: The ironies of household technology from the open hearth to the microwave.* New York: Basic Books.

Currie, D. H. (1999). *Girl talk: Adolescent magazines and their readers.* Toronto: University of Toronto Press.

Davis, F. J. (1991). *Who is black? One nation's definition.* University Park: Pennsylvania State University Press.

Davis, G. F. (2003). American cronyism. *Contexts, 2*(3).

Davis, K. (1940). Extreme social isolation of a child. *American Journal of Sociology, 45,* 554–565.

Davis, K., & Moore, W. E. (1944). Some principles of stratification. *American Sociological Review, 10*(2), 242–249.

Davis, L. (2011). Race, gender, and class at a crossroads: A survey of their intersection in employment, economics, and the law. *Journal of Gender, Race & Justice.*

Death Penalty Information Center. (2013). Facts about the death penalty. Retrieved from www .deathpenaltyinfo.org/documents/FactSheet.pdf

De Baca, L. C. (2011, May 23). Labor trafficking in troubled economic times: Protecting American jobs and migrant human rights. Office to Monitor and Combat Trafficking in Persons Statement before the Commission on Security and Cooperation in Europe (U.S. Helsinki Commission), Washington, DC. Retrieved from www.state.gov/g /tip/rls/rm/2011/164657.htm

DeNeve, C. (1997, Winter). Hispanic presence in the workplace. *The Diversity Factor,* 14–21.

Denizet-Lewis, B. (2004, May 30). Friends, friends with benefits, and the benefits of the local mall. *The New York Times Magazine.* Retrieved from www .nytimes.com/2004/05/30/magazine /30NONDATING.html?ex=1216353600&en=68ca 79c485d7e207&ei=5070

DeParle, J. (2004). *American dream: Three women, ten kids and a nation's drive to end welfare*. New York: Viking.

De Vos, G., & Wagatsuma, H. (1966). *Japan's invisible race: Caste in culture and personality*. Berkeley: University of California Press.

DiMaggio, P. J. & Powell, W. (1983). The iron cage revisited: Institutional isomorphism and collective rationality in organizational fields. *American Sociological Review, 48*, 149.

Dinnerstein, L., et al. (1996). *Native and strangers: A multicultural history of Americans*. New York: Oxford University Press.

Domhoff, G. W. (2010). Wealth, income, and power. *Who rules America?* Retrieved from www2.ucsc.edu /whorulesamerica/power/wealth.html

Dove. (2006). *Real women have real curves*. Retrieved from www.campaignforrealbeauty.com/flat3.asp?id= 2287&src=InsideCampaign_firming

Du Bois, W. E. B. (1903). *The souls of black folk*. Paris: A.C. McClurg & Co.

Duncan, G. J., et al. (2005). Peer effects in drug use and sex among college students. *Journal of Abnormal Child Psychology, 33*(3), 375–385. Retrieved from www.gse .uci.edu/person/duncan_g/docs/11peerdrugs.pdf

Durkheim, É. (1951; orig. 1897). *Suicide: A study in sociology* (G. Simpson & J. A. Spaulding, Trans.). New York: Free Press.

Durkheim, É. (1972; orig. 1893). The forced division of labor. In A. Giddens (Ed.), *Selected writings* (p. 181). Cambridge: Cambridge University Press.

Durkheim, É. (1995; orig. 1917). *The elementary forms of religious life* (K. E. Fields, Trans. and Intro.). New York: Free Press.

Durkheim, É. (1997; orig. 1893). *The division of labor in society* (L. A. Coser, Intro.; W. D. Halls, Trans.). New York: Free Press.

Duvall, M. L. (1991). *Feeding the family: The social organization of caring as gendered work*. Chicago: University of Chicago Press.

Dyer, G. (1985). *War*. New York: Crown.

Easterly, W., & Levine, R. (2002). *Tropics, germs, and crops: How endowments influence economic development* (NBER Working Paper No. W9106).

Edgerton, R. (1995). "Bowling alone": An interview with Robert Putnam about America's collapsing civic life. *American Association for Higher Education Bulletin, 48*(1).

Edin, K., & Lein, L. (1997). *Making ends meet: How single mothers survive welfare and low-wage work*. New York: Russell Sage Foundation.

Ehrenreich, B. (2001). *Nickel and dimed: On (not) getting by in America*. New York: Metropolitan Books.

Ehrenreich, B., & Hochschild, A. R. (Eds.). (2004). *Global woman: Nannies, maids and sex workers in the global economy*. New York: Macmillan Holt.

Eisenberg, D., et al. (2013, November). Peer effects on risky behaviors: New evidence from college roommate assignments. *Journal of Health Economics, 33*, 126–138. doi:10.1016/j.jhealeco.2013.11.006

Enloe, C. H. (2000). *Maneuvers: The international politics of militarizing women's lives*. Berkeley: University of California Press.

Epstein, C. F. (1988). *Deceptive distinctions: Sex, gender, and the social order*. New Haven: Yale University Press.

Eriksen, S., & Jensen, V. (2006). All in the family? Family environment factors in sibling violence. *Journal of Family Violence, 21*(8), 497–507.

Erikson, K. (2005; orig. 1966). *Wayward puritans: A study in the sociology of deviance* (Rev. ed.). Boston: Pearson/ Allyn & Bacon.

Essman, E. (2007). The American people: Social classes. *Life in the USA: The complete guide for immigrants and Americans*. Retrieved from www.lifeintheusa.com

Estabrook, B. (2009, March). Politics of the plate: The price of tomatoes. *Gourmet*. Retrieved from www .gourmet.com/magazine/2000s/2009/03/politics -of-the-plate-the-price-of-tomatoes

Eyerman, R. (2001). *Cultural trauma: Slavery and the formation of African American identity*. Cambridge: Cambridge University Press.

Fagan, J., et al. (2003, March 31). Reciprocal effects of crime and incarceration in New York City neighborhoods. *Fordham Urban Law Journal, 30*, 1551–1602. doi:10.2139/ssrn.392120

Fausto-Sterling, A. (2000). *Sexing the body: Gender politics and the construction of sexuality* (1st ed.). New York: Basic Books.

Federal Bureau of Investigation. (2003). *Facts and figures 2003*. Retrieved from www.fbi.gov/libref /factsfigure/wcc.htm

Federal Bureau of Investigation (2013). Uniform crime report: Crime in the United States, 2012. Retrieved from www.fbi.gov/about-us/cjis/ucr/crime -in-the-u.s/2012/crime-in-the-u.s.-2012/tables /1tabledatadecoverviewpdf/table_1_crime_in_the _united_states_by_volume_and_rate_per_100000 _inhabitants_1993-2012.xls

Ferber, A. L. (1999). *White man falling: Race, gender, and white supremacy*. Lanham, MD: Rowman & Littlefield.

Figlio, D. N. (2007, September). Boys named Sue: Disruptive children and their peers. *Education Finance and Policy, 2*(4), 376–394.

Fink, S., et al. (2006). Mammalian monogamy is not controlled by a single gene. *Proceedings of the National Academy of Sciences of the United States of America, 103*(20), 10956–10960. Retrieved from www.pnas.org/content/103/29/10956

Fischer, P. M., et al. (1991, December). Brand logo recognition by children aged 3 to 6 years: Mickey Mouse and old Joe the Camel. *Journal of the American Medical Association, 266*, 3145–3148.

Fortin, J. (2013, January 26). Women in combat: Now it's official, but they were already fighting. *International Business Times.* Retrieved from www.ibtimes.com/women-combat-now-its-official-they-were-already-fighting-1040702

Foss, R. J. (1994). The demise of homosexual exclusion: New possibilities for gay and lesbian immigration. *Harvard Civil Rights–Civil Liberties Law Review, 29,* 439–475.

Foster, D. (2006, February 19). Mind over splatter. *The New York Times.* Retrieved from www.nytimes.com/2006/02/19/opinion/19foster.html?scp=1&sq=february+19%2C+2006+foster&st=nyt

Foucault, M. (1977). *Discipline and punish: The birth of the prison.* New York: Pantheon Books.

Foucault, M. (1978). *The history of sexuality.* New York: Pantheon Books.

Foucault, M. (1980). *Power/knowledge: Selected interviews and other writings, 1972–1977* (C. Gordon, Ed.). New York: Pantheon Books.

Francis, D. R. (2005, November). Changing work behavior of married women. *NBER Digest.* Retrieved from www.nber.org/digest/nov05/w11230.html

Franklin, J. H. (1980). *From slavery to freedom* (5th ed.). New York: Knopf.

Frederick, C. (2010). A crosswalk for using pre-2000 occupational status and prestige codes with post-2000 occupation codes. Center for Demography and Ecology, University of Wisconsin-Madison. Data files retrieved from www.ssc.wisc.edu/cde/cdewp/OccCodes.zip

Fredrickson, G. M. (2002). *Racism: A short history.* Princeton, NJ: Princeton University Press.

Friedan, B. (1997; orig. 1963). *The feminine mystique.* New York: W. W. Norton.

Fry, R., & Cohn, D. (2011). Living together: The economics of cohabitation. Pew Research Center. Retrieved from http://pewresearch.org/pubs/2034/cohabitation-rate-doubled-since-mid-90s-only-more-educated-benefit-economically

Fryer, Jr., R. G. (2010, August 10). *Racial inequality in the 21st century: The declining significance of discrimination* (NBER Working Paper No. 16256). Retrieved from www.nber.org/papers/w16256

Gans, H. (1979a). *Deciding what's news: A study of CBS Evening News, NBC Nightly News, Newsweek and Time.* New York: Vintage.

Gans, H. (1979b). Symbolic ethnicity: The future of ethnic groups and cultures in America. *Ethnic and Racial Studies, 2,* 1–19.

Garfinkel, H. (1967). *Studies in ethnomethodology.* Englewood Cliffs, NJ: Prentice-Hall.

Garrett, J. T. (1994). Health. In M. B. Davis (Ed.), *Native Americans in the 20th century* (pp. 233–237). New York: Garland.

Gates, G., & Newport, F. (2012). Special report: 3.4% of US adults identify as LGBT. Gallup poll. Retrieved from www.gallup.com/poll/158066/special-report-adults-identify-lgbt.aspx

Geertz, C. (1973). *The interpretation of cultures.* New York: Basic Books.

Gerson, K. (1985). *Hard choices: How women decide about work, career, and motherhood.* Berkeley: University of California Press.

Gerson, K. (1993). *No man's land: Men's changing commitments to family and work.* New York: Basic Books.

Gilbert, D. (1998). *The American class structure in an age of growing inequality.* Belmont, CA: Wadsworth.

Gilligan, C. (1982). *In a different voice: Psychological theory and women's development.* Cambridge, MA: Harvard University Press.

Glassner, B. (1999). *The culture of fear: Why Americans are afraid of the wrong things.* New York: Basic Books.

Glaze, L. E., & Parks E. (2012, November). Correctional populations in the United States, 2011. *Bureau of Justice Statistics Bulletin.* Retrieved from www.bjs.gov/content/pub/pdf/cpus11.pdf

Glazer, N., & Moynihan, D. P. (1963). *Beyond the melting pot: The Negroes, Puerto Ricans, Jews, Italians, and Irish of New York City.* Cambridge, MA: MIT Press.

Glenn, E. N. (1986). *Issei, Nisei, war bride: Three generations of Japanese American women in domestic service.* Philadelphia: Temple University Press.

Goffman, E. (1959). *The presentation of self in everyday life.* New York: Doubleday.

Goffman, E. (1961). *Asylums: Essays on the social situation of mental patients and other inmates.* New York: Doubleday Anchor.

Goffman, E. (1963). *Stigma: Notes on the management of spoiled identity.* Englewood Cliffs, NJ: Prentice-Hall.

Goodman, S. W. (2010, November). Naturalisation policies in Europe: Exploring patterns of inclusion and exclusion. Retrieved from http://eudo-citizenship.eu/docs/7-Naturalisation%20Policies%20in%20Europe.pdf

Gordon, M. M. (1964). *Assimilation in American life: The role of race, religion, and national origins*. New York: Oxford University Press.

Gould, J. (2010, January 3). Commander softens punishment for pregnancy. *Army Times*. Retrieved from www.armytimes.com/article/20100103 /NEWS/1030309/Commander-softens-punishment -pregnancy

Gourevitch, P. (1998). *We wish to inform you that tomorrow we will be killed with our families: Stories from Rwanda*. New York: Farrar, Straus & Giroux.

Gramsci, A. (1971). *Selections from the prison notebooks*. London: Lawrence and Wishart.

Granovetter, M. (1973). The strength of weak ties. *American Journal of Sociology, 78*, 1360–1380.

Granovetter, M. (1974). *Getting a job: A study of contacts and careers*. Chicago: University of Chicago Press.

Grant, M. (1936; orig. 1916). *The passing of the great race* (4th rev. ed.). New York: Charles Scribner's Sons. Retrieved from www.archive.org/stream/passingof greatra00granuoft/passingofgreatra00granuoft_djvu .txt

Gray, J. (1992). *Men are from Mars, women are from Venus: A practical guide for improving communication and getting what you want in your relationships*. New York: HarperCollins.

Gray, M. (2009). *Out in the country: Youth, media, and queer visibility in rural America*. New York: NYU Press.

Gray, N., & Nye, P. S. (2001). American Indian and Alaska Native substance abuse: Co-morbidity and cultural issues. *American Indian and Alaska Native Mental Health Research, 10*(2), 67–84. Retrieved from www.ucdenver.edu/academics/colleges /PublicHealth/research/centers/CAIANH/journal /Documents/Volume%2010/10(2)_Gray _Substance_Abuse_67-84.pdf

Greenhouse, S. (2013, July 27). Fighting back against wretched wages. *The New York Times*. Retrieved from www.nytimes.com/2013/07/28/sunday-review /fighting-back-against-wretched-wages.html

Greer, C. (2006, April). *Black ethnicity: Political attitudes, identity, and participation in New York City*. Institute for Social and Economic Research and Policy, Columbia University. Retrieved from www.iserp.columbia.edu /news/articles/black_ethnicity.html

Grosz, E. A. (1994). *Volatile bodies: Toward a corporeal feminism*. Bloomington: Indiana University Press.

Hacker, J. (2006). *The great risk shift: The assault on American jobs, families, health care and retirement and how you can fight back*. New York: Oxford University Press.

Haley, A. (1976). *Roots: The saga of an American family*. New York: Doubleday.

Han, J. (2006). *"We are Americans too": A comparative study of the effects of 9/11 on South Asian communities*. Cambridge, MA: Discrimination and National Security Initiative, Harvard University. Retrieved from www.pluralism.org/affiliates/kaur_sidhu /We_Are_Americans_Too.pdf

Haney López, I. F. (1995). White by law. In R. Delgado (Ed.), *Critical race theory: The cutting edge* (pp. 542–550). Philadelphia: Temple University Press.

Hannaford, I. (1996). *Race: The history of an idea in the West*. Washington, DC: The Woodrow Wilson Center Press.

Harding, S. (1987). *Feminism and methodology: Social science issues*. Bloomington: Indiana University Press.

Harris, A. R., et al. (2002). Murder and medicine: The lethality of criminal assault, 1960–1999. *Homicide Studies, 6, 128*.

Harris, D. R., & Sim, J. J. (2002, August). Who is multiracial? Assessing the complexity of lived race. *American Sociological Review, 67*(4), 614–627.

Hartmann, H. (1981). The unhappy marriage of Marxism and feminism. In L. Sargent (Ed.), *Women and revolution: A discussion of the unhappy marriage between Marxism and feminism* (pp. 1–43). Boston: South End Press.

Hawley, A. (1968). Human ecology. In D. Sills (Ed.), *International encyclopedia of the social sciences* (pp. 327–337). New York: Macmillan.

Hays, S. (2003). *Flat broke with children: Women in the age of welfare reform*. New York: Oxford University Press.

Hegewisch, A., et al. (2013). The gender wage gap: 2012. Institute for Women's Policy Research. Retrieved from www.iwpr.org/publications/pubs/the-gender -wage-gap-2012/

Heilbroner, R. L. (1999). *The worldly philosophers*. New York: Simon & Schuster.

Herbert, W. (2011, June 7). Virginity and promiscuity: Evidence for the very first time. *Association for Psychological Science*. Retrieved from www .psychologicalscience.org/index.php/news/full -frontal-psychology/virginity-and-promiscuity -evidence-for-the-very-first-time.html

Herdt, G. H. (1981). *Guardians of the flutes: Idioms of masculinity*. New York: McGraw-Hill.

Hernandez, D. J. (1993). Figure 2.2, Percentage of children aged 0–17 living in four types of families, 1790–1989. In D. J. Hernandez, *America's children: Resources from family, government, and the economy*. New York: Russell Sage Foundation.

Hernandez, D. J., et al. (2007, April). Children in immigrant families in the U.S. and 50 states: National origins, language, and early education. *Children in*

America's newcomer families. Child Trends and the Center for Social and Demographic Analysis, State University at Albany, SUNY 2007 Research Brief Series.

Herrnstein, R. J., & Murray, C. (1994). *The bell curve: Intelligence and class structure in American life*. New York: Free Press.

Hetherington, E. M., & Kelly, J. (2002). *For better or for worse: Divorce reconsidered*. New York: W. W. Norton.

Ho, M. K. (1987). *Family therapy with ethnic minorities*. Newbury Park, CA: Sage.

Ho, V. (2009, March 12). Native American death rates soar as most people are living longer. *Seattlepi.com*. Seattle, Washington. Retrieved from www.seattlepi.com/local/403196_tribes12.html

Hochschild, A. R. (1989). *The second shift: Working parents and the revolution at home*. New York: Viking.

Hochschild, A. R. (2003). *The commercialization of intimate life: Notes from home and work*. Berkeley: University of California Press.

hooks, b. (1984). Black women: Shaping feminist theory and feminism: A movement to end sexist oppression and the significance of the feminist movement. In *Feminist theory from margin to center* (pp. 1–17). Boston: South End Press.

Hout, M. (1983). *Mobility tables: Quantitative applications in the social sciences*. Beverly Hills, CA: Sage.

Howe, L. K. (1977). *Pink collar workers: Inside the world of women's work*. New York: Putnam.

Human Rights Watch. (2006). Building towers, cheating workers. Report. Retrieved from www.hrw.org/sites/default/files/reports/uae1106webwcover.pdf

Hurley, D. (2005, April 19). The divorce rate: It's not as high as you think. *The New York Times*. Retrieved from www.nytimes.com/2005/04/19/health/19divo.html?scp=1&sq=&st=cse

Hurtado, A. (1995). Variations, combinations, and evolutions: Latino families in the United States. In R. E. Zambrana (Ed.), *Understanding Latino families: Scholarship, policy, and practice* (pp. 40–61). Thousand Oaks, CA: Sage.

Hymowitz, K. S., et al. (2013). *Knot yet: The benefits and costs of delayed marriage in America*. Retrieved from http://nationalmarriageproject.org/wp-content/uploads/2013/04/KnotYet-FinalForWeb-041413.pdf

Intersex Society of North America (ISNA). (2006). *What's wrong with the way intersex has traditionally been treated?* Retrieved from www.isna.org/faq/concealment

Isaacs, H. (1975). *Idols of the tribe: Group identity and political change*. New York: Harper & Row.

Jackson, R. M. (1998). *Destined for equality*. Cambridge, MA: Harvard University Press.

Jacobs, J. (1961). *The death and life of great American cities*. New York: Random House.

Jacobson, M. F. (1998). Anglo-Saxons and others, 1840–1924. In *Whiteness of a different color: European immigrants and the alchemy of race* (pp. 39–90). Cambridge, MA: Harvard University Press.

Johnston, D. C. (2005, June 5). Richest are leaving even the rich far behind. *The New York Times*. Retrieved from www.-nytimes.com/2005/06/05/national/class/HYPER-FINAL.html?scp=1&sq=Richest%20are%20leaving%20even%20the%20rich%20far%20behind&st=cse

Kanter, R. M. (1977). *Men and women of the corporation*. New York: Basic Books.

Kaplan, E. A. (2003, October 3–9). Black like I thought I was: Race, DNA, and a man who knows too much. *L. A. Weekly*. Retrieved from www.alternet.org/story.html?StoryID=16917

Karen, D. (2002, July). Changes in access to higher education in the United States: 1980–1992. *Sociology of Education, 75*(3), 191–210.

Kelling, G. L., & Sousa, Jr., W. H. (2001). Do police matter? An analysis of the impact of New York City's police reforms. *Civic Report, 22*.

Kilbourne, J. (1979). *Killing us softly: Advertising's image of women* [Videorecording]. Belmont, MA: Cambridge Documentary Films.

Killewald, A. (2013, August). Return to *Being Black, Living in the Red*: A race gap in wealth that goes beyond social origins. *Demography, 50*(4), 1177–1195. Retrieved from http://link.springer.com/article/10.1007/s13524-012-0190-0

Kim, S. (2001). Hegemony and cultural resistance. In N. J. Smelser & P. B. Baltes (Eds.), *International encyclopedia of the social & behavioral sciences*. New York: Elsevier.

Kimmel, M. S. (1996). *Manhood in America: A cultural history*. New York: Free Press.

Kimmel, M. S. (2000). *The gendered society*. New York: Oxford University Press.

Kinsey, A. C. (1948). *Sexual behavior in the human male*. Philadelphia: Saunders.

Klein, M. (1949). *The psycho-analysis of children* (3rd ed.). London: Hogarth Press.

Klein, N. (2000). *No logo: Taking aim at the brand bullies*. New York: Picador.

Klinenberg, E. (2013). *Going solo: The extraordinary rise and surprising appeal of living alone*. New York: Penguin.

Knobel, D. T. (1986). *Paddy and the republic: Ethnicity and nationality in antebellum America.* Middletown, CT: Wesleyan University Press.

Kohn, M. L., & Schooler, C. (1983). *Work and personality: An inquiry into the impact of social stratification.* Norwood, NJ: Ablex.

Kraybill, D. B. (Ed.). (1993). *The Amish and the state.* Baltimore, MD: Johns Hopkins University Press.

Kraybill, D. B., & Nolt, S. (1995). *Amish enterprise: From plows to profits.* Baltimore, MD: Johns Hopkins University Press.

Kreider, R., & Ellis, R. (2011). Number, timing, and duration of marriages and divorces: 2009. Current population reports, U.S. Census Bureau. Retrieved from www.census.gov/prod/2011pubs/p70-125.pdf

Kremer, M., & Levy, D. (2008). Peer effects and alcohol use among college students. *Journal of Economic Perspectives, 22*(3), 189–206.

Krugman, P. (2005, September 16). Not the new deal. *The New York Times.* Retrieved from www.nytimes.com/2005/09/16/opinion/16krugman.html?scp=6&sq=Not%20the%20new%20deal%20krugman&st=cse

Kulick, D. (1998). *Travesti: Sex, gender, and culture among Brazilian transgendered prostitutes.* Chicago: University of Chicago Press.

Kuruvil, M. C. (2006, September 3). 9/11: Five years later. Typecasting Muslims as a race. *San Francisco Chronicle.* Retrieved from www.sfgate.com/cgi-bin/article.cgi?f=/c/a/2006/09/03/MNG4FKUMR71.DTL

Lamont, M. (1992). *Money, morals, and manners.* Chicago: University of Chicago Press.

Laqueur, T. (1990). *Making sex: Body and gender from the Greeks to Freud.* Cambridge, MA: Harvard University Press.

Lareau, A. (2002). Invisible inequality: Social class and child-rearing in black families and white families. *American Sociological Review, 67,* 747–776.

Lareau, A. (2003). *Unequal childhoods: Class, race, and family life.* Berkeley: University of California Press.

Lareau, A., et al. (2006, July). *Social class and children's time use* (working paper). University of Maryland Department of Sociology.

Lasch, C. (1977). *Haven in a heartless world: The family besieged.* New York: Basic Books.

Lasch, C. (1991). *The true and only heaven: Progress and its critics.* New York: W. W. Norton.

Lee, F. R. (2006, March 28). In Utah, Hollywood seems oversexed. *The New York Times.* Retrieved from http://query.nytimes.com/gst/fullpage.html?res=98 06E3D91430F93BA15750C0A9609C8B63&sec=&spon=&pagewanted=2

Lever, J. (1976). Sex differences in the games children play. *Social Problems, 23,* 478–487.

Lewis, C., et al. (1992). Sex stereotyping of infants: A re-examination. *Journal of Reproductive and Infant Psychology, 10,* 53–61.

Lieberson, S. (1961). A societal theory of race and ethnic relations. *American Sociological Review, 26,* 902–910.

Lieberson, S., & Mikelson, K. S. (1995). Distinctive African American names: An experimental, historical, and linguistic analysis of innovation. *American Sociological Review, 60,* 928–46.

Lifeway Research. (2013). Same-sex marriage is civil rights issue. Retrieved from www.lifeway.com/article/research-same-sex-marriage-civil-rights-issue-americans-say?cid=jdw-VOCUS

Livingston, G., & Cohn, D. (2010). Childlessness up among all women; down among women with advanced degrees. Pew Research Center, Social & Demographic Trends. Retrieved from www.pewsocialtrends.org/2010/06/25/childlessness-up-among-all-women-down-among-women-with-advanced-degrees/

Lorber, J. (1994). *Paradoxes of gender.* New Haven: Yale University Press.

Lui, M. (2004). Doubly divided: The racial wealth gap. In C. Collins et al. (Eds.), *The wealth inequality reader.* Cambridge, MA: Economic Affairs Bureau.

MacKinnon, C. (1983). Feminism, Marxism, method and the state: Toward feminist jurisprudence. *Signs: Journal of Women in Culture and Society, 8,* 635.

MacMaster, N. (2001). *Racism in Europe 1870–2000.* Basingstoke, Hampshire: Palgrave.

Malinowski, B. (1913). *The family among the Australian Aborigines.* London: University of London Press.

Maltz, M. D. (2001). *Recidivism.* Orlando, FL: Academic Press. (Original work published 1984.) Retrieved from www.uic.edu/depts/lib/forr/pdf/crimjust/recidivism.pdf

Maraniss, D. (1995). *First in his class: The biography of Bill Clinton.* New York: Simon & Schuster.

Martin, J. A., et al. (2010). Births: Final data for 2008. Centers for Disease Control and Prevention, National Center for Health Statistics. *National Vital Statistics Report, 59*(1). Retrieved from www.cdc.gov/nchs/data/nvsr/nvsr59/nvsr59_01.pdf

Martin, J., et al. (2013). Births: Final data for 2012. Centers for Disease Control and Prevention, National Center for Health Statistics. *National Vital Statistics Reports, 62*(1). Retrieved from www.cdc.gov/nchs/data/nvsr/nvsr62/nvsr62_09.pdf

Martineau, H. (1837). *Theory and practice of society in America.* London: Saunders & Otley.

Martineau, H. (1838). *How to observe morals and manners.* London: Charles Knight & Company.

Marx, A. W. (1998). To bind up the nation's wounds: The United States after the Civil War. In *Making race and nation: A comparison of South Africa, the United States, and Brazil* (pp. 120–157). Cambridge: Cambridge University Press.

Marx, K. (1999; orig. 1890–91). Critique of the Gotha programme. In *Marxists Internet archive.* Retrieved from www.marxists.org/archive/marx/works/1875/gotha/index.htm

Marx, K., & Engels, F. (1998; orig. 1848). *The communist manifesto.* New York: Penguin Group.

Massey, D. S. (1995). The new immigration and ethnicity in the United States. *Population and Development Review, 21,* 631–652.

Massey, D. S., & Denton, N. A. (1993). *American apartheid: Segregation and the making of the underclass.* Cambridge, MA: Harvard University Press.

Mathur, A., et al. (2013). The mysterious and alarming rise of single parenthood in America. *The Atlantic.* Retrieved from www.theatlantic.com/business/archive/2013/09/the-mysterious-and-alarming-rise-of-single-parenthood-in-america/279203/

McCloskey, D. (1999). *Crossing: A memoir.* Chicago: University of Chicago Press.

McIntosh, P. (1988). *White privilege and male privilege: A personal account of coming to see correspondences through work in women's studies.* Wellesley, MA: Wellesley College Center for Research on Women.

McMillan, C. (2011, July 14). State budget shortfall forces UC fee increase for 2011 [press release]. University of California Office of the President. Retrieved from http://newsroom.ucla.edu/stories/uc-regents-vote-tuition-increase-210662

Mead, G. H. (1934). *Mind, self, and society from the standpoint of a social behaviorist* (C. W. Morris, Ed.). Chicago: University of Chicago Press.

Mead, M. (1928). *Coming of age in Samoa.* New York: Morrow.

Meckler, L. (2002, July 24). Divorce, American style. Study: Certain couples more likely to split up than others. *CBS News.* Retrieved from www.cbsnews.com/stories/2002/07/24/national/main516165.shtml

Media Matters for America. (2005). *The "truth" according to Limbaugh.* Retrieved from www.mediamatters.org/items/200508160001

Meier, R. F. (1982). Perspectives on the concept of social control. *Annual Review of Sociology, 8,* 35–55.

Merton, R. (1938). Social structure and anomie. *American Sociological Review, 3,* 672–682.

Merton, R. (1949). Discrimination and the American creed. In R. M. MacIver (Ed.), *Discrimination and national welfare; a series of addresses and discussion* (pp. 99–126). New York: Institute for Religious and Social Studies.

Milkman, R. (1987). *Gender at work: The dynamics of job segregation by sex during World War II.* Urbana: University of Illinois Press.

Mills, C. W. (1959). *The sociological imagination.* New York: Oxford University Press.

Mills, C. W. (2000; orig. 1956). *The power elite.* New York: Oxford University Press.

Mishel, L., & Shierholz, H. (2013). *A decade of flat wages: The key barrier to shared prosperity and a rising middle class.* Economic Policy Institute. Retrieved from www.epi.org/publication/a-decade-of-flat-wages-the-key-barrier-to-shared-prosperity-and-a-rising-middle-class/

Molnar, A., & Sawicky, M. B. (1998, April). *The hidden costs of Channel One: Estimates for the 50 states.* Tempe, AZ: Commercialism in Education Research Unit.

Montesquieu, C., Baron de. (1750; orig. 1748). *The spirit of the laws* (Vols. 1–2, Thomas Nugent et al., Trans.), 1777.

Morning, A. (2004). *The nature of race: Teaching and learning about human difference.* Ph.D. dissertation, Department of Sociology, Princeton University.

Morrison, D. R., & Coiro, M. J. (1999). Parental conflict and marital disruption: Do children benefit when high-conflict marriages are dissolved? *Journal of Marriage and the Family, 61,* 626–637.

Moskovitz, D. (2006, September 8). Anti-Muslim incidents on rise in state, watchdog group says. *Miami Herald.* Retrieved from www.miami.com/mld/miamiherald/15465296.htm

Moynihan, D. P. (1965). *The Negro family: The case for national action.* Washington, DC: Office of Policy Planning and Research United States Department of Labor.

Murray, C. A. (1984). *Losing ground: American social policy, 1950–1980.* New York: Basic Books.

Murray, S. (2009, May 9). The curse of the Class of 2009. *The Wall Street Journal.* Education section. Retrieved from http://online.wsj.com/article/SB124181970915002009.html#

Myrdal, G. (1944). *An American dilemma: The Negro problem and modern democracy.* New York: Harper & Brothers.

Nanda, S. (1990). *Neither man nor woman: The hijras of India.* New York: Wadsworth. [2nd ed. published in 1999].

National Center for Educational Statistics. (2012). Total fall enrollment in degree-granting institutions, by level of enrollment, sex of student, level and control of institution, and attendance status of student: 2011. *Digest of Education Statistics: 2012 Tables and Figures*, Table 228. Retrieved from http://nces .ed.gov/programs/digest/d12/tables/dt12_228.asp

National Center for Education Statistics. (2013a). Immediate transition to college. *Digest of Education Statistics*. Retrieved from http://nces.ed.gov /programs/coe/pdf/coe_cpa.pdf

National Center for Education Statistics. (2013b). Institutional retention and graduation rates for undergraduate students. *Digest of Education Statistics*. Retrieved from http://nces.ed.gov/programs/coe /pdf/coe_cva.pdf

Nelson, D. J., & Rogers, D. C. (2004). *A national analysis of diversity in science and engineering faculties at research universities*. Retrieved from www.now.org/issues /diverse/diversity_report.pdf

Nelson, M. K. (1990). *Negotiated care: The experience of family day care providers*. Philadelphia: Temple University Press.

New York City Department of Public Health. (2009). Don't drink yourself fat [Public service poster]. Retrieved from www.nytimes.com /imagepages/2009/09/01/nyregion/01fat.ready .html

New York State Division of Parole (2007, September). *New York State parole handbook* (NYSPH). Retrieved from http://parole.state.ny.us/Handbook.pdf

Nissle, S., & Bshor, T. (2002). Winning the jackpot and depression: Money cannot buy happiness. *International Journal of Psychiatry in Clinical Practice, 6*(3), 183–186.

Oakley, A. (1972). *Sex, gender, and society*. London: Maurice Temple Smith.

O'Barr, W. (1995). *Linguistic evidence: Language, power and strategy in the courtroom*. San Diego, CA: Academic Press.

Oliver, J. E. (1993). Intergenerational transmission of child abuse: Rates, research and clinical implications. *American Journal of Psychiatry, 150,* 1315–1324.

Oreopoulos, P., & Salvanes, K. (2009). How large are returns to schooling? Hint: Money isn't everything. *NBER Working Paper Series*. Cambridge, MA: National Bureau of Economic Research. Retrieved from www.nber.org/papers/w15339.pdf

Orfield, G. (1996). Turning back to segregation. In G. Orfield & S. E. Eaton (Eds.), *Dismantling desegregation: The quiet reversal of Brown v. Board of Education* (pp. 1–22). New York: New Press.

Orfield, G., et al. (2012). E pluribus . . . separation: Deepening double segregation for more students. The Civil Rights Project at the University of California-Los Angeles. Retrieved from http:// civilrightsproject.ucla.edu/research/k-12-education /integration-and-diversity/mlk-national/e-pluribus... separation-deepening-double-segregation-for-more -students.

Ortner, S. (1974). Is female to male as nature to culture? In M. Z. Rosaldo & L. Lamphere (Eds.), *Woman, culture, and society* (pp. 67–88). Stanford, CA: Stanford University Press.

Oyěwùmí, O. (1997). *The invention of women: Making an African sense of Western gender discourses*. Minneapolis: University of Minnesota Press.

Pager, D. (2003). Blacks and ex-cons need not apply. *Contexts, 2*(4), 58–59.

Pareto, V. (1983; orig. 1935). *The mind and society* (A. Livingston, Ed.; A. Bongiorno & A. Livingston, Trans.). New York: AMS Press.

Pareto, V., & Finer, S. E. (1966). *Sociological writings*. New York: Praeger Sociology.

Parker, I. (2007, July 30). Our far flung correspondents: Swingers. *The New Yorker*. Retrieved from www .newyorker.com/reporting/2007/07/30/070730fa _fact_parker

Parsons, T. (1951). *The social system*. Glencoe, IL: Free Press.

Pascoe, C. J. (2007). *Dude, you're a fag: Masculinity and sexuality in high school*. Berkeley: University of California Press.

Pettit, B., & Western, B. (2004). Mass imprisonment and the life course: Race and class inequality in U.S. incarceration. *American Sociological Review, 69*(2), 151–169.

Pew Research Center. (2011a). Muslim American survey. Retrieved from www.people-press.org/2011/08/30 /section-1-a-demographic-portrait-of-muslim -americans/

Pew Research Center. (2011b). Pew Research Center's social & demographic trends (July 26). Wealth gaps rise to record highs between whites, blacks and Hispanics. Retrieved from http://pewresearch .org/pubs/2069/housing-bubble-subprime -mortgages-hispanics-blacks-household-wealth -disparity

Pew Research Center. (2011c). Multi-race Americans and the 2010 Census (April 5). Retrieved from www .pewsocialtrends.org/2011/04/05/multi-race -americans-and-the-2010-census/

Pew Research Center. (2012). Diverse origins: The nation's 14 largest Hispanic-origin groups. Retrieved

from www.pewhispanic.org/2013/06/19/
diverse-origins-the-nations-14-largest-hispanic-ori
gin-groups/

Pew Research Center. (2013a, July 18). Welcome to the
global middle-class surge. Retrieved from www
.pewresearch.org/2013/07/18/welcome-to-the
-global-middle-class-surge/

Pew Research Center. (2013b). Changing attitudes on
gay marriage. Pew Religion and Public Life Project.
Retrieved from http://features.pewforum.org
/same-sex-marriage-attitudes/

Pierce, J. L. (1995). *Gender trials: Emotional lives in
contemporary law firms* (Intro. and Chap. 3–6). Berkeley:
University of California Press.

Pipher, M. B. (1994). *Reviving Ophelia: Saving the selves of
adolescent girls*. New York: Putnam.

Plath, S. (1971; orig. 1963). *The bell jar*. New York:
Harper & Row.

Portes, A. (1969). Dilemmas of a golden exile:
Integration of Cuban refugee families in Milwaukee.
American Sociological Review, 34, 505–518.

Portes, A., et al. (1985). After Mariel: A survey of the
resettlement experiences of 1980 Cuban refugees in
Miami. *Estudios Cubanos* (Cuban Studies), *15*, 37–59.

Portes, A., & Zhou, M. (1993). The new second
generation: Segmented assimilation and its variants.
*Annals of the American Academy of Political and Social
Science, 530*, 74–96.

Posner, R. A. (1992). *Sex and reason*. Cambridge, MA:
Harvard University Press.

Public Agenda. (2012, October 1). Hard work is
essential for achieving the American dream, but is it
enough? Americans are divided according to a new
survey. Retrieved from www.publicagenda.org/press
-releases/hard-work-is-essential-for-achieving-the
-american-dream-but-is-it-enough-americans-are
-divided-according-to-a-new-survey

Putnam, R. D. (2000). *Bowling alone: The collapse and revival
of American community*. New York: Simon & Schuster.

Quadagno, J. (1996). *The color of welfare: How racism
undermined the war on poverty*. New York: Oxford
University Press.

Radway, J. (1987). *Reading the romance: Women, patriarchy,
and popular literature*. Chapel Hill: University of North
Carolina Press.

Ralli, T. (2005, September 5). Who's a looter? In
storm's aftermath, pictures kick up a different kind
of tempest. *The New York Times*. Retrieved from
www.nytimes.com/2005/09/05/business/05caption
.html

Ramey, V. A., & Francis, N. (2006). *A century of work
and leisure*. Cambridge, MA: National Bureau of
Economic Research.

Read, J. (2008, February). Muslims in America. *Contexts*.
Retrieved from http://contexts.org/articles/fall
-2008/muslims-in-america/

Reardon, S. F. (2013, May). The widening income achievement gap. *Educational Leadership, 70*(8), 10–16. Retrieved
from http://nppsd.fesdev.org/vimages/shared
/vnews/stories/525d81ba96ee9/SI%20-%20The%20
Widening%20Income%20Achievement%20Gap.pdf

Reardon, S. F., et al. (2012, August 3). Race, income,
and enrollment patterns in highly selective colleges,
1982–2004. Center for Education Policy Analysis,
Stanford University. Retrieved from http://cepa
.stanford.edu/sites/default/files/race income %26
selective college enrollment august 3 2012.pdf

Reddy, G. (2005). *With respect to sex: Negotiating hijra identity
in South India*. Chicago: University of Chicago Press.

Remez, L. (2000). Oral sex among adolescents: Is it sex
or is it abstinence? *Family Planning Perspectives, 23*(6).
Retrieved from www.guttmacher.org/pubs
/journals/3229800.html

Reskin, B., & Roos, P. (1990). *Job queues, gender queues*.
Philadelphia: Temple University Press.

Rich, A. (1980). Compulsory heterosexuality and lesbian
existence. *Signs: Journal of Women in Culture and Society,
5*, 631–660.

Rios, V. (2011). *Punished: Policing the lives of black and
Latino boys*. New York: NYU Press.

Risman, B. J. (1998). *Gender vertigo: American families in
transition*. New Haven: Yale University Press.

Roberts, S. (2010, January 5). No longer majority black,
Harlem is in transition. *The New York Times*. NY/
Region section. Retrieved from www.nytimes
.com/2010/01/06/nyregion/06harlem.html

Rosaldo, M. Z. (1974). Woman, culture
and society: A theoretical overview.
In M. Z. Rosaldo & L. Lamphere (Eds.), *Woman,
culture, and society* (pp. 17–42). Stanford, CA: Stanford
University Press.

Rosenhan, D. L. (1973). On being sane in insane places.
Science, 179, 25–58.

Rousseau, J.-J. (2004; orig. 1754). A dissertation on the origin
and foundation of the inequality of mankind. In *Discourse
on inequality*. Whitefish, MT: Kessinger Publishing.

Rubin, G. (1975). The traffic in women: Notes on the
"political economy" of sex. In R. R. Reiter (Ed.),
Toward an anthropology of women (pp. 157–210).
New York: Monthly Review Press.

Russell, S. T., & Joyner, K. (2001). Adolescent sexual
orientation and suicide risk: Evidence from a

national study. *American Journal of Public Health, 91*, 1276–1281.

Sacerdote, B. (2001). Peer effects with random assignment: Results for Dartmouth roommates. *Quarterly Journal of Economics, 116*.

Sachs, J. D. (2001). *Macroeconomics and health: Investing in health for economic development.* Report of the Commission on Macroeconomics and Health. Geneva: World Health Organization.

Sadker, M., & Sadker, D. (1994). *Failing at fairness: How America's schools cheat girls.* New York: Touchstone.

Sadler, A. G., et al. (2003). Factors associated with women's risk of rape in the military environment. *American Journal of Industrial Medicine, 43*(3), 262–273.

Saez, E. (2010). Striking it richer: The evolution of top incomes in the United States. Retrieved from http://elsa.berkeley.edu/~saez/saez-UStopincomes-2008.pdf

Saez, E. (2013). Striking it richer: The evolution of top incomes in the United States. Retrieved from http://elsa.berkeley.edu/~saez/saez-UStopincomes-2012.pdf

Sahr, R. C. (2010, September 30). Inflation conversion factors 1774 to estimated 2019. Retrieved from http://oregonstate.edu/cla/polisci/sahr/sahr

Salai-i-Martin, X. (2002). *The disturbing "rise" of global income inequality* (NBER Working Paper No. 8904). Retrieved from www.nber.org/papers/w8904

Salganik, M. J., et al. (2006, 10 February). Experimental study of inequality and unpredictability in an artificial cultural market. *Science, 311*(5762), 854–856.

Sanday, P. R. (1990). *Fraternity gang rape: Sex, brotherhood, and privilege on campus.* New York: New York University Press.

Sander, T. H., & Putnam, R. D. (2005, September 10). Sept. 11th as a civics lesson. *The Washington Post*, p. A23. Retrieved from www.washingtonpost.com/wp-dyn/content/article/2005/09/09/AR2005090901821.html

Sander, T. H., & Putnam, R. D. (2010). Still bowling alone? The post-9/11 split. *Journal of Democracy, 21*(1), 9–16.

Santa Ana, O. (2004). Is there such a thing as Latino identity? *American family: Journey of dreams.* Retrieved from www.pbs.org/americanfamily/latino2.html

Schackner, B. (2002, September 27). College course focuses on the wealthy minority. *Post-Gazette.* Retrieved from www.post-gazette.com/localnews/20020929wealthy6.asp

Scharf, S. A., & Flom, B. A. (2010, October). Report of the fifth annual national survey on retention and promotion of women in law firms. *National Association of Women Lawyers.* Retrieved from www.aauw.org/learn/research/upload/NewVoicesPayEquity_NAWL.pdf

Scott, J. W. (1988). Women's history and gender: A useful category of analysis. In *Gender and the politics of history* (pp. 28–50). New York: Columbia University Press.

Shah, D. (2004). Defense of Marriage Act: An update. Washington, DC: U.S. General Accounting Office. Retrieved from www.worldcat.org/title/defense-of-marriage-act-update-to-prior-report/oclc/56121746&referer=brief_results

Shaheen, J. G. (1984). *The TV Arab.* Bowling Green, OH: Bowling Green State University Popular Press.

Shore, B. (1998). *Culture in mind: Cognition, culture, and the problem of meaning.* New York: Oxford University Press.

Simmel, G. (1950). Quantitative aspects of the group. In Kurt Wolff (Comp. and Trans.), *The sociology of Georg Simmel* (pp. 87–180). Glencoe, IL: Free Press.

Skocpol, T. (2004). Civic transformation and inequality in the contemporary United States. In K. Neckerman (Ed.), *Social inequality* (pp. 731–769). New York: Russell Sage Foundation.

Skogrand, L., et al. (2004, July). Understanding Latino families: Implications for family education family resources. *Family Resources.* Retrieved from http://extension.usu.edu/diversity/files/uploads/Latino02-7-05.pdf

Smedley, A. (1999). *Race in North America: Origin and evolution of a worldview.* Boulder, CO: Westview Press.

Snowden, F. M. (1983). *Beyond color prejudice: The ancient view of blacks.* Cambridge, MA: Harvard University Press.

Sommers, C. H. (2000). *The war against boys: How misguided feminism is harming our young men.* New York: Simon & Schuster.

Sorokin, P. (1959; orig. 1927). *Social and cultural mobility.* New York: Free Press.

Spock, B. (1998; orig. 1946). *Baby and child care.* New York: Pocket Books.

Spohn, C., & Holleran, D. (2002). The effects of imprisonment on recidivism rates of felony offenders: A focus on drug offenders. *Criminology, 40*(2), 329–358.

Spurlock, M. (2008). *30 days with Muslim Americans* [Television show]. FX network.

Stacey, J. (1987). Sexism by a subtler name? Postindustrial conditions and postfeminist consciousness in the Silicon Valley. *Socialist Review, 96*, 7–28.

Stacey, J. (1996). *In the name of the family: Rethinking family values in the postmodern age.* Boston: Beacon Press.

Stacey, J. (1997). Neo-family-values campaign. In R. N. Lancaster & M. di Lionardo (Eds.), *The gender/sexuality reader: Culture, history, political economy* (pp. 453–472). New York: Routledge.

Stacey, J. (2004). Cruising to familyland: Gay hypergamy and rainbow kinship. *Current Sociology, 52*(2), 181–197.

Stacey, J., & Thorne, B. (1985). The missing feminist revolution in sociology. *Social Problems, 32,* 301–316.

Stack, C. B. (1974). *All our kin: Strategies for survival in a Black community.* New York: Harper & Row.

Stack, C. B., & Burton, L. M. (1994). Kinscripts: Reflections on family, generation and culture. In E. N. Glenn et al. (Eds.), *Mothering: Ideology, experience, and agency* (pp. 33–44). New York: Routledge.

Steele, C. M., & Aronson, J. (1998). Stereotype threat and the test performance of academically successful African Americans. In C. Jencks and M. Phillips (Eds.), *The black-white test score gap* (pp. 401–427). Washington, DC: Brookings Institution Press.

Stevens, J. (2006). Pregnancy envy and the politics of compensatory masculinities. *Gender and Politics, 1,* 265–294.

Swanson, S. A., et al. (2011, March 7). Prevalence and correlates of eating disorders in adolescents: results from the National Comorbidity Survey Replication Adolescent Supplement. *Archives of General Psychiatry.* Retrieved from www.nimh.nih.gov/science-news/2011/most-teens-with-eating-disorders-go-without-treatment.shtml

Thomas, W. I., & Thomas, D. S. (1928). *The child in America: Behavior problems and programs.* New York: Knopf.

Triester, R. (2005, July 22). "Real beauty"—or real smart marketing? *Salon.com.* Retrieved from http://dir.salon.com/mwt/feature/2005/07/22/dove/indexl.html

Truth, S. (1851). Ain't I a woman? Speech delivered at the Women's Convention in Akron, Ohio. *Feminist.com.* Retrieved from www.feminist.com/resources/artspeech/genwom/sojour.html

Unah, I., & Boger, J. C. (2001, April 16). *Race and the death penalty in North Carolina.* Retrieved from www.common-sense.org/pdfs/NCDeathPenaltyReport2001.pdf

UNICEF. (2007). *The state of the world's children 2007: Women and children: The double dividend of gender equality.* New York: UNICEF.

United Nations High Commissioner for Refugees. (2014). *Law No. 26 of 1975 Concerning Egyptian Nationality.* Retrieved from www.refworld.org/docid/3ae6b4e218.html

U.S. Census Bureau. (1993). We the First Americans. U.S. Department of Commerce Economics and Statistics Administration. Retrieved from www.census.gov/apsd/wepeople/we-5.pdf

U.S. Census Bureau. (2010a). Nation's foreign-born population nears 37 million (October 19). Retrieved from www.census.gov/newsroom/releases/archives/foreignborn_population/cb10-159.html

U.S. Census Bureau. (2010b). Population Finder fact sheet. 2006–2008 American Community Survey 3-year estimates. Data profile highlights. Retrieved from http://factfinder.census.gov/servlet/ACSSAFFFacts?_sse=on

U.S. Census Bureau. (2010c). 2012 statistical abstract: Income, poverty, & wealth. Retrieved from www.census.gov/compendia/statab/cats/income_expenditures_poverty_wealth.html

U.S. Census Bureau. (2011a). Income, poverty and health insurance coverage in the United States: 2010. Retrieved from www.census.gov/newsroom/releases/archives/income_wealth/cb11-157.html

U.S. Census Bureau. (2011b). The black population: 2010 (September). Retrieved from www.census.gov/prod/cen2010/briefs/c2010br-06.pdf

U.S. Census Bureau. (2011c). The Hispanic population: 2010. 2010 Census briefs. (May). Retrieved from www.census.gov/prod/cen2010/briefs/c2010br-04.pdf

U.S. Census Bureau. (2011d). Overview of race and Hispanic origin: 2010. 2010 Census briefs (March). Retrieved from www.census.gov/prod/cen2010/briefs/c2010br-02.pdf

U.S. Census Bureau. (2011e). The 2012 statistical abstract: Births, deaths, marriages, & divorces: Life expectancy. Retrieved from www.census.gov/compendia/statab/cats/births_deaths_marriages_divorces/life_expectancy.html

U.S. Census Bureau. (2011f). Race and Hispanic origin of the foreign-born population in the United States: 2010. American Community Survey reports (January). Retrieved from www.census.gov/prod/2010pubs/acs-11.pdf

U.S. Census Bureau. (2011g). Age and sex composition: 2010 Census brief (May). Retrieved from www.census.gov/prod/cen2010/briefs/c2010br-03.pdf

U.S. Census Bureau. (2012a). The American Indian and Alaska Native population. Retrieved from www.census.gov/prod/cen2010/briefs/c2010br-10.pdf

U.S. Census Bureau. (2012b). Selected population profile in the United States: 2012 American Community Survey 1-year estimates. Retrieved from http://factfinder2.census.gov/faces

/tableservices/jsf/pages/productview.
xhtml?pid=ACS_12_1YR_S0201&prodType=table

U.S. Census Bureau. (2012c). Hispanic or Latino origin by specific origin. 2012 American Community Survey 1-year estimates. Retrieved from http://factfinder2.census.gov/faces/tableservices/jsf/pages/productview.xhtml?pid=ACS_12_1YR_B03001&prodType=table

U.S. Census Bureau. (2012d). Median income in the past 12 months (in 2011 inflation-adjusted dollars). 2009–2011 American Community Survey 3-year estimates. Retrieved from http://factfinder2.census.gov/faces/tableservices/jsf/pages/productview.xhtml?pid=ACS_11_3YR_S1903&prodType=table

U.S. Census Bureau. (2012e). Table 4: Projections of the population by sex, race, and Hispanic origin for the United States: 2015 to 2060 (NP2012-T4).

U.S. Census Bureau. (2013a). Arab households in the United States: 2006–2010. Retrieved from www.census.gov/prod/2013pubs/acsbr10-20.pdf

U.S. Census Bureau. (2013b). America's families and living arrangements: 2012. Retrieved from www.census.gov/prod/2013pubs/p20-570.pdf

U.S. Census Bureau. (2013c). Census Bureau reports 21 percent married households have at least one foreign-born spouse. Retrieved from www.census.gov/newsroom/releases/archives/foreignborn_population/cb13-157.html

U.S. Citizenship and Immigration Services. (2004). Citizenship in the United States. Retrieved from www.ilw.com/resources/Citizenship_United_States.pdf

U.S. Citizenship and Immigration Services. (2014). Citizenship through naturalization. Retrieved from www.uscis.gov/us-citizenship/citizenship-through-naturalization/

U.S. Department of Commerce. (2009, May 15). Confirmation hearing for Robert Groves, chaired by Senator Thomas Carper (D-DE). Retrieved from www.census.gov/newsroom/releases/pdf/confirmation_transcript.pdf

U.S. Department of Health and Human Services. (2013). 2013 Poverty guidelines. Office of the Assistant Secretary for Planning and Evaluation. Retrieved from http://aspe.hhs.gov/poverty/13poverty.cfm

U.S. Department of Justice, Civil Rights Division. (2007). Enforcement and outreach following the September 11 terrorist attacks. Retrieved from www.usdoj.gov/crt/legalinfo/discrimupdate.html

U.S. Department of State, Bureau of Consular Affairs. (2013). Intercountry adoption statistics. Retrieved from http://adoption.state.gov/about_us/statistics.php

U.S. Senate, Subcommittee on Immigration and Naturalization of the Committee on the Judiciary. (1965, February 10). Washington, D.C., pp. 1–3.

Waite, L., & Gallagher, M. (2000). The case for marriage: Why married people are happier, healthier, and better off financially. New York: Doubleday.

Wallerstein, J., et al. (2000). The unexpected legacy of divorce. New York: Hyperion.

Wang, W. (2012). The rise of intermarriage. Pew Research: Social and Demographic Trends. Retrieved from www.pewsocialtrends.org/2012/02/16/the-rise-of-intermarriage/

Wang, W., & Parker, K. (2011, August 17). Women see value and benefits of college; men lag on both fronts, survey finds. Pew Research Center. Retrieved from http://pewsocialtrends.org/2011/08/17/women-see-value-and-benefits-of-college-men-lag-on-both-fronts-survey-finds/

Warren, J. W., & Twine, F. W. (1997). White Americans, the new minority? Non-blacks and the ever-expanding boundaries of whiteness. Journal of Black Studies, 28, 200–218.

Washington, E. (2008). Female socialization: How daughters affect their legislator fathers' voting on women's issues. American Economic Review, 98(1), 311–332.

Watts, D. (2003). Six degrees: The science of a connected age. New York: W. W. Norton.

Weber, M. (1968; orig. 1922). Economy and society: An outline of interpretive sociology (G. Rothe & C. Wittich, Eds.; E. Fischoff et al., Trans.). New York: Bedminster Press.

Weber, M. (2003; orig. 1904). The Protestant ethic and the spirit of capitalism. Oxford: Blackwell.

Wegener, B. (1991). Job mobility and social ties: Social resources, prior job, and status attainment. American Sociological Review, 56(1), 60–71.

West, C., & Zimmerman, D. (1987). Doing gender. Gender & Society, 1(2), 125–151.

Wilgoren, J. (2003, March 28). A nation at war: Women in the military: A new war brings new role for women. The New York Times. Retrieved from http://query.nytimes.com/gst/fullpage.html?res=9B01E2D61F30F93BA15750C0A9659C8B63

Williams, C. (1995). Still a man's world: Men who do women's work. Berkeley: University of California Press.

Williams, C. (2013). The glass escalator, revisited. Gender & Society, 27(5), 609–629.

Williams, S. (2005). Million dollar blocks. Public service announcement [Digital presentation]. Columbia University, Spatial Information Design Lab.

Retrieved from www.spatialinformationdesignlab
.org/movie.php?url=MEDIA/PSA_01.avi

Wilson, J. Q., & Kelling, G. L. (1982). Broken windows: The police and neighborhood safety. *The Atlantic Monthly, 249*(3), 29–37.

Wilson, W. J. (1978). *The declining significance of race: Blacks and changing American institutions.* Chicago: University of Chicago Press.

Wilson, W. J. (1987). *The truly disadvantaged: The inner city, the underclass, and public policy.* Chicago: University of Chicago Press.

Winant, H. (2001). *The world is a ghetto: Race and democracy since World War II.* New York: Basic Books.

Wirth, L. (1938). Urbanism as a way of life. *American Journal of Sociology, 44*(1), 1–24.

Wood, W., et al. (2002). Sources of information about dating and their perceived influence on adolescents. *Journal of Adolescent Research, 17*, 401–417.

Wuthnow, R. (1998). *Loose connections: Joining together in America's fragmented communities.* Cambridge, MA: Harvard University Press.

Young, L., & Hammock, E. (2007). On switches and knobs, microsatellites and monogamy. *Trends in Genetics, 23*(5), 209–212.

Young, L., & Wang, Z. (2004). The neurobiology of pair bonding. *Nature Neuroscience, 7*(10), 1048–1054. Retrieved from www.ecfs.org/projects/pchurch /AT%20BIOLOGY/PAPERS%5CNeurobiology% 200f%20Pair%20Bonding.pdf

Zelizer, V. A. (2005). *The purchase of intimacy.* Princeton, NJ: Princeton University Press.

Zernike, K. (2006, April 23). College, my way. *The New York Times.* Retrieved from http://query .nytimes.com/gst/fullpage.html?res=9E01E1DB1F3 0F930A15757C0A9609C8B63

Zickuhr, K., & Smith, A. (2013). Home broadband 2013. Pew Internet and American Life Project. Retrieved from www.pewinternet.org/Reports/2013 /Broadband.aspx

Zimbardo, P. (1971). *Stanford prison experiment: A simulation study of the psychology of imprisonment conducted at Stanford University.* Retrieved from www .prisonexp.org

Zimbardo, P. (2007). *The Lucifer effect: Understanding how good people turn evil.* New York: Random House.

Zukin, S. (2003). *Point of purchase: How shopping changed American culture.* New York: Routledge.

CREDITS

TEXT

Chapter 1: From the book *Pulp Fiction: A Quentin Tarantino Screenplay* by Quentin Tarantino. Copyright © 1994 Quentin Tarantino. Reprinted by permission of Miramax Books. All Rights Reserved.

FIGURES & TABLES

Chapter 2: **Figure 2.3**: From Babbie, *The Practice of Social Research*, 11E. © 2007 South-Western, a part of Cengage Learning, Inc. Reproduced by permission. www.cengage.com/permissions.

Chapter 5: **Figure 5.3**: Originally from "Studies of independence and conformity: A minority of one against a unanimous majority," by Asch, S.E. *Psychological Monographs* 70 (9), 1–70. doi:10.1037/h0093718. **Figure 5.5**: Figure 2, "Structure of Romantic and Sexual Contact at Jefferson" from "Chains of Affection: The Structure of Adolescent Romantic and Sexual Networks" by Peter S. Bearman, James Moody, and Katherine Stovel, *American Journal of Sociology*, Vol. 110, No. 1, July 2004, pp. 44–91. Copyright © 2004, The University of Chicago Press. Reprinted by permission of the publisher. **Figure 5.6**: from "Chains of Affection: The Structure of Adolescent Romantic and Sexual Networks" by Peter S. Bearman, James Moody, and Katherine Stovel, *American Journal of Sociology*, Vol. 110, No. 1, July 2004, pp. 44–91. Copyright © 2004, The University of Chicago Press. Reprinted by permission of the publisher.

Chapter 7: **Figure 7.1**: Figure from "Power in America: Wealth, Income, and Power" by G. William Domhoff. September 2005, updated February 2013. Reprinted by permission of G. William Domhoff—www.whorulesamerica.net. **Table 7.2**: Figure from *Mobility Tables: Quantitative Applications in the Social Sciences* by Michael Hout. Copyright © 1983 by Sage Publications, Inc. Books. Reproduced with permission of Sage Publications, Inc.

Books in the format Textbook via Copyright Clearance Center.

Chapter 9: **Table 9.1**: Figure "Gordon's Stages of Assimilation," *Assimilation in American Life: The Role of Race, Religion, and National Origins* by Milton M. Gordon, p. 71. Copyright © 1964, Oxford University Press, Inc. Reprinted by permission of Oxford University Press, Inc.

Chapter 10: **Figure 10.1**: Figure 1 from Cohen, Philip. (2014) "Recession and Divorce in the United States, 2008–2011." *Population Research and Policy Review*. Reprinted with permission of Springer Science & Business Media.

PHOTOS

Table of Contents: **p. vi**: Yaroslava Mills; **p. vii**: infusny-244/INFphoto.com/Newscom; **p. viii**: Mark Peterson/Redux; **p. x**: Q. Sakamaki/Redux; **p. xi**: Abbie Trayler-Smith/Panos Pictures; **p. xiii**: Sean Justice/Taxi/Getty Images.

Chapter 1: **p. 2**: Katrina Wittkamp/Getty Images; **p. 5**: Yaroslava Mills; **p. 7**: Miramax/Photofest; **p. 11 (left)**: AP Photo/Paul Sakuma; **(right)**: Daily Mail/Rex/Alamy; **p. 14 (left)**: Spencer Platt/Getty Images; **(right)**: Getty Images; **p. 16 (from left to right)**: SuperStock; Granger Collection; Granger Collection; **p. 17 (clockwise from top)**: Granger Collection; Bridgeman Art Library; Bridgeman Art Library; **p. 18 (left)**: Underwood & Underwood/Corbis; **(right)**: Corbis; **p. 19 (from left to right)**: Bridgeman Art Library; Granger Collection; Bentley Historical Library The University of Michigan; Getty Images; **p. 20 (both)**: Granger Collection; **p. 21 (from left to right)**: Granger Collection; Granger Collection; Granger Collection; Getty Images; **p. 22 (from left to right)**: University of Pennsylvania University Archives Digital Image Collection Photo by Frederick A. Meyer; Getty Images; Time Life Pictures/Getty Images; Courtesy Ann Oakley; **p. 23 (from left to right)**: Newscom; Courtesy Anthony

Giddens; Newscom; American Sociological Association; **p. 27:** Underwood & Underwood/Corbis; **p. 30:** Bettmann/Corbis; **p. 31:** Bob Krist/Corbis; **p. 33:** Fox Photos/Getty Images; **p. 34:** Courtesy of Erica Rothman, Nightlight Productions and Dalton Conley; **p. 35:** Alamy.

Chapter 2: p. 42: Angel Nieto/ddp images/Sipa USA; **p. 48:** AP Photo/Julie Jacobson; **p. 54:** Ovie Carter; **p. 56:** Chang W. Lee/The New York Times/Redux; **p. 58:** AP Photo; **p. 59:** Time Life Pictures/Getty Images; **p. 63:** Time Life Pictures/Getty Images; **p. 64:** Ducklau/dpa/Corbis; **p. 65:** Courtesy Matthew Salganik.

Chapter 3: p. 72: AP Photo/Yossi Aloni; **p. 74:** It Gets Better Project and Daniel Arzola; **p. 76 (clockwise from top left):** Greg Gawlowski Photography; Lester Lefkowitz/The Image Bank/Getty Images; Rose Hartman/Corbis; Werner Forman/Corbis; **p. 77:** Granger Collection; **p. 78:** Réunion des Musées Nationaux/Art Resource, NY; **p. 81 (from left to right):** Mitch Kezar/Stone/Getty Images; Atlantide Phototravel/Corbis; Rudy Sulgan/Corbis; **p. 83:** Library of Congress; **p. 84:** Wolfgang Kaehler/Corbis; **p. 86 (left):** Peter Endig/dpa/Corbis; **(right):** Christian Kober/Robert Harding World Imagery/Corbis; **p. 88:** Images Distribution/Newscom; **p. 89 (left):** Corbis; **(right):** John Springer Collection/Corbis; **p. 90 (from left to right):** Bridgeman Art Library/Getty Images; Corbis; CNN via Getty Images; **p. 91:** AP Photo; **p. 94:** Julia Xanthos/New York Daily News; **p. 96:** Bettmann/Corbis; **p. 97 (top):** CBS/Photofest; **(bottom):** ABC/Photofest; **p. 99:** Newscom; **p. 100 (left):** AP Photo; **(right):** Chris Graythen/Getty Images; **p. 101:** Media Education Foundation; **p. 102:** Ruby Washington/The New York Times/Redux; **p. 104:** Courtesy of Erica Rothman, Nightlight Productions and Dalton Conley; **p. 106 (both):** Adbusters; **p. 108:** infusny-244/INFphoto.com/Newscom.

Chapter 4: p. 112: Joe Fornabaio/The New York Times/Redux; **p. 115:** Jose Luis Pelaez/Iconica/Getty Images; p. 117: Jose Luis Pelaez, Inc./Corbis; p. 119: Steve Skjold/Alamy; p. 121: Red Images, LLC / Alamy; p. 122: Courtesy of Erica Rothman, Nightlight Productions and Dalton Conley; **p. 125:** Darren McCollester/Newsmakers/Getty Images; **p. 126:** Everett Collection; **p. 127:** Scott Olson/Getty Images; **p. 128 (left):** http://helloblueivycarter.tumblr.com; **(right):** John Ricard/FilmMagic/Getty Images; **p. 129:** AFP/Getty Images/Newscom; **p. 130:** Mark Peterson/Redux; **p. 131:** Courtesy of Erica Rothman, Nightlight Productions and Dalton Conley; **p. 133:** AP Photo/Courtesy Zucker

Public Relations; **p. 133:** Photo: Jacqueline Hyde. CNAC/MNAM/Dist Réunion des Musées Nationaux/Art Resource, NY. © 2014 The Pollock-Krasner Foundation/Artists Rights Society (ARS), New York; **p. 134:** Kevin Foy/Alamy; **p. 135 (clockwise from top left):** Stephanie McGehee/Reuters; Michael Dwyer/Alamy; Eric Vidal/AFP/Getty Images; **p. 137:** Copyright © Us Weekly LLC 2009. All Rights Reserved. Used by Permission; **p. 140:** 20th Century Fox/Photofest; **p. 143:** Piotr Redlinski/The New York Times/Redux; **p. 145:** AP Photo.

Chapter 5: p. 148: Benoit Decout/REA/Redux; **p. 150:** Kate Rich/Feral Trade; **p. 153:** Mark Leong/Redux; **p. 154:** Dawn Villella/The New York Times/Redux; **p. 157 (left):** Kelly-Mooney Photography/Corbis; **(right):** Zefa RF/Alamy; **p. 158:** Newscom; **p. 163:** Mark Peterson/Redux; **p. 165:** Courtesy of Erica Rothman, Nightlight Productions and Dalton Conley; **p. 166:** Lee Celano/The New York Times/Redux; **p. 167:** Richard Perry/The New York Times/Redux; **p. 168:** AP Photo/The Ledger Independent, Terry Prather; **p. 169:** AP Photo/Patriot-News, Paul Chaplin; **p. 170:** Doug Pensinger/Getty Images for AFL; **p. 171:** Courtesy of Erica Rothman, Nightlight Productions and Dalton Conley; **p. 173:** Lauren Greenfield/INSTITUTE.

Chapter 6: p. 184: Lluis Real/Agefotostock; **p. 186:** Courtesy of Erica Rothman, Nightlight Productions and Dalton Conley; **p. 188 (left):** New York Public Library/Art Resource, NY; **(right):** Bettmann/Corbis; **p. 189:** AP Photo/David J. Phillip; **p. 190 (both):** Bettmann/Corbis; **p. 191:** Three Lions/Getty Images; **p. 192:** AP Photo/Greg Wahl-Stephens; **p. 195:** SuperStock; **p. 198:** Granger Collection; **p. 202 (conformist):** Jack Hollingsworth/Corbis; **(ritualist):** Anthony-Masterson/Riser/Getty Images; **(innovator):** Seth Wenig/Reuters/Corbis; **(retreatist):** Buddy Mays/Corbis; **(rebel):** Joseph Scherschel/Time Life Pictures/Getty Images; **p. 204:** Ruth Fremson/The New York Times/Redux; **p. 206:** PGZimbardo Inc.; **p. 207:** AP Photo; **p. 208:** Allied Artists/Photofest; **p. 210:** Courtesy of Erica Rothman, Nightlight Productions and Dalton Conley; **p. 211:** PGZimbardo Inc.; **p. 214:** Timothy A. Clary/AFP/Getty Images; **p. 218:** Columbia University Graduate School of Architecture, Planning and Preservation; **p. 220:** Q. Sakamaki/Redux; **p. 222:** Mary Evans Picture Library/Alamy; **p. 224:** Bettmann/Corbis; **p. 228:** Brant Ward/San Francisco Chronicle/Corbis.

Chapter 7: p. 232: Anna Schori/Camera Press/Redux; **p. 235:** Bridgeman Art Library/Getty Images; **p. 239:** AP

Photo/Themba Hadebe; **p. 240:** AP Photo/Kevork Djansezian; **p. 242:** Ted Streshinsky/Corbis; **p. 243:** Ben Stechschulte/Redux; **p. 245:** Reuters/Corbis; **p. 246:** AFP/Getty Images; **p. 247:** AP Photo; **p. 252:** Roger L. Wollenberg/UPI/Newscom; **p. 258:** Courtesy of Erica Rothman, Nightlight Productions and Dalton Conley; **p. 261:** Courtesy of Erica Rothman, Nightlight Productions and Dalton Conley; **p. 262:** Q. Sakamaki/Redux; **p. 267:** Katherine Taylor/The New York Times/Redux; **p. 269:** Granger Collection.

Chapter 8: **p. 272:** Abbie Trayler-Smith/Panos Pictures; **p. 274:** Wikimedia Commons; **p. 276:** Time Life Pictures/Getty Images; **p. 279:** Reuters/Corbis; **p. 281:** M. C. Escher Foundation; **p. 283:** Sam Panthaky/AFP/Getty Images; **p. 284:** SuperStock; **p. 287:** Getty Images; **p. 289:** Janine Wiedel Photolibrary/Alamy; **p. 291:** Corbis; **p. 292:** AP Photo; **p. 294:** Ashmolean Museum, University of Oxford/Bridgeman Art Library; **p. 297:** Alamy; **p. 298:** Reuters; **p. 299:** Alamy; **p. 300:** Courtesy of Erica Rothman, Nightlight Productions and Dalton Conley; **p. 302:** Andy Kropa/Redux; **p. 306:** The Advertising Archives; **p. 309:** AP Photo/Fremont Tribune, Matt Gade; **p. 310:** Courtesy of Erica Rothman, Nightlight Productions and Dalton Conley; **p. 312:** Ted Banks/U.S. Navy via Getty Images; **p. 313:** Granger Collection; **p. 314:** Time Life Pictures/Getty Images.

Chapter 9: **p. 318:** SuperStock/Agefotostock; **p. 321:** The Ohio State University Billy Ireland Cartoon Library & Museum; **p. 323:** Reproduced by courtesy of Mauricio

Hatchwell Toledano. www.facsimile-editions.com; **p. 325:** SPL/Science Source; **p. 326:** Hulton-Deutsch Collection/Corbis; **p. 327:** National Park Service, Statue of Liberty National Monument; **p. 328:** Wikimedia Commons; **p. 329:** Keith Bedford/The New York Times/Redux; **p. 331:** Simon Rawles/Alamy; **p. 332:** Courtesy of Erica Rothman, Nightlight Productions and Dalton Conley; **p. 333:** Reuters; **p. 334:** Reuters; **p. 336:** Reuters/Jonathan Ernst; **p. 337:** Mario Villafuerte/Redux; **p. 340:** Cheryl Senter for the Boston Globe; **p. 343:** AP Photo/The Sun Herald, Sean Loftin; **p. 348:** National Archives; **p. 349:** Bettmann/Corbis; **p. 350:** Bettmann/Corbis; **p. 352:** Reuters; **p. 356:** Getty Images; **p. 358:** Library of Congress; **p. 362:** Courtesy of Erica Rothman, Nightlight Productions and Dalton Conley; **p. 364:** Keith Dannemiller/Corbis.

Chapter 10: **p. 368:** Tomas Van Houtryve/VII Photo; **p. 370:** Photofest; **p. 372:** Time Life Pictures/Getty Image; **p. 374 (top):** Reed Kaestner/Corbis; **(center):** Tami Blumenfeld; **(bottom):** Jenny Matthews/Alamy; **p. 377:** Time Life Pictures/Getty Images; **p. 379:** Bettmann/Corbis; **p. 381:** Louis Edmond Pomey/Fine Art Photographic/Getty Images; **p. 382:** Bert Hardy/Getty Images; **p. 384:** Alamy; **p. 385:** Everett Collection/Newscom; **p. 389:** Getty Images; **p. 391:** Sean Justice/Taxi/Getty Images; **p. 395:** Ozier Muhammad/The New York Times/Redux; **p. 397:** AP Photo; **p. 399:** Ed Kashi/Corbis; **p. 402:** Courtesy of Erica Rothman, Nightlight Productions and Dalton Conley; **p. 407:** Paul Buck/EPA/Landov; **p. 408:** Alex Wong/Getty Images.

INDEX

aristocracy, 251
Aristotle, 323
Arnaz, Desi, 97
Arnold, Matthew, 77
Aronson, Joshua, 360
art, representation of ideal in, 78
artificial intelligence, 114
Asch Test, 160
ascribed status, 129
Asian Americans, 334, 339–41, 347, 361, 362; as model
    minority, 341, 347, 363; outmarriage of, 407;
    socioeconomic status of, 340, 358, 362
Aslett, Don, 390
assets, 237, 268, 357, 358, 359
assimilation, 26, 120, 344–48; of African Americans,
    338; of Asian Americans, 341; of Irish immigrants,
    320; of Muslim Americans, 332; of Native
    Americans, 336
attention, 157, 158; and civil inattention, 138
Australia, Aboriginals of, 245, 336, 373

Baby and Child Care (Spock), 392
baby boom, 382
backstage experiences in dramaturgical theory, 32,
    136–37, 354
Baek, Bliss, 145
Bali, 83–84, 85
Balkin, Amy, 150
Ball, Lucille, 97
banking and financial industry. *See* financial industry
Barth, Ernest, 346
baseball, 84–85
beanpole family structure, 380–81
Bearman, Peter, 173, 175, 176
beauty, feminine, 284–85
Becker, Howard S., 204–5
Begay, Annie, 233
Bell, Daniel, 22
Bell Curve, The (Herrnstein and Murray), 29
Bell Jar, The (Plath), 200
Ben-Dor Benite, Zvi, 38
Benedict, Ruth, 82
Bentham, Jeremy, 223, 224
Berbrier, Mitch, 343
Berk, Sarah Fenstermaker, 385
Bernard, Jessie, 385
Bernier, François, 324
Beyond the Melting Pot (Glazer and Moynihan), 345

bias, 216, 360, 376
Big Brothers Big Sisters program, 172
bio-logic, 293
biological determinism, 281, 288, 319
biology, 37, 65; sex differences in, 276, 277, 278, 281
birth order, 244–45, 401
birthrates, 382, 383–84, 396
Bitch magazine, 101
black Americans. *See* African Americans
black feminism, 291–93
Blackman, Laura, 243
Blau, Peter M., 22, 249, 250, 265, 267
blended families, 376, 405
Blumenbach, Johann Friedrich, 324
Blumer, Herbert, 31, 203
Blythe, William Jefferson, IV, 400
Boas, Franz, 82, 329
Bobo, Lawrence, 350
body size, and ideal feminine beauty, 284
Borat, 140
Bordo, Susan, 293
Born Rich, 232
Bourdieu, Pierre, 23
bourgeoisie, 248
bourgeois society, 242
bowling, 167
Bowling Alone (Putnam), 166
boyd, danah, 43, 67
Boys Don't Cry, 74
Brahmin caste, 246
Brazil, *travesti* in, 283, 299
breaches in social interactions, 137–38, 139–41, 145
breadwinner and homemaker roles in families, 370–71,
    378, 381, 392
British Broadcasting Company, 102
broken windows theory of deviance, 211–12
Browning, Elizabeth Barrett, 407
Brown v. Board of Education, 349
Brubaker, Rogers, 63–64
Buffon, Comte de, 324, 343
Bukowski, Ken, 368
bullying, 74, 131–32, 305
Burakumin, 330–31, 338
burakus, 331
Bureau of Inverse Technology, 149
Burt, Ronald, 164
Bush, George H. W., 69
Bush, George W., 82, 173, 359, 403

busing of students for school integration, 349
Butler, Judith, 293
Buy Nothing Day, 106

Calhoun, Craig, 114
Camel cigarette ads, 106
Campaign for Real Beauty, 101–2
capital: human, 249; social, 165–72
capitalism, 23–24; class system in, 248; corporations in, 179; equality of opportunity in, 242; family in, 380; free-market ideology in, 92; gender roles in, 290; limited liability in, 88; and patriarchy, 290, 291
capital punishment, 101–92, 193, 222, 225–27
caregiving, gender roles in, 289
Carrington, Christopher, 391
Carroll, Tara, 123–24
Case for Marriage, The (Waite and Gallagher), 404
case studies, 59
caste system, 235, 245–46, 251, 372
Castro, Fidel, 339
Catholics, 197–98, 396
causality, 46–50
cell phones, 103
census, 59, 67–69, 68, 180, 361
change, social, 30
Channel One, 104
chat rooms, online, 141
Chauncey, George, 299
Cherlin, Andrew, 402, 403, 405
Chicago School, 25–27, 28–29
childbirth, 377
Child Development (Brooks-Gunn), 384
child rearing: cultural differences in, 375; gender roles in, 288, 375, 380, 381, 387–93; and maternal employment, 384, 387–93; as second shift responsibility, 387–93; in single-parent families, 399
children: abuse of, 387; adoption of, 377–78; advertising targeting, 95, 103, 104–5; in blended families, 376, 405; in breadwinner–homemaker model of families, 371; divorce of parents, 403–4; families of, 120–24; firstborn, 153, 154–55, 401; gender roles of, 130–32; historical roles of, 132; intersex, 278–79; media influence on, 95, 98, 126; peer influence on, 125–26, 131–32; play of, 118, 130–31, 132, 289; in preindustrial era, 379–80; of same-sex couples, 405; schools of, 123, 124–25 (*See also* schools); in single-parent families, 377, 378; socialization of, 117–26; with working mothers, 384

China, 82, 235, 262, 339, 340, 364; media descriptions of population in, 98–99
Chinatowns, 340
Chinese Exclusion Act (1882), 340
Chodorow, Nancy, 288, 289, 290
Christianity, 246
Citigroup, 252
citizenship, 64, 321, 328, 363–64, 408–9
civic participation and engagement, 166, 167, 170–71; political (*See* political participation)
civil inattention, 138
civil rights, 91, 92, 348–50
Civil Rights Act (1964), 306, 307
Clark, Gregory, 233, 234, 235
classical sociological theories, 21–25
class system, 247–49. *See also* social class
climate, and racial differences, 325, 326
Clinton, Bill, 252, 311, 405; family of, 400–401; immigration policies of, 364; and sampling-adjusted census count, 68; and welfare policies, 399
Clinton, Roger, 400–401
Clinton, Virginia, 400
closings in social interactions, 138–39
Cloward, Richard, 213
cocaine, 217, 360
cockfighting, 83–84, 85
code-switching, 355
coffee trade, 149–50
cohabitation, 376
Cohen, Sacha Baron, 140
Coleman, James, 23
Coleman Report, 22
collective conscience, 190
collective resistance, 355
college, 8–12; affirmative action programs of, 242–43, 266–68; cost of attending, 8–9, 258; diploma and credentials awarded by, 4, 11–12; diversity in, 269; ethical guidelines on research in, 66, 67; gender differences in enrollment, 303–4; hook-up culture in, 300–301; motivation for attending, 4, 8; norms and values in, 87; roommates in, 142–44; as social institution, 12–13, 14–15; and socioeconomic status, 123–24, 257–58
Collins, Patricia Hill, 292, 394
Collins, Randall, 11, 12
Collins, Susan, 69
colonialism, 260, 261, 262, 323, 324
Columbus, Christopher, 335

combat, women in, 311–13

Coming of Age in Samoa (Mead), 83

communication, 139, 141

Communism, 22, 24, 82, 243, 339

Communist Manifesto (Marx and Engels), 17

community: of African Americans, 394–95; of Amish, 168–69; civic participation and engagement in, 166, 167, 170–71; housing values in, 268; incarceration of members affecting, 218–19; neighborhood watch groups in, 194; police in, 213; in preindustrial era, 379; residential segregation in, 350–52; social capital in, 166–67; social control in, 194–95

comparative research, 61, 63–64

competition, 30

Comte, Auguste, 15–19, 21, 25, 38

condition, equality of, 242–43

condom use, 301

conflict, 30; in gender relations, 290, 291; in inequality, 236; in marriage, 404; Marx on, 22–23, 30; and power, 290; racial, 352–53; between roles, 129, 136; social change in, 30; in triads, 154–55

conformity, 125, 131–32, 160, 201, 202

consent, informed, 66–67

consumerism, 103–4, 105–6

content analysis, 64–65, 93

contradictory class locations, 248

control, social, 185–231; in homosexuality, 297–98

Cookson, Peter W., Jr., 124

Cooley, Charles Horton, 18, 19, 20, 26, 27, 117, 159

Coontz, Stephanie, 378, 383

Coptic Christians, 235

Corbin, Margaret, 312

corporate crime, 214

corporations, 177–80; contradictory class locations in, 248; crimes committed by officers of, 214; in elite–mass dichotomy system, 251, 252–53; glass ceilings in, 308–10; as legal persons, 177; limited liability of, 88

correlation of variables, 46–50

Cortés, Hernán, 77

Coser, Lewis, 30

costs of college education, 8–9, 258

Counter-Reformation, 33, 34

Cowan, Ruth Schwartz, 390

crack cocaine, 360

Cranston, Alan, 142

credentialism, 11–12

Credential Society, The (Collins), 11

crime, 212–29; in adolescence, 304; broken windows theory of, 211–12; corporate, 214; death penalty for, 191–92, 193, 222, 225–27; definition of, 187; and double consciousness, 28; homosexuality as, 297–98; and Internet technology, 141–42; labeling theory on, 204, 208–9, 219; media affecting, 95, 98; in poor neighborhoods, 186; racism in media images of, 99–100; stigma of, 209–11

Critique of the Gotha Programme (Marx), 243

Crossing (McCloskey), 273–75

cross-national studies, 64

cross-sectional surveys, 62

Cuba, 338, 339

Cuckoo's Calling, The (Galbraith), 88

Cucolo, Anthony, 312

cult of domesticity, 381, 384, 385, 387

culture, 73–111; anthropology of, 35–36; definitions of, 74–78, 85; and ethnic identity, 345; experimental research on, 65–66; and food choices, 133; and gender, 283–84; of Native Americans, 80–81; in nativism, 327; organizational, 178; and race, 329; and racism, 356, 357; relativism of, 82–85; research on, 64, 82–85; and sexuality, 294–95; and social construction of reality, 133; sociology of, 25, 26; subcultures in, 85–86; and symbolic interactionism, 134

Culture and Anarchy (Arnold), 77

culture jamming, 105–6

Culture of Fear, The (Glassner), 100

Currie, Dawn, 101

Dahrendorf, Ralph, 30

Dalits or untouchables, 246

Damiens, Robert François, 221, 222, 223

Darwin, Charles, 326

Darwinism, social, 326

Das Kapital (Marx), 18

data collection, 56–66

dating relationships, 301

Davis, F. James, 329

death penalty, 191–92, 193, 222, 225–27

death rates, 304

de Beauvoir, Simone, 286

deception in research, 67

Deciding What's News (Gans), 93–94

deductive approach, 45, 46

Defense of Marriage Act (DOMA), 405

democracy, ideology of, 82

Democratic Party, 68

Denton, Nancy, 23, 350

DeParle, Jason, 122

dependency, mutual, 240

dependent variables, 50, 51

depression, 209

desegregation of schools, 349

determinism, biological, 281, 288, 319

deterrence theory of crime control, 217–19, 227

deviance, social, 185–229. *See also* social deviance

dialectic, 239–41

dialects, compared to language, 15

Dictionary of the Social Sciences, 114

differential opportunity theory, 213

DiMaggio, Paul, 179, 180

Diné Bikéyah, 336

diploma and credentials in college education, 4, 11–12

discipline, 223, 224, 298

Discipline and Punish (Foucault), 221

discrimination, 348–52, 355–57; sexual harassment in, 306–7; statistical, 360

dissimilarity index, 350–51

divide and conquer *(divide et impera)*, 154, 155

division of labor, 24–25, 29, 193; gender roles in *(See* gender roles); by same-sex couples, 391; in second shift of household responsibilities, 387–93; social cohesion in, 189–90; and social sanctions, 193

Division of Labor in Society, The (Durkheim), 19, 24, 189, 193, 196

divorce, 376, 382, 384, 392, 402–4; after birth of first child, 153, 154–55; in same-sex marriage, 406

DNA testing, 227, 329–30

doctors: common names in directories of, 233–34; medical education of, 11

Dodds, Peter, 65

"doing gender," 290–91, 385

domestic abuse, 83, 386–87

domesticity, cult of, 381, 384, 385, 387

domination, 92, 286, 333, 353–55

Dominican Republic, 338

"do no harm" rule in research, 66

"don't ask, don't tell" military policy, 108, 311

double consciousness, 28, 355

Douglas, Alfred, 297

Dove, advertising campaign of, 101–2

Down's syndrome, 280

dramaturgical theory, 32, 135–39, 291, 354

drug industry, 178–79

drug use: incarceration for, 218, 225, 360; of marijuana, 204–5; media images of, 96; rehabilitation in, 192, 218; and War on Drugs, 217, 225

dual-income families: divorce in, 392; gender roles in, 386, 387–93

Du Bois, W. E. B., 18, 19, 22, 27–28, 355, 394

Duke, David, 343

Duncan, Otis Dudley, 22, 249, 250, 265, 267

Duncan scale, 249–50

Duneier, Mitchell, 52–54

Durkheim, Émile, 21, 24–25, 38; on division of labor, 24–25, 193; functionalist approach of, 29, 189, 203; on religion, 25; on social cohesion, 189, 190–91, 229; on social sanctions, 193, 221, 224; on suicide, 25, 196–200; in timeline of sociology, 17, 19, 20

Duvall, Marjorie, 385

dyads, 152–53, 156, 158

eating disorders, 284, 304

Ebbers, Bernard, 202

economics, discipline of, 37

economy: corporations in, 252–53 *(See also* corporations); differential opportunities in, 213; legitimate and illegitimate, 213; political, 102–6; power elite in, 251, 252–53; social, 151

Economy and Society (Weber), 20, 24

Edin, Kathryn, 395, 397

education: affirmative action programs in, 242, 243, 266–68; Coleman Report on, 22; college, 8–12 *(See also* college); financial returns in, 8, 9, 10; gender differences in, 303–4, 305–6; inequalities in, 305–6, 348–50, 360; institutional racism in, 360; medical, 11; of middle class, 257–58; parent involvement in, 123–24; parent level of, 268; and poverty, 51, 186; primary and secondary system of, 14–15; in private schools, 124–25; in schools *(See* schools); segregation and discrimination in, 348–50; social class affecting, 123–25, 266–68; in socialization process, 114–15, 123, 124–25; status-attainment model on, 265

Educational Testing Service, 15

egoistic suicide, 197

Egypt, 364

Ehrenreich, Barbara, 398

elderly, 381, 387, 389

elections, 82; voting in, 82, 170–71, 245

Electoral College, 82

Elementary Forms of Religious Life, The (Durkheim), 20, 25 elite-mass dichotomy system of stratification, 251–53

embeddedness in social networks, 162–64

emerging adulthood, 133

emoticons, 79

employment: of African Americans, 395; of Asian Americans, 341; and contradictory class locations, 248; as farm workers, exploitation in, 240–41; in industrial era, 380; minimum wage in, 398; in post-World War II era, 381–82; and race of job candidates, 210, 360; sexual harassment in, 306–7; of single mothers, 397–98, 399; and status hierarchy system, 249–50; stigma affecting, 210; of tokens, 309, 310; of women, 306–11, 314, 381–84, 387–93, 397–98; of working poor, 259

endogamy, 372

England, 80, 88

England, Paula, 173, 300, 301

English language, 15

Enlightenment, 17, 236–39, 244

Enron, 252

entrepreneurs, 163, 164, 168–69

Epstein, Cynthia Fuchs, 285

equality: affirmative action programs for, 242–43, 266–69; in breadwinner and homemaker roles, 392; of condition, 242–43; cultural concept of, 86–87; in dyads, 153, 158; economic, 357–60; gender affecting, 295, 305–11, 392; global, 259–62; historical views of, 235–41; ontological, 325–26; of opportunity, 241–42, 277; of outcome, 243–44; in small groups, 158; standards of, 241–44

equity inequality, 358

Erikson, Kai, 214–15

Escher, M. C., 281

essentialism, 281, 290, 305

Essman, Elliot, 255

estate system, 245

estate tax, 359

ethical issues in social research, 66–67

ethnicity, 333–42; and cultural practices, 26; and minority–majority group relations, 344–53

ethnocentrism, 77, 324

ethnomethodology, 139–41

eugenics, 326–28

Evans, Phyllis, 58

evolution, 37, 326

exceptionalism, American, 63

exchange mobility, 265

exogamy, 372, 406–7

experimental methods in research, 65–66

experimenter effects, 52–54

extended families, 375

face, saving of, 137–38

Facebook, 44, 142, 149, 171

face-to-face interactions, 157, 158, 159

"fag discourse," 131–32

Failing at Fairness (Sadker and Sadker), 305

Fair Sentencing Act (2010), 360

families, 369–411; of African Americans, 393–95; birth order in, 244–45, 401; breadwinner and homemaker roles in, 370–71, 378, 381, 392; domestic abuse in, 386–87; dual-income, 386, 387–93; employment of mothers in, 314, 384, 387–93; firstborn children in, 153, 154–55, 401; gender roles in, 287, 370–71, 380–81, 384, 385–86, 387–93; matrifocal, 393–94; media images of, 74, 96–97, 369–70; middle class, 259; in modern societies, 375–83; pecking order among siblings in, 400–402; in poverty, 396–99; power in, 385, 389; as primary group, 159; psychoanalytic theories of, 288; second shift responsibilities in, 387–93; siblings in, 120 (*See also* siblings); size of, 382; in socialization process, 114, 115, 120–24, 159, 385

farm workers, 240–41, 264–65

Fascism, 33, 34, 92

fatalistic suicide, 200

fathers, 375, 389

Fausto-Sterling, Anne, 280

Feeding the Family (Duvall), 385

Feinberg, Kenneth, 390, 391

feminine beauty, 284–85

Feminine Mystique, The (Friedan), 22, 292, 385

femininity, 284–85, 286, 288, 291

feminism, 20, 30–31, 83; black, 291–93; on equality of opportunity, 277; on family, 385–86; and gender, 30–31, 277, 285–86, 291–93; on housework, 390; Marxist, 295; and media images of women, 101; radical, 290; research methods in, 55, 66; on socialization, 120; on suicide, 200

Feral Trade, 150–51

Ferber, Abby, 343

Ferguson, Jesse Tyler, 97

fertility: and birthrates, 382, 383–84, 396; treatments increasing, 377

feudalism, 234, 245

Figlio, David, 108

financial crisis (2008), 253, 306

financial industry: in elite–mass dichotomy system, 252–53; social influences on, 66; upper class in, 255; white-collar crime in, 213–14

firstborn children in family, 153, 154–55, 401

Fittje, Ryan, 309

fixed effects, 273

Flat Broke with Children (Hays), 399

Fong, Jeanne, 408

food, 48–49, 133

food stamps, 397, 398

For Better of for Worse (Hetherington and Kelly), 404

Ford Motor Company, 252

formal deviance, 187. *See also* crime

formal social sanctions, 194–95

formal sociology, 25

Foster, Don, 132

Foucault, Michel, 221–24, 296, 297, 298

France, 63–64, 79–80; name choices in, 107; prison life in, 223; punishment of Damiens in, 221, 222, 223

Francis, Neville, 388

free rider problem, 244

French Revolution, 235

Freud, Sigmund, 288, 289, 290

Friedan, Betty, 22, 292, 385

Friendster, 44

front stage experiences in dramaturgical theory, 32, 136–37, 354

Fryer, Roland, Jr., 268

functionalist approach, 29, 30; to families, 373; to inequality, 29, 30; to sex roles, 287–88; to social deviance and control, 188–202, 203

Future of Marriage, The (Bernard), 385

Gaddis, Michael, 171–72

Gagnon, Ralph, 234

Galbraith, Robert, 88

Galileo, 81, 82

Gallagher, Maggie, 404

Galton, Francis, 327

games in childhood, 118–19

Gans, Herbert, 93–94, 334

Garfinkel, Harold, 139

Garner, Tyron, 189

Gates, William Henry "Bill," Jr., 234, 244, 253

Gay New York (Chauncey), 299

gay population. *See* homosexuality

gay pride parades, 298

Geertz, Clifford, 83, 84, 85, 345

Geithner, Timothy, 253

gender, 273–317; and academic achievement, 305; of early sociologists, 28–29, 55; and education, 303–4, 305–6; and equality, 295, 305–11; and feminism, 30–31, 277, 285–86, 291–93, 386–87; and mortality rates, 304; and name choices, 108; and outmarriage, 407; roles related to (*See* gender roles); and sexism in media, 100–102; stereotypes related to, 100–102, 274–75, 309–10; stratification by, 244–45

"Gendergate," 303

gender roles, 130–32, 282, 285, 286–94; in African American families, 393–94; in breadwinner–homemaker model of families, 370–71, 378, 381, 392; in child rearing, 288, 375, 380, 381; and combat roles of women, 312; conflict theories on, 290, 291; and cult of domesticity, 381, 384, 385, 387; deceptive distinctions in, 285, 305, 309; in dual-income families, 386, 387–93; feminist approach to, 30–31, 277, 286, 291–93, 385–86; in industrial era, 380–81; in Latino families, 396; media images of, 305–6, 369–70; and natural sex differences, 278; and occupations, 304, 305, 306, 307–11, 314; in play, 130–31, 289; same-sex parental role models of, 384; in second shift responsibilities, 387–93; socialization of, 130–32, 288; and spending patterns of family income, 386; and suicide, 200; unpaid work of women in, 296, 380–81, 387, 390–91

generalizability, 52, 59

generalized other, 27, 119, 120

General Social Survey (GSS), 62, 330

genetics: in monogamy, 373; and race, 326–27, 329–30

genitalia: of intersex children, 278–80; mutilation in females, 83; in psychoanalytic theories, 288

genocide, 353

geography: and global inequality, 260–61; race categories based on, 324, 330

German Americans, 354

Germany, 63–64, 86, 328

Gerson, Kathleen, 383

gestures, 139

ghettos, 350–52

Giddens, Anthony, 23

Gilbert, Dennis, 254–55

Gilligan, Carol, 288–89, 290, 304

"girl crisis," 304

Giuliani, Rudy, 103, 212

given gestures, 139

given off gestures, 139

glass ceilings, 308–10

glass escalators, 310–11

Glassner, Barry, 100

Glazer, Nathan, 345

global inequality, 259–62

globalization, 36, 259–62

Goddard, H. H., 327

Goffman, Alice, 56

Goffman, Erving, 22, 32; dramaturgical theory of, 32, 135–39, 291, 354; on masculinity, 285; on total institutions, 219–21

Goldman Sachs, 252

Google, 103, 108, 143

Gordon, Milton, 344

Gore, Al, 82

goth culture, 85–86

graffiti, 212

Graham, Billy, 300

Gramsci, Antonio, 92, 99

Granovetter, Mark, 162, 179

Grant, Madison, 327

Gray, John, 276, 283

Gray, Mary, 73

Great Depression, 67–68, 180

great man theories of history, 33

Great Migration of African Americans, 26, 322, 353–54

Great Risk Shift, The (Hacker), 258

Greece, 322, 364

green cards, 364

greenhouse gas emissions, 95

green revolution, 260–61

Grosz, Elizabeth, 281

groups, 152–61, 183; and endogamy, 372; and exogamy, 372; informal social sanctions of, 194; minority–majority group relations, 344–53; response to domination, 353–55; Simmel on, 25, 152, 153, 154, 156, 157, 158; social mobility of, 263; in status hierarchy system, 249–50

Groves, Robert, 69

Guess Who's Coming to Dinner, 97

Guevara, Ernesto "Che," 202

Gulf War, 311

Gutenberg, Johannes, 90

Guthrie, Doug, 36

Haiti, 33, 34, 338, 347–48, 364

Haley, Alex, 334

Hamlin, Melanie, 123

Hamme, Kimberly, 169

hara-kiri, 198

Harding, Sandra, 55

Harris, David R., 143

Hart, Owen, 144–45

Hart-Cellar Act, 180

Hartmann, Heidi, 290

Haven in a Heartless World (Lasch), 400

Havrilla, Rebekah, 311

Hays, Sharon, 399

Hays Code, 98

health: and height, 48–49; socioeconomic status affecting, 46–47, 49; water quality affecting, 48–49

health care, 64, 83

Heerwig, Jennifer A., 144

Hegel, Georg Wilhelm Friedrich, 239–41

hegemony, 92, 99, 285, 356

height, and health, 48–49

helplessness, learned, 199

Herdt, Gilbert, 294

Herrnstein, Richard J., 29

"herstory" approach to history, 290

Hetherington, E. Mavis, 404

higher education. *See* college

hijra identity, 283

Hinduism, 198

Hippocrates, 323

hiring patterns, 210, 360

Hispanics. *See* Latinos

history, 33–35; "herstory" approach in, 290; Marx on, 22–23; research on, 33–34, 62–65; of sociology theories, 16–29

History of Sexuality, The (Foucault), 296

History of White People, The (Painter), 342

Hitchcock, Alfred, 97

Hitler, Adolf, 33, 34

HIV infection and AIDS, 175

Hobbes, Thomas, 17

Hochschild, Arlie, 23, 387, 388, 391, 392

Holocaust, 353

home ownership, 352, 357, 358, 359

Home Owners' Loan Corporation (HOLC), 352

homicides, 96, 216–17, 226

homophobia, 131–32

homosexuality, 74, 296–99; as crime, 187–88, 189; cultural differences in, 294–95, 296; and division of household chores by same-sex couples, 391;

historical views of, 294; identity in, 294, 296, 298, 299; media images of, 74, 97; military policy on, 108, 311; and out-groups, 160; and peer influence in gender-role socialization, 131–32; same-sex marriage in, 298, 405–6

hooks, bell, 293

hook-up culture of teenagers, 172, 173, 300–301

horizontal social mobility, 263

hormones, 44

hospitals, mental, 205, 208, 219

Houghton, Katharine, 97

households, 36, 409; composition of, 375–76; division of labor in, 380–81, 387–93; in preindustrial era, 379; spending decisions in, 386

housework, 380–81, 387–93

housing: and asset inequality, 359; loans for, 352; and net worth, 357, 358; in public housing projects, 352; and residential segregation, 350–52, 355, 359

Hout, Michael, 258

Howe, Louise, 307

How to Observe Morals and Manners (Martineau), 17, 20

Hull House, 28

human nature, 115, 116–17

Human Nature and the Social Order (Cooley), 19, 117

human trafficking, 240–41, 286

humor in breach of script, 137–38

Hurricane Katrina, 99–100, 170

Hutu, 352–53

hypothesis testing, 32, 38, 50–51

I, concept of, 117

identity, 13–14, 279, 282, 345; homosexual, 294, 296, 298, 299; racial, 319, 331–32, 361, 363; stigma affecting, 209–11; in total institutions, 220

ideology, 81–82, 86, 88, 92

Iksil, Bruno, 214

illness, water quality as factor in, 49

I Love Lucy, 97

imagination, sociological, 4–12, 15, 41

Imbens, Guido, 366

imitation, 118

immigration, 26, 345–48, 361, 363–65; from Africa, 337, 338; of Asians, 340, 341; assimilation in, 26, 120, 320, 344–48; of farm workers, 240–41; Hart-Cellar Act on, 180; intelligence testing in, 327; of Irish, 320–21; of Latinos, 338–39, 362, 395–96; quotas on national origin in, 180, 321; racial issues in, 320–21, 322, 327

Immigration Act (1924), 321, 329

Immigration and Nationality Act Amendments, 180

impression management, 135, 137

inattention, civil, 138

incarceration, 217–29. *See also* prisons

incest, 286

income, 247–48, 253, 254; and affirmative action, 268; and consumer culture, 105; in dual-income families, 386; education affecting, 8–10; in equality of outcome, 244; gender inequality in, 307, 308, 310–11, 384; global inequality in, 259–62; and health, 46–47, 49; intergenerational patterns in, 234; of middle class, 256, 257, 258–59; in poverty, 51, 259; and socioeconomic status, 254 (*See also* socioeconomic status); status-attainment model on, 265; of upper class, 254, 256–57

independent variables, 50, 51

index of dissimilarity, 350–51

Index of Occupational Status, 249

India, 198, 235, 261–62, 283; caste system in, 246, 372

inductive approach, 45–46

industrialization, 380–81

Industrial Revolution, 16, 380–81; and capitalism, 23; and global inequalities, 260; and limited liability, 88

inequality, 233–71; affirmative action programs in, 242–43, 266–69; conflict theory on, 30, 290; and double consciousness, 28; economic, 357–60; in education, 305–6, 348–50, 360; in employment, 306–11, 314; in equity, 358; feminist theory on, 31; functionalist approach to, 29, 30; and gender, 295, 305–11; global, 259–62; historical views of, 235–41; in sibling relationships, 400–402

infections: causal relationships of, 49; and global inequality, 260, 261, 262; HIV infection and AIDS, 175; malaria, 261; of Native Americans, 336; of teenagers, sexually transmitted diseases in, 172–76, 301–2; waterborne, 49

infertility treatments, 377

inflation, 8

informal deviance, 187

informal social sanctions, 194–95

informed consent, 66–67

Ingres, Jean Auguste Dominique, 78

in-groups, 160–61

innovators, 201, 202

institutionalism, 180

institutions, 179–80; economic, 251, 252; racism of, 359–60; social, 12–15 (*See also* social institutions); total, 127, 219–21

mathematics skills, 304

matriarchy in African American families, 393–94

McCain, John, 403

McCandless, Christopher Johnson, 201

McCarty, Oseola, 247

McCloskey, Deirdre/Donald, 273–75, 276

McGlaun, Jenni, 397

McGregor, Jena, 163

McIntosh, Peggy, 342

McNamara, Robert, 252

McRobbie, Angela, 101

McVeigh, Timothy, 191–92

me, concept of, 117

Mead, George Herbert, 18, 20, 21, 26, 27, 117, 118, 119

Mead, Margaret, 36, 83, 158

means-ends theory of deviance, 201

Mears, Ashley, 310–11

measurements, validity and reliability of, 52

mechanical social sanctions, 191, 193, 221

mechanical solidarity, 189, 190

media, 73–74, 90–108, 111; family images in, 74, 96–97, 369–70, 393; gender roles in, 305–6; homosexual relationships in, 74, 97; in socialization process, 126; television (*See* television); violence in, 95, 98, 101, 126

mediator role in triads, 154, 155

Medicaid, 268

medical education, 11

men: college enrollment of, 303, 304; as fathers, 375, 389; glass escalators for, 310; housework and child care responsibilities of, 388–89

Men and Women of the Corporation (Kanter), 309

Men Are from Mars, Women Are from Venus (Gray), 276

mental health, labeling on, 205, 208, 209

mental hospitals, 205, 208, 219

meritocracy, 251

Merton, Robert, 21, 32, 128, 201, 202, 203, 213, 355

Mexico, 339, 363, 364–65

microinteractions, 25, 290–91

micropenis, 279

microsociology, 31, 39, 203

middle class, 247, 255–59; education of, 257–58; socialization process in, 121–24; working class compared to, 256

Middle Eastern Americans, 341–42

midrange theory, 32

migration of African Americans, 26, 322, 353–54

Mikelson, Kelly S., 107–8

Milgram, Stanley, 165

military order in elite–mass dichotomy system, 251, 252

military service, 127, 144, 199, 313; of homosexuals, 108, 311; of women, 311–13

Milkman, Ruth, 314

Mill, John Stuart, 17

Mills, C. Wright, 4–5, 8, 20, 21, 22, 30, 179, 251–52

Mind, Self, and Society (Mead), 21, 27

Mind and Society, The (Pareto), 251

minimum wage, 398

minority groups, 344–53; and Asian Americans as model minority, 341, 347, 363; suicide in, 200

miscegenation, 329, 371, 406

MIT Center for Future Civic Media, 103

mobility: loss of civic life in, 167; social (*See* social mobility)

Möbius strip, 281–82

model minority, Asian Americans as, 341, 347, 363

Modern Family, 97

modern societies: family in, 375–83; liquidity of, 167; organic solidarity in, 189; punishment in, 221–24; race and racism in, 323–26, 328–30; social networks in, 167, 171; social sanctions in, 193

modern sociological theories, 29–32

Molina, Florencia, 240

Money, John, 278–79, 280

Money, Morals, and Manners (Lamont), 60–61

monogamy, 372, 373

monogenism, 326

Monroe, Rose, 314

Montesquieu, 260, 324–25

moral issues, 16

Moretti, Franco, 38

More Work for Mother (Cowan), 390

Morgan, Stephen, 36

Mormons, 372

Morning, Ann, 64–65

mortality rates, 304

mortgage loans, 352

Moss, Kate, 106

mothers: in African American families, 393–94; age at first childbirth, 377; and cult of domesticity, 381, 384; cultural differences in role of, 375; employment and child rearing of, 314, 384, 387–93; as single parents, 377, 378, 396–99; as supermom, 387–93; time spent with children, 389

movie industry, Production Code of, 96–97, 98

Moynihan, Daniel Patrick, 345, 393, 394

Mozart, Wolfgang Amadeus, 88

Ms. Magazine, 101

multiculturalism, 348

multiple births, 377

multiracial families, 406–7

multiracial identity, 361, 363

Multiracial March, 361

murders, 96, 216–17, 226

Murray, Charles, 29, 398–99

music, 65–66, 85, 87, 88–89, 95

Music Lab experiment, 65–66

Muslims, 246, 331–33, 341

Mussolini, Benito, 33

Myrdal, Gunnar, 357

MySpace, 44

nadle, 283

names: changed in passing response, 354; choice of, 107–8; in physician directories, 233–34; and social mobility, 233–34

Nanda, Serena, 283

Na people, 375

narratives in social networks, 161–62

National Association for the Advancement of Colored People (NAACP), 20, 27, 28, 348

National Association for the Advancement of White People (NAAWP), 343–44

National Longitudinal Survey of Adolescent Health, 173, 302

National Organization of Women, 171

National Origins Acts (1924), 322

Native Americans, 80–81, 334, 335–37; equity inequalities affecting, 358; gender concept of, 283; on reservations, 336; social outcomes for, 357; socioeconomic status of, 336, 357, 358; surnames of, 233

nativism, 327

naturalization, 321, 363–64

natural selection, 326

nature: and culture, 75; and influence of nurture, 115, 144, 278

Navajo, 283, 336

Nazism, 328, 349, 353, 371

Negro Family, The (Moynihan), 393

neighborhood watch groups, 194

Nelson, Margaret, 386

networks, 149–52, 161–77, 183; analysis of, 44, 172–77; institutional isomorphism in, 179–80; kinship, 375, 379; social (*See* social networks)

net worth, 357

New Deal era, 63

New Guinea, 294–95

New Moon Girls, 101

news programs on television, 91, 92, 94

Newsweek, 99

New York Federal Reserve, 253

New York State Parole Handbook, 222–23

Nichols, Nichelle, 97

1984 (Orwell), 184

Nixon, Richard M., 181, 217, 349

Noel, Donald, 346

No Logo (Klein), 104

nonmaterial culture, 78–79, 81–82

nonverbal communication, 139

normalization, 298

normal science, 38

normative theory of suicide, 196–200

norms, 87, 88, 120; deviance from, 187; gender roles in, 130, 131, 285; residential segregation affecting, 350; on romantic relationships of teenagers, 176–77; social control for compliance with, 194; and suicide, 196–200

Northern Exposure, 74

nuclear family, 373, 378, 381, 385–86

nurture versus nature debate, 115, 144, 278

nutrition, 48–49, 133

Oakley, Ann, 22, 30

Obama, Barack, 69, 108, 252, 311, 335, 360, 371

O'Barr, Jean, 305

O'Barr, William, 305

observation, participant, 60, 66–67

occupation: common names associated with, 233–34; gender differences in, 304, 305, 306, 307–11, 314; of middle class, 256, 257; and social mobility, 263, 264–65; status of, 249–50, 265; of working class, 256

Oglala Nation, 336

Ohlin, Lloyd, 213

Ojibwe tribe, 335

Olivetti girls campaign, 306

Olivier, Laurence, 89

one-drop rule, 329, 371

On the Natural Varieties of Mankind (Blumenbach), 324

ontological equality, 325–26

openings in social interactions, 138

operationalization, 50–51

opportunity: and differential opportunity theory, 213; equality of, 241–42, 277; in legitimate and illegitimate economies, 213

opportunity costs in college education, 9

oppression, 353–55

organicism, 29

organic solidarity, 189, 190

organizations, 177–80; corporate (*See* corporations); as legal persons, 177; voluntary, 166, 167, 170–71

orgasms, 280

Orszag, Peter, 252

Ortner, Sherry, 286, 287

Orwell, George, 184

Othello, 154

other, concept of, 27, 117–20

outcome equality, 243–44

out-groups, 160–61

outmarriage, 406–7

overpopulation, 237–39

Oyěwùmí, Oyèrónké, 293

Pager, Devah, 209–10, 219

Painter, Nell Irvin, 342

Pakistan, 246

Palestinian territories, 341

Panel Study of Income Dynamics (PSID), 62

panopticons, 223–24

Paradoxes of Gender (Lorber), 277

paralegals, 309–10

parents: birth of first child, 153, 154–55; cultural differences in role of, 375; divorce of, 403–4; education level of, 268; fathers, 375, 389; income and social class of, 121–24, 234, 358; involvement in education of children, 123–24; mothers (*See* mothers); psychoanalytic theories on relationships with, 288; same-sex, 405; second shift responsibilities of, 387–93; in single-parent families, 377, 378, 396–99; in socialization process, 120–24; time spent with children, 389

Parent Trap, The, 155

Pareto, Vilfredo, 251, 252

Pareto Principle, 251

Park, Robert, 26, 329, 344, 345, 346

parole system, 217, 218, 222–23

Parsons, Talcott, 19, 21, 29, 30, 287–88, 373

participant observations, 56, 60, 66–67

parties, 158

Pascoe, C. J., 131, 132

passing, as response to racial oppression, 354

patriarchy, 286, 290, 291, 373

Patterns of Culture (Benedict), 82

Pattillo, Mary, 60

Pecking Order, The (Conley), 384, 400, 404

pecking order among siblings, 400–402

peekaboo game, 117, 118

peer influence, 125–26, 131–32, 142–44

penis, 279, 288

Persell, Caroline Hodges, 124

Personal Responsibility and Work Opportunity Reconciliation Act (PRWORA), 399

Philip Morris Company, 13, 14

phrenology, 324, 325

physical inequality, 235–36

physicians: common names in directories of, 233–34; medical education of, 11

physics, social, 15, 18, 38

physiognomy, 324, 325

Pickett, Abbie, 313

Pierce, Jennifer L., 309

Pine Ridge Indian Reservation, 336

pink-collar jobs, 307

Pinterest, 149

Piper, Charles F., 59

Pipher, Mary, 304

Pitcher, Molly, 312

Plath, Sylvia, 200

Plato, 77–78

play, 118, 130–31, 132, 289

Plessy v. Ferguson, 329, 348

pluralism, 345–48

Point of Purchase (Zukin), 103

Poitier, Sidney, 97

Poland, 353

police, 185, 186, 195, 213

political economy, 102–6

political order in elite–mass dichotomy system, 251, 252

political participation: land ownership required for, 245; terrorism affecting, 170–71; voting in, 82, 170–71, 245

political science, 37

politics: and census calculations, 67–69; and ideology of democracy, 82; in triads, 154

Pollock, Jackson, 132

polyandry, 372

polygamy, 372

polygenism, 326

polygyny, 372

poor population, 259; socialization of, 121–24; social mobility of, 185–87; working, 259

population, 58; of foreign born in U.S., 346–47, 361; growth rate of, 237–39; sample of, 58–59, 67–69

Portes, A., 347

Portugal, 364

positivism, 15, 16, 25, 38, 55–56

postmodern societies, 31, 32, 293–94, 409

posttraumatic stress disorder of women veterans, 313

poverty, 259; and education, 51, 186; families in, 396–99; hypothesis testing on, 50–51; income in, 51, 259; policing strategies in, 185, 186; population in, compared to upper class population, 254; and residential segregation, 350; single-parent families in, 396–99; social mobility in, 185–87

Powell, Walter, 179, 180

power: and conflict, 290; in dyads, 153; in elite-mass dichotomy system, 251–52; in families, 385, 389; feminist theory on, 31, 293; and group response to domination, 353–55; of in-groups and out-groups, 160–61; in organizations, 178; political science of, 37; of racial groups, 333; and sexuality, 294, 295–96; in sociology research, 54–55; in total institutions, 220–21, 224; in triads, 153, 154; of upper class, 254–55; of women in military, 313

Power Elite, The (Mills), 251

pregnancy: during military service, 312; psychoanalytic theories of, 289; of teenagers, 382

preindustrial era, 378–80

prejudice, 355–57

premodern societies, 189, 190, 193, 280

Preparing for Power (Cookson and Persell), 124

Presentation of Self in Everyday Life, The (Goffman), 22, 32, 135

Presley, Lisa Marie, 372

primary deviance, 209

primary education, 14–15

primary groups, 159–60

primordialism, 345

printing press invention, 90

prisons, 217–29; drug offenders in, 218, 225, 360; habitual offenders in, 213; race of population in, 225, 226, 338, 352, 360, 395; rape in, 294; rehabilitation in, 218, 219, 222–23, 224, 227–29; and Stanford Prison Experiment, 206–7, 220–21; as total institutions, 127, 219–21

private property, 80–81, 235, 236, 237

private schools, 124–25

Production Code of movie industry, 96–97, 98

proletariat, 248

property ownership, 80–81; of homes, 352, 357, 358, 359; inequality in, 235, 236, 237; and women as property, 286

prostitution, 240, 299

Protestant Ethic and the Spirit of Capitalism, The (Weber), 19, 24

Protestant Reformation, 24, 323

Protestants, 197, 335

psychoanalytic theories on sex roles, 288–90

psychology compared to sociology, 36, 37

public housing projects, 352

public service announcements, 95

Puerto Rico, 338, 339

Pugh, Allison, 103, 104, 105

Pulp Fiction, 6–7

Punished (Rios), 186

punishment, 187, 188, 191–94, 221–29; death penalty in, 191–92, 193, 222, 225–27

Punjabi, 332

Puritans, 214–15

Putnam, Robert, 166, 167, 171

Quadagno, Jill, 63

qualitative research, 38, 39, 45, 56; case studies in, 59; participant observation in, 60; reflexivity in, 52, 54

quantitative research, 38, 39, 45, 56

quota system in immigration restrictions, 180, 321

race, 319–67; and affirmative action programs, 266, 267, 268; biological concept of, 65; and black feminism, 291–93; and class divisions, 267, 268; of college roommate, 143; content analysis method of research on, 64–65; and culture, 80, 329; and death penalty, 225–26; and double consciousness, 28; and genetics, 326–27, 329–30; and in-groups and out-groups, 160–61; and interracial marriage, 97, 329, 357, 371–72, 406–7; media images of, 96, 97, 98–100; and multiracial families, 406–7; one-drop rule on, 329, 371; of prison population, 225, 226, 338, 352, 360, 395; as social construction, 65, 320, 343, 363; and social mobility, 234–35; stereotypes on, 98–100, 210; stigma of, 210

racialization, 331–33

racism, 321–22, 324, 328; cultural, 356, 357; and ethnocentrism, 77, 324; and global inequality, 260, 261; historical research methods on, 63; in immigration restrictions, 320–21; institutional, 359–60; in media, 98–100; prejudice and discrimination in, 355–57

Radway, Janice, 93

Ramey, Valerie A., 388
rape, 294, 295, 313
rational actor model, 37
Read, Jen'nan, 331, 332
reading by women, 93, 101
Reading the Romance (Radway), 93
Reagan, Ronald, 349, 397
reality, social construction of, 27, 132–42
Reardon, Sean, 267
rebels, 202
recidivism, 217, 219
Reddy, Gayatri, 283
reference groups, 161
reflection theory, 87–90
reflexivity, 52, 54
rehabilitation in social deviance, 192; parole in, 222–23;
    prisons in, 218, 219, 222–23, 224, 227–29
Reimer, David, 278–79
relativism, cultural, 82–85
reliability, 52
religion: of Amish, 168–69; and caste system, 245–46;
    Comte on, 16–17; and culture, 83; Durkheim on,
    25; as ideological framework, 82; of Latinos, 396;
    and race, 323–24, 326; and racialization of Muslims,
    331–33; and social deviance, 214–15; and suicide,
    197–98; Weber on, 24
remarriage, 376, 405
Renoir, Pierre-Auguste, 194, 195
reporting bias in crime, 216
Republic (Plato), 77–78
research, 43–71; on culture, 82–85; ethnomethodology
    in, 139–41; on historical issues, 33–34, 62–65;
    sociological imagination in, 4–8
residential segregation, 350–52, 355, 359
resistance, 354–55
Reskin, Barbara, 308
resocialization, 126–27
resources, inequality in, 237
response rate in survey research, 61–62
restitutive sanctions, 192–93
retreatists, 201, 202
returns to schooling, 8, 9, 10
reverse causality, 49–50
Reviving Ophelia (Pipher), 304
revolution: agricultural, 259, 260–61; Industrial, 16, 23,
    88, 260, 380–81
Reynolds, William Bradford, 349
Rezaee, Rosia, 272
Rich, Adrienne, 296

Rich, Kate, 149–51
rights, civil, 91, 92, 348–50
Rios, Victor, 185–87
riots in racial conflicts, 354
Risman, Barbara, 385, 392
ritualists, 201, 202
Roberts, John G., Jr., 32
Robeson, Paul, 348
roles, 128–32, 135–36; gender-related (*See* gender roles);
    online, 141; in prisons, 206–7, 219–21; in small
    groups, 158; in social institutions, 13; status in, 128,
    129–30, 158; in triads, 154–55
romantic relationships, 96, 97, 371–73; of teenagers,
    172–77, 301–2
Rome, ancient, 322
roommates in college, 142–44
Roos, Patricia, 308
Roosevelt, Franklin D., 63
Roots (Haley), 334
Rosaldo, Michelle, 286
Roseanne, 74
Rosenhan, David L., 208
Rosie the Riveter, 314
Rousseau, Jean-Jacques, 17, 77, 235–36, 243–44
Rowling, J. K., 88
Rubens, Peter Paul, 284
Rubin, Donald, 366
Rubin, Gayle, 278, 286
Russia, 80
Rutgers, Jeff, 233
Rwanda, 352–53

Sacerdote, Bruce, 143, 366
Sachs, Jeffrey, 238, 239, 261
Sadker, David, 305
Sadker, Myra, 305
Salai-i-Martin, Xavier, 262
salary, 248, 256–57, 258–59; and breadwinner–
    homemaker model of families, 378; gender
    differences in, 304, 305; and occupational status,
    250; and social mobility, 263
Salganik, Matthew, 65
Sambia, 294–95
same-sex couples, 298, 405–6, 407–8
Samoa, 83
sample population, 58–59, 62, 67–69
sanctions, social, 191–93, 194–95, 221
sanskritization, 246
Sapir-Whorf thesis, 80

variables, 50, 51

varna system, 246

Veblen, Thorstein, 254

vengeance for social deviance, 191

Verstehen (understanding), 24, 38

vertical social mobility, 263

Victim Compensation Fund Final Rule, 391

Vietnam War, 91–92, 311

violence, 215–17; in advertising images of women, 101; intimate partner, 387; in media, 95, 98, 101, 126; in prisons, 222; between siblings, 386; in song lyrics, 87, 95

virginity pledge, 173, 302

voluntary organizations, 166, 167, 170–71

voting, 82, 170–71, 245

wages, 15; gender inequality in, 307, 308, 310–11, 384; minimum wage, 398

Waite, Linda, 404

Wallerstein, Judith, 404

Wall Street, 252

War (Dyer), 127

War against Boys, The (Sommers), 304

War on Drugs, 217, 225

Washington, Denzel, 233

Washington, Ebonya, 120

water supply, 48–49

Watts, Duncan, 65, 66, 67, 165

Wayward Puritans (Erikson), 214–15

Way We Never Were, The (Coontz), 378

wealth, 253, 254; and affirmative action, 268; and equity inequality, 358; global inequality in, 259–62; and net worth, 357; racial inequality in, 357–60

Webb, Jim, 312

Weber, Max, 24; on class, 248–49; on status groups, 249; in timeline of sociology, 18, 19, 20, 21

Weingarter, Eliot, 122

welfare, single-parent families on, 396–99

West, Candace, 130, 291

West, Kanye, 107, 108

West, Mae, 96

white coat effects, 52

white-collar crime, 213–14

white flight, 351–52, 355

whiteness, 321, 322, 328, 342–44

White Patriot (Duke), 343

Whyte, William Foote, 21

WikiLeaks, 94

Wilde, Oscar, 297

Will and Grace, 97

Williams, Alexander, 123

Williams, Christine, 310

Willis, Paul, 22

Wilson, William Julius, 23, 267, 394

Wimberly, Marcia Felts, 399

Winant, Howard, 356

Winthrop, Patricia, 233

Wirth, Louis, 26

withdrawal response of oppressed groups, 353–54

"woman question," 286–94

women: in African American families, 393–94; college enrollment of, 303–4; in combat, 311–13; domestic responsibilities of, 381, 385, 387–93; employment of, 306–11, 314, 381–84, 387–93, 397–98; feminine beauty of, 284–85; and feminism (*See* feminism); glass ceilings affecting, 308–10; and ideological changes, 82; media images of, 97, 100–102, 306; as mothers (*See* mothers); in prison, 225; reading by, 93, 101; suicide of, 200; and textual analysis of media, 93; unpaid work of, 296, 380–81, 387, 390–91

Woods, Tiger, 137

work. *See* employment

working class, 121–24, 247–48, 256

working poor, 259

WorldCom, 252

World War II: employment of women during, 314; Japanese Americans during, 358; Navajo service during, 336; racism during, 98–99, 329, 349; and social change, 5; and withdrawal response to oppression, 353

World Wrestling Federation, 144–45

Wright, Erik Olin, 248

Wuthnow, Robert, 166–67, 171

xenophobia, 6

Yazzie, John, 233

Yelp, 143

Yoruba, 293

Zaloom, Caitlin, 36

Zambia, 375

Zelizer, Viviana, 386, 388, 390

Zhou, M., 347

Zimbardo, Philip, 206–7, 211, 212, 220

Zimmerman, Don, 130, 291

Zuckerberg, Mark, 9, 11, 142

Zuckerman, Ethan, 103

Zukin, Sharon, 103